CHARMING
FRENCH
RESTAURANTS

CHARMING FRENCH RESTAURANTS

EDITED BY

Fiona Duncan & Leonie Glass

Interlink Books
An imprint of Interlink Publishing Group, Inc.
New York • Northampton

First published in 2003 by
Interlink Books
An imprint of Interlink Publishing Group, Inc.
46 Crosby Street, Northampton, Massachusetts 01060
www.interlinkbooks.com

This title is conceived, designed and produced by Duncan Petersen Publishing Ltd.,
31 Ceylon Road, London W14 OPY

Editorial Director Andrew Duncan
Editors Fiona Duncan and Leonie Glass
Contributing Editors Nicola Davies and Juliet Young
In-house Editor Sarah Boyall
Designer Don Macpherson
Maps Eugene Fleury

Library of Congress Cataloging-in-Publication Data

Charming French restaurants / edited by Fiona Duncan & Leonie Glass.
    p. cm. - - (Charming restaurant guides)
    ISBN 1-56656-499-9
    1. Restaurants - - France - - Guidebooks. I. Duncan, Fiona. II. Glass,
Leonie III. Series.
    TX910.F8C47 2003
    647.9544 - - dc21
                                                2003000187

Printed and bound in Italy

To request our complete 40-page full-color catalog, please call us toll-free at 1-800-238-LINK,
visit our website at www.interlinkbooks.com or send us an e-mail: info@interlinkbooks.com

THE CONTRIBUTORS

OUR WARMEST THANKS TO

●**BRETAGNE** Elizabeth James, *lives Ploerdut, Morbihan, Brittany.*
●**BASSE-NORMANDIE**
Gaynor Wingham, *journalist, maison secondaire in Orne*; Lyn Lawrence, *runs vegetarian restaurant in Orne*; Mélanie Langlois and family (especially her father), *runs B & B in Catteville, Manche.*
●**HAUTE-NORMANDIE** Nicola Davies, *Duncan Petersen editor, maison secondaire near Forges-les-Eaux*; Peter Avis, *journalist and chief contributor to* A Taste of Dieppe.
●**PICARDIE** Chrystelle Fevre, *lives Oise*; Richard Williams, *château-hôtel manager, Somme.*
●**NORD-PAS-DE-CALAIS** Janey and Patrick Harpur, *run the idiosyncratic Hôtel de France in Montreuil-sur-Mer;* and Nicola Davies.
●**PARIS AND ILE-DE-FRANCE** Brent Gregston, *American travel writer, food writer and journalist, lives in Paris;* and Sharon Sutcliffe, *wine and food writer, lives in Paris.*
●**CHAMPAGNE-ARDENNE** Brent Gregston and Sharon Sutcliffe.
●**LORRAINE** Brent Gregston and Sharon Sutcliffe.
●**ALSACE** Brent Gregston and Sharon Sutcliffe.
●**PAYS DE LA LOIRE** Maggie Mortimer, *maison secondaire in Mayenne*
●**CENTRE** Erica Williams, *radio journalist*
●**BOURGOGNE** main contributor, Martin Raeburn, *wine exporter, lives Beaune*
●**FRANCHE-COMTE** Leonie Glass, *Duncan Petersen editor and writer*
●**POITOU-CHARENTES** William Rees, *journlist and former hotel owner; lives Vienne*
●**LIMOUSIN** William Rees
●**AQUITAINE** Jan Dodd, *travel writer, lives Riguepeu, Gers*; and Edward Landau, *runs catering business, lives Maubourguet, Hautes Pyrénées*
●**MIDI-PYRENEES** Alan Thornton, *university teacher, maison secondaire in Vercors;* and Barbara Thomas, *maison secondaire in south-west France*
●**AUVERGNE** Leonie Glass
●**RHONE-ALPES** Juliet Young, *marketing consultant, lives Tourves, Var*
●**LANGUEDOC-ROUSSILLON** Carolyn Marill, *travel writer, lives Bessan, Hérault*
●**PROVENCE-ALPES-COTE-D'AZUR** Juliet Young

●**COLOUR SECTIONS**
Fiona Duncan, *Duncan Petersen editor and writer*

Our thanks also to François Bergez, Christelle Clement, Mélanie Delplanque, Anjana Devoy, Capucine d'Halluin and Sarah Poulain for additional recommendations; to Kevin Grant-Dalton, Christopher Birrell, Jonathan Marland and George Pownall; and to Syndicats d'initiative all over France.

CONTENTS

REGIONS OF FRANCE

THE REGIONS — THEN AND NOW

The government regions of France shown on this map and used in this contents list are the modern, official face of France. Often enough, they describe areas of France that everyone knows, and has always known - Britanny, for example, or Alsace. But many a foreign traveller thinks of many a French region by other, often older names – and looking at this map, will wonder where they have gone. Here are some of the answers:

'The Dordogne' – the Dordogne river valley runs through the *département* of Dordogne in Aquitaine.

'The Lot' – the Lot river valley runs through Aquitaine.

Perigord – in *département* of Dordogne in Aquitaine.

Normandy – two regions, Basse- and Haute-Normandie.

The Loire – runs through Centre and Pays de la Loire; the famous part of the Loire valley, with its châteaux, is in Centre.

Quercy – in *départements* of Lot and Tarn-et-Garonne in Midi-Pyrénées.

Gascony – region of south-west France, spanning the *départements* of Gers and Landes in Aquitaine.

Languedoc – part of Languedoc-Roussillon

Provence – part of Provence-Alpes-Côte d'Azur

Côte d Azur – part of Provence-Alpes-Côte d'Azur

EDITORS' INTRODUCTION

I n 20 years of travel publishing, we've not often felt as excited about a new project as we do about this. The world overflows with travel guides to France, but we believe that this one really does deserve its place on the shelves.

Why? Although France is *the* land and the French are *the* guardians of culinary genius, the real French eating experience gets harder by the year to track down. Bureaucracy, and obsession with the bottom line have made the tinned, the frozen, the bottled and the re-heated much too common. Fewer and fewer restaurants seem to be interested in producing honest but delicious food that might have come - or nearly might have come - from the kitchen at home.

This guide is not a complete newcomer. It is, of course, the first cousin of our *Charming Small Hotel Guide* to France: that guide, now in its 20th year, is all about escaping standardization, and we've found our philosophy applies just as neatly to eating as to lodging. And we hope that this new guide fills, for travellers both sides of the Atlantic, the gap left by the recent end of the English language editions of *Gault Millaut and Bottin Gourmand*.

This was a particularly daunting book to put together. No single person has the knowledge, of course, to report on eating places throughout such a large country. So instead we recruited and commissioned a group of more than 20 contributors. Some were British, some American food writers, with a far reaching knowledge of France and French food. Of these we should perhaps make special mention of the three individuals who did the largest sections of the book. Paris and Ile-de-France is the work of Brent Gregston and Sharon Sutcliffe. Brent, American, and Sharon, English, are both travel and food writers who live in the French capital, know it back to front and have, we believe, created the most stimulating selection of eating places in Paris that you can find anywhere. The guide also owes much to Juliet Young, our Provence and Rhône-Alpes contributor, who gave us invaluable help working out the initial concept. We think her selections in the south are, like Brent and Sharon's in Paris, hard to beat.

Many of our other contributors were English and Americans, or French, with homes or holiday homes all over France, keen to try their hand at restaurant reviewing. We can't thank them enough for sharing their local knowledge, for telling us many of their secrets and for searching out via friends, many more. A full list of contributors is on page 5.

We took care to communicate our selection criteria clearly to each and every contributor, but there's no denying that the strength, and the weakness, of a compilation such as this is its reliance on individual opinion. Not all the restaurants will be as good as each other (even making allowances for price and area). We hope you'll be as indulgent as you can of this first edition. With the help of our network of contributors, and, equally important, of readers, we believe we can make it better with each new edition. The readers' comments paragraph at the end of each description is there for this purpose, so even if you have three words of comment on a restaurant - good or bad - scribble it on a postcard and send it on to us. (For more information on reporting to the guide, see page 157.)

Fiona Duncan and Leonie Glass

USING THIS GUIDE

FINDING A RESTAURANT

EITHER browse the master maps covering all France, pages 10-15. They show places where the restaurants are located, and page numbers.

OR if you're on a French motorway, try the maps on pages 16-19, marked with places and page numbers of restaurants within 20 minutes of the motorway.

OR if you'are in a specific locality, browse the detailed maps at the start of each section, again marked with places and page numbers.

OR if you want to know if there is a restaurant at a certain place, search the alphabetical listing starting on page 378.

HOW THE BOOK IS ORGANIZED

The restaurant listings are in 21 sections corresponding to the 21 government regions of mainland France (excluding Corse). Full list, page 6. They follow in geographical order, starting in north-west France and ending in south-east France.

Within these sections, restaurants follow in alphabetical order by city, town or village in which, or near which, the restaurant is located.

READING AN ENTRY

Beutin
◆ Auberge de la Canche
€ Fr

3 RN39, 62170 Beutin, Pas-de-Calais
Tel 02 31 68 76 03 Fax 02 31 68 63 58

Newly restored and run by a family from Montreuil, the Auberge de la Canche is the answer to a prayer for somewhere with a terrace and a pretty garden, overlooking a stream, where you can park without fuss, and get a decent meal (from a comprehensive menu and a good wine list), pleasantly served. Then make a note to come back in winter when the big fireplace might just have blazing logs in it – which it will.

❛ *Great fun ... the place was full of locals* ❜

CLOSED Mon, Tue
CARDS MC, V

First comes the city, town or village in which, or near which, the restaurant is located.

Next comes the name of the restaurant

Next comes its price band

€   less than 30 euros
€€   30-50 euros
€€€   over 50 euros
– based on menu prices without wine.

Prices were correct when the guide went to press, but can change at short notice.

Next comes our Fr symbol, if applicable, given to restaurants where menus offer *cuisine du terroir*, classical French dishes, or regional dishes with an emphasis on fresh ingredients.

Next comes the address and telephone number.

Next comes the description.

In some cases this is followed by diners' comments, if available. These are informal, subjective views collected from people who have eaten at the restaurant.

Finally, closing times and credit cards accepted.

● Occasionally the editors have added some extra addresses - introduced by a bullet point, which readers may find useful if our main selections are closed or booked solid.

Please remember: if enjoyment of your day is going to depend on getting a table and paying a certain price, reserve a table in advance and check the price first.

MASTER MAP–THE NORTH

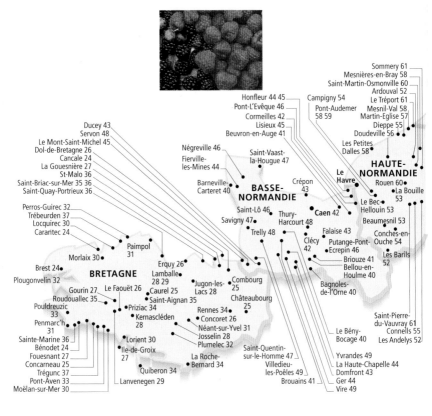

Sommery 61
Mesnières-en-Bray 58
Saint-Martin-Osmonville 60
Ardouval 52
Honfleur 44 45   Campigny 54   Le Tréport 61
Pont-L'Evêque 46   Pont-Audemer   Mesnil-Val 58
Cormeilles 42   58 59   Martin-Eglise 57
Lisieux 45   Dieppe 55
Beuvron-en-Auge 41   Doudeville 56
Ducey 43   Les Petites
Servon 48   Négreville 46   Saint-Vaast-   Dalles 58
Le Mont-Saint-Michel 45   Fierville-   la-Hougue 47   **HAUTE-**
Dol-de-Bretagne 26   les-Mines 44   Le   **NORMANDIE**
Cancale 24   Crépon   **Havre**   Rouen 60
La Gouesnière 27   Barneville-   43   La Bouille
St-Malo 36   Carteret 40   Le Bec-   53
Saint-Briac-sur-Mer 35 36   **BASSE-**   Helouin 53
Saint-Quay-Portrieux 36   **NORMANDIE**   **Caen** 42   Beaumesnil 53
Saint-Lô 46   Thury-   Conches-en-
Perros-Guirec 32   Savigny 47   Harcourt 48   Falaise 43   Ouche 54
Trébeurden 37   Trelly 48   Putange-Pont-   Les Barils
Locquirec 30   Clécy   Ecrepin 46   52
Carantec 24   Paimpol   42   Briouze 41
Morlaix 30   31   Bellou-en-
Erquy 26   Houlme 40
Brest 24   **BRETAGNE**   Lamballe   Combourg   Bagnoles-
Plougonvelin 32   28 29   Jugon-les-   25   de-l'Orne 40
Gourin 27   Le Faouët 26   Caurel 25   Lacs 28   Châteaubourg   Saint-Pierre-
Roudouallec 35   Saint-Aignan 35   25   du-Vauvray 61
Pouldreuzic   Priziac 34   Rennes 34   Connells 55
33   Kernascléden   Concoret 26   Le Bény-   Les Andelys 52
Penmarc'h   28   Néant-sur-Yvel 31   Bocage 40
31   Lorient 30   Josselin 28
Sainte-Marine 36   Ile-de-Groix   Plumelec 32   Yvrandes 49
Bénodet 24   27   La Roche-   Saint-Quentin-   La Haute-Chapelle 44
Fouesnant 27   Bernard 34   sur-le-Homme 47   Domfront 43
Concarneau 25   Villedieu-   Ger 44
Trégunc 37   Quiberon 34   les-Poêles 49   Vire 49
Pont-Aven 33   Lanvenegen 29   Brouains 41
Moëlan-sur-Mer 30

Madelaine-sous-Montreuil 75
Le Touquet 78 79
Wimereux 79
Hardelot-Plage 74
Saint-Folquin 77
Gravelines 74
Beutin 73
Blendecques 73
Houlle 75
Clairmarais 73
Steenvoord 78
Inxent 75
Arques 72
Aire-sur-la-Lys 72
Attin 72 Montreuil 76
Sorrus 77
Hesdin 74 Arras 72
Fort-Mahon 67
Quend 68
Rue 69
Etroeungt 73
NORD-PAS-DE-CALAIS
Etréaupont 67
Aumale 52 Amiens 64
Caulières 65
Gerberoy 67
PICARDIE
Signy-l'Abbaye 136
Berry-au-Bac 65
Saint-Jean-aux-Bois 69
Mouzon 135
Thionville 142
Itterswiller 149
Osthouse 151
Mittelbergheim 150
Erstein 147
Ottrott 151 152
Obernai 151
Strasbourg 154 155
Marlenheim 150
Mittelhausen 150
Brumath 146
Saverne 154
Agnetz 64
Courcelles-sur-Vesle 66
Tinqueux 137
Le Fossé 56
Apremont 64
Gisors 57
Neuilly-Saint-Front 68
Reims 135 136
Saint-Imoges 136
Norroy-le-Veneur 142
Metz 141
Baerenthal 140
Chantilly 65
Coye-la-Fôret 66
Champillon-Bellevue 134
Hinsingen 148
Fourges 56
Vinay 137
LORRAINE
Saint Ouen 83
Neuilly 83
Le Perreux-sur-Marne 83
Epernay 134
Révigny sur Orain 142
Nancy 141 142
Lunéville 141
PARIS 82-192
Issy-les-Moulineaux 82
Versailles 84
Bar-le-Duc 140
Turquestein-Blancrupt 143
ALSACE
ILE-DE-FRANCE
Moissy Cramayel 83
CHAMPAGNE-ARDENNE
Le Valtin 143
Bergheim 146
Barbizon 82
Troyes 137
Gérardmer 140
Bas-Rupts 140
Xonrupt-Longemer 143
Illhaeusern 148
Fontainebleau 82
Flagy 82
Langres 134
Artzenheim 146
Thannenkirch 156
Ribeauvillé 152
Riquewihr 152 153
Hunawir 148
Zellenbergl 156
Lapoutroie 149
Colmar 147
Wihr-au-Val 156
Eguisheim 147
Diefmatten 147
Rouffach 153

MASTER MAP
–CENTRAL FRANCE

MASTER MAP–THE SOUTH

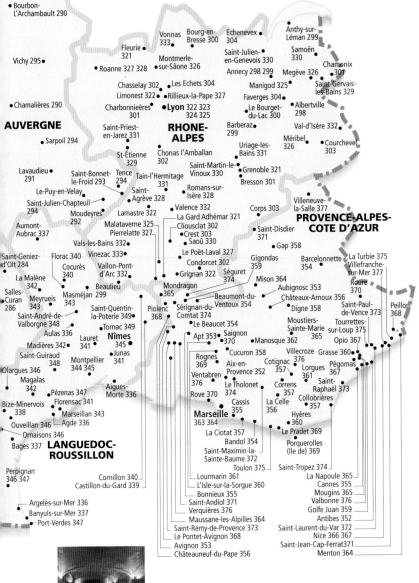

Bourbon-L'Archambault 290

Vonnas 333

Bourg-en-Bresse 300

Echenevex 304

Anthy-sur-Léman 299

Fleurie 321

Saint-Julien-en-Genevois 330

Samoën 330

Vichy 295

Montmerle-sur-Sâone 326

Roanne 327 328

Annecy 298 299

Megève 326

Chamonix 301

Saint-Gervais-les-Bains 329

Chasselay 302

Les Echets 304

Manigod 325

Limonest 322

Rillieux-la-Pape 327

Faverges 304

Albertville 298

Chamalières 290

Charbonnieères 301

Lyon 322 323 324 325

Le Bourget-du-Lac 300

AUVERGNE

Saint-Priest-en-Jarez 331

RHONE-ALPES

Barberaz 299

Val-d'Isère 332

Méribel 326

Courcheve 303

Sarpoil 294

St-Étienne 302

Chonas l'Amballan

Uriage-les-Bains 331

Saint-Martin-le-Vinoux 330

Grenoble 321

Lavaudieu 291

Saint-Bonnet-le-Froid 293

Tence 294

Tain-l'Hermitage 331

Bresson 301

Le-Puy-en-Velay

Saint-Agrève 328

Romans-sur-Isère 328

Saint-Julien-Chapteuil 294

Moudeyres 292

Lamastre 322

Valence 332

Corps 303

Villeneuve-la-Salle 377

Aumont-Aubrac 337

Malataverne 325

Pierrelatte 327

La Gard Adhémar 321

PROVENCE-ALPES-COTE D'AZUR

Vals-les-Bains 332

Cliousclat 302

Crest 303

Saint-Disdier 371

Saint-Geniez-d'Olt 284

Florac 340

Vinezac 333

Saoû 330

Gap 358

La Malène 342

Cocurès 340

Vallon-Pont-d'Arc 332

Le Poët-Laval 327

Condorcet 302

Gigondas 359

Barcelonnette 354

La Turbie 375

Villefranche-sur-Mer 377

Salles-Curan 286

Meyrueis 343

Masméjàn 299

Beaulieu

Grignan 322

Séguret 374

Mison 364

Aubignosc 353

Roure 370

Saint-André-de-Valborgne 348

Saint-Quentin-la-Poterie 349

Piolenc 368

Sérignan-du-Comtat 374

Mondragon 365

Beaumont-du-Ventoux 354

Châteaux-Arnoux 356

Digne 358

Saint-Paul-de-Vence 375

Peillon 368

Aulas 336

Tornac 349

Le Beaucet 354

Moustiers-Sainte-Marie 365

Tourrettes-sur-Loup 375

Madières 342

Lauret 341

Nîmes 345

Apt 353

Saignon 370

Manosque 362

Opio 367

Saint-Guiraud 348

Junas 341

Cucuron 358

Villecroze 376

Grasse 360

Olargues 346

Montpellier 344 345

Rognes 369

Aix-en-Provence 352

Cotignac 357

Lorgues 361

Pégomas 367

Magalas 342

Pézenas 347

Aigues-Morte 336

Ventabren 376

Le Tholonet 374

Correns 357

Saint-Raphaël 373

Bize-Minervois 338

Florensac 341

Rove 370

Cassis 355

La Celle 356

Collobrières 357

Ouveillan 346

Marseillan 343

Agde 336

Marseille 363 364

Hyères 360

Ornaisons 346

Bages 337

LANGUEDOC-ROUSSILLON

La Ciotat 357

Le Pradet 369

Perpignan 346 347

Cornillon 340

Bandol 354

Porquerolles (Ile de) 369

Castillon-du-Gard 339

Saint-Maximin-la-Sainte-Baume 372

Argelès-sur-Mer 336

Toulon 375

Saint-Tropez 374

Banyuls-sur-Mer 337

Lourmarin 361

La Napoule 365

Port-Verdes 347

L'Isle-sur-la-Sorgue 360

Cannes 355

Bonnieux 355

Mougins 365

Saint-Andiol 371

Valbonne 376

Verquières 376

Golfe Juan 359

Maussane-les-Alpilles 364

Antibes 352

Saint-Rémy-de-Provence 373

Saint-Laurent-du-Var 372

Le Pontet-Avignon 368

Nice 366 367

Avignon 353

Saint-Jean-Cap-Ferrat 371

Châteauneuf-du-Pape 356

Menton 364

RESTAURANTS 20 MINUTES FROM THE MOTORWAYS –THE NORTH

Steenvoord 78
Aire-sur-la-Lys 72
Arques 72
Clairmarais 73
Houlle 75
Gravelines 74
Saint-Folquin 77
Blendecques 73
Beutin 73
Wimereux 79
Hardelot-Plage 74
Le Touquet 78 79
Madelaine-sous-Montreuil 75
Inxent 75
A16
Attin 72
A26
Sommery 61
Montreuil 76
Mesnières-en-Bray 58
Sorrus 77
Saint-Martin-Osmonville 60
Hesdin 74
Fort-Mahon 67
Rue 69
Ardouval 52
Abbeville
Quend 68
Doudeville 56
A28
Amiens 64
A29
Les Petites Dalles 58
Aumale 52
Caulières 65
A16
Pont-Audemer 58 59
Campigny 54
HAUTE-NORMANDIE
Le Fossé 56
Honfleur 44 45
Gerberoy 67
Pont-L'Evêque 46
Le Havre
Rouen 60
Agnetz 64
Cormeilles 42
La Bouille 53
Creil
BASSE-NORMANDIE
Crépon 43
A13
Connells 55
Apremont 64
Le Bec-Hellouin 53
Fourges 56
Chantilly 65
Caen 42
Beuvron-en-Auge 41
Lisieux 45
Saint-Pierre-du-Vauvray 61
Coye-la-Fôret 66
Saint-Lô 46
A13
Saint Ouen 83
Savigny 47
Le Bény-Bocage 40
Thury-Harcourt 48
Les Andelys 52
Neuilly 83
Trelly 48
A13
Clécy 42
PARIS 84-131
Villedieu-les-Poêles 49
Vire 49
Versailles 84
Le Mont-Saint-Michel 45
Saint-Quentin-sur-le-Homme 47
Issy-les-Moulineaux 82
Servon 48
Ducey 43
Le Perreux-sur-Marne 83
Dol-de-Bretagne 26
Moissy Cramayel 83
Combourg 25
A84
Neufchâtel-en-Saosnais 168
Chartres 179
A11
Barbizon 82
Châteaubourg 25
St-Georges-le-Gaultier 170
A28
Mezangers 167
Sille-le-Guillaume 173
La Ferté-Bernard 163
Illiers-Combray 182
BRETAGNE
Neau 168
Ste-Suzanne 172
Vibraye 173
A10
Laval 165
A81
Loué 166
Le Mans 166
CENTRE
Olivet 186
Saulges 172
Baule 176
Sable-sur-Sarthe 170
Tavers 188
Marcilly-en-Villette 184
St-Denis d'Anjou 170
A11
La Flèche 163
Blois 177
PAYS DE LA LOIRE
Briollay 161
St-Sylvain d'Anjou 171
A10
Angers 160
Chênehutte-les-Tuffeaux 162
Azay-le-Rideau 176
Vouvray 189
A71
A11
Chemillé 162
Saumur 172 173
Bléré 177
Nantes 167 168
Chinon 181
A85
Saché 187
Montbazon 184
Cholet 163
L'Ile Bouchard 182
A10
Cussay 182
Veuil 189
A71
Levroux 183
Issoudun 182
Naintre 218
Leigné-les-Bois 216
Buzançais 179
Bruère Allichamps 178
Lencloitre 216
A20

16

Itterswiller 149
Osthouse 151
Mittelbergheim 150
Erstein 147
Ottrott 151 152
Obernai 151
Strasbourg 154 155
Marlenheim 150
Mittelhausen 150
Brumath 146
Saverne 154

A25

Arras 72

NORD-PAS-DE-CALAIS

Compiegne
Saint-Jean-
aux-Bois 69

A26

Berry-au-Bac 65

Courcelles-
sur-Vesle 66   Tinqueux 137

PICARDIE

Neuilly-Saint-
Front 68   Saint-Imoges 136   A4

Reims 135 136

Champillon-Bellevue

Vinay
137   Epernay   Châlons-en-
134   Champagne

**ILE-DE-
FRANCE**

A5

A4

A26

**CHAMPAGNE-
ARDENNE**

Fontainebleau 82

Troyes 137

Flagy 82

A5

A31

Thionville 142

Norroy-le-
Veneur 142   A4

Metz 141

LORRAINE

Nancy
141 142   Sarrebourg

St-Nicolas-   Lunéville 141
de-Port

Baerenthal 140

Hinsingen
148

ALSACE   A35

Saverne 154

Thannenkirch 156

Bergheim
146

Le Valtin 143

Gérardmer 140   Illhaeusern
Bas-Rupts 140   148

Xonrupt-Longemer 143

Ribeauvillé 152   Artzenheim 146

Riquewihr 152 153   Hunawir 148

Lapoutroie 149   Zellenbergl 156

Colmar 147   Diefmatten 147

A6

Langres 134

BOURGOGNE

Mailly-le-
Château 197   Nitry 198

L'Isle-sur-
Serein 196

Quarré-les-
Tombes 200   **Dijon** 196

Chavignol 180

Sancerre 188

Vougeot 201   Gevrey-
Chambertin 196

Ladoix-Serrigny 197

Arnay-le-Duc 192   Auvillars-
Saône 192

Beaune 192 193

Chagny 193 194   Saint-Gervais-
Rully 200   en-Vallière 201

Mercurey 198   Courlans 206

Mellecey 197   Chalon-sur-
Saône 194

Nevers 198

A6

A31

A39

**FRANCHE-
COMTE**

Baume-les-
Dames 205   A36   Wihr-au-Val 156

Besançon 205

Amondans
204

Dole 207

Arbois 204

Baume-les-Messieurs 205

Châtillon 206

Rouffach 153
Eguisheim 147

17

RESTAURANTS 20 MINUTES FROM THE MOTORWAYS –THE SOUTH

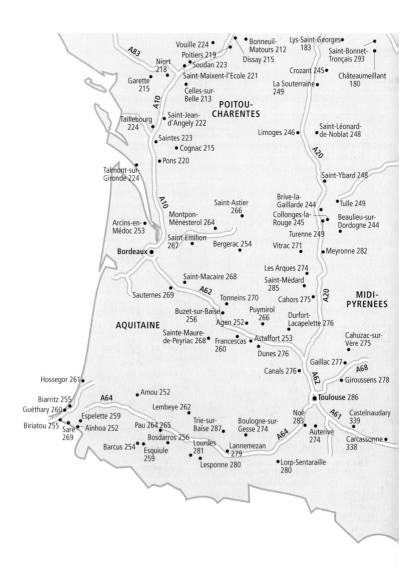

Vouille 224
Bonneuil-Matours 212
Lys-Saint-Georges
183
Saint-Bonnet-Tronçais 293
Poitiers 219
Dissay 215
Niort 218
Soudan 223
Crozant 245
Châteaumeillant 180
Garette 215
Saint-Maixent-l'Ecole 221
La Souterraine 249
Celles-sur-Belle 213
POITOU-CHARENTES
Taillebourg 224
Saint-Jean-d'Angely 222
Limoges 246
Saint-Léonard-de-Noblat 248
Saintes 223
Cognac 215
Pons 220
Talmont-sur-Gironde 224
Saint-Ybard 248
Saint-Astier 266
Brive-la-Gaillarde 244
Tulle 249
Montpon-Ménesterol 264
Collonges-la-Rouge 245
Beaulieu-sur-Dordogne 244
Arcins-en-Médoc 253
Saint-Emilion 267
Bergerac 254
Turenne 249
Vitrac 271
Meyronne 282
Bordeaux
Saint-Macaire 268
Les Arques 274
Saint-Médard 285
Sauternes 269
Tonneins 270
Cahors 275
MIDI-PYRENEES
Buzet-sur-Baïse 256
Puymirol 266
Durfort-Lacapelette 276
AQUITAINE
Agen 252
Cahuzac-sur-Vère 275
Sainte-Maure-de-Peyriac 268
Francescas 260
Astaffort 253
Dunes 276
Gaillac 277
Canals 276
Giroussens 278
Hossegor 261
Amou 252
A68
Biarritz 255
Lembeye 262
Noé 283
Castelnaudary 339
Guéthary 260
A64
Toulouse 286
Espelette 259
Trie-sur-Baïse 287
Boulogne-sur-Gesse 274
Biriatou 255
Aïnhoa 252
Pau 264 265
Auterive 274
Carcassonne 338
Sare 269
Bosdarros 256
Lourdes 281
Lannemezan 279
Barcus 254
Esquiule 259
Lesponne 280
Lorp-Sentaraille 280

A83
A10
A10
A62
A20
A62
A61
A64

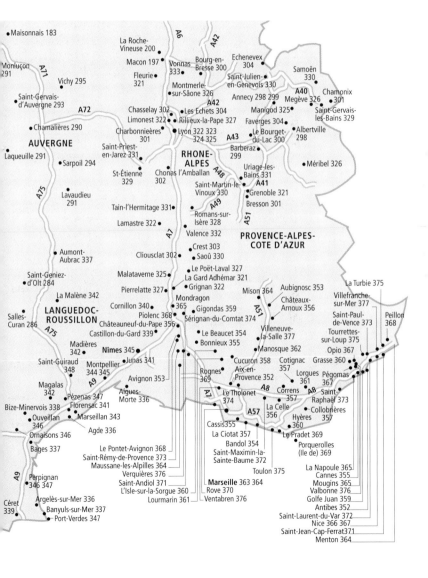

Maisonnais 183

La Roche-Vineuse 200
A6
A42

Macon 197
Vonnas 333
Bourg-en-Bresse 300
Echenevex 304

Monluçon 291
A71

Vichy 295
Fleurie 321
Saint-Julien-en-Genevois 330
Samoën 330

Saint-Gervais-d'Auvergne 293
A72
Montmerle-sur-Saône 326
Annecy 298 299
A40
Mégève 326
Chamonix 301

Chamalières 290
Chasselay 302
Les Echets 304
Manigod 325
Saint-Gervais-les-Bains 329

AUVERGNE
Limonest 322
Rillieux-la-Pape 327
Faverges 304

Laqueuille 291
Charbonnières 301
Lyon 322 323 324 325
A43
Le Bourget-du-Lac 300
Albertville 298

Saint-Priest-en-Jarez 331
RHONE-ALPES
Barberaz 299

Sarpoil 294
St-Étienne 329
Chonas l'Amballan 302
Uriage-les-Bains 331
Méribel 326

A75
Lavaudieu 291
Saint-Martin-le-Vinoux 330
A41
Grenoble 321

Tain-l'Hermitage 331
A49
Bresson 301

Lamastre 322
A7
Romans-sur-Isère 328
A51

Valence 332
PROVENCE-ALPES-COTE D'AZUR

Aumont-Aubrac 337
Crest 303

Cliousclat 302
Saoû 330

Saint-Geniez-d'Olt 284
Malataverne 325
Le Poët-Laval 327
La Gard Adhémar 321
La Turbie 375

La Malène 342
Pierrelatte 327
Grignan 322
Mison 364
Aubignosc 353
Villefranche-sur-Mer 377

LANGUEDOC-ROUSSILLON
Cornillon 340
Mondragon 365
Gigondas 359
A51
Châteaux-Arnoux 356
Saint-Paul-de-Vence 373
Peillon 368

Salles-Curan 286
A75
Piolenc 368
Sérignan-du-Comtat 374
Villeneuve-la-Salle 377
Tourrettes-sur-Loup 375

Châteauneuf-du-Pape 356
Le Beaucet 354
Opio 367

Madières 342
Castillon-du-Gard 339
Bonnieux 355
Manosque 362
Grasse 360

Nîmes 345
Junas 341
Cucuron 358
Cotignac 357
Pégomas 367

Saint-Guiraud 348
Montpellier 344 345
Rognes 365
Aix-en-Provence 352
Lorgues 361

Magalas 342
Avignon 353
A7
Correns
A8
Saint-Raphaël 373

Bize-Minervois 338
Aigues-Morte 336
Le Tholonet 374
La Celle 356
Collobrières 357

Pézenas 347
Florensac 341
A57
Hyères 357

Ouveillan 346
Marseillan 343
Cassis 355
360

Ornaisons 346
Agde 336
La Ciotat 357
Le Pradet 369

Bages 337
Le Pontet-Avignon 368
Bandol 354
Porquerolles (Ile de) 369

Saint-Rémy-de-Provence 373
Saint-Maximin-la-Sainte-Baume 372
La Napoule 365

Maussane-les-Alpilles 364
Toulon 375
Cannes 355

Verquières 376
Mougins 365

A9
Perpignan 346 347
Saint-Andiol 371
Marseille 363 364
Valbonne 376

L'Isle-sur-la-Sorgue 360
Rove 370
Golfe Juan 359

Céret 339
Argelès-sur-Mer 336
Lourmarin 361
Ventabren 376
Antibes 352

Banyuls-sur-Mer 337
Saint-Laurent-du-Var 372

Port-Verdes 347
Nice 366 367

Saint-Jean-Cap-Ferrat 371

Menton 364

MENU DECODER

Abats	offal
Aiglefin, aigrefin, eglefin	haddock
Ail	garlic
Airelles	cranberries, whortleberries, bilberries
Allache	large sardine
Alsacienne, à la	with choucroute, ham and frankfurter sausages
Ananas	pineapple
Andouillettes	small chitterling sausages, usually served hot with mustard
Ange de mer, angelot	angel fish, resembling skate
Anguille	freshwater eel
Araignée de mer	spider crab
Arapède	limpet
Arlésienne à l'	fish or meat with tomatoes, onions and olives
Armoricaine à l'	fish or lobster with brandy, white wine, herbs, tomatoes and onions
Baie de ronce	blackberry
Bar, badèche, cernier, bézuque, loup de mer	sea bass
Barbue	brill
Baudroie	monkfish
Bécasse, bécasseau	woodcock
Bécassine	snipe
Belon	breton oyster
Bergère, à la	chicken or meat with ham, mushrooms, onions and potatoes
Betterave	beetroot
Bonite	bonito fish, resembling tuna
Bordelaise, à la	in red wine sauce with shallots, tarragon and bone marrow
Boudin noir	black pudding
Bouillabaisse	mediterranean fish stew
Boulangère, à la	oven baked, with potatoes
Boule de neige	sponge or ice-cream covered with whipped cream
Bourgeoise, à la	braised meat or chicken with bacon, carrots and onions
Bourride	white fish stew
Brandade de morue	dried salt cod mousse
Bretonne, à la	in onion sauce with haricot beans
Bretonneau	turbot
Brochet	pike
Brochet de mer	barracuda
Broufado	beef stew with vinegar, capers and anchovies
Cabillaud	cod
Caille, cailleteau	quail
Camarguaise, à la	with tomatoes, garlic, herbs, orange peel olives and wine or brandy
Canard, caneton, canardeau	duck
	cranberry
Cardeau, celan	plaice
Carrelet	pork, mutton or lamb, cooked with haricot beans, bacon and
Cassoulet	sausage
Cèpe	wild boletus mushroom
Cervelas	smoked pork sausage with garlic
Cervelle	brain
Chasseur	with wine, mushrooms and shallots
Chèvre	goat
Chevreuil	venison
Chicon	chicory
Chou-navet	swede
Ciboule	spring onion
Citrouille	pumpkin
Civet	thick meat stew, thickened with blood
Clafoutis	baked cherry batter pudding
Colin	hake
Coquillages	shellfish
Coquille Saint-Jacques	scallops
Cotriade	fish stew with onions, potatoes and cream
Couissinet	cranberry
Crème Anglaise	egg custard
Crevette	shrimp, prawn
Croque Monsieur	toasted ham and cheese sandwich
Crudités	raw vegetables
Cuisseau	leg of veal
Cuisses de grenouille	frogs' legs

Darne	thick fish steak
Daube	braised meat in red wine, herbs, carrots and onions
Daurade, dorade	sea bream
Dieppoise, à la	fish, often sole with shellfish, in white wine sauce
Dinde	turkey
Ecrevisse	crayfish
Encornet	squid
Espadon	swordfish
Esquinade	spider crab
Estouffade	pot-roasted meat
Faisan, faisandeau	pheasant
Faux-filet	sirloin steak
Fermiére, à la	meat or chicken braised with vegetables
Flétan	halibut
Galantine	loaf-shaped chopped meat, fish or vegetables set in natural jelly
Galette	breton buckwheat pancake
Garbure	soup with root vegetables and bacon
Gibier	game
Gigot	leg of lamb
Grecque, à la	mushrooms, aubergines and other vegetables poached in oil and herbs
Grenade	pomegranate
Groseille	redcurrant
Hareng	herring
Homard	lobster
Huître	oyster
Langue	tongue
Lièvre	hare
Lotte de mer, baudroie	monkfish
Lyonnaise, à la	with onions
Maquereau	mackerel
Merlan	whiting
Merluche	hake
Mode, à la	marinated meat braised in wine with bacon, calf's foot and vegetables
Mouclade	mussel stew
Myrtille	bilberry
Palombe	woodpigeon
Palourde	clam or cockle
Pamplemousse	grapefruit
Perdreau	partridge
Persil	parsley
Pintade	guinea fowl
Pipérade	scrambled egg with red peppers, onions and tomatoes
Plie	plaice
Pochade	freshwater fish stew with carrots
Poireau	leek
Potirol	pumpkin
Poulpe	octopus
Pouvron	sweet pepper
Praire	clam
Prune	plum
Pruneau	prune
Quenelle	poached, chopped fish or white meat, like dumplings
Ramereau, ramier	woodpigeon
Rave	turnip
Reine, à la	with chicken
Rillettes	shredded, potted meat
Ris	lamb or veal sweetbreads
Rognon	kidney
Rouget	red mullet
Salmis	game casserole
Sanglier	wild boar
Soupe au pistou	vegetable soup with basil paste
Tarte Tatin	upside down apple pie
Thon	tuna
Truffado	potatoes with garlic, bacon and cheese
Veau	veal
Vigneron, à la	in wine sauce, with grapes

BRETAGNE

The westernmost region of France pushes into the windswept Atlantic like a giant peninsula, with 750 miles (1,200 km) of dramatic coastline. The *département* of Finistère is in the extreme west and includes Brest and Quimper, while Côtes-d'Armor in the centre includes the lovely Côte du Granit Rose and Saint-Brieuc. Ile-et-Vilaine stretches east as far as Mont-Saint-Michel (just in Normandy), incorporating Saint-Malo, Dinard and the regional capital, Rennes. To the south-east, Morbihan includes the lovely bay of the same name, and the town of Vannes. The *département* of Loire-Atlantique, including Nantes and the Parc Naturel de Brièr, though always considered Breton, is nowadays part of the Pays de la Loire region.

Golfe de St-Malo

Saint-Briac-sur-Mer 35 36

St-Malo 36

● Cancale 24

● Erquy 26

La Gouesnière 27

N176

BASSE-
NORMANDIE

D768

● Lamballe 28 29

N176

Dol-de-
Bretagne 26

D155

● Jugon-les-Lacs 28

D766

● Combourg 25

N164

A84

N137

N12

D178

N12

Rennes 34 ●

N157

Néant-
sur-Yvel 31

D766

● Concoret 26

N24

Châteaubourg
25

D163

Josselin 28

N137

● Plumelec 32

D121

N165

La Roche-
Bernard 34

PAYS DE
LA LOIRE

Bénodet
◆ La Croisette €€

*3 avenue de l'Odet, 29950 Bénodet,
Finistère*
Tel 02 98 57 06 39 Fax 02 98 57 18 94

Monsieur Texia, the proprietor of this modern blue and white marina restaurant with panoramic views over the sea, specialises – naturally enough – in sea food – *poissons, fruits de mer, crustaces* – as well as *grillades*. You might indulge in a steaming *bouillabaisse* or crustaceans served, Breton fashion, with plenty of white bread and accompanying sauces. The *fruits de mer* will be washed down with a crisp white Bordeaux or Muscadet.

CLOSED never
CARDS AE, DC, MC, V

Brest
◆ Amour de Pomme de Terre € Fr

*23 rue des Halles-Saint-Louis, 29200 Brest,
Finistère*
Tel 02 98 43 48 51 Fax 02 98 43 61 88

Afficionados of the king of vegetables won't be able to resist. This jolly, tightly packed bistro behind the covered market, imbued with the humourous personality of its owner, is devoted to the potato – solely to the 'samba' variety in fact. You wouldn't believe what you can do with a potato until you come here, and you needn't miss out on other ingredients, as it comes with cheese, meat, fish and shellfish and more.

CLOSED Christmas, New Year
CARDS MC, V

Brest
◆ Le Nouveau Rossini
€€€

*22 rue Commandant Drogou, 29200 Brest,
Finistère*
Tel 02 98 47 90 00 Fax 02 98 47 90 00

Annie and Maurice have run this lovely restaurant, which opens on to delightful grounds, since 1975 and pride themselves on their creative cuisine and a genuinely warm welcome. As a result, an atmosphere of chic, tranquillity and gentle *bonhomie* pervades in this listed granite building in the heart of Brest, facing the church. Specialities include salad of asparagus and artichokes prepared in their special way, but fish and seafood predominate – with happy results.

❝ I had the galette of sea fish flavoured with rosemary – delicious ❞

CLOSED Sun dinner, Mon; mid-Mar, late Aug
CARDS AE, MC, V

Cancale
◆ Continental € – €€ Fr

*4 quai Albert-Thomas, port de la Houle,
35260 Cancale, Ile-et-Vilaine*
Tel 02 99 89 60 16 Fax 02 99 89 69 58

There are plenty of restaurants to choose from in Cancale, famous for its oysters, including the romantic, top-flight *relais gourmande* of chef Olivier Roellinger at Maisons de Bricourt (which incorporates a hotel, Les Rimains). The Continental is a fine period residence situated on the old harbour of La Houle, with a bustling backdrop of oyster boats coming and going and people passing by. In a calm atmosphere, amidst panoramic views, you can enjoy excellent Breton seafood, including the local fish stew, *cotriade*, as well as *ragoût de homard* and *nage de Saint-Pierre au cidre et légumes*. Sweet crêpes appear among the desserts, as well as an excellent *gratin* of figs in season.

CLOSED Mon, Tue (except dinner Jul, Aug); mid-Nov to mid-Mar
CARDS AE, DC, MC, V

Carantec
◆ Le Cabestan
€ – €€ Fr

7 rue du Port, Carantec, 29660 Finistère
Tel 02 98 67 01 87 Fax 02 98 67 90 49

Here is a quaint little restaurant facing the sea in the old port of Carantec. It has been in the hands of the same proprietor, M. Godec, full of good cheer, for more than thirty years. The menus include traditional dishes as well as more electic ones, and diners can enjoy a variety of seafood dishes (including *à la Thailandais*) as well as meat dishes. Michelin award a 'Bib Gourmand'. Next door is La Cambuse – under the same management – a lively bar/brasserie with loud music.

CLOSED Mon Sep-Jun, Tue; Nov to mid-Dec
CARDS MC, V

Caurel
◆ Beau Rivage € – €€€

Lac de Guerlédan, 22530 Caurel, Côtes d'Armor
Tel 02 96 28 52 15 Fax 02 96 26 01 16

Driving along the N164 you come across the huge Lac de Guerlédan, in fact a chain of lakes with a barrage that can be walked across. With its wooded banks, its boat trips, watersports, nature walks and the nearby ruins of Abbaye de Bon Repos this is a local beauty spot that attracts plenty of vistors, particularly families. Along its shores are many little restaurants, pizzerias, crêperies and stopping places. Best bet for a decent meal is the floating Beau Rivage, part of a small, plain but comfortable hotel run by the Boscher family since 1971.

CLOSED Sun, Mon dinner, Tue; mid to late Oct, late Feb
CARDS MC, V

Châteaubourg
◆ Ar Milin' €€

30 rue de Paris, 35220 Châteaubourg, Ile-et-Vilaine
Tel 02 99 0030 91 Fax 02 99 00 37 56

Ar Milin' means 'mill' in Breton, and this hotel and restaurant, a former mill on the banks of the river Vilaine makes a lovely setting, in its own wooded park which includes an arboretum. These are delightful surroundings in which to spend a whole day or perhaps a weekend, enhanced by the culinary triumphs of M. Burel. Regional specialities are offered alongside imaginative dishes plush a wonderful array of sweets.

❝ Magical...The food was a delight on the eye as well as the stomach ❞

CLOSED Sun dinner winter; mid-Dec to mid-Jan
CARDS AE, DC, MC, V

Combourg
◆ Hôtel du Château

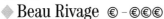

€ – €€€

1 place Chateaubriand, 352701 Combourg, Ile-et-Vilaine
Tel 02 99 73 00 38 Fax 02 99 73 25 79

At the foot of the prestigious building – a 14th to 15thC fortress, remodelled in Romantic style in the late 19th century – which was the childhood home of the writer Chateaubriand, on the shores of Lac Tranquille, this hotel and restaurant has views over the château, gardens and lake. Christian, the chef and host, prepares a range of mouthwatering dishes, which combine specialities from sea and land. Half way between Rennes and Dinan, this makes a good place to stop for lunch if you are exploring the Emerald Coast and its interior.

CLOSED Sun dinner except Jul, Aug, Mon lunch, Mon dinner Oct-Apr; mid-Apr, mid-Dec to mid-Jan
CARDS AE, DC, MC, V

Concarneau
◆ Chez Armande €€ Fr

15 avenue Docteur-Nicolas, 29900 Finistère
Tel 02 98 97 00 76 Fax 02 99 97 00 76

In a great position facing Concarneau's delightful Ville Close, a tiny harbour island enclosed by walls, Chez Armande is the first choice for locals, with food that's refreshingly above expectations. The local fish stew, *cotriade*, is the speciality, but there are other excellent choices on the *carte*, such as a *salade de langoustines*, and the fixed priced menu is a good bet too. Michelin awards Armande a Bib Gourmand. Predominantly fish, as you would expect.

❝ This is our favourite place in Concarneau. The food can be very good ❞

CLOSED Tue (except Jul, Aug), Wed; last week Aug, mid-Dec to Jan, mid-Feb to Mar
CARDS AE, MC, V

Concoret
◆ Chez Maxime € – €€ Fr

place de l'Eglise, 56430 Concoret,
Morbihan
Tel 02 97 22 63 04 Fax 02 97 22 67 12

This delightful, ivy-covered building is a hotel and restaurant from where diners look out on to the equally pleasing church in a village of red stone and slate buildings. East of Mauron and north-east of Ploermel, the village stands on the doorstep of the Fôret de Brocéliande, steeped in Arthurian legend. Tuck into a seafood platter to start, followed perhaps by venison, or the excellent local pork or veal. The puddings are not to be missed, especially the seasonal fruit soufflé, which must be ordered half an hour in advance.

❛ Very picturesque, with a wonderful
ambience ❜

Closed Tue dinner, Wed winter; early to mid-Jul
Cards AE, MC, V

Our price bands
Rather than giving actual prices (which are prone to change) we indicate the cost of a three-course meal for one person, without wine, by means of price bands. They are as follows: € under 30 euros €€ 30-50 euros €€€ over 50 euros. Where we give more than one price band, for example €– €€€, this indicates that in that restaurant a meal can be had at a range of prices. As well as the cost of *prix fixe* menus, our price bands also take into account the cost of an average selection from the *à la carte* menu.

Dol-de-Bretagne
◆ La Bresche Arthur €

36 boulevard Deminiac, 35120 Dol-de-Bretagne, Ile-et-Vilaine
Tel 02 99 48 01 44 Fax 02 99 48 16 32

Just off the centre of this lovely old town with its quaint shops and immense cathedral, the hotel and restaurant Bresche Arthur has been in the hands of chef Philippe Martel and his wife since 1989. The three well-priced menus and the à la carte

list are somewhat limited in scope, tending towards fish and shellfish (try the *mouclade de moules de bouchots de la Baie du Mont-Saint-Michel*), with a couple of chicken and lamb dishes as alternatives, or perhaps pigeon with blackcurrent and ginger), and the desserts, though again limited, are excellent, especially the *crème brûlée à la vanille, caramélisée à la cassonade*.

Closed Sun dinner, Mon winter; Jan
Cards AE, MC, V

Erquy
◆ Beauséjour €

21 rue de la Corniche, 22430 Erquy, Côtes-d'Armor
Tel 02 96 72 30 39 Fax 02 96 72 16 30

In a lovely traditional building, full of character, M. Thibault has been dispensing typical Breton hospitality for more than 30 years. Regular visitors to this beautiful part of Brittany make a point of returning to the Hôtel Beauséjour and its restaurant year after year to enjoy the wonderful view over the sea and the speciality of the house, *coquilles Saint Jacques*.

Closed Sun dinner, Mon mid-Sep to mid-Jun; mid-Dec to mid-Jan
Cards MC, V

Fr French regional or classical French dishes on menu.

Le Faouët
◆ Au Pied de Sainte-Baube €

Le Grand Pont, 56320 Le Faouët, Morbihan
Tel 02 97 23 20 84

On the roadside between Peiziac and Le Faouët, this tiny bar is reminiscent of a quaint Cornish establishment. The host, Karim Hassouna, is unusual: he speaks several languages and loves to chat to his customers and offer them warm hospitality. He says cooking is an art that one has to love as he does. He prepares all his recipes in the traditional manner, eschewing short cuts and using home-made stocks to enhance their flavour. They include delicious potatoes baked with cheese, and original North African dishes. He will also offer you the use of his hookah!

Closed Mon
Cards MC, V

Fouesnant
◆ La Cale ⓔ **Fr**

34 rue Glénan, 29170 Finistère
Tel 02 98 94 17 18 Fax 98 94 43 66

This is a simple hotel and restaurant, typically Breton, where you can enjoy honest local cooking. The white, slate-roofed house with flowers and veranda in front stands just a short walk back from the port and beaches, with bedrooms overlooking the sea. The famous local cider is on offer.

Closed closed Wed winter
Cards MC, V

Our price bands
ⓔ under 30 euros ⓔⓔ 30-50 Euros
ⓔⓔⓔ over 50 euros for a menu

La Gouesnière
◆ Château de Bonaban
ⓔⓔ

rue Alfred de Folliny, 35350 La
Gouesnière, Ile-et-Vilaine
Tel 02 99 58 24 50 Fax 02 99 58 24 50

In the heart of Malouin country, with a fine park bordering the bay of Cancale, this hotel is a beautifully restored 17thC château complete with chapel and magnificent staircase. Here you can choose from an excellent gourmet menu that might include stuffed lamb and salmon, followed by a *crème brulée vanille Bonaban*. Later you could regain your appetite by exploring the park with its magnificent sea views and rural atmosphere: fishing, tennis, walking and cycling are available.

Closed phone for details
Cards AE, MC, V

Gourin
◆ Crêperie du Moulin
ⓔ – ⓔⓔ

Moulin de Kerbiquet, 56110 Gourin,
Morbihan
Tel 02 97 23 64 81

Denise Massé is the chef, and her husband the man about the house. They bought this old mill eight years ago, and have been restoring it themselves ever since. In the rustic dining room, or at simple tables on the terrace by the river (or as takeaway) Denise offers crêpes with all types of fillings (they are not *galettes*, she stresses, but the type of crêpes specific to her area). "We do not want to be a large business," she says, "just enough to keep us going and enable us to continue the restoration of this lovely old building". Well signposted.

Closed phone for details
Cards MC, V

● *Crêperies worth seeking out in Morbihan include l'Hermine at Crach (tel 02 97 30 01 17); La Chaloupe at Le Palais on Belle-Ile (tel 02 97 31 88 27); La Campagnarde at Pontivy (tel 02 97 35 23 07); La Duchesse Anne at Saint-Malo (tel 02 97 30 49 33); and Steredenn at Saint-Thégonnec (tel 02 98 79 43 34)*

Ile-de-Groix
◆ Hôtel de la Marine ⓔ

7 rue du Général-de-Gaulle, 56590 Ile-de-Groix, Morbihan
Tel 02 97 86 80 05 Fax 02 97 86 56 37

A 45-minute ferry ride (or 30 minutes by taxi boat) from Lorient, Enez or Groac'h brings you to this sunny island, a flat undulating plateau girdled by cliffs rising from the sea. Situated high above the port, the neat little Hôtel de la Marine is a characterful two-star establishment with a cosy, antique-filled interior. The pretty dining room has stone walls and a large fireplace, pictures, attractive pottery and a shell-encrusted clock. Or you can eat on the sunny terrace, shaded by the oldest tree on the island. Either way, the food should not disappoint and might include fish and shellfish *couscous*, cod *parmentier* with kidney beans, and *crème brulée* with *marrons glacés*, all at extremely reasonable prices.

CLOSED phone for details
CARDS MC, V

Josselin
◆ Hôtel du Château
€ – €€

1 rue Général-de-
Gaulle, 56120 Josselin, Morbihan
Tel 02 97 22 20 11 Fax 02 97 22 34 09

Accessed from behind Josselin's splendid château (home of the Ducs de Rohan since the 13th century) and situated on a little bridge, the attractive dining room of this hotel, run by Claire and Bernard Bonimeux, overlooks the Nantes/Brest canal and the château. If you dine here on Bastille Day, you can watch an impressive firework display as you eat. The *boeuf Wellington* is excellent, the wine list is varied, and the puddings are mouthwatering: you can even plump for an *assiette* of them, a small piece of several. Good cheeses too.

❛ You can eat relatively cheaply here; the middle-priced menus offer the best value, with an excellent choice of dishes ❜

CLOSED Christmas, New Year; Feb
CARDS AE, MC, V

Jugon-les-Lacs
◆ L'Ecu
€ – €€

place du Martray, 22270 Jugon-les-Lacs,
Côtes-d'Armor
Tel 02 96 31 61 41

In the heart of this little 'Cité de Charactère' situated on the N176 between Dinan and Lamballe, L'Ecu is a pretty *auberge* offering a wide selection on its menus, with starters that include her-

rings and oysters. The traditional cuisine matches the cosy and attractive rustic decoration of the dining room. Main courses include leg of lamb, paella, rabbit and a good *boeuf Bourguignone*. The small selection of wines includes Gamay, and there are good cheeses and puddings.

❛ Charming little place, with a warm ambience ❜

CLOSED Mon
CARDS MC, V

Kernascléden
◆ Orée du Bois € – €€ Fr

Kerchopine, 56540 Kernascléden,
Morbihan
Tel 02 97 51 61 51

The chic and charming *patronne* (who is also a dressmaker specialising in silk) of this endearing little establishment has owned the building since 1975, later converting part of it into a bar and restaurant when she married a professional cook. The beamed, tile-floored restaurant, with vases of fresh flowers, is neat and pleasing to the eye, and the chef's home cooking, using local produce from land and water, is good value for money.

❛ Good foie gras and smoked duck and cheeses'..."We had strawberries from their garden which were succulent and tasty ❜

CLOSED Wed
CARDS MC, V

Lamballe
◆ Manoir de la Ville Gourio € – €€€

22400 Lamballe, Côtes-d'Armor
Tel 02 96 31 02 05 Fax 02 96 32 75 68

In a local beauty spot just 2 miles (4 km) from the sea and the coast of Penthièvre, this rural restaurant set in a 17thC manor house offers a choice of simple dishes – grilled meats, fish and pizzas – as well as more traditional ones. Conviviality and tranquility are the keywords, and golfers especially will be drawn: it has a nine-hole golf course. The *patronne*, Mme Guihot, has been running the place for nearly 25 years and has recently added hotel facilities.

CLOSED winter – phone for details
CARDS AE, MC, V

Lamballe
◆ Philippe Le Mercier €

10 rue Saint-Martin, 22400 Lamballe,
Côtes-d'Armor
Tel 02 96 31 02 05

Not a restaurant, but such a rare find in Brittany – a place where one can have a cup of tea or coffee and a snack (and what a snack) – that we felt compelled to include it. Philippe Le Mercier's lovely tea-shop offers an extensive and mouthwatering array of *pâtisserie*, chocolates and breads: mousses, *charlottes, bavaroises, tartes* and *tartelettes*, croissants, quiches, biscuits and so on. What to choose? The *charlotte aux amandes*, perhaps – utterly delicious. There is another branch of this excellent *pâtissier, chocolatier* and *boulanger* in Lamballe's place du Marché.

CLOSED public holidays
CARDS MC, V

Please send us reports
A guide such as this thrives on reader's reports. If you send us five usable reports, we will send you a free copy of any title in our *Charming Small Hotel Guides* series (see page 241 for France titles in the series).

The five reports should contain at least two new restaurants; the rest can be comments on restaurants already in the guide.
1 Tell us about your experiences in restaurants already in this guide.
2 Send us new reports. New reports should give the following information:
- **Region** – City, town, village or nearest village.
- **Name of restaurant** – Please double check the spelling, it's surprisingly easy to make a mistake.
- **Address** – including *département*
- **Telephone number** – plus fax and e-mail if available. Double check this information.
- **Objective description** – Try to explain simply why it should be in the guide. Remember that the guide is very selective - our entries are those one-in-five places that combine
- **interesting food with**
- **character and charm, in the building, the setting or both.**
The guide hates tourist traps, and pretentious, dressed-up food. We like places where the French go.

We favour places in the lower and middle price bands but there are plenty of expensive places that have our qualities, and we list those too.
- **Diner's comments** – These should be short, personal comments on features that strike you. They can be your comments, or others'.
- **Closing times**
- **Credit cards accepted**
Don' t forget to date your report and add your name and address.
Send reports to Charming Restaurant Guides, Duncan Petersen Publishing, 31 Ceylon Road, London W14 0PY.

Lanvenegen
◆ Auberge de Kérizac
€ Fr

route Le Faouët-Scaër, 56320 Lanvenegen,
Morbihan
Tel 02 97 34 44 57 Fax 02 97 34 44 57

Up hill and down dale to this picturesque converted farm (with outbuildings now serving as *gîtes*) run by the welcoming and helpful Le Meur family. The cuisine is carefully presented *à la mode*, but its roots are traditional, and the chef prides himself on using only local produce, including salads and vegetables from his own garden. His annual certificates proclaiming that this is a Restaurant du Terroir are proudly displayed. On the menu at the Auberge you might find lamb cooked in red wine and served (most unusually in France) with baked jacket potatoes, courgettes, baked tomatoes with a crunchy garlic topping and an excellent *crème caramel maison* to follow. Specialities of the house include *salade d'andouille chaude, jambon braisé, émincé de poulet à la bière Bretonne, foie gras maison*, and *terrine maison*.

CLOSED Mon summer, Mon to Fri winter
CARDS none

Locquirec
◆ Grand Hôtel des Bains
€€ – €€€

*15 bis rue Eglise, 29241 Locquirec,
Finistère
Tel 02 98 67 41 02 Fax 02 98 67 44 60*

The special feature of this imposing Belle Epoque hotel are the gardens and terraces that run down to the sea between the Côte Sauvage and Côte de Granit Rose at the characterful little port of Locquirec. Recently restored, the hotel features a balneotherapy health spa, heated salt water swimming pool, steam baths and Jacuzzis. The cooking in the spacious, rather grand dining room with picture windows overlooking the sea is similarly health-oriented. The ingredients (seafood and vegetables predominate) are organic wherever possible, and the carefully presented dishes are cooked to a high standard. Excellent service.

CLOSED lunch Mon-Fri in winter; mid-Jan to mid-Feb
CARDS AE, DC, MC, V

Please send us reports
A guide such as this thrives on reader's reports. If you send us five usable reports, we will send you a free copy of any title in our *Charming Small Hotel Guides* series (see page 241 for France titles in the series).
   The five reports should contain at least two new restaurants; the balance can be comments on restaurants already in the guide. **Send reports to** Charming Restaurant Guides, Duncan Petersen Ltd, 31 Ceylon Rd, London W14 0PY.

Lorient
◆ Le Pic € – €€   Fr

*2 boulevard Franchet-d'Esperey, Morbihan
Tel 02 97 21 18 29 Fax 02 97 21 92 64*

This simple bistro – or rather wine bar – is known primarily for its extraordinary

cellar of more than 15,000 bottles. The patron, Pierre Le Bourhis, is an award-winning connoisseur and his wines are drawn from all over France. To accompany them, bistro-type dishes, such as *pied de porc* stuffed with oxtail, sautéed veal kidneys and cod with *aïoli*, are available.

CLOSED Sat lunch, Sun
CARDS MC, V

Moëlan-sur-Mer
◆ Les Moulins du Duc
€€ – €€€

*29350 Moëlan-sur-Mer, Finistère
Tel 02 98 96 52 52 Fax 02 98 96 52 53*

In the wooded hills of Finistère, just above the lowest tidal reaches of the Belon, this is an old mill that is still in the food business, but has rocketed upmarket since it became a restaurant, with Thierry Quilfen, who started off as head chef, now the owner as well. You arrive to find manicured gardens around a small lake and apparently no building big enough to house a restaurant, let alone a 27-room hotel. The mill is below the dam that traps the water that used to turn its grindstone, and from a small cottage-like entrance perched on top of the dam, the mill expands downwards and outwards in an almost extra-dimensional way. At the lowest level, almost in the river (with big sliding windows open in summer) you can dine very seriously at the pink linen-covered tables. M. Quilfen majors, not surprisingly given its location near the coast, on seafood in sophisticated dishes such as *moelleux de crabe au millefeuille d'artichaut* and *blanc de chapon lardé cuit au bouillon et parfumé au miel*, but meat dishes are also available, and tempting desserts.

CLOSED Mon lunch, Tue lunch May-Sep; Sun dinner, Mon Sep-May; mid-Nov to mid-Dec, Jan-Mar
CARDS AE, DC, MC, V

Morlaix
◆ Bistro des Bains Douches €

*45 allée du Poan-Ben, 29600 Morlaix,
Finistère
Tel 02 98 63 83 83*

Generations of Morlaisiens and their visitors have taken advantage of the pure waters of these town centre 'shower baths'. The building's façade is crowned in glass, which bathes the place in light, showing off the green and white tiles inside to advantage. A charming bridge over the river gives entry to the restaurant – in the style of a Parisian *bistrot* – from the Allée du Poan-Ben. Chef-patron Tony Pilon changes the *menu du jour* regularly, and accompanying wines are usefully offered by the glass as well as by the bottle.

CLOSED Sun, Mon
CARDS MC, V

Néant-sur-Yvel
◆ Auberge de la Table Ronde € Fr

56430 Néant-sur-Yvel, Morbihan
Tel 02 97 93 03 96 Fax 02 97 93 05 26

This authentic *auberge* in the centre of an attractive old village just off the D766 between Mauron and Ploërmel has been in the same family since 1895, passing through four generations and resting, at present, with Marie-Madeleine and Philippe Morice. Photographs from every generation show that few changes – apart from a less severe façade added mid-century – have taken place over the years. Just to the left of the main door is the long, beamed dining room, while the bedrooms above are basic. The ambience, and the excellence of the home-cooking – including a delicious *confit de porc* – is not in doubt. Menus are well presented and the food is carefully prepared; vegetables are served with imagination.

CLOSED Mon; Sun dinner Sep-Jun; mid-Sep, mid-Jan to mid-Feb
CARDS MC, V

Paimpol
◆ Le Barbu € - €€

Pointe de l'Arcouest, 22620 Ploubazlanec, Paimpol, Côtes d'Armor
Tel 02 96 55 86 98 Fax 02 96 55 73 87

The headland of l'Arcouest juts out into the sea facing the Ile de Bréhat – island of flowers and pink rocks. Here, with its feet in the water, nestles the hotel-restaurant Le Barbu, an institution since 1892 when the family Barbu created the bar and restaurant (the hotel was added in 1920). Today, Mme Dimeglio offers *homard sauce Barbu* as well as grilled cutlets and crustaceans of all sorts. This is a tourist trap – each year more than 2,000 visitors pass through to visit the Ile de Bréhat – but a good one, where you can relax and contemplate the breathtaking panorama of the Bay of Launay.

❨ Worth a visit for the sheer beauty of the place ❩

CLOSED mid-Nov to Mar
CARDS AE, MC, V

Paimpol
◆ Le Repaire de Kerroc'h €€

29 quai Morand, 22500 Paimpol, Côtes-d'Armor
Tel 02 96 20 50 13 Fax 02 96 22 07 46

Built at the end of the 18th century by Corouge Kersau, a famous local corsair, this attractive, practical hotel looks out over Paimpol's bustling yacht marina. The flagged ground floor is mostly given up to eating and drinking. At one end there is a fine cosy restaurant that spills out towards the harbour in summer. Oysters, lobster, *coquilles*, salmon, pork and veal all put in an appearance somewhere on the menu, deftly treated in M. Trebaol's kitchen and well presented by friendly staff. The wine list is extensive but sensibly includes a fine selection of modestly priced wines (reds from Graves and the Loire amongst them). There is also a small bistro at the other end of the hotel, open for lunch and dinner and offering excellent value on a short menu.

CLOSED never
CARDS MC, V

Penmarc'h
◆ Le Doris €€ Fr

Port de Kérity, 29760 Penmarc'h, Finistère
Tel 02 98 56 60 92 Fax 02 98 58 58 16

This little harbour-front restaurant, run by a local fishing family, has an excellent reputation for simple, traditional fish and seafood, serving it absolutely fresh, perhaps plainly grilled, or *en brochette*, or with *beurre blanc*, or to a local recipe. There are meat dishes too, such as lamb and duck breast. Excellent spot, popular with locals.

CLOSED Wed winter
CARDS MC, V

Perros-Guirec
◆ Le Feux des Iles €€ – €€€

53 boulevard Clemenceau, 22700 Perros-Guirec, Côtes-d'Armor
Tel 02 96 23 22 94 Fax 02 96 91 07 30

Perched on the heights of the Perros-Guirec coast road, this hotel and restaurant enjoys a privileged and panoramic location. Dating from the 1930s, the stone-built house faces the ocean. which opens out beyond well-tended grounds. From balconies, terraces and picture windows, guests can watch the changing shapes and colours of the sea. M. Le Roux, the chef, relies on the best of local produce: freshly caught fish and shellfish.

❢ Good food at reasonable prices in a spectacular setting ❢

CLOSED phone for details
CARDS AE, DC, MC, V

Perros-Guirec
◆ Le Manoir du Sphinx
€€€

chemin de la Messe, 22700 Perros-Guirec, Côtes-d'Armor
Tel 02 96 23 25 42 Fax 02 96 91 26 13

On the shoulder of the steep headland that sets it well apart from the bars and nightlife of Perros-Guirec, this well-appointed hotel (nothing 'olde worlde' about it; furniture and fittings are modern and in good repair) is reached by a small seaside lane and looks out across the bay of Tristignel. The deeply comfortable, well-polished restaurant, dressed in pale blue linen and with the emphasis on peace and quiet, is the setting for patron M. Le Verge's cooking,

which offers mainly seafood and fish dishes.

CLOSED Mon, Fri lunch; Sun dinner winter; early Jan-Feb
CARDS AE, MC, V

---

charmingsmallhotels.co.uk
Visit Duncan Petersen's travel website, the best online search tool for places to stay that combine character and charm. Currently features Britain, France, Italy and Ireland, with other destinations being continuously added.

Plougonvelin
◆ Hostellerie Saint-Mathieu €€ – €€€

Pointe-Saint-Mathieu, 29217 Plougonvelin, Finistère
Tel 02 98 89 00 19 Fax 02 98 89 15 68

Here is another exceptional setting in which to enjoy a meal. The *hostellerie* stands between a beacon and the stone ruins of the Abbaye Saint-Mathieu on this headland near Brest, surrounded by the unpredictable sea, with views across to the Ile d'Ouessant. Here you can tuck into regional fare such as chicken cooked in cider, as well as lobster, crab, king prawns, *langoustines* and seaweed, all prepared to chef Philippe Corre's own recipes. Despite its recent bland modern makeover, the interior of the stone building has impressive centuries-old doors and staircase and a vast stone fireplace.

CLOSED mid-Jan to mid-Feb
CARDS MC, V

Plumelec
◆ Le Moulin de Callac
€€ – €€€

Callac, 56420 Plumelec, Morbihan
Tel 02 97 67 12 65 Fax 02 97 67 12 65

Comprising eight guest bedrooms and a dining room seating 50 with a huge granite fireplace, this is a simple, beautifully restored old stone building on the edge of a lake, surrounded by thickly wooded grounds.

The restaurant specialises in traditional *galettes* and crêpes made with organic flour and other ingredients. On display is an interesting collection of porcelain. Régine Theroine is the host and service is courteous and friendly.

❝ Typically Breton' …We enjoyed our fireside table and beautiful views ❞

CLOSED Tue dinner, Wed
CARDS AE, MC, V

Pont-Aven
◆ Les Ajoncs d'Or € – €€

1 place de l'Hôtel de Ville, 29930 Pont-Aven, Finistère
Tel 02 98 06 02 06 Fax 02 98 06 18 91

This matronly white-painted, blue-shuttered, slate-roofed hotel stands at the heart of picturesque Pont-Aven, famous for its associations with Gauguin and the school of artists who followed him there. Its a charming place for a stroll before lunch, with its pretty walks over little bridges across the river Aven, dotted with water wheels, sluices and mills. The hotel is run by a young, English-speaking couple who make a great effort and are extremely helpful. Though the smart, newish decoration (there are two restaurants, one in, one out) is hardly characterful, you will eat fine *fruits de mer* here.

CLOSED Nov
CARDS AE, DC, MC, V

Pont-Aven
◆ Moulin du Grand Poulguin € – €€

2 quai Théodore Botrel, 29930 Pont-Aven, Finistère
Tel 02 98 06 02 67 Fax 02 98 06 08 55

IN a 14thC building on the banks of the Aven with a huge water wheel on one wall and a slightly smaller one on the other is this popular pizzeria with a lot going for it. The stone-walled dining room is nicely decorated and the young owners are enthusiastic and welcoming. From 11.30 in the morning onwards hungry visitors can tuck into *galettes* with a variety of fillings as well as

crisp, freshly made pizzas (takeaway available). The Moulin is also a museum, offering the chance to see an original water mill.

CLOSED never
CARDS AE, DC, MC, V

Pont-Aven
◆ Moulin de Rosmadec €€

Venelle de Rosmadec, 29930 Pont-Aven, Finistère
Tel 02 98 06 00 22 Fax 02 98 06 18 00

Tucked at the end of a lane between two branches of the river, this family-run old stone mill makes a delightful choice for a meal and perhaps for an overnight stay in one of the four small but neat bedrooms. The mill wheel still turns and an atmosphere of peace pervades in the lovely dining room that spills on to the terrace and the riverside garden, making a perfect setting for good fish dishes, grilled Rosmadec lobster and their special dessert, delicious crêpes soufflées.

CLOSED Sun dinner (winter), Wed; 2 weeks Nov, Feb
CARDS MC, V

Pouldreuzic
◆ Breiz-Armor € – €€

Plage de Penhors, 29710 Pouldreuzic, Finistère
Tel 02 98 51 52 53 Fax 02 98 51 52 30

Standing right by the beach at Penhors, with splendid views across 13 miles (20 km) of seashore around the Audierne bay, this is a breezy hotel, modern in construction but traditional in style, and appreciated by visitors for its warm welcome and the food in its restaurant, a cut above the normal tourist fare. Choose your fish from the seawater tank and it will be prepared with aplomb; or plump for *moules marinières, palourdes farcis, crabe gratin*, lobster casserole flambéd with whiskey, or, if you prefer, ostrich steaks and, to end the meal, Madame's special strawberry pudding. Wash it down with Muscadet by the bottle or glass.

CLOSED Nov-Mar
CARDS MC, V

Priziac
◆ Le Cheval Blanc ⓔ Fr

5 rue Albert Saint-Jalmes, 56320 Priziac,
Morbihan
Tel 02 97 34 61 15 Fax 02 97 34 63 10

At first aquaintance, this ordinary, old-fashioned Logis de France in the middle of the village of Priziac is unprepossessing. Stick to your resolve: you will be rewarded. In the large, tile-floored dining room with ladder-back chairs and flowery tablecloths you will eat simple, home-cooked, regional food of a refreshingly high standard. Such staples as *magret de canard, terrine maison*, and *fruits de mer* are offered, while the *menu de terroir* includes *bolée de cidre 'yeed-mad'* at a very reasonable price. But you may not want to miss the steaks: cooked in herb butter they melt in the mouth. The village is in the heart of the Roi Morvan region, close to the Lac de Bel Air, popular with families, so you can combine the two and make a day of it.

❜ Never judge a book by its cover. Personally, I'd rather eat here than many a more expensive place I can think of ❜

CLOSED Nov
CARDS AE, DC, MC, V

Looking for somewhere to stay? See page 241.

Quiberon
◆ La Chaumine ⓔ – ⓔⓔ Fr

36 place du Manémeur, 56170 Manémeur,
Quiberon, Morbihan
Tel 02 97 50 17 67 Fax 02 97 50 17 67

In a pretty setting in Quiberon's fishing port, this is a delightful little spot, close to the action, yet tranquil, relaxing and refreshingly simple. The cheapest set menu, served at lunch Monday to Saturday, is just 13 euros (at the time of going to press). Or you can choose from the carte. Either way, its all about fish and seafood, prepared with simplicity and best accompanied by a glass of Muscadet. Excellent value (Michelin

awards a Bib Gourmand); plenty of locals.

CLOSED Sun dinner, Mon; Nov to mid-Dec; early to mid-Mar
CARDS MC, V

Rennes
◆ Les Agapes ⓔ – ⓔⓔⓔ

22 place de l'Eglise, 35520 La Mézière,
Rennes, Ile-et-Vilaine
Tel 02 99 69 39 27 Fax 02 99 69 32 42

In a former girls' school some six miles (10 km) northwest of Rennes (on the N137 and D28) a young chef called David Etcheverry is making waves, and has already been identified by Gault Millau as a *'grand de demain'*. He brings a refreshing *élan* to *cuisine gourmande* and ensures that his cool, spacious, brick-walled restaurant, his enthusiastic young staff and his prices are both easy-going and approachable. His remarkable food is inventive in the best sense of the word, full of good ideas, but using local produce where appropriate. And the prices are astonishing for such quality.

CLOSED Sun dinner, Mon
CARDS AE, MC, V

La Roche-Bernard
◆ Auberge Bretonne
ⓔⓔⓔ

2 place Duguesclin, 56130 La Roche-Bernard, Morbihan
Tel 02 99 90 60 28 Fax 02 99 90 85 00

For years the pretty Auberge Bretonne in the partly medieval town of La Roche-Bernard has featured in our *Charming Small Hotel Guide to France*, which qualifies its top-flight restaurant (two Michelin stars; 19/20 from Gault Millau) to be included amongst this list of Brittany's charming restaurants. The philosophy of the owners since 1980, Solange and Jacques Thorel, is simple: to offer the finest and rarest wines they can find, the best possible food to accompany them and then a really comfortable bed for the night. The dining room, pale yellow sponge walls and cool tiled floor, stretches round a little vegetable garden ready for the kitchen. Jacques Thorel's cooking is sublime: mackerel pickled with ginger;

a featherlight beetroot mousse; *coquilles Saint-Jacques* sprinkled with chopped truffles until invisible and then covered with fresh cream of asparagus; sea bass virtually unadored; *brochette* of duck served with dates; strawberries and cream – except the cream turns out to be weightless elderflower froth. The wine list is exceptional and although some of the prices look heavy, you are being offered vintages no longer available on the open market.

❢ One dinner I won't forget ❣

CLOSED Mon lunch, Tue lunch, Fri lunch and Thur; mid to late Nov, early to mid-Jan
CARDS AE, DC, MC, V

Roudouallec
◈ Le Bienvenu € – €€

*84 rue Nicolas-le-Grand, 56110 Roudouallec, Morbihan
Tel 02 97 34 50 01 Fax 02 97 34 54 90*

A straightforward establishment in a pretty part of the countryside between Quimper and Gourin, close to the border of Morbihan with Finistère. M. Spegagne's imaginative country-based cuisine has a firm local following. Plenty of meat and game dishes (including ostrich – there are several ostrich farms in these parts) to balance the local fish and shellfish on the menu.

❢ Not much ambience, but we've eaten very well here – the food can be excellent ❣

CLOSED Tue dinner, Wed
CARDS MC, V

Saint-Aignan
◈ L'Anse de Sordan € Fr

*65480 Saint-Aignan, Morbihan
Tel 02 97 27 52 36 Fax 02 97 27 52 36*

On the shores of Lac de Guerlédan, bordered by the Fôret de Quénécan, this is a simple, modern bar and restaurant with large picture windows in the dining room and a terrace for sunny days. It caters for the campers and day visitors who flock to the lake to swim and hire canoes and pedalos, and would be unremarkable were it not for the fact that, apart from the usual crêpes, pizzas and ice creams, it also offers honest local cooking, including excellent steaks and local pork, as well as *poulet de Rennes*, much as you might find in a more traditional rural *ferme-auberge* specialising in *cuisine bourgoise*. Escargots in herb butter are also on the menu. Although the restaurant is officially only open in summer, bookings are taken out of season by prior arrangement.

CLOSED Nov-Mar except by prior arrangement
CARDS AE, MC, V

Saint-Briac-sur-Mer
◈ L'Hernine €

*Le Chemin, 35800 Saint-Briac-sur-Mer, Ile-et-Vilaine
Tel 02 99 88 36 59*

Brittany and the crêpe (or *galette*) are synonymous: wherever you go you aren't far from the ubiquitous crêperie, and although you may cry out for something else on your holiday, it does make an excellent way of feeding the family, whether savoury – as a main course or sweet – as a pudding. Here, in the little seaside town of Saint-Briac, is one such whose proprietor – it has been in the same family since 1975 – prides herself on quality. She and her husband share the duties of cooking and serving, and the setting is a large garden with ponds, water features and animals.

CLOSED Mon, Tue winter
CARDS MC, V

●*A good crêperie in Côtes-d'Armor is le Saint-Germain in the village of the same name near Matignon (tel 02 96 41 08 33); and Hamon in Perros-Guirec (tel 02 98 89 00 19). In Finistère, there's a great traditional Breton crêperie close to the chapel and calvary of Notre Dame de Tronoën (tel 02 98 82 02 40). Other traditional crêperies in Finistère worth seeking out: Le Blé Noir at Guilers, near Brest (tel 02 98 07 57 40); Les Salines at Carhaix-Plouguer (tel 02 98 99 11 32); and Ti à Dreux on Ile d'Ouessant (tel 02 98 89 00 19).*

Saint-Briac-sur-Mer
 Les Voiles Rouges

€ – €€

7 Grande-Rue, 35800 Saint-Briac-sur-Mer,
Ile-et-Vilaine
Tel 02 99 88 04 44

Right by the seaside in this charming lit-tle Côte d'Eméraude fishing village with its original church and narrow old streets, Les Voiles Rouges is a pretty restaurant where one can choose *'entre terre et mer'* while watching the sea and the gulls wheel-ing in the sky.

CLOSED Nov
CARDS MC, V

Saint-Malo
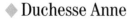 Le Chalut €€

8 rue de la Corne-de-Cerf, 35400 Saint-Malo, Ile-et-Vilaine
Tel 02 99 56 71 58 Fax 02 99 56 71 58

This intimate, well-worn, friendly, supremely fishy restaurant inside the ramparts sets high standards, and is fre-quented by locals and tourists alike. The fish on offer is displayed on ice on the pavement outside, as well as live in the fish tank in the marine-themed dining room. It is, not sur-prisingly, very fresh and dishes include excellent *coquilles Saint-Jacques au jus de truffe* (in season), *filet de Saint-Pierre à la coriandre* and *filet de bar au champagne*. Michelin awards a star.

CLOSED Mon, Tue dinner (except summer)
CARDS AE, MC, V

Saint-Malo
◆ Duchesse Anne

€€ – €€€

5 place Guy-La-Chambre, 35400 Saint-Malo, Ile-et-Vilaine
Tel 02 99 40 85 33 Fax 02 99 40 00 28

In the same hands for three generations, this traditional restaurant may no longer hold its Michelin star, but it is still much appreciated by its many regulars for its dependablity, its wonderful position tucked into the ramparts with superb views, and its

old-style dishes, predominantly fish. Favourites include *turbot Florentine, gratin de langoustines à l'estragon* and *noix de Saint-Jacques au beurre blanc*. A good wine list accompanies.

> ❛ My favourite restaurant in Saint-Malo – comfortingly old-fashioned'... 'Just the place for a treat ❜

CLOSED Sun dinner winter, Mon lunch, Wed; Dec, Jan
CARDS MC, V

> ● *At Saint-Lunaire, near St-Malo, the Restaurant du Décollé (tel 02 99 46 01 70) has very good seafood and wonderous views, with a useful crêperie next door for the children.*

Saint-Quay-Portrieux
 Hôtel Ker-Moor €€

13 rue du Président-Le-Sénécal, 22410 Saint-Quay-Portrieux, Côtes-d'Armor
Tel 02 96 70 50 49 Fax 02 96 70 50 49

Close to the charming villages of Binic and Etables-sur-Mer, the lively fishing port of Saint-Quay-Portriuex, overlooking the Golfe de Saint-Malo, is delightfully pic-turesque. The strikingly flamboyant Ker-Moor stands high on a clifftop with spectac-ular views across the sea, creeks and islands of Armor. The various menus feature local scallops in different guises as well as *meli-melo* of artichokes and *langoustine* tails. Finish with pears from the orchards of Anjou, flavoured with vanilla and pistachios.

CLOSED mid-Dec to mid-Jan; Sun Oct-Mar
CARDS AE, DC, MC, V

Sainte-Marine
◆ Sainte-Marine €€

19 rue du Bac, 29120 Sainte-Marine, Combrit, Finistère
Tel 02 98 56 34 79 Fax 02 98 51 94 09

Close to the water's edge in the charming little cove of Sainte-Marine, overlooking the sail-filled Odet estuary and Bénodet, is this delightful, breezy hotel-restaurant decked out in nautical colours and *trompe l'oeuil* murals in the bedrooms. Diners can sit either in the simple, elegant dining room or better still, outside on the terrace where they can watch the world go by. The seafood – Creuse oysters, crab, cod with curry and ginger and so on, is augmented by a regional menu that features the local pudding *far Breton* with prunes, and by a few meat dishes including ostrich with blueberries.

Our family love coming here. We stick the children in the pizza place next door, and get on with our piles of shellfish in peace

Closed mid-Nov to mid-Dec
Cards MC, V

Trébeurden
◆ Manoir de Lan Kerellec
€€ – €€€

allée Centrale, 22560 Trébeurden, Côtes-d'Armor
Tel 02 96 15 47 47 Fax 02 96 23 66 88

Lan Kerellec, a Relais et Chaâteaux hotel and a stalwart of our *Charming Small Hotel Guide to France*, is a gem. Quietly situated on a wooded promontory to the west of Lannion, it is sheltered from the open sea by its own archipelago of shoals, rocks and islets that curves round it on all three sides. Not content with this stunning position, the hotel has style as well. The timbered roof of the restaurant looks like an upturned boat: come here on a cool autumn night and you can dine by an open fire and drink your coffee in the *salon* by another one. In cold weather or hot, you will be extremely well fed: *presse d'homard et foie gras, dos de bar sur un lit de chou rouge, tarte aux poires avec glace au lait de brébis....* Fine wines accompany.

Closed Mon and Tue lunch; mid-Nov to mid-Mar
Cards AE, DC, MC, V

Trébeurden
◆ Ti Al-Lannec €€ – €€€€

14 allée de Mezo-Guen, 22560 Trébeurden, Côtes-d'Armor
Tel 02 96 15 01 01 Fax 02 96 23 62 14z

Another highly recommended hotel (which also features in our *Charming Small Hotel Guide to France*) in the resort of Trébeurden on the 'pink granite coast'. The handsome house stands high above the sea with a path down to the beach; it's south-facing terrace has a splended view over the bay of Lannion. It's a deeply comfortable place, with that elusive private-house feel, but also welcoming to families. The dining room has the sea view, and is crisp and fresh with rich drapes and old stone walls. Danielle Jouanny, who owns the hotel with her husband Gérard, is in charge of the kitchen. Expect the menu to feature *foie gras*, *coquilles Saint Jacques* with truffles, excellent fish and good meat dishes, as well as a delicious *tarte aux pommes*. Bordeaux features prominently on the wine list.

Consistently delicious'...' Children are genuinely welcome

Closed mid-Nov to mid-Mar
Cards AE, MC, V

Trégunc
◆ Auberge Les Grandes Roches €

29910 Trégunc, Finistère
Tel 02 98 97 62 97 Fax 02 98 50 29 19

Between Concarneau and Pont-Aven, a carefully converted group of attractive (partly thatched) farm buildings comprise an honest restaurant and bedrooms which are perfect for an overnight stay. The farm is surrounded by flowery gardens and parkland dotted with dolmens and menhirs. New owners are recently installed, and as we went to press a swimming pool was on its way. The menu features *filet mignon*, smoked salmon, grilled goat's cheese served on a bed of apples, Brie stuffed with marscapone, apricots and plums... There is as good wine list, as well as the local cider and beer.

We were told about this place by a discerning Frenchman, and were not disappointed

Closed MC. V
Cards AE, MC, V

BASSE-NORMANDIE

Normandy is divided into two government regions: Haute-Normandie and Basse-Normandie, with 600 km (375 miles) of varied coastline and a rich agricultural countryside carpeted with meadows and forests, and decorated by brown-and-white cows, black-and-white timber buildings and orchards of apple and pear. In Basse-Normandie, the coast stretches from Le Havre to the Cotentin Peninsular, passing charming Honfleur and Deauville and the unforgettable D-Day Landing beaches around

Arromanches on the way. At the head of the peninsula stands Cherbourg, and then the coast drops south to reach Avranches and Mont-Saint-Michel, where Normandy and Brittany meet. Inland from the D-Day beaches are Bayeux and its tapestry, and Caen, the regional capital. All around lies quintessential dairy and cider-producing Norman countryside in the areas known as Pays d'Auge, Suisse Normande (so named for its resemblance to Switzerland) and Bocage Normande.

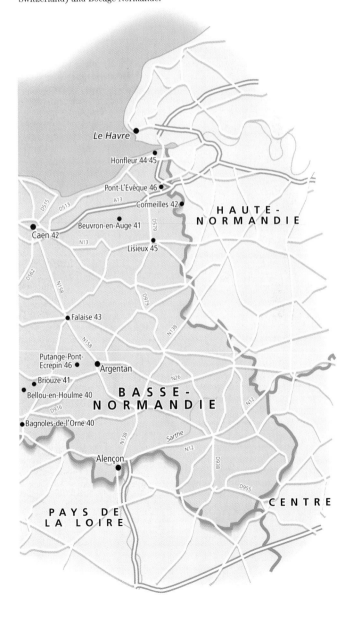

Bagnoles-de-l'Orne
◆ Manoir du Lys

€ – €€€

*la Croix Gauthier, route de Juvigny, 61140
Bagnoles-de-l'Orne, Orne
Tel 02 33 37 80 69 Fax 02 33 30 05 80*

The Quinton family own and run this delightful, typically Norman half-timbered hunting lodge with geraniums at its foot and dripping from its balconies. Marie-France oversees the smart dining rooms overlooking peaceful gardens through floor-to-ceiling windows. Here you can enjoy her son Franck's delicious Michelin-starred cooking, which is rooted in local tradition but respects contemporary trends. He likes to use mushrooms or truffles in his recipes (*poulet de ferme et croustillant à la crème de lait et truffes*, for example), and the family organizes popular 'mushroom weekends' for their hotel guests, during which up to 120 varieties may be picked in the surrounding woods. In summer you can dine comfortably outside; in winter, have a *digestif* in the cosy and polished little bar/salon with its huge open fire and grand piano (which is played on Friday nights).

CLOSED Sun dinner, Mon; early Jan to mid-Feb, Nov to Easter
CARDS AE, DC, MC, V

Barneville-Carteret
◆ Hôtel de la Marine

€ – €€€

*11 rue de Paris, 50270 Barneville-Carteret, Manche
Tel 02 33 53 83 31 Fax 02 33 53 39 60*

On the edge of Cartaret, and overlooking the tidal estuary that serves the neighbouring yacht marina, Hôtel de la Marine has itself been watched over by five generations of the Cesne family. In its current incarnation it presents a quite modern face to the littoral world but the service and food are far from casual – from the *beignet de foie gras en vinaigrette de betterave* to the *brioche aux pommes confites*, you know that you are in very capable hands indeed; those of Laurent, the Cesnes' son. His distinctive blend of innovation and delicacy has

won him many admirers. It's no surprise that the majority of his specialities, ranged over three menus, feature fish or seafood. The restaurant's wrap-around windows mean that diners can enjoy the view of the harbour to the full. As it's a very firm favourite in the area, you should be sure to book for dinner or for Sunday lunch.

❛ The best sea bass I've ever eaten ❜

CLOSED Mon lunch and Thu lunch Apr-Jul and Sep, Sun evening, Thu lunch and Mon Oct to mid-Nov, Mar; mid-Nov to Mar
CARDS AE, MC, V

Bellou-en-Houlme
◆ Le Grand Turc € Fr

*Bellou-en-Houlme, 61220 Briouze, Orne
Tel 02 33 66 00 53*

Le Grand Turc is difficult to miss: look for the pretty 13thC church in the centre of the village and the restaurant is smack opposite. In summer it is festooned with flower baskets. Very much an integral part of a working village, this is where the locals will meet for a drink, families will celebrate birthdays and anniversaries and newly-weds will hold their wedding reception – there are a few bedrooms for those who have travelled too far, eaten too well or celebrated too effectively to want to go home that night. None of the food, though, has travelled far to get to your table.

CLOSED never
CARDS MC, V

● *A great place to try is La Glycine (02 31 44 61 94) in Benouville (about 5 km from Ouistreham port). It's a real find, with stylish looks, delicious food and a warm welcome, just 10 minutes away from the ferry.*

Le Bény-Bocage
◆ Le Castel Normand

€ – €€

*14350 Le Bény-Bocage, Calvados
Tel 02 31 68 76 03 Fax 02 31 68 63 58*

Half way between Mont-Saint-Michel and Caen, Le Castel Normand inhabits a tall granite house, its outline softened by Virginia creeper, in the middle of the village. Good antiques, fine china and sparkling crystal conspire with the warmth of the welcome to make you instantly sure that you've done the right thing by coming here. The food complements the surroundings – it is imaginative and cooked with a delicate touch – so it's no wonder that the restaurant has nailed its reputation firmly to the gastronomic mast. In fine weather tables spill out into the lovely flower-filled garden, and on chilly days a fire will be burning in the massive stone fireplace.

CLOSED Sun evening, Mon, Tue lunch; one week late Aug
CARDS MC, V

Beuvron-en-Auge
◈ Auberge de la Boule d'Or € – €€

14450 Beuvron-en-Auge
Tel 02 31 79 78 79 Fax 02 31 39 61 50

South of the Normandy beaches, Beuvron-en-Auge is an almost-too-good-to-be-true timber-framed village, which could probably earn a decent municipal living as a film set. Regrettably, influxes of French and foreign tourists alike can raise the population to an uncomfortable level. Although it is in the main square, la Boule d'Or pitches itself at serious foodies rather than those who want to grab a bite and dash on to the next attraction. Mussels with a hint of chilli in their butter sauce can liven up your palate in order to appreciate what should be a memorable visit - especially if you finish with the chocolate mousse. Wines are quite steeply priced at this restaurant, but the food is good enough to justify a bit of recklessness as you plan your meal.

CLOSED Tue evening and Wed Sep-Jul; Jan
CARDS MC, V

● *In a restored market building in Beuvron-en-Auge (one of the prettiest villages in the area), Le Pavé d'Auge (02 31 79 26 71) is an attractive restaurant, serving elegant Norman cuisine.*

Briouze
◈ Hôtel Sophie € – €€ **Fr**

5 place Albert 1er, 61220 Briouze,Orne
Tel 02 33 62 62 82 Fax 02 33 62 82 83

The trouble with running a small hotel-bar-restaurant opposite a popular cattle market is that you can never let the quality and freshness of your ingredients drift: every Monday (for this is market day) the clientele, being experts themselves, are likely to give you a sharp reminder of the standards they expect. Happily the Hôtel Sophie needs no reminders and uses excellent local produce for its good Norman offerings. Do try the fish in sorrel sauce and don't pass up the excellent selection of local cheeses. The modern French decoration includes the obligatory television, so drive on if this is likely to bother you. We thought it worth staying for the *trou Normand* – a Calvados sorbet of considerable power that appears between courses.

❛ *Attentive and efficient service, and a charming, voluble chef* ❜

CLOSED Fri; Aug (variable closing times: phone for details)
CARDS MC, V

Fr French regional or classical French dishes on menu.

Brouains
◈ Auberge du Moulin € – €€

Moulin de la Sees, 4 Moulin de Brouains, 50150 Brouains, Manche
Tel 02 33 59 50 60 Fax 02 33 59 50 60

On the country road between Sourdeval and Brouains, a tall factory chimney proclaims the utilitarian past of this converted mill sandwiched between the road and the river Sees. Locals come here for special occasions - not least because the food and decoration are both comfortably above the ordinary, yet Yannick Baron and his wife have kept their prices within reach of ordinary mortals. Four can eat (and drink, for the wine is included) the evening set menu for a little over 100 euros. The wild salmon *crêpes* and *filet de porc* in a light pastry parcel are outstanding, and, although the menu offers no obvious vegetarian options, delicious alternatives will appear as if by magic.

Closed Tue evening and Wed evening Nov to mid-Mar, Sun evening, Mon; late Dec to late Jan
Cards MC, V

Caen
◆ Le Dauphin € – €€€

29 rue Gémare, 14000 Caen, Calvados
Tel 02 31 86 22 26 Fax 02 31 86 35 14

A scant three minutes' walk from William the Conqueror's castle, this former priory doesn't really reveal its age until you get inside. Exposed stone walls, beams and the stone staircase all show the kind of restoration that is more preoccupied with quality than with cost: the building is probably in better shape now than it was 200 years ago. Sylvie and Stéphane Pugnat (he is the chef) make a lively team and give the place a very welcoming atmosphere. The excellent cuisine is Norman, and Stéphane scores extra points by leaving space in his menus for any fish that appealed to him at the market. Crisp white linen, high-backed red velvet chairs, fresh flowers and a thoughtful wine list will keep you company in the restaurant while you wait for your food.

❛ The sole was absolutely fresh and beautifully cooked❜ ... ❛Such friendly people, we had a great evening ❜

Closed Sat lunch, Sun; 2 weeks Feb, mid-Jul to early Aug
Cards AE, DC, MC, V

Clécy
◆ Moulin du Vey € – €€

Le Vey, 14570 Clécy, Calvados
Tel 02 31 69 71 08 Fax 02 31 69 14 14

Whether the river took its name from the settlement or vice versa is moot, but what is sure is that the creeper-clad Moulin du Vey stands in an idyllic position among rolling hills and overlooking a lazy stretch of the river Clécy. Inside you are treated to the warmest of welcomes – and an astonishing array of yellow wallpapers that has skipped almost none of the pages in the pattern book. Served in a half-timbered, barn-like restaurant, across a courtyard from the main building, and popular with the French (both local and visiting), the best of Norman produce is treated with a light, artistic hand that creates that rare, happy coincidence of taste and presentation. There are three or four menus to choose from, each of at least four courses, of which one, inevitably in Normandy, is cheese.

❛ Excellent restaurant, friendly service ❜

Closed Sun evening low season; Dec-Feb
Cards AE, DC, MC, V

---

charmingsmallhotels.co.uk
Visit Duncan Petersen's travel website, the best online search tool for places to stay that combine character and charm. Currently features Britain, France, Italy and Ireland, with other destinations being continuously added.

Cormeilles
◆ Auberge du Président
€ – €€

2 rue Paul Guilbaud, 27190 Conches-en-Ouche, Eure
Tel 02 32 30 20 60 Fax 02 32 30 45 73

The Romans, who used to pass through Cormeilles on their way from Lisieux to Pont-Audemer, would probably have appreciated the Auberge du Président. Modern trout fishermen who are making a pilgrimage to the revered waters of the nearby Calonne certainly do. Timbered buildings surround the village's attractive main square, and the inn's traditionally housed dining room has had to sprout a modern companion to house the attendant bedrooms. Try the *croustillant de Camembert sur méli-mélo de salads, de pomme et de volailles* and the *soufflé glace à la confiture de lait et sa crème Anglaise caramélisée parfumée au Calvados*.

Closed Mon and Wed evening low season, Sun evening; Jan
Cards AE, DC, MC, V

Crépon
◈ Ferme de la Ranconnière ⓔ – ⓔⓔ **Fr**

route d'Arromanches, 14480 Crépon,
Calvados
Tel 02 31 22 21 73 Fax 02 31 22 98 39

This fortified farm, well placed for visiting the D-Day beaches, is no smallholding. The oldest building is 13thC and the final touches were added sometime in the 15th century. The buildings form three sides of an enormous courtyard, and the fourth side, on the road, is guarded by a crenellated wall – obviously a safe haven for the farmers and their stock in more troubled times. Even out of season, you are likely to find both atmospheric, rustic dining rooms (one beamed, the other barrel-vaulted) bursting with French families, attracted by Bruno Champion's regional food, that is plentiful, and of good quality and value. Specialities based on pork, veal and duck feature strongly on his pair of menus.

❮ *All the flavours of the region* ❯

CLOSED never
CARDS AE, MC, V

Domfront
◈ La Grange ⓔ

2 rue de la Gare, 61700 Domfront, Orne
Tel 02 33 38 94 17

Most restaurants welcome (well-behaved) children, but the reverse is not always true. La Grange, on the outskirts of Domfront, should meet with the approval of most children not least because it's probably open when their hunger pangs start to bite: unlike the small window of opportunity affected by some restaurants, La Grange has longer opening hours than many others in the area. Limited menus (but including a specific children's menu) and a short wine list conspire to reduce initial dithering to a minimum and the good, friendly service will whisk the chosen items to you in short order. Stone walls and interesting farm implements combine to give the place an attractive rustic look.

CLOSED never
CARDS MC, V

Ducey
◈ Auberge de la Sélune ⓔ – ⓔⓔ

2 rue Saint-Germain, 50220 Ducey,
Manche
Tel 02 33 48 53 62 Fax 02 33 48 90 30

Of the two conventional dining rooms in this village hotel, one is less formal than the other and gives on to an attractive terrace with tables and chairs, from which you can enjoy the pretty, flowery garden with a river burbling in the background. The food is well regarded, with *pie au crabe* being their *pièce de résistance*. Prices are honest and the staff friendly and eager to please. The *auberge* occupies two old buildings, connected by a rather soulless modern glass and metal lobby, and has 21 simple, but pleasant, colourful bedrooms.

CLOSED Mon low season; mid-Jan to mid-Feb
CARDS AE, DC, MC, V

Our price bands
ⓔ under 30 euros ⓔⓔ 30-50 euros
ⓔⓔⓔ over 50 euros for a menu.

Falaise
◈ La Fine Fourchette
ⓔ – ⓔⓔ

52 rue Georges Clémenceau, 14700 Falaise,
Calvados
Tel 02 31 90 08 59

Famous as the birthplace of William the Conqueror, Falaise was cruelly battered during the Battle of Normandy in 1944. Now restored and revived, its castle is one of Normandy's most rewarding historical sites. Just outside the town, on the road to Argentan and very near the Château de la Fresnaye, La Fine Fourchette offers a warm welcome to its glowing dining room. Typical Norman dishes are given a metropolitan twist by a chef who keeps himself inspired and *au fait* with trends and innovations through regular visits to fellow chefs in the capital. The results easily justify his train fares: try his *pressé de foie de volaille et pintade confite à la purée d'oignons* followed, perhaps, by *corolle de thon minute à la Provençale*.

CLOSED Tue evening low season; first 2 weeks Feb
CARDS AE, DC, MC, V

Fierville-les-Mines
◆ Auberge du Moulin € Fr

50580 Fierville-les-Mines, Manche
Tel 02 33 93 05 05 Fax 02 33 93 05 05

Don Quixote would have found it difficult to relax here: there's a working windmill next door. But, for many, the rustic calm of this thatched cottage, the modest prices and the honest approach to the traditional Norman dishes conspire to make it something of a favourite. A broad choice is offered, but if you have trouble making decisions, try the *tripes* (cooked in cider), the *rumsteck au livarot*, *galettes* (pancakes) or the *beignets au Camembert*. If you haven't yet tried it, *teurgoule* is the most famous Norman dessert. The service here is friendly, and quite without airs and graces.

❛ Good robust regional food at unbeatable prices ❜

CLOSED Mon and Tue winter
CARDS MC, V

Ger
◆ Bar-Restaurant Normand € Fr

50210 Savigny, Manche
Tel 02 33 07 60 32 Fax 02 33 46 25 28

Opposite the church, and next to the town square, this is a very basic, very popular restaurant – especially on Sundays (and it's always advisable to book). When the place is full, you are all sitting cheek by jowl, so it's not the place for quiet discussion of some dark family secret – nor is it the place to go if you're in search of *haute cuisine*. But you will get good value out of all five courses on offer (excellent salads, omelettes, steak, chips, *crème brûlée*, *tarte tatin* and local specialities: tripe, *tête de veau*, *andouille* and *tarte Normande*), and you can buy wine by the jug to wash them down with.

CLOSED Mon, Fri evening
CARDS none

La Haute-Chapelle
◆ Le Pont de Caen € Fr

61700 La Haute-Chapelle, Orne
Tel 02 33 38 65 51

If you don't speak any French, blow the dust off your phrase book before you walk into this small country hotel. Part of a hamlet, surrounded by woods, it is as typically French as you can get. This is where the locals come to eat, gossip and celebrate. The decoration is basic, the staff friendly and welcoming, and the food uncompromisingly Norman: don't expect any Mediterranean flourishes. What you will get is what the locals expect: well-prepared, good quality, local produce at easily affordable prices. The cheeses, pâtés and vegetables in particular are all top quality. Opening and closing times, and days, seem to vary on a slightly random basis so it's always best to check by telephone ahead of time.

❛ Friendly local restaurant in a peaceful country setting ❜

CLOSED variable closing times; phone for details
CARDS MC, V

Our traditional French cuisine symbol
So many of our readers enjoy seeking out the genuinely French eating experience that we have used Fr to mark restaurants which offer *cuisine du terroir*, classical French dishes or regional dishes with an emphasis on local ingredients, and traditional recipes.

Honfleur
◆ La Chaumière €€ – €€€

route du Littoral, Vasouy, 14600 Honfleur, Calvados
Tel 02 31 81 63 20 Fax 02 31 89 59 23

Strictly speaking a *chaumière* is a thatched cottage, but the Normans seem to have put tiles on this very handsome half-timbered house tucked into its manicured seaside meadow on the Seine estuary, minutes west of Honfleur. Compared to the stratospherically upmarket Ferme Saint-Siméon 2 km (one mile) away, also owned by the Boelen family, this hotel and restaurant is a smaller, more relaxed stablishment with nothing else between it and the sea. Run by a manager, it is a little difficult to forget that this is a business and not a vocation. Standards are high and so are prices, but the position alone goes a long way towards justifying the cost. The cosy beamed and tiled restaurant has a view out over the estuary and a consistently high-class output, strong on seafood and fresh local produce and with a wine list to remember. In summer, tables are set on a sheltered sunny terrace guarded by flower beds and fruit trees.

CLOSED Tue, Wed lunch, Thu lunch; 2 weeks Jan, 2 weeks early Dec
CARDS AE, MC, V

---

charmingsmallhotels.co.uk
Visit Duncan Petersen's travel website, the best online search tool for places to stay that combine character and charm.
Currently features Britain, France, Italy and Ireland, with other destinations being continuously added.

Honfleur
◆ Le Manoir du Butin
€€ – €€€

phare du Butin, 14600 Honfleur, Calvados
Tel 02 31 81 63 00 Fax 02 31 89 59 23

You get a firm impression that time runs a little more slowly than usual at this 18thC half-timbered Norman manor tucked into a wooded hillside just outside Honfleur. As well as a view across the Seine estuary, you are offered peace and quiet and the kind of welcoming atmosphere where no one would think it at all remarkable if you took a rug and a book out on to the gently sloping sunny lawn for a sleep after lunch. The light and attractive restaurant, decorated in pale yellow, offers an excellent regional cuisine on shortish, changing menus, where you might find such delicacies as *blanc de Saint-Pierre rôti, boudin d'encornets au fenouil et tomates séchées* or *langoustines*

rôties à la graisse d'oie, as well as a serious selection of old Calvados.

CLOSED Wed, Thu, Fri lunch; 2 weeks Jan, 3 weeks Nov
CARDS AE, MC, V

Lisieux
◆ Le Patio €

67 avenue Henry Cheron, 14100 Lisieux,
Calvados
Tel 02 31 31 25 37

Right in the centre of Lisieux, opposite the cathedral, Le Patio is just the sort of place to have lunch when you have already made grand plans for dinner. It's a modern, child-friendly pavement café, bar and restaurant with tables both inside and out, where you can have a full meal or just a cup of coffee, a cocktail or an ice cream. They offer a reasonable set menu but their real skills (and best value) lie in their individual salads and omelettes. They don't seem to need much sleep here in Lisieux – the opening hours are from seven in the morning to one o'clock the following morning.

❝ *An excellent place to watch the world go by* ❞

CLOSED never
CARDS MC, V

Our price bands
€ under 30 euros €€ 30-50 euros
€€€ over 50 euros for a menu.

Le Mont-Saint-Michel
◆ Auberge Saint-Pierre
€ – €€ Fr

BP16, Grande Rue, 50116 Le Mont-Saint-Michel, Manche
Tel 02 33 60 14 03 Fax 02 33 48 59 82

This agreeably rustic 15thC *auberge* is conveniently close to the causeway (all cars have to be parked outside the walls surrounding the Mont). Although its busy street-level restaurant is large, it has a cosy atmosphere, done out in typical Norman style with wood-backed, rush-seated chairs and red and white checked tablecloths. In keeping with the decoration, the food leans towards solid regional specialities. The Mont is at its best when the crowds are thinner in the evening and early morning and, if you're looking for somewhere to stay, the *auberge* has 21 bedrooms with a calmer atmosphere than the sometimes frenetic restaurant.

CLOSED never
CARDS AE, DC, MC, V

Négreville
◆ Le Mesnilgrand €–€€

50260 Négreville, Manche
Tel 02 33 95 09 54 Fax 02 33 95 20 04

Not far from Rocheville but in deep, deep countryside, this traditional Norman farmhouse was rescued and then carefully and tastefully rehabilitated by an English-French duo (James and Pascale) who have created a now highly popular restaurant-with-rooms. The peace and quiet of the country, the lovely garden, the warm atmosphere and the creative and original cuisine fill the place at weekends, and it's now starting to fill up during the week as well – so be sure to book well in advance. The menu changes, but don't ignore the spinach and mushroom salad or raspberry tart if they are offered. It's so rural that it can be difficult to find: you should take the Saint-Joseph exit off the RN13 in the direction of Rocheville, and look for signs to Le Mesnilgrand.

❛ Imaginative food and a wonderfully rural setting' ... 'The place was packed with locals ❜

CLOSED Sun dinner, Mon
CARDS MC, V

Pont-L'Evêque
◆ Auberge de l'Aigle d'Or €–€€

68 rue Vaucelles, 14130 Pont-L'Evêque, Calvados
Tel 02 31 65 05 25 Fax 02 31 65 12 03

On the main road that cuts across Pont L'Evêque from east to west, this 16thC *relais de poste* positively bristles with beams both inside and out. Meals are served in three snug dining rooms, where you might have a view out to the pretty garden or find yourself sitting by the inglenook fireplace; all have great character. There are three menus (*terroir*, *gourmand* and *de L'Aigle*) and a *carte*. Only available at lunchtimes (not Sundays or bank holidays), the set *menu terroir*, a bargain at 25 euros, might consist of *saumon fumé aux trois façons*, *blanc de poularde fermière façon pays d'Auge, paillasson de pommes de terre*, followed by sorbet or *tarte tatin* with *crème au Calvados*. If you opt for either of the more expensive menus or the *carte*, there is a choice of other irresistible desserts.

CLOSED Sun evening Nov to Easter, Tue evening, Wed; late Jun to early Jul, Feb hols
CARDS MC, V

Putange-Pont-Ecrepin
◆ Hôtel du Lion Verd
€–€€

61210 Putange-Pont-Ecrepin, Orne
Tel 02 33 35 01 86 Fax 02 33 39 53 32

River-crossings seem to attract people. In this case the river is the Orne, and the Lion Verd has a beautiful setting, with its own pretty riverside terrace, by the bridge in the centre of the town. Some people may just be tempted by the view, but the knowledgeable amongst them (mostly hotel residents and local families) eat here because they know that the menus may be limited but the food is superb. Unusually for France there are specific vegetarian dishes included in the menus, but the carnivores would do well to head for the steak in Camembert sauce. One excellent regional variation on offer is the *tiramisu* made with Calvados. The wine list is excellent though its prices might make your eyes water slightly.

CLOSED Sun evening, Fri evening and Mon Oct-Apr; mid-Dec to early Feb
CARDS MC, V

Saint-Lô
◆ La Gonivière €–€€ Fr

rond-point du 6 Juin, 50000 Saint-Lô, Manche
Tel 02 33 05 15 36 Fax 02 33 05 01 72

Though badly battered during World War II, Saint-Lô on the Vire river has been restored and its imposing ramparts and Notre-Dame are well worth seeing. Handily placed for the sights and close to the river, La Gonivière is a large, airy first-floor dining room with a welcoming atmosphere, generally regarded as one of the best addresses in Saint-Lô. It is decorated in soothing pastel shades, brightened by the modern paintings on the walls. The cuisine is based on produce fresh from the market, used in traditional regional dishes, such as *carpaccio de Saint-Jacques à l'huile de noisette, ragoût de moules et andouille de Vire*, lamb and pigeon from la Suisse Normande, on menus priced between 18 and 45 euros. Below the restaurant, on the ground floor, is a fun, popular bistro called La Cigale (on the same telephone number), renowned for its good service, tasty meat and interesting wine list.

CLOSED Sun
CARDS AE, MC, V

❛ *At Saint-Pierre-de-Semilly, 7 km (4 miles) from Saint-Lô, Les Glycines (02 33 05 02 40) blends the old and the new in its range of traditional dishes that are given a new slant; a restaurant with panache.* ❜

Saint-Quentin-sur-le-Homme
◈ Le Gué du Holme
€ – €€€

14 rue des Estuaires, 50220 Saint-Quentin-sur-le-Homme, Manche
Tel 02 33 60 63 76 Fax 02 33 60 06 77

Michel and Annie Leroux (he is the chef) own and run this spic-and-span restaurant-with-rooms opposite the church in the little village of Saint-Quentin. She prides herself on always being the first to open the doors in the morning and the last to lock up at night; he prides himself (justifiably) on his devotion to local produce from field, river and, above all, the sea. On the menu you will find lobster, turbot, bass and most of their friends and relations, all treated with a light hand to make sure that they are not robbed of their flavour. The wine list makes just as good reading as the menu. The

restaurant itself greets you with soft, warm colours, gentle lighting, starched white linen and fresh flowers. There is also a pretty, quiet garden filled with roses, where, if you decide to stay the night, breakfast is served in summer.

CLOSED Fri and Sat lunch Oct to mid-Apr; Jan
CARDS AE, DC, MC, V

Saint-Vaast-la-Hougue
◈ Hôtel de France et des Fuchsias € – €€€

20 rue Maréchal Foch, 50550 Saint-Vaast-la-Vaast, Manche
Tel 02 33 54 42 26 Fax 02 33 43 46 79

The emphasis is on the restaurant at this perennially popular halt for Cherbourg ferry passengers (French and British alike). The expressions of delight at the superb seafood platters, or the wonderfully presented produce from the Brix family (the owners) farm, prove that the customers are happy, although one ultra critical and well-travelled couple recently found the food good but unexceptional. The wine list offers plenty of half bottles and good-value options, the service is friendly and efficient, the atmosphere warm – whether in the cosy dining room or in the conservatory, decorated by a local *décorateur anglais*. There is a delightful English-style garden, where free chamber music concerts are held at the end of August.

❛ *Enticing conservatory, where we ate memorable, beautifully presented food* ❜

CLOSED Mon and Tue lunch low season; early Jan – late Feb
CARDS AE, DC, MC, V

Savigny
◈ La Voisinière
€ – €€

50210 Savigny, Manche
Tel 02 33 07 60 32 Fax 02 33 46 25 28

La Voisinière is east of the D52 on the D380 – not in Savigny at all, despite its address. It's obvious when you get there why this is the case: it's a farmhouse. It is also, now, a very charming restaurant-with-rooms, filled with antique regional furniture, set in an immaculate garden and a very comfortable distance from the madding crowd. The food is essentially Norman (entirely so if you choose the *menu du terroir*), but you can very safely branch out with *poëllée de langoustines aux arômes d'oranges* or the *fricasée de pintade aux raisins et aux baies de genièvre*. La Voisinère guarantees excellent value in very congenial surroundings.

CLOSED Sun evening, Mon, Tue lunch; first 2 weeks Jan, Feb, late Oct to early Nov
CARDS MC, V

Our price bands
Rather than giving actual prices (which are prone to change) we indicate the cost of a three-course meal for one person, without wine, by means of price bands. They are as follows: € under 30 euros €€ 30-50 euros €€€ over 50 euros. Where we give more than one price band, for example €–€€€, this indicates that in that restaurant a meal can be had at a range of prices. As well as the cost of *prix fixe* menus, our price bands also take into account the cost of an average selection from the *à la carte* menu.

Servon
◆ Auberge du Terroir
€ **Fr**

Le Bourg, 50170 Servon, Manche
Tel 02 33 60 17 92 Fax 02 33 60 35 26

Leave the N175 to the east of Pontorson for the village of Servon and this charming *auberge*, where you will be greeted warmly by Annie or Thierry Lefort. It occupies two distinct houses: one is the old school house, the other, which contains the enticing restaurant, has a rather un-Gallic Presbyterian history. Here imaginative dishes from Périgord, such as fillet of pork with apples and cider, duck thigh with *l'imperceptible jus de truffe* and duck breast with honey, fill menus from 15 to 40 euros. It has a large garden with tennis courts.

❮ *Try the duck - it was succulent and delicious* ❯

CLOSED Wed mid-Sep to Jul, Sat lunch; Feb, late Nov to early Dec
CARDS MC, V

Thury-Harcourt
◆ Le Relais de la Poste
€ – €€€ **Fr**

route de Caen, 14200 Thury-Harcourt, Calvados
Tel 02 31 79 72 12 Fax 02 31 39 53 55

The 12 bedrooms, decorated in the style of Louis XV and XVI by Nathalie Frémond, are restful and attractive, but it's the restaurant, overseen by Nathalie's husband, Jean-François, that really makes this old ivy-clad coaching inn a great place to visit. An elegant long room, with a remarkable pitched timber roof and a huge picture window which looks out to the garden at one end, it has a formal air, upholstered chairs and beautifully laid tables, covered in floor-length pink and white cloths. Jean-François specializes in traditional Norman fare: pigeon, duckling, and seafood, including lobster and crayfish - all carefully prepared and cooked with delicacy.

❮ *Delectable hot apple tart, served with thick Normandy cream* ❯

CLOSED Sun evening and Mon Oct-Apr, Mon; late Dec to late Jan
CARDS AE, MC, V

Trelly
◆ Verte Campagne
€ – €€€

50660 Trelly, Manche
Tel 02 33 47 65 33 Fax 02 33 47 38 03

Elegantly rustic on the inside (with stone walls, exposed beams and a scattering of knick-knacks) and truly rural on the outside, this cosy and welcoming restaurant inhabits an ivy-covered 17thC Norman farmhouse. An excellent choice of well-prepared and presented dishes is spread over a wide enough range of menus to suit most pockets. The cook is Pascal Bernou, whose specialities include *vinaigrette de rouget et langoustines*, *pigeonneau rôti aux épices* and *agneau de pré-salé* (salt-meadow lamb).

CLOSED Sun evening and Wed lunch Sep-Jul, Mon; 2 weeks Jan, one week Dec
CARDS MC, V

Villedieu-les-Poêles
◆ Ferme de Malte

€ – €€€

11 rue Jules Tétrel, 508000 Villedieu-les-Poêles, Manche
Tel 02 33 91 35 91 Fax 02 33 91 35 90

In the valley of the Sienne, Villedieu-les-Poêles owes its name to the manufacture of hammered copper tools, which was the principal occupation of its inhabitants for several centuries. Owned by the Knights of Malta – who certainly have a long connection with the town – this former farmhouse is now a very attractive restaurant with a solid reputation and a sensible range of menus, priced between 23 and 55 euros. There are two dining rooms to choose from, one dressed rustically and dotted with curios and the other, which opens on to the lovely garden, in a cooler, more contemporary style.

CLOSED Sat lunch, Sun dinner and Mon Sep-Jun; first 2 weeks Oct, late Jan to mid-Feb
CARDS AE, MC, V

Please send us reports
A guide such as this thrives on reader's reports. If you send us five usable reports, we will send you a free copy of any title in our *Charming Small Hotel Guides* series (see page 241 for France titles in the series).
   The five reports should contain at least two new restaurants; the balance can be comments on restaurants already in the guide. **Send reports to** Charming Restaurant Guides , Duncan Petersen Publishing, 31 Ceylon Rd, London W14 0PY.

Vire
◆ Manoir de la Pommeraie € – €€€

14500 Roullours, Vire, Calvados
Tel 02 31 68 07 71 Fax 02 31 67 54 21

On the road from Vire to Tinchebray, which sounds a little like a relic of the 'auld alliance', the Manoir de la Pommeraie is an imposing building which has had plenty of thought and money spent on its elegant interior. Diners are not seated in a grand salon but scattered through a series of smaller, more intimate rooms. This may slow the service a little but the beautifully prepared and presented food more than makes up for it. The style of cooking is sophisticated Norman: try the *saumon aux endives confites* or *le poulet au cidre*.

❢ Expensive surroundings' ... 'Stunning food ❩

CLOSED Sun evening, Mon
CARDS AE, DC, MC, V

Looking for somewhere to stay?
See page 241.

Yvrandes
◆ Le Relais d'Yvrandes
€ Fr

61800 Saint-Cornier-des-Landes, Yvrandes, Orne
Tel 02 33 64 80 05

This is a small, family-run, classic bar-restaurant on the border between Manche and Orne, concentrating on principally honest country fare (but with touches of real style and knowledge); even the lowest priced menu (13 euros) offers a choice between three starters, three main courses and six desserts (or cheese). Portions are generous and, if you have praise or criticism to offer, save it for the chef, Roland Yzeux, who pops out of his kitchen every now and then to see how everyone is doing. There's a good range of regional specialities – *tête de veau* and *andouillette*, for example – but, if you have a taste for the mildly exotic, try a locally produced bison steak (on the 23-euro menu). Service is fast and efficient.

❢ Excellent value ... thoroughly enjoyable' ... 'Packed with locals ❩

CLOSED Mon
CARDS MC, V

HAUTE-NORMANDIE

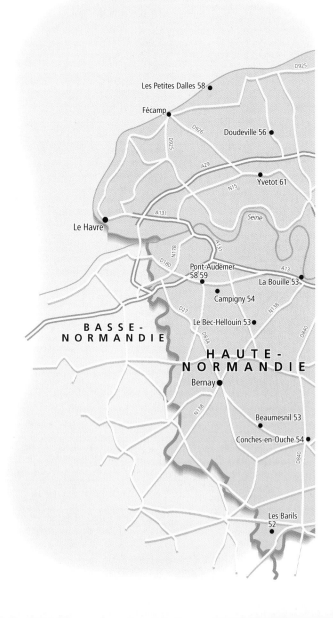

N ormandy is divided into two government regions: Haute-Normandie and Basse-Normandie, with 600 km (375 miles) of varied coastline and a rich agricultural countryside ,carpeted with meadows and forests, and decorated by brown-and-white cows, black-and-white timber buildings and orchards of apple and pear. In the centre of Haute-

Les Petites Dalles 58

Fécamp

D925

D926

Doudeville 56

D925

A29

N15

Yvetot 61

A131

Seine

Le Havre

A131

N178

D180

Pont-Audemer
58 59

A13

La Bouille 53

Campigny 54

N138

D27

Le Bec-Hellouin 53

D840

D834

**BASSE-
NORMANDIE**

**HAUTE-
NORMANDIE**

Bernay

N138

Beaumesnil 53

Conches-en-Ouche 54

D840

Les Barils
52

Normandie stands France's fourth-largest port, Rouen, with its great cathedral. From here, the river Seine flows in great loops to the English Channel at Le Havre. To the north of Le Havre, on the coast of Seine-Maritime, lie Etretat, Fécamp and Dieppe, while to the south of the Seine, Evreux is the principal town of Eure, whose southern border lies not far west of Paris.

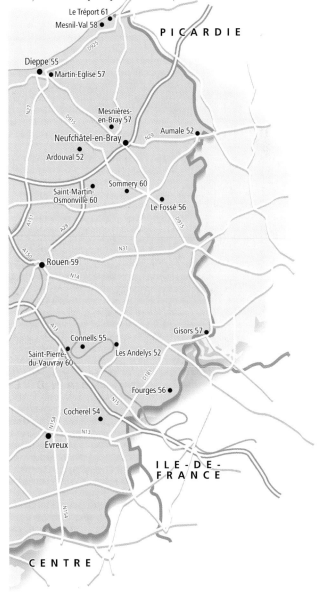

Les Andelys
◆ **Le Chaîne d'Or**

€ – €€€

27 rue Grande, 27700 Les Andelys, Eure
Tel 02 32 54 00 31 Fax 02 32 54 05 68

Under an hour from Paris, on a lazy curve in the Seine and overlooked by the pale remains of Richard the Lionheart's 12thC Château Gaillard, the cares of the world start to recede as soon as you pull into the peaceful gravelled courtyard of this 18thC inn. Owned by Mme Foucault for the last 17 years, it has a young, enthusiastic and professional staff, and despite being only a stone's throw from the centre of this little town, it could not be closer to the Seine without falling in. Not surprisingly, the restaurant looks out over it. Raw beams, warm yellow rough-plastered walls, fresh flowers and a massive stone fireplace surround the tables that stand on the black-and-white tiled floor. Excellent food on a range of menus (including the very reasonably priced *menu détente*), with the quality lasting through the salad and into the cheese and puddings, and a full, but by no means ruinous wine list, should satisfy the pickiest of diners.

❛ Not cheap, but well worth it' ... 'If you're in the neighbourhood, look no further ❜

CLOSED Sun dinner, Mon and Tue low season
CARDS AE, DC, MC, V

Ardouval
◆ **La Ferme Auberge d'Eawy** € **Fr**

2 place de l'Eglise, 76680 Ardouval, Seine-Maritime
Tel 02 35 93 02 42 Fax 02 35 94 06 97

Ardouval is a sleepy hamlet nestling in the Forêt d'Eawy, between Dieppe and Neufchâtel-en-Bray. It's not difficult to find if you follow the road signs off the D915 between Les Grandes Ventes and Neufchâtel. As you approach the village, look out for the sign *ferme auberge*. The farm inn is one of a cluster of redbrick buildings that make up the farm. Françoise Alard

has created an elegant setting for her restaurant, enhancing the old Norman interior and recently adding a terrace for outdoor dining. Specialities on the typically country menu include *poulet au calvados* and *pintade au cidre*.

❛ Succulent, beautifully cooked chicken ... great value for money ❜

CLOSED Sun dinner, Mon
CARDS MC, V

Our price bands
€ under 30 euros €€ 30-50 euros
€€€ over 50 euros for a menu.

Aumale
◆ **La Villa des Houx** € – €€ **Fr**

6 avenue du Général de Gaulle, 76390 Aumale, Seine-Maritime
Tel 02 35 93 93 30 Fax 02 35 93 03 94

Between Rouen and Amiens, Aumale is a pleasing little town with some useful shops and several decent restaurants. La Villa des Houx is an impressive, rather daunting-looking building in typical Norman style; timbered, with steep roofs perched on top like a collection of tall hats. It's a three-chimney *logis*, with 14 bedrooms and an agreeable restaurant. From here – or the summer terrace – you can admire the peaceful, pretty, flower-filled grounds, bordered by a stream. The food is regional, and specialities vary according to the season.

CLOSED Sun dinner mid-Oct to mid-Mar; 2 weeks Jan
CARDS MC, V

Les Barils
◆ **L'Epicier Normand** € – €€ **Fr**

2 rue de Verneuil, 27130 Les Barils, Eure
Tel 02 32 60 05 88 Fax 02 32 60 27 60

This little *épicerie* and restaurant is the perfect place to come after visiting the pretty fortified hilltop town of Verneuil-sur-Avre or the 17thC Abbaye Saint-Nicolas (one of the very few Norman abbeys to have survived), where they still hold religious services with Gregorian chant. However it's a good idea to telephone L'Epicier before you set out, as they occasionally stage live musical events or theatrical entertainments here. As you might expect, the cooking is firmly anchored in the region and the *épicerie* is an ideal place to stock up for picnics or presents. There is a tempting array of local produce – from home-made pâtés and *foie gras* to pickles, chutneys and jams made from all varieties of vegetable and fruit. To find Les Barils, turn left off the N26 west of Verneuil-sur-Avre on to the D166. L'Epicerie is opposite the church.

(*A unique place for a fun evening*)

CLOSED Mon dinner, Tue; last 2 weeks Jan
CARDS MC, V

Fr French regional or classical French dishes on menu.

Beaumesnil
◆ L'Etape Louis XIII
€ – €€€ Fr

2 route de la Barre-en-Ouche, 27410 Beaumesnil, Eure
Tel 02 32 44 44 72 Fax 02 32 45 53 84

A stone's throw from the magnificent Louis XIII Château de Beaumesnil (now a bookbinding museum) with its amazing garden designed by La Quintinie, this delightful restaurant occupies a former presbytery dating from 1612. A typical Norman timbered building, it has two dining rooms with huge fireplaces, rustic decoration and a welcoming, convivial atmosphere, generated – no doubt – by Christian and Christine Ravinel, the charming owners. In his cooking, Christian uses local produce, and his menus (ranging from 22 to 55 euros) and *carte* feature many Normandy favourites containing seafood, cheese, apples, cream, cider and Calvados. A pleasant garden and terrace provide the perfect spot for summer eating in this historic setting.

CLOSED Tue, Wed Sep-Jul; Feb school hols
CARDS AE, MC, V

Le Bec-Hellouin
◆ Auberge de l'Abbaye
€ – €€ Fr

Le Bec-Hellouin, 27800 Brionne, Eure
Tel 02 32 44 86 02 Fax 02 32 46 32 23

This exquisite geranium-decked 18thC inn, squarely in the centre of a row of half-timbered houses, looks across the village green to the entrance of the abbey of Notre-Dame du Bec, from which it takes its name. Open to the public, the abbey's well-tended gardens are well worth the short walk needed to get to them. The Sergent family have been here for 40 years and the present relaxed and welcoming team is mother and son. Everything about the place is in apple-pie order: the tiled floors are polished and the furniture gleams. The beamed dining room has immaculate stone walls and the traditional red-and-white checked tablecloths. In summer, tables are set under parasols in the central courtyard, and tables and benches for informal meals are ranged along the raised terrace at the front. Snails, lobster, fish, game and cider-based dishes feature on the menu and the *tarte aux pommes* has an almost international reputation.

(*For everyone who appreciates tradition and quality*)

CLOSED Mon dinner, Tue winter; Jan
CARDS MC, V

---

charmingsmallhotels.co.uk
Visit Duncan Petersen's travel website, the best online search tool for places to stay that combine character and charm. Currently features Britain, France, Italy and Ireland, with other destinations being continuously added.

La Bouille
◆ Le Saint-Pierre €

4 place du Bateau, 76530 La Bouille, Seine-Maritime
Tel 02 35 18 01 01 Fax 02 35 18 12 76

An hour from Paris, and a few minutes less from Le Havre, Le Saint-Pierre is at the centre of a picture-postcard village squeezed between the Seine and the high bluffs to the south. Beyond the river wall, a small car ferry plies back and forth, dodging the other river traffic, to save people the long drive in either direction for a bridge. Inside the restaurant, the deep-pile carpet and the muted greens, sponged yellows and attractive watercolours on the walls complement the broad views over the river. White linen and upholstered chairs in the dining room, and cane chairs and parasols on the large terrace are the winter and summer settings for a stream of original and popular combinations of flavours and textures from Arnaud Lindivat's kitchen. If you can't make up your mind what to choose, there is always the *menu dégustation* to fall back on.

CLOSED Sun dinner, Mon
CARDS AE, DC, MC, V

Campigny
◆ Le Petit Coq aux Champs €€€

la Pommeraie-Sud, Campigny, 27500 Pont-Audemer, Eure
Tel 02 32 41 04 19 Fax 02 32 56 06 25

A thatched house with its own heliport – it sounds unlikely, but convention counts for little at this smart, secluded retreat, in rolling meadows and sweeping forests in the Risle valley. Le Petit Coq offers an intriguing mix of the rustic, the sophisticated and the downright idiosyncratic. The building, mostly 19thC, has two main wings with a spacious, airy, modern extension in bet-ween. Subtly lit and handsomely furnished with antiques, the beamed restaurant has a vast open fireplace at one end. Jean-Marie Huard, who returned to his Norman roots after some years in highly reputed restaurants in Paris, pays serious attention to detail, presentation and local tradition in his cooking – with impressive results. The *pot-au-feu de foie gras aux choux croquants* and *salade de langouste aux pousses d'épinards à l'huile vierge* are irresistible. An intimate piano bar has been squeezed into the new building.

◗ Great dinner, romantic setting ◗

CLOSED Jan
CARDS AE, DC, MC, V

Cocherel
◆ La Ferme de Cocherel
€€ – €€€ Fr

route de la Vallée d'Eure, 27120 Cocherel, Eure
Tel 02 32 36 68 27 Fax 02 32 26 28 18

Pierre and Danielle Delton have turned their country home in the peaceful village of Cocherel on the banks of the river Eure into a delightful restaurant with two rustic-style bedrooms. They quickly established a reputation for really excellent food, which continues to grow. Pierre not only cooks but also shops, picking the freshest and the best ingredients, and travelling some distance – if necessary – to find them. Seafood comes from Normandy, lobsters from Brittany, vegetables and poultry from small local suppliers, and cheeses from all over France, which grace a board that deserves its splendid reputation. From a typical (34-euro) menu, you might choose *filet de rouget avec petites legumes*, followed by *canard de Barbarie*, then warm goats' cheese with salad and finish with a *tarte aux pommes*.

◗ The cheese board was spectacular ◗

CLOSED Tue, Wed
CARDS AE, DC, MC, V

Conches-en-Ouche
◆ Le Cygne € Fr

2 rue Paul Guilbaud, 27190 Conches-en-Ouche, Eure
Tel 02 32 30 20 60 Fax 02 32 30 45 73

A favourite stopping place for pilgrims en route to Santiago de Compostella, Conches-en-Ouches, with its medieval houses, church and extraordinary underground chambers, is still an excellent spot to break your journey. Try to plan it so that you arrive in time for lunch at this lovely Norman *relais de poste*. Its white-painted exterior looks charming, with flowers brightening the first-floor balcony and tables set outside on all but the chilliest days. The country atmosphere filters through to the inside, where they serve fresh regional food, according to 'tradition *et terroir*'. The kind of choice you might be faced with on the bargain 15-euro menu is between cod, chicken and lamb. There are delicious fruity desserts to follow, and two alternative, but pricier menus and a *carte*.

CLOSED Sun dinner, Mon
CARDS MC, V

Connelles
◆ Le Moulin de Connelles €€

route d'Amfreville-sous-les-Monts, 27430 Connelles, Eure
Tel 02 32 59 53 33 Fax 02 32 59 21 83

Scarcely a quarter of an hour from Monet's garden at Giverny, Le Moulin de Connelles is a fairy-tale sort of a place with turrets and gables, beams and arches. It even has its own private island with – if you can find them hidden in its gardens – a heated swimming pool and tennis courts. And, as if the location wasn't enough, Hubert and Luce Petiteau have also made a deeply comfortable, beautifully presented 13-room hotel and an excellent restaurant, which – spanning the mill-stream as it does – seems to be hovering over the water. Steamed salmon parcels, baked sea bass, kidneys cooked in three kinds of mustard are sometimes part of the offering from a highly-regarded kitchen. Sitting under the terrace awning, looking down at the mill's reflection and the lily pads floating in the quiet water, it is difficult to imagine wanting to be anywhere else on a summer evening.

❛ A beautiful riverside dining room ... sea bass cooked to perfection ❜

CLOSED Sun-Tue lunch May-Sep, Sun dinner and Mon Oct-May; early Jan to early Feb
CARDS AE, DC, MC, V

Dieppe
◆ Bistrot de Pollet €

23 rue Tête-de-Boeuf, 76200 Dieppe, Seine-Maritime
Tel 02 35 84 68 57

Even though this little restaurant, in the heart of the old fishermen's quarter between the Ango and Colbert bridges, is not in the thick of things over on the quai Henri IV or in the town centre, it is always busy and, as it only seats 24, you must book a table for lunch or dinner. Its attractions are many. Filled with warmth and bonhomie, it seems to have taken on the character of its welcoming owner, and is prettily decorated, its plain walls hung with old photographs. Prices are just as attractive for the lashings of fresh grilled fish and *fruits de mer* that fill the menus (the 10.37-euro weekday menu is superb). On Friday evenings and Saturdays, you choose specialities from the blackboard. If it's available, the *foie gras du pêcheur* is highly recommended.

CLOSED Sun, Mon; 2 weeks Mar, Aug
CARDS MC, V

Our traditional French cuisine symbol
So many of our readers enjoy seeking out the genuinely French eating experience that we have used Fr to mark restaurants which offer *cuisine du terroir*, classical French dishes or regional dishes with an emphasis on local ingredients, and traditional recipes.

Dieppe
◆ Les Tourelles €

43 rue du Commandant-Fayolle, 76200 Dieppe, Seine-Maritime
Tel 02 35 84 15 88

Of Dieppe's 100 or so restaurants, most tourists pick one along the refurbished quai Henri IV. But, if you're willing to leave the beaten track, walk up the pedestrian-only Grande Rue to the Café des Tribunaux, turn right and hunt out Les Tourelles behind the ancient seafront towers. You can't miss its Art Deco façade in blue and white. The Larsonneurs serve copious and inventive dishes in a charming, old-fashioned setting with a clock whose chimes punctuate your meal. The basic menu costs a mere 9 euros, or you could give yourself a three-course treat for 12 euros. Fish dishes predominate, and the *assiette du pêcheur* makes a generous starter. A wine buff, Guy Larsonneur will guide you through his interesting list.

CLOSED Sun dinner, Mon, Tue dinner
CARDS MC, V

Doudeville
◆ Relais du Puits Saint-Jean €€ - €€€ Fr

rue Henri Delanos, 76560 Doudeville, Seine-Maritime
Tel 02 35 96 50 99 Fax 02 39 95 61 82

Hearty fare is the order of the day at this simple restaurant with plenty of character, which occupies a large brick building in solid Norman style. Traditional local dishes are the ones they do best, so go for pressed duck, *terrine maison au lin accompagnée d'une confiture à l'oignon* (served with a glass of homemade cider), lobster, *pot-au-feu de l'océan* or *poulet fermier rôti à la graine de lin, cuit au lait entier, à la crème et monté au beurre*. There may be few surprises here, but the ingredients are fresh from the farm or the sea.

❝ Robust home-grown and cooked food ... worth a small detour if your appetite is large enough ❞

CLOSED part of Feb
CARDS MC, V

La Fossé
◆ Auberge du Beau-Lieu €€ - €€€

76440 Le Fossé, Forges-les-Eaux, Seine-Maritime
Tel 02 35 90 50 36 Fax 02 35 90 35 98

You wouldn't necessarily expect a roadside inn (on the main A15 Paris-Dieppe road) to serve superb, adventurous cuisine, but the Beau-Lieu defies expectation. A restaurant with a couple of rooms, it has rustic decoration and a snug atmosphere, partly due to the wood fires, lit in winter months, and partly to the friendly hostess's warm welcome. As far as the cooking is concerned, eating here is an event with nothing left to chance. Every dish looks immaculate; the style is traditional Norman but with inventive, contemporary dash. So you might spot *marinade de Saint-Jacques Dieppoise*, monkfish in cider, or *gratin de poire à la frangipane* on the menu. Choose from a long, interesting wine list as an accompaniment. Not surprisingly this *auberge* has a

large and faithful clientele. It is just before Forges-les-Eaux travelling towards the D915, and is approached through quite a pretty little garden.

❝ If you're celebrating, go for the menu gastronomique ❞

CLOSED Mon dinner, Tue, Thu lunch
CARDS AE, DC, MC, V

Our price bands
Rather than giving actual prices (which are prone to change) we indicate the cost of a three-course meal for one person, without wine, by means of price bands. They are as follows: € under 30 euros €€ 30-50 euros €€€ over 50 euros. Where we give more than one price band, for example €-€€€, this indicates that in that restaurant a meal can be had at a range of prices. As well as the cost of *prix fixe* menus, our price bands also take into account the cost of an average selection from the *à la carte* menu.

Fourges
◆ Le Moulin de Fourges €€ - €€€

38 rue du Moulin, 27630 Fourges, Eure
Tel 02 32 52 12 12 Fax 02 32 52 92 56

It's hard to imagine a more exquisite or typically Norman setting for a meal than this ivy-covered picture-postcard-pretty mill on the banks of the river Epte, within striking distance of Monet's garden at Giverny and Roche-Guyon castle. On sunny days, you can enjoy the setting to the full and eat outside by the river, whilst in winter you dine in the cosy dining room beside an open fire. Cathy and Jérôme Crépatte serve inventive regional cuisine, preferring local ingredients for their three seductive menus. Rabbit and vegetable *pâté*, followed by kidney chowder with cider and apples or sea bream stuffed with chicory preserve might be typical of the *menu du moulin*. However, if you're feeling slightly richer and more adventurous, you might choose the lobster salad or the duo of *foie gras*, one cooked with port wine, the other marinated with lavender, and then veal medallions, Livarot cream cheese and fresh pasta, or the tenderest beef with marrow, garlic, potatoes and corn, one of their classics, from the *menus gourmand* or *gastronomique*.

❛ Memorable meal, great setting ❜

CLOSED Sun dinner, Mon Feb-Jul, Sep-Jan
CARDS MC, V

Gisors
◈ Château de la Rapée
€€

Bazincourt-sur-Epte, 27140 Gisors, Eure
Tel 02 32 55 11 61 Fax 02 32 55 95 65

Agrandly conceived but small-scale period piece, this is more 19thC Gothic mansion than château, in a peaceful setting at the end of a long, rutted forest track from Bazincourt. Inside, original features have been carefully preserved and the house has been pleasantly furnished with antiques and reproductions. At first glance the elegant dining room might seem rather formal, with its high beamed ceiling, white tablecloths and straight-backed upholstered chairs. But this isn't really the case: fresh flowers grace every table, it is decorated in warm colours and on cold winter evenings a log fire roars in the hearth. Here, Pascal and Philippe Bergeron take their cooking seriously – classic dishes, with some regional influences and occasional original flourishes. The 36-euro menu stands out for its quality, including *coquilles Saint-Jacques Dieppoise* and *pieds d'agneau farcis à la Rouennaise*. After your meal, you might take a turn around the pretty flower garden.

CLOSED Wed; Feb; last 2 weeks Aug
CARDS AE, MC, V

Martin-Eglise
◈ Auberge du Clos Normand €€ – €€€ **Fr**

22 rue Henri IV, 76370 Martin-Eglise,
Seine-Maritime
Tel 02 35 04 40 34 Fax 02 35 04 48 49

The outskirts of Dieppe are only a few minutes' drive away from this charming country inn, but you would never know it.

The only real imponderable about this place is whether the dining room is in the kitchen – or the other way round. Either way the result is cosy and cheerful. Scooting around the flagged floor on his chef's stool, M. Hauchecorne has been exercising his culinary skills in public for 25 years. When asked about the staples of his menu, "*Tarte aux moules*, turbot, sole, *barbue*, *foie gras de canard*," he beams, "plenty of cream and butter – and the wines of the Loire." A sign on the road says 'Enter lightly', but it's unlikely that you'll be able to leave in the same fashion. The menu card was illustrated by his son, an artist who has a small *atelier* in Dieppe. Outside the river Eaulne flows between the large garden and the pasture beyond, the view for the nine modest bedrooms in a separate annexe.

CLOSED Mon dinner, Tue; mid-Nov to mid-Dec
CARDS AE, MC, V

Our traditional French cuisine symbol
So many of our readers enjoy seeking out the genuinely French eating experience that we have used Fr to mark restaurants which offer *cuisine du terroir*, classical French dishes or regional dishes with an emphasis on local ingredients, and traditional recipes.

Mesnières-en-Bray
◈ L'Auberge du Bec Fin €€– €€€

rue du Château, 76270 Mesnières-en-Bray,
Deux-Sèvres
Tel 02 35 94 15 15 Fax 02 35 94 42 14

If you look around this restaurant in the attractive village of Mesnières, you'll see a refreshing mix of people at the other tables from large family gatherings to romantic young couples. Its compelling blend of the traditional – wooden beams, panelling, mullioned windows – and smart formal style – lavish displays of fresh flowers, striped yellow wallpaper, silver candlesticks and cutlery, starched white napkins – clearly appeals to everyone. Eric Autun is the chef. He offers five menus as well as a *carte*, all imaginative and original. His salmon and duck dishes are particularly recommended. Some menus include a cheeseboard so enormous it has to be wheeled to your table on a trolley. Puddings are unusual and delicious, and must be ordered with the rest of your meal. Beware, the wine list is pricey, but the house red is both drinkable and affordable.

❛ The best confit de canard I've eaten ❜

CLOSED Mon (except public hols)
CARDS DC, MC, V

Fr French regional or classical French dishes on menu.

Mesnil-Val
◆ La Vieille Ferme
€ – €€

76910 Mesnil-Val, Seine-Maritime
Tel 02 35 86 72 18 Fax 02 35 86 12 67

Book well ahead at this popular, black-and-white timbered hotel-restaurant in the tranquil little village of Mesnil-Val. It has a low sloping roof, dotted with dormer windows, each one decorated with a box spilling over with geraniums. Run efficiently by the amiable M. and Mme Maxime, intuitive hosts, eager to put their guests at ease. The restaurant is well-regarded, specializing in typical Norman cuisine, with the emphasis on *fruits de mer* – hardly surprising when you consider how close it is to the sea. There is a delightful small beach nearby, and an enchanting, flowery garden, behind hedges, to eat, drink and relax in. They have a well-stocked cellar and, if you can't tear yourself away, there are 31 pretty bedrooms, some of which have views of the sea.

CLOSED Sun dinner, Mon; early Dec to early Jan
CARDS AE, DC, MC, V

Les Petites Dalles
◆ La Plage €

92 rue Joseph-Heuzé, 76540 Les Petites Dalles, Seine-Maritime
Tel 02 35 27 40 77

Oysters and mussels are the specialities at this substantial brick hotel-restau-rant a pebble's skim from the beach, although the requirements of meat-lovers are never ignored. Les Petites-Dalles is a small seaside resort between Fécamp and Saint-Valery-en-Caux, and a wonderfully tranquil spot in low season. Surprisingly, you won't have to reach too deep into your pockets for such mouthwatering dishes as *moules de Normandie mitonées dans une crême de ferme au Neufchâtel, avec cidre et vinaigre de cidre, le tout parfumé avec des pleurotes et légumes des maraîchers de la vallée de la Durdent*. As this implies, the owners support small local producers, and hand-pick their ingredients, which are of a consistently high quality.

❛ Modest prices for fine dining at this seaside location ❜

CLOSED Mon dinner, Sun, Mon lunch and Wed low season; Christmas and Feb school hols
CARDS MC, V

Looking for somewhere to stay? See page 241.

Pont-Audemer
◆ Auberge du Vieux Puits
€ – €€€ **Fr**

6 rue Notre-Dame-du-Pré, 27500 Pont-Audemer, Eure
Tel 02 32 41 01 48 Fax 02 32 42 37 28

Although war-damaged Pont-Audemer still has a charming historic centre, it is rather dwarfed by the nondescript suburbs that have grown up around it. The Vieux Puits shines out like a beacon – all crooked beams and leaded windows. Inside, it is a medievalist's dream, with twisting wooden stairs and dark beams hung with shining copper and ancient pewter. The simple, restrained decoration brings out the best in the building. The dining rooms are carefully furnished with antiques and decorated with fresh flowers. The kitchen maintains exceptionally high standards, and the seasonal menus and *carte* feature interesting dishes, many based on traditional recipes (for example, *canard aux cerises* and *truite Bovary au Champagne*).

CLOSED Mon, Tue low season; late Dec to late Jan
CARDS MC, V

Pont-Audemer
 Belle Ile sur Risle

€ – €€€

*112 route de Rouen, 27500 Pont-Audemer,
Eure
Tel 02 32 56 96 22 Fax 02 32 42 88 96*

If your heart sinks slightly as you drive along the unpromising suburban road towards Belle Ile for the first time, don't worry: the charming owner, Madame Yazbeck, felt exactly the same. When you cross the little bridge to the romantic setting of a private wooded island, your spirits will lift, and they will positively soar as you step into the elegant interior. Rescued from dereliction, this mid-19thC mansion has become a thoroughly well-equipped hotel and restaurant, without losing the welcoming feel of a private house. Period furniture is mixed with oriental touches, and the food is served in a raised conservatory with a wonderful view of the river, particularly at sunset. The new chef, Laurent Trontin, has already won a glowing reputation for his contemporary, subtly spiced cooking.

❛ The pastilla de lapin was absolutely delicious ❜

CLOSED Wed mid-Mar to mid-Jun; Jan to mid-Mar, mid-Nov to late Dec
CARDS AE, DC, MC, V

● *For a splendidly filling meal in pretty medieval Les Préaux – dubbed 'the Venice of Normandy' because of its canals – try La Cressonnière (02 32 42 10 60), where the food is in keeping with the traditional timbered building.*

Please send us reports
A guide such as this thrives on reader's reports. If you send us five usable reports, we will send you a free copy of any title in our *Charming Small Hotel Guides* series (see page 241 for France titles in the series).
The five reports should contain at least two new restaurants; the rest can be com-

ments on restaurants already in the guide.
1 Tell us about your experiences in restaurants already in this guide.
2 Send us new reports. New reports should give the following information:
- **Region** – City, town, village or neaest village.
- **Name of restaurant** – Please double check the spelling, it's surprisingly easy to make a mistake.
- **Address** – including *département*.
- **Telephone number** – plus fax and e-mail if available. Double check this information.
- **Objective description** – Try to explain simply why it should be in the guide. Remember that the guide is very selective - our entries are those one-in-five places that combine
  ● **interesting food with**
  ● **character and charm, in the building, the setting or both.**
  The guide hates tourist traps, and pretentious, dressed-up food. We like places where the French go.
  We favour places in the lower and middle price bands but there are plenty of expensive places that have our qualities, and we list those too.
- **Diner's comments** – These should be short, personal comments on features that strike you. They can be your comments, or others'.
- **Closing times**
- **Credit cards accepted**
  Don't forget to date your report and add your name and address.
Send reports to Charming Restaurant Guides, Duncan Petersen Publishing, 31 Ceylon Road, London W14 OPY.

Rouen
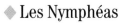 **Les Nymphéas**

€ – €€€

*7-9 rue de la Pie, 76000 Rouen, Seine-Maritime
Tel 02 35 89 26 69 Fax 02 35 70 98 81*

In a quiet street off Rouen's place du Vieux Marché with its grotesquely 'reptilian' church, Les Nymphéas has a Michelin rosette and a secluded garden terrace, raising it a notch above other restaurants in the city, and making it an excellent choice for a summer lunch or dinner. The dining room is attractive, but the terrace, with its shrubs, pots of colourful flowers and striped parasols, is a really special place to eat. The restaurant is favoured by locals (you see few tourists here), drawn principally by the imaginative cuisine, perhaps the delicious *foie gras*, pigeon and wide selection of fish in particular (apparently the *sandre* is superb). Very occasionally, they seem to try too hard as in a dessert of red fruits, garnished with olives. The wine list is extensive but not overpriced, and the service is friendly and helpful.

> ❛ *A serious restaurant' ... 'beguiling amuse-bouches and patisseries with coffee* ❜

CLOSED Sun evening, Mon; one week Feb, late Aug to early Sep (annual closure varies: phone to check)
CARDS MC, V

● *For a lively bistro in Rouen, look no further than Le P'tit Zinc (02 35 89 39 69), where Maud Simon is an enthusiastic proponent of cuisine bourgeoise.*

Saint-Martin-Osmonville
◆ L'Auberge de la Varenne
€ – €€ **Fr**

2 route de la Libération, 76680 Saint-Martin-Osmonville, Seine-Maritime
Tel 02 35 95 08 13 Fax 02 35 34 59 82

Eight years ago Pierre Davoine and Frédéric François teamed up to open this successful restaurant in an enchanting village near Bosc-sur-Buchy. Housed in an old inn with beams and wood panelling, it is cheerfully decorated in yellow and blue with a fruit design frieze. The walls of the main dining area are half-panelled with an apricot colour above. Focal points are a grand old stone fireplace and a tableau of wines, proudly displayed on gravel behind glass. The three perfectly pitched menus and *carte* are evidence that the proprietors know exactly what their customers want – excel-

lently cooked and presented, reasonably priced regional dishes – and can give it to them. Perennial favourites include *feuilleté Normand sur salade*, *foie gras de canard en terrine au vin doux*, *merlan vapeur sur purée de poix casses*, *magret de canard au cidre* and *gigot d'agneau rôti au thym*, *servi eminćé sur crème d'ail*.

CLOSED Sun evening, Mon; late Dec to early Jan
CARDS MC, V

Saint-Pierre-du-Vauvray
◆ Hostellerie Saint-Pierre €€

chemin des Amoureux, 27430 Saint-Pierre-du-Vauvray, Eure
Tel 02 32 59 93 29 Fax 02 32 59 41 93

An ideal stopover on the banks of the Seine and only a short drive from the Paris-Rouen motorway, this family-run hotel-restaurant is a bizarre concoction architecturally: a modern building, triangular in plan with a turret on one corner and half-timbered like a traditional Norman manor house. It sounds naff, but don't dismiss it. Not the least of its attractions is the cuisine – classical in style but inventive and light in approach, and of excellent quality, with the emphasis on fish and seafood: witness the enormous tank of *langoustes* and other consumables dominating the heavily decorated dining room (which has big picture windows looking on to the river). Its other bonuses are friendly service, 14 comfortable, well-equipped bedrooms, and a garden, which stretches down to the water's edge and is a relaxing place to sit.

CLOSED Tue lunch; early Jan to mid-Mar, mid-Nov to late Dec
CARDS MC, V

Sommery
◆ Le Relais du Bec Fin
€ – €€

La Cavée, 76440 Sommery, Seine-Maritime
Tel 02 35 09 61 30

Don't be put off by the blue neon strips outside this restaurant, or the too-bright yellow and blue colour scheme and framed black-and-white photos of film stars inside, it is the sister of Le Bec Fin at Menières (see page 10) and, despite these rather tacky touches, serves seriously good food. You get four courses on the 15-euro menu, starting perhaps with a choice of *salade océane* (a mixture of prawns, melon, beans and tomatoes) or *terrine de Saint-Jacques*. You could have *brochette d'agneau, mariné à l'Orientale* or duck as a main course, followed by salad or cheese. The choice of puddings typically includes *gratin de framboises au Sabayon, tarte fine aux poires caremélisées et sa glace vanille* and *crème brûlée à la fleur d'orange*. With a religious conviction, the blue decorative theme has been carried outside to the small patio garden, which comes into its own in summer.

❨ *Lively and friendly' ... 'serves a good choice of delicious, modestly priced food* ❩

CLOSED Mon; early Jul, end Aug
CARDS MC, V

Our traditional French cuisine symbol
So many of our readers enjoy seeking out the genuinely French eating experience that we have used Fr to mark restaurants which offer *cuisine du terroir*, classical French dishes or regional dishes with an emphasis on local ingredients, and traditional recipes.

Le Tréport
◆ Le Comptoir de l'Océan €–€€

46 quai François 1er, 76470 Le Tréport, Seine-Maritime
Tel 02 35 86 24 92 Fax 02 35 86 59 27

Le Tréport is famed for its quayside restaurants, whose proprietors have only to walk to the market across the road to obtain the freshly caught fish that are the glory of their menus. Le Comptoir de l'Océan is much favoured by the locals, including the mayor, all well trained in gastronomic appreciation. François Lavoine's menus are superb, though not cheap – try a succulent duck dish if you want a change from fish – and the service is impeccable (if you allow

for a short wait on a busy day). The wine list is impressive and your coffee may be accompanied by a plate of liqueur-soaked cherries instead of the usual tablet of chocolate. The menus start at 14.80 euros and extend to the gastronomic at 45 euros.

❨ *Splash out on the most expensive, luxurious, delectable menu* ❩

CLOSED never
CARDS AE, DC, MC, V

Our price bands
€ under 30 euros €€ 30-50 euros
€€€ over 50 euros for a menu.

Yvetot
◆ Auberge du Val au Cesne €–€€ Fr

le Val au Cesne, 76190 Yvetot, Seine-Maritime
Tel 02 35 56 63 06 Fax 02 35 56 92 78

In a quiet wooded valley south-east of Yvetot, this half-timbered inn springs out at you from an otherwise unremarkable roadside, looking slightly as if the Norman builder had suddenly developed Swiss leanings. Although the owner, Jérôme Carel, has created five boldly decorated bedrooms, Val au Cesne started life as a restaurant, with beams, log fires in winter, acres of family photos and a cuisine that is both regional and seasonal – the stuffed filet of sole and escalope of turkey are both highly recommended. A modestly priced *logis de France* menu is always available too. The original snug dining room flows round a stone chimney breast into another room and, as its popularity has grown, space on the first floor has been brought into play to extend the seating capacity of the restaurant, whilst outside cats, dogs, ducks, parakeets and prize poultry compare lengthy pedigrees with one another in the flower-filled garden.

❨ *Certainly worth a detour to discover this old inn buried in the country' ... 'The set menu is unbeatable* ❩

CLOSED Mon, Tue; 3 weeks Jan, late Aug to early Sep
CARDS AE, DC, MC, V

Fort-Mahon 67
Quend 68
Rue 69

Abbeville

D925
A16
A28
D1015
N25
D929

HAUTE-
NORMANDIE

D901

Amiens 64
N29
A29
A1

Caulières 65

PICARDIE

D9158

N1

Gerberoy 67

A16

D901

Beauvais

D916

Compiegne
D200

Agnetz 64
N31
N17

B981

Creil
A16
N1

Chantilly 65 66
Apremont 64
Coye-la-Fôret 66

ILE-DE-FRANCE

PARIS

PICARDIE

Picardy lies just north of Paris and Ile-de-France, touching the English Channel around the bays of the Somme and Authie, and stretching to Champagne to the west. To the north lies the Nord-Pas-de-Calais region, and the border with Belgium. There are plenty of fine sights among Picardy's flat, misty plains and valleys – the cathedrals of Amiens, Beauvais and Senlis, the medieval town of Laon, high on its hill overlooking the Champagne plain, Senlis, Chantilly, Compiègne, Ermenonville and Soissons --- and, of course, the impeccably maintained cemeteries and war memorials of the Somme, which sear the landscape with their memories.

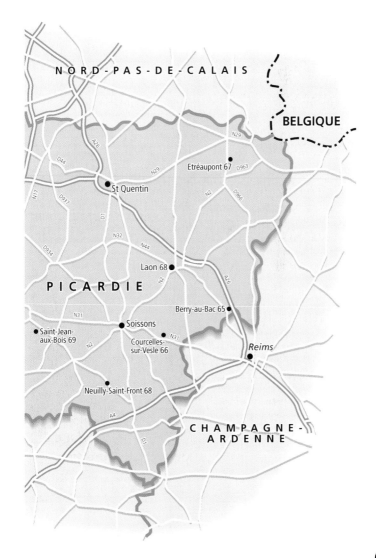

Agnetz
◆ Auberge de Gicourt
€ – €€ Fr

466 avenue Fôret de Hez, 60600 Agnetz,
Oise
Tel 03 44 50 00 31 Fax 03 44 50 42 29

On the edge of Hez-Froidment forest, 2 km (one mile) west of Clermont, the little town of Agnetz is worth a detour both for its interesting church, part of which dates back to the 13th century, and for a pit stop at this attractive, comfortable inn. Usually packed with locals, it offers two affordable menus featuring regional specialities mostly from the south west: *thon rouge confit à l'huile d'olive, boudin noir de canard, noisette d'agneau en piperade, gâteau Basque à la marmelade de cerises noires.*

(*We had a delicious confit de canard' ... 'The menu de terroir was a bargain at 17 euros*)

Closed Sun evening, Mon, Wed evening
Cards AE, MC, V

Our price bands
Rather than giving actual prices (which are prone to change) we indicate the cost of a three-course meal for one person, without wine, by means of price bands. They are as follows: € under 30 euros €€ 30-50 euros €€€ over 50 euros. Where we give more than one price band, for example €–€€€, this indicates that in that restaurant a meal can be had at a range of prices. As well as the cost of *prix fixe* menus, our price bands also take into account the cost of an average selection from the *à la carte* menu.

Amiens
◆ Le Bouchon € – €€ Fr

10 rue Alexandre-Fatton, 80000 Amiens,
Somme
Tel 03 22 92 14 32 Fax 03 22 91 12 58

Done out just like a traditional Lyon *bouchon* with red banquettes and a zinc-topped bar, this small, bustling restaurant near Tour Perret is convenient if you want a break from exploring the old town. In keeping with the decoration, the menus feature a number of traditional Lyonnais dishes (*charcuterie, pied de cochon, andouillette à la ficelle*), together with more local specialities, including their *spécialité de la maison*, a snail stew cooked with thyme, and delicious, simply grilled fish. Menus are reasonably priced, but the wine list, though impressive, is overpriced. The waiters wear genial smiles, and the ambience is refreshingly informal and low-key.

Closed Sun
Cards AE, DC, MC, V

Apremont
◆ La Grange aux Loups
€ – €€€

8 rue du 11 Novembre, 60300 Apremont,
Oise
Tel 03 44 25 33 79 Fax 03 44 24 22 22

A surprise lies in store in this sleepy country village: a rustic, welcoming inn that offers *cuisine gastronomique*. Inside, you'll find rough stone walls, exposed beams, wood tables and, most impressive of all, a huge chimney, where a cheerful fire crackles in winter. (Summer meals are served on the terrace.) Jean-Claude Jalloux welcomes his visitors with enormous enthusiasm. You are literally taken in hand the moment you walk through the door into the reception. His warm personality, brilliant smile and love of his work make him a real ambassador for French gastronomy. He refuses to serve a dish without giving detailed descriptions of its ingredients, and never misses an opportunity to heap praise on his chef, whose cuisine you can sample without worrying unduly about your pocket by sticking to the good-value 25 or 34-euro menus. If you want to push the boat out, the *menu dégustation* (48 euros, including wine) is unbeatable. It includes cold and hot *entrées*, a main course, cheese (try the delicious *fourme d'Ambert*) and a dessert (go for the wonderful *sabayon de poire au miel mille fleurs*).

(*A regional restaurant with a great reputation*)

Closed Sat lunch, Sun
Cards MC, V

Berry-au-Bac
◆ La Côte 108 € – €€€

02190 Berry-au-Bac, Aisne
Tel 03 23 79 95 04 Fax 03 23 79 83 50

Serge Courville is something of a celebrity chef in Picardie, and this is his Michelin-starred restaurant. In stylish surroundings, he changes his imaginative menus with the season. An instinctive cook with a streak of adventure, he doesn't ignore the classic dishes, but likes to introduce some truly innovative, contemporary ones too. His style is always lively and very appealing, evident in his *millefeuille de tourteau au parmesan, langoustines rôties au beurre d'agrume, carré d'agneau rôti aux épices douces* and *crème brûlée à la bergamote*. The *sommelier* will help you to choose just the right wines from the serious list.

❬ The best meal we had in France ❭

CLOSED Sun evening, Mon, Tue evening; mid- to late Jul, late Dec to mid-Jan
CARDS AE, MC, V

Caulières
◆ Auberge de la Forge
€ – €€€

14 rue de la 49ème-BCA, 80290 Caulières, Somme
Tel 03 22 38 00 91 Fax 03 22 38 08 48

In a beautiful timbered building off the RN 29, the Grebonvils are a successful and talented husband-and-wife team. Sylvie is front of house with a young and dynamic force of helpers, who not only give their guests a warm welcome, but are always ready to offer excellent advice on menu choices. Patrick is the chef. He only uses seasonal ingredients for his regional gastronomic cuisine, and specializes in fish and seafood. The *menu gourmand* at 32 euros is hard to resist. You might choose *la mousseline d'huitres au saumon fumé* to start, followed by *les escalopes de saumon, lotte et Saint-Jacques truffées au Champagne*. Then freshen the palate with an apple sorbet *au marc de Bourgogne*, before a choice of veal, duck, lamb, monkfish or salmon dishes. You could finish with cheese and salad, and some mouthwatering desserts. If you can't cope with every course, variations are possible, and there is the alternative *menu du terroir*, which changes according to the season. You must book for dinner.

CLOSED Wed evening
CARDS MC, V

Our traditional French cuisine symbol
So many of our readers enjoy seeking out the genuinely French eating experience that we have used Fr to mark restaurants which offer *cuisine du terroir*, classical French dishes or regional dishes with an emphasis on local ingredients, and traditional recipes.

Chantilly
◆ Aux Gouters Champêtres €

parc du Château de Chantilly, Le Hameau, 60500 Chantilly, Oise
Tel 03 44 57 46 21 Fax 03 44 57 28 23

As you approach this delightful straw-thatched building, deep in the park belonging to the Château de Chantilly, between groves and box hedges and by a little stream, you are likely to be greeted by the ducks who wander freely around the grounds and the wonderful scents of aromatic herbs grown in its little herb garden. This is a restaurant with a history: originally the dairy for the Princes of Condé, it was the place where the famous Chantilly cream was first made, and is still produced to the same recipe by M. and Mme Duda, who are dedicated to carrying on the tradition. The feeling that you could be in the middle of the country is reinforced inside, where walls are wood-panelled and, from 11am to 7pm, the Dudas produce wholesome snacks and lunches. (They don't serve dinner because the gates to the château grounds close at 7pm.) Although the dishes vary, they always offer a range of puddings, tarts, sorbets and cakes, to accompany their Chantilly cream. If you decide you can't live without it, you can buy the recipe on a postcard. On Sunday afternoons between the middle of May and early September, the waiters and waitresses dress in 18thC costume and serve specialities of the period.

CLOSED dinner; mid-Nov to mid-Mar
CARDS MC, V

Chantilly
◆ Le Goutillon
€ Fr

61 rue du Connétable, 60500 Chantilly, Oise
Tel 03 44 58 01 00 Fax 03 44 53 52 76

Its proximity to the race course quickly landed this restaurant its unofficial role as meeting place of aficionados and those passionate about horses. Almost everyone here seems to be a jockey, trainer, polo player or, at the very least, a punter. It's a memorable place: a bustling, friendly, traditional, typically French café-restaurant, where you will be welcomed by smiling Mamy or shy Bernard. Apart from the stone walls and red leather banquettes, everything is wood – the bar, the stools, the fridges, which form the background for Bernard's eclectic collection of bric-à-brac, including ancient iron plaques, colanders and worn leather satchels. Every centimetre of wall and ceiling space is filled. There are few frills (the vinyl tablecloths are worn) and no menu (dishes of the day are written on a blackboard), but you come here first and foremost for Michel Marteau's food. Having honed his skills in large Paris restaurants, he has moved to the country with the confidence to introduce 100-year-old recipes to the 21stC palette. Everything is simple, home-made (even the Scottish salmon is steeped in whisky and smoked on the premises) and exquisitely cooked: try *poulet aux écrevisses*, *filet de boeuf au poivre*, *tarte à l'abricot* or one of his delectable patisseries.

❛ A unique restaurant' ... 'relaxed atmosphere' ... 'terrific traditional food ❜

CLOSED never
CARDS AE, MC, V

Courcelles-sur-Vesle
◆ Château de Courcelles
€€ – €€€

8 rue de Château, 02220 Courcelles-sur-Vesle, Aisne
Tel 03 23 74 13 53 Fax 03 23 74 06 41

The management seems to be doing something quite special here. It is a graceful, not intimidatingly large, late 17thC, Louis XIV-style château set in a small park in a peaceful backwater of the Vesle between Reims and Soissons; and, of course, it has a history – Napoléon and Rousseau were guests. But it is not the magical surroundings that strike guests, so much as the remarkably warm welcome and impressive food. Head chef here since 1998, Eric Samson trained in Switzerland, then with Jean Bardet in Tours and Jacques Cagna in Paris before spending time perfecting his skills with fish and seafood in Brittany and Canada. He offers tasting, business (Mon-Fri lunch) and regional menus as well as a *carte*. Served in three dining rooms, specialities of the house include *petits boudins de brochet truffés, beurre mousseux d'écrevisses* and *la Charlotte de langoustines aux aubergines confites coulis de crustacés*. The château also has a particularly fine cellar.

CLOSED never
CARDS AE, DC, MC, V

Coye-la-Fôret
◆ Auberge Les Etangs
€ – €€

1rue des Clos des Vignes, 60580 Coye-la-Fôret, Oise
Tel 03 44 58 60 15 Fax 03 44 58 75 95

The Colagiacomos have been running this cosy *auberge* in the forest of Chantilly for 23 years, never losing their passion or their enthusiasm. It is their commitment and good humour as well as the first-class, yet modestly priced, traditional food they love to see produced that has ensured its reputation as *une très bonne addresse*. Madame is the interior decorator: she has done out a series of beamed dining rooms in Louis XIII style, with hand-made lace lampshades, English porcelain and fresh flowers, even in winter. There is an enchanting terrace, sheltered from the street by a high hedge, shaded by a lime tree and overlooking the pretty flowered garden. For the past ten years, the Colagiacomos have been blessed in having Christian Caux as their chef. Using only the freshest ingredients for what he sees as his art, he produces two menus: a *touristique* and a *gastronomique*. Specialities that set the tastebuds zinging include *terrine de bre-bis frais aux poivrons et aubergines, pavé de sandre à la Bordelaise, grenadin de veau aux girolles* and *tarte Isabella, poire et amande.*

❛ A fantastic place to eat - I recommend it without hesitation ❜

CLOSED Mon, Tue; 2 weeks late Jul, 2 weeks late Jan, one week Feb
CARDS AE, DC, MC, V

Etréaupont
◆ L'Auberge du Val de l'Oise €€ – €€

8 rue Albert Ledant, 02580 Etréaupont, Aisne
Tel 03 23 97 40 18 Fax 03 23 97 48 92

Marie-Lise and Dominique Trokay have created this stylish restaurant in a well-established small hotel, Le Clos du Montvinage, which occupies a *bourgeois* house of the mid-19th century. It is full of character and set in lovely, leafy grounds. The menu is interesting and well priced, with plenty of choice and some adventurous touches (for example, *la moussaka d'avocat farci de veau au coulis Richelieu*) and – unusually for France – a large selection of vegetarian dishes. Particular recommendations include the *ris de veau aux cèpes et à la vieille prune, sauté de Saint-Jacques et homard coulis oursins* and *clafoutis au Maroilles, compôte mijoté de Saint-Jacques, homardine, vacherin glacé au cassis.*

CLOSED Sun evening, Mon lunch; first week Jan, one week Feb, one week Aug
CARDS AE, DC, MC, V

Fort-Mahon
◆ La Mouette €€ – €€€ Fr

1176 avenue Plage, 80790 Fort-Mahon, Somme
Tel 03 22 27 70 53

La Mouette is a restaurant in two parts, and the great thing about it is that you can choose to dine either at one of the scrubbed tables in the relaxed brasserie or in the more formal surroundings of the restaurant itself. Here the tables are cov-

ered in crisp white cloths, separated by trellises, and lit by chandeliers. From the walls, the occasional stag's head surveys the scene. Perhaps not surprisingly for a restaurant so close to the shore, the seafood is superb, and the menu includes an impressive selection of local *fruits de mer*, alongside a wide choice of other traditional dishes. The excellence of the food is only surpassed by the charm and warmth of the owners.

❛ Memorable seafood ... wonderful welcome ❜

CLOSED phone for closing times
CARDS MC, V

Please send us reports
A guide such as this thrives on reader's reports. If you send us five usable reports, we will send you a free copy of any title in our *Charming Small Hotel Guides* series (see page 241 for France titles in the series).

The five reports should contain at least two new restaurants; the balance can be comments on restaurants already in the guide. **Send reports to** Charming Restaurant Guides, Duncan Petersen Publishing, 31 Ceylon Rd, London W14 0PY.

Gerberoy
◆ Ambassade de la République de Montmartre € Fr

2 allée du Jeu du Tamis, 60380 Gerberoy, Oise
Tel 03 44 82 16 50 Fax 03 44 82 67 35

Gerberoy is considered to be one of the 100 most beautiful villages in France and the Ambassade, at the foot of its ancient ramparts, is one of its most attractive buildings – half-timbered, light and rustic inside, with exposed beams. You are assured a genuine welcome from Jean-Pierre His, a real character, dressed all in black (including his hat), except for the red scarf knotted round his neck - and the atmosphere is as jovial as Jean-Pierre's personality. While you are sipping your aperitif, you can study the display of paintings by local artists and Danièle His' home-made regional products. Danièle is the cook, and an exceptionally talented one too, but she prefers to stay behind the scenes in her kitchen. She bases her cuisine on local ingredients, and makes almost everything herself. She doesn't offer a large choice, but her two set menus provide excellent balance and quality at a good price. *Marbré de foie gras de canard aux pommes et au Loupiac, l'aumonière de l'ambassadeur (foie gras poêlé et Saint-Jacques)* and *filet mignon de porc* are her signature dishes. There is a charming summer terrace with room to seat 30 and a view of the forest of Caumont.

❛ Taste Saint Rieul here – the only beer brewed in the Oise region ❜

CLOSED Sun evening, Mon, Tue evening
CARDS MC, V

Laon
◆ La Petite Auberge
€ – €€

45 boulevard Brossolette, 02000 Laon, Aisne
Tel 03 23 23 02 38 Fax 03 23 23 31 01

Willy-Marc Zorn, the son of the owner, is the chef, whose delicate interpretation of *cuisine du terroir* has put La Petite Auberge on the map. You are bound to be seduced by his *noix de Saint-Jacques à la crème de topinambour* or his *picatta de veau sauce à la truffe*, served with polenta *frites*, from a choice of menus at 20, 23 and 34 euros plus a *carte*.

CLOSED Sat lunch, Sun, Mon evening; Feb and spring school hols, first 2 weeks Aug
CARDS AE, MC, V

Neuilly-Saint-Front
◆ L'Auberge de la Cloche € Fr

11 rue Saint-Rémy-au-Mont, 02740 Neuilly-Saint-Front, Aisne
Tel 03 23 71 10 97 Fax 03 23 71 10 97

Just off the Champagne tourist trail near Villiers-Cotterêts, Alexandre Dumas' home town, the outside of this inn gives lit-

tle clue of what you will find inside. It's an intimate, rustic place. The low ceiling is beamed and the well-spaced tables (they can seat 80) are covered with flowery cloths. Floor-to-ceiling windows, overlooking a large covered terrace and wooded gardens beyond, ensure that the room is always bright and airy, and the terrace makes a glorious setting for lunch or dinner when the weather is warm. The good-value menus include traditional specialities of the region, with an emphasis on fish. *Saint-Jacques au Noilly, foie gras de canard maison, pavé de boeuf chatelaine* and *délice à l'orange et de l'estragon frais* are perennial favourites, and the *carte des vins* impresses with its strong selection from the Loire. The Izambards, who own and run the inn, are very friendly and welcoming people.

❛ A slice of the real, rural France … We had a splendid dinner here ❜

CLOSED Sun dinner, Mon lunch; 3 weeks Aug, late Dec to early Jan
CARDS MC, V

Quend
◆ Auberge Le Fiacre
€ – €€ Fr

Routhiauville, route de Fort-Mahon, 80120 Quend, Somme
Tel 03 22 23 47 30 Fax 03 22 27 19 80

If you come to this rustic restaurant on a Sunday at midday, you will find it packed with locals, out for lunch *en famille*. A typical country inn, it's charming in a rather outmoded way, the kind of place that changes little over the years. Although quite formal, the welcome is generous and friendly and, when coupled with a fine menu that concentrates on the local *terroir* and a reasonable selection of wines, it justifies a considerable detour. Among the most tempting dishes on the menu are *magret de canard aux pêches* and *salade de lapin à l'huile de noix*.

❛ A lovely old-fashioned inn' … 'Smiling service, excellent food ❜

CLOSED Tue lunch; 3 weeks Jan
CARDS MC, V

Rue
◆ Bonne Pâte € Fr

rue des Frères, Caudron,80120 Rue, Somme
Tel 03 22 25 65 16

There are three reasons for visiting this restaurant in the attractive village of Rue: exceptional food, outstandingly good prices, and the warmest of welcomes. Of the delicious dishes that fill the menu (most from Italy), you might try the wonderful *misto di pasta*, made with tasty, market-fresh ingredients and firm, perfectly cooked pasta, followed by a classic Italian pudding. They mix French and Italian cuisine in a dish such as *contrefilet* in a peppercorn sauce with penne. At 6-7 euros for a main course, you are unlikely to find any other restaurant locally that offers such good value for money. Finally, owners Pascal and Maryse Picot welcome you to their restaurant as friends: they say they like you to feel as if you are eating at their table in their home.

CLOSED Mon
CARDS MC, V

Rue
◆ Le Lion d'Or € – €€

5 rue de la Barrère, 80120 Rue, Somme
Tel 03 22 25 74 18 Fax 03 22 25 00 66

In a handsome beamed building, this *logis de France* is a popular choice for holidaymakers from the seaside resorts of Le Crotoy, Quend and Fort-Mahon-Plage (all just a few kilometres away) and for those en route to and from Calais. The restaurant is large (90 covers), congenial and bright with cheerful blue and yellow tablecloths, but otherwise decorated in a somewhat bizarre mish-mash of styles. There seems to be a country theme struggling to assert itself in the natural beams, collection of stuffed birds (some rather the worse for wear) and a paddle, hung with copper saucepans. There is also a little terrace (complete with astroturf) for summer dining. But it's the food that draws the crowds. Specialities from a range of menus and the *carte* are home-made *foie gras de canard, coquilles Saint-Jacques, moules* and fish (according to the season), accompanied by unusually generous helpings of vegetables. The meat dishes tend to be less reliable, but the home-

made ice-cream is delicious without fail.

❝ The pavé de saumon à la sauce crevettes was excellent ❞

CLOSED Sun low season; mid Dec to early Jan
CARDS AE, DC, MC, V

● *Try the restaurant that occupies the former stable block of the Château du Brontel (03 22 25 75 07), set back from the main street in the pretty village of Rue.*

Saint-Jean-aux-Bois
◆ Auberge à la Bonne Idée €€ – €€€

60350 Saint-Jean-aux-Bois, Oise
Tel 03 44 42 84 09 Fax 03 44 42 80 45

In a very pretty village on the edge of the huge Compiègne forest, this inn makes a charming and gastronomic stopover. Decorated in a rustic yet refined style, the dining room has a low ceiling with rafters, stone walls, wrought-iron wall lights, and large bay windows, elegantly dressed with heavy ivory curtains. The high-backed chairs are upholstered in smart striped fabric, and the small round tables impeccably laid. The service is careful but not overbearing, with helpful, friendly waiters. A young chef with a bright future ahead of him, Baptiste Biziaux has already excited interest with dishes such as *magret de canard à l'acacia, bar en croûte de sel, canette aux épices, cassolette de Saint-Jacques, nid de pigonneau* and *le chocolat chaud coulant au lait d'amandes douces*. There is a vast, tempting cheese trolley, which sits majesterially in the middle of the room. If money's no object, order the menu *à la bonne idée* (for 58 euros). It's exceptional. The shady terrace at the back is a lovely place to sit, relax and enjoy your coffee. Afterwards, you can take a stroll around the nearby abbey, an impressive building encircled by delightful little houses.

❝ If you're celebrating, go for the menu gastronomique ❞

CLOSED mid-Jan to mid-Feb
CARDS AE, MC, V

NORD-PAS-DE-CALAIS

Bordering both the English Channel and Belgium, this small region contains just two *départements*: Nord and Pas-de-Calais. It is the first port of call for many thousands of visitors to France, and for day-trippers it's very often the only one. Apart from the shopping opportunities of Calais and Boulougne, however, the region offers some unexpected delights: the magnificent Grand' Place in Arras; dynamic Lille (the regional capital); the picturesque town of Bergues and the windmill-dotted landscape of French Flanders; the pretty countryside of Avesnois around Maroilles and Bavay; and the Côte d'Opale between Calais and Boulogne.

BELGIQUE

Lille

NORD-PAS-DE-CALAIS

Etroeungt 73

PICARDIE

Aire-sur-la-Lys
◆ Trois Mousquetaires
€ – €€ **Fr**

27 rue du Fort de la Redoute, 62120 Aire-sur-la-Lys, Pas-de-Calais
Tel 03 21 39 01 11 Fax 03 21 39 50 10

An eccentric mixture of stone-and-brick stripes and pseudo-timbering beneath a steep slate roof, set in a large wooded garden with ponds and streams, this is a family-run *hostellerie* with a solid restaurant. The Venets are in charge – Madame looks after the hotel side, while her husband and son are the cooks. Their food has a regional bias, prepared and served from a spotless, open-to-view kitchen. The interior is traditionally grand in style, with 33 spruce bedrooms.

Closed mid-Dec to mid-Mar
Cards AE, DC, MC, V

Arques
◆ La Grande Sainte-Catherine € – €€ **Fr**

51 rue Adrien Danvers, 62510 Arques, Pas-de-Calais
Tel 03 21 38 03 73 Fax 03 21 38 17 39

You might have struck lucky, and, while gazing deep into a crystal masterpiece at the huge Verrerie-Cristallerie d'Arques, seen a sign that you should visit this excellent family hotel in the centre of the village – or you might have intended to take pot luck somewhere else. Either way, the traditional restaurant in this beautifully renovated 17thC *relais de poste* is well worth your attention. In winter you will sit in an elegant dining room, and in finer weather be offered a table on the very pretty garden terrace. The cuisine is unashamedly regional and well executed, and the service is flawless. For faster more economical fare there is also a cheerful, beamed bistro that offers a dish from each of France's ten regions – a kind of gastronomic Tour de France.

❢ *Fine regional food in an atmospheric former coaching inn* ❢

Closed Sat lunch, Sun evening
Cards AE, DC, MC, V

Arras
◆ L'Univers € – €€

3-5 place de la Croix Rouge, 62000 Arras, Pas-de-Calais
Tel 03 21 71 34 01 Fax 03 21 71 41 42

Don't miss out on Arras. The famous *places* (squares) in the town centre are spectacular, with their beautiful old gabled buildings, and a good reason to choose the town as a stopping place (the Channel Tunnel is less than an hour away by car). Another is the Hôtel de L'Univers, awkward to find in the backstreets behind the Hôtel de Ville, but worth the effort. Behind an arch off a pretty little square the handsome buildings, an old Jesuit college, form a peaceful quadrangle of their own, pleasantly apart from the bustle. Inside, exposed brickwork contrasts with white Picardy stone giving the pleasing striped effect that is traditional hereabouts, evident in the cosy bar where you can have drinks. In the restaurant, a handsome room with solid brick walls and smart striped curtains and matching chairs, you can sample the distinguished regional cooking with flashes of brilliance that is their speciality: *rôti de lotte à l'huile de noisettes* or *tournedos de veau au cidre, laqué aux épices*.

❢ *Superb wines ... calorific but irresistible puddings* ❢

Closed Sun dinner
Cards AE, MC, V

Attin
◆ Le Bon Accueil € – €€

62170 Attin, Pas-de-Calais
Tel 03 21 06 04 21 Fax 03 21 06 04 21

Between Le Touquet and Montreuil this family-run restaurant has been around for years. There has been no decline in standards though, as it exhibits what is almost a gold-backed guarantee of steady good value: it is consistently filled with French diners. The thoughtful, varied menu doesn't seem to change much but neither do the excellent, reasonably priced wines or the polite, professional service.

Closed Mon, Tue
Cards MC, V

Beutin

◆ Auberge de la Canche © Fr

3 RN39, 62170 Beutin, Pas-de-Calais
Tel 02 31 68 76 03 Fax 02 31 68 63 58

Newly restored and run by a family from Montreuil, the Auberge de la Canche is the answer to a prayer for somewhere with a terrace and a pretty garden, overlooking a stream, where you can park without fuss, and get a decent meal (from a comprehensive menu and a good wine list), pleasantly served. Then make a note to come back in winter when the big fireplace might just have blazing logs in it – which it will.

6 The place was full of locals 9

CLOSED Mon, Tue
CARDS MC, V

Our traditional French cuisine symbol
So many of our readers enjoy seeking out the genuinely French eating experience that we have used Fr to mark restaurants which offer *cuisine du terroir*, classical French dishes or regional dishes with an emphasis on local ingredients, and traditional recipes.

Blendecques

◆ Le Saint Sébastien © – ©© Fr

2 place de la Libération, 62575 Blendecques, Pas-de-Calais
Tel 03 21 38 13 05 Fax 03 21 39 77 85

South of Saint-Omer, showing a rather pleasing face to Blendecques' place de la Libération, this quiet *logis de France* is a warmly welcoming country hostelry. You are most likely to be welcomed by Mme Duhamel (Benoît will be in his kitchen) who will see you into the dining room of the moment. Of these, there are two, both decorated in rustic style, one twice the size of the other. If, up to now, you've carefully avoided *tête de veau*, or *pied de porc farci* for fear of making an expensive mistake then now's your chance: both are house specialities. If

you lose your nerve you can always settle for their excellent *brochette de lotte et de Saint-Jaques au beurre blanc*.

CLOSED Sat lunch, Sun evening, Mon
CARDS MC, V

● *For a wonderful place to eat, try Les Mauves (03 21 32 96 06), a delightful small hotel-restaurant in Cap Gris-Nez. It comes very highly recommended.*

Clairmarais

◆ Le Relais du Romelaëre © Fr

chemin du Grand Saint-Bernard, 62500 Clairmarais, Pas-de-Calais
Tel 03 21 38 95 95 Fax 03 21 38 95 99

Northeast of Saint-Omer, in the *marais audomarois* (Pas de Calais' equivalent of the fens in East Anglia), this comfortable and rustic establishment has brought fine, traditional and unfussy Flemish cuisine south of the Belgian border: they are particularly proud of their *carbonade* and *pot-jevlesh*. And, in traditional Flemish style, there are more beers to taste than you'd find at the average German *bierfest*. Once you get your feet firmly under the table you may be tempted to stay for a day or two – no problem as there are cheerful, simple rooms to be had.

CLOSED phone for closing times
CARDS MC, V

Etroeungt

◆ Auberge de la Capelette ©© Fr

Lieu-dit la Capelette, 59219 Etroeungt, Nord
Tel 03 27 59 28 33 Fax 03 27 59 28 72

If you mislaid your calendar on your travels and lost all track of time, you could get a pretty good approximation of the date by examining the menu at Naf and Dany Delmée's *ferme-auberge* in this pleasing little village south of d'Avesnes. Always moving with the seasons, and using the best and freshest of local ingredients, the result is superb regional cooking. Duck, lamb, guinea-fowl and suckling-pig all appear in the pleasant dining room at their appointed time. From the terrace there are panoramic views of the countryside – and it's worth taking a stroll before or after the pleasures of the dining table to get a closer look. You must book in advance.

CLOSED Jan
CARDS none

Gravelines
◆ Hôtel-Restaurant l'Alexandra

€ – €€

14 avenue de la Mer, 59820 Gravelines, Nord
Tel 03 28 51 30 00 Fax 03 28 65 32 77

Handy for Calais, and crowded to bursting point during the summer months, this is an unprepossessing building in a fine location overlooking the wide, sandy beach at Gravelines. Once inside, there is a marked improvement in looks, and the procession of seafood emerging from the kitchen is a joy to behold: mountains of *moules*, a wonderful variety of fish and vast platters of *fruits de mer*. If you need an extra excuse to be beside the sea, the impressive fortifications in the neighbourhood can be added to your reasons for stopping here. There are bedrooms to be had if you feel like making a night of it.

❢ *The best seafood we've eaten in France* ❟

CLOSED never
CARDS MC, V

Hardelot-Plage
◆ L'Océan

€ – €€

100 boulevard de la Mer, 62152 Hardelot-Plage, Pas-de-Calais
Tel 03 21 83 17 98 Fax 03 21 83 34 74

Should you need to resolve the conflicting demands in your party – of lunch for the grown-ups and extended bucket-and-spade hours for the younger members, then you could do worse than settle in to L'Océan, a typical French lunch spot. It's one of the few restaurants that are smack, bang right on the beach so you can safely tuck into your pre-prandial drink while keeping an eye on your children. The menus are well constructed with fish in most but not all of the starring roles, but service is pretty leisurely so there's no need to call in the sandcastle builders until your food actually appears on the table.

❢ *Great for families with children* ❟

CLOSED never
CARDS MC, V

Please send us reports
A guide such as this thrives on reader's reports. If you send us five usable reports, we will send you a free copy of any title in our *Charming Small Hotel Guides* series (see page 241 for France titles in the series).

The five reports should contain at least two new restaurants; the balance can be comments on restaurants already in the guide. **Send reports to** Charming Restaurant Guides, Duncan Petersen Ltd, 31 Ceylon Rd, London W14 0PY.

Hesdin
◆ Au Fil du Temps €

4 avenue Sainte-Austreberthe, 62140 Hesdin, Pas-de-Calais
Tel 03 21 86 83 08

The maple leaves are a substantial clue to the nationality of the chef, and the menus of this attractive brasserie-restaurant are larded with Québecois dishes amongst the more expected French ones. There is a brisk and faithful lunchtime trade, brought in by the thoughtful treatment given to the best of local produce – indeed they proudly announce their style as being *la cuisine des marchés*. Lunch is such a speciality that Au Fil du Temps is only open for dinner on Friday and Saturday nights. Good wines can be had by the glass, and you ignore at your peril the *plats du jour* chalked up on the blackboard: they will almost certainly be some of the wonderful dishes that you see being carried to the other tables.

❢ Francis and Danny are great hosts' ... 'Good value food and wine ❣

CLOSED Sun evening, Mon-Thu evening, Tue lunch
CARDS MC, V

● A restaurant with bags of character and an interesting menu, L'Ecurie (03 21 86 86 86) occupies some old stables in Hesdin and is a great place for lunch after the market on Thursday mornings.

Houlle
◆ L'Auberge de l'Étang Poupart €

*12 impasse des Etangs, 62910 Houlle, Pas-de-Calais
Tel 02 31 93 05 26 Fax 02 31 93 05 26*

If your passionate interest in gin has brought you down the river Houlle to La Distillerie Persyn, one of the oldest gin makers in the region, then, once you've sharpened your appetite, head for this low-built, lime-washed little house close to the mere from which it takes its name. Inside are tiles and beams and a large open fire for winter, and outside is a pleasant flower-decked summer terrace. Local produce and fish feature largely on Jérôme Delplace's menus (which change every day) and even the gin gets a look in as flavouring for some dishes.

CLOSED Sun evening, Tue evening
CARDS MC, V

Inxent
◆ L'Auberge d'Inxent
€ – €€

*318 rue de la Vallée, 62170 Inxent, Pas-de-Calais
Tel 03 21 90 71 19 Fax 03 21 86 31 67*

The trout caught in traps in the stream by this attractive 18thC *auberge* don't have

long to ponder their fate before they are whisked into the kitchen and prepared for the table in any one of four different ways. The same stream may well provide the cress and even the duck, which are combined to make an unusual and excellent soup. This is regional cooking with a light touch and just inventive enough to stay true to its roots without being dull and repetitive. Add to that a lovely position in this small village and you have an establishment well worth the detour.

CLOSED Mon lunch, Tue lunch, Tue dinner and Wed low season; mid-Dec to Feb
CARDS MC, V

Lépinoy
◆ Relais de la Forge € Fr

*RN39, 62990 Lépinoy, Pas-de-Calais
Tel 03 21 81 39 26*

Although in a course of a day the average tourist will probably whiz past a hundred places that look like the Relais de la Forge, this one is worth slowing down for. The decoration isn't especially impressive, but the scent of logs in the big, open fire in winter, or the smell of the charcoal grill outside in summer, both bring on a serious appetite. Full of locals, it is owned and run by a welcoming couple, the Wacheux. They also turn out excellent local dishes: *coq au vin, andouillette* with pepper and mustard sauce, duck and apple tart (the last is one of a long list of homemade desserts). Service is friendly and both the food and the thoughtful selection of wines are excellent value.

❢ Good-value regional cuisine' ... 'Cheerful, friendly atmosphere ❣

CLOSED Mon, Tue evening
CARDS MC, V

Madelaine-sous-Montreuil
◆ Auberge de la Grenouillère €€ – €€€

*La Madelaine-sous-Montreuil, 62170 Montreuil, Pas-de-Calais
Tel 03 21 06 07 22 Fax 03 21 86 36 36*

In a unique setting under the magnificent ramparts of Montreuil, by a trout stream, the Grenouillère, decorated throughout with froggy motifs, catches more than its fair share of English, and is known to many of them as the Froggery. But it catches them fairly with the services of a top-drawer chef and a well-stocked cellar. The spacious gravel terrace is an excellent spot for lunch, and on a summer evening, the late sun streaming through the trees on to the water is a magical sight. In winter and on chilly evenings you'll find gleaming brass and polished wood inside this low Picardy-style farmhouse. The menus change with the seasons and quality is consistently high. More expensive than most of its local competitors, but worth a visit just to be able to say you've been there.

CLOSED Tue, Wed Sep-Jul; Jan
CARDS AE, DC, MC, V

Our price bands
Rather than giving actual prices (which are prone to change) we indicate the cost of a three-course meal for one person, without wine, by means of price bands. They are as follows: € under 30 euros €€ 30-50 euros €€€ over 50 euros. Where we give more than one price band, for example €- €€€, this indicates that in that restaurant a meal can be had at a range of prices. As well as the cost of *prix fixe* menus, our price bands also take into account the cost of an average selection from the *à la carte* menu.

Montreuil
◆ Château de Montreuil €€€

4 chausée des Capuchins, 62170 Montreuil, Pas-de-Calais
Tel 03 21 81 53 04 Fax 03 21 81 36 43

This substantial, luxurious country house, dating from the 1930s, is a well-established favourite with British travellers. It is immaculately done out, with great taste throughout. There's a snug brick-and-beams bar, where you can have a drink before or after dinner in the elegant dining room. Christian Germain's cooking aims high and hits the target (the restaurant does not rely on English custom but has a loyal French following). *Pêche de petits bâteaux*, grouse

(in season) and *homard bleu à la bière ambrée et au gingembre* (for two people, on request) are his signature dishes. Although you're quite close to the town centre, the setting is quiet and the glorious English-style gardens secluded.

CLOSED mid-Dec to Feb
CARDS AE, DC, MC, V

Montreuil
◆ Le Darnétal €- €€€

place Darnétal, 62170 Montreuil, Pas-de-Calais
Tel 03 21 06 04 87 Fax 03 21 86 64 67

It's difficult to be sure whether Le Darnétal bought its furniture new, and they've both grown old gracefully together, or whether the impressive collection of pieces arrived more recently from conventional sources. Either way they seem to belong exactly where they are: on a small, peaceful square in the old section of the town. There's a marine bias to the impressive menu and one of the perennial favourites is warm oysters in Champagne. If you want to stay here, there are four large but slightly Spartan bedrooms to choose from.

❢ Often packed with English people
... Lisa is a very genial hostess ❟

CLOSED Mon, Tue; late Jun to mid-Jul
CARDS AE, DC, MC, V

Montreuil
◆ Relais du Roy €- €€

rue Pierre-Ledent, 62170 Montreuil, Pas-de-Calais
Tel 03 21 81 53 44

The French don't have monarchs any more but, when they did, this was a regular royal stop on journeys to and from the Channel ports. Victor Hugo stayed next door in the Hôtel de France while he was writing *Les Misérables*. Standing on the cobbled street that joins the upper and lower squares, the Relais du Roy has a great atmosphere, full of colour and fresh flowers. It offers classic French cooking at its best, but also caters for jaded palates by constantly supplementing the mainstream menus with daily specials to introduce interesting alternatives. There is a beautiful flow-ered courtyard for summer meals, and in winter a huge log fire burns inside. It's always busy, so it's a good idea to book.

6 Good-value specialities every day 9

CLOSED Tue, Wed
CARDS MC, V

Saint-Folquin
◆ Auberge de la Scierie
€€ – €€€

3739 route de Gravelines, 62370 Saint-Folquin, Pas-de-Calais
Tel 03 28 65 29 44 Fax 03 28 23 14 93

You might have lunch here by yourself, but there's no chance at all that you'll be alone in the evening: Auberge de la Scierie stays firmly shut at dinner time unless a minimum of eight people have booked in advance. If you can't raise a party of eight, seize any opportunity you can to piggy-back on other parties. Opposite a canal on the outskirts of Gravelines, this low roadside restaurant, brightly yellow-painted on the outside and beamed and wooden-floored on the inside, offers *cuisine du marché*: the menu is driven by what they feel is worthy of their undoubted and refined skills, and changes every two to three weeks. Their *terrine de la maison*, served with a selection of homemade bread and a salad, is known throughout the region. Both their butcher and their fishmonger are given prominent credits on the menu.

6 The parmentier de turbotin au jus corsé was superb – a kind of luxury fish pie 9

CLOSED Sat, Sun, evenings (unless pre-booked for groups); one week Feb, Easter, 2 weeks Aug, late Dec to early Jan
CARDS AE, MC, V

Please send us reports
A guide such as this thrives on reader's reports. If you send us five usable reports, we will send you a free copy of any title in our *Charming Small Hotel Guides* series (see page 241 for France titles in the series).

The five reports should contain at least two new restaurants; the rest can be comments on restaurants already in the guide.
1 Tell us about your experiences in restaurants already in this guide.
2 Send us new reports. New reports should give the following information:
- **Region** – City, town, village or neaest village
- **Name of restaurant** – Please double check the spelling, it's surprisingly easy to make a mistake
- **Address** – including *département*
- **Telephone number** – plus fax and e-mail if available. Double check this information.
- **Objective description** – Try to explain simply why it should be in the guide. Remember that the guide is very selective - our entries are those one-in-five places that combine
  ● **interesting food with**
  ● **character and charm, in the building, the setting or both.**
  The guide hates tourist traps, and pretentious, dressed-up food. We like places where the French go.
  We favour places in the lower and middle price bands but there are plenty of expensive places that have our qualities, and we list those too.
- **Diner's comments** – These should be short, personal comments on features that strike you. They can be your comments, or others'.
- **Closing times**
- **Credit cards accepted**
  Don' t forget to date your report and add your name and address.
Send reports to Charming Restaurant Guides, Duncan Petersen Publishing, 31 Ceylon Road, London W14 OPY.

Sorrus
◆ Auberge Mon Onc' Victor €

268 route de Montreuil, 62170 Sorrus, Pas-de-Calais
Tel 03 21 86 34 29

An ordinary looking roadside inn has been transformed into a very handsome restaurant, where everything seems to be made of wood: the floor, tables, chairs, the counter and stools in the small bar – even the ceiling has exposed beams. It is family run with a lovely, intimate atmosphere, partly due to the clever lighting from a series of wide-based low-hanging ceiling lights, and partly to the throng of locals that regularly fills the bar, where a fire often burns on chilly days. The food is simple fare, offered on a great-value 13-euro daily menu. The choice is usually between a salad and a starter, two main courses, which might be chicken *aux épices*, *carbonade* or turkey, with endives and ham on the side, followed by a home-made tart (apple, apricot or chocolate), rice pudding (a novel dish in France) or a selection of ice-creams. They always serve *chilli con carne* on Friday evenings, and have a superior *carte de vins*.

CLOSED Sun, Mon, Tue-Thu evenings
CARDS MC, V

Our price bands
€ under 30 euros €€ 30-50 Euros
€€€ over 50 euros for a menu

Steenvoorde
◆ Auberge du
Noordmeulen €€

route de Wormhout, 59114 Steenvoorde, Nord
Tel 03 28 48 11 18 Fax 03 28 49 77 69

Students of Flemish architecture would recognize many of the buildings in Steenvoorde as fine examples of their kind. The Auberge du Noordmeulen is itself a typical Flemish farmhouse, trimmed with blue shutters and loaded with flowers. Inside, it is beautifully done out with old country furniture and lace, presided over by a capacious fireplace. Lovers of traditional Flemish cooking seem to move around *en famille* here, as there always seem to be large, jolly groups of relatives tackling their food (and each other) with gusto. The kind of dishes that you will be asked to choose from are *coq à la bière des trois monts*, *lapin aux pruneaux et raisins*, *potch vlesh* and *watersoï de poulet*. If you have a penchant for looking at windmills, this is the

place for you as there are quite a few working in the neighbourhood, but it's best to avoid the first weekend in October when the local *fête* is held.

CLOSED never
CARDS none

Please send us reports
A guide such as this thrives on reader's reports. If you send us five usable reports, we will send you a free copy of any title in our *Charming Small Hotel Guides* series (see page 241 for France titles in the series).
   The five reports should contain at least two new restaurants; the balance can be comments on restaurants already in the guide. **Send reports to** Charming Restaurant Guides, Duncan Petersen Ltd, 31 Ceylon Rd, London W14 OPY.

Le Touquet
◆ Brasserie Le Nemo
€ – €€

67 rue de Metz, 62520 Le Touquet,Pas-de-Calais
Tel 03 21 90 07 08 Fax 03 21 90 07 09

One of the surprisingly few places in Le Touquet where you can eat overlooking the sea, this lively brasserie has a number of other attractions too. One is its seductive terrace where the tables seem to be laid at the merest hint of sunshine. Another is its opening hours, from 9am to midnight (10pm in winter), so – if you had nothing better to do – you could come for breakfast and stay all day. Inside it's decked out like Captain Nemo's submarine, presumably to get you in the mood for their excellent fish: turbot, sole and perch all crop up on the three-course daily menu (good value at 18 euros), together with the catches of the morning. If you're not a fish-lover, their duck, steaks and salads are all recommended alternatives.

❛ Good wine list ... genial service ❜

CLOSED never
CARDS DC, MC, V

Le Touquet
◈ Cosi Piu €

74 rue de Hiltz, 62520 Le Touquet,Pas-de-Calais
Tel 03 21 05 32 32

If you fancy a change from French food, Cosi Piu is a fantastic, family-run Italian restaurant, where you can sit outside in the sunshine, sip a something, and watch Le Touquet go by. Conveniently close to the shops, casinos and the beachfront, it has a genuine Italian flavour. Almost all the food is home-cooked – and what isn't is imported from Italy. If you only feel like a light lunch, they do a terrific plate of anti-pasti and garlic bread, though their numerous pasta dishes are excellent too. The icing on the cake is that prices are very reasonable. In typically Italian style, they love children – so it's a splendid place to feed the family.

❛ Italian food, wine and service' ... 'Friendly local Italian just off the main drag ❜

CLOSED Tue, Wed
CARDS MC, V

---

charmingsmallhotels.co.uk
Visit Duncan Petersen's travel website, the best online search tool for places to stay that combine character and charm. Currently features Britain, France, Italy and Ireland, with other destinations being continuously added.

Le Touquet
◈ Pérard au Touquet
€ – €€€€

67 rue de Metz, 62520 Le Touquet,Pas-de-Calais
Tel 03 21 05 13 33 Fax 03 21 05 62 32

Ignore the neon and brash look of this very French fish restaurant, with its picture window walls and its ceiling hung with fishing nets; it's well worth it. You can eat all sorts of fresh fish, but it's best to take advice on what the morning catches were, or choose your dinner from the tank in the splendid adjoining fish market. Alternatively you can never go far wrong with a huge plateau of *fruits de mer*. Pérard's *soupe de poissons* – also excellent – which is now bottled and for sale in delicatessens in the UK, is made here. If you're planning some entertaining, you can buy the soup from the *poissonnerie* next-door, plus *rouille*, croutons, and some fresh fish, prawns and mussels, so that nobody guesses you haven't made it yourself.

❛ Fantastic fish' ... 'Has a terrific buzz about it ❜

CLOSED Mon
CARDS AE, DC, MC, V

Our traditional French cuisine symbol
So many of our readers enjoy seeking out the genuinely French eating experience that we have used Fr to mark restaurants which offer *cuisine du terroir*, classical French dishes or regional dishes with an emphasis on local ingredients, and traditional recipes.

Wimereux
◈ La Liégeoise € – €€

Digue de Mer, 62930 Wimereux, Pas-de-Calais
Tel 02 33 54 42 26 Fax 02 33 43 46 79

If you are visiting the charming resort of Wimereux (and its ruined 19thC Fort de Croy), you couldn't do better for lunch than this restaurant in the imposing Atlantic Hôtel right on the seafront. Under the aegis of Alain Delpierre, a master chef who not surprisingly draws his inspiration from the sea, it is a stylish room where every table has a view through large windows. Alain's many delicious fishy specialities include striped mullet, flavoured with thyme and served with *foie gras*, and fillet of turbot with *morilles*. For hardened carnivores, he also cooks an excellent fillet of beef with a shallot and vinegar sauce; the bonus of eating meat is that you can go to town on the list of superb red wines. If you can't cope with a full meal, the hotel also has a useful brasserie where you can give your stomach a rest and just have a salad, soup or plate of *fruits de mer*.

CLOSED Sun evening, Mon lunch; Feb
CARDS AE, DC, MC, V

PARIS AND ILE-DE-FRANCE

T he French capital, divided into *arrondissements*, or districts, forms the hub of the government region of Ile-de-France. Most of the recomnmendations in this section are in Paris itself, but there are some useful addresses outside the city, too, in the four *départements* that circle the city, and make up the rest of the region.

Le Bouclard 131
Petrus 129 **17** La Fourchette des Anges 130
Olivier & Co 130
Caves Pétrissans 130
Le Grenadin 115 Bar Romain 116
Le Stubli 131 Le Clovis 114 A.G. Le Poete 113
La Grande Cascade 128 Le Café d'Angel 130 Café Jacquemart-André 114
Le Jardin 116 Granterroirs 115 Le Roi du pot-au-feu 118
8
L'Etoile 127 Le Copenhague 114 Le Celadon 86
Les Jardins de Bagatelle 128 Le Petit Retro 129 Asian 113 L'Envue 115
Le GR5 128 Xu 116 Le Carré des Feuillants 85
Le Chalet des Iles 127 **16** Le Scheffer 129 Brasserie de la Poste 127 Chez Savy 114 **1**
Le Totem 129 L'Affriolé 96
La Gare 128 La Fontaine de Mars 113
Le Galion 127 Le Bistro des Vignes 126 Au Bon Accueil 96 **7**
Le Florimond 96
La Cigale 96
Le Bistro de Breteuil 96 **6**
Café des Delices 94
Le Belisaire 125 Le Parc aux Cerfs 95
Dix Vins 126 Wadja 95
Bistro 121 125 **15** Le Bistrot de Cancale 125 Ti-Jos 125
Ty Breiz 126

14

PICARDIE

HAUTE-NORMANDIE

Mantes-la-Ville
Neuilly 83 Saint Ouen 83 Meaux
PARIS Le Perreux-sur-Marne 83
Versailles 84 Issy-les-Moulineaux 82 Coulommiers
ILE-DE-FRANCE
CHAMPAGNE-ARDENNE
Rambouillet Moissy Cramayel 83
Melun
Etampes Barbizon 82
Fontainebleau 82
Flagy 82

CENTRE

BOURGOGNE

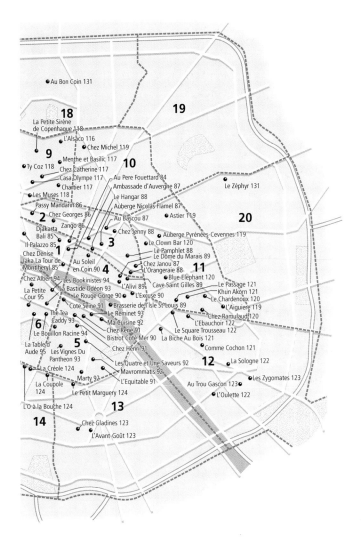

Au Bon Coin 131

18

La Petite Sirène
de Copenhague 118

19

L'Alsaco 116

Chez Michel 119

9

Menthe et Basilic 117

10

Ty Coz 118   Chez Catherine 117

Casa Olympe 117   Au Pere Fouettard 84

Chartier 117   Ambassade d'Auvergne 87   Le Zéphyr 131

Les Muses 118   Le Hangar 88

Passy Mandarin 86   Auberge Nicolas Flamel 87

2   Chez Georges 86   Astier 119   **20**

Zango 86   Au Bascou 87

Djakarta
Bali 85   Chez Jenny 88

Il Palazzo 85   **3**   Le Clown Bar 120

Chez Denise   Auberge Pyrénées-Cevennes 119

(aka La Tour de   **1**   Au Soleil   Le Pamphlet 88
Montlhery) 85   en Coin 90   Le Dôme du Marais 89   **11**

Chez Albert 94   Les Bookinistes 94   **4**   Chez Janou 87
       L'Orangeraie 88

La Petite   La Bastide Odéon 93   L'Alivi 89   Cave Saint Gilles 89   Le Passage 121
Cour 95   Le Rouge Gorge 90   L'Excuse 90   Khun Akorn 121

Cote Seine 91   Brasserie de l'Isle St Louis 89   Le Chardenoux 120

The Tea   Le Réminet 93   L'Aiguiere 119
Caddy 93   Ma Cuisine 92   Chez Ramulaud 120

6   Chez Rene 91   L'Ebauchoir 122

Le Bouillon Racine 94   Bistrot Coté Mer 90   La Biche Au Bois 121   Le Square Trousseau 122

La Table d'   **5**   Chez Henri 91
Aude 95   Les Vignes Du   Les Quatre et Une Saveurs 92   Comme Cochon 121
Pantheon 93

12   La Sologne 122

La Créole 124   Mavrommatis 92
Marty 92

La Coupole   L'Equitable 91   Au Trou Gascon 123   Les Zygomates 123
124   Le Petit Marguery 124   L'Oulette 122

L'O à la Bouche 124   **13**

14   Chez Gladines 123

L'Avant-Goût 123

Blue Elephant 120

81

Barbizon
◆ Auberge du Grand Veneur €€ – €€€

63 rue Gabriel-Séailles, 77630 Barbizon
Tel 01 60 66 40 44 Fax 01 64 14 91 20

This rustic, utterly quaint hunting lodge makes a perfect stop in the tiny village of Barbizon, a place that exerted a powerful charm over 19th century painters including Corot and Millet. It is dominated by a massive fireplace on which the chef prepares the house speciality, *grillade* (grills). *Gibier*, game, is usually on the menu from October to February. After eating, you can walk through the vast forest of Fontainebleau. Service is friendly.

Closed Wed eve, Thurs; first week of Jan, first three weeks of Aug
Cards AE, V

Our price bands
Rather than giving actual prices (which are prone to change) we indicate the cost of a three-course meal for one person, without wine, by means of price bands. They are as follows: € under 30 euros €€ 30-50 euros €€€ over 50 euros. Where we give more than one price band, for example €– €€€, this indicates that in that restaurant a meal can be had at a range of prices. As well as the cost of *prix fixe* menus, our price bands also take into account the cost of an average selection from the *à la carte* menu.

Flagy
◆ Hostellerie du Moulin €€

2, Rue du Moulin, 77940 Flagy, Seine et Marne
Tel 01 60 96 67 89 Fax 01 60 96 69 51

Set in a 13thC flour mill on the outskirts of the picturesque village of Flagy, one hour's drive from Paris, this restaurant is a pure delight. In summer you can eat out in the garden overlooking the Orvanne river, in winter opt for a table next to the monumental fireplace. The food is classical French

and the platter of different types of regional brie is itself worth the visit. Booking is essential, particularly at weekends. Several pretty beamed bedrooms are available.

' Lovely old beamed bar complete with library'...'Peace and quiet '

Closed Sun evening and Mon
Cards AE, DC, V

Fontainebleau
◆ Le Caveau des Ducs € – €€

24 rue de Ferrare, 77300 Fontainebleu
Tel 01 64 22 05 05 Fax 01 64 22 05 05

Just around the corner from the château of Fontainebleu, you can dine beneath the arches of magnificent 18thC cellars with furniture to match. José Perreire's *cuisine du marché* features plenty of seafood, and Mediterranean influences in dishes such as *alliance de saumon et de sandre à la bisque de langoustines* and *mijoté de baudroie à la provençale*. Or you can choose heartier fare such as *magret de carnard mulard au vinaigre de cidre et pommes caraélisées*. Portions are generous.

Closed first two weeks of Aug, first week of Jan
Cards AE, V

Issy-les-Moulineaux
◆ Issy Guinguette €

113bis, Av de Verdun, 92130 Issy-les-Moulineaux, Hauts de Seine
Tel 01 46 62 04 27 Fax 01 46 38 89 57
Metro Gare de l'Est

What a delight to discover this wonderful place off a nondescript road just outside Paris. The archway adjacent to Yves Legrand's wine boutique leads to the charming restaurant standing in the middle of a beautifully kept and fully-functioning vineyard. Dine on the terrace in the shade of a fruit-laden quince tree, next to the olive and medlar trees looking out onto the chardonnay vines. The terrine of spring vegetables and chicken with olive purée is just right for a summer's day. Yves is a respected wine dealer, consequently his list of bottles is perfect. He also has 800 metres of cellars in which he organizes wine tasting evenings.

CLOSED first two weeks of Aug, first week of Jan
CARDS AE, V

Moissy Cramayel
◆ La Mare au Diable
€€ Fr

Parc Plessis Picard, 77550 Moissy-Cramayel, Seine et Marne
Tel 01 64 10 20 90 Fax 01 64 10 20 91

This charming 15thC manor house/hotel, which used to belong to the writer George Sand, lies just 30 minutes from Paris via the N6. A visit can easily be combined with looking around the romantic candle-lit Château Vaux-le-Vicomte. The extensive, wooded gardens provide an idyllic setting for summer dining, but when the weather grows colder the ideal place to be is in the historic beamed dining room next to the log fire. The menu carries mainly seasonal produce, so you may find lobster salad, sander cooked in bacon, sea bass in meat juices, lamb with tarragon and of course the flagship dishes: pan-fried *foie gras* with cider and honey, and duck flamed in armagnac. Michèle Eberwein is a charming hostess.

❛ Delicious home-cooked bread'...'Enchanting gardens ❜

CLOSED Sat lunch, Sun; Aug
CARDS AE, V

Neuilly
◆ Durand Dupont
€€

14, place du Marché, 92200 Neuilly, Hauts de Seine
Tel 01 41 92 93 00

Five minutes from Porte Maillot, this is a favourite haunt of the well-heeled darlings of upmarket Neuilly, and with French actors and footballers. They come for the friendly, modern attitude and atmosphere; and to toy with a salad by the huge bay windows that look out on to a flower-bedecked patio. Open from 10 am to 2 am, Durand Dupont tries to be all things to all people:

tapas, cocktail or music bar, restaurant; and it does Sunday brunch from noon to 4.30 pm. Choose from Thai prawn salad, roasted monkfish, lamb tagine, *magret de canard*, grilled sole or simply the ageless chic of a pot of caviar.

❛ Perfect for people-spotting'...'Sumptuously creamy rice pudding ❜

CLOSED never
CARDS AE, MC, V

Le Perreux-sur-Marne
◆ Blue Marning €€

44, quai de l'Artois, 94170 Le Perreux-sur-Marnem, Val de Marne
Tel 01 43 24 11 05

One could not wish for more romantic a setting just a ten-minute drive from the city. This glass-fronted summer house stands literally on the Marne river opposite lovely Ile aux Loups. Portuguese owners Aurea and Manuel Alves have made such an effort to integrate the restaurant into its natural surroundings that they had part of it built around a tree that now towers above. The first course of grilled sardines is always a good bet in season; or try the salted codfish with red peppers. Ask Manuel for one of his excellent Portuguese wines kept for special customers. Don't miss the picturesque port of Nogent-sur-Marne just a short stroll away along the riverbank. In winter, you eat in the old beamed house across the road.

❛ Ducks swim just a few feet from the table'...'Tranquil bucolic setting'... 'Feels like rural France ❜

CLOSED Wed; annual holiday closure depends on the weather forecast
CARDS V

Saint Ouen
◆ Le Soleil €€

109 avenue Michelet, 93400 Saint Ouen
Tel 01 40 10 08 08 Fax 01 40 10 16 85
Metro Porte de Clignancourt

You come here because it is the best place to recover from a spree in the main Paris flea market, just next door. Eating in this friendly, elegant dining room will restore your spirits, though not your wallet. Owner Louis-Jacques Vannucci knows his ingredients and always includes seasonal shell fish on the menu as well as *filets de hareng* served with *pommes de terre rattes*, almost a meal in itself, a perfectly cooked entrecôte or rognon de veau and an awesome *baba geant au rhum a l'ancienne*. The wine list is limited but adequate.

CLOSED Open daily but not for dinner Sun to Wed
CARDS V

Versailles
◆ Le Boeuf a la Mode
€

4 rue au Pain, 78000 Yvelines
Tel 01 39 50 31 99 Fax 01 30 21 27 66

Tourists visiting the palace of Versailles tend to overlook the city itself and its superb farmer's market - its main attraction for French visitors, who come from far and wide to shop here. This tiny, traditional bistro is right on the marketplace and benefits from the market's cornucopia. Fresh produce shows up in dishes such as the *farci de pommes au chevre et noix, pave de veau en roquefort* and *filets de daurade aux baies roses*. For dessert, go for the *crème caramel* or a *crumble aux pommes et fruits rouges*. As we went to press the two course lunch menu, with wine and coffee included, cost 22 euros.

CLOSED never
CARDS V

◆ La Brasserie du Theatre €€ **Fr**

15 rue Réservoirs, 78000 Versailles
Tel 01 39 50 03 21

Almost everything is from another era here: the antique enamel advertisements, travel posters and autographed celebrity photos, the carefully preserved pre-war interior and the menu itself. Brasserie standards are well prepared using fresh ingredients from the oysters to the *choucroute, onglet de boeuf*, sole and *pêche melba*. The wine list is strong on Bordeaux

and there is an excellent cheese assortment, from brie to goat cheese to Roquefort.

CLOSED Christmas Day
CARDS AE, V

◆ Le Potager du Roi
€ – €€

1 rue du MI-Joffre, 78000 Versailles
Tel 01 39 50 35 34 Fax 01 30 21 69 30

A five-minute walk south from the main entrance to Versailles, the 'king's vegetable garden' is mostly about tradition: silky *foie gras maison* or densely flavoured *jarret de veau* or *veau sautée* with pan-fried artichokes. More unexpected is *charlotte d'aubergine* with lamb. Come with a royal appetite. Note that the king's original *potager* still exists across from the restaurant and adjacent to the chateau, but is only open to groups by appointment.

CLOSED Sat lunch, Sun evening, Mon
CARDS AE, V

Paris, 1st Arrondissement
◆ Au Pere Fouettard €

9, rue Pierre-Lescot, 75001 Paris
Tel 01 42 33 74 17
Metro Etienne-Marcel

Traditional wine bar steeped in the nostalgia of old Les Halles. Man-sized slabs of terrine, bowls of mussels and huge steaks are a perfect match for the larger-than-life atmosphere. Unfortunately, the wine list is crammed with the kind of spelling mistakes which appear to be a trademark of many of Paris' wine bars. Still, the service is good-humoured and the delicious home-made tarts, loaded with fruit, are reminiscent of those for which Alsace is famous. (In Alsace, Le Père Fouettard is a kind of bogeyman who accompanies Saint Nicholas on visits to naughty children.) As we went to press, one person could eat two courses here for around 12 euros. Wines were, on average, 3 euros a glass.

Closed Christmas Day
Cards AE, V

◆ Le Carre des Feuillants €€€ **Fr**

14, rue de Castiglione, 75001 Paris
Tel 01 42 86 82 82 Fax 01 42 86 07 71
Metro Tuileries

Just off the luxurious Place Vendôme, Chef Alain Dutournier's two-star restaurant stands at the end of a discreet flowery courtyard which opens out on to two soberly elegant dining rooms. The emphasis is on the best produce from Dutournier's native Gascony prepared with his touch of genius: eel and morel *cassolette*, truffled *foie gras en croûte*, milk-fed Pyrenean lamb, scampi with Espelette pepper. Prepare to be bowled over by his desserts: a divine *violet bombe glacée* with gariguette strawberries and the delicate lychees in rose jelly. The wine list is bible-thick and full of France's finest crus, and a breathtaking range of old armagnacs.

❛ *Horrendously expensive wines'...'Understated decoration* ❜

Closed Sat lunch, Sun; Aug
Cards AE, DC, MC, V

◆ Chez Denise (aka La Tour de Montlhery) €€ **Fr**

5 rue Prouvaires, 75001 Paris
Tel 01 42 36 21 82 Fax 01 45 08 81 99
Metro Chatelet

This all-night, no frills bistro is a throwback to the days when the Les Halles quarter was known as the 'belly of Paris' - a name it bore for centuries until the central food market was evicted to a suburb in the 1960s. The specialities are hearty onion soup, followed by oversize lamb chops, medieval portions of *haricot de mouton, pot-au-feu* (on Thur), or plate-

sized *entrecôtes* and *cotes de boeuf* with homemade *béarnaise* sauce. Superb *crème caramel* beckons at the end. Beaujolais flows from a barrel at the front of the bar.

Closed Sat, Sun; mid-July to mid-Aug
Cards V

◆ Djakarta Bali €€ – €€€

9 rue Vauvilliers, 75001 Paris
Tel 01 45 08 83 11
Metro Halles

The only Indonesian restaurant of note in the French capital, Djakarta Bali is run by a sister and brother team. Service is so pleasant and attentive that one has the impression of an invitation to a private house. The Hanafis are quick to point out that the Indonesian archipelago is made up of over three thousand islands so their food is predictably varied in style and they try to make it as authentic as possible. The *Nasi Goreng* (spicy fried rice with chicken, shrimps and vegetables) is outstanding, as are the various *satés*. The reasonably-priced wines make eating at this pretty restaurant light on the pocket.

Closed Mon
Cards MC, V

◆ Il Palazzo €€

Normandy Hotel, 7 rue de l'Echelle, 75001 Paris
Tel 01 42 60 91 20 Fax 01 42 60 45 81
Metro Palais-Royal

The huge Napoleonic dining room with its 7-metre-high ceiling complete with painted fresques makes Il Palazzo a fitting neighbour for the Louvre and Palais Royal. Contemporary touches have recently been added such as the massive light-reflecting steel domes and the purist lines of Bernardaud porcelain. "I'm developing a classical but modernistic style of Italian cuisine," says chef Thierry Barot. His food is certainly creatively presented: the *compotée* of sardines takes the form of a tin of sardines; the lobster, shellfish and vegetable stew is layered into glass jars in the manner of a traditional preserve. Each Saturday, from 1.30 pm to 5.30 pm, the pastry chef lays on an all-you-can-eat dessert buffet based on chocolate in winter and fruit in summer: 27.50 euros as we went to press.

❬ Plum-coloured decoration won't suit every taste'...'Well situated ❭

CLOSED Sun Mon; Aug
CARDS AE, DC, MC, V

◆ Zango €

15 rue du Cygne, 75001 Paris
Tel 01 40 26 27 27
Metro Etienne-Marcel

One of a rash of theme bar/restaurants to hit the capital, Zango caters for an eclectic crowd of Parisian globetrotters. Every detail suggests travel, from the sand-filled glass tables ('from beaches and deserts the world over') and photos of far-off lands to the exotic music and wide selection of maps, travel guides and magazines to flip through at the bar. Naturally, world cuisine predominates: stuffed vine leaves, Serrano ham, pastrami, moussaka, teryaki, colombo and risotto. As we went to press, the basic 'Explorer's' menu cost 12.50 euros.

❬ Great for holiday-planning'...'Out-of-Africa feel'...'Simple dishes ❭

CLOSED Sun eve
CARDS AE, V

Paris, 2nd Arrondissement

◆ Le Celadon €€€

Hôtel Westminster, 15 rue Daunou, 75002 Paris
Tel 01 42 61 77 42
Metro Opéra

Apart from the world's most famous names in jewellery, Rue de la Paix houses a number of the capital's luxury hotels. Standing next to Cartier, the Westminster's tastefully decorated restaurant looks as if it might belong to a super-rich haut-couturier. Arrive early in the evening to enjoy the delicious but all too-rare spider-crab or the Pyrenean baby lamb when in season. The hotel's Austrian manager, Volker Zach,

makes sure that the wine menu lists his country's top bottles while sommelier Richard Rahard has managed to unearth some of the Rhône's rarest whites such as the Clos des Grives. This is one of the few very expensive restaurants in the guide - average price of a meal without wine was more than 70 euros as we went to press. Singer most nights.

❬ Don't miss the fresh raspberry soufflé'...'The bar is very British ❭

CLOSED Sat, Sun
CARDS AE, DC, MC, V

◆ Chez Georges €€ **Fr**

1 rue du Mail, 75002 Paris
Tel 01 42 60 07 11
Metro Bourse or Sentier

The menu here sounds familiar, but the quality sets it apart. The *oeuf mayonaise, onglet de boeuf,* or *baba au rhum* is just so much better than you expected. The tender *coeur de filet grillé* comes with a taragon-rich *béarnaise* and the *steak de carnard* is piled with mushrooms stirred in a cream sauce. The wine list matches the food like a fist in a glove, starting with the house Brouilly. Service, food and decoration are pre-war.

❬ No place to go on a diet or in a hurry ❭

CLOSED Sun, first three weeks of Aug
CARDS AE, V

◆ Passy Mandarin €€ – €€€

6 rue d'Antin, 75002 Paris
Tel 01 42 61 25 52 Fax 01 42 60 33 92
Metro Opéra

Two minutes from the Opera and Place Vendôme, this charming, elegant Chinese restaurant has earned itself a solid reputation for quality and commitment to authenticity. Owner Vong Vai Kuan had already made a name for himself with the immensely popular Chez Vong at Les Halles. Here the decoration is even more refined and the service just as attentive and courteous. All of the dishes here are faultless, particularly the perfect, caramelised Peking duck. As well as Cantonese and other regional Chinese dishes, there is a selection of Thai specialities.

❦ Refined'...'Fabulous dim sum'...'Professional, deferent service ❧

CLOSED Sun in Aug
CARDS AE, DC, MC, V

Paris, 3rd Arrondissement
◈ Ambassade d'Auvergne € – €€ Fr

22 rue du Grenier-Saint-Lazare, 75003 Paris
Tel 01 42 72 31 22 Fax 01 42 78 85 47
Metro Rambuteau

Extremely popular, this rustic, two-storey restaurant, its beams hung with country hams and sausages, oozes conviviality. This is the place to enjoy genuine Auvergnat specialities made with ingredients brought direct from the region. Not to be missed are the memorable sausages served with hunks of country bread, hearty *potée d'Auvergne*, authentic *aligot*, Salers beef, and warm salads of Puy lentils. The cheese platter features the region's coarsely flavoured Laguiole, Fourme d'Ambert, Saint-Nectaire and Roquefort and this is one of the few places to offer the unusual wines of Aveyron: Saint-Pourçain, Chanturgue, Marcillac and Madargue. The charming owner Françoise Petrucci is always on hand with a smile.

❦ Cosy, friendly and countrified ❧

CLOSED Sun in Aug
CARDS AE, MC, V

◈ Au Bascou €€

38 rue Réaumur, 75003 Paris
Tel 01 42 72 69 25
Metro Arts et Métiers

Chef Jean-Guy Lousteau is on a mission to convince us that his native Basque country has the best food in the world. If you give him an afternoon or evening of your time, he

might well succeed. His classics include smoked tuna, *chipirons a l'encre* (baby squid), *pimentoes del piquillo farcie* (sweet stuffed peppers), *pipérade*, and the finest lamb from the Pyrénèes. Lousteau, a sommelier by training and inclination, also has a notable wine list with an excellent choice of Madiran, Irouléguy and so on.

CLOSED Sat lunch, Sun, Mon lunch; Christmas week; three weeks in Aug
CARDS AE, V

◈ Auberge Nicolas Flamel €€

51, rue de Montmorency, 75003 Paris
Tel 01 42 71 77 78
Metro Rambuteau

It may come as a surprise to some that Nicolas Flamel, the philosopher of Harry Potter fame, actually existed in real life. Built in 1407, the house once belonged to this celebrated alchemist and local benefactor, and was converted into a restaurant two centuries ago. It has retained its original façade and now boasts the most charming of proprietors, Natan Hercberg, formerly of Paris' most fashionable nightclub, Les Bains. The food at the 'oldest house in Paris' fits the context: classic and olde France. Don't miss the *gigot de sept heures* or the delicious *tatin de foie gras aux pommes caramel*. Ask Natan to show you the magical Salon des Anges before you decide whether to dine upstairs or down.

❦ Like dining in a time warp'...'Faultless service ❧

CLOSED Sat lunch, Sun
CARDS AE, DC, MC, V

◈ Chez Janou €

2 rue Roger Verlomme, 75003 Paris
Tel 01 42 72 28 41
Metro Bastilleov or Chemin-Vert

It doesn't hurt to be located on one of the most charming squares in Paris, but this bistro is more than just a pretty face. It is also friendly, and the dynamic team in the kitchen shows great sensitivity in its use of ingredients whether in the simple *salade d'épinards au chèvre*, the *thon à la provençal*, or well-executed standards like *rougets grillés à la tapenade* and *daube provençale*. As for desserts, the *blanc-manger au citron* is smooth and subtle. The heady wines are from côtes de Rousillon and Lubéron. Book ahead, but it's first-come-first-serve for tables on the leafy terrace.

Closed Christmas, New Year
Cards none

◆ Chez Jenny €€

39 bd du Temple, 75003 Paris
Tel 01 42 74 75 75
Metro Republique, Filles du Calvaire,
Temple or Oberkampf

There are two main attractions at this hugely popular, historic brasserie located just off buzzing Place de la République: the superb marquetry by celebrated cabinetmaker Charles Spindler, and the enormous platters of seafood and choucroute ferried around the vast dining room by waitresses in Alsatian costume. What makes the choucroutes so special is that instead of the usual boiled ham-hock they carry a whole knuckle of roasted pork taken from the rows of spits by the door. This is one of the few Parisian restaurants to have a useful no-smoking area.

Closed never
Cards AE, DC, MC, V

◆ Le Hangar €

12 Impasse Berthaud, 75003 Paris
Tel 01 42 74 55 44
Metro Rambuteau

Hidden in an alley, just steps from the Pompidou and honking horns, this is a friendly refuge with a terrace and minimalist, art gallery interior. The simple, classic food is all about attention to detail and the time of year - say a *gaspacho d'avocats*, cool squash soup or quivering pan-fried *foie gras* with puréed potatoes. Desserts are the forte here and you must choose between the signature *gateau au chocolate fondant*, a superb chocolate soufflé, or *crème catalan*.

Generous wine prices start at 9 euros a bottle (mostly from the Loire and Languedoc). It fills up quickly so reserve if possible. Find Le Hangar by walking north of the Pompidou on the east side of rue du Renard, taking the first right after Rambuteau.

❛ *Spartan but convivial atmosphere* ❜

Closed Sun, Mon; three weeks in Aug
Cards none

◆ L'Orangeraie

€€ – €€€

Hôtel Villa Beaumarchais, 5 rue des
Arquebusiers, 75003 Paris
Tel 01 40 29 14 00 Fax 01 40 29 14 01
Metro St Sébastien Froissart

This charming little hotel in a quiet street between the Place des Vosges and the Bastille creates an immediate feeling of intimacy. Downstairs, the Orangeraie restaurant is bathed in light thanks to its glass roof. The glass-fronted kitchen leaves you in no doubt about its standard of hygiene. Tables are arranged around a pleasant inner garden and the decoration seems to be inspired by Provence or Tuscany. Thierry Bourbonnais is the young, creative chef with a real flair for presentation: his line-caught sea bass with girolles can claim to be a work of art. Chef *sommelier* Cyril Jaegle has a judiciously selected wine list: a highlight is the little-known Menetou-Salon Cuvée Pierre Alexandre, resembling a top burgundy for a fraction of the price.

❛ *Well-spaced tables'...'Great for*
tête-à-têtes'...'Interesting colour
and flavour combinations ❜

Closed Sat lunch, Sun, Mon; Aug
Cards AE, DC, MC, V

◆ Le Pamphlet €

38, rue Debelleyme, 75003 Paris
Tel 01 42 72 39 24
Metro Filles du Calvaire or St Sébastien
Froissart

Despite his rapid rise to fame, the chef at this rustic little restaurant, stashed away in a winding street in the Marais, has kept a level-headed approach to success. Dishes on the succinct menu are still based on products that arrive fresh every morning and, happily, the beamed 17thC dining room with its round tables conducive to conversation remains free of any attempt at modernisation. In his small, impeccable kitchen Alain Carrère works on the best produce from his native south-west: tuna from Saint-Jean-de-Luz, farmhouse pigeons, Salers beef and sheep cheese from the Pyrénées.

❛ *A cosy place you can really settle into'...'Friendly service'...'Sensational amuse-bouche of potato purée with caviar* ❜

CLOSED Sat, Sun and Mon lunch
CARDS MC, V

Paris, 4th Arrondissement
◆ L'Alivi ©© Fr

27 rue du Roi de Sicile, 75004 Paris
Tel 01 48 87 90 20
Metro St Paul

In the heart of the Marais lies a small corner of 'Ile de Beauté'. With its wooden tables, beams, thick stone walls, polyphonic music and Corsican newspapers it is worth seeking out just for the cultural experience. Gruff service from the waiters perfectly reproduces the atmosphere at one of the island's splendid ferme-auberges. As rustic as the decoration, the food is true shepherd's fare - hearty country soup, *tarte aux herbes*, roasted kid and a fine selection of Corsican cheeses. Top Corsican wines.

❛ *A must for anyone who loves Corsica'...'Great Corsican aperitifs and beer* ❜

CLOSED Sun eve
CARDS MC, V

◆ Brasserie de l'Isle St-Louis ©

55 quai de Bourbon, 75004 Paris
Tel 01 43 54 02 59 Fax 01 46 33 18 47
Metro Pont-Marie

Nothing has changed in this brasserie for decades, certainly not the menu or the stuffed swan above the bar. The view from the tables outside looking up to Notre-Dame's soaring buttresses hasn't changed in centuries. The homey interior sports hunting trophies and endearing Alsatian bric-à-brac. Tourists rub elbows at the long tables with French rugby fans and residents of the little island. The hearty Alsatian menu offers *tarte à l'oignon* as a starter and the succulent *jarret de porc aux lentilles* or *choucroute garni as a main*. Wines are reasonable (from 13E a bottle) but skip the overpriced coffee and ice cream. Instead, walk across the street and buy your own.

CLOSED Wed, Thur lunch; Aug
CARDS MC, V

◆ Cave Saint Gilles ©

4, rue St Gilles, 75004 Paris
Tel 01 48 87 22 62
Metro Chemin-Vert

This place is a real find in the so-so restaurant zone that separates the Bastille from Place des Vosges. Not many tourists have yet discovered this archetypal bodega with authentic Spanish food. However, more and more Parisians are passing the word so it is best to book a table, particularly at weekends. Excellent selection of meats and fish à *la plancha*. Exceptional *chipirones en su tintaand*. Don't miss the celebrated *pata negra* ham.

❛ *Boisterous atmosphere'...'The waiters know their wines* ❜

CLOSED never
CARDS none

◆ Le Dôme du Marais
©© – ©©©

53 bis, rue des Francs Bourgeois, 75004 Paris
Tel 01 42 74 54 17
Metro St Paul

This 18thC dining room, topped with a glass dome, is quite simply unique. It is hard to believe that such a romantic place was once a state-owned pawnbroker's shop.

Enjoy the *cuisine inventive* of Breton chef Pierre Lecoutre: quick-cured *foie gras marbré de figues sèches*, a gamey *pintade fermière aux morilles*, and desserts like *biscuit moelleux à l'orange maltaise*. Two course lunch menu for 15 euros as we went to press.

6 Few remain indifferent to the majestic setting 9

Closed Sun, Mon
Cards AE, MC, V

◆ L'Excuse €€

14 rue Charles-V, 75004 Paris
Tel 01 42 77 98 97
Metro St Paul

On a quiet street in the historic Marais quarter, this tiny bistro occupies the ground floor of a 17thC mansion. The 20s decoration invites 'mirror, mirror on the wall' reflection while waiting for the arrival of an intriguing starter such as *raviolis aux langoustines* or *picatta de saumon petits raisins et romarin*. Mains include *bar aux noisettes* or *suprême de volaille fermière avec nems croustillants de foie gras aux noisettes*; Desserts include *macarons au chocolat glace au lait*, a joyous finale.

Closed Sun, Mon
Cards MC, V

◆ Le Rouge Gorge
€ – €€€

8, rue St Paul, 75004 Paris
Tel 01 48 04 75 89
Metro Sully-Morland

At the heart of the antique dealers' quarter, this small wine bar, all wooden beams and exposed stone, exudes Parisian charm. François Briclot makes each and every client feel like part of the family as he lines up sample bottles on your table. Wine themes change every three weeks; recently there was an interesting Corsican white by esteemed producer Etienne Suzzoni. The tasty food complements the wine and is copiously served, particularly the large bowl of *rillons confits* from Hardouin that you

can delve into at will. Wines are also available for take-away. You can eat here (wine excluded) for as little as 16 euros.

6 A little expensive'...'charming façade 9

Closed Sun eve; two weeks Aug
Cards MC, V

◆ Au Soleil en Coin €

21 rue Rambuteau, 75004 Paris
Tel 01 42 72 26 25
Metro Rambuteau

Unpretentious and inexpensive, this 'sunny corner' functions as a friendly neighbourhood canteen. There is a blackboard where local residents write announcements - concerts, offers to sell or exchange, looking for love, and so on. The short and sweet menu begins with a starter, perhaps *salade d'haricots verts et pétoncles marinées* or *huitres tièdes aux poireaux et à la vanille*. To follow you might well be offered the *Gigot poêlé aux herbes* or *blanquette de veau à l'ancienne*. The home-made desserts don't disappoint.

6 Lunchtime is crowded'...'Evenings (except Saturday) relaxed 9

Closed Sat lunch, Sun; Aug
Cards AE, DC, MC, V

Paris, 5th Arrondissement
◆ Bistrot Coté Mer
€ – €€

16 boulevard St Germain, 75005 Paris
Tel 01 43 54 59 10
Metro Maubert-Mutualité

It's no wonder that this affordable Left Bank 'seaside' bistro is always full. Given the often exorbitant price of fish restaurants in Paris, the *prix-fixe* menus here offer real value for money. In terms of atmosphere, the blue and yellow dining room feels like a family-run pension. In fact, it is supported by Michelin-starred chef Michel Rostang (his daughter started and runs it). First courses such as *ravioles de Romans au homard*, could be followed by a relatively simple main course of plump filet of Saint Pierre (John Dory) or a more rustic *gratin de macaroni au vieux jambon*. The *tarte soufflée au chocolat amer* is an intense third act.

CLOSED never
CARDS AE, V

◆ Chez Henri €–€€ **Fr**

9, rue de la Montagne Sainte-Geneviève, 75005 Paris
Tel 01 43 29 12 12
Metro Maubert-Mutualité

Chez Henri stands at the crossroads between the Latin Quarter and Boulevard Saint Germain and rue Monge, famous for its market. With its turn-of-the-century decoration, complete with brown banquettes, bevelled mirrors and long-aproned waiters, this is the snug, archetypal bistrot you were hoping to find. Menus don't come much more traditional than here, with *canard à l'orange, boeuf bourguignon, blanquette de veau, gigot de sept heures*, bone-marrow toasts, lemon tart and *confiture de vieux garçon*.

❛ *Totally Parisian'...'Exceedingly friendly owner and staff* ❜

CLOSED never
CARDS MC, V

Fr French regional or classical French dishes on menu.

◆ Chez René €

14 Boulevard St Germain 75005 Paris
Tel 01 43 54 30 23 Fax 01 43 26 43 92
Metro Maubert-Mutualité

This corner bistro, two blocks from the Seine, fully deserves its reputation as a *grande classic* where nothing has changed in decades. And why should it? There's no point in tampering with a perfect *coq au vin*, a memorable *entrecôte Bercy* for two, or a *turbot frais meunière* that flakes perfectly. The *plateau de frommages* offers everything from fresh, moist *chèvre*, to perfect

raw-milk Camembert, to Beaufort aged two years. There is a small, but pleasant, outdoor terrace.

CLOSED Sun, Mon, ten days at Christmas and in Aug
CARDS MC, V

◆ Cote Seine €€

45 quai des Grands Augustins, 75005 Paris
Tel 01 43 54 49 73
Metro St Michel

Standing on the banks of the Seine, between ever vibrant Place St Michel and the oldest bridge in Paris, this little bistro looks as if it has emerged from a fifties' film-set. Black and white photos of classic movie stars line the walls and the red moleskin banquettes lend an air of Paris in an earlier decade. Ladies come to this romantically-located bistro as much to admire the dark good looks of owner Remus Nica as for the food, which is best described as decent but nothing special. The rump steak with fat homemade fries and old-fashioned beef bourguignon stand out from an otherwise unadventurous menu. Ask for the window-seat from which you will be able to dine with a view of Notre-Dame.

❛ *Great view, particularly in the evening'...'Maigret-style charm'...'Tables too close together* ❜

CLOSED Mon lunch
CARDS AE, V

◆ L'Equitable €

1, rue des Fossés Saint-Marcel, 75005 Paris
Tel 01 43 31 69 20
Metro Censier-Daubenton

A few steps from the Grand Mosquée de Paris and the Jardin des Plantes, l'Equitable stands on the site of a former stables. The thick stone walls and heavy beams lend an air of a country auberge which belies the fact that it was used as a Gestapo headquarters during the war. Owner and chef Yves Mutin named the restaurant for his collection of old scales dotted around the dining room. The menu changes depending on the chef's mood, but his two flagship dishes are almost always available: *filet de canard au caramel d'épices* and *marbré de porc confit et foie gras*. Lunch menu, just over 20 euros as we went to press.

❝ Charming, smiling service from the two young waitresses'...'Plates searingly hot ❞

CLOSED Sun eve, Mon.
CARDS AE, V

◆ Ma Cuisine €€ Fr

26 boulevard St Germain, 75005 Paris
Tel 01 40 51 08 27 Fax 01 40 51 08 27
Metro Maubert Mutualité

A delightful little restaurant near the Institut du Monde Arabe with attractively simple blue and white decoration. The name, Ma Cuisine, clearly reflects the philosophy of owner/chef Jean Louis Huclin: a personal interpretation of traditional bourgeois cookery. This is the place Parisians frequent to bring to life childhood memories of *cuisine de grand-mère: mussels marinière*, thick veal cutlets with wild mushrooms, *blanquette*, *turbot* in champagne sauce, *choucroute* and triple chocolate tart. The warm atmosphere and service completes the back-home experience.

❝ Cosy'...'A little expensive' ... 'Traditional comfort food ❞

CLOSED Sun eve, Mon.
CARDS V

◆ Marty €€ – €€€

20 avenue des Gobelins, 75005 Paris
Tel 01 43 31 39 51 Fax 01 43 37 63 70
Metro Gobelins

L ocated next to the historic Gobelins tapestry workshops, Marty opened in 1913 as a coaching inn and has become a veritable institution. Its authentic 1930s decoration, complete with leopardskin upholstery, is a talking point amongst diners. The chef comes from the illustrious Tour d'Argent and his experience shows not only in the range of brasserie classics (juicy thick-cut fillet steak with *frites*, *navarin* of lamb) but also in more contemporary offerings such as the crisp filo pastry basket

filled with colourful spring vegetables. The people at the next table confirmed the freshness and quality of their heavily-laden seafood platters. As we went to press menus ranged from 33 to 90 euros

❝ An up-market brasserie'...'Great wine list'...'Full even on a hot mid-August lunchtime ❞

CLOSED never
CARDS AE, DC, MC, V

◆ Mavrommatis €€

5 rue du Marché des Patriarches, 75005 Paris
Tel 01 43 31 17 17
Metro Censier-Daubenton

W ith its rather understated decoration - a classic blend of wood and neutral colours, enlivened by black and white photos of old Cyprus and a few discreetly-placed silvery olive trees, Mavrommatis is light years away from the tourist-trap Greek canteens of the nearby Quartier Latin. The food is as select as the clientele. *Mega pikilia* features no less than ten traditional starters, but the warm octopus salad with lemon and olive oil is also hard to resist. Main courses include *sheftalia*, minced lamb pancakes, and the colourfully-named Cypriot 'resistance fighter' leg of lamb. The wine list includes what is probably the best retsina outside Greece, but possibly a more original choice would be the full-bodied Domaine Mercouri.

❝ Refined Greek cuisine'...'Friendly service ❞

CLOSED Sun eve, Mon; Aug
CARDS MC, V

◆ Les Quatre et Une Saveurs €

72, rue du Cardinal-Lemoine, 75005 Paris
Tel 01 43 26 88 80
Metro Cardinal Lemoine

T he strengths of this vegan, smoke-free Left Bank restaurant are freshness of flavour and simple presentation; and it is a stunning value when you compare it to the trendy restaurants that are now 'discovering' vegetarian-organic food. The macrobiotic menu offers rich and fragrant miso soup, stimulating vegetable *voloutés* and well-rounded *assiettes complètes* (with tofu or tempura) - all organic and delivered to the table in bento boxes. For drink you can choose between organic wine, beer, fruit juice or an herbal infusion.

CLOSED Mon
CARDS None

◆ Le Réminet
€ – €€€

3, rue des Grands Degrés, 75005 Paris
Tel 01 44 07 04 24 Fax 01 44 07 17 37
Metro Maubert-Mutualité

Norman chef Hugues Gournay packs every dish with subtle flavours. From ravioli of sea and burgundy snails to deluxe comfort food such as the *entrecôte* paired with roasted shallots and grated potato pancakes with herbs. He can also dream up truly original desserts, say a *mousse au the earl grey, feuilles craquantes d'aubergines, tuile au sesame, essence de bergamote.* As we went to press the weekday lunch menu was a remarkable three courses for 14 euros of whatever Hugues was cooking that day. Wines are fairly priced.

❝Outstanding value'...'Practically in the shade of Notre Dame ❞

CLOSED Mon, Tue; two weeks in Aug, three weeks in Jan
CARDS MC, V

◆ The Tea Caddy €
14, rue Saint-Julien-le-Pauvre, 75005 Paris
Tel 01 43 54 15 56
Metro St Michel

Adorable little tea-room standing opposite Notre Dame and looking out on to the oldest church in Paris, Saint-Julien-le Pauvre, built in 507. Several generations of Parisians have been coming to take tea in this genteel little room since it was opened by Miss Kinklin, former housekeeper to the Parisian bourgeoisie. Installed in front of the old fireplace, you can sip one of a carefully selected range of teas from Blue Willow

china while savouring a home-made pastry or a light lunch of salad or scrambled eggs.

❝At the heart of the Latin Quarter ❞

CLOSED evenings after 7 pm; 21 July to 24 Aug
CARDS AE, V

◆ Les Vignes Du Pantheon
€–€€€

4, rue des Fossés Saint-Jacques, 75005 Paris
Tel/Fax 01 43 54 80 81
Metro Luxembourg

A little restaurant full of character next to the Panthéon. It seems to have stepped out of another era, with its painted ceiling, wood-panelled walls lined with bevelled mirrors, old tiled floor and original zinc bar. Just the place in which to linger over dinner and lose yourself in deep conversation: time seems to stand still here. This impression is confirmed by a menu that includes such ageless bistro classics as bonemarrow on toast, *úufs meurette*, smoked herrings with warm potatoes, kidney in mustard sauce and tripe. The time-travel experience is completed with a choice of soul-comforting desserts such as home-made profiteroles, *crème caramel* served in a deep, earthenware terrine, wine-soaked prunes and *Óle flottante*. Prices are reasonable and Marie-Josèphe Malière extends a warm, smiling welcome.

❝Old Paris atmosphere'...'Very friendly service ❞

CLOSED Sat, Sun (but open Sat eve on request)
CARDS V

Paris, 6th Arrondissement
◆ La Bastide Odéon
€–€€€

7 rue Corneille, 75006 Paris
Tel 01 43 26 03 65 Fax 01 44 07 28 93
Metro Odéon

This nouveau bistro, near the théâtre de l'Odéon, is where chef Gilles Ajuelos offers the simple but inspired food you associate with Provence. The menu is light, delicious, reasonably priced, and varies seasonally. Sensual flavours kick in with a *tarte feuilletée à la tomate et chèvre chabichou à la sarriette*; Mediterranean fish dishes such as a *poêlée de rascasse et asperges vertes aux patates douces écrasées* are offered alongside Provençale peasant fare such as roast suckling pig or *pieds et paquets d'agneau à la Provençale*. Imaginative desserts include a *pain d'épices poêlé et gingembre confit au miel*.

CLOSED Sun, Mon
CARDS AE, DC, V

◆ Les Bookinistes
€€ Fr

53, quai des Grands Augustins, 75006 Paris
Tel 01 43 25 45 94 Fax 01 43 25 23 07
Metro St Michel

Opened in 1994, this offshoot of Guy Savoy's gastronomic empire attracts a crowd of faithful followers, not least due to the superb location. A self-proclaimed supporter of genuine farm produce - "supermarkets are vectors of trends and false prophets of pleasure" - he correspondingly offers a range of relatively simple dishes based on seasonal products: grilled *andouille* with cauliflower cream, Salers beef and a wonderful shepherd's pie made with oxtails… and for dessert the perennial almond and hazelnut macaroon with chestnut ice-cream or chocolate tart. The wood and steel decoration in the spacious, sun-coloured dining room aims to reflect a combination of past (the historic area) and present (Savoy's innovative cuisine).

❛ Service a little offhand'…'Crowded at lunchtime ❜

CLOSED Sat lunch, Sun
CARDS AE, DC, MC, V

◆ Le Bouillon Racine
€€

3 rue Racine , 75006 Paris
Tel 01 44 32 15 60 Fax 01 44 32 15 61
Metro Cluny-La-Sorbonne or Odéon

This art nouveau monument historique is guaranteed to induce reverie as you stare at chandeliers reflected in mirrored walls and sip the world's best beer. Poured out in oddly shaped glasses, the Belgian brews - blonde, brown or amber - have names that evoke sin (*Duvel*, 'Devil') and its consequences (*Mort Subite*, 'Sudden Death'). *Palm Spéciale* is on tap. For food, choose between the restaurant or the cheaper, more informal café. *Waterzooi de poulet fermier à la gantoise* is a speciality - chicken poached in broth, cream and vegetables; there is also a fish version. If ravenous, try the suckling pig roasted in beer.

CLOSED Sun, Mon
CARDS AE, DC, MC, V

◆ Café des Delices €€

87, rue d'Assas, Paris 75006
Tel 01 43 54 70 00 Fax 01 43 54 42 05
Metro Vavin

The menu here lives up to is sensual motto: *Couleurs et Parfums*. Chef Gilles Choukroun gave up one-star cooking in Chartres to try out new ideas in a new setting near Luxembourg Gardens. His gift for original combinations shows in a *Saint-Jacques et boudin noir au Balsamique et au cacao* and a *crème brûlée de foie gras aux cacahuètes*. He also has a passion for updating French classics, floating a tender *jarret de porc* in a delicate broth. The vaguely oriental decoration is relaxed but uninspiring.

❛ lunch formule is a real bargain ❜

CLOSED Sun, Mon
CARDS MC, V

◆ Chez Albert €

43 rue Mazarine, 75006 Paris
Tel 01 46 33 22 57
Metro Odéon

This intimate family restaurant stands out in a much-visited area increasingly dominated by anonymous eateries. The fresh seafood stands out too as it lands on your table grilled, marinated or steamed. A glorious paella for two comes heaped with *fruits de mer.* Beef arrives sizzling *à la plancha*. The excellent wines come from the Dão region of Portugal, reflecting the origins of the chef and his wife. It is usually full to overflowing so reserve your table. As we went to press the lunch menu was 15 euros.

CLOSED Sun, Mon; July
CARDS MC, V

◆ Le Parc aux Cerfs
€€

50 rue Vavin, 75006 Paris
Tel 01 43 54 87 83 Fax 01 43 26 42 86
Metro Vavin

Crayons are on the table so diners can doodle in this skylit Montparnasse bistro, a former artist's atelier that still feels private thanks to a cosy mezzanine and interior courtyard. Young Corsican chef Martine Maille-Battestini shows plenty of sun-kissed flair in her short Mediterranean menu with starters such as *mousse de courgettes aux safran* and main courses such as *râble de lapin aux pruneaux et haricots tarbais au jus* or a *tajine d'agneau aux olives niçoises*. Many of her desserts are graced by home-made ice cream - *au lait d'amande and au caramel* - or *sorbet à la mirabelles*. Owner Paul Hayat is a wine connoisseur and his wine list shows it, in fact it's a model of value for money.

CLOSED Aug
CARDS MC, V

Our price bands
€ under 30 euros €€ 30-50 Euros
€€€ over 50 euros for a menu

◆ La Petite Cour €€

8 rue Mabillon, 75006 Paris
Tel 01 43 26 52 26
Metro Mabillon

Right at the heart of Saint-Germain-des-Près, the terrace at La Petite Cour is set on a slightly lower level than the road. Parisians and tourists jostle for a table all summer long as this is one of the few restaurants in the area to offer a garden setting

and to serve dinner until as late as 11pm The home-style cooking with a light touch goes well with the flowery surroundings here. There is game on the menu in season.

❛ *Gets crowded - use the carpark'...'Cooking erratic, especially at the height of the season* ❜

CLOSED never
CARDS AE, V

◆ La Table d'Aude € Fr

8 rue de Vaugirard, 75006 Paris
Tel 01 43 26 36 36 Fax 01 43 26 90 91
Metro Odeon

The seasonally changing menu of chef Bernard Patou spans the cuisine of Aude, a departement in the Languedoc region stretching between the Massif Central and the Mediterranean. He and his wife, Veronique, deliver their regional fare inside a tiny, cosy restaurant near the Luxembourg gardens. They will happily introduce you to the earthy pleasures of an *Aude chicken facon grand-mère, coq au vin*, or an exemplary *cassoulet de Castelnaudary* (white beans, grilled pork sausages, duck or goose *confit*) married to powerful, berry-filled wines such as Minervois, Fitou, Corbières. In winter, there is *pigeon paté* and *sanglier* (wild boar). A we went to press the weekday lunch menu was 12 euros.

CLOSED Sun; Aug
CARDS AE, V

◆ Wadja €

10 rue de la Grande-Chaumière, 75006 Paris
Tel 01 46 33 02 02
Metro Vavin

The decoration here was the latest thing - in 1930. You could not ask for a pleasanter patronne or a better, cheaper, market fresh lunch menu (*cuisine du marché*). The wine list is informative - and complete with maps - but you can also just ask for a recommendation. A la carte takes over in the evenings: try starting with a *fricassée de pleurotes et pancetta rotie* or *terrine de carnard sauvage et figues* followed by a garlicky *gigot â sept heures* or *blanquette de lotte minute et croustillant d'oignons carmélisés*. Dessert could be a simple baked apple with honey, or something fancier such as *tiramisu à la menthe poivrée*. The three-course lunch menu at 13.15 euros is one of the best for value on the Left Bank.

CLOSED Sat-Sun; Aug
CARDS MC, V

Paris, 7th Arrondissement
◆ L'Affriolé ⓔ – ⓔⓔ

17 rue Malar, 75007 Paris
Tel 01 44 18 31 33 Fax 01 44 18 91 12
Metro Invalides

On a narrow street just off the Seine, behind a 1930s façade, lies this quirky bistro, usually packed with locals who appreciate the kitchen's finesse coupled with a sense of adventure. Start with the *feuilletés d'escargots* before moving on to a richly flavoured *chausson de lapin aux oignons et romarin*, or a *vapeur de raie, compotée de choux et girolles*. The coffee, served with *petit fours*, is practically a dessert unto itself. The bread is from Poujauran, the favourite baker of French presidents.

CLOSED Sun to Mon; two weeks in Aug
CARDS MC, V

◆ Au Bon Accueil ⓔ – ⓔⓔ

14 Montlessuy , 75007 Paris
Tel 01 47 05 46 11
Metro Alma-Marceau

Sitting outside beneath the awning, you'll see the Eiffel Tower loom up, Godzilla-like, just a couple of hundred metres away. Despite the location, this second-generation bistro is mostly a local hangout for people who have the time to linger (smoking at intervals) over an exquisite, deboned *pigeonneau rôti*, or a fresh *sole de Saint-Gilles-Croix-de-Vie au beurre de crustacés*. The cosy dining room, decorated with wine paraphernalia and a grinning Bacchus, reminds you this is also a wine bistro. The daily menu, using fresh produce, is a highlight.

CLOSED Sat and Sun, 15 days in Aug
CARDS V

◆ Le Bristro de Breteuil ⓔ **Fr**

3 Place de Breteuil, 75007 Paris
Tel 01 45 67 07 27 Fax 01 42 73 11 08
Metro Sèvres-Lecourbe

Standing on one of the discreet 7th Arrondissement's most elegant squares, the Bistro de Breteuil might be in some quiet provincial town. The wide terrace looking out onto a statue of Louis Pasteur is perfect for a leisurely lunch between visits to nearby Invalides and the Eiffel Tower. Chef Marc Nouveau used to work at the prestigious Crillon hotel. He has fashioned a menu based on seasonal produce that is inclusive of aperitif, wine and coffee and cost 29 euros as we went to press. Choose from *ravioles d'écrevisse, salade de haddock, magret de canard* or *rôti de lotte*.

CLOSED never
CARDS AE, MC, V

◆ La Cigale ⓔ

11 bis, rue Chomel, 75007 Paris
Tel 01 45 48 87 87
Metro Sèvres-Babylone

Gerard Idou is the king of soufflé and many Parisians are happy to cross the city to enjoy his speciality. He's also a hero of what is known in France as the price/quality ratio. Depending on the time of year (the menu changes monthly) there are 60 to 80 kinds of soufflés, many of them vegetarian. In autumn, you can eat a *soufflé aux morilles* and in summer a *soufflé aux apricots*. Non-soufflé dishes include *Filet de boeuf à la moelle* or a *Dorade au four sauce vierge*.

❛ *Soufflé heaven* ❜

CLOSED Sat lunch, Sun
CARDS MC, V

◆ Le Florimond ⓔ

19 avenue de la Motte-Picquet, 75007 Paris
Tel 01 45 55 40 38 Fax 01 45 55 40 38
Metro Ecole-Militaire

Continued on page 113

NORTHERN FRANCE

THE REGIONAL CUISINES

● BRETAGNE ● HAUTE- AND BASSE-NORMANDIE ●
● PICARDIE ● NORD-PAS-DE-CALAIS ●
● PARIS AND ILE-DE-FRANCE ●
● CHAMPAGNE-ARDENNE ● LORRAINE ● ALSACE ●

BRETAGNE

Think of typical Breton cuisine and you probably imagine a regal *plateau de fruits de mer* accompanied by a bottle of crisp, dry white wine. Perhaps you are on an island in the Golfe du Morbihan, with boats bobbing in the harbour, whitewashed houses framed by banks of wild hydrangeas, and a clear blue sky. Or maybe you are in a simple village crêperie where delicate, wafer-thin pancakes, wrapped, perhaps, around ham, cheese, sardines or sausage, are served with jugs of powerful local cider.

Crêperies come in all shapes and sizes in Brittany: some traditional ones provide nothing but the pancakes themselves, and locals bring extra ingredients – usually nothing more than a bottle of lait ribot (buttermilk) for dipping – plus cutlery and plates.

Today's sophisticated Breton crêpe, or *galette*, has its roots in buckwheat (which grows well in the granite soil) kneaded into a dough with salt and water, and baked on stones. In times past, this was an

Below: Fast food – Breton style.

essential staple of local diet.

With its earthy, mysterious character and its sense of independence, Brittany has no tradition of *haute cuisine*. Its excellence lies in the freshness and simplicity of its best produce – notably seafood, vegetables and pork. Hours-old fish and shellfish – including sardines, tuna, monkfish, lobster and the famous Breton oysters – are mostly served unadorned, and where possible raw or in the shell. Look out too for *palourdes farcies* (stuffed clams) and the traditional fish stew *cotriade*. Like its southern counterpart, *bouillabaisse*, this mixture of oily and white fish augmented by potatoes and mussels, originated as a way of using up the leftovers from the day's catch.

Superb pork means superb *charcu*

sweet and sour cream beaten thick and served sprinkled with sugar with fruit. Few cheeses are made; they include Crémet Nantais, Campéneac and the rind-washed Saint-Paulin.

The vineyards around Nantes, in the neighbouring Pays-de-la-Loire region, produce Brittany's favourite wine, Muscadet, a perfect accompaniment to seafood. As well as a Muscadet de Sèvres et Maine (of which the finest is Muscadet-sur-Lie) a Loire Sancerre or Pouilly-Fumé, or a light red Chinon or Saumur will do the trick. Connoisseurs of dry white wine will want to try the ultra-dry, almost bitter Gros Plant. Its only, and some say, perfect, match is seafood.

While the best cider is from

terie – wonderful ham, *andouille*, *andouillette*, *boudin noir* and *blanc caillettes* (rissoles) and *casse* (*terrine* of ham in a caul).

Sweet dishes, apart from crêpes, are a speciality. Several small factories in Brittany make biscuits using the excellent local salted butter, while *kouign aman*, sold from market stalls, is a delicious concotion of yeast dough, butter and sugar. Look out too for the pudding far Breton, made with prunes, and for *Mingaux*,

Top: Cidre bouché.
Above: Fresh vegetables assembled for the pot at Beau Rivage, Caurel.

Normandy, Breton ciders – of which there are many varieties – can be good, especially the sparkling *cidre bouché*: names such as Fouesnant and Beg-Meil are notable. Brittany's version of Calvados is *eau-de-vie de cidre*; if you are offered a glass of 'fearsome' Lambig, give it a try.

HAUTE- AND BASSE-NORMANDIE

S everal of the distinguishing features of Breton produce crop up in neighbouring Normandy, but here the lush, fertile landscape and even climate provides something extra: the rich dairy produce and apple and pear orchards that are central to the Norman cuisine and way of life. Fat brown and white cows grazing in the pastures, bowls of cream and slabs of butter, apples, Calvados and cider - it may be a cliché, but they are the cornerstones of Norman food. A dish of the superb local pork with cream and caramelised apples – *filet mignon de porc Normande* – followed by a *tarte Normande*, a Camembert and a Calvados makes the perfect apples-and-dairy menu. Ideally, you should drink cider with your meal, preferably from the Pays d'Auge, which also produces the best, most intense Calvados. Normandy is too fertile for the grape: you will have to look outside the region for wine.

Amongst meat and fowl, there are plenty of local specialities to seek out. *Canard à la Rouennais* is gamey, unbled Rouen duck served in a red wine sauce, while Caen's *tripe à la mode* is a mixture of cow's stomach, calf's feet and pig's skin cooked in cider with vegetables and sealed with a paste of flour and water. Tripe also appears *à la Ferte-Macé* in skewered bundles, and in Coutances with cream. Amongst andouilles (smoked tripe sausages) those from Vire are said to be the best in France: try them cooked with apples, or with sorrel and cream. Fans of black pudding will note Mortagne-au-Perche, on the southern border, where a *boudin fest* takes place each spring. Inimitable *agneau de pré-salé* is lamb raised on the sea-lapped marshes near Mont Saint-Michel, which comes with a natural and delicate flavouring of salt. If it's in season and on the menu it shouldn't be missed, perhaps cooked in a ragoût with spring vegetables. And not forgetting Alençon's braised goose, pig's feet *à l'Argentan*, anything described as Vallée d'Auge (with cream and cider), rabbit *en papillote* from Le Havre ... and the much-vaunted *omelette de la Mère Poulard*.

Below: The Normandy coast on the western Cherbourg Peninsula.

Like Brittany, Normandy enjoys a long coastline and seafood is a highlight. Here, inevitably, it is served with less simplicity, as in *sole Normande*, poached in cream with shrimps and mussels. Fish stews called *matelotes* or *marmites* are popular, especially *marmite Dieppoise*, flavoured with the spices that became popular when brought back by merchant ships returning from the East. Dieppe is also home to *lisettes de Dieppe*, baby mackerel cooked in cider or white wine, while Fécamp is known for its salt cod (*morue*) and herrings.

But it's the butter – creamy, fragrant Beurre d'Isigny and Sainte-Mère-Eglise –

Above: Red mullet, occasionally on northern menus, imported from the south.

and bulgy, but does not run when cut.

Normandy is also quite well known for *pâtisserie*: the melting *brioches* and *gâches* (flat yeast bread) are exceptional, as are the delicate butter biscuits, *sablés*, *bourdelots* (apple dumplings), and *douillons* (pear dumplings).

And yet ... Normandy's cuisine has never quite matched its superlative produce. It's location made it the premier supplier – of fish, pork, vegetables, dairy produce – to Paris, yet it was the

Above: Le Petit Coq au Champs, Campigny, Haute-Normandie.

Above: Le Saint-Pierre, La Bouille, Haute-Normandie. Centre: rustic Normandy.

the cream, the unctuous crème fraîche, and the cheese that lingers longest in the memory. There is Camembert, of course, but also Bondon, Brillat-Savarin, Pont-l'Evêque, Livarot, Neufchâtel. The perfect Camembert is considered to be soft, pale

Parisians, not the Normans, who took the ingredients and created fire-works in their restaurants. A little cream and apples and pork is fine, but anyone who has stayed in the region for some time knows that they go a long way.

101

PICARDIE & NORD-PAS-DE-CALAIS

Above: Ambassade de la République de Montmartre, Gerberoy, Picardie

Most travellers slice through the flat, damp and misty plains of the north as fast as they can. They miss such unexpected delights as Arras's show-stopping Grand Place, the great cathedral at Amiens, the pretty countryside of the Avesnois or the Authie Valley, and the impeccably maintained cemeteries and war memorials, which bring you up short with the memories they stir.

While finding good food to eat in restaurants is trickier in these parts than most – taking pot luck does not often pay dividends – the produce from the fertile plains is plentiful and excellent and the regional cuisine is far from meagre. Some of the most popular dishes — *carbonnade de boeuf* (beef cooked in beer) and *water zooï* (freshwater fish or chicken stew) originated in nearby Flanders, and the Belgian appetite for, amongst other things, beer, chips, herrings and eels, is understandably shared over the border. The emphasis in these parts has always been on food for celebrations – feast days and festivals – and on hearty, warming food to keep the workers going. Another typically filling dish is *hochepot*, a mixed meat (beef, pork, mutton and oxtail) and vegetable stew, again originating in Flanders.

Apart from beer (the climate is too cool for wine), the regional drink is gin flavoured with juniper berries (*genièvre*).

Like beer, it crops up in the cooking, as in *rognons au genièvre*, where the kidneys are likely as not served on a bed of sautéed potatoes (crisp on the outside, soft inside, just how the locals like them). Strong flavours (witness the pungent local cheese, Maroilles) are preferred here, hence rabbit with prunes, braised veal with dried apricots, chicken in beer and anything with onions.

As well as onions and potatoes, two other vegetables that get plenty of attention are the chicory or Belgian endive and the leek. The plump white heads of endive are best braised, either as an accompaniment for meat or, with ham and cheese, as a meal in themselves. Leeks appear in *flamiche aux poireaux*, a cousin of the better-known quiche, as well as in soups. Cabbage, too, is popular, and white asparagus, served as in Belgium and The Netherlands, with hard-boiled eggs.

Boulogne is one of the country's largest fishing ports, so seafood has always been on the menu here, but its influence is not as great as you might expect, with the exception of the herring. Boulogne's excellent mussels, often served in a cream sauce, are prized, while *anguilles au vert* (eels with herbs) are popular, as well as a sea fish stew known as *caudière*. But it's the nutritious herring, raw, smoked, salted, pickled or soused, that has been the northeners' staple for centuries. Try them lightly smoked (*harengs saurs*) with a hot potato salad. The smoking is an art: in Boulogne a mixture of oak and beech is used, while Dunkirk's *craquelots* are smoked over walnut.

Centre: Ambassade de la République de Montmartre, Gerberoy, Picardie - "a jovial atmosphere".
Below: Domesticated geese graze on a farm near Calais.

PARIS AND ILE-DE-FRANCE

The attitude in Paris towards eating has changed little since Brillat-Savin wrote more than a century ago that 'the way in which mealtimes are passed is most important to what happiness we find in life'.

When Parisians seek such happiness in a restaurant, they usually don't opt for *haute cuisine*, le fast food or any of the designer places where you will get a meal much like you would get in London or New York. What they look for is creative cooking that might or might not be regional in inspiration, served in a casual setting, probably a bistrot, at prices that are *doux* ('sweet', i.e. value for money) or at least *correct* ('fair').

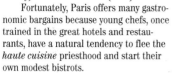

Fortunately, Paris offers many gastronomic bargains because young chefs, once trained in the great hotels and restaurants, have a natural tendency to flee the *haute cuisine* priesthood and start their own modest bistrots.

So what can you expect to eat in the French capital?

Depending on what restaurant you take a table in, it might be simple regional fare: Alsatian *choucroute*, an Auvergnat cheese platter, *saucisson de Lyon*, *gigot* from the Pyrénées, *daube Provençale*, *boeuf bourguignon*, *Basque pipérade*, *cassoulet au canard confit* from the Southwest, *poulet* from Bresse, quiche Lorraine, or fondue from Haute-Savoie.

All French roads don't meet in Paris but just about all French products and dishes do. It is remarkable to what extent you can find the gastronomic abundance of an entire French region - fresh farm products, aged cheeses and at least decent wines - packed into one small corner *bistrot* in Paris.

But the regional element is simply one of many possible sources of inspiration. Despite globalisation, the City of Light still hungers incessantly for what is naturally in season. So the daily *plat du jour* lives on, against all odds, with chefs creating *cuisine du marché* and scrawling something new on their ardoise (chalkboard) each day.

In spring, it might be asparagus or fresh goat's cheese or a *grande salade de légumes*. Autumn is a time to indulge in truffles and mushrooms such as *cèpes*, *chanterelles*, *girolles*, *pleurottes* and *morilles*. *Gibier* (game) is on the menu of many restaurants in Paris and the Ile-de-France from October through to February: pheasant paté, grilled baby boar, venison ragoût and the legendary *lièvre* (hare) *à la royale*. Summer is a season for super-ripe melon and figs, fresh-fruit sorbets and *soupe aux fruit rouges*.

Of course, there are things to eat in Paris and the Ile-de-France that have little to do with the time of year and nothing to do with novelty, starting with the humble baguette (invented by a Parisian baker). Many traditional bistros take pride in serving good aged beef in the form of an *onglet*, *entrecôte*, *bavette* or *filet*. And what could be more Parisian than a *pot-au-feu*, the simmered beef and vegetable stew often served in two courses, followed perhaps by a big bowl of *île flottante* with great mounds of soft meringue or a towering Grand Marnier soufflé?

Centre and opposite: Le Parc aux Cerfs in Paris' 6th Arrondissement has been carved out of a former artist's atelier. Well presented seafood platters feature on the menu.

CHAMPAGNE-ARDENNE

IN 1961 MADAME LILY BOLLINGER WAS ASKED HOW SHE ENJOYED HER OWN CHAMPAGNE. SHE REPLIED:

'I drink it when I'm happy and when I'm sad. Sometimes I drink it when I'm alone. When I have company I consider it obligatory. I trifle with it if I'm not hungry and drink it when I am. Otherwise I never touch it – unless I'm thirsty.'

The Champagne region is known for one thing and one thing only, so much so that it's difficult to imagine what would have distinguished it in the visitor's mind had Dom Pérignon not discovered those precious bubbles back in the 17th century. As far as the menu is concerned, you are more likely to find dishes adopted from elsewhere, although the region is not without its local specialities.

When one thinks of Champagne, it's usually the great central plain that comes to mind, plus of course the vineyards and villages of the Route du Champagne between Reims and Vertus. There are also forests and lakes, (including France's largest, Der Chantecoq) fertile valleys, and beautiful cities: Laon, Troyes, Reims and Langres.

The pretty village of Hautvillers, where Don Perignon was cellar master, may like to have you believe that he suddenly discovered bubbles in a blinding, almost religious revelation, but the truth,

involving a series of complex experiments, is somewhat more prosaic. At any rate, the monk seems to have been the first, or one of the first, to blend grapes systematically and to induce a second fermentation and its resulting fizz. Champagne is made from a blend (*cuvée*) of grapes from different vineyards and different years, and is therefore known by its brand names rather than by the name of the vineyard. Vintage champagne is the exception, using grapes solely from the same excellent year. Dom Pérignon's *méthode Champenoise* means that, after a first fermentation, cane sugar and yeast is added to induce a second fermentation and bubbles. The wine is then allowed to mature in the bottle for anything up to five years. Visits to the vast cellars (Moët et Chandon have 16 miles / 25km of them) of the great champagne houses are always

Centre: Stained glass window in the cathedral at Rheims.

106

rewarding, as is buying direct from smaller family firms at kind prices.

Returning to regional food, Sainte-Menehould's stuffed pig's feet have been a speciality since the time of Louis XV. Troyes is famous for its *andouillette*, served piping hot with potatoes, fried onions or red beans, Troyes is also known for smoked lamb or sheep's tongues (*langues fumées*) and for *petits pâtés chauds* (pastry encased pâtés). Other dishes which find favour in Champagne are chicken in pastry (*coq en pâté*), *potée Champenoise* (pork and cabbage stew), *jambonnneau* (breaded ham hock), and *boudin blanc*. Champagne is used in the cooking of such dishes as poached pike or salmon and braised chicken, but it's more likely to be a still white Champagne that's used – there is no point in wasting precious fizz in cooking. Local confectionary includes *rocaillons* (chocolate pebbles) from Sedan, marzipan from Reims and *biscuits de Reims*, excellent with a glass (*un coupe*) of Champagne, almond meringues from Bar-sur-Aube and Wassy and *nougat de miel* from Langres. Cheeses range from the strong – washed-rind Langres – to the more usual mild, such as the soft skimmed milk cheeses Barberey and Cendré de Champagne. Chaorce, with its pure white crust and smooth texture, has been made since the 14th century.

Top and centre: L'Assiette Champenoise at Tinqueux

107

LORRAINE

Lorraine is often overlooked, both in culinary terms and in what it has to offer the visitor, who thinks of a battle-scarred landscape thick with the acrid smoke of heavy industry. Both sentiments are unfair. Lorraine has a fine, if placid, culinary tradition – albeit found more at home than in the relatively few restaurants. And as well as the World War battlefields and the factories, it has meadows and forests, a beautiful national park, castles and churches, the cathedral of Metz, and Domrémy, Joan of Arc's birthplace.

The region's most famous dish – quiche Lorraine – is a clue to the inhabi-tants' (who are traditionally hard-working and loyal Frenchmen) favourite ingredients: bacon, eggs and dairy produce (although not cheese, with the exception of Munster). It has graced local tables since the 16th century. Bacon also makes an appearance in *potée Lorraine*, an excellent one-pot mix of pork, dried beans and vegetables served with mustard. As in Alsace, pork is the preferred meat, a throwback to the days when every family

Below: Pastoral Lorraine contrasts with industrial Metz and Nancy.

kept a pig, although geese and game come a close second. As well as bacon and *charcuterie*, pork is found in pastry-encased *pâté de Lorraine* and is roasted with plums (*mirabelles* or *quetsches*). Freshwater fish, such as pike (*brochet*) is also enjoyed; again plums, in the form of brandy, may be used in the cooking. Alongside the adored yellow *mirabelle*, fruits of all sorts – *quetsches* (purple plums), *reine-claudes* (greengages), *myrtilles* (bilberries), *cerises* (cherries) *merises* (wild cherries), pears, strawberries, raspberries, blackberries, whortleberries – feature in tarts and as *eaux-de-vie* and fruit liqueurs to rival those of Alsace.

As well as its fruit liqueurs, Lorraine has a few fine wines, notably the dry, perfumed and delicate rosés (known as *gris*) and whites of the Côtes de Toul and Côtes de Moselle. Beer is widely drunk, as in Alsace, although the many interesting individual breweries of bygone days have been replaced by a few vast factories.

Apart from the ubiquitous quiche, confectionery is perhaps Lorraine's strongest point. The region can lay claim to the rum baba, said to have been created by former Polish king, Duke Stanislas of Lorraine in the 18th century, the *madeleine* (from Commercy) so beloved of Marcel Proust, and the macaroon, first produced in Nancy by two Benedictine nuns in around 1793. Nancy's other speciality is the *bergamot*, a glistening transparent gold sweet made with sugar and essence of bergamot pear.

Centre and below: Lorraine produce including quiche and bottled greengages.

ALSACE

Two distinct influences ensure that Alsatian cooking is the most unusual of all the regional cuisines of France. The first, and greatest, is of course that of its neighbour, Germany; the second emanates from the substantial Jewish population that long ago took root in and around Strasbourg.

Bordered by the eastern slopes of the Vosges on one side, and by the Rhône on the other, Alsace stands at the geographical hub of Europe, in the past a pawn in the political struggle between the Great Powers, now the site of the European Parliament at Strasbourg. It feels quite different from the rest of France, with half-timbered houses, romantic castles perched on hilltops and *winstubs* (wine taverns, but more like beer cellars) full of hearty locals grouped round their *stammtisch* (regulars' table). The local Germanic dialect is widely spoken, with many variations up and down the region. A tour of Alsace might begin in Strasbourg with its two identities – one cosmopolitan and international, the other Alsatian and charmingly provincial. Then you might wander off along the famous Route des Vins with its picture-perfect villages strung out along vine-covered hillsides, punctuat-

Below: Classic Alsatian landscape: spreading vineyards bordered by hills.

ed by Colmar and the astonishing Issenheim Altarpiece. The return journey can be made along the spine of the Vosges mountains, the Route des Crêtes. On the way, whether in restaurants or private homes, you will find no lack of traditional Alsatian dishes to eat: in fact it's difficult to eat much else.

Above: The typical fluted shape of Alsace wine and liqeur bottles.
Below: The Auberge Au Vieux Pressoir at Rouffach has a vineyard and makes its own wine - not unusual in Alsace.

Just as Alsatian wines have a delicacy all their own, so the food has a surprising finesse, despite its hearty nature and huge, Germanic portions. Take *baeckaoffe* (spelt in a variety of other ways). Traditionally cooked overnight in the baker's oven and served on Monday wash-day, this casserole of potatoes and mixed meat marinated in wine is prepared with great care and lovingly presented. Then there is the Alsatian version of that great German staple, *sauerkraut*, or *choucroute* as it is called in French. The salt-pickled cabbage, whose correct preparation is the subject of much debate, is often served *garni* or *Alsacienne* with pork and sausages. Another favourite is *spaetzli*, curly noodle dumplings, while the region's greatest delicacy is fattened goose liver, *foie gras*. The goose also turns up roasted with apples, especially in November. Not forgetting excellent game, *truite au bleu*, *kugelhopf*, the cake with a hole, and fruit tarts.

The Jewish population has influenced the cooking of goose, for example *cou d'oie*

Above: L'Ami Fritz at Ottrott.
Below: The Maison Kamerzell, Strasbourg landmark, serving traditional dishes.

Nowhere else in Northern France does the wine and the food impress in equal measure. Alsatian white wines are known by their seven grape varieties, as follows: Sylvaner, light, fresh and fruity; Pinot Blanc, well-balanced and supple; Riesling, delicately fruity with a fine bouquet; Muscat d'Alsace, dry and fresh; Tokay Pinot Gris, opulent and robust;

Above: On the dessert trolley at Auberge Au Vieux Pressoir, Rouffach.

Gewurztraminer, distinctively spicy and fairly full-bodied; Pinot Noir, the only red (and rosé) which is dry, with a cherry-flavoured fruitiness. As well as the grape variety, individual vineyards may also appear on the wine label. Alsace wines should be drunk young (between one and five years after harvest) and chilled, but not too cold. Alsace is also known for its beer, and for its fruit liqueurs and *eaux-de-vie*.

farci (stuffed necks, often with *foie gras*). And on fish: witness the well-known *carpe à la juive*, which was traditionally eaten cold on the Sabbath. Excellent local chocolate, a liking for spices, especially cumin, and pretzels, available everywhere, are further reminders.

Continued from page 96

Perhaps the best way to get over a visit to Napoleon's tomb, the world's most pompous after the pyramids, is to lunch on a plate of Pascal Guillaumin's stuffed cabbage, *chou farcie de ma grandmere*. You won't find a more authentic version in Paris. The chef has his own wonderful recipes, too, from starters such as *ravioles de homard* to desserts such as the sublime *millefeuille à la vanille*. It serves as a lunch canteen for people working at the neighbourhood's government ministries (also UNESCO). Rare is the tourist who knows about it.

❛ *Perfect stuffed cabbage, cooked grandmother's way* ❜

Closed Sat lunch, Sun; Aug
Cards MC, V

◆ La Fontaine de Mars
€€ – €€€ **Fr**

129 Rue St-Dominique, 75007 Paris
Tel 01 47 05 46 44 Fax 01 47 05 11 13
Metro Ecole Militaire

This archetypal Paris bistro is complete with lace curtains, checked-gingham table cloths, attentive waiters, fabulous food - and locals who treat it like home. Follow their example and tuck into the *plat de jour fois gras chaud et lentilles*, *magret de canard au miel des Pyrénées* or *turbot sauce hollandaise*. The house speciality, *véritable cassoulet au canard confit*, is the real thing and so is the *île flottante Fontaine de Mars*. On the wine list is an excellent Cahors house wine at 11 euros.

Closed New Year's Eve, Christmas
Cards AE, MC, V

Paris, 8th Arrondissement
◆ A.G. Le Poete €€

27, rue Pasquier, 75008 Paris
Tel 01 47 42 00 64 Fax 01 47 42 48 55
Metro St Lazare

This romantic little haven lies in the quiet rue Pasquier just behind the Madeleine.

The setting is ideally suited to tête-à-têtes between lovers, perhaps unsurprising when you consider that chef Antoine Gayet is also an accomplished poet. The small dining room is brightened with large mirrors and plenty of bouquets and service takes place with a certain amount of pomp as each course arrives under a silver cover. The menu leans towards seasonal fish, the perennial speciality being *sole waterzoï*.

❛ *Excellent fresh daily special menu'…'Soothing decoration'…* ❜

Closed Sat lunch, Sun
Cards AE, MC, V

Please send us reports

A guide such as this thrives on reader's reports. If you send us five usable reports, we will send you a free copy of any title in our *Charming Small Hotel Guides* series (see page 241 for France titles in the series).

The five reports should contain at least two new restaurants; the balance can be comments on restaurants already in the guide. **Send reports to** Charming Restaurant Guides, Duncan Petersen Ltd, 31 Ceylon Rd, London W14 0PY.

◆ Asian € – €€

30 avenue George V, 75008 Paris
Tel 01 56 89 11 00 Fax 01 56 89 11 01
Metro George V or Alma Marceau

Welcome to a world of super chic, oriental relaxation. This is a new concept at one of the most coveted addresses in Paris, a few steps from the Champs Elysées. The de-stress experience begins with the long entrance hall where birdsong and gentle music lead you to the airy, elegant bar furnished with teak, soft light emanating from luminous columns. Downstairs, the restaurant is just as smart and also offers dishes from throughout the Asian world. Go Chinese with a crispy 'sour' royal bream, Vietnamese with crab dumplings, Thai with the plump salt 'n' pepper giant prawns or bass fillet in banana leaves. Japan is represented with a *sashimi* and sushi menu. The market menu was 58 euros as we went to press- wines are in our lower and middle price bands.

> ❛ *Incredibly different'...'Totally zen, a great place to unwind'...'State-of-the-art crispy duck* ❜

CLOSED Sat lunch
CARDS AE, DC, MC, V

◆ Café Jacquemart-André €

158 Boulevard Haussmann, 75008 Paris
Tel 01 45 62 04 44
Metro Miromesnil

Built in the Belle Epoque's most magnificent boulevards, this 1870 dreamhouse evokes the Second Empire and the exquisite world of Charles Swann, the protagonist of Proust's Remembrance of Things Past. It is now a museum strong on the French and Italian Renaissance. The charm of its sumptuous café pulls in local residents as well as museum goers, and is surely the only place where you can eat with a Gobelin tapestry at your elbow. While waiting for your salad to arrive (served with smoked salmon or breast of duck), look up at the trompe l'oeil ceiling by Tiepolo - and its gallery of 17th-century faces staring down at you from a painted banister. As we went to press, the *plats de jour* were ten to 16 euros.

CLOSED for dinner every day; lunch 11.30am-5.30pm
CARDS V

◆ Chez Savy € – €€

23 rue Bayard, 75008 Paris
Tel 01 47 23 46 98 Fax 01 47 23 54 93
Metro Franklin Roosevelt

Paris' answer to London's Simpson's on the Strand is a firm favourite with the media barons from neighbouring radio stations and newspaper groups. With its original Art Deco surroundings, moleskin banquettes, and mirrored booths reminiscent of the carriages in an old steam train, Savy is light years from the ultra-snob theme restaurants of nearby Avenue Montaigne. The owner is from the Auvergne province in central France, famous for sturdy pork

sausage, Salers beef and Cantal cheese. You will not regret ordering a plate of his *saucisse d'Auvergne pommes pailles, farçou aveyronnais* or the *côte de boeuf grillée à la moelle*. Famed for its thick-cut, juicy *Aubrac de Laguiole* rump-steaks accompanied by home-made fries, the menu also offers the hearty, no-nonsense specialities of Aveyron, including *farçou* and authentic *aligot*, not to mention superb Cantal *charcuteries*.

> ❛ *Best in the evening'...'Lunch brings a crush of suits* ❜

CLOSED Sat, Sun; mid-Aug to Sep
CARDS AE, MC, V

◆ Le Clovis €€€

Hôtel Sofitel, 2 avenue Bertie Albrecht, 75008 Paris
Tel 01 53 89 50 53
Metro George V

Two minutes' walk from the Arc de Triomphe, Le Clovis has attracted much attention since chef Bruno Turbot was awarded his first Michelin star in 1998. *Canette de Challans* is the star attraction, with the bird's wings, breast and legs presented in three successive courses. He is also the first chef to present a special 'business woman's lunch': *amuse-bouche*, tiger prawns and a plate of mini desserts accompanied by water and a glass of wine (As we went to press 50 euros). Sommelier Arnaud Fatôme has established a superb wine list by the glass which includes such gems as the Coteaux du Layon from Soulez and the Domaine de la Pinte's Macvin.

> ❛ *The rhubarb wine is better than it sounds'...'Chic decoration. Competent sommelier* ❜

CLOSED Sat, Sun; Aug
CARDS AE, DC, MC, V

◆ Le Copenhague €€ – €€€

142 avenue des Champs-Elysées, 75008 Paris
Tel 01 44 13 86 26 Fax 01 42 25 83 10
Metro Ch. de Gaulle Etoile

It may come as a surprise to stumble across a Danish restaurant right at the top of the Champs Elysées but Le Copenhague has been there so long that it is now part of the scenery. Regulars have always found it consistent. The first-floor restaurant *commands* a magnificent view of the 'most beautiful avenue in the world'; downstairs the airy patio is a pure delight in spring and summer. Chef Georges Landriot, formerly of the prestigious Goumard, serves precisely executed dishes that have earned the restaurant its well-deserved reputation for quality. Fish is the star attraction, particularly the *saumon à l'unilateral*. The wine list features an incredible number of top names at emminently reasonable prices.

❝ *Splendid view'…'Top crus at knockdown prices* ❞

CLOSED Sat lunch, Sun; two weeks Aug
CARDS AE, MC, V

---

charmingsmallhotels.co.uk
Visit Duncan Petersen's travel website, the best online search tool for places to stay that combine character and charm.
Currently features Britain, France, Italy and Ireland, with other destinations being continuously added.

◆ **L'Envue** €-€€

39 rue Boissy d'Anglas, 75008 Paris
Tel 01 42 65 10 49
Metro Concorde

Between Place de la Concorde and La Madeleine, ultra-fashionable, ultra contemporary L'Envue is the latest place to be seen. Opened in summer 2002, it immediately attracted followers from the nearby Embassies and chic shoppers from rue du Faubourg Saint Honoré and Rue Royale. Owner Valerie Balard created her elegant rose, grey and mauve decoration from ideas gleaned in Greece, Italy and Germany and poached the chef from jet-set darling Costes. He definitely has the edge for minimalist but delicious dishes such as the *langoustine ravioli* and the beef fillet with perfect *pont neuf* potatoes. The *Tout en Vue* snack or starter menus offer a prettily presented

range of four appetizers served with a glass of wine. As we went to press, breakfast was 12 euros; snacks 7; four appetisers with wine were 26 euros.

❝ *A happening place'…'The most incredibly contemporary toilets in Paris* ❞

CLOSED never
CARDS AE, DC, MC, V

◆ **Granterroirs** €

30, rue de Miromesnil, 75008 Paris
Tel 01 47 42 18 18 Fax 01 47 42 18 00
Metro Miromesnil

Extremely popular with office workers from nearby Champs Elysées, this ultra-chic delicatessen set inside a luxury grocery store is the fashionable place to be seen in at lunch. Oak dressers lined with hand-made biscuits and bottles of wine and two country-style *tables d'hôte* where diners are seated cheek-by-jowl on long benches make for a convivial, out-of-town atmosphere. Products used in the freshly made, copiously-served dishes are also on sale in the boutique and include oil scented with white truffle, muscat vinegar, *rillettes* by Hardoin and salted butter caramels from Ile de Ré.

❝ *Extra-fresh salads'…'Convenient, take-aways'…'Great for presents for foodie friends* ❞

CLOSED Sat, Sun and weekday evenings; Aug
CARDS AE, MC, V

◆ **Le Grenadin**
€€-€€€

44-46 rue de Naples, 75008 Paris
Tel 01 45 63 28 92 Fax 01 45 61 24 76
Metro Europe

Innovation, creativity, and modernity are the bywords here. Chef Patrick Cirotte trained with three-star Guy Savoy and Taillevent, then worked as the personal chef to music giant Eddy Barclay. Don't be put off by the rockstar-style decoration, Cirotte's talent for making the most of prime products makes a visit here well worthwhile. He manages to create happy marriages from radically different textures and flavours in such dishes as haddock and avocado on granny smith *coulis*, sea bream in chocolate sauce, rhubarb crumble with curry ice-cream and his signature *chef-d'oeuvre*, the *millefeuille minute*.

❛ Surprising use of unusual vegetables'…'A fun food experience ❜

Closed Sat lunch, Sun, Mon eve; one week in July, one week Aug
Cards AE, MC, V

◆ Le Jardin €€€

Hôtel Royal Monceau, 37 avenue Hoche 75008 Paris
Tel 01 42 99 88 00 Fax 01 42 99 89 90
Metro Ternes or Courcelles

Two blocks away from the Arc de Triomphe, Le Jardin's French windows open out on to the beautifully-kept, flower-bedecked gardens of the luxurious Hôtel Royal Monceau. You can eat outside, weather permitting, but the dining room is always bright and cheerful. The talents of pedigree chef Bruno Cirino with his penchant for Mediterranean cuisine, and those of the aimiable sommelier, Stéphane Lochon, result in a delightfully relaxing gourmet experience in the sunniest of surroundings. Specialities include the *araignée de mer de casier, encornet sauvages,* and *onglet de veau de lait.* Menus start at 50 euros.

❛ Creative cooking'…'Fresh flavours of the South'…'Convenient for the Champs Elysées ❜

Closed Sat, Sun
Cards AE, DC MC, V

◆ Xu €€

19 rue Bayard, 75008 Paris
Tel 01 47 20 82 24 Fax 01 47 20 20 21
Metro Alma-Marceau

Frequented by top models from the world-famous fashion houses lining Avenue Montaigne, Xu offers an ultra-trendy pop-art-inspired atmosphere of multicoloured lamps, vibrant cloths and a huge crystal chandelier. The emphasis is as heavily on world cuisine as it can be in a French-owned

restaurant, with ostrich, *gnocchi*, *nems* and *gaspacho* all flying the flag for their respective homelands. Xu's music bar is perfect for flaunting your cool whilst seated on one of the bright purple *settees* with a plate of oriental tapas.

❛ Wannabe paradise'…'Fun for people-watching ❜

Closed Sun lunch
Cards AE, MC, V

Paris, 9th Arrondissement
◆ L'Alsaco € Fr

10 rue Condorcet, 75009 Paris
Tel 01 45 26 44 31
Metro Poissonnière

It may be the size of a railroad car, but this jovial Alsatian Winstub does better *choucroute garni* than any grand brasserie. The poached sausages and roast and steamed pork, nestling in a bed of nicely acid *sauerkraut*, are a carnivore's dream. A mug of Alsatian beer is the classic accompaniment. Equally satisfying is the *bäckaofa*, a thick, three-meat stew. For a lighter meal, ask the ruddy-faced waitresses for a *flammenkueche*, an Alsatian 'pizza' topped with bacon, cream, onions and cheese. The wine cellar offers 150 of Alsatian's best wines (Ostertag, Domanine Faller, Trimbach, and so on) and potent *eau de vie*.

Closed Sat lunch; last two weeks July, Aug
Cards MC, V

◆ Bar Romain €€

6, rue de Caumartin, 75009 Paris
Tel 01 42 68 07 89
Metro Havre-Caumartin

Sumptuously decorated bar-cum-restaurant near the Madeleine. Apart from the superb mahogany bar and woodwork, mosaic floor and the Sienna marble columns, the focal point here remains the superb murals painted by Gustave Surand in 1903 on the theme of ancient Rome. This is one of Paris' oldest bars, and has always been a favourite with actors and theatre-goers from the nearby Olympia, with which it used to be linked via an underground passage. There is jazz or piano music on certain evenings - check for details. *Steak tartare* is the flagship dish.

6 Great for post-theatre dinners'... 'Simple menu'... 'Huge choice of cocktails 9

CLOSED Sat lunch, Sun; Aug
CARDS AE, MC, V

◆ Casa Olympe €€

48 rue St Georges, 75009 Paris
Tel 01 42 85 26 01
Metro St Georges

In an area where a number of small restaurants vie for attention on a busy street, this one is particularly good value. Local regulars crowd in at lunchtime to soak up the convivial atmosphere and enjoy Olympe's down-to-earth cooking. Many of the dishes are inspired of her Corsican origins, such as the herb-crusted leg of lamb which arrives at the table whole, still sizzling in its oven dish. Not that Olympe is any stranger to sophistication: she used to be the darling of the jet-set at her former establishment in the 15th Arrondissement. Now notoriously media-shy, she still attracts a faithful following of in-the-know Parisians.

6 Simple decoration' ... 'Generous portions' ... 'Convivial atmosphere' ... 'Excellent value 9

CLOSED Sat, Sun; Christmas and New Year; one week in May, three weeks in Aug
CARDS AE, MC, V

◆ Chartier € Fr

7 rue du Faubourg-Montmartre, 75009 Paris
Tel 01 47 70 86 29
Metro Rue Montmartre

No visit to Paris is complete without a visit to Chartier. Two centuries ago this was a *bouillon*, a workers' serving. Bought by Edouard Chartier in 1896 this cavernous restaurant still caters to anyone on a tight budget or who is looking for basic fare such as house pâté, snails, egg mayonnaise, steak and chips, *sole meunière*... The decoration is listed – revolving doors, antiquated mirrors and brass coat stands – nothing has

changed since the beginning of the 20th century. It's as popular as ever - diners still have to share a table and wait to be seated. Noisy, boisterous and immortal.

6 A golden oldie' ... 'Character and prices from another age 9

CLOSED never
CARDS MC, V

◆ Chez Catherine €€ Fr

65 rue de Provence, 75009 Paris
Tel 01 45 26 72 88
Metro Chaussée d'Antin

People who like warm, explosive flavours will appreciate Catherine Guerraz's bistro in the otherwise nondescript rue de Provence. The Art Deco dining room is a cosy place to enjoy the good things in life, particularly her chicken *fricassée de sot-l'y-laisse*, the *filet de sandre au pistou de légumes* and - as an encore - the sublime *crème brûlée à la pistache et aux poires caramélisées*. In winter, try the *cassoulet* - a dish from Catherine's native south-western France. The wine list is moderately priced and the magnificent bar at the entrance offers a rainbow of aperitifs, liqueurs and *digestifs*. It's best to reserve ahead.

6 Bankers come here to forget about the profit and the loss 9

CLOSED Sat, Sun, Mon evening; Aug
CARDS MC, V

◆ Menthe et Basilic €

6 rue Lamartine, 75009 Paris
Tel 01 48 78 12 20 Fax 01 48 78 12 21
Metro Cadet

Sparsely decorated but welcoming, this restaurant offers many pleasing variants on Provençal cuisine with plenty of fresh fish and wonderful pastas. There are tender *escargot brochettes*, or *tatin de tomates tièdes* with the basil cream (a house speciality) and *chantilly au basilic*. A typical main course is the *filet de Dorade grise en papillotte* or *suprême de sandre et son sabayon au poivre et à la tomate.* There are intense sorbets for dessert and a wicked *fondant au chocolat chaud.*

CLOSED Sat lunch, Sun; three weeks in Aug, one week in Feb
CARDS MC, V

◆ Les Muses €€€ Fr

Hôtel Scribe, 1 rue Scribe, 75009 Paris
Tel 01 44 71 24 24 Fax 01 42 65 39 97
Metro Opéra

Not only is Les Muses superbly located – it stands within the triangle formed by the Opéra, the Madeleine and Place Vendôme - it now houses one of the capital's most up-and-coming young chefs. "I love classic French cuisine so I take my cue from Escoffier and Bocuse," says Yannick Alléno, who learned his art at Paris' top restaurants and was recently awarded a second Michelin star. His menus always include a selection of *grande cuisine* dishes with a personal touch such as the majestic *Lièvre à la Royale* in the game season. This is also one of the few restaurants outside Brittany to serve *abalone.* The lunch menu was 41 euros as we went to press.

❛ Knowledgeable sommelier, high-class food'…'Discreet dining room'…'Friendly, professional service'…'Well-situated ❜

CLOSED Sat, Sun, Mon
CARDS AE, DC, MC, V

◆ La Petite Sirène de Copenhague €€

47 rue Notre-Dame-de-Lorette, 75009 Paris
Tel 01 45 26 66 66
Metro St Georges

This franco-Danish bistro is the sort of quintessential *bonne address* that Parisians share with friends. Come here for the best smoked salmon served in Paris. The perfectionist chef Peter Thulstrup, who has worked at the Crillon and La Tour d'Argent, limits the menu to a few starters such as the *omelette norvègienne à l'anis,* and mains such as *fricadelles au curry, lotte aux bet-*

teraves, selle d'agneau aux pruneaux. The excellent wine list includes a margaux chateau Palmier and a 1988 chassagne Montrachet. Reservations are a must here in the evening.

❛ Friendly service ❜

CLOSED Sun, Mon; 3 weeks in summer
CARDS none

◆ Le Roi du pot-au-feu € Fr

34 rue Vignon, 75009 Paris
Tel 01 47 42 37 10
Metro Havre-Caumartin

This place is so firmly rooted in tradition that it feels timeless. Trends will come and go, but Parisians will always eat *pot-au-feu* in that pre-war interior with slow-motion waiters. The classic beef and vegetable stew, served with pickles and grain mustard, is a substantial and appetising meal that forms a nice duo with a house *gamay d'Anjou.* But you can add a starter, say the greaseless *bol de bouillon* or *l'os à moelle* (bone marrow) on toast and/or a desert: *crème caramel, tarte Tatin, mousse chocolate* or the more adventurous *sorbet pomme au calvados.*

CLOSED Sun; 15 Jul-15 Aug
CARDS MC, V

Our price bands
€ under 30 euros €€ 30-50 Euros
€€€ over 50 euros for a menu

◆ Ty Coz €€ Fr

35 rue St Georges, 75009 Paris
Tel 01 48 78 42 95
Metro N.D. de Lorette or Le Peletier

Delightful Breton-style restaurant serving impeccable seafood. The thick fillet of smoked haddock in butter sauce was an exercise in style and the whole crab served on a bed of fresh seaweed is delicious. The setting reproduces the atmosphere of a mariner's cottage, complete with wooden beams, crockery dresser and a superb model ship. Warm service from the staff and perfectly chilled white wines make this a connoisseur's address.

CLOSED Sun, Mon; two weeks in Aug
CARDS AE, MC, V

Paris, 10th Arrondissement
◆ Chez Michel €€

10 rue de Belzunce, 75010 Paris
Tel 01 44 53 06 20 Fax 01 44 53 61 31
Metro Gare-du-Nord or Poissonière

Rare is the chef who straddles the line between tradition and invention with the finesse of Thierry Breton. Given the low price (30 euros as we went to press) of his gourmet menu, he also merits the title of a public benefactor. He gleefully experiments with the best ingredients in a classic bistro setting near the Gare du Nord train station. The result can claim to be a sort of new regional cuisine. Dishes such as *lasagnes de chèvre et artichaut breton au pistou*, and *milllefeuille de betteraves et foie gras poêlé* are genuinely original. For dessert, try the traditional *Kouing Amman*, a stack of ultrathin pastry leaves filled with butter and sugar. Be sure to book.

❛ *Indulge your gourmet instincts at a reasonable price* ❜

CLOSED Sun, Mon; Christmas week; Aug
CARDS MC, V

Paris, 11th Arrondissement
◆ L'Aiguiere €€

37 bis rue de Montreuil, 75011 Paris
Tel 01 43 72 42 32 Fax 01 43 72 96 36
Metro Faidherbe Chaligny or Rue des Boulets

Formerly a coaching inn serving the royal musketeers, l'Aiguière is now a romantic little restaurant offering candlelit dinners a short metro ride from the centre of town. Owner Patrick Masbatin has brought back to life a forgotten dish originally created at the Tour d'Argent when Napoleon received the Tsar of Russia : the *tournedos Yella*. Patrick is an expert on wine and spirits and often organises special cognac and cigar evenings.

❛ *A little out of the way'... 'Matches wine and food well* ❜

CLOSED Sat lunch, Sun
CARDS AE, DC, MC, V

◆ Astier € **Fr**

44, rue Jean-Pierre Timbaud, 75011 Paris
Tel 01 43 57 16 35
Metro Parmentier or Couronnes

With its firmly-established reputation as a true bargain, Astier epitomizes the great-value Paris neighbourhood bistrot. Every weekday, devoted regulars sit elbow to elbow in the nondescript dining room for the sake of this copiously served, tasty, traditional food. Not the place to come if you don't have a healthy appetite. Astier's menu depends on the season and what was available at market. If you're lucky you will find freshly-caught sole, calf liver with bilberries or rabbit in mustard sauce with a side-basket of thick-cut chips. But leave some room to delve into the platter of cheeses that will take up most of your table. The wine list offers some excellent bottles at reasonable prices. As we went to press, the cheapest menu was 19.50 euros.

❛ *Incredible portions'...'Go early - it can get smoky'...'Buzzing area near République* ❜

CLOSED Sat, Sun; Easter, Aug, Christmas
CARDS MC, V

◆ Auberge Pyrénées-Cevennes € - €€ **Fr**

106 rue de la Folie Mericourt, 75011 Paris
Tel 01 43 57 33 78
Metro Republic

An eclectic crowd comes here with one thing in common: a (big) appetite for French *terroir* soul food from Lyon and the Southwest. For a starter try the *caviar du Puy* (green lentils in vinaigrette) or *Lyonnais endive salads* topped with chunky bacon. The humble *cassoulet* is elevated to a pedestal here along with perfectly aged *entrecôte* and *Sabodet* sausage. The runny Saint-Marcellin cheese is exquisite. Good value wines from Morgon. Among desserts, the *Tarte Tatin* takes pride of place. Possibly the only restaurant in Paris with hams and sausages hanging from the ceiling.

CLOSED Sat lunch, Sun; 15 Jul to 15 Aug
CARDS V

◆ Blue Elephant €€

43, rue de la Roquette, 75011 Paris
Tel 01 47 00 42 00
Metro Bastille

Fabulous Thai 'village' on busy rue de la Roquette next to Bastille. Massive bunches of imported orchids, teak walls and furniture, waterfall complete with giant carp and waitresses in vibrant silk render the enchantment real. The whole concept is in line with the taste one would expect of the elegant antiquarian owner Karl Steppe. Head Chef Nopporn Siripark specializes in Royal Thai Cuisine featuring classics and personal creations such as the red and green curries, delicious banana flower salad, Thai fish cakes, prawn and lemongrass soup, jasmin tart and the unusual sweet 'n' sour dessert, Sod Sai. Most ingredients are imported direct from Thailand and degrees of spiciness are indicated by elephant symbols. The impeccable wine list is put together by international expert Manuel de la Motta Veiga. Several regional Thai festivals are celebrated throughout the year.

❛ Magical'…'Marvellous attention to detail'…'Superb presentation ❜

CLOSED Sat lunch
CARDS AE, DC, V

◆ Le Chardenoux €€ Fr

1 rue Jules Vallès, 75011 Paris
Tel 01 43 71 49 52
Metro Charonne

If you are looking for an typical, turn-of-the century bistro with film-set decoration of tiled floors, engraved glass room screens, bevelled windows and authentic marble and zinc bar, this is the place to come. Classified a historic monument in 1904, Chardenoux gives life to the expression *Tout change, rien ne change*: the quality of the classic

French food remains constant as does the unhurried service. Try the lentil soup, homemade terrines, thick-cut veal chop and veal kidneys in mustard sauce.

❛ Amazing that nothing ever changes here'…'Authentic decoration ❜

CLOSED Sat lunch, Sun; Aug
CARDS AE, DC, MC, V

◆ Chez Ramulaud € Fr

269 rue du Faubourg Saint-Antoine, 75011 Paris
Tel 01 43 72 23 29
Metro Faidherbe-Chaligny or Nation

Forget eating out in Bastille (just down the road) and come here instead for a night to remember. The seasonally changing menu celebrates fresh produce and regional dishes. The *maraichère de légumes nouveau* or a *chaussons de chèvre* are straightforward combinations, exquisitely prepared; ditto mains such as the *filet mignon de porc a la marjolaine* or a *palombe au jus simple*; desserts include an ultra-rich *mi-cuit au chocolat*. Owner Monsieur Gillou shares his knowledge and passion for wine in a bargain-priced connoisseur's list including the Morgon Cote-du-Py 99 (Jean Foillard Patrimonio), and Grotte di Sole 98 (Antoine Arena). On Sundays, there is ballroom dancing. There's a 12 euro lunch menu.

CLOSED Sat lunch, Sun
CARDS none

◆ Le Clown Bar €

114 rue Amelot, 75011 Paris
Tel 01 43 55 87 35
Metro Filles-du-Calvaire

This Art Nouveau gem, full of clown and circus memorabilia, will evoke childhood fantasies of running away to join the circus. Perhaps it's not too late, the Cirque d'Hiver is just next door and real-life clowns often drink at the zinc bar. They have a savvy selection of wines by the glass to choose from. The food is simple *cuisine solide* and reliably good: *assiette de charcuteries*, a delicious *oeufs en meurette* (eggs in wine sauce), *mignon de porc à l'ancienne* or tender *noisettes d'agneau à l'estragon*.

CLOSED Sun lunch, third week of Aug
CARDS none

◆ Khun Akorn €€

8 avenue de Taillebourg, 75011 Paris
Tel 01 43 56 20 03 Fax 01 40 09 18 44
Metro Nation

This tropical gourmet island lies in the middle of one of Paris' most densely populated areas. Oak floors, carved wood, elegant ornamentation and waitresses in traditional costume all contribute to a feeling of serenity. But the highlight of eating at Khun Akorn is the fact that dishes are inspired of a chef who was born in the service of the Thai royal family and established Thailand's first cookery school. The cuisine is entirely classical, and precisely executed. The prawn and lemon grass soup and duck in red curry are particularly good. The upstairs terrace is extremely popular, particularly on a summer's evening, so book a week in advance.

❜ *Food not quite spicy enough'…'Spacious dining room'…'Convenient for Nation* ❜

CLOSED Mon
CARDS AE, V

◆ Le Passage €

18 passage de la Bonne-Graine, 75011 Paris
Tel 01 47 00 73 30
Metro Ledru-Rollin

It is snugly hidden in the elbow of an alley only steps from the busy Bastille crossroads. Technically, it is a wine bar - with a formidable list of Rhone Valley and Burgundy crus; it would take hours to read the wine list - so ask for advice. The Breton owner finds room on his menu for the eight verions of the earthy *andouillette*, served grilled, as well as trendier dishes like seafood risotto or pasta. The trio of *pots de crème* makes a perfect finale. To find the passage, walk south from the crossroads of Charonne and Ledru-Rollin, on the right-hand side of Ledru-Rollin Renard, taking the first left.

❜ *Friendly staff'…'Very savvy wine selection* ❜

CLOSED Sat lunch, Sun
CARDS V

Paris, 12th Arrondissement
◆ La Biche Au Bois
€ Fr

45 avenue Ledru Rollin, 75012 Paris
Tel 01 43 43 34 38
Metro Quai de la Rapée

A candidate for the title of best-value-for-money in Paris, this small restaurant near the Gare de Lyon is always full. Parisians come for the copiously served, home-style cooking and decent wines, but also to be part of the ambient *bonhomie*. Nowhere else in town will you encounter this quality and choice at such a bargain price. The Biche really comes into its own during the game season, when you will often find grouse, venison, partridge and wild boar on the menu. Always on offer are the state-of-the-art *coq au vin*, *bœuf bourguignon*. A huge platter of perfectly-ripened cheeses plus dessert are included in the price. Booking is essential. As we went to press the single menu cost just over 20 euros.

❜ *Truly amazing value'…'Waiters keep on smiling despite the constant stream of hungry diners'…'French provincial cooking at its best* ❜

CLOSED Sat, Sun; end July to third week of Aug
CARDS AE, DC, MC, V

◆ Comme Cochon €

135 rue de Charenton, 75012 Paris
Tel 01 43 42 43 36
Metro Gare de Lyon

This is a 'grand bistro', a canteen for the neighbourhood around Gare de Lyon. It hums with a local crowd who appreciate the bargain lunch menu (14 euros as we went to press) and dishes such as the ultra-fresh *turbotin braisé et marmelade de fenouil*, the hit-the-spot *fois de veau au cassis* and a delicate *crêpe soufflée au pralin*. The big terrace is a great place for people watching and browsing an impressive and honestly priced range of wines. For a high-level view of eastern Paris, take a walk along the nearby Promenade Plantée, the former railway tracks planted with roses and shrubs.

CLOSED Sun
CARDS V

◆ L'Ebauchoir ⊜ **Fr**

43 rue de Citeaux, 75012 Paris
Tel 01 43 42 49 31
Metro Faidherbe-Chaligny

You could hardly ask for a more traditional looking Paris bistro - worn tile floors, huge gilt mirrors, a menu scrawled in chalk on a blackboard. But the classic French cooking also comes with many original touches. If *L'espadon* (swordfish) is on the menu, *à l'émulsion de vanille et noisette* or *au beurre de citron et gingembre*, order it. Prices are fair and wines are accessibly priced. The bargain lunch menu nourishes a horde of temperamental Bastille locals, including artists and media types. Lunch menu was 13 euros as we went to press.

CLOSED Mon lunch, Sun
CARDS MC, V

◆ L'Oulette ⊜ – ⊜⊜

15 place Lachambeaudie, 75012 Paris
Tel 01 40 02 02 12
Metro Bercy

L'Oulette was a pioneer in this now supertrendy area of the capital and has a faithful following of diners. The widely-spaced tables guarantee confidential conversation and the warm but unobtrusive service and imaginative takes on the cooking of South-West France keep Parisians coming back. The generous evening menu includes two half bottles of very decent white and red wine. From the à la carte menu choose from duck terrine with *foie gras* in *Jurançon* jelly, *millefeuille de sardines*, duck *confit* and for dessert, the featherlight apple *tourtière*. The informed wine list features a number of quality sherries, and coffee is chosen

from a menu arranged by country.

*⟨ Delightful'… 'Far from the crowds'
…'Chic but homey decoration ⟩*

CLOSED Sat lunch, Sun
CARDS AE, DC, MC, V

◆ La Sologne ⊜ – ⊜⊜

164 avenue Daumesnil, 75012 Paris
Tel 01 43 07 68 97 Fax 01 43 44 66 23
Metro Daumesnil

As the name suggests, this classic stalwart next to the fountains of Place Daumesnil serves *cuisine de terroir*, particularly from the eponymous region. Think Sologne, think game goes the saying, and here the chef really comes into his own during the game season. Wild boar, duck, partridge, hare, venison… Didier Maillet offers the whole range, except pheasant. "It is impossible to find good-quality pheasant today, so we just refuse to sell it." He used to have a wine shop, so he knows all the best producers and now his wine list offers such rarities as Overnoy's Arbois Pupillin 85, a Rayas 97 and a superb Fixin Domaine Fougeray de Beauclair 98.

*⟨ Excellent home-made
bread'… 'Simple, almost boring
decoration ⟩*

CLOSED Sat lunch, Sun
CARDS AE, MC, V

◆ Le Square Trousseau
⊜ – ⊜⊜

1 rue Antoine Vollon, 75012 Paris
Tel 01 43 43 06 00 Fax 01 43 43 00 66
Metro Ledru-Rollin

It would be hard to exaggerate the nostalgic charm of this corner bistro-brasserie dating from 1900. You will be tempted to linger in front of your carafe of wine long after the generous portions of *agneau parfumé au thym* and *clafoutis aux clémentines* are finished. It overlooks a lovely square - Trousseau - at the heart of the 12th arrondissement. An interesting wine list features full-bodied Rhône reds from Domaine Gramenon. After lunch, be sure to visit the nearby Place d'Aligre food and flea markets.

CLOSED Sun, Mon; Aug
CARDS V

◆ Au Trou Gascon €€

40, rue Taine, 75012 Paris
Tel 01 43 44 34 26 Fax 01 43 07 80 55
Metro Daumesnil

Alain Dutournier's second restaurant, tucked well off the beaten track, is the place to go for a taste of the top chef's superb food at half the price you would pay at the luxurious Carré des Feuillants. The dining room has recently been redecorated to provide a neutral backdrop for a number of paintings by internationally-recognized artists, but the 16kg ham holding court in the centre of the room leaves you in no doubt as to the restaurant's main vocation: traditional cuisine from South-West France, using only the finest farmhouse produce - such as Chalosse chicken and beef, and cassoulet with genuine Tarbais beans. The extraordinary selection of Armagnacs dates from 1929.

❛ Unchanging dishes'... Worth crossing town for ❜

CLOSED Sat lunch, Sun; Aug; 25 Dec to 2 Jan
CARDS AE, MC, V

◆ Les Zygomates
€€ – €€€

7 rue de Capri, 75012 Paris
Tel 01 40 19 93 04 Fax 01 44 73 46 63
Metro Daumesnil or Michel-Bizot

The zygomatic muscles of the lower cheek are used for two of pleasurable activities - smiling and chewing - and this bistro is a place to do both. It was a delicatessen in the 1920s, which explains the pre-war interior of marble counters, painted etched glass, and polished, walnut-moulded windows and doors. Starters include a luscious goat-cheese cannelloni. Typical of main dishes is the *crépinette de faison farci au chou et*

foie, a roll of sliced pheasant, with crispy skin on the outside, stuffed with cabbage and duck liver. As we went to press there was a 14 euro lunch menu.

CLOSED Sat lunch, Sun; Aug
CARDS V

Paris, 13th Arrondissement
◆ L'Avant-Goût
€ – €€

26 rue Bobillot, 75013 Paris
Tel 01 53 80 24 00 Fax 01 53 80 00 77
Metro Place d'Italie

This is the best restaurant in Butte-aux-Cailles, a village-like enclave of small houses and gardens and arguably the most charming unknown neighbourhood in Paris. Noisy and crowded, it's not a place for quiet reflection, but for savouring, in convivial communion, the inventive cuisine of chef Christophe Beaufront. A starter might be *tajine des legumes à la graine de fenouil*, followed by the house speciality, *pot-au-feu de cochon aux épices* or, in season, *sanglier à sept heures*. The wine list is original and affordable. Lunch menu for 14 euros as we went to press.

CLOSED Sun, Mon; first week of Jan and May; three weeks Aug
CARDS V

◆ Chez Gladines €

30 rue des Cinq-Diamants, 75013 Paris
Tel 01 45 80 70 10
Metro Corvisart

This Basque restaurant is a friendly neighbourhood *table de quartier*, always crowded and incredibly cheap. The house speciality is an immense salad with a citrus vinaigrette served in an earthenware bowl. You choose what to add: *jambon de Bayonne*, duck, potatoes, and so on. Or you can go for Basque chicken, *piperade* or, in winter, *pot-au-feu*, accompanied by full-blooded wines from the south-west. Finish with a slice of sheep's cheese or the fine home-made desserts, such as a cherry-filled *Gateau de Basque*. You can eat here for around ten euros without wine. Dinner menu 16 euros as we went to press.

6 Enormous salads 9

CLOSED never
CARDS none

◆ Le Petit Marguery

€€ – €€€ **Fr**

9 boulevard de Port-Royal, 75013 Paris
Tel 01 43 31 58 59
Metro Les Gobelins

The three Cousin brothers from Poitiers (Alain, Michel and Jacques) have turned this Belle Epoque dining room into a gourmet's paradise. In autumn, they serve a legendary *La Lièvre à la royale* and a menu *dégustation, special gibier* that includes pheasant, wild boar and venison. Alternatives to game are the *poêlée de coquilles Saint-Jacques aux cèpes, raviolis de pétoncles aux champignons des bois, blanc de turbot aux fines herbes* or *raie rôtie à la graine de moutarde*. It's normally full of middle-aged French couples who've been coming here for years for a meal that frequently ends in a *soufflé au Grand Marnier*. The wine list is strong on affordable wines from Burgundy.

CLOSED Sun, Mon
CARDS V

Paris, 14th Arrondissement
◆ La Coupole €€

102 bd du Montparnasse, 75014 Paris
Tel 01 43 20 14 20 Fax 01 43 35 46 14
Metro Vavin

Generations of Parisians have dined, danced and romanced at La Coupole which is as much a part of the history of Montparnasse as the Bohemian poets, musicians and artists who made it their own at the turn of the 20th century. Despite its huge size, this 'food hall' fills up with a crowd of Parisians, suburbanites and tourists every meal time. The wait for a table often exceeds half an hour in the evening, but still they come to people-watch, admire the Art Deco and experience one of the liveliest restaurants in Paris. Be sure that this is the charm of La Coupole, rather than

interesting food. As in all brasseries, seafood tops the bill but the extensive menu also offers such timeless favourites as snails, onion soup, *foie gras*, *steak tartare* and *châteaubriand*.

6 Part of the Paris experience - you have to go there at least once'
…'Jokey waiters'…'Factory-like 9

CLOSED Sun
CARDS AE, DC, MC, V

◆ La Créole €€ – €€€

122 bd du Montparnasse, 75014 Paris
Tel 01 43 20 62 12
Metro Vavin

This is the nearest you will get to the French Caribbean without leaving Paris. Smiling, friendly waitresses clad in colourful *damas* and lace, white wrought-iron or wicker furniture and huge bouquets of vibrant tropical flowers offer a faithful reproduction of the Antilles. Peep though the curtain of green plants which all but obscure the windows and you might just remember you are in Paris. Owner Charlie will explain the differences between the dishes of Martinique and Guadeloupe from a menu that includes such stalwarts as *féroce*, stuffed crab, cod fritters, *chatrou* (octopus stew) and a delicious *colombo* (lamb or pork curry. Charlie is president of the Rum Academy so can be relied upon to unearth that old vintage you have been longing to try.

6 Caribbean ambiance but not over-the-top 9

CLOSED never
CARDS AE, DC, MC, V

◆ L'O à la Bouche
€ – €€

124 bd de Montparnasse, 75014 Paris
Tel 01 56 54 01 55 Fax 01 43 21 07 87
Metro Vavin

Before striking out on his own, Chef Frank Paquier learned his trade in a couple of Paris' best places, the Troisgros and the Savoy, and it shows. The pleasures of his ambitious menu include his signature *salade multicolore de gambas au sesame* and mains including *tarte feuilletée au rouget-barbet* and a *daurade en écailles écrasée de pommes ratte et jus de langoustine*. Attracting a mixed Left Bank crowd, it is joyfully noisy in the best bistro tradition. The intelligent wine list is fairly priced, but service is on the slow side.

CLOSED Sun, Mon, one week in Jan, second week of April, first three weeks of Aug
CARDS MC, V

◆ Ti-Jos €

30 rue Delambre, 75014 Paris
Tel 01 47 34 96 12
Metro Montaparnasse or Edgar Quinet

All feels right in the world after you've eaten your fill of Breton crêpes and quaffed a couple of bowls of vitamin-rich cider in this small dining room, full of old oak cupboards, pew-like wooden benches and Breton bric-à-brac. There is live Celtic music (Breton or Irish) in a cellar on Fridays. As we went to press, you could eat here à la carte without wine for 15 euros; menus 11 euros (lunch) and 13 euros (dinner).

CLOSED Tue eve, Sat, Sun; Aug
CARDS AE, MC, V

Paris, 15th Arrondissement
◆ Le Belisaire €

2, rue Marmontel, 75015 Paris
Tel 01 48 28 62 24
Metro Convention

Just the kind of place you were hoping to stumble upon in this tiny street at the heart of Paris' most extensive Arrondissement. The essential elements of the quintessential old bistro are still there –polished wooden floors and bar, Art Deco lighting, mirror panels, snowy-white tablecloths – but Matthieu Garrel, the 31-year-old Breton chef, has rejuvenated the menu, lending an innovative touch to the classics: saffron mussels, black sausage *nems*, green pepper *vichyssoise, feuilleté d'andouille*, artichokes *barigoule* with *foie gras*, and for dessert… chocolate and pepper cake.

❛ Lovely atmosphere'…'good house wine in pitchers'…'Enthusiastic chef anxious to please ❜

CLOSED Sat lunch, Sun; three weeks Aug
CARDS V

◆ Bistro 121 €€

121, rue de la Convention, 75015 Paris
Tel 01 45 57 52 90 Fax 01 45 57 14 69
Metro Boucicaut

Formerly a favourite haunt of Orson Welles and François Mitterand, Bistro 121 has kept the warm atmosphere and rich mahogany tones of its original decoration designed by the ubiquitous Slavik. It now caters for an almost exclusively Parisian clientèle, particularly from the residential 15th Arrondissement. Chef Igor Sterenfeld serves a blend of *cuisine du terroir* and lighter, more contemporary dishes. According to the season his menu may include such monuments as *tête de veau sauce gribiche* or *pot au feu*, but also *gratin de langoustines* or *artichauts Lucullus*.

❛ Good atmosphere cosy winter get-togethers'…'Food erratic ❜

CLOSED never
CARDS DC, MC, V

◆ Le Bistrot de Cancale € Fr

30-32 bd de Vaugirard, 75015 Paris
Tel 01 43 22 30 25 Fax 01 43 22 45 13
Metro Montparnasse Bienvenüe

A recent addition to the Breton enclave around Montparnasse station, this out-sized *bistrot* extending over three levels plus a terrace, is distinguished by the quality of its fish dishes. Young chef Gaël Allais started out working with three-star Olivier Roellinger in his native Brittany where he learned how to select the very best of the day's catch. The ultra-fresh seafood platters at the Cancale feature oysters, shrimps, prawns, cockles and a whole crab, or you can go for the elite of the oyster world: a dozen Belons on the half-shell. The lunchtime menu is unbeatable value for the area, and includes a starter or dessert and main course plus a choice of wine, beer or cider.

❛ *Like Brittany'…'Handy for the train station'…'Restricted choice of wines* ❜

CLOSED Sun and Sat in Aug
CARDS AE, MC, V

◆ Dix Vins €

57 Falguière, 75015 Paris
Tel 01 43 20 91 77
Metro Pasteur

The ridiculously low-priced menu of this bistro gem features starters such as *calamars à la plancha, sardines grillées*, followed by *filets de rouget grillés pistou, pintade* with *crème de fois gras, onglet de boeuf sauce camembert*, and, for dessert, a *tarte au chocolat* or *crème brulèe*, redolent with real vanilla. But you could come here for the wine list alone. The place is often hectic but the busy blonde patronne runs a tight ship with a smile and, on weekends, help from her son, who was twelve years old when we went to press.

CLOSED Sun, Mon
CARDS none

◆ Ty Breiz €

52 Boulevard de Vaugirard
75015 Paris
Tel 01 43 20 83 72
Metro Pasteur or Montparnasse

In the shadow of Tour Montparnasse, the City of Light's only skyscraper, you will find this homey, wood-panelled *creperie*, one of the best cheap eateries in Paris. Lacey, thin buckwheat pancakes (*galettes*) are served, simply with salted Breton butter, or filled with ingredients. One house speciality is *la Normande* (chicken, crème sauce and mushrooms). Earthenware bowls of bubbling cider or thick *lait Ribot* (Breton buttermilk) are happy partners. For dessert, don't miss *la crêpe de froment Ty Breiz*, stuffed with apples, whipped cream and homemade ice-cream.

CLOSED Sun, Mon
CARDS MC, V

Paris, 16th Arrondissement
◆ Le Bistro des Vignes € – €€

1 rue Jean-Bologne, 75016 Paris
Tel 01 45 27 76 64
Metro La Muette or Passy

You have to show up regularly here to fully appreciate Chef Eric Corailler's commitment to *cuisine du marché*. He prints a new menu every month and writes out daily specials on the blackboard in his friendly corner bistro, located off chic Passy street. Choice depends on season, a wintry starter might be *cassolette de champignons sauvages et d'escargots à bourguignonne* or, in summer, *fines crêpes d'herbes fraîches aux écrevisses*. Don't miss the game classics in autumn or lamb in spring.

CLOSED Aug
CARDS AE, MC, V

Please send us reports
A guide such as this thrives on reader's reports. If you send us five usable reports, we will send you a free copy of any title in our *Charming Small Hotel Guides* series (see page 241 for France titles in the series).

The five reports should contain at least two new restaurants; the rest can be comments on restaurants already in the guide.
1 Tell us about your experiences in restaurants already in this guide.
2 Send us new reports. New reports should give the following information:
- **Region –** City, town, village or neaest village.
- **Name of restaurant –** Please double check the spelling, it's surprisingly easy to make a mistake.
- **Address –** including *département*.
- **Telephone number –** plus fax and e-mail if available. Double check this information.
- **Objective description –** Try to explain simply why it should be in the guide. Remember that the guide is very selective - our entries are those one-in-five places that combine
  ● **interesting food with**
  ● **character and charm, in the building, the setting or both.**

The guide hates tourist traps, and pretentious, dressed-up food. We like places where the French go.

We favour places in the lower and middle price bands but there are plenty of expensive places that have our qualities, and we list those too.

- **Diner's comments –** These should be short, personal comments on features that strike you. They can be your comments, or others'.
- **Closing times**
- **Credit cards accepted**
Don' t forget to date your report and add your name and address.
Send reports to Charming Restaurant Guides, Duncan Petersen Publishing, 31 Ceylon Road, London W14 OPY.

◆ Brasserie de la Poste ⓔ – ⓔⓔ

54 rue de Longchamp, 75016 Paris
Tel 01 47 55 01 31
Metro Trocadero

Only a couple of blocks from place Trocadero and stunning views of the Eiffel Tower, this is a friendly haven in a much-visited, upmarket area. An elegant bar dominates the entrance to the polished, 1930s wood and mirrored interior. A crowd of locals and suits pay homage to a seasonal menu ranging from *huîtres fines de claires* and *choucroute garni* in winter to a summer *salade d'herbes folles* and *Saint-Jacques à la provençale*. *Steak tartare* and the house *foie gras* are constants as well as a superb *crème brûlée* and on weekends all you can eat for 18.5 euros.

Closed never
Cards AE, V

◆ Le Chalet des Iles
ⓔ – ⓔⓔ

Lac du Bois de Boulogne, 75016 Paris
Tel 01 42 88 04 69 Fax 01 45 25 41 57
Metro Pte Dauphine

A short boat ride takes you to this glass-fronted haven on an island in the Bois de Boulogne. Originally built as a hunting lodge for Empress Eugenie, the restaurant features a wide terrace where you can dine with a view over the lake with the Eiffel Tower in the distance while peacocks strut around the lawn. Probably the most romantic setting in the capital. Tables overlooking the lake are distributed on a first-come-first-served basis, so come early. Food is expensive, but interesting, with a hint of the Pacific Rim, a relatively new concept in France : Prawn Colombo, Salmon steak marinated in saké.

❛ *Inconvenient for the metro. Take a taxi'… 'Ideal for a Paris proposal* ❜

Closed Sun evening in winter
Cards AE, V

◆ L'Etoile ⓔⓔ

12, rue de Presbourg, 75016 Paris
Tel 01 45 00 78 70
Metro Ch. de Gaulle Etoile

Installed inside a superb *hôtel particulier*, formerly the property of a Marshal of the Empire, this first-floor restaurant/piano bar is the only eating place in Paris to have a completely unobstructed view of the Arc de Triomphe. One might imagine that the food is secondary to the view, but manager Tony Gomez, former *enfant terrible* of the Paris night scene, insists on the best for the pampered jet setters who frequent his Elysian establishment: Charolais beef, line-caught bass, farmhouse cheeses… The crimson silk-taffeta curtans, red leather armchairs and sumptuous bouquets create a luxurious setting from which to observe Napoleon's triumphal arch.

❛ *Contemporary cosiness'… 'Comes into its own in the evening' … 'Expensive wine list* ❜

Closed Sat lunch, Sun
Cards AE, MC, V

◆ Le Galion
ⓔⓔ – ⓔⓔⓔ

10 Allée du Bord de l'Eau, 75016 Paris
Tel 01 44 14 20 00 Fax 01 44 14 20 00
Metro Pte Dauphine

Anchored in the Bois de Boulogne, opposite Longchamp racetrack, the 170 ft ship-cum-restaurant looms incongruously on the Seine. Every detail has been taken care of to make it look like a real sixteenth-century galleon and the place has a Disney-like fascination for Parisian children whose parents bring them in droves on Sundays when entertainment is specially laid on. Food is inspired by Alain Raichon, chef at the nearby Jardins de Bagatelle, with the emphasis on simplicity : coddled eggs with asparagus, fillet of beef with hand-cut fries and saddle of lamb with fennel. Lunch menu 39 euros.

(Wonderfully kitsch'…'Convenient for the Bois de Boulogne camping site)

CLOSED never
CARDS AE, V

◆ La Gare €−€€

19 Chaussée de la Muette, 75016 Paris
Tel 01 42 15 15 31 Fax 01 42 15 15 23
Metro La Muette

A reminder of times past, this railway station is now a stylish brasserie. The tables occupy where once there were platforms and rails and the waiting room is now a bar. The house speciality is spit-roasted *poulet de bresse, agneau, veau* or *faux filet*. For starters, try the *caviar d'aubergines* or *pancetta à la provençale*. It also serves large mixed salads with a nicely citrus vinaigrette and a wicked *moelleux au chocolat amer sauce caramel*. Wines from Bordeaux and the Loire go well with the food. Best to eat lunch here on a fine day and combine it with a visit to the Marmottan museum or Bois de Boulogne.

CLOSED Christmas, New Year
CARDS MC, V

◆ Le GR5 €

19 rue Gustave Courbet, 75116 Paris
Tel 01 47 27 09 84
Metro Rue de la Pompe

The GR5 is a hiking trail that crosses the shoulder of Mont Blanc. It is also a cosy bistro in the middle of the 16th, decorated with clunky ski paraphernalia and posters from the 1930s. A mostly local crowd indulges in hearty bistro fare and the cheesy specialities of the Alpine Savoy region such as a tangy and perfectly melted *fondue, raclette* served with Alpine *charcuterie, tartiflette au reblochon* or a *gratinée de vacherin* (served in the evening only).

CLOSED Sun
CARDS none

◆ La Grande Cascade €€€ Fr

Allée de Longchamp, Bois de Boulogne, 75016 Paris
Tel 01 45 27 33 51 Fax 01 42 88 99 06
Metro les Sablons

Located at the Porte Maillot entrance to the Bois de Boulogne, La Grande Cascade is one of Paris' few remaining *haute bourgeoisie* French restaurants. The service still carries all the pomp and ceremony of the Second Empire that was, when this lavish pavillion was built. However, with its intricate ironwork and gold-leafing, the crescent-shaped dining room is the epitomy of Belle Epoque. The cuisine is correspondingly elaborate,as indeed are the prices: *foie gras confit, scallop gratin* with truffles, *caneton en croûte*. One of the most expensive places in the guide, as we went to press the avergae price of an à la carte meal for one without wine was 110 euros. Menus started at 54, rising to 129 euros.

(Perfect for a romantic evening'…'Luxury at a price'…'Silver salver service)

CLOSED end Jan to end Feb
CARDS AE, DC, MC, V

◆ Les Jardins de Bagatelle €€−€€€

Parc de Bagatelle, Route de Sèvres à Neuilly, 75016 Paris
Tel 01 40 67 98 29
Metro Pte Dauphine

Summer or spring are the best times to enjoy a leisurely lunch at delightful Bagatelle park deep at the heart of the Bois de Boulogne. Tables are set out in the shade of the century-old trees next to the delightful scented rose garden. Chef Alain Raichon comes from the Jura, so expect to sample traditional regional dishes such as chicken with morels cooked in *vin jaune*. He also makes his own *foie gras*. Combine eating here with a visit to the park's folly, built in just 64 days as a bet between Marie-Antoinette and her brother-in-law, the Comte d'Artois.

❦ A little expensive but worth it to sit in the lovely garden ❞

CLOSED evenings mid-Sept to 1st May; 24 and 31 Dec
CARDS AE, MC, V

◆ Le Petit Retro €

5 rue Mesnil, 75116 Paris
Tel 01 44 05 06 05 Fax 01 44 05 06 05
Metro Victor Hugo

A bar and two tiny rectangular rooms are all there is to this turn-of-the-century bistro. The classic bistro food has some whimsical touches such as the *oeufs pochés a la crème de chorizo* or the *raviole de crabe au curry*. The *blanquette de veau à l'ancienne* is, in the best tradition, satisfyingly robust and tender. Dessert lovers will adore the *rioche rotie au miel et glace au pain d'épices*. An interesting choice of wines and perky service add to the pleasure.

CLOSED Sat lunch, Sun, three week in Aug
CARDS none

◆ Petrus €€€

12, place du Maréchal-Juin, 75016 Paris
Tel 01 43 80 15 95
Metro Pereire

The denizens of this 'desirable-residence' part of the 17th arrondissement frequent this glass-fronted restaurant for the excellent quality of the fish. A native of Savoie, Jean-Pierre Barrié visits Rungis every morning to pick out the best of the catch. The dishes are as expensive as the restaurant's illustrious namesake, but the impeccable flavour of the top-quality fish and shellfish remains unspoiled by superfluous sauces: salt

cod, Scottish salmon, line-caught bass, squid.

❦ Off the beaten track'...'Interesting white wine list'... 'Attentive service ❞

CLOSED first two weeks of Aug
CARDS AE, MC, V

◆ Le Scheffer €

22 rue Scheffer, 75116 Paris
Tel 01 47 27 81 11
Metro Trocadero or Passy

A happy, family-run *bistro de quartier* hides behind red-and-white chequered curtains on a sidestreet off place Trocadero. Simple and unpretentious, it serves sturdy bistro classics to a crowd of often packed-in regulars, many of whom, alas smoke. Starters run from a *terrine de lapin aux pleurotes* to *salade d'epinard frais oeuf poché*, while main courses feature a first-rate *navarin d'agneau aux petits legumes*, *filets de rouget* and *foie de veau*, either *rosé au vinaigre de Xéres* or *au miel d'acacia*. Some of the desserts pack an alcoholic punch: try *cerises à l'eau de vie* or prunes soaked in either cassis or armagnac.

CLOSED Sun; Christmas, New Year
CARDS none

Please send us reports
A guide such as this thrives on reader's reports. If you send us five usable reports, we will send you a free copy of any title in our *Charming Small Hotel Guides* series (see page 241 for France titles in the series).
  The five reports should contain at least two new restaurants; the balance can be comments on restaurants already in the guide. **Send reports to** Charming Restaurant Guides, Duncan Petersen Ltd, 31 Ceylon Road, London W14 0PY.

◆ Le Totem €€

Musée de l'Homme, 17 place du Trocadéro, 75016 Paris
Tel 01 47 27 28 29 Fax 01 47 27 53 01
Metro Trocadero or Passy

There is no better terrace from which to view the Eiffel Tower. Le Totem is at the Palais de Chaillot, its tables overlooking the Trocadero fountains and gardens. Inside, the decoration is a curious mixture of objects from the American Indian world, with two gigantic Canadian totem poles taking pride of place. The contemporary French food with a slight exotic bent draws an eclectic mix of 16th arrondissement bourgeois ladies-who-lunch, businessmen, actors and tourists. Booking essential.

❮ *Spectacular panorama'…'Long bar with a selection of world beers'…'Between pub and bistro* ❯

Closed never
Cards AE, DC, V

Paris, 17th Arrondissement
◆ Le Café d'Angel €

16 rue Brey, 75017 Paris
Tel 01 47 54 03 33 Fax 01 47 54 03 33
Metro Charles-de-Gaulle-Etoile

Only a couple of blocks from the Arc de Triomphe, this bistro possesses an intimate charm in a mostly grandiose neighbourhood. It attracts a well-dressed local crowd but few tourists. Tasty starters include *tartare d'avocats et crevettes* and *soupe veloutée de lentilles et croutons*; mains such as *veau sauce romarin*; desserts of *gateau au chocolat maison*. You can buy jars of home-made *confiture* to take home with you. The wine list, unlike the food, is not a bargain.

❮ *Splendid view'…'Top crus at knockdown prices* ❯

Closed Sat to Sun; Christmas week, three weeks in Aug
Cards MC, V

◆ Caves Pétrissans
€€ – €€€

30 bis, avenue Niel, 75017 Paris
Tel 01 42 27 52 03 Fax 01 40 54 87 56
Metro Ternes or Pereire

Wine and classic bistro cuisine are a marriage made in heaven - especially in places like this Bacchic 1895 dining room graced by no less than 500 vintages. They are a perfect fit for *produits du terroir* such as *quenelles de brochet, côtes de veau aux petits pois frais* and *gigot de Pyrénées*. The *crème brulée à la cassonade* is a wonderful finale. There are always at least a dozen wines on hand that cost less than 15 euros a bottle. The patron scouts out wines all over France to keep his regular customers happy.

Closed Sat, Sun; Aug
Cards AE, DC, MC, V

◆ La Fourchette des Anges
€ – €€

17 rue Biot, Paris, 75017 Paris
Tel 01 44 69 07 69
Metro Place-de-Clichy

Only a few metres from the honking horns of Place Clichy, the 'angels' fork' is a very popular bistro, which has kept its soul intact - simple, charming and still relatively cheap. Unroll your papyrus scroll menu beneath grinning plaster-of-Paris cupids and look for starters such as *cassolette de ravioles* or *mille-feuille de légumes à la mozzarella*. Mains include *émincé de bœuf* and *magret de canard aux figues*. For dessert, there is a truly divine *poire pochée au caramel épicé*. Reservations advised, particularly in the evening.

Closed Sun; Aug
Cards MC, V

◆ Olivier & Co €

8, rue de Lévis, 75017 Paris
Tel 01 53 42 18 04 Fax 01 53 42 18 15
Metro Villiers

Olivier Baussan shot to fame with his Provençal-style boutiques dedicated to Mediterranean olive oils made by top small producers. Now he has opened his first bistro/shop in the chic 17th arrondissement. Run by Mario Pontarolo, formerly a sommelier at the Tour d'Argent, the restaurant is an ode to all things olive-based. Before you eat he will run you through a tasting of a selection of oils which you can follow up with a simple choice of three *tians*. The stuffed bell peppers and artichoke and fennel mousse are particularly recommended. For dessert, the pineapple in hibiscus syrup.

> ❢ *The lovely boutique is just made for browsing'…'Mario comments on the oils as he would on wines'…'Fascinating'…'Simple dishes* ❢

CLOSED Sun, Mon, Tue, Wed eve; three weeks in Aug
CARDS AE, V

◆ Le Stubli €

11, rue Poncelet, 75017 Paris
Tel 01 42 27 81 86
Metro Ternes

Just off the main axis of Avenue des Ternes, rue Poncelet is one of the Parisian's favourite places to shop for quality foodstuffs. This little coffee shop's Austro/German wooden façade fits nicely into the profusion of fruit, cheese and wine displays lining the street. Black Forest gateau, an *Apfelstrudel*, and Viennese hot chocolate are served on the first floor; downstairs the Delikatessen offers *charcuterie* and *wienerschnitzel* to homesick Germanic residents. *Gemütlichkeit* guaranteed.

> ❢ *Crowded but cosy* ❢

CLOSED Mon
CARDS AE, V

Paris, 18th Arrondissement
◆ Au Bon Coin €

1, rue des Cloÿs, 75018 Paris
Tel 01 46 06 91 36
Metro Larmarck-Caulaincourt

From the outside, you would never guess that this ordinary-seeming café is an awarding winning ('Bouteille d'Or') bistro. The third-generation owner, Jean-Louis Bras, is its heart and soul, gathering the *produits du marché* each morning for a couple of tasty *plats du jour* (*saucisson de Lyon à beaujolais, tartiflette*) and pairing them with just the right, ready-to-drink *vins de*

soif. Prepare to meet local people who call this café home for at least part of the day.

CLOSED Sat dinner, Sun; Aug
CARDS MC, V

◆ Le Bouclard € – €€

1 rue Cavallotti , 75018 Paris
Tel 01 45 22 60 01 Fax 01 45 22 00 47
Metro Place Clichy

Amicable Michel Bonnemort, an osteopath turned *bistrotier*, honours the memory of his grandmother Rosalie - he even has her picture on the wall - in this corner bistro on a tourist-free street behind Montmartre cemetery. By all accounts, she was an extraordinary cook and it is only fitting that everything is cooked her way (*façon grand-mère*) from the *macaronis au foie gras* and *fricasée de poulet à la vanille estragon* to her special chocolate fondant cake. The three-course lunch menu (22 euros), including a glass of wine and coffee, is rare value.

CLOSED Sat lunch, Sun
CARDS AE, MC, V

Paris, 20th Arrondissement
◆ Le Zéphyr € – €€

1 rue du Jourdain, 75020 Paris
Tel 01 46 36 65 81
Metro Jourdain

This Art Deco gem is well worth seeking out in the up-and-coming 20th Arrondissement. You can combine the lunch menu - one of the best value for money in Paris - with a walk in either the Buttes Chaumont or Parc Belleville, two of Paris' loveliest parks. The food displays original touches without being off-the-wall: witness the *canard sauvage roti au miel de lavande* accompanied by a *polenta épicée*. Desserts are classic - go for the *fondant tiède au chocolat sauce vanille* or whichever *crème brulée* is on offer (with coffee and cardoman or figs and cinnamon ice-cream). The wine list is good, if not thrilling. It fills up most evenings with neighbourhood residents, so best to reserve ahead.

CLOSED Sat lunch, Sun; Aug
CARDS AE, DC, MC, V

CHAMPAGNE-ARDENNE

A region of forests, lakes, fertile valleys and fine old cities, Champagne's reputation is dominated by its greatest product – Champagne. In the north, the industrialized Meuse valley and its principal town, Charleville-Mézières, co-habit alongside the peaceful Ardennes forest. Reims, with its great cathedral, stands at the heart of the region, and the Route du Champagne stretches south from there to Vertus. East of here is the regional capital, Chalons-sur-Marne and, nearby, the basilica of l'Epine. To the south are the 16thC houses and fine stained glass that distinguish Troyes, and the fortified city of Langres.

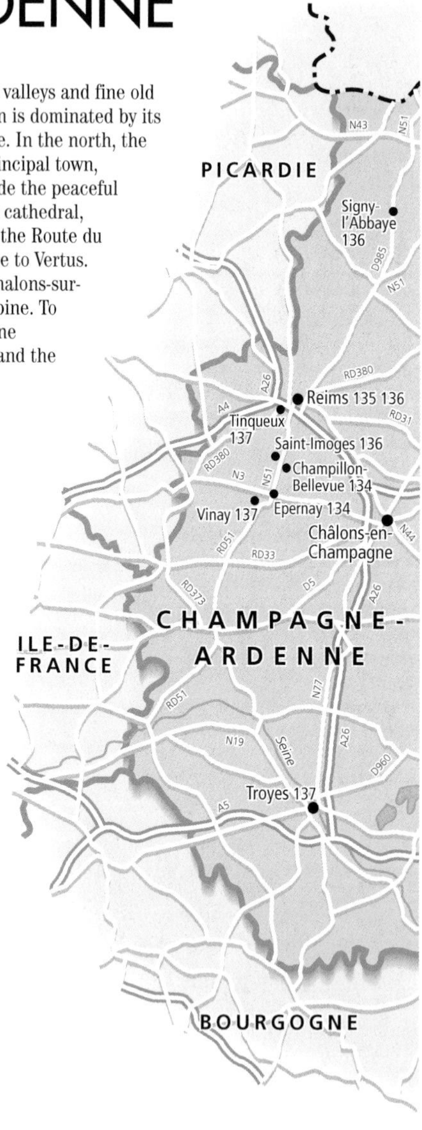

PICARDIE
N43
N51
Signy-l'Abbaye 136
D985
N51
RD380
A26
Reims 135 136
RD31
A4
Tinqueux 137
Saint-Imoges 136
RD380
N3
N51
Champillon-Bellevue 134
Vinay 137
Epernay 134
Châlons-en-Champagne
N44
RD51
RD33
RD373
D5
A26
CHAMPAGNE-ARDENNE
ILE-DE-FRANCE
N77
RD51
N19
Seine
A26
D960
Troyes 137
A5
BOURGOGNE

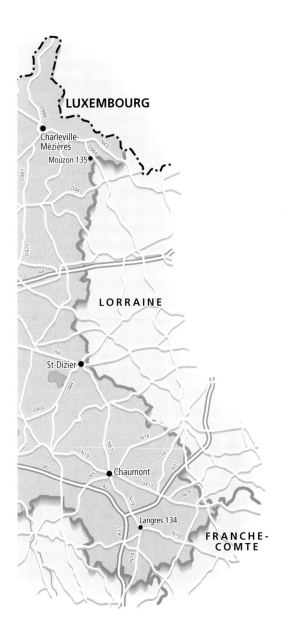

LUXEMBOURG

Charleville-
Mèzières

Mouzon 135

LORRAINE

St-Dizier

Chaumont

Langres 134

**FRANCHE-
COMTE**

D988
D43
D964
D947
D987
D977
A4
N4
D384
D400
N19
N67
N74
D74
A5
D65
A5
D417
N19
A31
D429
A31
N19
N74

Champillon-Bellevue
◆ Le Royal Champagne
€€€

route du Vignoble, 51160 Champillon-Bellevue, Marne
Tel 03 26 52 87 11 Fax 03 26 52 89 69

This 18thC post house stands surrounded by the lush Pinot Noir vineyards of the Montagne de Reims. The charming restaurant and chalet bedrooms command a sweeping view over a sea of vines with Epernay in the distance. Fresh from stints in the kitchens of Switzerland and Alsace, young chef Christophe Dufossé has united his *savoir-faire* with that of experienced manager Alain Guichaoua to create a luxuriously comfortable style of dining with the emphasis on tradition. Menus often include a superb farmhouse chicken in a salt crust (guaranteed to linger in the memory), roast scampi with morels, and fillet of John Dory with herb-stuffed ravioli, and several delicious and artistically-presented desserts.

❛ Impeccable service'...'Book well in advance for a table by the window ❭

CLOSED 2 weeks Feb
CARDS AE, DC, MC, V

Epernay
◆ Hôtel Les Berceaux
€€€ **Fr**

13 rue des Berceaux, 51200 Epernay, Marne
Tel 03 26 55 28 84 Fax 03 26 55 10 36

Just down the road from the world-famous names on prestigious avenue de Champagne, chef Patrick Michelon offers a choice of informal, inexpensive wine bar meals or traditional Champenois fare in his Michelin-starred restaurant. That old regional favourite, pig's trotter, is served in a potato crust with onion 'jam', the spinach cannelloni in meat juices and the chicken and snail *blanquette* comes in Champagne sauce. Considering Michelon's experience – ten years at the magnificent Château de Fère in Tardenois followed by the Armes de Champagne at l'Epine – you can hardly fail to leave your table satisfied. It's just a pity that the *sommelier* has ideas above his sta-

tion. If you want to stay the night, the bedrooms are small but cosy.

CLOSED wine bar: Sat, Sun; restaurant: Mon, Tue; three weeks Feb, two weeks Aug
CARDS AE, DC, MC, V

Epernay
◆ La Table Kobus
€€ **Fr**

3 rue du Docteur Rousseau, 51200 Epernay, Marne
Tel 03 26 51 53 53 Fax 03 26 58 42 68

Serge Herscher recalls his dream: "My Grandmother was cook to the wealthy bourgeoisie; I have always wanted to run my own restaurant." And now it has come true after working for three-star chef Gérard Boyer. Located behind Notre Dame church, this chic, 'old-style' bistro offers a choice of classic favourites at bargain prices: *foie gras*, haddock and chicory salad, sea bream, duck breast, Salers beef, nougat *glacé* and chocolate *fondant* with pears. The young chef's most inspired move was to allow diners to bring their own wine at no extra charge, an idea much appreciated by his daily clientele of Champagne house executives. An excellent place for opening that special bottle without breaking the bank.

❛ Good value'... 'Down-to-earth cuisine' ...'A bargain bistro ❭

CLOSED Sun dinner, Mon, Thu dinner
CARDS AE, MC, V

Langres
◆ Restaurant Diderot
€€

4 rue l'Estres-F, 52200 Langres, Haute-Marne
Tel 03 25 87 07 00 Fax 03 25 87 23 13

The charm of Langres, a fortress city that has changed little since the Enlightenment philosopher Diderot grew up here in the 18th century, is enhanced by the opportunity to savour the creative cooking of chef Patrick Durdan at Restaurant Diderot, part of a small hotel, Le Cheval Blanc. Dishes that stand out most on the seasonally changing menu include the *foie gras poêlé au miel d'épices*, the *noix de Saint-Jacques à la vinaigrette de pommes vertes* and a *ragout de morilles a l'oeuf cassé*. For dessert, there is the highly imaginative *soupe chaude des fruits rouges en vapeur de violette*.

CLOSED Tue dinner, Wed lunch Sep-Jul; last two weeks Nov
CARDS AE, MC, V

Mouzon
◆ Les Echevins €

33 rue Charles-de-Gaulle, 08210 Mouzon, Ardennes
Tel 03 24 26 10 90 Fax 03 24 29 05 95

Diners with a sense of history as well as an appetite will find it hard not to fall in love with this 17thC inn built by the Spaniards when they ruled the Meuse region. The kitchen never skips a beat from a bright and inspired entrée of *asperges et poireaux ravigotes* to deeply satisfying *rosace de veau poché à la fleur de sel sauté de courgettes au chèvre frais*. The service is both cordial and efficient.

❧ Amuse-bouches and petit-fours suddenly appear on the table as if by magic ❧

CLOSED Sun dinner, Mon; 2-3 weeks Jan, late Jul to late Aug
CARDS MC, V

Reims
◆ Boyer 'Les Crayères'
€€€

64 boulevard Henry-Vasnier, 51100 Reims, Marne
Tel 03 26 82 80 80 Fax 03 26 82 65 52

One of France's most sumptuous hotel-restaurants, Les Crayères occupies the chateau that was once home to the widow Pommery. This is Champagne at its most opulent. The truly magnificent dining room looks out through huge bow windows on to a terrace and century-old trees in the parkland beyond. From the thick-pile carpet to the beautiful furniture, every element of three-star chef Gérard Boyer's establishment is designed for comfort and to please the eye. Unbridled luxury extends, of course,

to the food and Boyer's signature dishes testify to his ultra-classic style: pig's trotter stuffed with *foie gras* and served with truffle *vinaigrette*, line-caught sea bass with spring vegetables, noisettes of lamb with a date and *foie gras purée* to name but a few.

CLOSED Mon, Tue lunch; late Dec to mid-Jan
CARDS AE, DC, MC, V

Our price bands
€ 15 Euros or less €€ 30-50 Euros
€€€ 50+ Euros for a menu.

Reims
◆ Les Charmes €€

11 rue Brûlart, 51100 Reims, Marne
Tel 03 26 85 37 63 Fax 03 26 36 21 00

Located near the city's Champagne cellars, this tiny bistro is one of its best bargains for lunch or dinner. It is run by a charming couple, chef Jacques Goyeux and his wife, Sylvie. Specialities of the house, skilfully executed, include *foie gras maison* served with *compotée de melon au ratafia à déguster avec le pain d'épices du chef*, *ris de veau braisés au porto*, *escalope de saumon mi-fumé maison et sa crème fouettée à la truffe*. For a *digestif*, there is a fine selection of whiskies.

CLOSED Sat lunch, Sun
CARDS MC, V

Reims
◆ Le Petit Comptoir €€

17 rue de Mars, 51100 Reims, Marne
Tel 03 26 40 58 58 Fax 03 26 47 26 19

The Petit Comptoir is the latest 'happening' place in Reims. Its designer decoration attracts the city's bright young things, while chef Fabrice Maillot keeps the gourmets happy. He trained with 3-star Gérard Boyer and has developed an eye for the finest, freshest products, which he infuses with his talent for invention. The pigeon *tagine*, with feather-light couscous, juicy meat and a touch of preserved lemon, the herb ravioli in walnut oil and the astonishing ice-cream list (including parmesan with olive oil and roquette) are all witness to this up-and-coming chef's creativity. There's a reasonably-priced Champagne list too.

‹ *Convenient for the Champagne houses. Inventive and surprising food* ›

CLOSED Sat lunch, Sun; 2 weeks Aug, end Dec to mid-Jan
CARDS MC, V

Reims
◆ La Vigneraie €€

14 rue de Thillois, 51100 Reims, Marne
Tel 03 26 88 67 27 Fax 03 26 40 26 67

Chef Hervé Badier's *cuisine créative et légère* is a marvellous way to begin or end a tour of Reims' glorious cathedral, which is only a stone's throw away. He lures local and out of town gourmets to his pretty little bistro with dishes like a delicate *fricassé de homard* on top of a *coulis au Sauternes façon cappuccino* or *filet de boeuf* with a wine and beef marrow sauce. Service is brisk and friendly.

CLOSED Sun dinner, Mon, Wed lunch; late Feb to early Mar, 3 weeks Aug
CARDS AE, MC, V

---

charmingsmallhotels.co.uk
Visit Duncan Petersen's travel website, the best online search tool for places to stay that combine character and charm. Currently features Britain, France, Italy and Ireland, with other destinations being continuously added.

Reims
◆ Le Vigneron
€€ Fr

place Paul-Jamot, 51100 Reims, Marne
Tel 03 26 79 86 86 Fax 03 26 79 86 87

This country-style tavern-cum-bistro is full of regional atmosphere and has a fascinating 'museum' in a series of windowed rooms, showing how life used to be for the region's grapegrowers. Antique Champagne posters, some of which date back to 1850, line the wood-panelled walls and provide a great talking-point, while the

menu concentrates heavily on *terroir*. This is the place to come if you are looking for solid, regional dishes such as Reims ham encased in flaky pastry, pig's trotter Sainte-Menehould, pike in champagne butter, *andouillette de Troyes*, and poached eggs in Maroilles cream. There is an extensive (and expensive) list of Champagnes including a number of old vintages. The patron can sometimes act like a bear with a sore head.

‹ *Has real atmosphere'... 'Serves robust country food* ›

CLOSED Sat lunch, Sun; 2 weeks Aug, late Dec to early Jan
CARDS MC, V

Saint-Imoges
◆ La Maison du Vigneron €€ Fr

RN 51, 51160 Saint-Imoges, Marne
Tel 03 26 52 88 00 Fax 03 26 52 86 03

This maison is a friendly spot in the idyllic *forêt du parc naturel de la Montagne de Reims,* near the classic Champagne vineyards and a short drive from the windy banks of the Marne or the cathedral city of Reims. Chef André Bougy's menus, served in a dining room bedecked with flowers, are composed of lovingly prepared recipes, designed to be the perfect foil for the region's characteristic wines. Excellent regional specialities include a *poêlée d'escargots de Champagne beurre rouge, petit flan de persil, poitrines de pigeonneau aux cèpes* and a *suprême de turbot rôti réduction au Champagne.*

CLOSED Wed
CARDS AE, MC, V

Signy-l'Abbaye
◆ Auberge de l'Abbaye €€ Fr

2 place Aristide-Briand, Signy-l'Abbaye 08460, Ardennes
Tel 03 24 52 81 27 Fax 03 24 53 71 72

In the middle of a fortified village overlooking a valley criss-crossed by ancient hedgerows and patches of forest, this inn has been in the hands of the Lefebvre family since the Revolution. The highlight of a meal in their rustic dining room, warmed by a real fire, is succulent beef from a breed called 'les blondes', which happens to be raised by the multi-talented Lefebvres, and is usually served with vegetables from the family garden.

CLOSED Wed; mid-Jan to early Feb
CARDS MC, V

Tinqueux
◆ L'Assiette Champenoise €€€

40 avenue Paul-Vaillant-Couturier, 51430 Tinqueux, Reims, Marne
Tel 03 26 84 64 64 Fax 03 26 04 15 69

Talented Arnaud Lallement who trained with three-star chefs Alain Chapel and Michel Guérard has taken over from his much-respected father at the helm of the Château Hôtel de la Muire, a luxurious establishment just outside Reims centre. Its restaurant, L'Assiette, is a favourite with executives from the nearby Champagne houses thanks to the unceremonious but professional service and Arnaud's refreshing interpretations of France's star products: frog's legs, Breton scampi, lobster, turbot and sea bass, lamb, veal, duck and pigeon. The wild mushrooms with crayfish in liquoriced meat juice and the turbot served with salted pork and Château Chalon sauce are particularly recommended, though every dish carries this young chef's original touch.

❜ Superb hotel with a warm, friendly atmosphere and an enthusiastic, dynamic young chef ❜

CLOSED Tue, Wed lunch
CARDS AE, DC, MC, V

Troyes
◆ Le Valentino €€ Fr

35 rue Palliot-de-Montabert, 10000 Troyes, Aube
Tel 03 25 73 14 14 Fax 03 25 73 74 04

This restaurant is in the heart of the ancient capital of Champagne, Troyes, a city of crooked half-timbered mansions, which bulge at strange angles, and with a skyline of ancient belfries and steeples. The dining room occupies a picturesque 16thC mansion where chef André Gilles conjures up a *millefeuille de betterave rouge et mousse de chèvre frais* or *cannelloni d'asperges vertes*, served with scallops grilled on bay leaves. In autumn, don't miss out on the venison *ragout* or grilled *marcassin* (baby wild boar).

❜ Game, when it's available, is outstanding ❜

CLOSED Sun, Mon; mid Aug to early Sep
CARDS AE, MC, V

Our traditional French cuisine symbol
So many of our readers enjoy seeking out the genuinely French eating experience that we have used Fr to mark restaurants which offer cuisine du terroir, classical French dishes or regional dishes with an emphasis on local ingredients, and traditional recipes.

Vinay
◆ Hostellerie La Briqueterie €€€

4 route de Sézanne, Vinay, 51530 Epernay, Marne
Tel 03 26 59 99 99 Fax 03 26 59 92 10

Blending perfectly into the vineyards on the flanks of the Côte des Blancs, this refined hotel-restaurant, housed in a former brickyard, is a paradise of peace and quiet. With its pink tablecloths, flowery curtains and upholstered chairs, it epitomizes genteel, provincial French dining. Chef Christophe Bernard had already exercised his talents with legendary three-star chefs Paul Bocuse and Alain Ducasse before settling here in the heart of Champagne. The result is a classic, refined style of cooking and an extensive menu featuring veal stuffed with *foie gras* in ratafia sauce, smoked duck breast with honeyed fruits, turbot in Champagne and whole grilled sole.

❜ Romantic neo-classical setting ❜

CLOSED one week Dec
CARDS AE, MC, V

LORRAINE

Bordered by the Vosges mountains and Alsace to the east, Franche-Comté to the south, Champagne-Ardennes to the west, and Luxembourg to the north, Lorraine is a battle-scarred region which combines heavy industry with a quiet green countryside of thick forests, ploughed fields, meadows, rivers and lakes. The fierce battles of the World Wars are commemorated principally at Verdun, while walkers and hikers find peace in the Lorraine National Park and the Vosges mountains. The regional capital of Metz has a superb cathedral and Nancy is distinguished by its elegant place Stanislas. In the south of the region, near Epinal, are the well-known thermal stations of Contrexéville and Bains-les-Bains.

DEUTSCHLAND

N3

A4

N74

N56

N62

Baerenthal 140

D955

N74

D955

D914

Sarrebourg

N4

St-Nicolas-de-Port

N4

Turquestein-
Blancrupt 143

Lunéville 141

ALSACE

N59

N59

St-Dié

N420

N57

D166

N415

Epinal

Le Valtin 143

N57

Gérardmer 140

Bas-Rupts 140

Xonrupt-
Longemer 143

N66

FRANCHE-
COMTE

Mulhouse

Baerenthal
◆ L'Arnsbourg €€€

*Lieu-dit Untermuhlthal, 57230 Baerenthal,
Moselle*
Tel 03 87 06 50 85 Fax 03 87 06 57 67

At the end of a long forest road, deep in the heart of the Northern Vosges mountains, L'Arnsbourg has earned itself a reputation for quality that extends far beyond the frontiers of Lorraine. Arriving at this cosy old village *auberge*, with its traditional antique furniture and painted façade, gives the impression of coming across the seven dwarves' cottage, but its folksy look and isolated location belie the sophistication of the cuisine. The Klein family cooks are as inventive and as demanding about the quality and freshness of their ingredients as any Paris chef. The sumptuous *baeckeoffe* of truffled farmhouse chicken, the John Dory in salt crust, and the scallops with pine nuts would alone justify their two Michelin stars. As for desserts, the wild strawberries with preserved olives in vanilla olive oil are particularly excellent.

❛ *A perfect place to unwind'...'Cathy Klein is a wonderful hostess* ❜

CLOSED Tue, Wed; Jan, end Aug to mid-Sep
CARDS AE, DC, MC, V

Fr French regional or classical French dishes on menu.

Bar-le-Duc
◆ La Meuse Gourmande €€ Fr

*1 rue François-de-Guise, 55000 Bar-le-Duc,
Meuse*
Tel 03 29 79 28 40 Fax 03 29 45 40 71

This restaurant occupies an enchanting 18thC priory and garden at the heart of the Renaissance part of town, near the Gothic church of Saint-Pierre, which houses the curious 'skeleton' statue of one of the Princes of Orange. Franck and Frédérique Damien are the charming hosts, always eager to please and ready with a smile. You wash down the traditional cuisine with regional wines from the Meuse and Côtes de Toul. Be sure to visit the famous redcurrant jam makers of Bar-le-Duc. First documented in 1344, the jam was a favourite gift at court. Even today the redcurrants are still deseeded by hand using a goose feather.

CLOSED Sun dinner, Wed; Feb, end Aug
CARDS AE, MC, V

Bas-Rupts
◆ Hostellerie des Bas-Rupts €€ – €€€ Fr

88400 Bas-Rupts, Vosges
Tel 03 29 63 09 25 Fax 03 29 63 00 40

In the heart of the Vosges mountains, on the road from La Bresse ski resort and the beautiful glacial lake at Gérardmer, Les Bas-Rupts is one of the region's gastronomic hotspots. Everybody here looks noticeably happy, and a general feeling of bonhomie reigns in this pretty restaurant. The breathtaking view over the pine-covered slopes could have something to do with it. The two covered terraces are full both in summer and winter, and when it's sunny, tables are set out in the lovely gardens. Michel Philippe who holds the title 'Maître Cuisinier de France' turns out elegant, *terroir*-based dishes, such as warm terrine of goose *foie gras* with potatoes, tripe in mustard sauce, arctic *char* with herb butter, game in season and desserts using the local mountain honey or forest fruits. A stay at the Hostellerie is particularly enchanting in April when the surrounding villages host the wild daffodil fair. Don't miss the bed and table linen factory shops in the pretty town of Gérardmer, where everything is sold for less than half the normal retail price.

❛ *Lovely, flower-bedecked façade - everyone was friendly and welcoming'...'Divine bilberry tart* ❜

CLOSED never
CARDS AE, MC, V

Gérardmer
◆ A la Belle Maré €€

*144 route de la Bresse, 88400 Gérardmer,
Vosges*
Tel 03 29 63 06 83 Fax 03 29 63 20 76

Hidden away in the middle of the Vosges pine forests, this well-priced fish and seafood restaurant is a welcome find. Trout is the speciality, fished from Marie-Laurence Galli's own waters. However you like it cooked, the chef will prepare it to your taste: 'blue', grilled, roast, smoked, with almonds, wrapped in bacon, or poached in butter. Inside, mahogany fittings recreate the atmosphere of a 19thC ship while the terrace has a fresh 'back-to-nature' feeling.

❢ Delicious ultra-fresh trout'...'Cosy and snug inside ❣

CLOSED Sun dinner, Mon
CARDS AE, MC, V

Lunéville
◆ Château D'Adomenil
€€€

Rehainviller, 54300 Lunéville, Meurthe-et-Moselle
Tel 03 83 74 04 81 Fax 03 83 74 21 78

In all its 18thC glory, complete with moat, swans and a vast, romantic park, the former Duke of Lorraine's *'petit* Versailles' is a dream setting for chef Michel Million's dream cuisine. He is loyal to regional ingredients, but daring with their preparation, as shown in happy combinations such as the *croustillant de porcelet* paired with herbed *spaetzele* (dumpling noodles) or a *pot au feu* of squab accompanied by a *vinaigrette de truffes*. In season, wild game takes pride of place in dishes such as the *noisettes de biche aux figues*, or the *filet de râble de lièvre*. Moment-of-truth desserts include a riveting *déclinaison de chocolat jivara lactée et caramel*.

CLOSED Sun dinner, Mon, Tue lunch winter
CARDS AE, MC, V

Metz
◆ Pont Saint-Marcel € Fr

1 rue du Pont-Saint-Marcel, 57000 Metz, Moselle
Tel 03 87 30 12 29

The dining room here looks out on to the immense cathedral of Metz from a 17thC building constructed on oak piles driven into the Moselle river. Lorraine terroir cooking reigns supreme from a huge wedge of light, custardy quiche Lorraine to a rib-sticking *coquelet farci de la 'Mamiche'* or *lapin forestière*. For true Metz peasant fare, start with headcheese, suckling pig *en gelée*, or lard soup. The folksy atmosphere – the staff sport regional costumes – is part of the fun, and the local wine list is a joy. Try a Gris de Toul, an oaked Pinot Noir from Bruley or sparkling wine from Vezon.

CLOSED Sun dinner, Mon
CARDS MC, V

Metz
◆ Les Roches €€

29 rue des Roches, 57000 Metz, Moselle
Tel 03 87 74 06 21 Fax 03 87 75 40 04

Les Roches is a lovers' dream restaurant. Standing opposite the theatre and hard by Metz's medieval cathedral with its marvellous stained-glass windows, the romantic terrace is on a level with the gently flowing Moselle. Inside, the low timbered ceilings and stone walls lend themselves to declarations of love or, at the very least, *dîners à deux*. The food is fairly traditional and well-presented. You might be tempted, for example, by the excellent *presskopf* of red mullet and trout, followed by the marvellous *mirabelle soufflé*.

❢ A lovers' paradise - take the ring with you'...'Good traditional, regional food ❣

CLOSED Sun dinner, Mon dinner
CARDS AE, DC, MC, V

Nancy
◆ L'Excelsior € Fr

50 rue Henri-Poincaré, 54000 Nancy, Meurthe-et-Moselle
Tel 03 83 35 24 57 Fax 03 83 35 18 48

A 'monument historique', this Art Nouveau brasserie displays the brilliance of two of the city's finest turn-of-the-century craftsmen, working in cloudy glass and sinuous wood. After a visit to the Musée de l'Ecole de Nancy, come here for post-museum reverie and sustenance. The classic menu scores well with starters such as the *tourte de pigeon* and main courses such as *saumon à l'oseille*, *magret de canard mulard* or an appetizing *choucroute paysanne*. People-watching, over coffee, is part of the fun – it attracts all sorts of local power brokers, politicos and wannabes.

❢ *Almost unchanged since it opened its doors in 1910* ❢

Closed never
Cards AE, MC, V

Nancy
◆ La Mignardise €

28 rue Stanislas, 54 000 Nancy, Meurthe-et-Moselle
Tel 03 83 32 20 22 Fax 03 83 32 19 20

In the heart of Nancy, just off place Stanislas, one of the most illustrious squares in France, lies this discreet but popular bistro. Newly renovated by local designer Gilles Schmitt, the decoration is a cross between Louis XVI and Philippe Starck. Chef Didier Metzelard acquired his *savoir-faire* in several Michelin-starred restaurants before striking out on his own. His *filet de boeuf* comes *flambéed à la mirabelle* in the local plum brandy, and accompanied by *compoté de choux nouveaux au lard paysan et de pommes mignonnette*. Desserts such as the *légèreté à la rhubarbe* are equally impressive.

Closed Sun dinner, Mon
Cards MC, V

Norroy-le-Veneur
◆ Chez Yvette €€ Fr

41 Grand-Rue, 57140 Norroy-le-Veneur, Moselle
Tel 03 87 51 34 60 Fax 03 87 51 21 05

An old *auberge* that looks as though it has tumbled out of another era, with a rambling garden and a sweeping view over the Moselle valley. In summer tables are set up outside among the flowers; inside you have to negotiate Yvette Lorentz's kitchen in order to reach the comfortable dining room. Not surprisingly in such rustic surroundings the cuisine follows no-nonsense traditional lines according to the season, with delicious, plump frogs' legs

and fat stalks of asparagus. In summer the delectable desserts made with the region's golden mirabelle plums are a must. Norroy-le-Veneur is 18 km (11 miles) from Metz.

❢ *It feels like dining with the family'...'A gorgeous view* ❢

Closed Mon, Tue dinner; mid-July to early Aug
Cards AE, DC, MC, V

Révigny sur Ornain
◆ Les Agapes €€€

6 place Henriot-du-Coudray, Révigny-sur-Ornain, Meuse
Tel 03 29 70 56 00 Fax 03 29 70 59 30

The village of Révigny-sur-Ornain, a brief stop on the Paris-Strasbourg rail line, has two claims to fame: trout-fishing and a restaurant that lures gourmets from all over France. The building it occupies, a former retreat of the Dukes of Lorraine, is now home to chef Jean-Marc Joblot who learned his trade with Alain Dutournier. Representative of his classical and regional fare are a kind of lake fish soup, *omble-chevalier mitonnée de légumes à la coriandre et crevettes grises*, and young pigeon, deboned, grilled and surrounded by a *coulis de cresson et gnocchi*. The *pain perdu à la rhubarbe et son sorbet* must be one of the most creative ways of serving the humble rhubarb.

Closed Sun dinner, Mon lunch; first 2 weeks Aug
Cards AE, MC, V

Thionville
◆ Les Sommeliers € Fr

25 place de la République, 57100 Thionville, Moselle
Tel 03 82 53 32 20 Fax 03 82 53 47 85

A former bank in a turn-of-the-century Haussmann-style building provides the setting for this wine bar/bistro, run by one of France's best *sommeliers*. Brigitte Gallois keeps her best crus locked away in the old strongroom. All France's wine regions are well represented on her list but Brigitte's preference for the Langeudoc-Roussillon shows with such treasures as a Domaine Gauby Les Rocailles or Vieilles Vignes, Domaine Alquier Les Bastides and the voluptuous Jardins de Bouscassé by

Brumont. Dishes of the day, which may include game in season or such down-to-earth fare as sausage and mash or quiche Lorraine, are marked up on blackboards placed around the room.

❛ *A relaxed atmosphere, and an excellent selection of wine by the glass* ❜

CLOSED Sat lunch, Sun; late Dec to early Jan
CARDS MC, V

Turquestein-Blancrupt
◆ Auberge du Kiboki
€€ Fr

route de Donon, 57560 Turquestein-Blancrupt, Moselle
Tel 03 87 08 60 65 Fax 03 87 08 65 26

If you are passing through the bleak town of Baccarat where the only thing that shines is the world-famous glassworks, it is worth pressing on 48 km (30 miles) further to this wonderful, quiet little *auberge* deep in woody Sarre Blanche valley. Its fairy-tale setting, on the banks of the river, lends itself to peaceful reflection – it's easy to understand why it belongs to the 'Relais du Silence' group. Owner Roger Schmitt, who seems gruff at first, but is in fact friendly underneath, serves hearty, regional fare such as frog leg pie, river trout, Lorraine pâté, *coq au vin blanc* and bilberry sorbet and pie. The 16 bedrooms are warm and cosy, and there is a delightful pool.

❛ *Perfect peace and relaxation'...'Arrive with an appetite – the food is very filling* ❜

CLOSED Tue lunch, Wed; Feb-Apr
CARDS MC, V

Le Valtin
◆ Auberge du Val Joli € Fr

12 bis Le Village, 88230 Le Valtin, Vosges
Tel 03 29 60 91 37 Fax 03 29 60 81 73

The restaurant is housed inside an old timbered building on the main street of Le Valtin, a lovely village (750 metres above

sea level) 13 km (8 miles) north east of Gérardmer. The rustic dining room has enough wooden beams to satisfy the most demanding medievalist, and the modern, glass-walled annexe, though less charming, has plunging views of the Vosges mountains. Menus live up to names like 'tradition' and '*terroir*'. The *paté Lorrain* is homemade and the trout is smoked on the premises. From the menu, you might choose *blanc de poulet cuit au Riesling,* followed by Munster cheese and *tarte aux myrtilles*. To get here from Gérardmer, take the road to Saint-Die, turn right on to the D23 towards Colmar, and at Xonrupt, turn left to Le Valtin.

CLOSED second week Jan, one week Mar, 2 weeks Dec
CARDS MC, V

Xonrupt-Longemer
◆ Lapôtre € Fr

9937 route de Colmar, 88400 Xonrupt-Longemer, Vosges
Tel 03 29 60 09 57 Fax 03 29 60 08 77

A long and winding road leads to this magnificent, family-run chalet strategically located (1100 m/3600 ft above sea level) deep in the *parc naturel des ballons des Vosges* – a region of meadows, wildflowers and misty forests. Its restaurant lures locals and hikers, as well as guests, for unfussy *terroir* cooking, created by Olivier Lapôtre with regional products and vegetables from his garden. Everything, from the *terrine de potée Lorraine* to the *cuisse de canard confite sur choucroute légère,* is served in generous portions. It is 7 km (4 miles) northeast of Gérardmer on the D417; then follow signs for Col de la Schlucht-Munster.

❛ *Clean mountain air'...'Honest home cooking* ❜

CLOSED Wed (except school hols)
CARDS AE, MC, V

ALSACE

At the eastern border of France, in the heart of Europe, the long slither of forests, lakes, vineyards and picturesque villages of half-timbered houses that makes up Alsace is flanked on the west by the Vosges mountains and on the east by the Rhine and Germany's Black Forest. The famous Route du Vin winds its way through the centre of the region's two *départements,* Haut-Rhin and Bas-Rhin for about 75 miles (120 km), while Strasbourg, at the hub of European life, and Colmar are the region's principal towns.

Hinsingen 148

LORRAINE

Saverne 154 ● ● Brumath 146

Mittelhausen 150

Marlenheim 150

Strasbourg
154 155

Ottrott
151 152 ● Obernai 151

ALSACE

Erstein 147

Mittelbergheim 150

Itterswiller 149 ● Osthouse
151

Thannenkirch
156 ● Sélestat

Ribeauvillé 152 ● Bergheim 146

Hunawir 148 ● ● Illhaeusern 148

Riquewihr 152 153 ● Zellenberg
156

Artzenheim
146

DEUTSCHLAND

Lapoutroie 149 ●

Wihr-au-Val
156 ● Eguisheim 147

Colmar 147

Rouffach 153 ●

Mulhouse

Belfort ● ● Diefmatten 147

FRANCHE-
COMTE ● Basèl

SCHWEIZ
SUISSE

145

Artzenheim
◆ Auberge d'Artzenheim
€€ Fr

30 rue du Sponeck, 68320 Artzenheim,
Haut-Rhin
Tel 03 89 71 60 51 Fax 03 89 71 68 21

Really good values are not choc-a-bloc on the much-trodden Alsatian Wine Route but this *auberge* is one that still continues to hold them. It excells at the traditional food for which the region is justly famous. Even a small wedge of *presskopf* (pork terrine) is delicately prepared here. The *foie d'oie poelé accompagné de pommes acidulées et porto* is a classic starter. *Baeckeoffe*, often on the menu in Alsace, and sometimes unappetizing, is here an excellent herb-infused mélange of lamb, beef and pork with potatoes and onions served in a floral baking dish. You can also opt for *suprême de blanc de volaille aux morilles spaetzle*. If you like *strudel*, try their classic version, made with apples and raisins and laced with rum.

CLOSED mid-Feb to mid-Mar
CARDS AE, MC, V

Our price bands
Rather than giving actual prices (which are prone to change) we indicate the cost of a three-course meal for one person, without wine, by means of price bands. They are as follows: € under 30 euros €€ 30-50 euros €€€ over 50 euros. Where we give more than one price band, for example €– €€€, this indicates that in that restaurant a meal can be had at a range of prices. As well as the cost of *prix fixe* menus, our price bands also take into account the cost of an average selection from the *à la carte* menu.

Bergheim
◆ Winstub du Sommelier
€ Fr

451 Grand'Rue, 68750 Bergheim, Haut-Rhin Tel 03 89 73 69 99 Fax 03 89 73 36 58

This quaint *winstub* serves delicious regional dish such as *jambonneau* in a white wine sauce with wonderful *knepfla* (a dumpling of flour, egg and milk boiled and then baked to a light brown crispness). The owner is a former *sommelier* with an unsurpassed knowlege of local vintages. His cellar is filled with the wine treasures of Alsace including bottles from many smaller producers and older vintages; better still, he offers them for prices you will not easily come across elsewhere.

❛A classic Alsatian establishment'
...'If you love Alsatian wine, you
must come here ❜

CLOSED Sun, Mon; mid-Jan to early Feb
CARDS MC, V

● *Chez Norbert in the charming village of Bergheim (tel 03 89 73 31 15) is a typically Alsatian place in which to eat and stay. It was recommended by a local man who seemed to know what he was talking about.*

Fr French regional or classical French dishes on menu.

Brumath
◆ L'Ecrevisse €€

4 avenue de Strasbourg, 67170 Brumath,
Bas-Rhin
Tel 03 88 51 11 08 Fax 03 88 51 89 02

A solidly traditional hotel-restaurant by the river Zorn that has been attracting customers for over 150 years. This is a father-to-son business and current chef Michel Orth represents the sixth generation, offering a modernised version of Alsace *terroir* classics with the emphasis on fish. He is famed for his takes on the regional speciality, crayfish (*écrevisse*) which you might find on the menu doused in champagne, in a salad with *foie gras*, in a well-seasoned *court bouillon* or, unusually, in a rich *lasagne*. The hotel bedrooms are dollhouse pretty with the added attraction of a swimming pool and health centre. Major excavation work is underway on the Gallo-Roman remains in the surrounding area.

The village of Brumath itself suffered dramatically from the 1870 war.

❝ *Jovial wine waiter...delicious, juicy crayfish.* ❞

CLOSED never
CARDS AE, DC, MC, V

Colmar
◆ La Maison des Têtes
€€€

19 rue des Têtes, 68000 Colmar, Haut-Rhin
Tel 03 89 24 43 43 Fax 03 89 24 58 34

Dating from 1609, La Maison des Têtes is known for the 105 carved wooden faces that adorn its façade. As testimony to its former vocation as a wine exchange, the statue of a cooper stands on the gables, sculpted by Colmar-born Auguste Bartholdi (sculptor of the Statue of Liberty). The house was originally designed to bear witness to the affluence of the merchant classes and indeed, the architecture and sumptuous decoration are the main attraction here. Inside, the dining room has retained its gorgeous frescoes by Eggemann, and staine-glass windows. As for the food, traditional Alsatian dishes reign supreme, with several interpretations of *foie gras*, snails, *choucroute*, spiced roast duck, pike dumplings and for dessert, *kugelhopf* or chocolate fritters. The hotel has recently been renovated by owners Carmen and Marc Rohfritsch.

❝ *The setting is great, the food decent but unexciting* ❞

CLOSED Sun dinner, Mon; Feb
CARDS AE, DC, MC, V

Diefmatten
◆ Le Cheval Blanc
€€€

17 rue de Hecken, 68780 Diefmatten, Haut-Rhin
Tel 03 89 26 91 08 Fax 03 89 26 91 08

Welcome to Hansel-and-Gretel country, also known as the Sundgau, the sleepy southern corner of Alsace that belonged to Austria for a couple of centuries. Third-gen-

eration chef Patrick Schlienger offers creative, mostly regional cuisine at his *auberge* in the little town of Diefmatten (the lobster *gratin* is so good you won't care where you are eating it). Order the *grande assiette de tous les foies gras* and you will land in *foie gras* heaven. For dessert, there is an unusual variation of the traditional Alsatian pastry *kugelhopf,* served with local Morello cherries. Be sure to take time for a post-prandial stroll through the countryside.

CLOSED Jan to mid-Feb
CARDS AE, MC, V

Eguisheim
◆ Caveau d'Eguisheim
€€

3 place du Château, 68420 Eguisheim, Haut-Rhin
Tel 03 89 41 08 89 Fax 03 89 23 79 99

In the best Alsatian tradition, chef Jean-Christophe Perrin's cooking is earthy but subtle, drawing inspiration from the impressive bounty of his native region. Witness a starter like the Alsatian headcheese known as *presskopf,* which he pairs with shrimp, or melt-in-you mouth squab *rôti au cumin* and served with salsify. The sense of perfectionism extends to serving the best and most perfectly ripe Munster cheese and a wicked *tendre de chocolat avec une glace à la pistache*. The decoration, like the cooking, is a happy marriage of the rustic and refined.

❝ *The excellent wine list proudly ignores anything that is not local* ❞

CLOSED Mon, Tue; mid-Jan to mid-Feb
CARDS AE, MC, V

Erstein
◆ Jean-Victor Kalt €€

43 avenue de la Gare, 67150 Erstein, Bas-Rhin
Tel 03 88 98 09 54 Fax 03 8898 83 01

It's well worth the slight detour from the Route du Vin to spend an afternoon or evening with chef Kalt and his wife (she is in charge of the dining room). He is the sort of cook who can turn the simplest ingredients into a memorable experience. There are excellent themed menus and specialities like the *salade tiede de pigeonneau* or *rognonnade de veau*. Servings are generous, but should there be room for dessert, plump for the buttery-crisp apple *streusel* tart. The wine list, from the chilled Gewerztraminer to the top-quality *eau-de-vie* selection is a happy way to extend the meal.

CLOSED Sun eve, Mon
CARDS AE, MC, V

Hinsingen
◆ La Grange du Paysan
€ Fr

8 rue Principale, 67260 Hinsingen, Bas-Rhin
Tel 03 88 00 91 83 Fax 03 88 00 93 23

Immediately over the border from the province of Lorraine, you need look no further for Alsatian *cuisine paysanne*, served here in astonishing portions in a former barn (or in summer on a vast, flower-bedecked terrace) in the centre of town. Two excellent standards are *poularde au Riesling* or *porcelet grillé au feu de bois*. On weekends, the kitchen roasts an entire piglet and produces *flammekueche*, Alsatian 'pizza' cooked in a wood-fired oven. If you really want to go native, order the *boudin maison aux pommes* sautéed with *raifort maison* (homemade horseradish) or *estomac de porc farci* – stuffed pig's stomach.

❝ A great place - service is friendly and efficient ... *' We couldn't fault our meal, or the service, but we needed a good long walk to get over it ❞*

CLOSED Sun, Mon; 2 weeks Feb, early to mid-Aug
CARDS MC, V

Hunawir
◆ Winstub Suzel
€ Fr

2 rue de l'Eglise, 68150 Hunawir, Bas-Rhin
Tel 03 89 73 30 85

Hunawir is a relatively untouristy wine-growers' village with magnificent Rhine views and a 14thC fortified church. This charming little wine pub, serving appetising

local fare, is another reason to stop. Tuck into the rich and custardy *tarte à l'oignon* or a fat slab of the garlic-laced *pâté en croûte* – either one with a pair of fresh vegetable salads – and that's just for starters. There is a superb terrace for summer meals with a view of the old church tower. On Sunday evenings, they serve *flammekueche* (*tartes flambées*), the Alsatian 'pizza' made of paper-thin dough with cream cheese on top. Excellent *cave* with reasonable prices.

CLOSED Tue
CARDS MC, V

---

charmingsmallhotels.co.uk
Visit Duncan Petersen's travel website, the best online search tool for places to stay that combine character and charm. Currently features Britain, France, Italy and Ireland, with other destinations being continuously added.

Illhaeusern
◆ Auberge de l'Ill €€€

2 rue de Collonges, 68150 Illhaeusern, Haut-Rhin
Tel 03 89 71 89 00 Fax 03 89 71 82 83

World-famous three-star restaurant in an idyllic, tranquil setting on the banks of the river Ill. Dining outside by the weeping willows in this sleepy little village not far from Colmar is an unforgettably magical experience, not least for the quality of the food. The Haeberlin family has based its international reputation on a suble combination of *terroir* and *haute cuisine* via such gastronomic monuments as the *saumon soufflé* and roasted Bresse chicken with truffled *baeckoffe*. The impressive wine list is compiled by unassuming wine expert Serge Dubs, holder of the prestigious title of 'Best Sommelier in the World'. There's something quaintly old-fashioned about the dining room, which only adds to the charm. There is nothing old fashioned, though, about the hotel that goes with the restaurant. Called the Hôtel des Berges and standing a little apart in a garden on the river Ill, it is run by family member Marco Baumann and is, like the restaurant, luxurious in an understated way, decorated in immaculate taste and full of natural materials – kelims, much use of wood, almost nothing metallic or shiny . It makes the perfect place to stay the night after dinner at the *auberge*.

❢ Worth every penn... smiling welcome' ... 'A true classic that stands the test of time ❢

CLOSED Mon, Tue; Jan-Mar
CARDS AE, DC, MC, V

Itterswiller
 Arnold € Fr

98 route des Vins, 67140 Itterswiller, Bas-Rhin
Tel 03 88 85 50 58 Fax 03 88 85 55 54

Here is a clever package of hotel, restaurant and shop – a blend of the best of the old and the new, aimed at today's traveller, who appreciates a traditional ambience but wants everything convenient. The slick accommodation is in a pleasing timber and yellow-painted Alsatian house standing in its own vineyards; the restaurant (and shop) is just 50 paces up the road, where local residents mingle with hotel guests, there is a happy buzz and the hearty regional food is way above average. The Arnold's friendly young owner, Bruno Simon, has a head for the market, attention to detail and a liking for people – and it shows. The Arnold has its own wines – try the Oscar Riesling, available in the restaurant and for sale in the shop.

CLOSED Jan, mid to late Feb, one week Jun
CARDS AE, MC, V

Please send us reports
A guide such as this thrives on reader's reports. If you send us five usable reports, we will send you a free copy of any title in our *Charming Small Hotel Guides* series (see page 241 for France titles in the series).

The five reports should contain at least two new restaurants; the rest can be comments on restaurants already in the guide.
1 Tell us about your experiences in restaurants already in this guide.
2 Send us new reports. New reports should give the following information:
– **Region –** City, town, village or neaest village.
– **Name of restaurant –** Please double check the spelling, it's surprisingly easy to make a mistake.
– **Address –** including *département*
– **Telephone number –** plus fax and e-mail if available. Double check this information.
– **Objective description –** Try to explain simply why it should be in the guide. Remember that the guide is very selective - our entries are those one-in-five places that combine
• **interesting food with**
• **character and charm, in the building, the setting or both.**
The guide hates tourist traps, and pretentious, dressed-up food. We like places where the French go.
We favour places in the lower and middle price bands but there are plenty of expensive places that have our qualities, and we list those too.
– **Diner's comments –** These should be short, personal comments on features that strike you. They can be your comments, or others'.
– **Closing times**
– **Credit cards accepted**
Don' t forget to date your report and add your name and address.
Send reports to Charming Restaurant Guides, Duncan Petersen Publishing, 31 Ceylon Road, London W14 0PY.

Lapoutroie
 Les Alisiers € Fr

5 rue Faudé, 68650 Lapoutroie, Haut-Rhin
Tel 03 89 47 52 82 Fax 03 89 47 22 38

Welcoming hosts Ella and Jacques Degouy are proud of their mountain *auberge* with its panoramic view of the Vosges mountains and Rhine valley from 700 metres above sea level. Generosity is part of the appeal here, particularly in the restaurant prices and portions. Regional specialities are thoughtfully prepared, from the *salad de choucroute* – mounded with grilled, garlicky *cervelat* (cured pork sausage) – to the *filet de truite saumonée à l'oseille*. A meaty *jarret de porc braisé au four* is simple, and soul-satisfying. This place is a stalwart of our *Charming Small Hotel Guide* to France.

❧ Comfort food doesn't get any more comforting than the potatoes au Munster fondu' ... 'relaxed family atmosphere, iwth children and dogs allowed in the dining room ❧

CLOSED Mon dinner, Tue (except for hotel guests on half-board); Christmas, Jan, one week end Jun
CARDS MC, V

Marlenheim
◆ Le Cerf €€€

*30 rue du Général-de-Gaulle, 67520 Marlenheim, Bas-Rhin
Tel 03 88 87 73 73 Fax 03 88 87 68 08*

This flower-bedecked village inn remains as compelling as ever for visitors who like the cooking of Alsace as much as its wines. Michel Husser carries on the gastronomic tradition of his father Robert; Michelin awards two stars and Gault Millau 18/20 for such house specialities as *presskopf de tête de veau en croustille, sauce gribiche* and *choucroute au cochon de lait et foie gras fumé*. Bedrooms are not particularly luxurious, but well-furnished and comfortable. There is a cobbled courtyard for drinks and breakfast.

❧ Good wine list, with plenty of bearable prices to choose from' ... 'Service was slow on our visit – maybe it was an off day ❧

CLOSED Tue
CARDS MC, V

Mittelbergheim
◆ Winstub Gilg
€€ Fr

*1 route du Vin, Bas-Rhin
Tel 03 88 08 91 37 Fax 03 88 08 45 17*

It is easy to understand why Mittelbergheim was voted one of France's hundred prettiest villages. Easily identified from afar by the high spire of its chapel, it features a medieval tithe barn and colour-washed wine-makers' houses line the steep sloping roads. The town hall was built in the 16th century, just before this storybook *winstub* complete with timbered walls, geranium-bedecked windows, ancient wine cellar and a dining room that oozes refined rusticity. The menu changes with the seasons but young chef Vincent Reuschlé, who trained at three-star Auberge de l'Ill may be offering roasted veal with truffled *baeckoffe,* scallops, saddle of venison with fruits of the forest and cabbage or onion tart, rounded off with his speciality: nougat *glace* with pine honey. Wines not to be missed come from the surrounding vineyards like the easy-drinking Sylvaner from nearby Zotzenberg.

❧ Particularly genial atmosphere. Warm welcome ❧

CLOSED Tue, Wed; Jan, late Jun to mid-Jul
CARDS AE, MC, V

Our price bands
Rather than giving actual prices (which are prone to change) we indicate the cost of a three-course meal for one person, without wine, by means of price bands. They are as follows: € under 30 euros €€ 30-50 euros €€€ over 50 euros. Where we give more than one price band, for example €– €€€, this indicates that in that restaurant a meal can be had at a range of prices. As well as the cost of *prix fixe* menus, our price bands also take into account the cost of an average selection from the *à la carte* menu.

Mittelhausen
◆ A L'Etoile €€ Fr

*12 rue de la Hey, 67170 Mittelhausen, Bas-Rhin
Tel 03 88 51 28 44 Fax 03 88 51 24 79*

In the old village of Mittelhausen, 20 minutes from Strasbourg, L'Etoile is just the sort of cosy, picturesque inn where you feel at home as soon as you walk in. This pleasantly old-fashioned *auberge* has been in the Bruckmann family since 1888 and is simply furnished with plenty of wooden fittings in typical Alsatian style. Classically French, the food carries regional touches: rabbit *presskopf,* veal kidney in mustard sauce, duck *choucroute* and a speciality dessert: *mousse au marc de Gewurztraminer.* Unsurprisingly for this superb wine-producing region, Alsace figures heavily.

CLOSED Sun dinner, Mon; early to mid-Jan, Jul
CARDS AE, MC, V

Obernai
◆ Le Parc
€€

*169 rue Général-Gouraud, 67210 Obernai,
Bas-Rhin
Tel 03 88 95 50 08 Fax 03 88 95 37 29*

At the foot of Mont-Sainte-Odile, famous for its convent and pilgrim centre, Obernai is the archetypal 'toytown' Alsatian village featuring spick-and-span timbered houses dripping with geraniums, a neat little town hall with oriel windows, a medieval chapel and a charming fountain...Le Parc fits perfectly into this fairytale setting: a characterful, immaculately-kept inn standing just outside the village, set in beautiful gardens with indoor and outdoor swimming pools. Roland Schaeffer, chef to the Wucher family of owners for 'longer than he cares to remember' offers a classical choice of dishes that attract diners from over the border, particularly on Sundays when they come for the superb Alsatian brunch, which may include pike dumplings, veal sweetbreads, warm Munster cheese with potatoes.

❝ Tasteful decoration ... family-friendly hotel and restaurant ❞

CLOSED Tue-Sat lunch, Sun dinner, Mon; early to mid-Jul, Dec to mid-Jan
CARDS AE, MC, V

Looking for somewhere to stay? See page 241.

Osthouse
◆ A L'Aigle d'Or €€

*67150 Osthouse, Bas-Rhin
Tel 03 88 98 06 82 Fax 03 88 98 81 75*

In the calm little village of Osthouse, this is a charming restaurant where Jean-Philippe Helmann presents sophisticated, imaginative and flavoursome dishes such as *cassolette de gambas, terrine de poissons avec une salade de fèves* and *croustillant aux fruits rouges dans un strudel au cacao*. Jean-Philippe and his wife Brigitte have also converted an old family farmhouse in the village, painting the exterior a brilliant powder blue and decorating the interior to make seven guest bedrooms and a breakfast room with great flair. You can therefore dine and sleep in Osthouse very well.

CLOSED Mon, Tue; third week Aug
CARDS MC, V

Please send us reports
A guide such as this thrives on reader's reports. If you send us five usable reports, we will send you a free copy of any title in our *Charming Small Hotel Guides* series (see page 241 for France titles in the series).
   The five reports should contain at least two new restaurants; the balance can be comments on restaurants already in the guide. **Send reports to** Charming Restaurant Guides, Duncan Petersen Ltd, 31 Ceylon Road, London W14 OPY.

Ottrott
◆ L'Ami Fritz €€

*8 rue des Châteaux, 67530 Ottrott-le-Haut, Bas-Rhin
Tel 03 88 95 80 81 Fax 03 88 95 84 85*

L'Ami Fritz is picture postcard material. The lovely ochre-tinted façade, with spruce white shutters and a profusion of geraniums at each window predispose to good humour. Inside, the atmosphere is so cheerful and the welcome so friendly that one immediately has the impression of being a regular. Flagship dishes include a flavoursome duck *choucroute* and *presskopf `a l'ancienne*. The fillet of beef with bone marrow and shallots provides an excellent excuse for quaffing some *rouge d'Ottrott* for which this neat little village is famous. The Fritz family produces its own wine, which you can sample with your meal.

❝ Easy-going atmosphere. Luxury style winstub ❞

Closed Tue lunch, Wed; last week Jun
Cards AE, DC, MC, V

Ottrott
◆ Beau Site €€ Fr

place de l'Eglise, 67530 Ottrott-le-Haut,
BGas-Rhin
Tel 03 88 95 80 61 Fax 03 88 48 14 18

At the heart of the pretty little village of Ottrott, overlooking a sea of vines, the Hôtel Beau Site is Alsace just as you imagined it. This is especially true in the evening when its tastefully-illuminated façade draws regulars like moths to a flame. The main dining room is adorned with marquetry fashioned by Charles Spindler and the snug *winstub* has kept all its original character. As soul-warming as the place itself, dishes are likely to include thick split-pea soup, traditional onion tart, duck breast with blackcurrants, chicken doused in Riesling and game when in season. The mouth-watering *baeckoffe* is cooked for hours on end according to tradition and must be ordered at least 48 hours in advance.

❛ Quintessentially Alsatian ❜

Closed Sun dinner, Mon; Feb
Cards AE, MC, V

---

charmingsmallhotels.co.uk
Visit Duncan Petersen's travel website, the best online search tool for places to stay that combine character and charm. Currently features Britain, France, Italy and Ireland, with other destinations being continuously added.

Ribeauvillé
◆ Zum Pfifferhüs €€ Fr

14 Grand Rue, 68150 Ribeauvillé, Haut-Rhin
Tel 03 89 73 62 28 Fax 03 89 73 80 34

A charming, authentic little *winstub* installed in a 14thC house, complete with wooden beams and walls and cosy little booths that hark back to how *winstubs* came into being (originally a room in a farmhouse where wine was served to friends). The food is as traditional as the decoration and the menu reads like a comprehensive list of Alsace specialities: *choucroute, presskopf, kassler en croûte, coq au Riesling*, smoked goose... A wise selection of fine regional wines is complemented by pitchers of gluggable Edelzwicker. Zum Pfifferhüs is an excellent choice for non-smoker as smokers are kindly requested to take their custom elsewhere.

Closed Wed, Thu; Jan to late Feb; early Jul
Cards MC, V

● *If you know where to go, and avoid the tourist traps, you can eat superbly in the restaurants, winstubs and auberges of Alsace, and you will have the best chance of eating proper, un-mucked-up regional food in all France. Some great places to visit, amongst many, include Hostellerie du Rosenmeer in Rosheim (tel 03 88 50 43 29) and Bürestubel in Pfulgriesheim (tel 03 88 20 48 97).*

Riquewihr
◆ Le Sarment d'Or €€

4 rue du Cerf, 68340 Riquewihr, Haut-Rhin
Tel 03 89 86 02 86 Fax 03 89 47 99 23

Known to locals as 'the pearl of Alsace vineyard', the medieval village of Riquewihr is the stuff of fairytales, particularly out of season. The cobbled main street winds upwards between ancient geranium-festooned houses with their oriel windows towards the Dolder Gate built in 1291. The Sarment d'Or is a characterful little hotel with old beams and thick walls and an appealing restaurant where you can dine by firelight on cool evenings. Gilbert Merchling cooks classic dishes such as frogs' legs, *foie gras*, breast of duck and *filet de veau aux arômes des truffes et un gratin d'agrumes*. The cheapest menu is a good bet here.

Closed Sun dinner, Mon, Tue lunch; mid-Jan to mid-Feb, first week Jul
Cards MC, V.

Riquewihr
◆ La Table du Gourmet

5 rue de l'Armée, 68340 Riquewihr, Haut-Rhin
Tel 03 89 49 09 09 Fax 03 89 49 04 56

La Table du Gourmet is a low-beamed restaurant dating from the 16th century but there is nothing old-fashioned about the cooking. Chef Jean-Luc Brendel attracts a fair part of his clientele from among the region's myriad wine producers with his truly inventive cuisine that makes full use of rare flowers, roots and wild herbs after the fashion of three-star Michel Bras and Marc Veyrat. Each season brings new ideas and you might have a choice of smoked sander in genever, milk-fed veal with truffled potato *baeckoffe*, chubby frogs' legs with wild garlic, wild turbot cooked in verbena, bitter chocolate cake with sakura tea, cherry and iced gentian mousse. Whatever you choose, it is likely to be an ephemeral work of art.

❜ Luscious, unusual dishes - extraordinary use of herbs' ... 'Dolls' house setting ❜

Closed Tue and Wed, Thur lunch Apr to mid-Nov; Tue, Wed mid-Nov to Apr; Jan to mid-Feb
Cards AE, MC, V.

Our traditional French cuisine symbol
So many of our readers enjoy seeking out the genuinely French eating experience that we have used Fr to mark restaurants which offer *cuisine du terroir*, classical French dishes or regional dishes with an emphasis on local ingredients, and traditional recipes.

Rouffach
◆ Château d'Isenbourg
€€

68250 Rouffach, Haut-Rhin
Tel 03 89 78 58 50 Fax 03 89 78 53 70

About 15 miles (25 km) from Mulhouse and its fascinating automobile museum, and 9 miles (15 km) from Colmar, the hotel Château d'Isenbourg's dining room and terace enjoy a magnificent view over one of Alsace's rare walled vineyards and the tiled roofs of the ancient town of Rouffach. Beyond lie the foothills of the Vosges and in the distance, the Rhine Valley and the Black Forest. The château, which used to belong to the bishops of Strasbourg, was built over 14thC vaulted cellars, which now contain the many wines on the restaurant's extensive list. The quiet terrace, with its wrought ironwork, is particularly enchanting at sundown. Didier Lefeuvre serves classical cuisine with a touch of regional colour, ideally accompanied by the elegant wines of the Clos Isenbourg or those of nearby Cave de Pfaffenheim.

❜ Magnificent collection of wines' ... 'Luxurious open air and indoor swimming pools...very relaxing and elegant ❜

Closed Wed lunch, Sat lunch; late Jan to Mar
Cards AE, DC, MC, V

Please send us reports
A guide such as this thrives on reader's reports. If you send us five usable reports, we will send you a free copy of any title in our *Charming Small Hotel Guides* series (see page 241 for France titles in the series).

The five reports should contain at least two new restaurants; the balance can be comments on restaurants already in the guide. **Send reports to** Charming Restaurant Guides, Duncan Petersen Ltd, 31 Ceylon Road, London W14 0PY.

Rouffach
◆ Au Vieux Pressoir
€€ **Fr**

Domaine du Bollenberg, 68250 Rouffach, Haut-Rhin
Tel 03 89 49 67 10 Fax 03 89 49 76 16

Installed in what used to be a former farmhouse belonging to Sainte Appoline convent, this splendidly atmospheric inn is well worth a visit to the pretty town of Rouffach. Take time out to discover the Renaissance corn house, the witches' tower and cathedral-like Notre Dame before settling in amongst a wealth of copper kettles, period furniture, earthenware plates and collection of old weapons. Food is typical of the region with trout or chicken in Riesling, *feuilleté* of Munster cheese, pig's trotter, home-prepared *foie gras*, and according to the season, wild boar or a plateful of the juicy, thick white stalks of asparagus for which Alsace is rightly famous. Excellent wine list.

CLOSED Wed; Jan
CARDS AE, MC, V

Saverne
◆ La Taverne Katz
€ Fr

80 Grande Rue, 67700 Saverne, Bas-Rhin
Tel 03 88 71 16 56

This restaurant occupies the 1605 dreamhouse built in late German Renaissance style for an archbishop's tax collector; its bulky beams are sculpted into bare-breasted maidens and vines heavy with ripe grapes. The menu is a recital of earthy, impeccably prepared local dishes, from starters like *salade de gruyère* (cheese and shallots in a mustardy *vinaigrette*) to mains like *timbale de poulette fermière sous croûte*, a rich chicken stew sealed under a lid of golden puff pastry.

❛ *There is not a more authentic place to dine in all Alsace* ❜

CLOSED never
CARDS MC, V

Strasbourg
◆La Choucrouterie
€ Fr

20 rue Saint-Louis, 67000 Strasbourg, Bas-Rhin
Tel 03 88 26 52 87

Local colour is guaranteed here. The building has been a welcoming place since it opened its doors as a coach station in the 18th century. Perhaps never more so than now. The current patron Roger Siffer is

an Alsatian folk singer who has hung old musicial instruments on the walls. The back room is a cabaret with folk or gypsy music (sometimes jazz) most nights. The food is also reliably good. Most diners, once seated at one of the communal tables in the front room, opt for *choucroute*. Other dishes include thick *bratwurst*-like *saucisse de Strasbourg* with crisp sautéed potatoes.

❛ *A good place to come for food, wine and folklore* ❜

CLOSED Sun; early Jan; 3 weeks Aug
CARDS MC, V

Looking for somewhere to stay? See page 241.

Strasbourg
◆ Le Clou € Fr

3 rue du Chaudron, 67000 Strasbourg, Bas-Rhin
Tel 03 88 32 11 67 Fax 03 88 75 72 83

A visit to this traditional *winstub*, a sort of Alsatian bistro/wine pub, will help explain why gourmands the world over hold this region in such high regard. The old-fashioned, low-beamed establishment with lacey tablecloths has existed for more than a hundred years. It is on a little side street just off Strasbourg's place du Château, in front of the city's majestic cathedral. The menu proudly ignores anything that is not local. The *choucroute garni*, accompanied by a generous dollop of good local mustard and a glass of Pinot Blanc or Riesling, is flat out delicous.

CLOSED Wed lunch, Sun
CARDS MC, V

Strasbourg
◆ Au Crocodile €€€

10 rue de l'Outre, 67000 Strasbourg, Bas-Rhin
Tel 03 88 32 13 02 Fax 03 88 75 72 01

There are more Michelin-starred chefs in Alsace than in any other region and gently-spoken Emile Jung is the most modest of them all. Apart from the astonishing sight of a 200-year old, 3-metre long stuffed crocodile at the entrance, everything about the Crocodile speaks of discretion, from the luxurious but understated decoration to the discreet service. The stars of the show are most definitely on your plate and in your glass. After over 30 years in the business Jung still attracts gourmets from the world over, and you can hear as many different languages as there are tables when you dine there. Legendary dishes include the quail stuffed with *foie gras*, truffle *feuilleté*, poached whole *foie gras* with truffle juice, turnips and potatoes. Your choice of Au Crocodile's 2000 wines, presented on a beautifully illustrated *carte*, is served by self-effacing *sommelier* Gilbert Mestrallet or his delightful assistant, Guillaume Robuchon.

Closed Sun, Mon; Jul, Aug
Cards AE, DC, MC, V

Our price bands
Rather than giving actual prices (which are prone to change) we indicate the cost of a three-course meal for one person, without wine, by means of price bands. They are as follows: € under 30 euros €€ 30-50 euros €€€ over 50 euros. Where we give more than one price band, for example €– €€€, this indicates that in that restaurant a meal can be had at a range of prices. As well as the cost of *prix fixe* menus, our price bands also take into account the cost of an average selection from the *à la carte* menu.

Strasbourg
◆ Maison Kamerzell
€€ **Fr**

16 place de la Cathédrale, 67000 Strasbourg, Bas-Rhin
Tel 03 88 32 42 14 Fax 03 88 23 03 92

Built in 1427, Maison Kamerzell is a listed building and the city's pride and joy. It is situated at the foot of Strasbourg's magnificent Gothic cathedral with its monumental astronomical clock (arrive before 12.30 pm) and 142-metre high chiselled stone spire. Kamerzell's beautifully sculpted façade gives an idea of the enchanting, cosy deco-

ration inside: wood panelling, vaulted ceilings, frescoes and coloured, bottle-bottom windows make this a snug winter reteat from the snowy world outside. Guy-Pierre Baumann has turned this restaurant into a conservatory of tradition as witnessed by the state-of-the-art fish *choucroute*, pigeon breast in chestnut crust, duck *foie gras* and apple *strudel* with caramel ice-cream.

Closed Chirstmas eve
Cards AE, DC, MC, V

Strasbourg
◆ S'Munstertuewel €€

8 place du Marché aux Cochons de Lait, 67000 Strasbourg, Bas-Rhin
Tel 03 88 32 17 63

It may have an unpronouceable name but this *winstub* offers a warm and cheerful welcome and a virtuoso chef in Patrick Klipfel (he started the Michelin-starred Auberge du Kochersberg). One of his specialities is the *pied de porc désossé maison en baeckeoffe farci aux trois viandes* (boned and stuffed pig's trotters); his classic *choucroute* is excellent, as are his unusual variations – such as lightly sautéed shrimp tails on a bed of *choucroute caramélisée au meil*. For dessert – *kouglof glace au marc de Gewurztraminer* is a winner. The restaurant has a formidable wine cellar and dispenses delicious white wine by the carafe.

Closed Sun, Mon; 2 weeks Feb, early to mid-Aug
Cards AE, MC, V

Strasbourg
◆ La Vieille Enseigne
€€

9 rue des Tonneliers, 67000 Strasbourg, Bas-Rhin
Tel 03 88 32 58 50 Fax 03 88 75 63 80

Chef Jean-Christophe Langs has been honoured (by Michelin among others) for his successful marriage of regional and *nouvelle* cuisine. Feasting in this 17thC inn in the medieval heart of Strasbourg on roast bream stuffed with crunchy fennel (and paired with an aniseed veal reduction) or squab braised with spiced bread is not your everyday dining experience. Desserts such as a *millefeuille de crêpes aux bananes, glace aux sucre roux*, are equally impressive.

CLOSED Sat lunch, Sun
CARDS AE, MC, V

Thannenkirch
◆ Auberge La Meunière
ⓔ Fr

30 rue Sainte-Anne, 68590 Thannenkirch.
Haut-Rhin
Tel 03 89 73 10 47 Fax 03 89 73 12 31

A charming Alsatian village inn that looks downright Swiss. Antique Alsatian plates decorate the walls; and lace and flowers round out the decoration. It has a distant view of the surrounding forest and Haut-Koenigsbourg. The menu represents regional cooking without fuss or pretention and always includes fish dishes like a *medaillon de lotte sur lit de choux*. In autumn, goose features prominently on the menu as well as *noisettes de marcassin* (wild baby boar). If dessert beckons, the *linzertorte*, spiced with cinnamon and filled with raspberry jam, is a delight. The bedrooms upstairs can provide a cosy and comfortable place to stay the night; two of the rooms have balconies with splendid views across to Haut-Koenigsbourg, and there are just as good views from the terrace, where meals are served on sunny days.

CLOSED Mon and Tue lunch; mid-Dec to mid-Mar
CARDS AE, MC, V

Wihr-au-Val
◆ La Nouvelle Auberge ⓔ

9 route Nationale, 68230 Wihr-au-Val,
Haut-Rhin
Tel 03 89 71 07 70

Chef Bernard Leray and his wife Martine have been restoring this former coachhouse near Munster for the last eight years. He is schooled in the cuisine of Bernard Loiseau and generous with his culinary *savoir-faire*. Witness the 17 euro menu (at the time of going to press), an exceptional bargain that recently included a *cervelas de brochet* (pike sausage), *coq au Riesling* and a *sorbet citron de marc Gewurztraminer*. Add to that a cosy, rustic dining room, a friendly reception

and fairly priced wines by the bottle, carafe or glass. La Nouvelle Auberge is located 5 miles (9 km) east of Munster, five minutes from the centre of Wihr-au-Val.

CLOSED Mon dinner, Tue
CARDS MC, V

Please send us reports
A guide such as this thrives on reader's reports. If you send us five usable reports, we will send you a free copy of any title in our *Charming Small Hotel Guides* series (see page 241 for France titles in the series).

The five reports should contain at least two new restaurants; the balance can be comments on restaurants already in the guide. **Send reports to** Charming Restaurant Guides, Duncan Petersen Ltd, 31 Ceylon Road, London W14 0PY.

Zellenberg
◆ Maximilien ⓔⓔⓔ

19a route d'Ostheim, 68340
Zellenberg, Haut-Rhin
Tel 03 89 47 99 69 Fax 03 89 47 99 85

L ocals and tourists alike come here for the impressive view over the vineyards and the plain of Alsace. Standing on Zellenberg hill, Maximilien offers a simple interior, thereby emphasising the spectacular panorama outside. Son of a grape-grower, Jean-Michel Eblin learned his craft with the elite of the gastronomic world in Alsace and Paris: three-star Haeberlin and Taillevent. No wonder then that his cuisine uses only fresh produce and needs no superfluous garnishes to boost the flavour. The majority of dishes are simply presented, such as the warm leeks in *vinaigrette* with *foie gras*, the miniature *baeckeoffe* of snails with a hint of garlic, the *tartare* of smoked trout and frog's legs, gingered lamb or the luscious pigeon with lobster.

❛ Efficient service...a classic address ❜

CLOSED Fri lunch, Sun dinner, Mon; mid-Aug to early Sep; mid-Feb to Mar.
CARDS AE, DC, MC, V

PLEASE SEND US REPORTS

A guide such as this thrives on reader's reports. If you send us five usable reports, we willsend you a free copy of any Duncan Petersen guide (which include the *Charming Small Hotel Guides*) - see page 241 for France titles in this series.

The five reports should contain at least two new restaurants; the rest can be comments on restaurants already in the guide.

1 Tell us about your experiences in restaurants already in this guide.

2 Send us new reports. New reports should give the following information:

– **Region –** City, town, village or nearest village.

– **Name of restaurant –** Please double check the spelling, it's surprisingly easy to make a mistake.

– **Address –** including *département*.

– **Telephone number –** plus fax and e-mail if available. Double check this information.

– **Objective description –** Try to explain simply why it should be in the guide. Remember that the guide is very selective - our entries are those one-in-five places that combine

● **interesting food with**

● **character and charm, in the building, the setting or both.**

- The guide hates tourist traps, and pretentious, dressed-up food. We like places where the French go.
- We favour places in the lower and middle price bands, but there are plenty of expensive places that have our qualities, and we list those too.

– **Diner's comments –** These should be short, personal comments on features that strike you, They can be your comments, or others'.

– **Closing times**

– **Credit cards accepted**

Don' t forget to date your report and add your name and address.
Send reports to Charming Restaurant Guides, Duncan Petersen Publishing, 31 Ceylon Road, London W14 0PY.

PAYS DE LA LOIRE

The government region of Pays de la Loire, lying to the south of Brittany and north of Poitou-Charentes, surrounds the western reaches of France's longest river where it finally empties into the Atlantic ocean. (The region called Centre is the one that encompasses the most famous stretch of the river, from Orléans to Tour). Pays de la Loire covers the *départements* of Vendée, Loire-Atlantique, Maine-et-Loire, Mayenne and Sarthe and includes 300 km of Atlantic coastline. The regional capital is Nantes, in Loire-Atlantique, formerly part of Brittany, and still considered Breton. Other principal towns are Le Mans, renowned for its annual car race, Angers and Saumur.

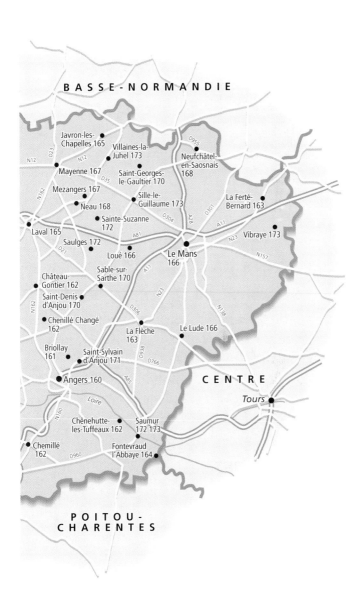

BASSE-NORMANDIE

Javron-les-
Chapelles 165
Villaines-la-
Juhel 173
Neufchâtel-
en-Saosnais
168
Mayenne 167
Saint-Georges-
le-Gaultier 170
Mezangers 167
Sille-le-
Guillaume 173
La Ferté-
Bernard 163
Neau 168
Sainte-Suzanne
172
Laval 165
Saulges 172
Vibraye 173
Loué 166
Le Mans
166
Sable-sur-
Sarthe 170
Château-
Gontier 162
Saint-Denis
d'Anjou 170
Chenillé Changé
162
La Flèche
163
Le Lude 166
Briollay
161
Saint-Sylvain
d'Anjou 171
Angers 160

CENTRE

Tours

Chênehutte-
les-Tuffeaux 162
Saumur
172 173
Chemillé
162
Fontevraud
l'Abbaye 164

POITOU-
CHARENTES

Ancenis
◆ La Toile à Beurre € Fr

82 rue Saint-Pierre, 44150 Ancenis, Loire-Atlantique
Tel 02 40 98 89 64 Fax 02 40 96 01 49

Once a major wine-shipping port, Ancenis now relies on light industry, with the added interest of a fine old *château* and a 500m suspension bridge across the Loire. The town is a fishing centre, and freshwater fish feature large on the menu: the house speciality (May-Sep) is eel (try *le croustillant d'anguilles de Loire*, a mixture of eels and vegetables in a pastry base. Chef Jean-Charles Baron boasts of no less than 26 local producers supplying him with his ingredients, which he serves simply, with a modern touch, in such dishes as *poissons de Loire au beurre blanc* and *rognons de veau au Chinon*.

❛ *Charming treasure trove of knick-knacks'...'In the style of an old-fashioned little café, but with modern ambience and excellent service* ❜

CLOSED Sun dinner, Mon; first two weeks Feb, first two weeks Sep
CARDS DC, MC, V

Our traditional French cuisine symbol
So many of our readers enjoy seeking out the genuinely French eating experience that we have used Fr to mark restaurants which offer *cuisine du terroir*, classical French dishes or regional dishes with an emphasis on local ingredients, and traditional recipes.

Angers
◆ Club 1925 € – €€

4 rue Anjou, 49100 Angers, Maine-et-Loire
Tel 02 41 87 62 36 Fax 02 41 25 11 59

As the name suggests, this restaurant in the old part of this university city – also a centre for flowers and of the arts – harks back to the Roaring Twenties in its decoration. The bistro-style cuisine is presented in a selection of fixed price menus. *Fruits de mer* are a speciality, but snails in garlic cream are also popular, or you could plump for an excellent grilled steak. .

❛ *The decoration is great fun. Fixed priced menus really good value* ❜

CLOSED Sat lunch, Sun
CARDS MC, V

Bernerie-en-Retz
◆ Château de la Gressière €€

rue de la Noue-Fleurie, 44760 Bernerie-en-Retz, Loire-Atlantique
Tel 02 51 74 60 06 Fax 02 51 74 60 02

In an idyllic position on a hill overlooking the sea, with Ile de Noirmoutier in the distance, the *château*, recently converted into a hotel, is surrounded by wooded parkland. It was bought by Jean-Luc Denieul as a retirement project after a career in technology. The lavishly decorated restaurant, with sea views, serves '*cuisine gastronomique*' of a traditional nature. Fish and shellfish predominate, along with an excellent selection of wines.

CLOSED never
CARDS AE, DC, MC, V

Blain
◆ Cochin €€ Fr

6 quai Surcouf, 44130 Blain, Loire-Atlantique
Tel 02 40 79 01 22 Fax 02 40 79 89 32

On the banks of the Nantes-Brest canal at Blaine, Cochin takes part in the Restaurants du Terroir scheme, offering high quality regional cooking. A requirement of the scheme is that food is freshly made from local produce. The Cochin family have owned the restaurant for 35 years; the chefs are Marc Cochin and his son Olivier. Meals can be taken in the dining room or on the patio. Beef, chicken and fish dishes are all well represented, along with a cellar of over 200 wines.

❛ *A restful setting* ❜

CLOSED phone for details
CARDS MC, V

Briollay
◆ Château de Noirieux
€€ – €€€

26 route du Moulin, 49125 Briollay, Maine-et-Loire
Tel 02 41 42 50 05 Fax 02 41 37 91 00

Not a grand *château*, more an extremely comfortable country house hotel in a tranquil riverside setting surrounded by woods. Non-residents are welcome for lunch or dinner, though it would be prudent to reserve a table. Chef Gerard Côme serves delicious fresh food, and you eat either on the sunny terrace or in the cool, restful dining room, decorated in creamy lemon and white. As befits the recent award of a Michelin star, meals are beautifully presented on fine china: indeed it often seems a shame to dig in and spoil the picture on the plate. Local game features on the menu, or you might choose *carré d'agneau de Lozère* or *dos de bar grillé sur sa peau*, followed by *soufflé chaud au Cointreau et citron vert*. Good list of Loire wines.

Closed Sun, Mon; mid-Feb to mid-Mar; first two weeks Nov
Cards AE, MC, V

---

charmingsmallhotels.co.uk
Visit Duncan Petersen's travel website, the best online search tool for places to stay that combine character and charm. Currently features Britain, France, Italy and Ireland, with other destinations being continuously added.

Challans
◆ Auberge de la Coétière € – €€

route des Sables, 85300 Challans, Vendée
Tel 02 51 93 16 45 Fax 02 51 93 35 87

This is an anodyne modern building with off-white plastered walls and red tiled roof in the 'traditional' style of so many suburban developments in the region. The dining room is a similarly unexceptional rectangular room with exposed timberwork. Still, it's a spacious and pleasant enough place – and family-run – in which to enjoy the fruits of the surrounding countryside. Being on the southern edge of the Vendée/Breton *marais* (sea marshes), expect such specialities as *canard de Challans, cuisses de grenouilles, brochette de Saint-Jacques* and *foie gras de canard*.

❛ I can't quite put my finger on it, but to me this place sums up the local area ❜

Closed never
Cards AE, DC, MC, V

Champtoceaux
◆ Le Champalud
€€ Fr

promenade du Champalud, 49270 Champtoceaux, Maine-et-Loire
Tel 02 40 83 50 09 Fax 02 40 83 53 81

In this pretty riverside town, Le Champalud is a hotel-restaurant offering a variety of menus at very reasonable prices. The dining room is light and spacious with attractive paintings on exposed stone walls. Chef Claude Rabu offers a bargain price *menu terroir*, and if that doesn't appeal, there is a wide range of other menus from which to choose. For light snacks, there is also a *pub menu*. Just the place for lunch after a walk around town.

❛ Pleasant setting for excellent food ❜

Closed never
Cards MC, V

Châteaubriant
◆ Le Poëlon d'Or €€

30 bis rue 11-Novembre 1918, 44110 Chateaubriant, Loire-Atlantique
Tel 02 40 81 43 33 Fax 02 40 81 43 33

A pretty converted *maison bourgeoise*, elegantly decorated, is the setting for this appealing restaurant. Strong emphasis is placed on presentation and attention to detail, such as home-made bread. Staff are courteous and service excellent. Chef Serge Arboli produces some memorable dishes, such as lobster ravioli in ginger butter, as well as a succulent steak *en croûte*. Chateaubriant itself is a rural market town where livestock markets have been held since the Middle Ages. Its 15thC château was the scene of the execution of 21 political detainees in October 1941, after the murder of the German commander at Nantes.

CLOSED Sun dinner, Mon; Feb school hols, 3 weeks Aug
CARDS MC, V

Château-Gontier
◆ La Brasserie
€ – €€

2 avenue Joffre, 53200 Château-Gontier,
Mayenne
Tel 02 43 09 60 00 Fax 02 43 09 60 01

There is much to explore in this bustling market town, which holds the largest cattle market in the region. The 11th-century church of Saint-Jean-Baptiste is a gem, and there are many half-timbered houses. The quayside gardens are filled with magnificent trees and even the tourist office is a boat. La Brasserie makes a pleasant place for lunch or dinner, and the *chef-patron*, Jacques Pinon, a disciple of Escoffier, relies on locally-sourced produce and fresh ingredients. Look out for fish dishes, and for the local beef.

CLOSED phone for details
CARDS MC, V

> **Fr French regional or classical French dishes on menu.**

Chemillé
◆ Auberge de l'Arrivée € – €€ Fr

15 rue de la Gare, 49120 Chemillé,
Maine-et-Loire
Tel 02 41 30 60 31 Fax 02 41 30 78 45

Mme Gimenez is in charge in the beamed, well-lit and comfortable dining room of the Auberge de l'Arrivée. Her husband is the chef, and he consistently turns out traditional regional dishes with

some light touches. Duck and rabbit are featured, along with a recent addition – ostrich. The menu changes at least four times a year. The area around Chemillé, between Angers and Cholet, is renowned for its medicinal plants.

> ❛ *Mme Gimenez is helpful and efficient* ❜

CLOSED Sun dinner
CARDS MC, V

Chênehutte-les-Tuffeaux
◆ Le Prieuré
€€ – €€€

49350 Chênehutte-les-Tuffeaux,
Maine-et-Loire
Tel 02 41 67 90 14 Fax 02 41 67 92 24

A luxurious *château-hôtel* in the Loire Valley near Saumur. The two elegant dining rooms overlook the hotel's parkland and the river. Classically-trained chef Jean-Noel Lumineau adapts traditional recipes to suit the modern lighter approach. He makes use of regional wines, and the food is complemented by a cellar of over 10,000 bottles. Dishes such as *raviolis de langoustines à la crème de truffes*, and *moelleux au chocolat au coeur fondant de banane verte* give a clue to the sophisticated menu.

CLOSED Jan, Feb
CARDS AE, MC, V

Chenillé-Changé
◆ La Table du Meunier
€ – €€ Fr

49200 Chenillé-Changé, Maine-et-Loire
Tel 02 41 95 10 98 Fax 02 41 95 10 52

A pretty waterside village which prides itself on its floral displays and attractive gardens, Chenillé-Changé makes a lovely place for a gentle stroll, especially at night when it is prettily lit. An old watermill, still functioning, is home to La Table du Meunier. It also offers a *bateau-restaurant* on the Mayenne, but the mill is the find here. Simple food, well-cooked, using local products, is served in a thoughtfully converted dining room enlivened by works by local artists.

⟨ Simple French food, properly cooked – perfect ⟩

CLOSED Mon eve, Tue; Wed winter; first two weeks Jan, Feb
CARDS MC, V

Cholet
◆ Château de la Tremblaye
€€ – €€€

route des Sables, 49300 Cholet, Maine-et-Loire
Tel 02 41 58 40 17 Fax 02 41 58 20 67

A 19thC lakeside château set amidst parkland, and close to Puy Dufou, one of the grandest of *son et lumières*. Chef Thierry Guimard serves the freshest local produce, cooking to order. High ceilings, chandeliers and candlelight all contribute to the atmosphere, helped by beautifully laid tables. *Foie gras* is big on the menu, which also has a wide choice of puddings: Thierry's English wife, Allyson, is a *chef-pâtissier*.

CLOSED never
CARDS AE, DC, MC, V

Le Croisic
◆ Au Fin Gourmet
€ – €€€ Fr

1 place du Pilori, 44490 Le Croisic, Loire-Atlantique
Tel 02 40 23 00 38 Fax 02 40 62 96 27

T he pretty fishing port of Le Croisic – known for its catches of sardines, prawns oysters and mussels – has a remarkable number of good restaurants, an indication of the quality of the fish that comes in fresh each day. Au Fin Gourmet keeps things simple, relying on the freshness of the fish to speak for itself. A 16th-century house, decorated without pretension, it draws many locals – always a good sign. The oysters and whelks are wonderfully fresh. The sea bass is also highly recommended.

CLOSED Sun dinner winter, Mon; mid-Dec to Feb
CARDS MC, V

Ernée
◆ Le Grand Cerf
€€

17-19 rue Aristide-Briand, 53500 Ernée, Mayenne
Tel 02 43 05 13 09 Fax 02 43 05 02 90

W ord has it that a new, young chef has revitalized the menus at Le Grand Cerf, a restaurant to watch. There is something for all tastes, from robust dishes such as pigs' trotters to fresh tuna served with *tagliatelli*, followed perhaps by a *sorbet gentiane*. The market town of Ernée was built around a *château* that was replaced, in 1697, by a church.

⟨ Seems to be improving all the time'...'Friendly, welcoming.' 'Excellent wine list ⟩

CLOSED Sun dinner, Mon; mid to late Jan
CARDS AE, MC, V

La Ferté-Bernard
◆ Le Dauphin
€€

3 rue d'Huisne, 72400 La Ferté-Bernard, Sarthe
Tel 02 43 93 00 39 Fax 02 43 71 26 65

T he river Huisne runs through this charming small medieval town, the church of Notre-Dame-des-Marais has beautiful windows, and the nearby Halles date from the 16th century. There is a folk festival in July. Boat trips, starting near the tourist office, make a relaxing way to pass the time, and Le Dauphin, in the pedestrianised part of town, makes a good place to eat. There are set menus, as well as *à la carte*. Regional specialities are given a contemporary lift, and Loire Valley wines are much in evidence.

⟨ Stylish. The setting complements the food ⟩

CLOSED Mon
CARDS MC, V

La Flèche
◆ Le Moulin des Quatre Saisons
€ – €€

2 rue Gallieni, 72200 La Flèche, Sarthe
Tel 02 43 45 12 12 Fax 02 43 45 10 31

An old converted mill on the banks of the Loire has been sympathetically modernised to become a peaceful restaurant, with a terrace for summer eating. The emphasis is on seasonal food from the area and the cellar is outstanding, with knowledgeable advice on hand.

CLOSED mid-Jan, 3rd week Oct
CARDS AE, MC, V

Fontenay-le-Comte
◆ Auberge de la Rivière
€€

Fontenay-le-Comte, 85770 Velluire, Vendée
Tel 02 51 52 32 15 Fax 02 43 45 10 31

There could hardly be anything more typical of the Marais Poitevin than this ivy-clad complex of old riverside buildings. Forming its own cul-de-sac and surrounded by the gentle river, the trees and an arched stoned bridge, it makes a delightful and tranquil setting that is the perfect precursor for a memorable meal. In the large, warm, gently rustic rectangular dining room with windows almost dipping into the adjoining waterway the two set menus are fairly priced and feature interesting dishes prepared as much as possible from local produce – perhaps fresh salmon in sorrel sauce or *lapin rex du Poitou* in thyme.

❛ *Be prepared for a languid meal; despite its proximity to the Nantes-Bordeaux motorway this is not a place for a quick getaway* ❜

CLOSED Sun eve, Mon Mar-Jun, Sep-Dec; Mon lunch Jul, Aug; mid-Dec to Mar
CARDS MC, V.

Looking for somewhere to stay? See page 241.

Fontevraud-l'Abbaye
◆ La Licorne €€ – €€€

allée Sainte-Catherine, rue Robert d'Abrissel, 49590 Fontevrau- l'Abbaye, Maine-et-Loire
Tel 02 41 51 72 49 Fax 02 41 51 70 40

The final resting place of the Plantagenets – Henry II of England, Eleanor of Aquitaine and Richard the Lionheart amongst others – is the largest and most complete abbey in France, a superb example of Romanesque architecture. In its role as a cultural centre, concerts are held year round. La Licorne attracts a well-heeled clientele amongst visitors with its imaginative, modern cookery (witness, for example, *filet de boeuf au gingembre et cardamome* or *tarte gratinée à la rhubarbe, sorbet fraise*) carefully presented in stylish surroundings near the abbey. There is a good selection of Loire wines. The restaurant has a Michelin star.

CLOSED Sun dinner, Mon; mid-Dec to Feb
CARDS AE, DC, MC, V

Le Gavre
◆ Auberge de la Fôret
€ – €€€

La Maillardais, 44130 Le Gavre, Loire-Atlantique
Tel 02 40 51 20 26 Fax 02 40 79 08 31

Set in the Forêt du Gavre, with its shady walks and cycle paths, the Auberge de la Fôret has the look of a hunting lodge, particularly in one of its two dining rooms which has heavy beams and a stone floor. The other is more elegant in style, decorated in pale shades, with blue table linen. The chef, Bertrand Pouland, combines *cuisine gastronomique* with traditional regional cooking. He makes a particular feature of local game and fish, and, in season, of the wild mushrooms which attract many fungi hunters to the forest in autumn. A good place for a walk in the cool, followed by a leisurely lunch.

CLOSED never
CARDS MC, V

Les Herbiers
◆ Mont des Alouettes €

route de Cholet, 85500 Les Herbiers, Vendée
Tel 02 51 67 02 18 Fax 02 51 67 03 22

Set on the edge of an escarpment overlooking a vast, often misty, expanse of the Vendéen countryside, this unattractive glass-fronted roadhouse is separated from the viewpoint, two distinguishing windmills and a 19thC chapel by an extensive car park. Don't be deterred, however, by the unlikely - looking venue and visions of mass roadside catering: Mont des Alouettes (skylarks) is distinctly French, even Vendéen. Far from succumbing to the lowest common denominator, this bar/restaurant offers four set menus with numerous choices on each. The wine list features a short section of Vendée wines, including Pissotte, Mareuil and a Brem *cuvé special* matured in oak.

CLOSED check with restaurant
CARDS MC, V

Please send us reports
A guide such as this thrives on reader's reports. If you send us five usable reports, we will send you a free copy of any title in our *Charming Small Hotel Guides* series (see page 241 for France titles in the series).

The five reports should contain at least two new restaurants; the rest can be comments on restaurants already in the guide.
1 Tell us about your experiences in restaurants already in this guide.
2 Send us new reports. New reports should give the following information:
- **Region** – City, town, village or neaest village.
- **Name of restaurant** – Please double check the spelling, it's surprisingly easy to make a mistake.
- **Address** – including *département*
- **Telephone number** – plus fax and e-mail if available. Double check this information.
- **Objective description** – Try to explain simply why it should be in the guide. Remember that the guide is very selective - our entries are those one-in-five places that combine
- interesting food with
- character and charm, in the building, the setting or both.
The guide hates tourist traps, and pretentious, dressed-up food. We like places where the French go.
We favour places in the lower and middle price bands but there are plenty of expensive places that have our qualities, and we list those too.
- **Diner's comments** – These should be

short, personal comments on features that strike you. They can be your comments, or others'.
- **Closing times**
- **Credit cards accepted**
Don't forget to date your report and add your name and address.
Send reports to Charming Restaurant Guides, Duncan Petersen Publishing, 31 Ceylon Road, London W14 0PY.

Javron-les-Chapelles
◆ La Terrasse
€ – €€€

30 Grande- Rue, 53250 Javron-les-Chapelles, Mayenne
Tel 02 43 03 41 91 Fax 02 43 04 44 94

La Terrasse is the star of its village, and can be spotted by the bright baskets of flowers hanging from its façade. There is also a 16th-century church nearby, which is worth a visit. The whole feel of the place is typically French, and so you may be surprised to discover that La Terrasse is run by an English couple, chef Michael Greenaway and his wife Alison. In an elegant, modern setting, they offer both *prix fixe* and *à la carte* menus which are changed regularly.

❛ *Excellent list of Loire wines including a good range of half bottles* ❜

CLOSED Tue dinner, Wed
CARDS AE, MC, V

Laval
◆ Bistro de Paris €€

67 rue du Val-de-Mayenne, 53000 Laval, Mayenne
Tel 02 43 56 98 29 Fax 02 43 56 52 85

The charming, old-fashioned *brasserie* style of La Bistro de Paris belies the fresh, contemporary food that is served by the *chef-patron* Guy Lemercier. The *menu-dégustation* is a good way to sample his skills, and very good value too. Service is swift and courteous. The wine list specialises in Burgundy and Bordeaux. Laval, established in the 13th century by Flemish weavers, has many historic buildings.

CLOSED Sat lunch, Sun dinner, Mon; 2 weeks mid-Aug
CARDS AE, MC, V

Loué
◆ Ricordeau €€ – €€€€

*11-13 rue de la Libération, 72540 Loué,
Sarthe
Tel 02 43 88 40 03 Fax 02 43 88 62 08*

The village of Loué, some 20 miles (30 km) from Le Mans, is well known for the quality of its poultry and for the annual poultry fair held here at the beginning of December. Jean-Yves Herman, *chef-patron* of this former coaching inn overlooking delightful gardens quite rightly makes a feature of *poulet de Loué*, but there are plenty of other choices: how about *langoustines rôties à la verveine* or *tartare de canard aux huîtres*? Corinne Herman oversees front-of-house, with happy results. Special prices are offered for guests who would like to stay overnight.

❛ *Very agreeable' … 'Excellent winelist, with plenty of choice and a good range of prices* ❜

CLOSED Sun dinner, Mon; three weeks Jan, Feb
CARDS AE, MC, V

Le Lude
◆ La Renaissance
€ – €€

*2 avenue Libération, 72800 Le Lude, Sarthe
Tel 02 43 94 63 10 Fax 02 43 94 21 05*

Surprisingly, considering the press of visitors to the *château's* extravagant *son et lumière* (involving 350 actors and 300 fountains as well as fireworks), there are few decent restaurants in Le Lude. Le Renaissance is the exception, offering good food at reasonable prices. The decoration is light, airy and unpretentious, and the chef produces some imaginative dishes which are also, mostly, successful. Try, for example, sander poached with rhubarb – not at all bad. Fish is featured widely on the menu.

CLOSED Sun dinner, Mon
CARDS MC, V

Le Mans
◆ Le Beaulieu €€ – €€€

*24 rue des Ponts-Neufs, 72000 Le Mans,
Sarthe
Tel 02 43 87 78 37 Fax 02 43 87 78 27*

With its Michelin star, Le Beaulieu is probably the best restaurant that Le Mans (celebrated for its motor sports, but well-worth visiting for Vieux Mans and the cathedral of Saint-Julien) has to offer. *Chef-patron* Olivier Boussard continues to visit the markets regularly to choose the finest produce on sale. His contemporary style of cooking matches the warm modern decoration, and tends towards the luxurious. Truffles and *foie gras* are liberally used in dishes such as *coquilles Saint-Jacques poêlées et julienne de truffes* and *foie gras poêlées dans une réduction au porto*. The excellent *poulet de Loué* also features: try *filet de volaille de Loué au Vin Jaune*. As you would expect, a good cellar accompanies the food.

CLOSED Sat, Sun; one week Feb or Mar, Aug
CARDS AE, MC, V

Le Mans
◆ Le Pantagruel
€€ – €€€

*place Saint-Pierre, 72000 Le Mans, Sarthe
Tel 02 43 24 87 63 Fax 02 43 77 00 58*

Not in the same culinary league as Le Beaulieu (see above), Le Pantagruel is nevertheless a very good choice, not least for its setting in Vieux Mans. It stands opposite the half-timbered former palace of the Counts of Maine, close to the delightful 18thC Hôtel de Ville. The cuisine here is definitely *gastronomique*, and is served in one of two welcoming dining rooms, both with huge fireplaces for use in winter, or on the terrace in summer. Specialities are fish and *fruits de mer*.

❛ *A great favourite; we always head here when we come in to town'…'Lovely in summer on the terrace* ❜

CLOSED Mon
CARDS AE, MC, V

Mayenne
◆ Beau Rivage €–€€

53100 Moulay, Mayenne. Mayenne
Tel 02 43 00 49 13 Fax 02 43 04 43 69

The location is key here, although the food is no let-down, with good value set menus featuring plenty of fish dishes. The *prix fixe* lunch menu, available Monday to Friday, also hits the spot, especially on a sunny day. The hotel-restaurant stands on the banks of the Mayenne, near a weir, opposite an old mill and lovely gardens. In summer meals are served on the tree-canopied river bank, but if you have to be indoors, the view can be enjoyed from the huge picture windows of the light and airy dining room. The Beau Rivage is signposted off the N162 Mayenne to Laval road, just outside Mayenne.

❛Perfect for a lazy lunch on a summer's day ❜

Closed Sun dinner, Mon; two weeks mid-Feb
Cards MC, V

Mayenne
◆ Le Grand Hôtel € – €€

2 rue Ambroise de Lore, 53100 Mayenne,
Mayenne
Tel 02 43 00 96 00 Fax 02 43 00 69 20

In the pretty, fairly quiet town of Mayenne, which straddles the river of the same name, this sturdy *hôtel-restaurant* on the river bank keeps up standards and provides a good choice for a meal. The spacious dining room, decorated in white and pastels, overlooks the river, and the food, using local produce, is elegantly presented. Mayenne is enjoyed by tourists who prefer to be off the beaten track. After lunch, if you like, you can go boating.

Closed Sat dinner winter; mid-Dec to Jan
Cards AE, MC, V

Mezangers
◆ Le Relais du Gué de Selle € – €€€

route de Mayenne, 53600 Mezangers,
Mayenne
Tel 02 43 91 20 00 Fax 02 43 91 20 10

Close to a forest, this is a delightful *hôtel-restaurant* in a carefully restored farm. It is surrounded by its own land including a large lake, and lovely countryside for walking. The Château de Rocher, which can be admired from the outside, is close by. On cooler days you eat in the large, high-ceilinged dining room with massive fireplace, while in summer there is a terrace. Chef Didier Peschard uses the best and freshest ingredients he can find. Fish is well represented and lobster is a great favourite here. The hotel is signposted on the D7 road from Mezangers to Mayenne.

❛ Oozes comfort and well-being ❜

Closed Sun dinner, Mon Oct to Apr
Cards AE, MC, V

Nantes
◆ L'Atlantide €€ – €€€

15 quai Ernest-Renaud, 44000 Nantes,
Loire-Atlantique
Tel 02 40 73 23 23 Fax 02 40 73 76 46

Much of the lovely city of Nantes – the 7th largest in France – can be seen from this slick, contemporary, air-conditioned fourth floor restaurant. L'Atlantide is part of the Tables de Saveurs de Bretagne scheme (Nantes was formerly capital of Brittany) in recognition of the quality of its food. Jean-Yves Guého is an inspired chef, adding far-flung twists to his dishes, such as turbot with Cantonese spices and seafood curry. Perhaps the highlight though, are the puddings – an incredible range, with emphasis on chocolate as well as fresh fruit. The cellar is just as strong as the food, as is the service.

❛ As memorable as the Pont de Saint-Nazare, slung 60 m above the Loire ❜

Closed Sat lunch, Sun; one week May, 3 weeks Aug
Cards AE, MC, V

Nantes
◆ Bateaux-Nantais €€

Parc Fluvial des Bateaux-Nantais, quai de la Motte-Rouge, place Waldeck-Rouseeau, BP50826, 44008 Nantes, Loire-Atlantique
Tel 02 40 14 51 14

Hardly a typical charming small restaurant, hardly memorable food, but we include Nantes' *bateaux-restaurants* to ring the changes, and because they work well and make a fun way to spend lunch or dinner while cruising the Erdre Valley. Music accompanies: classical, or a selection of flamenco, salsa and blues – and concerts and dinner dances are also arranged, as well as Disney treasure hunts for children. The cruise takes you past 20 or so châteaux, including the 15thC Gascheirie, as well as lovely *manoirs* and their gardens. The à la carte menu is varied and well-presented and includes quail, duck, *foie gras* and fish. There is also a children's menu.

CLOSED Mon-Fri Apr, May, Sep, Oct; never Jun-Aug
CARDS MC, V

Nantes
◆ Lou Pescadou €€

8 allée Baco, 44000 Nantes, Loire-Atlantique
Tel 02 40 35 29 50 Fax 02 51 82 46 34

Massive expansion and modernisation in recent years has meant that Nantes has a thriving business community, including the second largest Bourse in France after Paris. In the heart of the business quarter, opposite the old château, is this unashamedly fishy *bistrot*, packed with bits and pieces to do with fishing and seafaring. Chef Nicolas Barteau has a way with fish – lobster, turbot, sea bass and shellfish all feature. You might choose *turbot rôti aux grenailles de Noirmoutier, bar sauvage en croûte de sel*, or *marinière de homard au layon*. The wines are well-chosen, and particularly strong on Muscadet.

❛ *Try my favourite – sea bass baked in a salt crust* ❜

CLOSED Sun
CARDS MC, V

Neau
◆ La Croix Verte
€ – €€

2 rue Evron, 53150 Neau, Mayenne
Tel 02 43 98 23 41 Fax 02 43 98 25 39

The pretty medieval village of Neau, with its 13thC frescoes, is surrounded by unspoilt countryside featuring dolmen-like stones, reminiscent of Brittany. It makes a charming setting for La Croix Verte. Chef-patron Bertrand Boullier proudly offers regional specialities, and the restaurant is part of the *'goutez à la Mayenne'* scheme, aimed at promoting regional cooking and produce. There is a friendly atmosphere in the restaurant, which has rather unusual murals. Thick linen napkins and fine china set off the excellent food, which includes local beef and *pommeau*, an apple aperitif.

❛ *Moules au pommeau are to die for.* ❜

CLOSED Sun dinner
CARDS AE, MC, V

Neufchâtel-en-Saosnais
◆ Relais des Etangs de Guibert €€

Etangs de Guibert, 72600 Neufchâtel-en-Saosnais, Sarthe
Tel 02 43 97 15 38 Fax 02 43 33 22 99

This well-renovated farmhouse stands in the Forêt de Perseigne, not far from the ruined abbey of the same name. There is a lake stocked with pike and trout for fishing enthusiasts, and lovely countryside for walking. The relaxing, friendly restaurant has a large dining room with French windows opening on to a terrace, where meals can be taken in warm weather. Sit back and enjoy seasonal specialities prepared by *chef-patron* Gilles Gaultier.

CLOSED Sun dinner, Mon
CARDS MC, V

Noirmoutier-en-l'Ile
◆ Le Grand Four
€ – €€€

1 rue de la Cure, 85330 Noirmoutier-en-l'Ile, Vendée
Tel 02 51 39 61 97 Fax 02 51 39 61 97

The castle may have deterred unwanted guests in years gone by (particularly the English) but it can no longer resist discerning guests from Patrice Vétélé's table in the ivy-clad Grand Four. Both the establishment and the cuisine shine with brilliance and imagination. The welcoming table arrangement pairs slate blue-rimmed plates with strident tulips on white porcelain. Mme Vétélé, elegant and charming, promotes the menus and particularly her husband's speciality: wonderful desserts. On an island barely a kilometre wide, fresh local seafood features strongly (as it should), but this is not a seafood restaurant – it's much more. Try for example *jambon de parme avec l'anchoïade de coquillages* or *langoustines et chair d'araignnée sur la tête de veau*.

❛ The supreme indulgence: a five-course meal of Patrice's puds ❜

Closed Sun dinner, Mon
Cards MC, V

Please send us reports
A guide such as this thrives on reader's reports. If you send us five usable reports, we will send you a free copy of any title in our *Charming Small Hotel Guides* series (see page 241 for France titles in the series).

The five reports should contain at least two new restaurants; the balance can be comments on restaurants already in the guide. **Send reports to** Charming Restaurant Guides, Duncan Petersen Ltd, 31 Ceylon Rd, London W14 0PY.

La Plaine-sur-Mer
◆ Anne de Bretagne
€€ – €€€

Port de la Gravette, 44770 La Plaine-sur-Mer, Loire-Atlantique
Tel 02 40 21 54 72 Fax 02 40 21 02 33

Unusual festivals are a speciality of many towns and villages in France, and La Plaine-sur-Mer is no exception: every spring it hosts a Festival of Mussels and the Sea, celebrating the importance of both to this long-established fishing port. Chef Philippe Vételé and his wife Michèle, who is the *sommelier*, make an unbeatable combination in this terrific seafront hotel-restaurant.

Lobster lovers will simply have to plump for the *'menu d'homard'*; it's also hard to resist the warm oysters in white wine *zabaglione*. Puddings employ early strawberries from Plougastel in season, and cheeses come from M. Bellevaire, a master cheese-maker. There are also themed menus on offer, which showcase seasonal ingredients. The wine list is excellent, with a good range of prices. Michelin awards a star.

❛ Don't visit unless you are truly hungry – you will eat every morsel on your plate'...'One of our favourites ❜

Closed Sun dinner, Mon, Tue lunch, last week Feb
Cards AE, MC, V

La Roche-sur-Yon
◆ Auberge de la Borderie
€€ – €€€   Fr

Le Petit Bois Massuyeau, 85000 La Roche-sur-Yon, Vendée
Tel 02 51 08 95 95 Fax 02 51 62 25 78

Straw and sun hats decorate the cloakroom and loo in this unusual establishment which exudes charm and personality *je ne sais quoi*. The small restaurant and back-garden terrace has the suburban feel of an ordinary private house but the cuisine is the stuff of dreams for most householders. Dishes are beautifuly presented and very good. They may include – on the *menu du jour* – smoked ham surrounded by melon and avocado followed by turkey breast with wild mushrooms in a cream source and a mix of pears and other fruit in flaky pastry, as well as local *jambon de Vendée* with *mojettes* (white beans) and *pot-au-feu de la mer*. There is also a *menu entre terre et mer* (*gaspacho aux moules de Bouchot*) and a *menu gourmand* (*pressée de filets de sardines au citron*). At heart this is local country cooking – with panache. Take the old road to Sables d'Olonne, and at the roundabout at the western end of the Roche-sur-Yon bypass follow signs for Abbaye des Fontenelles.

Closed Sun and Wed dinner, Mon; 3 weeks Aug, 10 days late Feb, early Mar
Cards MC, V

Sable-sur-Sarthe
◆ Bateau le Sablésien

€€

S.A.R.L. Croisières Saboliennes, B.P. 56,
quai National, 72302 Sable-sur-Sarthe,
Sarthe
Tel 02 43 95 93 13 Fax 02 43 95 99 14

Enjoy a boat trip on the Sarthe, eating your dinner as the scenery – which could not be seen on foot – slips past. Four boats offer dinner cruises, each one with a different destination: Château de Beaucé, Avoise, Moulin d'Ignière and Malicorne. On board there is a choice of four menus, including wine, plus a children's menu. The food served in the comfortable dining area is very simple – pork in cider, grilled lamb and fish – but carefully presented.

CLOSED winter
CARDS MC, V

Our traditional French cuisine symbol
So many of our readers enjoy seeking out the genuinely French eating experience that we have used Fr to mark restaurants which offer *cuisine du terroir*, classical French dishes or regional dishes with an emphasis on local ingredients, and traditional recipes.

Les Sables d'Olonne
◆ Le Petit Pavillon €

22 quai Guiné, 85100 Les Sables d'Olonne,
Vendée
Tel 02 51 32 71 76 Fax 02 51 32 71 76

The name must hark back to some previous incarnation, for this glass-fronted quayside restaurant is more of a brasserie than a pavilion and hardly 'petit'. Set amongst a long line of restaurants, it has the advantage of being partly raised above street level, affording views across the harbour without the disturbance of promenaders jostling along the pavement. It offers a wide, even confusing, range of menus and options, mostly, not surprisingly, incorporating fish and seafood. Daily specials might include a memorable warm duo of scallops and *foie*

gras, followed by turbot with *hollandaise* sauce, then a fruit tart flambéed in Calvados.

> *A good meal; our quibble was with the steep mark-up on an inexpensive bottle of local Vendéen wine*

CLOSED never
CARDS MC, V

Saint-Denis d'Anjou
◆ La Maison du Roi
   René € – €€€

53290 Saint-Denis d'Anjou, Mayenne
Tel 02 43 70 52 30 Fax 02 43 70 58 75

Marie-Christine de Vaudernier is the chef here, and her husband manages the restaurant. Both are welcoming, as indeed is the small but charming dining room, with comfortable chairs and beautifully arranged tables. They make especially imaginative use of vegetables, including relatively unusual ones such as salsify. The wine list is interesting, strong, as you would expect, on the Loire, and Pierre de Vaudernier is always happy to suggest interesting bottles to accompany his wife's cooking. The medieval village of Saint-Denis d'Anjou is well worth an after-dinner stroll.

> *Well laid-out dining room' ...*
> *'Unusual and very welcome number of wines by the glass*

CLOSED never
CARDS MC, V

Saint-Georges-le-Gaultier
◆ Relais des Alpes
   € Fr

rue des Ardoises, 72130 Saint-Georges-le-
Gaultier, Sarthe
Tel 02 43 33 79 19

This is one of those little French restaurants that provide dream set lunches. As we went to press, 8.6 euros bought a selection from the huge buffet consisting of a hot *plat du jour*, cheese, dessert, wine and coffee. Unusually for such a simple place, the desserts are often freshly made by the young chef-patron, and the vegetables will be fresh too, not the ever-present tinned *petits pois*. The Relais des Alpes is set in an ordinary little market town, but it is close to the Alpes Mancelles, an area of lovely scenery - forests, streams and rocky outcrops.

CLOSED dinner; Sat, Sun
CARDS none

Saint-Joachim
◆ Auberge du Parc
€€–€€€

162 Ile de Fédrun, 44720 Saint-Joachim, Loire-Atlantique
Tel 02 40 88 53 01 Fax 02 40 91 67 44

Set in the mysterious, watery landscape of the Brière national park (you can reach the inn by boat as well as by car), this is a charming thatched inn with white walls and blue-painted shutters surrounded by a garden, and inside a cosy, low beamed dining room with dressers full of china and blue and white cloths on the prettily set tables. It's in the the hands of a young Parisian chef, Eric Guérin, so the traditional decoration has a modern touch (including the art on the walls), and so does the food, which takes traditional local dishes, and gives them an interesting twist, earning a Michelin star in the process. Specialities include *croquant de queue de boeuf et anguilles fumées* and *supr`eme de canard à la moutarde de salicorne*. Muscadet is the thing to drink.

CLOSED Sun dinner, Mon except Jul; Mar, Aug
CARDS AE, MC, V

Saint-Lyphard
◆ Auberge de Kerbourg
€€ Fr

route de Guérande, Kerbourg, 44410 Saint-Lyphard, Loire-Atlantique
Tel 02 40 61 95 15 Fax 02 40 61 98 64

St-Lyphard is in the Parc Naturel de Brière, a huge area of peaty plain, flooded in winter. Houses in the area typically have thatched roofs, adding to its charm for increasing numbers of visitors. Boat trips are popular too. The Auberge de Kerbourg is a charming bistro in one of these pretty

thatched cottages. It's a cut above too: chef-patron Bernard Jeanson cooks regional specialities such as Breton oysters, frogs and pigeon with tremendous style and flair, and has recently been awarded a well-deserved Michelin star as a result.

◆Service was friendly and relaxed'
...'Service was a bit slow – not a place for a quick visit ◆

CLOSED Sun, Mon, Tue Sep-Jun; never Jul-Aug; one week Oct, mid-Dec to mid-Feb
CARDS MC, V

Saint-Sylvain d'Anjou
◆ Le Clafoutis €€

La Lieue, 49480 Saint-Sylvain d'Anjou, Maine-et-Loire
Tel 02 41 43 84 71 Fax 02 41 34 74 80

On the N23, 3 miles (5 km) NE of the centre of Angers, Le Clafoutis is a popular choice for Angevins, who are for the most part a lively bunch thanks to the presence of the city's university: you'll usually find a crowd of locals creating a warm atmosphere in this attractive restaurant created by chef-patron Serge Lebert. His strong card is seasonal local produce, particularly fish from the Loire, typically zander and shad. The cellar specialises in local wines.

CLOSED Sat lunch, Sun, Mon dinner; one month Jul-Aug; Christmas holidays
CARDS MC, V

Saint-Vincent-sur-Jard
◆ Le Chalet Saint-Hubert € Fr

20 route de Jard, 85520 Saint-Vincent-sur-Jard, Vendée
Tel 02 51 33 40 33 Fax 02 51 33 41 94

Towards the south of Vendée's beach and holiday coastline, the popular restaurant of this cheerful establishment is housed in a considerable extension to the original 'chalet'. It's a jolly place, decorated with nautical nick-nacks, a set of antlers and a wide selection of brochures and posters about nearby attractions. There are three standard menus, but the holiday mood is best reflected in the Menu du Chalet which offers a choice of either fried eels (a local delicacy) or *assiette de fruits de mer* accompanied by a half bottle of Muscadet and followed by cheese and dessert.

CLOSED Sun dinner; Nov
CARDS MC, V

Sainte-Suzanne
◆ Beau Séjour ©© Fr

4 rue de la Libération, 53270 Sainte-Suzanne, Mayenne
Tel 02 43 01 40 31 Fax 02 43 01 46 21

Sainte-Suzanne, a *petite cité de charactère*, is a real find. The hilltop village is contained within a triangle of ramparts that overlook the river Erve, popular for fishermen. The hotel-restaurant Beau Séjour is quintessentially French, with lace curtains, pretty tablecloths and bentwood chairs. Stephane Huchet makes appropriate use of local produce, though there are some unusual additions: kangaroo steak recently appeared on one of the set menus.

CLOSED Sun dinner in winter
CARDS MC, V

Saulges
◆ L'Ermitage ©©–©©©

3 place Saint-Pierre, 53340 Saulges, Mayenne
Tel 02 43 64 66 00 Fax 02 43 64 66 20

Close to the church in this interesting Erve Valley village (two churches, one Romanesque, one 7thC; prehistoric caves; a swimming lake) L'Ermitage is a stone house standing in its own grounds. The dining room is sunny and spacious and overlooks the terrace and garden. Chef Thierry Janvier is the grandson of the restaurant's original chef-*patronne*, and he maintains standards well. The family is justifiably proud of the fresh local produce they serve 'with a modern twist'. You might choose *salade de maquereaux marinés aux herbes et citron vert*, followed by *blanc de volaille de Loué à la crème de chorizo*, then *crème brûlée à l'anis*, all reasonably priced.

❛ A calm, gentle place. We much enjoyed our lunch here ❜

CLOSED Sun dinner, Mon; Feb; first week Nov
CARDS AE, MC, V

Saumur
◆ Les Délices du Château ©© – ©©©

cour du Château du Saumur, 49400 Saumur, Maine-et-Loire
Tel 02 41 67 65 60 Fax 02 41 67 74 60

The restaurant is housed in the outbuildings of the medieval château of Saumur, which dominates the attractive riverside town that has been built up around it. In this superb setting, chef Pierre Millan makes imaginative use of local produce. Much of the menu is à la carte, but the weekday lunchtime *prix fixe menu d'affaires* is an absolute bargain.

❛ On a summer's day, there can be nothing better than visiting Les Délices du Saumur ❜

CLOSED Sun dinner, Mon, Tue dinner; mid-Sep to end May; never Jun to mid-Sep
CARDS MC, V

Our price bands
© under 30 euros ©© 30-50 Euros
©©© over 50 euros for a menu

Saumur
◆ Le Gambetta ©©

12 rue Gambetta, 49400 Saumur, Maine-et-Loire
Tel 02 41 67 66 66 Fax 02 41 50 83 23

Le Gambetta is a beautiful old house, painstakingly restored, with a shaded inner courtyard. It makes a very pleasant setting for lunch or dinner, and the food is both excellent and unusual, employing produce of a very high quality. M. Chesnoy's cooking is best described as French fusion food, combining regional produce with global tastes. You might find pigeon with Peking spices and dandelion salad, or seared tuna with risotto. Service under the present management is friendly and efficient, a great improvement on a couple of years ago.

The wine list is short, but includes some excellent Loire wines.

❝ *A delightful find' ... 'Steadily improving* ❞

CLOSED Sun dinner, Mon; Nov
CARDS AE, MC, V

Saumur
◆ Les Mariniers €€

*Loire Hôtel, rue du Vieux Pont, 49400
Saumur, Maine-et-Loire
Tel 02 41 66 22 42 Fax 02 41 67 88 80*

The Loire Hôtel, newly built in tradition-al style and so offering the best of both worlds, stands on a small islet in the Loire, opposite the old town and its magnificent château. Its air-conditioned restaurant, Les Mariniers, has views across the river to the château, dramatically floodlit at night. It's an elegant setting, with good quality linen on carefully-laid tables, and the service is smooth, friendly and unobtrusive. The chef, Gilles Doire, serves mainly tradi-tional dishes.

❝ *A truly superb position* ❞

CLOSED never
CARDS AE, MC, V

Sille-le-Guillaume
◆ Le Bretagne €–€€

*1 place Croix d'Or, 72140
Sille-le-Guillaume, Sarthe
Tel 02 43 20 10 10 Fax 02 43 20 03 96*

The pretty town of Sille-le-Guillaume is dominated by a huge 15thC château, while in the nearby Fôret de Sille a lake with beach provides fishing and water-sports. The restaurant is nondescript from the outside, and heavily beamed inside, though white walls and table linen help to offset the dark. Jean-Marie Fontaine cooks regional dishes with a light touch, comple-mented by a good wine list.

❝ *This restaurant is a joy to eat in'
...'Good value menu de terroir* ❞

CLOSED Sun dinner
CARDS MC, V

Vibraye
◆ Auberge de la Fôret
€–€€ Fr

*rue Gabriel Goussault, 72320 Vibraye,
Sarthe
Tel 02 43 93 60 07 Fax 02 43 71 20 36*

Vibraye is a little village in the Fôret d'Harcourt, which is excellent walking terrain. Fishermen are drawn to the Braye river, which flows gently near this *auberge*. The dining room is traditionally decorated, with candlelight adding to the cosy atmos-phere. Chef-patron Guy Renier offers a wide choice of meat dishes and local fish. Amongst the puddings, he is especially proud of his very own apple-based creation, *le petit Sarthois*.

❝ *We much enjoyed the cheeses from the local goat farm* ❞

CLOSED Sun dinner, Mon
CARDS MC, V

Villaines-la-Juhel
◆ Le Jardin Gourmand
€–€€€ Fr

*1 place Croix d'Or, 72140
Sille-le-Guillaume. Sarthe
Tel 02 43 20 10 10 Fax 02 43 20 03 96*

The small town of Villaines-la-Juhel bor-ders the beautiful Alpes Mancelles. Le Jardin Gourmand, despite its alluring name, is a modern hotel and restaurant, with bland and unremarkable decoration. It is, however, a member of the Goutez `a la Mayenne scheme, offering regional speciali-ties. Chef Auguste Maillot offers an excel-lent range of meals, from the *prix fixe* lunch to *cuisine gastronomique*. Particular favourites have been duck breast in a honey and lavender sauce, pigeon in walnut wine, and a seafood terrine. The excellent cheese-board is also a great treat.

❝ *A good range of reasonably priced wines, many also usefully avail-able in half bottles* ❞

CLOSED never
CARDS AE, MC, V

CENTRE

The government region with the least familiar title (named for its location in the heart of France) – and comprising six confusingly similar-sounding *départements* – Centre is dominated by the magnificent River Loire and criss-crossed by other charming rivers including the Cher, the Loir and the Indre. It is in fact the region of France that we refer to as The Loire Valley, with its many splendid châteaux, its great cathedrals at Bourges and Chartres, its troglodyte villages dug from the soft, chalky tufa and its market gardens. Encompassing the old regions of Touraine and Berry, it includes the cities of Orléans (the capital) and Tours.

HAUTE-NORMANDIE

BASSE-NORMANDIE

Montigny-sur-Avre 184
Nogent-le-Roi 185
Châteauneuf-en-Thymerais 180
Chartres 179
Illiers-Combray 182
Châteaudun 179

Le Mans

PAYS DE LA LOIRE

Baule 176
Vendôme 188
Tavers 188
Bracieux 178
Blois 177
Chitenay 181
Vouvray 189
Chissay-en-Touraine 181
Tours
Bléré 177
Pontlevoy 187
Azay-le-Rideau 176
Chenonceaux 180
Montbazon 184
Noyers-sur-Cher 186
Chinon 181
Saché 187
Veuil 189
L'Ile Bouchard 182
CENTRE
Cussay 182
Buzançais 179
Levroux 183
Le Petit-Pressigny 186
Châteauroux

POITOU-CHARENTES

Yzeures-sur-Creuse 189

LIMOUSIN

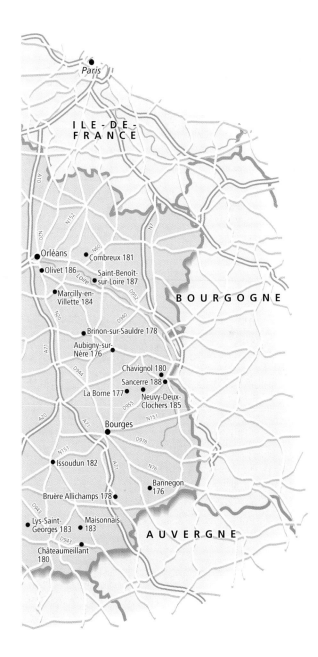

Paris

ILE-DE-
FRANCE

A10

N20

N152

N7

Orléans

Combreux 181

Olivet 186

Loire

Saint-Benoît-
sur-Loire 187

D952

BOURGOGNE

Marcilly-en-
Villette 184

N20

D940

A71

Brinon-sur-Sauldre 178

Aubigny-sur-
Nère 176

D944

Chavignol 180

Sancerre 188

La Borne 177

D955

Neuvy-Deux-
Clochers 185

A20

A71

Bourges

N151

D976

A71

N151

Issoudun 182

N76

Bannegon
176

Bruère Allichamps 178

D943

Lys-Saint-
Georges 183

Maisonnais
183

AUVERGNE

D943

Châteaumeillant
180

Aubigny-sur-Nère
◆ La Chaumière € – €€

2 rue Paul-Lasnier, 18700 Aubigny-sur-Nère, Cher
Tel 02 48 58 04 01 Fax 02 48 58 10 31

This pale stone building straddling the corner of a street doesn't give much away, but inside the dining room is gorgeous and oozes country character in the best sense. The pale pink brick of the walls, and the floor tiles, are beautifully highlighted by the deep coral and terracotta furnishings. The high ceilings make it very airy, and part of the rear wall has been glazed so there's lots of natural daylight. All the menus are tempting but the 17 euro (as we went to press) *menu du marché* (not available on Sundays or public holidays) is very good value. Everything is carefully prepared and presented, with the emphasis on fresh local produce.

CLOSED Sun dinner, Mon Sept–June; last week Aug, Feb
CARDS MC, V

Azay-le-Rideau
◆ L' Aigle d'Or € – €€€

10 rue Adelaide-Riche, 37190 Azay-le-Rideau, Indre-et-Loire
Tel 02 47 45 24 58 Fax 02 47 45 90 18

The garden here is an unexpected treat – there's no hint of it from the street, but it's a perfect place to eat on a summer's afternoon, in the dappled shade of its trees. You may even be lucky enough to enjoy snatches of an occasional rehearsal drifting on the breeze from the Ecole de Musique next door. Inside the beams are painted in blue-green colour which is traditional in the Touraine, with the stone fireplace well used in cooler months. The *chef-patron* and his wife are from Azay, and both fiercely proud of their region. Theirs is a mainly traditional menu with seasonal changes.

❛ *Faultless gazpacho served with lobster – perfect for a hot summer's afternoon* ❜

CLOSED Sun dinner, Wed; Tue dinner Sep–Jun; Mon dinner Dec–Mar
CARDS MC, V

Bannegon
◆ Auberge du Moulin de Chaméron € – €€ **Fr**

18210 Bannegon, Cher
Tel 02 48 61 84 48 Fax 02 48 61 84 92

Everything is made in the kitchen here – the bread, the aperitif pastries, the ice cream and sorbets, even the salmon is smoked on the premises. This would be an excellent restaurant, even without its picturesque setting, in the heart of *berrichone* Charolais country. The building itself dates back to 1767, and the old mill works can still be seen in a little museum on the upper floors. It's a sophisticated restaurant, which makes inventive use of good local produce, such as the beef, and the goat's cheese, but it still hasn't lost that rustic, cosy feel of being a mill, and the welcome is warm and genuine.

CLOSED Mon and Tue lunch; mid-Nov to Mar
CARDS AE, MC, V

Our traditional French cuisine symbol
So many of our readers enjoy seeking out the genuinely French eating experience that we have used Fr to mark restaurants which offer *cuisine du terroir*, classical French dishes or regional dishes with an emphasis on local ingredients, and traditional recipes.

Baule
◆ Auberge Gourmand € – €€€

RN 152, 45130 Baule, Loiret
Tel 02 38 45 01 02 Fax 02 38 45 03 08

You forget about the main road as soon as you step into either the cool, neutral dining room or on to the peaceful garden terrace, with its lavender, fuchsias and birdsong. Didier Benoit oversees the service, and his brother Gilles is expertly in charge of the kitchen. This is unpretentious cooking that allows all the seasonal flavours to come through, with the sort of attention to detail that has you reaching for the bread to wipe each plate. As for the desserts, they are delicious and original – witness, for example, the *gratinée* of melon with spiced ice cream.

❛ We found this place quite by chance, and spent a leisurely Sunday lunch feeling more and more smug about it ❜

CLOSED Sun and Mon dinner, Wed; one week Aug
CARDS AE, MC, V

Bléré
◆ Le Cheval Blanc
€€ – €€€

place de l'Eglise, 37150 Bléré, Indre-et-Loire
Tel 02 47 30 30 14 Fax 02 47 23 52 80

This 17thC building dominates the square at Bléré, looking like just another hotel until you step inside. The dining rooms are elegant, and the smaller one at the rear is particularly charming, with a medieval patterned wallpaper complementing the traditional stone fireplace and the beamed ceiling. It also overlooks the terrace brimming with flowers, where you can eat on sunny days. The food is a huge draw here – Michel Blériot has a well-deserved reputation (Michelin awards a star). His is a light touch that emphasises the flavours of the local produce, and his talent shines from the very start with a really tasty selection of *amuse bouches*. Make sure you leave room for dessert, which is likely to be a mini work of art.

CLOSED Sun dinner, Mon, Fri lunch except Jul, Aug; Jan to mid-Feb
CARDS AE, DC, MC, V

Blois
◆ L'Orangerie du Château €€ – €€€

1 avenue Jean-Laigret, 41000 Blois, Loir-et-Cher
Tel 02 54 78 05 36 Fax 02 54 78 22 78

You can't really miss this imposing building, with its half-timbered gallery that dates back to the 15th century. What you might not realise, thinking it's just another tourist trap, is that this is regarded as one of the best tables in the area (and has a Michelin star). Food is taken very seriously here, with great emphasis on flavours and using the best of local products – Jean-Marc Molveaux takes care of that, while his wife will make sure you're welcomed properly. The dining rooms are elegant, and the service professionally attentive. It's a place for indulgence, an escape from the hustle and bustle of the tourists outside.

CLOSED Sun dinner, Wed; Mon lunch Easter-Oct, Tue dinner Nov-Easter; mid-Feb to mid-Mar, one week Aug, one week Nov
CARDS MC, V

Blois
◆ Au Rendez-Vous des Pêcheurs
€ – €€€

27 rue du Foix, 41000 Blois, Loir-et-Cher
Tel 02 54 74 67 48 Fax 02 54 74 47 67

A lovely restaurant, which is well regarded throughout the region (and has a Michelin star to prove it). From the outside it doesn't look much, but as soon as you step through the heavy curtains behind the door, you know you have found somewhere special. The decoration is simple and elegant, with literary quotations stencilled on the walls of the rear room, and miniature florists's buckets of fresh flowers on each table. The service is discreetly attentive without being formal, but the food is the real star. Christophe Cosme's cooking is fresh and original, combining beautifully judged flavours with a light modern touch – everything is cooked and served to perfection. Fish is obviously the speciality. The *menu retour du marché* is very good value and changes every day.

CLOSED Sun, Mon lunch; three weeks Aug, early to mid-Jan
CARDS AE, MC, V

La Borne
◆ Epicerie Restaurant Salon de Thés €

La Borne, 18250 Henrichement, Cher
Tel 02 48 26 90 80

If you are after traditional French cuisine, then this is not for you. But if you are in a bohemian mood, and fancy something informal, laid back and well travelled – then you will love this place. The well-stocked grocery, the Salon de Thés and the restaurant are all part of one rambling building. There is only one menu, four course, with a choice of two main courses. Uncomplicated food, with fresh flavours. La Borne has a long tradition of earthenware and ceramics, revived in recent years by artisan potters and artists who have settled here. You might be interested to know that your tea and coffee will be served in a locally made cup. La Borne is on the D22, 1.5 miles (3 km) from Henrichement. The restaurant is signposted from the main road.

✦ Well worth a visit, if only to see what the French make of the cosmopolitan informality ✦

CLOSED Mon
CARDS MC, V

Bracieux
◆ Le Relais de Bracieux
€€ – €€€€

1 avenue de Chambord, 41250 Bracieux, Loir-et-Cher
Tel 02 54 46 41 22 Fax 02 54 46 03 69

A treat: everything – the welcome, the service and the wonderful food – in this former coaching inn, almost halfway between Chambord and Cheverny, is designed to make you feel special. Bernard Robin has a wholly deserved reputation as a master chef, and his essentially regional menus are original and inventive, layered with flavours of fresh, seasonal produce. The weekday *menu déjeuner* at 30 euros (at the time of going to press) is excellent value for this standard of cooking, with dishes such as Sologne white asparagus with mushroom sauce, bream fillet and rhubarb *millefeuille* with strawberry *compôte* and vanilla ice cream. The predominantly deep terracotta dining room overlooks the well cared-for garden.

CLOSED Tue, Wed; Sun dinner, Mon Dec-Mar; mid-Dec to mid-Jan
CARDS AE, DC, MC, V

Brinon-sur-Sauldre
◆ La Solognote €€

18410 Brinon-sur-Sauldre, Cher
Tel 02 48 58 50 29 Fax 02 48 58 56 00

A real hidden gem – be careful or you will drive straight past. It's just another ordinary Sologne red brick building in a perfectly ordinary street from the outside, but once you step inside, you start to notice the details that matter – the original terracotta floor tiles, the polished dark wood, the country doll collection, generous wine glasses on the table, fresh flowers... all in all a delightful ambience, with pretty, countrified bedrooms upstairs should you want to stay. And then there is the food: Dominique Girard is master of his kitchen, and creates memorable, elegant dishes. His wife Andrée is adeptly in charge of providing the warm welcome and making sure you have all you need.

CLOSED Tue, Wed Oct-May; Tue, Wed lunch Jul-Sep; 5 weeks Feb-Mar; one week May; one week Sep
CARDS MC, V

Please send us reports
A guide such as this thrives on reader's reports. If you send us five usable reports, we will send you a free copy of any title in our *Charming Small Hotel Guides* series (see page 241 for France titles in the series).
    The five reports should contain at least two new restaurants; the balance can be comments on restaurants already in the guide. **Send reports to** Charming Restaurant Guides, Duncan Petersen Ltd, 31 Ceylon Road, London W14 OPY.

Bruère Allichamps
◆ Les Tilleuls €– €€ Fr

18200 Bruère Allichamps, Cher
Tel 02 48 61 02 75 Fax 02 48 61 08 41

From the outside Les Tilleuls is a bland modern building, but we make no apologies for including this restaurant, which is beside the river Cher, on the road out to the stunning Abbey de Noirlac. Once inside, Françoise Dauxerre's warm welcome will immediately put you at your ease, and the other serious diners will reassure you that this is an establishment with a reputation for local cooking of a high standard. The menu changes seasonally, but specialities include guinea fowl with *foie gras* and Berry lentils, Ferté grain-fed pigeon and beef tournedos with Menetou Salon red wine sauce.

❨ Great food in the geographical heart of France ❩

Closed Mon; phone for details of other closing times
Cards MC, V

Buzançais
◈ Hermitage €€€ Fr

route d'Argy, 36500 Buzançais, Indre
Tel 02 54 84 03 90 Fax 02 54 02 13 19

Surrounded by a large park on the banks of the river Indre, this lovely old manor house is a simple family hotel with cooking, by Claude Sureau, that is well above average. Rooted in the region, and featuring plenty of Berry specialities, this is sophisticated home cooking: fish such as *terrine de carpe aux lentilles* and *salade d'anguilles*, game in season, and good poultry. Desserts feature *profiteroles au chocolat* and *charlotte au pain d'épices*. Local wines are given prominence on the short, well-judged *carte des vins*.

Closed Sun dinner, Mon Sep-Jun; mid-Sep, early to mid-Jan
Cards MC, V

Looking for somewhere to stay? See page 241.

Chartres
◈ Le Moulin de Ponceau
€€ – €€€

21-23 rue de la Tannerie, 28000 Chartres, Eure-et-Loir
Tel 02 37 35 30 05 Fax 02 37 35 30 12

It's worth booking ahead for a table overlooking the river: the Eure here just under the cathedral is beautiful. The waterside terrace stretches under striped awnings and under an old beamed washhouse, which were once common along here. Specialities include homemade *terrine de foie gras de canard* or *gambas royales*. A restaurant that suits families and couples alike.

Closed Sat lunch, Sun dinner; three weeks Feb
Cards AE, MC, V

Chartres
◈ Le Saint-Hilaire
€€ – €€€ Fr

11 rue du Pont Saint-Hilaire, 28000 Chartres, Eure-et-Loir
Tel 02 37 30 97 57 Fax 02 37 30 97 57

This former winemaker's house has to be *the* place to eat in Chartres. Be sure to book, because there are only eight tables, arranged on two prettily decorated floors. Benoit Pasquier is the second of three brothers to establish a restaurant in the Beuce (you'll have to go to Belgium to complete the hat trick), and he takes cooking seriously. Menus start at a remarkable 15 euros (at the time of going to press), reaching 38 euros for the *menu homard*, and including the exemplary regional *menu l'Eure-et-Loire à table*. The *à la carte* choice is deliberately limited – the emphasis is on fresh, seasonal produce, and Benoit is justifiably proud of his relationship with local producers. There's support for local artists too, with changing exhibitions.

❨ All restaurants should be like this: original, intimate and totally of their region ❩

Closed Sat lunch, Sun, Mon lunch; late Jul to mid-Aug, Christmas to mid-Jan
Cards MC, V

Châteaudun
◈ La Licorne €€ Fr

6 place du 18-Octobre, 28200 Châteaudun, Eure-et-Loir
Tel 02 37 45 32 32

Châteaudun is a convenient stopover en route for the Loire from Chartres, with ample parking within its narrow streets. La Licorne is a fuss-free location for lunch, very popular with locals. Don't be put off by the fact that it's in the main square – its location does not triumph over its warm welcome, and its simple but tasty and unpretentious food. Mme Lavouiray's motherly eye makes sure everything runs smoothly. This is sturdy cooking, and the weekday *petit menu* at 11 euros (at the time of going to press) is excellent value and more than adequate.

CLOSED Tue dinner, Wed
CARDS MC, V

Châteaumeillant
◆ Le Piet à Terre
€ – €€€

*21 rue du Château, 18370
Châteaumeillant, Cher
Tel 02 48 61 41 74 Fax 02 48 61 41 88*

Everything about Le Piet à Terre is designed to attack your senses. The building is dominated by the conservatory room, but that's nothing compared to the minimal but very purple and citrus yellow reception area. Compared to that, the dining room seems fairly plain and simple – it's the food you are here for after all. Thierry Finet's cuisine is locally renowned: innovative, original, modern, created with passion and presented with flair. The herbs and 'forgotten' vegetables are grown by the *auberge's* gardener, and flowers are grown by *grand-père* Piet. Sylvie, Thierry's wife, will make sure you're warmly welcomed.

CLOSED Sun dinner, Mon, Tue lunch; Jan, Feb
CARDS MC, V

Châteauneuf-en-Thymerais
◆ L' Ecritoire € – €€

*43 rue Emile-Vivier, 28170 Châteauneuf-en-Thymerais, Eure-et-Loir
Tel 02 37 51 85 80 Fax 02 37 51 86 87*

A former 16thC *relais de poste*, which became an inn in 1743 and has been called L'Ecritoire since 1745, is today lavishly framed by wistaria and blue shutters, and is the setting for Michelin-starred food. Chef-patron Luc Pasquier comes from a good pedigree – five generations of apiculturists, great uncles who were directors of the Tour d'Argent and Laserre in Paris, and two brothers who also own their own restau-

rants. He's worked as far afield as Egypt and Asia, and spices are used creatively in his cooking. Cumin with salmon in his hands is fusion food without the cliché. The cheeseboard is a delight – 15 or more varieties left on the table for you to help yourself.

CLOSED Sun dinner, Mon
CARDS AE, DC, MC, V

Chavignol
◆ La Côte des Monts Damnés € – €€

*Chavignol, 18300 Sancerre, Cher
Tel 02 48 54 01 72 Fax 02 48 54 14 24*

Goat's cheese and Sancerre wine are both good reasons to visit Chavignol, 2 miles (4 km) from Sancerre, but once you've eaten here, there will be plenty of other delights on the menu that will bring you hurrying back. The decoration is fresh and elegant, and the cooking, although drawing heavily on local produce, is refined, inventive and beautifully presented. Jean-Marc Bourgeois has perfect judgement when it comes to flavours, and you won't get better value for money anywhere in the region. There is a list of courses, and you can choose as many as you want up to five. Don't skip the cheese: you won't get a better opportunity to taste the different local *crottins de Chavignol*.

CLOSED Sun, Tue dinner, Wed; Feb
CARDS MC, V.

Chenonceaux
◆ Le Bon Laboureur
€€ – €€€

*6 rue du Docteur-Bretonneau, Indre-et-Loire
Tel 02 47 23 90 02 Fax 02 47 23 82 01*

Here is a former post-house that dates back to 1786. Today it looks very much the country inn, covered in creeper, which seems to insulate it from the hustle and bustle at the nearby château. Inside there is an elegant mix of old and new furnishings, with bright sunny colours in the bar and calm neutrals in the main dining room. You can also eat, on sunny days, in the pretty garden at the back. Traditional gourmet cooking is on offer, with specialities such as roast pigeon with figs and spiced bread, and, more unusually, roast lamb with *croquettes* of goat's cheese flavoured with curry.

CLOSED Tue, Thu, Sat lunch; mid-Nov to mid-Dec, mid-Jan to mid-Feb
CARDS MC, V

Chinon
◆ Au Chapeau Rouge
€ – €€€

Hôtel France, 49 place du Général-de-Gaulle, 37500 Chinon, Indre-et-Loire
Tel 02 47 98 08 08 Fax 02 47 98 37 03

Tucked away in the far corner of the square, it's the Art Nouveau lettering on the blind and sign that will first catch your eye, but there was a restaurant called Chapeau Rouge here as far back as 1577. Its 16thC origins are now evoked by the bare stone wall, and the occasional tapestry. It's part of the Hôtel de France, which also runs the busy (at lunchtimes) bistro next door. Far better to sit here, if you have the time, feeling superior and enjoying the excellent value *menu découverte.*

❛ *Flavours were well matched – fresh tomato coulis with avocado mousse, braised celery with scorpion fish* ❜

CLOSED Sun dinner, Mon; phone for further details
CARDS AE, DC, MC, V

Chissay-en-Touraine
◆ Château de Chissay
€€

41400 Chissay-en-Touraine, Montrichard, Loir-et-Cher
Tel 02 54 32 32 01 Fax 02 54 32 43 80

You are in château country, so why not dine in splendour. This one is the real thing, dating back to Charles VII and Louis XI – even de Gaulle stayed here in 1940. It's a little formal, but the welcome is genuine, even if you are hot and sticky from a long car journey. The dining room is full of character, with a Gothic vaulted ceiling, oak panelling, and windows that overlook the Italianate

inner courtyard, where you can take your pre-dinner drinks or your coffee. The cuisine is traditional, with fine judgement when it comes to combining flavours such as *mille-feuille* with veal and figs served with a caramelised *jus*. The lunchtime (except Sunday) *menu d'affaires* is good value.

CLOSED Mon, Tue lunch; mid-Nov to mid-Mar
CARDS AE, MC, V

Chitenay
◆ Auberge du Centre
€ – €€ **Fr**

place de l'Eglise, 41120 Chitenay, Loir-et-Cher
Tel 02 54 70 42 11 Fax 02 54 70 35 03

In the evenings – in particular in high season – this pretty, fresh-looking blue, yellow and white dining room is full of international tourists, but don't let that put you off. The restaurant has an excellent reputation, concentrating on dishes that are simple and uncomplicated, using local produce and fresh flavours. Even at the busiest times, the young team are unfailingly cheerful, warm and courteous and will do their best to help. Don't overdo the cheese – the dessert portions are generous.

CLOSED Sun dinner, Mon winter; Feb; phone for further details
CARDS AE, MC, V

Combreux
◆ L' Auberge de Combreux € – €€ **Fr**

35 route de Gâtinais, 45530 Combreux, Loiret
Tel 02 38 46 89 89 Fax 02 38 59 36 19

A delightful welcome – warmth is at the heart of what Madame does here. This is Sologne hunting country, so the season extends well into the autumn, when the fire is lit in the bar, and candles are placed on the tables in the cosy winter dining room. This is a 19thC coaching inn that has lost none of its character. In the summer you eat in the conservatory or the garden in fine weather. Menus are available in English, Dutch and German (although the translations are fairly original) – they have a regular international clientele stopping on their way south as well as a good local reputation. This is traditional cooking, specialising in game in season.

◆ Blink and you'll miss Combreux, but you'll be very glad you spotted this auberge ◆

CLOSED Mon lunch, mid-Dec to mid-Jan
CARDS AE, MC, V

Cussay
◆ Auberge du Pont Neuf € – €€€ Fr

37420 Cussay, Indre-et-Loire
Tel 02 47 59 66 37 Fax 02 47 59 67 53

Arrive early so that you can sit and drink your aperitif in the bar with the locals. Williams Gellot makes sure his small team extends a warm welcome, and he takes pride in preparing traditional cuisine with the best produce the market has to offer. Specialities include fish and shellfish, but the menu changes every two months. There is a small garden, but you may prefer the calm of the pretty pale green and pink dining room, because the *auberge* is on the main road. The lunchtime *menu confiance* is perfect for a stopover en route.

CLOSED Wed winter; Nov, Feb
CARDS MC, V

L' Ile Bouchard
◆ Auberge de L'Ile € – €€€ Fr

37220 l'Ile Bouchard, Indre-et-Loire
Tel 02 47 58 51 07

You will find this restaurant on the island as you cross the river: don't be put off by the huge painted Auberge de L'Ile as you cross the Vienne – the restaurant is far more sophisticated than the sign would have you believe. Inside, the cool, calm decoration is lifted by brightly painted contemporary art, and the terrace overlooking the river is a perfect vantage point from which to watch the world go by. Pierre Koniecko is fiercely proud of his wine list, but his traditional

cooking, served with a modern light touch is also worth a mention. Only fresh local produce is used, the chef taking over "where the *paysan* left off" – you won't find asparagus out of season here. Pierre's wife makes sure the service is attentive and professional.

CLOSED Tue, Wed; three weeks Jan, Feb
CARDS MC, V

Illiers-Combray
◆ Le Florent € – €€€ Fr

place du Marché, 28120 Illiers-Combray,
Eure-et-Loir
Tel 02 37 24 10 43 Fax 02 37 24 11 78

Don't worry about the 1970s glazed exterior when you arrive at Le Florent (just off the central place du Marché, by the church). This former hardware shop (look for the old photographs at the far end of the main room) was modernised before Elisabeth and Herve Priolet established a restaurant here ten years ago, and of the orignal shop front only the Art Nouveau tiles remain. Inside, pastel colours including pale green panelling give a light, airy feel, with the original black and white floor tiles adding character, and linking the two dining rooms. Takeaway *madeleines* (order at the beginning of your meal) are the most obvious reference to A La Recherche du Temps Perdue and Marcel Proust. The author spent his childhood holidays close by in the house of his aunt Léonie (now a museum).

◆ We were happily surprised by the quality of the food ◆

CLOSED Sun dinner, Mon, Wed dinner
CARDS AE. MC, V

Issoudun
◆ La Cognette € – €€€€

2 boulevard de Stalingrad, Issoudun,
Indre
Tel 02 54 03 59 59 Fax 02 54 03 13 03

This restaurant was immortalised by Balzac in La Rabouilleuse, and once you step inside you begin to believe you have been transported back to those days. The decoration is an amazing mix of Empire, Restoration and Louis-Philippe styles –

crammed full with antiques, dripping with luxurious curtains and drapes. This in itself is enough of a reason to eat here – that the food has such a high reputation (Michelin star, 16/20 from Gault Millau) is a bonus. Jean-Jacques Daumy 'Jeune Restaurateur d'Europe', cooks with passion. The cheapest menu (26 euros at the time of going to press) is very good value: well judged flavours, imaginatively put together. You will find La Cognette near the large market square. The hotel is signposted, although the restaurant is in a separate building a little further along the boulevard de Stalingrad.

❢ I'd choose to eat here in the evening, just to enjoy the candlelight casting shadows on the draped ceiling ❡

Closed Sun dinner, Mon, Tue Oct–Jun; Jan
Cards AE, DC, MC, V

Our price bands
Rather than giving actual prices (which are prone to change) we indicate the cost of a three-course meal for one person, without wine, by means of price bands. They are as follows: € under 30 euros €€ 30-50 euros €€€ over 50 euros. Where we give more than one price band, for example €– €€€, this indicates that in that restaurant a meal can be had at a range of prices. As well as the cost of *prix fixe* menus, our price bands also take into account the cost of an average selection from the *à la carte* menu.

Levroux
◆ Relais Saint-Jean
€ – €€

34 rue Nationale, 36110 Levroux, Indre
Tel 02 54 35 81 56 Fax 02 54 35 36 09

Here is an old coaching inn, decked out with flower-filled window boxes. Patron Claude Patry has gained a reputation as one of the best chefs in the area, and his wife Evelyne provides a *sympatique* welcome. Specialities include scallop ravioli with a *cep* sauce, fillet of beef with *foie*

gras, and a heavenly chocolate dessert. All the flavours are finely judged. A meal you are likely to remember.

Closed Sun dinner, Wed; Tue dinner Oct–May; mid–Sep to mid–Oct, three weeks Feb
Cards AE, MC, V

Lys-Saint-Georges
◆ Auberge La Forge
€ Fr

Le Bourg, 36230 Lys-Saint-Georges, Indre
Tel 02 54 30 81 68 Fax 02 532 49 80 09

Even if it were not the only restaurant in this little village of barely 200 inhabitants, La Forge would still be *the* place to eat. The village itself is delightful, with its own 15thC château, and the restaurant's summer garden, filled with birdsong, is the perfect place to enjoy the tranquil surroundings. In winter, a fire is lit inside, where you can appreciate the work of local artists arranged on the walls beneath sturdy beams. The simple, classic dishes on the menu change with the seasons. There is a good selection of cheeses to finish, and a kindly-priced wine list to accompany.

Closed Mon, Tue; early to mid–Jan, mid–Sep to mid–Oct
Cards MC, V

Maisonnais
◆ Prieuré d'Orsan €€

Les Jardins du Prieuré Notre-Dame d'Orsan, 18170 Maisonnais, Cher
Tel 02 48 56 27 50 Fax 02 48 56 39 64

Heaven is a good word to describe this lovely, original restaurant because it's in the restored medieval garden of a former priory. Everything is designed with the contemplative spirit of the place in mind, so although the menu is a touch expensive, you are buying into a soothing philosophy as well. The dining room is a vast restored space of stone and pale wood, with elegant Lloyd Loom chairs in dusky pink and green, and perfect service. There is only one menu, with two prices for two or three courses, and a couple of choices for each. The emphasis is on fresh fruit, vegetables and herbs from the garden. As well as the restaurant, a bookshop and reception centre, there are seven stylish, simple bedrooms overlooking the garden. You will find the Jardins du Prieuré Notre-Dame d'Orsan on the D65 between Lignières and Le Châtelet, well-signposted from all directions.

❜ Bring a book and spend the afternoon in a quiet corner of the gardens – they are so peaceful ❜

CLOSED Nov-Apr
CARDS MC, V

Marcilly-en-Villette
◆ Auberge de la Croix Blanche € – €€ **Fr**

118 place de l'Eglise, 45240 Marcilly-en-Villette, Loiret
Tel 02 38 76 10 14 Fax 02 38 76 10 67

This *auberge* dates back to the 17th century, and back then you could also have had your hair cut here. Keep an eye out for the original sign, which is still above the welcoming fireplace in the reception hall, as you step into the cosy dining room, with its traditional terracotta tiled floor. Chef Christophe Pinguet serves up traditional *cuisine du terroir*, with specialities such as game in season. There is also a nice selection of salads on the à la carte menu, such as *langoustines* with home smoked salmon and avocado mousse with lime. They have a motto of well-being and conviviality, reflected in the pleasant service.

CLOSED never
CARDS MC, V

Montbazon
◆ Domaine de la Tortinière €€ – €€€

Les Gués de Veigné, 37250 Montbazon, Indre-et-Loire
Tel 02 47 34 35 00 Fax 02 47 65 95 70

Another restaurant that is popular with locals. In fact, it is *the* venue for weddings in the summer, so make sure you book well in advance for weekends. It's well worth it, for this is a dream of a place. Don't be put off by photographs – this is *château sans*

snob, elegance without formality, and one of the warmest welcomes in the Loire. The restaurant , in the *orangerie* of this 19thC *château-hôtel*, is pretty in shades of yellow ochre and red, and the terrace has wonderful far reaching views south. Freddy Lefebvre's cuisine is classic, but inventive, relying heavily on the best local produce. La Tortinière is just north of Montbazon, signposted from the village of Les Gués.

CLOSED mid-Dec to Mar
CARDS MC, V

Montbazon
◆ Le Moulin Fleurie €€ – €€€ **Fr**

route de Ripault, 37250 Veigné, Montbazon, Indre-et-Loire
Tel 02 47 26 01 12 Fax 02 47 34 04 71

Very popular locally, this is a 16thC watermill in a perfect setting by the banks of the Indre. Mme Chaplin is a hospitable hostess, while her husband's skills in the kitchen do not disappoint. Enjoy the view from the peaceful terrace while you sip your aperitif (meals are served in the pretty dining room only) and study the menu. It changes seasonally but specialities include Loire whitebait, zander, *andouillette de Montbazon*, *rillons* and *Géline*, the local poultry. Make sure you also cast an eye over the wine list – Loire wines predominate of course, but with incredible vintages. Whatever your date of birth, you'll probably find it here.

CLOSED Mon and Thu lunch; Sun dinner winter; last week Dec, Feb to mid-Mar
CARDS AE, MC, V

Montigny-sur-Avre
◆ Moulin des Planches €€ – €€€

28270 Montigny-sur-Avre, Verneuil, Eure-et-Loir
Tel 02 37 48 25 97 Fax 02 37 48 35 63

The river Avre, which lies beside this beautifully restored watermill, once marked the boundary between Normandy and France, and was the site of many battles. As a consequence the original 11thC mill had to be rebuilt many times, but this is nowadays a truly peaceful and beautiful corner of the countryside. Inside, you will find a friendly welcome and traditional cooking in a smart dining room with views down to the river. The owners took two years to restore the building, lovingly preserving oak beams and exposed brickwork. A popular spot for weddings.

CLOSED Sun dinner, Mon; Jan
CARDS MC, V

Please send us reports
A guide such as this thrives on reader's reports. If you send us five usable reports, we will send you a free copy of any title in our *Charming Small Hotel Guides* series (see page 241 for France titles in the series).

The five reports should contain at least two new restaurants; the rest can be comments on restaurants already in the guide.
1 Tell us about your experiences in restaurants already in this guide.
2 Send us new reports. New reports should give the following information:
- **Region** – City, town, village or neaest village.
- **Name of restaurant** – Please double check the spelling, it's surprisingly easy to make a mistake.
- **Address** – including *département*
- **Telephone number** – plus fax and e-mail if available. Double check this information.
- **Objective description** – Try to explain simply why it should be in the guide. Remember that the guide is very selective - our entries are those one-in-five places that combine
- interesting food with
- character and charm, in the building, the setting or both.
The guide hates tourist traps, and pretentious, dressed-up food. We like places where the French go.

We favour places in the lower and middle price bands but there are plenty of expensive places that have our qualities, and we list those too.
- **Diner's comments** – These should be short, personal comments on features that strike you. They can be your comments, or others'.
- **Closing times**
- **Credit cards accepted**

Don' t forget to date your report and add your name and address.
Send reports to Charming Restaurant Guides, Duncan Petersen Publishing, 31 Ceylon Road, London W14 OPY.

Neuvy-Deux-Clochers
◆ Auberge La Vouivre

18250 Neuvy-Deux-Clochers, Cher
Tel 02 48 79 42 83 Fax 02 48 28 01 87

This little village restaurant takes its name from a sculpture of a man-eating viper in the 12thC tower in the village. Tradition has it that *la vouivre* lived in the Berry marshes. Lunchtimes, the set *menu du jour* served in the bar is the main business, but menus in the fresh and simply decorated dining room give the young chef an opportunity to be a little more adventurous (20 euros for four courses as we went to press) – goat's cheese tart with *lardons*, tomatoes and figs, red snapper with raspberry b*eurre blanc*, and a tempting choice of homemade desserts. This a a great find – an imaginatively-run restaurant with an enthusiastic young couple at the helm.

CLOSED dinner winter
CARDS none

---

charmingsmallhotels.co.uk
Visit Duncan Petersen's travel website, the best online search tool for places to stay that combine character and charm. Currently features Britain, France, Italy and Ireland, with other destinations being continuously added.

Nogent-le-Roi
◆ Relais des Remparts

2 place du Marché aux Légumes, 28210 Nogent-le-Roi, Eure-et-Loir
Tel 02 37 51 40 47 Fax 02 37 51 047

The inn must have once stood near the ramparts of this medieval market town, but all that remains now is the nearby moat. Pale yellow walls create a calm interior, which distracts you nicely from the passing traffic. A popular meeting place for local businessmen, the restaurant offers a very good value lunchtime menu, which might feature a well-judged *terrine de maison*, and a refreshing strawberry soup flavoured with mint for dessert. Children under 12 are treated with respect: half portions for half price of anything on the menu. Classic cuisine with an emphasis on seasonal produce.

Closed Sun and Tue dinner, Wed; two weeks Aug, two weeks Jan-Feb
Cards AE, DC, MC, V

Our traditional French cuisine symbol
So many of our readers enjoy seeking out the genuinely French eating experience that we have used Fr to mark restaurants which offer *cuisine du terroir*, classical French dishes or regional dishes with an emphasis on local ingredients, and traditional recipes.

Noyers-sur-Cher
◆ Hostellerie Le Clos du Cher €–€€

route de Saint-Aignan, 41140 Noyers-sur-Cher, Loir-et-Cher
Tel 02 54 75 00 03 Fax 02 54 75 03 79

First impressions are of a rather stately 19thC *maison de maître*, quite close to a busy road junction. But the restaurant is on the other side of the inner courtyard, and a delight. There are rustic touches – beams, a Sologne brick fireplace, some antique furniture – but otherwise it's the cheerful but rather sophisticated yellow decoration and bright floral curtains that will catch your eye. And to complete the picture, there is the superb cooking. The *menu d'affaires* (weekdays) is very good value, with everything cooked fresh to order – the warm Berry green lentil salad stands out.

❮ My profiteroles put all the others I've ever had to shame: totally tasty and the best value anywhere ❯

Closed Sun and Wed dinner, Thu mid-Oct to Apr; Jan to mid-Feb
Cards AE, MC, V

Our price bands
€ under 30 euros €€ 30-50 Euros
€€€ over 50 euros for a menu

Olivet
◆ Le Rivage €€

635 rue de la Reine-Blanche, 45160 Olivet, Loire
Tel 02 38 66 02 93 Fax 02 38 56 31 11

Position and food are the keys to this ordinary-looking hotel. It's in a peaceful spot on the banks of the Loiret, with a riverside terrace shaded by trees. The cooking of the chatty, friendly chef-patron Jean-Pierre Bereaud is regionally-based and features local produce: fish, game and the tender vegetables that thrive so well in the region's mild climate. You might start with pan-fried lamb's sweetbreads with warm vegetables served with carrot and orange *jus*, go on to striped mullet in layered cabbage with bone marrow served with Tarbes beans, and finish with a selection of iced red fruit with Vouvray wine and fresh thyme *cristalline*. Loire wines accompany.

Closed Sat lunch; Christmas to mid-Jan
Cards AE, DC, MC, V

● *For somewhere to eat in Orléans, try Eugène (24 rue Sainte-Anne; tel 02 38 53 82 64) and La Promenade (1 rue Adolphe-Crespin; tel 02 38 81 12 12). Both are reliable and inexpensive.*

Le Petit-Pressigny
◆ La Promenade €–€€

37350 Le Petit-Pressigny, Indre-et-Loire
Tel 02 47 94 93 52 Fax 02 47 91 06 03

This building used to belong to chef-patron Jacky Dallais' father, and was the village hotel-bar and smithy until he opened his restaurant here 18 years ago, and slowly set about making his establishment the very best in the area. The interior is contemporary, with exhibitions of remakably good art by local artists. Jacky's near-faultlesss cooking is refreshingly original – chocolate sorbet with olive oil and pineapple served with red pepper sauce feature among the desserts, but dishes change with the seasons. The *menu du marché* at 23 euros (at the time of going to press) is incredible value.

It was like driving to the heart of France to get there, and we didn't want to leave. We began to wish we lived close enough to eat there every week

CLOSED Sun dinner, Mon, Tue lunch (and Tue dinner winter); two weeks Sep-Oct, Jan
CARDS MC, V

Please send us reports
A guide such as this thrives on reader's reports. If you send us five usable reports, we will send you a free copy of any title in our *Charming Small Hotel Guides* series (see page 241 for France titles in the series).

The five reports should contain at least two new restaurants; the balance can be comments on restaurants already in the guide. **Send reports to** Charming Restaurant Guides, Duncan Petersen Ltd, 31 Ceylon Road, London W14 OPY.

Pontlevoy
◆ Restaurant-Hôtel de l' Ecole €€ – €€€

12 route de Montrichard, 41400 Pontlevoy, Loir-et-Cher
Tel 02 54 32 50 30 Fax 02 54 32 33 58

This much appreciated local restaurant, which was a former posthouse, not a school, stands on the main road in the proud village of Pontlevoy – birthplace of Auguste Poulain, the chocolate-maker, and site of an airport in 1910. The four course *menu à quatre saisons* is a snip, featuring only the chef's seasonal choice of dishes. This is a

sophisticated take on traditional cooking, prettily presented in generous portions and expertly served.

CLOSED Sun dinner, Mon
CARDS MC, V

Saché
◆ Auberge du XII Siècle
€ – €€€ **Fr**

Saché, 37190 Azay-le-Rideau, Indre-et-Loire
Tel 02 47 26 88 77 Fax 02 47 26 88 21

This is the place to eat in the area, one of the oldest inns in France, dating back to the 12th century, still with original beams and crooked half-timbered walls. Balzac used to drink here, when he stayed at the nearby château, which is now a museum. Inside the dining room, set down on every available surface, fresh flowers almost tumble out of their vases. You can also eat in the pretty garden. There are two *chefs de cuisine* – Zavier Aubrun takes charge of the fish, and Thierry Jiminez looks after the meat. This is excellent food, modern and original interpretations of traditional flavours – and incredible value.

I want to come back here for Christmas, for Easter, for my birthday...

CLOSED Mon, Tue lunch; three weeks Jan, first week Jun, first week Sep,
CARDS MC, V

Fr French regional or classical French dishes on menu.

Saint-Benoît-sur-Loire
◆ Le Grand Saint-Benoît
€ – €€€ **Fr**

7 place Saint-André, 45730 Saint-Benoît-sur-Loire, Loiret
Tel 02 38 35 11 92 Fax 02 38 35 13 79

The regualr clientele love this neat stone building with a correspondingly simple but sophisticated interior, with pale wood and deep terracotta walls. The weekday menu is excellent value, but you get a better idea of the chef's inventive touch with traditional cuisine by choosing the next option (24 euros at the time of going to press) with dishes such as roast zander with Chinon wine sauce, or veal chops with a *jus* flavoured with coriander to tempt you. The service is quiet and discreet, and the ambience is one of quiet satisfaction.

CLOSED Mon, Sat lunch, Sun dinner; one week Aug-Sep, mid-Dec to mid-Jan
CARDS MC, V

Our price bands
Rather than giving actual prices (which are prone to change) we indicate the cost of a three-course meal for one person, without wine, by means of price bands. They are as follows: € under 30 euros €€ 30-50 euros €€€ over 50 euros. Where we give more than one price band, for example €– €€€, this indicates that in that restaurant a meal can be had at a range of prices. As well as the cost of *prix fixe* menus, our price bands also take into account the cost of an average selection from the *à la carte* menu.

Sancerre
◆ Auberge Joseph Mellot
€ – €€

16 Nouvelle Place, 18300 Sancerre, Cher
Tel 02 48 54 20 53 Fax 02 48 54 20 53

Yes, this place is on the main square in Sancerre, and yes, it is very popular with tourists, but it's worth a visit for its *assiette du pays*. This is a way of promoting the produce of the area – here mainly goat's cheese – by offering a choice of main courses served with the wine or cider of the region. You can eat, for example, a warm goat's cheese salad with a glass of Sancerre, followed by a pear poached in red Sancerre for 10 euros (at the time of going to press). It isn't complicated food, but if you don't want to spend a long time over lunch, it's not a bad deal. Ask for a table inside – it's delightfully

rustic, dripping with antique country tools.

CLOSED Sun dinner, Mon
CARDS MC, V

Fr French regional or classical French dishes on menu.

Tavers
◆ La Tonnellerie € – €€

12 rue des Eaux-Bleues, Tavers, 45190 Beaugency, Loiret
Tel 02 38 44 68 15 Fax 02 38 44 10 01

La Tonnellerie, long-featured in our *Charming Small Hotel Guide to France*, was formerly a *maison de vin*, and wines, especially those of the Loire, still have an important role to play in the restaurant, acknowledged as the best place to eat in the Beaugency area. Inside there are huge vases of scented flowers, and attractive furnishings in warm colours. In summer, you can eat in the beautiful flower-filled garden, under the shade of the chestnut tree, or the parasols. The food is sophisticated, following the season, with something to tempt everyone: roast monkfish with saffron, veal with onion marmalade, *millefeuille* with strawberries and *praline* from Montargis.

❛ La Tonnellerie made a perfect stopover en route south last summer – a good meal and a comfortable bed in charming surroundings ❜

CLOSED Sat lunch, Mon; Jan-Mar
CARDS AE, MC, V

Vendôme
◆ Auberge de la Madeleine € – €€

6 place de la Madeleine, Vendôme, Loir-et-Cher
Tel 02 54 77 20 79 Fax 02 34 80 00 02

Vendôme is a charming town, entwined in the arms of the Loir, with many old buildings. This *auberge* stands on the place de la Madeleine in the old town with a pretty courtyard garden on the banks of the river and an attractive pink and white dining room for cooler days. Dishes are creative, with interesting vegetables – stuffed mushrooms, marrow in savoury custard – beautifully presented. Locals and those in the know flock here.

CLOSED Feb
CARDS MC, V

---

charmingsmallhotels.co.uk
Visit Duncan Petersen's travel website, the best online search tool for places to stay that combine character and charm. Currently features Britain, France, Italy and Ireland, with other destinations being continuously added.

Veuil
◆ Auberge Saint-Fiacre
€ – €€

Le Bourg, 36600 Veuil, Valençay, Indre
Tel 02 54 40 32 78 Fax 02 54 54 40 35 66

In a delightful flower-filled village, this is a lovely 17thC inn on the banks of a stream. In summer you can dine in the garden, under the shade of chestnut trees, while in winter the fire is lit in the cosy, rustic dining room, creating a warm atmosphere. Menus are changed seasonally, but the emphasis remains on light, tasty cooking. Specialities include apple with Valençay cheese and Berry honey sauce, pan-fried escalope of *foie gras* with figs, and a moist fig and almond tart with homemade vanilla ice cream.

CLOSED Sun dinner, Mon
CARDS MC, V

Vouvray
◆ Le Grand Vatel
€ – €€€

8 avenue Brulé, 37210 Vouvray, Indre-et-Loire
Tel 02 47 52 70 32 Fax 02 47 52 74 52

Teamwork is at the heart of this favourite restaurant. Frédéric Scicluna-Tulasne takes his cooking very seriously, making his own *foie gras*, and giving local produce

pride of place on the menu. His wife Laurence provides the warm welcome in their classy, high-ceilinged dining room, immediately putting you at ease. The most obvious local produce of course is Vouvray wines – there are two whole pages of them on the list, although maybe the easiest way to get to know them is to choose the *menu dégustation*, which includes a different glass of Vouvray with every course, from the *moelleux* (served with *foie gras*) through to the *méthode traditionelle*. There are other menus too – all representing superb value.

CLOSED Sun dinner, Mon
CARDS MC, V

Our traditional French cuisine symbol
So many of our readers enjoy seeking out the genuinely French eating experience that we have used Fr to mark restaurants which offer *cuisine du terroir*, classical French dishes or regional dishes with an emphasis on local ingredients, and traditional recipes.

Yzeures-sur-Creuse
◆ La Promenade
€ – €€ **Fr**

1 place du 11 Novembre, 37290 Yzeures-sur-Creuse, Indre-et-Loire
Tel 02 47 91 49 00 Fax 02 47 94 46 12

Here is a real village inn with a lovely dining room. In the heat of summer you can enjoy the coolness of the stone walls, and in winter, the warmth of the 18thC fireplace. The building was originally a coaching inn, but had fallen into disuse. It wasn't until Mme Geniève Bussereau bought it in 1978, and completed restoration, that it once again began to welcome travellers. The cooking is traditional, with great emphasis on seasonal produce, and using the best the market has to offer. Everything is proudly homemade, even the bread, and you are warned you may have to wait while your dessert is prepared. There is a vegetarian dish available on the à la carte menu.

CLOSED Mon winter, Tue: mid-Jan to mid-Feb
CARDS MC, V

ILE-DE-FRANCE

CENTRE

BOURGOGNE

AUVERGNE

Auxerre

Nitry 198

Mailly-le-Château 197

L'Isle-sur-Serein 196

Quarré-les-Tombes 200

Oulon 199

Ouroux-en-Morvan 199

Nevers 198

Poisson 199

Charolles 195

BOURGOGNE

J ust south-west of Paris, and en route for the south, Burgundy is richly endowed. Apart from its famous wines and cuisine, it has beautiful countryside, historic buildings (at Vézélay, Dijon, Fontenay, Beaune, Ancy-le-Franc to name but a few) and a network of delightful waterways and canals. Côte d'Or includes Beaune and the regional capital, Dijon, and the famous Côte d'Or vineyards in between. Saône-et-Loire stretches south to Macon, covering the Côte Challonais and Côte Maconnais vineyards and, to the west, the pastoral Brionnais region with its distinctive churches and Charollais cattle. Yonne includes Auxerre, Chablis, Vézélay and Avallon, while the quiet *département* of Nièvre has Nevers as its main town, surrounded by tranquil, unspoilt countryside. In the centre of Burgundy lies the Morvan, a region of forests, hills and lakes.

Our chief Bourgogne contributor is Martin Raeburn, a wholesaler of top French and Italian wines. He can arrange wine tastings, organize gastronomic visits around Bourgogne, or find that bottle you have been looking for. Be sure to ring ahead for an appointment: Amadeus Wines / Wine Portfolio Management 2 Petite rue St Nicolas, 21200 Beaune Tel 03 80 22 51 52 Fax 03 80 22 33 44

CHAMPAGNE-ARDENNE

Dijon 196
Vougeot 201
Gevrey-Chambertin 196
Ladoix-Serrigny 197
Auvillars-sur-Saône 192
Arnay-le-Duc 192
Beaune 192 193
FRANCHE-COMTE
Chagny 193 194
Saint-Gervais-en-Vallière 201
Mercurey 198
Rully 200
Mellecey 197
Chalon-sur-Saône 194
La Roche-Vineuse 200
Macon 197
RHONE-ALPES

Arnay-le-Duc
◆ Chez Camille €︎ – €︎€︎€︎

1 pl Edouard-Herriot, 21230 Arnay-le-Duc,
Côte-d'Or
Tel 03 80 90 01 38 Fax 03 80 90 04 64

This quaint, and slightly eccentric, village
is proud of its gastronomic heritage. The
Maison Régionale des Arts de la Table has
an exhibition on the culinary art from March
to November, and once a year the 'Confrérie
de la Poule au Pot' ('boiled chicken brother-
hood') meet at Arnay-le-Duc to promote the
cuisine of the region. The town's main claim
to fame, though, is that the largest ever *jambon persillé* (ham with parsley, in aspic) was
prepared here and is featured in *The
Guinness Book of Records*. Amongst the
spires and turrets of this historic town you
will find Chez Camille. The dining room is in
a conservatory, with wicker chairs, a jungle
of plants and green trellis archways. To one
side is the kitchen, open to view and adjoining the *pâtisserie*. "It's interesting for the
guests to see the kitchen staff at work," says
chef Armand Poinsot, "and just as interesting for the staff to see the guests." His team
appears to be faultless: one feels he has per-
fected the art of running a traditional
French restaurant. The waitresses wear long
white aprons and floral skirts, the food is
delicious, the service smooth. From the
three-course Menu Bandoit, the cheapest
option, you might try *jambon persillé maison* for a starter, *escalope de saumon au
beurre d'echalotes* for a main, and *fruits
rôtis en tartes paysannes* for dessert. M.
Poinsot makes good use of local produce and
traditional recipes, such as in his *raviole
ouverte d'escargots de Bourgogne sauce
mousseuse au beurre de persil* or the *estouffade de boeuf à la Bourguignon*. Children
are truly welcome here and can stay in your
room and eat for free.

Closed never
Cards AE, DC, MC, V

Auvillars-sur-Saône
◆ Auberge de l'Abbaye
€︎ – €︎€︎

*route de Seurre, 21250, Auvillars-sur-
Saône, Côte-d'Or*
Tel 03 80 26 97 37 Fax 03 80 26 92 25

The Auberge is in a beautiful spot, a short
walk from Citeaux Abbey, home of the
Cistercian order. Chef Jean-Michel
Réchard's repertoire includes an excellent
veal and chicken pie, spiced bread *terrine*
and bread and butter pudding. Exceptional
value for money. Children can eat for just
under 10 euros.

Closed Wed; Sun and Tue evening; 1 week July, 28 Aug
– 3 Sept; Feb holidays
Cards MC, V

---

charmingsmallhotels.co.uk
Visit Duncan Petersen's travel website, the
best online search tool for places to stay
that combine character and charm.
Currently features Britain, France, Italy
and Ireland, with other destinations being
continuously added.

Beaune
◆ Cave Madeleine €︎ –€︎€︎

*8 rue du Faubourg Madeleine, 21200
Beaune, Côte-d'Or*
Tel 03 80 22 93 30

Don't expect too much privacy during
your meal in this place. Long wooden
tables adorn this wine cellar. You'll undoubtedly be sat next to someone you've never
met in your life. The menu is classic and simple: duck, snails, Charollais steaks, so order
quickly then wander round the place to
choose the wines you're after, which adorn
the walls. Don't neccessarily go for the
Burgundies (try Rhones too as we're not that
far). This is the place for those in search of
ambience, relaxation and unobtrusive
French charm.

Closed Sun
Cards MC, V

Beaune
◆ Le Jardin des
   Remparts €︎ – €︎€︎€︎

10 rue Hôtel-Dieu, 21200 Beaune, Côte-d'Or
Tel 03 80 24 91 00

This Michelin-starred restaurant, run by
the dynamic and imaginative couple, M.

and Madame Chanliaud, boasts fine decoration, a very good wine list and tempting menus. M. Chanliaud is highly imaginative in his cooking. For starters try his raw beef tartar with oysters - divine and surprising, and his fish dishes are superb, his *foie gras* exquisite (with four different choices). The wine list is a tad pricey but don't hesitate on the Village Burgundies from Charlopin, and some premier crus from B Morey if you want to stay on the safe side. In summer try to get a table for lunch in their delightful garden.

❝ Even the toilets are the height of elegance! ❞

CLOSED Sun, Mon
CARDS MC, V

Our price bands
Rather than giving actual prices (which are prone to change) we indicate the cost of a three-course meal for one person, without wine, by means of price bands. They are as follows: € under 30 euros €€ 30-50 euros €€€ over 50 euros. Where we give more than one price band, for example €– €€€, this indicates that in that restaurant a meal can be had at a range of prices. As well as the cost of *prix fixe* menus, our price bands also take into account the cost of an average selection from the *à la carte* menu.

Beaune
◆ Ma Cuisine €

passage St Hélène, 21200 Beaune, Côte-d'Or
Tel 03 80 22 30 22

This restaurant boasts the finest wine list in Beaune and at reasonable prices. Take your time to read it and don't neccessarily stick to Burgundy. Apart from that, the cooking is really splendid, with fresh produce, lovely presentation and plenty to eat. It's done by one of Burgundy's great cooking families (Parra) and has really gone stellar over the last year or so. Try the raw tuna tartar, their salade gourmand, or the pigeon. If you're familiar with the names and faces of France's finest wine producers, you may well see one or two of them across the room from you. The decoration is simple - a mass of empty bottles around the place bearing glo-

rious names. You will be grateful that you can find those same bottles full in the cellar!

CLOSED weekends
CARDS MC, V

Our traditional French cuisine symbol
So many of our readers enjoy seeking out the genuinely French eating experience that we have used Fr to mark restaurants which offer *cuisine du terroir*, classical French dishes or regional dishes with an emphasis on local ingredients, and traditional recipes.

Beaune
◆ Le Petit Paradis €

25 rue du Paradis, 21200 Beaune, Côte-d'Or
Tel 03 80 24 91 00

Anne and Jean-Marie just make this restaurant arguably the best in Beaune. Great food, great ambience (intimate, no chichi) and a couple who you know are living their work. When asked why they didn't expand the operation (there are only about 30 places at the tables), they responded, "We're just fine as we are... don't want to spoil the experience". You'll find this gem is the only restaurant that resembles Beaune, down a backstreet just behind the main zone 'piétone'. A must for those who love food and are in search of restaurants that offer both charm and value for money. Reservations are essential.

CLOSED Mon, Tue; mid-Nov to mid-Dec, 2 weeks March, 1 week Aug
CARDS MC, V

Chagny
◆ L' Amigo €– €€ Fr

12 avenue de la République, 71150 Chagny, Saône-et-Loire
Tel 03 85 91 27 30

With a menu at around the 10 euro mark, this small restaurant, packed with contented locals, is the ideal spot for a quick lunch in town. The service is attentive and always with a smile, even when the ancient coffee machine breaks down. The dishes change every day, depending on what Madame feels like, but be it a fabulous *jambon persillé* or the super-rich, meltingly good *boeuf Bourgignon* you will always be more than content. One regret is that the wine list, which is less good, also depends on Madame.

❝ *Divine content* ❞

CLOSED Mon dinner, Thu
CARDS MC, V

---

charmingsmallhotels.co.uk
Visit Duncan Petersen's travel website, the best online search tool for places to stay that combine character and charm. Currently features Britain, France, Italy and Ireland, with other destinations being continuously added.

Chagny
◆ Lameloise €€€

place d'Armes, 71150 Chagny, Saône-et-Loire
Tel 03 85 87 65 65 Fax 03 85 87 03 57

Chagny is without doubt one of the scruffiest, most workaday and least attractive villages in Burgundy, and it makes a surprising venue for one of the great restaurants of France But then Lameloise began life in a humble way, and has passed from father to son, which is what makes it special. Its roots are still firmly in Burgundian tradition. The shuttered house itself is calm and sophisticated, a haven of low-key luxury. Best, if you can afford it, to stay the night in one of the extremely attractive and comfortable bedrooms, and prepare yourself for the wonderful breakfast the next day, followed, perhaps, by lunch. Jacques Lameloise richly deserves his three Michelin stars for his impeccable, classic food. What to choose? Perhaps the *côte de veau en cocotte* with spring vegetables, or the fried frogs' legs with aubergine. House specialities include ravioli of *escargots de Bourgogne* and pigeon with truffles. Leave room for the wonderful desserts. As for wine, the cellar is as impeccable as the food. They have some bottles – top vintage Jayer, Bonneau and Leflaive for example – that are in the vaults but not on the list. Try charming the *sommelier* if you want one. You can expect to

pay upwards of 150 euros per person excluding wine for dinner. Worth it.

❝ *A must for serious epicureans* ❞

CLOSED Tue and Thu lunch, Wed; mid-Dec to mid-Jan
CARDS AE, DC, MC, V

Chalon-sur-Saône
◆ La Ferme €–€€   Fr

2 rue du Four-des-Chênes, 71100 Chalon-sur-Saône, Saône-et-Loire
Tel 03 85 43 43 95

When you step into La Ferme, you feel you have entered a typical old Bresse farmhouse: scythes and other farm tools hang from old beams, and tables placed side by side to create a warm local atmosphere are covered in simple red-and-white check cloths. Once seated, the good smells from your neighbour's dishes begin to waft over, making you all the more eager to choose, order and eat. There are dishes to suit every budget on the menu, including local classics such as snails (a cloth will be wrapped around your neck to avoid stains in your enthusiasm to mop up the sauce with the delicious crusty house bread). Or try the Bresse chicken breasts cooked in cream – they just melt in your mouth. the wine list is limited but well chosen. Go for the local wines, such as a delicious Macon white 99/2000 from Fichet. La Ferme is in the Saint-Jean-des-Vignes *quartier* of Chalon, near the cemetary.

❝ *If you are a large party, there's a room upstairs seating 20 that can be reserved* ❞

CLOSED Sun
CARDS MC, V

Chalon-sur-Saône
◆ Le Verre Galant
€   Fr

8 place Saint-Vincent, 71100 Chalon-sur-Saône, Saône-et-Loire
Tel 03 85 93 09 87

This delightful informal restaurant is situated in the heart of Chalon, looking up to the magnificent spires of Cathédrale

Saint-Vincent. It is run by husband and wife Didier and Geneviève, who specialise in rich Burgundian dishes. The style is that of a *bistrot à vin*, with intimate tables, comfortable wooden benches and a wine list that overflows with the produce of small producers from all over France. For the local Côtes Chalonnais, it's without doubt the finest wine list in Chalon. Or try a glass of *vin surprise* – if you guess it, you can have it for free. As for the food, hearty stews are served directly at the table from heavy metal pans, or you could try *reniflette*, a *tartiflette* made with Morbier cheese or stewed game. Or *pain dans le groin: tartine de pain paillaisse à la tête de cochon grillée sur salade, le croustillant d'andouillette à la vinairgrette de champignons et les gratins de fromage.*

❢ Our favourite place in Chalon. Ask for a table on the terrace in summer when you book – it gets very full on Friday, market day ❩

Closed Sun, Mon; Easter, Nov
Cards MC, V

Please send us reports

A guide such as this thrives on reader's reports. If you send us five usable reports, we will send you a free copy of any title in our *Charming Small Hotel Guides* series (see page 241 for France titles in the series).

The five reports should contain at least two new restaurants; the rest can be comments on restaurants already in the guide.

1 Tell us about your experiences in restaurants already in this guide.

2 Send us new reports. New reports should give the following information:

- **Region** – City, town, village or neaest village.
- **Name of restaurant** – Please double check the spelling, it's surprisingly easy to make a mistake.
- **Address** – including *département*
- **Telephone number** – plus fax and e-mail if available. Double check this information.
- **Objective description** – Try to explain simply why it should be in the guide. Remember that the guide is very selective - our entries are those one-in-five places that combine

- **interesting food with**
- **character and charm, in the building, the setting or both.**

The guide hates tourist traps, and pretentious, dressed-up food. We like places where the French go.

We favour places in the lower and middle price bands but there are plenty of expensive places that have our qualities, and we list those too.

- **Diner's comments** – These should be short, personal comments on features that strike you. They can be your comments, or others'.
- **Closing times**
- **Credit cards accepted**

Don't forget to date your report and add your name and address.

Send reports to Charming Restaurant Guides, Duncan Petersen Publishing, 31 Ceylon Road, London W14 0PY.

Charolles
◆ Hotel de la Poste
€ – €€€

2 av de la Libération, 71120, Charolles, Saône-et-Loire
Tel 03 85 24 11 32 Fax 03 85 24 05 74

A prime example of a provincial hotel and restaurant doing a sound job. The white-painted building is immaculately maintained, as is the smart bar/salon, and the pale yellow panelled dining room is positively ritzy by small town standards. It is also possible to dine in the flowery internal courtyard. Moustachioed chef-patron Daniel Doucet and his son Frédéric work together in the kitchen. The focus is on fresh local produce, and Charolles is of course at the heart of a region with a reputation for the quality of its beef and veal. There is an excellent choice on the menu – the *côte de boeuf charolais à deux temps* and the croustillant of veal sweet-breads with chanterelle mushrooms and morels are particularly recommended. You might stop here after visiting the Charolais Institute, a museum dedicated to the breeding of the famous breed of cattle.

Closed Mon; Sun evening; mid-Nov to Dec
Cards AE, MC, V

Dijon
◆ Le Bistrot des Halles
€ Fr

10 rue Bannelier, 21000, Dijon, Côte-d'Or
Tel 03 80 49 94 15 Fax 03 80 38 16 16

Le Bistrot des Halles is across the street from the market in the centre of Dijon and always full of locals, so it is wise to book. You can sit on the terrace or inside the restaurant, which is decorated in the traditional bistro style, with mirrors in large wooden frames surrounding the dining room and the ubiquitous red-and-white checked tablecloths. Try something from the daily specials board, or one of the regional specialities - *jambon persillé* or the *Daube d'agneau* – a cold, tomato-based terrine of roasted lamb, olives, carrots and leaks. The *crème brûlée* stands out among the desserts. Free aperitif.

CLOSED Sun evening
CARDS MC, V

Our price bands
Rather than giving actual prices (which are prone to change) we indicate the cost of a three-course meal for one person, without wine, by means of price bands. They are as follows: € under 30 euros €€ 30-50 euros €€€ over 50 euros. Where we give more than one price band, for example €– €€€€, this indicates that in that restaurant a meal can be had at a range of prices. As well as the cost of *prix fixe* menus, our price bands also take into account the cost of an average selection from the *à la carte* menu.

Gevrey-Chambertin
◆ Chez Guy € Fr

3 pl de l'Hôtel-de-Ville, 21220 Gevrey-Chambertin, Côte-d'Or
Tel 03 80 58 51 51 Fax 03 80 58 50 39

Gevrey-Chambertin is one of the largest wine growing villages in France, producing world-famous red wines, and you'll find a good selection of them on the list at Chez Guy. Chef Joel Guillaud produces the region's favourite dishes from ingredients

that he selects daily from the local market. Traditional recipes are executed with flare. Try the *tartine d'epoisses gratinées et petite salade* for a starter, an *emincé de magret de canard aux cerises* for a main course, and *panacotta aux fraises et sorbet passion* for dessert. One menu is devoted entirely to Burgundy specialities. Coffee is free, in fact the place offers real value for money: as we went to press children could eat a main course and an ice cream for eight euros. There are occasional jazz concerts – check for dates.

' A lively place - great for groups '

CLOSED Wed; Tue off-season; Feb holidays
CARDS MC, V

Our traditional French cuisine symbol
So many of our readers enjoy seeking out the genuinely French eating experience that we have used Fr to mark restaurants which offer *cuisine du terroir*, classical French dishes or regional dishes with an emphasis on local ingredients, and traditional recipes.

L'Isle-sur-Serein
◆ Auberge du Pot d'Etain
€ – €€€

24 rue Bouchardat, 89440 L'Isle-sur-Serain, Yonne
Tel 03 86 33 88 10 Fax 03 86 33 90 93

If you are going to or from Noyers-sur-Serain, an interesting town to visit, with a turbulent history, this country inn makes a useful stopover. The three dining rooms and the flowery courtyard are all spacious, impeccably neat and tastefully decorated. Proprietors Catherine and Alain Péchery have developed a vast wine list, which, as you would expect, is strong on the local Chablis. Chef Didier Robert has a large repertoire featuring a healthy mixture of traditional French and inventive modern dishes, including *escalope de foie gras chaud aux asperges vertes, fricassée de sot-l'y laise et escargots aux oignons nouveaux*, and *gâteau de pommes de terre tiède à l'andouillette de Chablis*. As we went to press menus ranged from a modest

16.50 euros (Sundays only) to 49 euros; and children could eat for 8.50 euros. There are nine bedrooms.

CLOSED Mon and Sun evening (except July-Aug); Feb; 1 week Oct
CARDS MC, V

Ladoix-Serrigny
 ### Les Terrasses de Corton € – €€

21550 Ladoix-Serrigny, Beaune, Côte-d'Or
Tel 03 80 26 42 37 Fax 03 80 26 48 23

Nothing special as far as ambience is concerned, except that the roadside hotel backs on to the immortal vineyards of the Cote d'Or (Corton Charlemagne can be seen growing at the top of the hill). Eat on the terrace (prey to noise from the busy road) or in the dining room (dully decorated). Either way, you will enjoy swift, friendly service and simple, properly executed Burgundian cooking (*jambon persillé, escargots, coq au vin*) with a few Spanish dishes thrown in, such as a refreshing *gazpacho* to start .

CLOSED Tue dinner, Wed Oct-Mar; Feb
CARDS MC, V

Looking for somewhere to stay? See page 241.

Macon
Le Restique € Fr

56 rue Saint Antoine, 71000 Macon, Saône-et-Loire
Tel 03 85 38 38 76

A typical Lyonnais-style *bistrot* where the patron serves you with a cheeky joke and a twinkle in the eye. Regulars can tell that the chef here has bartered, contrived, swapped and swindled in local markets to find the best available produce with which to concoct his classic menus of regional cooking, for example *andouillette Maconnaise à la moutarde*, a local speciality. Between mouthfuls you can admire the amazing collection of hats and berets which make up the restaurant's decoration – each one has a story. The wine list is biased

toward the Maconnais Chardonnay, but when you have tried the Guillemot 2000 Viré Clessé in conjunction with the daily selection of fish you won't really mind.

CLOSED Sat dinner, Sun
CARDS MC, V

Mailly-le-Château
Le Castel €

pl de l'Église, 89660 Mailly-le-Château, Yonne
Tel 03 86 81 43 06 Fax 03 86 81 49 26

Built at the end of the 19th century, Le Castel is a large shuttered house lying in the shadow of the village church. It has a well-kept garden and a flowery terrace shaded by lime trees where you can eat or take drinks in warm weather. There are two dining rooms, separated by a small salon and a handsome fireplace. You get a free kir when you eat here and the menu is exceptional value for money. M. Breerette is a character and a good cook, and Madame is 'the perfect hostess'. The focus is on traditional regional cuisine – *coq au vin*, *escargots*, Charolais steak with mustard. Because the name and the house are rather grand, some visitors expect too much, but Le Castel is worth a visit if you want good food for little money. Menus start at 11 euros. Bedrooms here are also very cheap, and vary from the spacious, with touches of grandeur such as chandeliers and drapes over the bedheads, to much smaller and simpler rooms.

CLOSED Wed; mid-Nov to Mar
CARDS MC, V

Mellecey
Le Guide de Marioux € – €€ Fr

71640 Mellecey, Mercurey, Saône-et-Loire
Tel 03 85 45 13 03 Fax 03 85 45 28 46

Corinne (who serves) and Jean (who cooks) make a great team in this village restaurant, be it in the dining room or over the furnace. Charm, smiles, attentive service and excellent food. Jean has a talent for cooking fish as well as meat, and the quality of the produce is impeccable, with beautifully presented dishes. Save a place for his desserts too – they merit serious investigation. From the wine list, it's clear to anyone in the know that Jean's wine suppliers dine with him regularly as the list is laden with hard to find vintages, regional wines and his personal favourites from around the country.

❛ A must if you are a carnivore, and lover of frogs and wine'...'The tables are airily spaced, but the decoration may not be to your liking – keep sniggers to a minimum and enjoy the food'...'you should reserve for the evening; at midday you may have to enjoy a kir while waiting for a table ❜

Closed Mon, Thu dinner, Sun dinner
Cards MC, V

Please send us reports
A guide such as this thrives on reader's reports. If you send us five usable reports, we will send you a free copy of any title in our *Charming Small Hotel Guides* series (see page 241 for France titles in the series).

The five reports should contain at least two new restaurants; the balance can be comments on restaurants already in the guide. **Send reports to** Charming Restaurant Guides, Duncan Petersen Ltd, 31 Ceylon Road, London W14 0PY.

Mercurey
◆ Hôtellerie du Val d'Or

€ – €€€

*Grande-Rue, 71640 Mercurey, Côte-d'Or
Tel 03 85 45 13 70 Fax 03 85 45 18 45*

This 19thC coaching inn is on the main street of the prestigious but rather dull wine village of Mercurey. In the capable hands of chef-patron Jean-Claude Cogny and his wife Monique, it is a modest place that does its job well, with simple but impeccable accommodation and good food. It's easy to see what brings the customers back, especially in a region of culinary excellence and exorbitant prices, where many are daunted by the formal (or even pretentious) style of most hotels, and long to find some village-inn simplicity. The friendly Val d'Or obliges, and the tradition begun by Jean-Claude's great aunt in 1910 continues unbroken. There are two dining rooms; one rustic, with beamed ceiling, large fireplace and pretty floral curtains; the other more intimate and elegant; and a bar with neat tables and chairs. M. Cogny's cooking is a cut above: he has a Michelin star for such dishes as *millechou d'escargots et pied de porc au beurre rouge* and *la pochouse de sandre, grenouilles et ecrevisses à ma faço*n.

Closed Tue lunch; Mon; mid-March to April, mid-Dec to mid-Jan
Cards MC, V

Nevers
◆ La Cour Saint-Etienne

*33 rue St- Etienne, 58000 Nevers, Nievre
Tel 03 86 36 74 57 Fax 03 86 61 14 95*

A useful address in Nevers. The two dining rooms are decorated in low-key colours and service is adequate. On the seasonally changing menu you might find salmon stuffed with artichoke or supreme of chicken stuffed with ceps. For dessert, the croquant of pear with chicory is apparently superb. As we went to press, menus ranged from 14 (except Sat) to 24 euros. If the weather is fine you can eat on the terrace looking onto the lovely church of Saint-Etienne. Michelin awards it a Bib Gourmand (good food at moderate prices).

Closed Sun, Mon; 2 weeks Jan, 2 weeks Aug
Cards MC, V

Nitry
◆ Auberge la Beursaudière € – €€

*9 chemin de Ronde, 89310 Nitry, Yonne
Tel 03 86 33 69 69 Fax 03 86 33 69 60*

If you look up the amazingly sophisticated website, complete with contented snores of this country hotel and restaurant (www.beursaudière.com), you will see that it is a slick interpretation of rustic simplicity, complete with waiters and waitresses in traditional Morvan costume. The lovely old building, complete with medieval dovecote, sets the scene for this idyll. Inside, there are several interconnecting dining rooms with wooden tables and chairs and candlelight, while attractive bedrooms, each dedicated to a craft, such as lacemaking, have recently been added. There is also a splendid terrace for summer dining. The food is certainly real, and carefully presented: local dishes including snails, crayfish, *andouillette de Clamecy fait maison* and *pressé de jambonneau à la terrine d'andouillette*. A brick wood-fired oven, open to view, is responsible for much of the cooking. Good desserts.

Closed early to mid-Jan
Cards AE, DC, MC, V

Looking for somewhere to stay? See page 241.

Oulon
◆ Ferme-Auberge du Vieux Château
€ – €€ **Fr**

58700 Oulon, Nièvre
Tel 03 86 68 06 77

It's unlikely that you would ever find yourself in this lovely, undulating corner of Burgundy unless you were heading to this beautifully situated *ferme-auberge* run by the Fayolle-Tilliot family. The turreted old farm lies just outside the charming village of Oulon in a fold of green hills that stretch out on all sides. For overnight guests there are some very simple bedrooms, and a small swimming pool, while in the dining room you will be presented with a simple menu, often starting with the farm's own *foie gras*, followed perhaps by *côte d'agneau*, *pommes dauphinoise*, a tray of cheese and home-made crystallized fruit. Before leaving, you could buy a bottle of homemade *crème de cassis*.

❢ *Afterwards, seduced by the place, we walked in the countryside and, despite the lacklustre bedrooms, decided to stay the night* ❢

Closed Dec to Mar
Cards MC, V

Ouroux-en-Morvan
◆ Ferme-Auberge Chez Flo € **Fr**

Coeuzon, 58230 Ouroux-en-Morvan, Nièvre
Tel 03 86 78 21 87 Fax 03 86 78 25 81

Deep in the hilly, thickly wooded, lake-filled Morvan, this is another excellent ferme-auberge (see Le Vieux Château at Oulon, above). Ouroux is situated midway between Lac de Pannissière-Chaumard and the particularly lovely Lac des Settons. In the capable hands of Florence Berlo, you can feast, for a mere handful of euros, off high-quality home-cooking from a simple but satisfying set menu. Main courses might be *poulet à la crème, coq au vin, boeuf en cocotte* or *Bourgignone*. You must phone to reserve.

Closed phone for details
Cards none

Our traditional French cuisine symbol
So many of our readers enjoy seeking out the genuinely French eating experience that we have used Fr to mark restaurants which offer *cuisine du terroir*, classical French dishes or regional dishes with an emphasis on local ingredients, and traditional recipes.

Poisson
◆ La Poste € – €€€

Le Bourg, 71600 Poisson, Saône-et-Loire
Tel 03 85 81 10 72 Fax 03 85 81 64 34

The strangely-named village of Poisson lies on the borders of Charolais (famous for its white cattle) and Brionnais (noted for its Romanesque churches), both beautiful, little visited stretches of rolling countryside. When farmers walked their cattle to market in St. Christophe-en-Brionnais (still held every Thursday), they stopped to rest at the village inn, La Poste, which for the past 30 years has been the restaurant, specializing in Charolais beef and fish, of Denise and Jean-Noel Dauvergne. They have now bought the house next door and converted it into a small hotel (La Reconce). A door in the lobby of La Reconce connects with the bar of

La Poste, where locals gather. The restaurant is smartly decorated, with apricot walls, pale wicker chairs and white tablecloths, and a tank of tropical fish. In summer you can eat in the little garden under the shade of paulownia trees. While dainty and elegant Madame Dauvergne runs things up front, the hands-on chef, Jean-Noel, rarely emerges from the kitchen. Try his *petite salade aux escargots et saumon mariné à l'huile de noisettes* or his *canard sauvage, double cuisson, déglacé au vinaigre de figues.*

CLOSED Mon and Tue (except July – Aug); first 2 weeks Oct; Feb
CARDS AE, DC, MC, V

Our price bands
€ under 30 euros €€ 30-50 Euros
€€€ over 50 euros for a menu

Quarré-les-Tombes
◆ Le Morvan € – €€ Fr

6 rue des Écoles, 89630 Quarré-les-Tombes, Yonne
Tel 03 86 32 29 29 Fax 03 86 32 29 28

This cheerful hotel-restaurant in the Parc Naturel Régional du Morvan will help you unwind if you grow tired of looking at sarcophagi at the nearby l'Église Saint Georges. The welcome is warm and the dining room is brightly decorated, with cream walls and bright flower arrangements. The menu offers regional dishes, using fresh ingredients, and prices are fair. Michelin awards a Bib Gourmand. There are eight comfortable bedrooms.

CLOSED Mon and Tue (except July-Aug); 1 week Oct, Dec to Feb
CARDS AE, DC, MC, V

La Roche-Vineuse
◆ Le Bar des Sports
€ – €€ Fr

Le Bourg, 71960 La Roche-Vineuse, Saône-et-Loire
Tel 03 85 91 27 30

Here is a restaurant dedicated to local customers, with a tiny catchment area.

You have to be in the know – a passer-by wouldn't go near the place thinking, quite possibly, that it had been abandoned. Once you've ventured in beyond the old glass door, however, you will discover a fabulous old bar around which clients linger, chatting away and knocking back regular servings of one or other of the three drinks available: wine, beer or *pastis*. If you want water, the local well isn't far! The patron is the boss. He'll serve the unique 10 euro (at the time of going to press) menu himself, his shirt unbuttoned over his ample stomach: *entrée, plat, fromage, dessert, café et vin sans modération.* The tables touch, the conversation mingles and the food is genuine. The *entrecôte* is from the highly-prized *charollais* and cooked in the best tradition – quickly seared and still very red. The *andouillette fait maison* has the most divine stuffing. And then there are the *frites* – handmade by the patron's daughter, and just perfect. Pay in cash.

❛ *If you love simplicity, reality, La France profonde and home-made frites, come here* ❜

CLOSED Mon to Sun dinner
CARDS none

Fr French regional or classical French dishes on menu.

Rully
◆ Le Vendangerot
€ – €€ Fr

6 place Sainte-Marie, 71150 Vendangerot, Sâone-et-Loire
Tel 03 85 87 38 76 Fax 03 85 91 27 18

Armand and Marie Lollini will make your visit to Rully a special one. This charming hotel-restaurant (formerly the Hôtel du Commerce – the old sign still hangs outside) mixes class with sobriety and the service is always cheerful and efficient, even when the place is full. What to choose? The *queue de boeuf* and the *pavé de porc* are the specialities, and they are superb, but everything else is good too: freshwater fish, crayfish, pigeon with truffle sauce, *coq-au-vin* cooked in white wine. Wonderful *pain perdu,* undoubtedly homemade. There is a *menu du jour* at 15 euros (at the time of going to press), or you may be tempted by the *menu dégustation* at 37 euros. Excellent wine list – good on local wines, including of course Rully (which is also available by the glass) and vintages, whether red, white or bubbly. You can stay the night, should you wish, in one of 14 wooden-shuttered bedrooms in this large village house surrounded by a quiet garden.

❛ I won't forget sitting on the intimate terrace with a bottle of Crémant de Bourgogne and a refreshing bolée de fraise ❜

Closed Tue, Wed; early to mid-Jan, mid-Feb to mid-Mar
Cards MC, V

Please send us reports
A guide such as this thrives on reader's reports. If you send us five usable reports, we will send you a free copy of any title in our *Charming Small Hotel Guides* series (see page 241 for France titles in the series).

The five reports should contain at least two new restaurants; the balance can be comments on restaurants already in the guide. **Send reports to** Charming Restaurant Guides, Duncan Petersen Ltd, 31 Ceylon Road, London W14 0PY.

Saint-Gervais-en-Vallière
◆ Moulin d'Hauterive

71350, Saint-Gervais-en-Vallière, Côte-d'Or
Tel 03 85 91 55 56 Fax 03 85 91 89 65

The wheels of this converted mill were still turning 40 or so years ago. Only since 1977 has it enjoyed a new lease of life as an unusual country hotel with a good blend of comfort and rural seclusion. You have a choice of three cosy dining rooms, but the decoration is a little clustered and out-dated. Dishes on Christiane Moille's menu include *pot au feu de foie gras de canard au gros sel et mignonnette, ragoût de homard aux pommes de terre et échalotes confites sauce crustacées* and *gatinois et sa glace*

pain d'épices sauce caramel. If you decide to spend the night, you can unwind in the swimming pool or sauna, do some bodybuilding, go for a bike ride, or try the water therapy. Or you could just sit in the garden by the river and enjoy the view.

❛ The perfect place for a relaxing waterside meal ❜

Closed Mon and Tue lunch; lunch Sept to June (except weekends and public holidays)
Cards AE, DC, MC, V

Our price bands
Rather than giving actual prices (which are prone to change) we indicate the cost of a three-course meal for one person, without wine, by means of price bands. They are as follows: € under 30 euros €€ 30-50 euros €€€ over 50 euros. Where we give more than one price band, for example €– €€€, this indicates that in that restaurant a meal can be had at a range of prices. As well as the cost of *prix fixe* menus, our price bands also take into account the cost of an average selection from the *à la carte* menu.

Vougeot
◆ Château de Gilly
€€ – €€€

21640 Gilly-lès-Cîteaux, Côte-d'Or
Tel 03.80 62 89 98 Fax 03 8062 89 98

This is a magnificent château, with gardens, rooms, and a restaurant in a beautiful, enormous vaulted room (an old chapel). Its stone columns make you forget the size and find the intimacy you're after. The menu is full of classics and moderns. The *feuilleté* of frogs legs, parsley and ceps was divine, washed down with a Chambolle Musigny 1990 from C. Roumier. Ask the advice of waiter and *sommelier* to find out what's really happening in the cellar and the kitchen. If you want to stay in the hotel, its gorgeous, individually-decorated rooms will really let you get the most from the meal. You can also visit their 45000 bottle cellar.

Closed Feb
Cards AE, DC, MC, V

FRANCHE-COMTE

Between Alsace and Burgundy, and sharing borders with Germany and Switzerland, Franche-Comté is a beautiful, little-visited region covered by forests, innumerable rivers and waterfalls and 80 tranquil lakes. In the north of the region, the high valley of the Saône and the Vallée de l'Ognon (principal towns Vezoul and Belfort) create a rustic, gently undulating countryside, while in the south lie the wild, untamed mountains of the Jura. In Doubs, in the centre, lies the elegant regional capital, Besançon, famous for its September music festival.

CHAMPAGNE-
ARDENNE

N19

D70

D87

● Dijon

A36

N73

● Dole 207

D472

A39

Arbois 204
●

N5

Chalon-sur-Saône
●

Baume-les-
Messieurs 205

BOURGOGNE

Courlans
206

Châtillon 206
●

N78

A39

Bonlieu
206
●

RHONE-
ALPES

LORRAINE

ALSACE

Fougerolles 207

Mélisey 209

Mulhouse

Belfort

F R A N C H E -
C O M T E

Baume-les-Dames 205

Goumois 207

Besançon 205

Villers-le-
Lac 209

Amondans
204

Vernierfontaine
209

Malbuisson 208

SCHWEIZ
SUISSE

Genève

Amondans
◆ Château d'Amondans
€€ – €€€

*9 rue Louise-Pommery, 25330 Amondans,
Doubs
Tel 03 81 86 53 14 Fax 03 81 86 53 76*

On the edge of a plateau, in its own wood-ed park, this elegant château dates back to the 16th century, though most of the building has been reworked in the centuries since. During the late 1980s, gourmet chef Frédéric Médigue (from Bésançon, just 32 km/20 miles away) and his wife, Pascale, fell in love with it. Without a moment's hesita-tion, they bought it and have turned it into a comfortable, well-appointed hotel with a first-class, Michelin-starred restaurant, highly rated by locals. With its tiled floor, large bare wood-framed windows and stone fireplace, the handsome half-panelled main dining room is reminiscent of a Dutch inte-rior. Frédéric takes his cooking very serious-ly, baking bread twice a day and changing his menus weekly. His specialities (many based on fish and shellfish) are distinctive versions of local dishes. If the weather's fine, ask for your coffee in the garden.

CLOSED Sun evening, Wed Oct-Jun; early Jan to mid-Mar, one week Aug
CARDS AE, DC, MC, V

Arbois
◆ La Balance Mets et Vins €€ – €€ Fr

*47 rue de Courcelles, 39600 Arbois, Jura
Tel 03 84 37 45 00 Fax 03 84 66 14 55*

The brainchild of Thierry Moyne, this busy restaurant in the town centre does exact-ly what it says in its name: tries to achieve the perfect balance between food and wine. It is a showcase for wine-growers of the Jura, and you can order wines by the glass, in order to sample different vintages with each course. Thierry designs his menus around Chardonnays (some of which com-pare well with the lesser white Burgundies), the unique and powerful Savagnins, the excellent Arbois rosés, and a range of smooth red wines. His specialities (*salade de pétoncle aux pétales de Morteau, coq au vin jaune et morilles, saucisse de Morteau, pigeon rôti au vin de paille* and *croquant de pommes au Macvin*) combine culinary tradition with modern trends in an irre-sistible way. You can also eat on a very pleas-ant terrace.

❛ *Not to be missed if you're in Arbois'* ... *Terrific service* ❜

CLOSED Sun evening and Mon late Aug to mid-Jul, Tue and Wed Feb-Mar; early Dec to early Feb
CARDS MC, V

Our traditional French cuisine symbol
So many of our readers enjoy seeking out the genuinely French eating experience that we have used Fr to mark restaurants which offer *cuisine du terroir*, classical French dishes or regional dishes with an emphasis on local ingredients, and tradi-tional recipes.

Arbois
◆ Jean-Paul Jeunet
€€€

*9 rue de l'Hôtel-de-Ville, 39600 Arbois,
Jura
Tel 03 84 66 05 67 Fax 03 84 66 24 20*

In a 17thC former Carmelite convent, mas-ter chef Jean-Paul Jeunet took over this successful hotel and restaurant from his father, André. Jean-Paul has fitted out the hotel in a brutally modern style, in marked contrast to the old building, and it now appeals to a mainly business clientele. However the restaurant is still stunning, with its beams, open hearth, terracotta flagged floor, and walls, tablecloths and chairs, all in white or off-white. Even in André's day, it was considered a shrine to Jura cooking, and Jean-Paul carries on the tradition with great panache. Having trained under Jean Troisgros and Alain Chapel amongst others, he brings his experience and inspiration to the cuisine of the region and all that he learned from his apprentice-ship with his father. He offers three seduc-tively named, but pricey menus (*d'inspira-tion gourmande, terroir de pasteur* and *symphonie des parfums*). In comparison, the wine list almost seems good value.

Closed Tue, Wed lunch mid-Sep to Jul; Dec, Jan
Cards AE, DC, MC, V

Baume-les-Dames
◆ Le Charleston € Fr

10 rue des Armuriers, 25110 Baume-les-Dames, Doubs
Tel 03 81 84 24 07 Fax 03 81 84 79 76

Perhaps this bistro's food is so good and so popular because the chef is a former protégé of Marc Veyrat (see page 326). Classic dishes of the region, such as *millefeuille de saucisse de Morteau* and *escalopes de sandre au vin jaune*, are the draw to shoppers and sightseers in this attractive town of honey-stone buildings. On a central pedestrian street, it could be the perfect lunch spot. Inside the 17thC building, one of the few original features is the impressive stone fireplace, otherwise the decoration is determinedly *belle époque*.

❝ Central position ... very good food ❞

Closed Sun evening, Mon
Cards MC, V

Our price bands
€ under 30 euros €€ 30-50 euros
€€€ over 50 euros for a menu.

Baume-les-Dames
◆ Hostellerie du Château d'As € – €€€

26 rue du Château-Gaillard, 25210 Baume-les-Dames, Doubs
Tel 03 81 84 00 66 Fax 03 81 84 39 67

A stone's throw from the Swiss border, this town house and its large garden dominate the centre of Baume. Two brothers run the *hostellerie*. Both are excellent chefs, so they share the cooking. They offer imaginative dishes with snails, seafood and mushrooms as well as an exciting array of puddings. Their *gâteau au chocolat aux griottines de Fougerolles* has admirers on the other side of the border, willing to make the journey for a taste. Although the dining room is formal and sober-looking, with dark carpet and walls, the warmth of the service

compensates. The weekday lunchtime menu is by far the best value.

❝ Superb soupe de moules on a bed of saffron ❞

Closed Sun evening; mid-Jan to mid-Feb
Cards AE, DC, MC, V

● *Cinq Claire (04 73 37 10 31), a useful address in Clermont-Ferrand, is recommended for its honest regional cuisine – aiguillettes de canard, rouelle de porc, and a gigantic board of mainly local cheeses.*

Baume-les-Messieurs
◆ Les Grottes € Fr

aux Grottes, 39210 Baume-les-Messieurs, Jura
Tel 03 84 44 61 59 Fax 03 84 44 61 59

Though on the tourist trail, this restaurant (open for lunch only) is something special. Close to the salt roads, it can be reached the easy way (by road) or by horse, bike, or by intrepid walkers, exploring the cirque de Baume (one of the many examples of natural amphitheatre that occur in the Jura) and the surrounding mountains. Les Grottes stands right above a huge waterfall and at the end of the track near the caves, the attraction for most of the tourists. In a simple room with the obligatory red-check tablecloths and some grotto decoration, the house speciality is *écrevisses à la crème*. They keep the crayfish in tanks. In summer, the terrace is a great bonus.

Closed dinner, Wed Sep-Jul; Oct to Easter
Cards MC, V

Besançon
◆ Mungo Park
€€ – €€€

11 rue Jean-Petit, 25000 Besançon, Doubs
Tel 03 81 81 28 01 Fax 03 81 83 36 97

There's no getting away from it – this upmarket address in Besançon is expensive, but everybody loves it. With its country look, its beams, ceiling fans, copper pans, cosy round tables and the exquisite cuisine of Jocelyne Lotz-Choquart, it has what the French call *âme* (soul). Gault Millau even give it one of their prestigious hearts. Mme Lotz-Choquart is an intelligent, feminine cook, who concentrates on textures and subtly brings out flavours in specialities that always respect nature: among them, *escargots de Bourgogne en verdure, crème de raifort aux radis roses, pigeon fermier farci de ses abats, marmelade de potimarron au Macvin* and *léger vacherin aux griottines de Fougerolles, marmelade de citron et sauce griotte*. The wine list excels.

‘ Attractive surroundings ... mouthwatering food’ ... ‘The duck and chocolate mousse were delicious ’

CLOSED Sun, Mon; late Jul to mid-Aug, one week Nov
CARDS AE, DC, MC, V

---

charmingsmallhotels.co.uk
Visit Duncan Petersen's travel website, the best online search tool for places to stay that combine character and charm. Currently features Britain, France, Italy and Ireland, with other destinations being continuously added.

Bonlieu
◆ La Poutre € – €€ Fr

39130 Bonlieu, Jura
Tel 03 84 25 57 77 Fax 03 84 25 51 61

The name 'La Poutre' refers to the massive 17m (56ft) long beam that supports this charming house, typical of the Jura region and run as a hotel and restaurant by the Moureaux family. The pretty dining room is all beams and knick-knacks. The decoration – highly polished floor, primose-yellow tablecloths and faded floral upholstered chairs – is charmingly old-fashioned. Simple, well-cooked, appetizing regional dishes, such as *filet de truite, vol au vent de volaille et champignons, ragoût d'escargots aux morilles* and *escalope de veau*, arrive in hearty portions. There is an excellent wine list here, which is particularly strong on local vintages.

‘ We were looked after very well ’

CLOSED Mon, Tue; Nov to early May
CARDS MC, V

Châtillon
◆ Hotellerie du Pont Chez Yvonne € Fr

39130 Châtillon, Jura
Tel 03 84 25 70 82

Blissfully isolated, this *hostellerie* nestles into the meandering river Ain, not far from its source. The name recollects Yvonne Petier-Perret, a former owner, who – some years ago – was responsible for the award of a Michelin. The star was later relinquished but, apart from that, little seems to have changed *chez Yvonne* under the direction of M. and Mme Naudet. Regulars return here year after year just because things don't change; not the homely welcome, nor the traditional regional products that the Naudets provide at very modest prices: fresh trout and other river fish, mushrooms from the forests (*morilles* are a speciality), *foie gras* and excellent *poulet de Bresse* and other poultry. It is best to come here in summer, when you dine on a gorgeous terrace beside the river, looking out to the magnificent wooded gardens. And there are eight bedrooms and a pool, if you could do with a quiet break.

CLOSED Mon evening, Tue; Jan to mid-Feb
CARDS MC, V

Courlans
◆ Auberge de Chavannes € – €€

route de Châlon, 39570 Courlans, Jura
Tel 03 84 47 05 52 Fax 03 84 43 26 53

Here is a rarity: a one-Michelin-starred restaurant that doesn't charge astronomic prices. 'Simplicity' is the key word for chef-patron Pierre Carpentier, from his style of cooking to the clean lines of his pale, elegant dining room, and his honest prices. He admits that it's not easy to achieve: "C'est très difficile de faire simple, car faire simple, nécessite de faire juste." Drink wines from the Jura to accompany Pierre's specialities; his strengths lie in meat, game and fish dishes including *foie gras*, *poularde de Bresse*, *escargots en cassolette*, *pigeon rôti* and *rognon de veau*. Six km (3 miles) west of Lons-le-Saunier, Auberge de Chavannes is not a huge detour from the Lyons-Strasbourg *autoroute*.

> *Pierre Carpentier is an artist' ...
> Very impressive wine list*

CLOSED Sun evening, Mon, Tue lunch; Jan, late Jun to early Jul
CARDS MC, V

Dole
◆ La Chaumière
€ – €€€

346 avenue du Maréchal-Juin, 39100 Dole, Jura
Tel 03 84 70 72 40 Fax 03 84 79 25 60

Don't be put off this roadside restaurant by its rather unappealing looks, particularly the dull decoration. The young chef, son of the owners, the Pourcheresses, has a magician's touch in the kitchen. Despite his tender years, he has made such an impression on the critics that he has already won a Gault Millau heart for La Chaumière. He uses the best fresh ingredients, farm-reared poultry and delicate spices for his beautifully cooked and presented specialities. If it's on one of his selection of menus, try the *tourteau au gratin*, with a *polenta moelleuse au vin jaune et une rémoulade de céleri*. It's utterly delicious.

CLOSED Sat lunch, Sun dinner, Mon lunch Sep-Jun, Sun lunch; one week Apr, late Oct to early Nov, late Dec to mid-Jan
CARDS MC, V

● *With a children's play area and lovely shady terrace, Le Pic Vert (03 84 25 75 95) at Doucier is a great place to take the family for salads, crêpes and regional food.*

Fougerolles
◆ Au Père Rota   € – €€€

8 Grande-Rue, 70220 Fougerolles, Haute-Saône
Tel 03 84 49 12 11 Fax 03 84 49 14 51

Haute-Saône is something of a desert as far as restaurants go, so it's a real joy to find one of such quality as Au Père Rota. The chef-patron, Jean-Pierre Kuenz, a Maître Cuisinier de France, is passionate about his native region. He is extremely choosy when picking ingredients, concentrating on locally grown produce, which he prepares in an inspired way. His faithful customers won't let him remove his famous *terrine de canard aux griottines de Fougerolles, sa confiture d'oignons* from his menus. However, his real love is seafood, and you'll certainly find John Dory, turbot, zander, lobster or Saint Pierre, usually with *vin jaune du Jura*, on one of his menus. Light streams into the restaurant, which is quietly and tastefully decorated, with a calm atmosphere.

CLOSED Sun evening, Mon; 3 weeks Jan
CARDS AE, DC, MC, V

Our price bands
Rather than giving actual prices (which are prone to change) we indicate the cost of a three-course meal for one person, without wine, by means of price bands. They are as follows: € under 30 euros €€ 30-50 euros €€€ over 50 euros. Where we give more than one price band, for example €–€€€, this indicates that in that restaurant a meal can be had at a range of prices. As well as the cost of *prix fixe* menus, our price bands also take into account the cost of an average selection from the *à la carte* menu.

Goumois
◆ Taillard   € – €€

25470 Goumois, Doubs
Tel 03 81 44 20 75 Fax 03 81 44 26 15

In a wooded valley on the Swiss border, this pretty chalet has a delightful garden, wonderful views, a friendly atmosphere and delicious food. The house has its roots in the 18th century, and has been owned and run as a hotel and restaurant by the same family since 1875. The present M. Taillard is an artist as well as the chef, and some of his paintings decorate the walls. The dining room makes the most of the view, with elegantly laid tables placed around bay windows, thrown open in summer. M. Taillard's cuisine is excellent, typical of this mountain region, but never heavy. Ingredients that he favours include *jambon de montagne*, *foie gras*, trout from nearby rivers, *morilles* and the marvellous local cheeses. The colourful garden gives way to green pastures and then thickly forested hills which stretch over the border. In summer you can take in the breathtaking view over a coffee on the terrace.

❢ A beautiful place' ... The Taillards are such a delightful family ❣

CLOSED mid-Nov to mid-Mar
CARDS AE, DC, MC, V

Malbuisson
◆ Le Bon Accueil € – €€

25160 Malbuisson, Doubs
Tel 03 81 69 30 58 Fax 03 81 69 37 60

Specialities from Haut-Doubs with an avant-garde, contemporary twist are chef-patron Marc Faivre's stock in trade at this simple village inn. A typical meal might be *tarte fine à la saucisse de Morteau*, followed by *râble de lapin au Savagnin et cuisse en daube*, and *sorbet à la gentiane* to finish. Marc manages to keep prices low, and his wife, Catherine, is a smiling hostess.

CLOSED Sun evening Sep-Jul, Mon, Tue lunch; one week Apr, late Oct to early Nov, mid-Dec to mid-Jan
CARDS DC, MC, V

Please send us reports

A guide such as this thrives on reader's reports. If you send us five usable reports, we will send you a free copy of any title in our *Charming Small Hotel Guides* series (see page 241 for France titles in the series).

The five reports should contain at least two new restaurants; the rest can be comments on restaurants already in the guide.
1 Tell us about your experiences in restaurants already in this guide.
2 Send us new reports. New reports should give the following information:
– **Region** – City, town, village or neaest village.
– **Name of restaurant** – Please double check the spelling, it's surprisingly

easy to make a mistake.
– **Address** – including *département*
– **Telephone number** – plus fax and e-mail if available. Double check this information.
– **Objective description** – Try to explain simply why it should be in the guide. Remember that the guide is very selective - our entries are those one-in-five places that combine
● **interesting food with**
● **character and charm, in the building, the setting or both.**
The guide hates tourist traps, and pretentious, dressed-up food. We like places where the French go.
We favour places in the lower and middle price bands but there are plenty of expensive places that have our qualities, and we list those too.
– **Diner's comments** – These should be short, personal comments on features that strike you. They can be your comments, or others'.
– **Closing times**
– **Credit cards accepted**
Don't forget to date your report and add your name and address.
Send reports to Charming Restaurant Guides, Duncan Petersen Publishing, 31 Ceylon Road, London W14 0PY.

Malbuisson
◆ Le Lac € – €€

25160 Malbuisson, Doubs
Tel 03 81 69 34 80 Fax 03 81 69 35 44

Ten members of the Chauvin family run this traditional French hotel in a pastoral village, surrounded by trees and dairy country, with a view over the calm waters of Saint-Point lake. The view is particularly splendid from the spacious Louis XVI-style dining room, where the classic decoration and furniture is complemented by the classic French cuisine in which the Chauvin chefs specialize. They are so particular about their ingredients, that they think nothing of travelling half way across the country to buy just the right one; although many of their specialities are based on the fruits of the lake: *gratin d'écrevisses décortiquées à la bisque crèmée* and *truite belle comtoise au coulis d'écrevisses*. They pride themselves on the fact that everything is home-made, from bread and brioche to jam and *Viennoiseries*. The hotel has two other restaurants, whose names – 'du Fromage' and 'A la Ferme' – are self-explanatory.

CLOSED mid-Nov to late Dec
CARDS DC, MC, V

Mélisey
◆ La Bergeraine ⓔ – ⓔⓔ

27 route des Vosges, 70270 Mélisey, Haute-Saône
Tel 03 84 20 82 52 Fax 03 84 20 04 47

You wouldn't expect to find gastronomic cooking in this tiny village restaurant, but you will. It lives up to the excellent reputation it has gained for both food and price throughout the region and beyond. But in order to avoid being disappointed, you must book ahead. Attentive staff serve imaginatively cooked regional dishes: some featuring *morilles*; others *foie gras*; a number appear in a *vin jaune* sauce. The salmon smoked on the premises and the *fricassée de volaille à l'estragon* are universally acclaimed. The ambience is charming.

❝ *Excellent regional cooking in a rural village* ❞

CLOSED Sun eve, Tue eve, Wed Sep-Jul; one week Feb
CARDS AE, DC, MC, V

● *Le Mirabilise (03 84 48 24 36) at Mirabel is an utterly charming restored farmhouse, where the food is good and the atmosphere friendly.*

Vernierfontaine
◆ L'Auberge Paysanne ⓔ Fr

18 rue de Stade, 25580 Vernierfontaine, Doubs
Tel 03 81 60 05 21 Fax 03 81 60 05 21

You can be sure of generous helpings of robust country fare at this ancient farmhouse in an isolated rural village. There's a detectable Germanic influence in much of

it: a clue to the origins of the patron, who makes a mouthwatering apple strudel Beforehand, you could order a selection of locally-smoked *charcuterie*, followed by a *fondue*, made with regional cheeses. The inn is decorated in appropriately rustic fashion.

❝ *Make sure you come here with a healthy appetite* ❞

CLOSED Tue dinner, Wed, Thu; one week late Jun, early Nov to early Feb
CARDS MC, V

Please send us reports
A guide such as this thrives on reader's reports. If you send us five usable reports, we will send you a free copy of any title in our *Charming Small Hotel Guides* series (see page 241 for France titles in the series).

The five reports should contain at least two new restaurants; the balance can be comments on restaurants already in the guide. **Send reports to** Charming Restaurant Guides, Duncan Petersen Ltd, 31 Ceylon Road, London W14 0PY.

Villers-le-Lac
◆ France ⓔ – ⓔⓔⓔ

8 place Cupillard, 25130 Villers-le-Lac, Doubs
Tel 03 81 68 00 06 Fax 03 81 68 09 22

A hotel and restaurant in a similar mould to Le Lac at Malbuisson, but the France has the added attraction of Hughes Droz, a brilliant chef in his own right, though he comes from a long line. He plans his menus and *carte* with the utmost precision, and though fairly short, they are faultless. Subtly seasoned and spiced, his recipes draw the crowds from the other side of the border in Switzerland. You might start with one of his superb terrines (maybe the asparagus, with *foie gras* in balsamic vinegar),or with the snails cooked in *absinthe*. For a main course, the fish is always fresh and flaky, and there is an impressive list of local wines.

CLOSED Sun evening, Mon and Tue low season; one week Nov, Jan
CARDS MC, V

PAYS DE LA LOIRE

Nantes

Cholet

Mauléon 217

Bressuire 213

Moncoutant 217

Garette 215

Niort 218

Charron 214

Saint-Martin-de-Ré 222

La Rochelle 220 221

Surgères 223

Saint-Jean-d'Angély 222

Taillebourg 224

Saintes 223

Royan 221

Cognac 215

Pons 220

Talmont-sur-Gironde 224

Gironde

POITOU-CHARENTES

L ying midway along the Atlantic coast between the Loire and Bordeaux, mild and sunny Poitou-Charentes has 300 miles (480 km) of coastline, which includes the historic, lively port of La Rochelle and the islands of Oléron, Aix and Ré. Inland, a soothing landscape of vast, misty horizons stretch from the marshes and waterways of the Marais Poitevin and the regional capital of Poitiers in the north to the foothills of Charente, the city of Angoulême and the vineyards of Cognac in the south.

Thouars 224
Loudun 217
Oiron 219

CENTRE

Lencloitre 216
Naintre 218
Leigné-les-Bois 216
Angles-sur-l'Anglin 212
Dissay 215
Vouillé 224
Parthenay 219
Bonneuil-Matours 212
Poitiers 219
Chauvigny 214
Soudan 223
Saint-Maixent-l'Ecole 221
Celles-sur-Belle 213
Port de Salles 220

LIMOUSIN

POITOU-CHARENTES

Luxé 217

Limoges

Bourg Charente 213
Montbron 218
Jarnac 216
Angoulême 212

AQUITAINE

Chalais 214

Angles-sur-l'Anglin
◆ Le Relais du Lyon d'Or €

4 rue d'Enfer, 86260 Angles-sur-l'Anglin, Vienne
Tel 05 49 48 32 53 Fax 05 49 84 02 28

Angles-sur-l'Anglin is, by any measure, a very attractive village indeed. Perched on a hill, its medieval houses look out over the substantial ruins of both castle and abbey to the river below. Carvings discovered recently in caves near the river show that people have been coming here for around 15,000 years but the misfortune of these early visitors was that Guillaume and Heather Thoreau didn't arrive until 1994. They took a semi-derelict post house and transformed it, inside and out, making a delightful hotel, with 11 bedrooms and a highly successful restaurant that beats any big-city equivalent with the freshness and quality of its (local) ingredients, and wins the service match hands down with its warmth and friendliness. A large room with a high, beamed ceiling and a baronial stone fireplace at one end, it is still warm and intimate. Local wines are well represented on the short, excellent list, and there is a wide selection of half bottles so you can ring the changes.

CLOSED Mon, Tue lunch; Jan-Mar
CARDS AE, MC, V

Angoulême
◆ La Ruelle € – €€ Fr

6 rue de Trois Notre Dames, 16000 Angoulême, Charente
Tel 05 45 95 15 19 Fax 05 45 92 94 64

A street-side stone façade sets La Ruelle apart from the surrounding open-fronted cafés and restaurants in old Angoulême. The spacious interior is lit by ceiling spotlights, focused on the white-clothed tables, creating tableaux of the diners, crafted portraits reminiscent of Rembrandt, against the dim burgundy or stone walls. They may not be romantic, but at least the spotlights enable the older generation to see their food clearly (which is not always the case in some dimly-lit, atmospheric places), and it's certainly worthwhile seeing Cristophe

Combeau's specialities: among them, *filets de rouget poêlés sur sa fondue de tomates confites au basilic, canon d'agneau rôti aux poivrons doux, crème d'ail légère au romarin* and *fricassée de lapin au romarin et ses gnocchis de pommes de terre.* His menus and *cartae* deserve the high acclaim they unfailingly receive.

❛ *The dessert was a work of art* ❜

CLOSED Sat lunch, Sun; 2 weeks Aug
CARDS AE, DC, MC, V

Angoulême
◆ Tour des Valois
€ – €€ Fr

7 rue Masillon, 16000 Angoulême, Charente
Tel 05 45 95 23 64 Fax 05 45 38 14 55

This small restaurant in the café quarter stands out among its neighbours because it is so popular. In many, on a quiet mid-week evening, the staff seem to outnumber their guests, while a glance through the window of the Tour de Valois might suggest that there are no free tables. But their secret weapon is a first-floor dining room. One side of the ground floor is an impressive dressed-stone wall with alcoves for brandy bottles, lights and a fireplace. A participant in a local promotion, which offers a typical regional speciality (such as *escalope de sandre à la Charantaise*) each evening, the restaurant aims to give customers the opportunity to sample the tastes of the region.

❛ *A useful find in Angoulême's café quarter* ❜

CLOSED Sun dinner, Mon lunch; 2 weeks Feb, 2 weeks Aug-Sep
CARDS AE, MC, V

Bonneuil-Matours
◆ Le Pavillon Bleu €

route d'Espalion, 12340 Bozouls, Aveyron
Tel 05 65 44 92 27 Fax 05 65 48 81 40

Once a commercial building associated with the river port, Pavillon Bleu is stone-built and overlooks the Vienne river and a suspension bridge to the main part of the village. The only concession to its name is the blue painted exterior woodwork. Inside there are rugs on a terracotta floor, creamy tablecloths and much exposed stonework. For those rushing southwards (or dragging their feet back north), there is a bargain two-course lunch (starter and main course or main course and dessert) for 11.50 euros, including coffee, available from Tuesday to Friday. Otherwise, it's a leap from an economic four-course menu at 15 euros to a much more elaborate, nominally four-course version at 26 euros. Either way the range of attractive dishes, prepared by the chef, M. Ribaudière, and his team without too much pretension, constitutes remarkable value for money. To get here, take the D749, 16 km (10 miles) south of Châtellerault towards Chauvigny.

(Good food and tranquillity)

Closed Sun dinner, Mon; 2 weeks Oct
Cards MC, V

Our traditional French cuisine symbol
So many of our readers enjoy seeking out the genuinely French eating experience that we have used Fr to mark restaurants which offer *cuisine du terroir*, classical French dishes or regional dishes with an emphasis on local ingredients, and traditional recipes.

Bourg Charente
◆ La Ribaudière
€€ – €€€

16200 Bourg Charente, Charente
Tel 05 45 81 30 54 Fax 05 45 81 28 05

If Thierry Verrat is not at his stove, he's probably in the kitchen garden. Growing his own ingredients gives him the opportunity to pursue his passion, he says, for purity of taste. And it's this commitment that produces the outstanding food, served under the direction of his wife, Patricia, in their comfortable restaurant. It would be a winning formula anywhere, but when the establishment is in a quiet corner of a village among the Cognac vineyards – and when the dining room, terrace and ornamental garden are on the bank of the Charente – it's small

wonder that people make pilgrimages here from far and wide. Keep a close eye for the turning off the new standard N141 road. It's about 10 km (6 miles) east of Cognac towards Jarnac.

Closed Sun dinner, Mon, Tue lunch
Cards AE, DC, MC, V

Bressuire
◆ Le Bouchon € Fr

9 rue Emest Perochon, Bressuire, Deux-Sèvres
Tel 05 49 74 36 64 Fax 05 49 81 28 03

They say that cooking is art and if so Le Bouchon is theatre. Dominique Sorillet is certainly the leading lady, who dances among the tables joking with guests, while husband Alain pops out of his kitchen to help take orders and deliver food, with the regularity of the hero entering the wrong bedroom in a good old-fashioned farce. One diner recalled a visit on an unexpectedly busy Saturday lunchtime – the day-off for their staff. Alain took his order, and soon Dominique was offering him desserts while clearing away the plate off which he'd only just finished his starter. But they quickly put things to rights, bringing him his *côte du porc à la moutarde* amidst good-humoured laughter. Try the excellent Anjou red served in a jug.

(Excellent food'...'A great atmosphere)

Closed Sun, Mon; first week Feb, 3 weeks Aug
Cards MC, V

Celles-sur-Belle
◆ Hostellerie de l'Abbaye €

1 place des Epoux Laurent, 79370 Celles-sur-Belle, Deux-Sèvres
Tel 05 49 32 93 32 Fax 05 49 79 72 65

Curiously Celles-sur-Belle seems little rated in French guidebooks, but this medieval village and abbey is well worth the short detour from the D948; all the more so if the object of the exercise is to visit Catherine and Reynaud Robelin's busy *hostellerie*. A bistro area offers black-board-ed daily menus and a wide range of grills, salads and sandwiches. Elsewhere there is a dining room, a family dining room for those with young children and a terrace for summer moments. The fairly short menus are carefully crafted (for instance, *mesclun aux noix, émincé de râble de lapin confits*, followed by *médaillons de filet mignon, petits oignons grelots confits à l'estragon*, or *l'assiette de saumon fumé maison au bois de hêtre, quenelles de caviar d'aubergines*, followed by *magret de canard à la Florentine aux cerises confites*), and even the 'regional menu to savour' is within our most modest price band.

◖ A place to write home about ◗

CLOSED Sun dinner; mid-Feb to early Mar, late Oct to early Nov
CARDS DC, MC, V

Looking for somewhere to stay?
See page 241.

Chalais
◆ Relais du Château
€ Fr

16210 Chalais, Charente
Tel 05 45 98 23 58 Fax 05 45 98 00 53

Restaurant du Château is a common enough name and such places are generally to be found facing or near the local *château*. Here, you follow a winding narrow road to the fortress on the brow of the hill, and the restaurant lies beyond the drawbridge, within the castle walls. There are two rooms: the main one is a stone-walled, high-ceilinged and beamed hall, and a *petit salle*, reminiscent of a commodious cell with a round table that seats six. However, no prisoner could possibly expect such excellent service, and the food, cooked by the talented Christophe Vine, tastes as if it must have come from the baron's table itself. His classic menus might include *filet de loup aux herbes, mignon de veau gourmande, turbot rôti au beurre d'herbes* or *filet de boeuf au poivre*.

CLOSED Mon; Nov
CARDS AE, MC, V

Charron
◆ Theddy Moules €

72 rue de 14 Juillet, 17230 Charron,
Charente-Maritime
Tel 05 46 01 51 29 Fax 05 46 01 57 31

There's little enough reason for any stranger to go to Charron – a somewhat dispirited straggly village on the coastal edge of a muddy section of coastline – except for Theddy Moules. More of an experience than a restaurant, this awning on an extension of a veranda (or is it a barn?) is dedicated to sampling fresh seafood without any pretentious distractions. The tables are simple – little more than trestles – but crowded with devotees eager to savour the daily harvest of the sea. The speciality of the chef, *moules Theddy*, will set you back a mere 6 euros. A selection of local wines is offered mostly in carafes at equally attractive prices. *Plateau royal avec homard*, on the other hand, costs 38 euros – but will probably feed half a dozen and take an afternoon to eat. Charron is 10 km (6 miles) west of Marans on the D105.

◖ The perfect atmosphere (and prices) to enjoy a summer seafood feast ◗

CLOSED Oct-Apr
CARDS MC, V

Fr French regional or classical French dishes on menu.

Chauvigny
◆ Les Choucas € - €€

21 rue des Puys, 86300 Chauvigny, Vienne
Tel 05 49 46 36 42

In high summer Les Choucas provides meals on an open-air platform – almost a stage – between two of the lanes crowning the hilltop and ancient part of Chauvigny. The parent restaurant is just across one of the roads (follow the signs for *ville haut*) and has been shoehorned into a terrace of cottages, which were originally inside the fortifications of the nearby 11thC baronial castle. If you're looking around the ruins, where giant birds of prey have settled, and want a snack, you can buy *crêpes* and ice cream on the ground floor. For those in search of more serious food, there is a wide range of menus available for both lunch and dinner.

6 There's a real feeling of history about this restaurant 9

CLOSED Wed Sep-Apr; 2 weeks Nov
CARDS MC, V

Our price bands
Rather than giving actual prices (which are prone to change) we indicate the cost of a three-course meal for one person, without wine, by means of price bands. They are as follows: € under 30 euros €€ 30-50 euros €€€ over 50 euros. Where we give more than one price band, for example €–€€€€, this indicates that in that restaurant a meal can be had at a range of prices. As well as the cost of *prix fixe* menus, our price bands also take into account the cost of an average selection from the *à la carte* menu.

Cognac
◆ Le Parc € – €€

Parc Françoise 1er, 16100 Cognac, Charente
Tel 05 45 82 34 78

On an evening's riverside walk or short drive from the centre of Cognac you will find an archetypal Victorian park pavilion among tall trees. You might feel lucky to get an ice-cream or a coffee as the shadows gather and the steward seems to be closing the place for the night. But investigate further, and you'll find quite a large restaurant with a terrace, where you can eat almost on the river bank. Unfortunately, you may have to be tolerant of a fairly average meal, but that's somewhat parsimonious when you can enjoy such a lovely setting. Follow the road signs for Parc Françoise 1er and Base de Plein Air from the Pont Neuf, or the pedestrian signs for the river walk.

6 You only need boaters and blazers to complete the picture 9

CLOSED Mon dinner Nov-Mar
CARDS MC, V

● *Les Pigeons Blancs (05 45 82 16 36) is an old relais de poste with one of the best tables in Cognac.*

Dissay
◆ Le Clos Fleuri € – €€

86130 Dissay, Vienne
Tel 05 49 52 40 27 Fax 05 49 62 37 29

Hidden behind a roadside curtain wall, this restaurant makes much of an ancient chestnut tree within its flowered enclosure, features that are unfortunately almost eclipsed by the presence of parked cars. The cars, however, don't prevent it from being an excellent restaurant. Designed in two parts, it makes imaginative use of wall lighting and mirrors to disguise the fact that the interior room has no windows other than a glass screen, which separates it from the large conservatory. As in many establishments the *mise en bouche*, once a surprise taster, has become a standard element of the menu, whilst an *apéritif* is accompanied by tasty biscuits and olives. Conveniently to the north of Futuroscope, Dissay is just on the east side of the N10. At the village centre, leave the small château on your left and continue straight on for 500 m (550 yards). The restaurant is on your right.

CLOSED Sun dinner, Wed
CARDS MC, V

Garette
◆ Mangeux de Lumas
€ – €€

79270 Garette, Deux-Sèvres
Tel 05 49 35 93 42 Fax 05 49 35 82 89

Lumas are, reportedly, a particularly tasty variety of snail. Ten km (6 miles) west of Niort, in the heart of the Marais Poitevin – the extensive marshes on the Atlantic coast – and on the bank of a major stream, the Mangeux de Lumas is surrounded by the delicacy's perfect habitat. As you would expect, with fresh produce so near to hand, *lumas* feature prominently on the establishment's menus. Those who prefer to leave snails to the French will find plenty more conventional alternatives on the menus and will enjoy the restaurant's location, including a terrace above the water's edge. The village is pedestrianized in summer, and every other building in the single street seems to have an access to the heavily wooded river bank, a landing stage and craft that can be hired.

❛ Try one of the many dishes that include snails ❜

CLOSED Mon dinner, Tue Sep–Jul; 2 weeks Jan
CARDS MC, V

---

charmingsmallhotels.co.uk
Visit Duncan Petersen's travel website, the best online search tool for places to stay that combine character and charm. Currently features Britain, France, Italy and Ireland, with other destinations being continuously added.

Jarnac
◆ Restaurant du Château
€ – €€

15 place du Château, 16200 Jarnac, Charente
Tel 05 45 81 07 17 Fax 05 45 35 35 71

Approach from the west and you enter the centre of Jarnac by crossing the river Charente over an arched stone bridge. Although bisected by through-traffic and largely used for car parking, the place du Château is a spectacular open space, bounded by the Courvoisier Château on the right and, at the top left-hand corner, a tall and more homely ivy-clad building, which houses this restaurant. M. Destrieux, a tall, distinguished man, is justly proud of his immaculate restaurant, and extensive catering operation, which sometimes provides sumptuous meals for Cognac makers entertaining their guests in the deep wine cellars. In the restaurant you can sample a little of his expertise in the *chausson de pigeon sous bois*, *tartare de thon frais mariné*, *magret de canard aux pommes fruits et Cognac* or *rognon de veau rôti estragon, beurre rouge*.

❛ The proprietor's warm personality fills this restaurant ❜

CLOSED Sun dinner, Mon, Wed dinner; 2 weeks late Jan, 3 weeks Aug
CARDS AE, MC, V

Leigné-les-Bois
◆ Bernard Gautier
€ – €€

place de la Mairie, 86450 Leigné-les-Bois, Vienne
Tel 05 49 86 53 82 Fax 05 49 86 58 05

In a prominent building opposite the church in an almost Cotswold-like village, Bernard Gautier's small, cosy restaurant has beams, wooden tables and a hearth, where a fire cheers autumnal evenings. It is refreshingly unspoiled and peaceful, tucked away off the tourist track. Interestingly, a spread of four menus offers more courses but less choice as you advance up the scale. Dishes on the cheapest are both excellent and generous (*cabillaud demi-sel doré au four, aromates* is particularly fine), and it would be difficult to fault M. Gautier's execution and presentation of those on the most expensive menu (where you might be tempted by *tartare de saumon frais et crabe en écrin fumé* and *pigeon rôti aux épices et champignons*). Leigné-les-Bois is 15 km (9 miles) south-east of Châtellerault by the D14 towards Pleumartin, then the D15.

CLOSED Sun dinner, Mon; 2 weeks Feb, 2 weeks Nov
CARDS MC, V

Lencloitre
◆ Le Champ de Foire
€ – €€

18 place du Champ de Foire, 86140 Lencloitre, Vienne
Tel 05 49 90 74 91 Fax 05 49 93 33 76

An undistinguished building, overlooking the large, tree-shaded, market arena at Lencloitre, shelters a restaurant of distinction. In his introduction to the menus, chef-patron Richard Toix justifiably draws attention to the crispy homemade bread rolls that accompany a large choice of dishes from a standard menu, priced according to the number of courses taken. Two *menus saveurs* are available and differ from such gourmet *cartes* in many restaurants by being reasonably priced and by offering a minimum of choices (*terrine de foie gras de canard maison et sa confiture, filet de pageot aux girolles* and *tournedos de filet de boeuf au coulis de Saumur* might be some of them) – a sure sign of the chef's confidence and almost certainly the route to a memorable meal.

' A dull exterior conceals a gem of a restaurant' ... 'Expect to be more than pleasantly surprised. '

Closed Sun dinner, Mon, Tue dinner; school hols, Feb
Cards MC, V

Loudun
◆ Le Ricordeau €–€€

place de la Boeuffeterie, 86200 Loudun, Vienne
Tel 05 49 22 67 27 Fax 05 49 22 53 16

On one of Loudun's central squares, in a large and rather plain town house with a terrace, Isabelle and Jacques Boucher have created a restaurant of distinction. Isabelle, tall and very slim, is in charge of the high-ceilinged dining room, which is furnished mostly in cream with contemporary chairs, their backs, tall, narrow and creamy-yellow in colour. Jacques' menus span the lower price band, ranging from a simple daily *entrée* and *plat du marché*, to a modest selection of ambitious dishes in the more expensive (but still only four-course) menus. Here you might find *foie gras aux pommes et à la chapelure de pain d'épices, filet de sandre poêlé aux escargots*, or *médaillon de lotte au chorizo et au safran*. Perhaps the most unusual aspect of all is the soothing sound of birds, wildlife and the sea in the background.

Closed Sun dinner, Mon
Cards MC, V

Luxé
◆ Cheval Blanc €–€€

place de la Gare, 16230 Luxé, Charente
Tel 05 45 22 23 62 Fax 05 45 39 94 75

A somewhat nondescript building opposite a rural railway station, 6 km (4 miles) west of Mansle and 26 km (16 miles) north of Angoulême, gives little indication of the modest opulence of the restaurant it contains. For many guests the second surprise will be the unqualified opulence of the *menu du jour* (lunchtimes except Sundays and public holidays). To start, you will be served a creamed *potage*, not quite as exceptional as the pastry parcel of salmon and vegetables that might be the *entrée*. The trout, a possible main course, is often served with *sauté* potatoes and mixed vegetables. The cheese board is extensive and the dessert – perhaps an individual peach tart (with strawberries) – completes a bargain lunch, which would be astonishing even if the carafe of wine were not also included. The feast costs 12 euros – though they do charge 1.50 euro for coffee.

' Sets its own standards of value for money '

Closed Sun dinner, Mon, Tue dinner; Feb
Cards MC, V

Mauléon
◆ La Terrasse €

7 place de la Terrasse, 79700 Mauléon, Deux-Sèvres
Tel 05 49 81 47 24 Fax 05 49 81 65 04

Tucked away in the confusing geography of this hillside town, La Terrasse faces its own virtually private square with its inevitable car parking, a dominant plane tree and a large monumental crucifix. Although close to the N149, it is a very peaceful corner indeed. The cosy, rustic-style restaurant offers appropriately traditional regional cooking in a range of excellent value (bilingual) menus. The wine list includes a wide selection of Loire vintages together with moderately priced *pichets* of unusual 44 cl (14.6 fl. oz) and 22 cl (7.3 fl. oz) capacities.

Closed Fri dinner and Sat mid-Sep to Jun; Sun; late Apr to mid-May, first 2 weeks Aug
Cards AE, DC, MC, V

Moncoutant
◆ Le Saint Pierre €–€€

route de Niort, 79320 Moncoutant, Deux-Sèvres
Tel 05 49 72 88 88 Fax 05 49 72 88 89

You think of film sets, Art Deco and whether Bertie Wooster is hiding behind the aspidistra when you walk into this most modern of hexagonal wooden chalets. It's furnished rather than decorated with large urns of greenery and dominated by a central column topped with everlasting tropical flowers. The tables fill the spaces in between and are well served by efficient young women. Tuesday night is the night to come here for the specially promoted *menu du terroir* (Jun-Sep). Kir and appetisers might be followed by a *harlequin* of sea trout with citrus *vinaigrette* and then beef Parthenay. Cheese and desserts complete the picture, together with a short list of suggested wines from the adjacent regions of the Loire, Haut-Poitou and Vendée.

CLOSED Sat lunch (except for groups), Sun dinner
CARDS DC, MC, V

Please send us reports
A guide such as this thrives on reader's reports. If you send us five usable reports, we will send you a free copy of any title in our *Charming Small Hotel Guides* series (see page 241 for France titles in the series).
   The five reports should contain at least two new restaurants; the balance can be comments on restaurants already in the guide. **Send reports to** Charming Restaurant Guides, Duncan Petersen Ltd, 31 Ceylon Road, London W14 OPY.

Montbron
◆ Château Saint-Catherine €-€€

route de Marthon, 16220 Montbron, Charente
Tel 05 45 23 60 03 Fax 05 45 70 72 00

Driving through an arched gatehouse into the grounds of this rural pale stone château, once the residence of the Empress Joséphine, gives you a distinctly regal feeling, a mood that stays with you inside the building and in the grand, spacious restaurant. Nevertheless the *menu du terroir* – at 26 euros – is not entirely out of reach of those not blessed with a royal purse. There

is a wide selection of elegantly presented dishes with little ostentation. Although the menu contains such simple descriptions as 'a piece of salmon with sorrel' and 'slivers of duck flamed with Cognac', when they appear, they are astonishing masterpieces.

❛An excellent place to celebrate a special occasion❜

CLOSED Jan
CARDS AE, DC, MC, V

Naintre
◆ La Grillade €-€€ Fr

RN10, 86530 Naintre, Vienne
Tel 05 49 90 03 42 Fax 05 49 90 06 75

The focal point of this restaurant-in-the-round is an open grill area surmounted by a large copper cauldron and a stag's head. Although comfortably seating about 60, it's a surprisingly intimate setting, with people gathered around the warmth of a fire. However, most of the dishes come from the inner kitchen, including the hot *salade de gésiers*, which contains delicious morsels of meat, and the trout fillet – which looks as though it is a piece from near the tail of a large sea-trout. In addition to the unique ambience and excellent food, Annick and Jacques Chevré welcome their guests with menus illustrated with original coloured drawings. La Grillade is on the RN 10, just south of the Châtellerault south exit from the A10.

CLOSED Sun dinner
CARDS MC, V

Niort
◆ Table des Saveurs €-€€

9 rue Thiers, 79000 Niort, Deux-Sèvres
Tel 05 49 77 44 35 Fax 05 49 77 44 36

Surrounded by an impressive collection of public buildings, Table des Saveurs must see more than its fair share of *départemental* movers and shakers. The demands of a rush of diners leave the young waiters making rapid rhythms on the wooden staircase to the mezzanine as they dash up and down. This high-ceilinged restaurant, with beech wood furnishings and a gallery, is certainly a find in a county whose motto is 'a place to discover'. The Saveurs has a choice of four menus, ranging up to nearly 40 euros and leaves you wondering where else in the world you could find a city-centre restaurant serving a three-course meal for just 13 euros.

❢ A real find' ... 'Remarkable value for money ❢

CLOSED Sun
CARDS MC, V

Oiron
◆ Relais du Château €

place des Maronniers, 79100 Oiron, Deux-Sèvres
Tel 05 49 96 54 96 Fax 05 49 96 54 45

The name alludes to the imposing mansion close to this village on the southern fringes of Loire Châteaux country. The restaurant is in a building on the corner of the village square and opens on to a courtyard, whose builder must have had a penchant for verandas and pergolas – a delightful and sheltered spot for a summer meal. Toasted rounds of bread with a yoghurt dip are served before the middle-priced menu. It might feature a tomato and shrimp starter, in which apple provides a deliciously contrasting taste. The main course might be succulent slices of veal on a bed of assorted mushrooms, accompanied by boiled potatoes and haricots verts, presented in an unusual way for this part of France.

❢ A restaurant that will reward a special journey ❢

CLOSED Sun dinner, Mon; Feb
CARDS MC, V

Parthenay
◆ La Bergerie € Fr

104 rue de Sépulcre, 79200 Parthenay, Deux-Sèvres
Tel 05 49 64 24 56

A short drive, rather than a walk, from the town centre, this former farmhouse has a large bar that might seem the natural habitat of local farmers. The dining room is reminiscent of rural kitchens where neither

Wellington boots, Barbours nor overalls would be out of place, and the private car park will comfortably accommodate the Volvo and its trailer. Olivier Picaut's cooking is as comfortably homespun and traditional as the surroundings (*filet de boeuf* or *d'agneau*, *rognon de veau* or *magret de canard*) and will fortify you well for an afternoon's grappling with a recalcitrant boiler or other such physically demanding tasks. Follow the signs from the roundabout by the central Super U store.

CLOSED Sun; one week Feb, 3 weeks Aug
CARDS AE, MC, V

Poitiers
◆ Les Bons Enfants €

11 bis rue Cloche-Perse, 86000 Poitiers, Vienne
Tel 05 49 41 49 82

Tucked away on a corner between the Palais de Justice and the university and conveniently close to the main pedestrian shopping area, the Bons Enfants is an upmarket bistro, where you can expect to rub shoulders with economically minded 'legal eagles' or proud parents bearing *bon* offspring in outrageous tee-shirts. The pleasant service heavily promotes the *menu du jour* – no doubt mindful of what must be a tiny kitchen – which constitutes a satisfying three-course meal, two glasses of wine and coffee and a laudable bill of only 17 euros. The fish and seafood dishes are particularly recommended, and there is a popular *fondue*, prepared with local cheeses.

CLOSED Sun, Mon; Aug to early Sep , Christmas to Jan
CARDS MC, V

Poitiers
◆ Cellier Saint-Hilaire
€ – €€

65 rue T. Renaudot, 86000 Poitiers, Vienne
Tel 05 49 41 15 45 Fax 05 49 60 20 32

Behind a frontage masquerading as part of a modern block of flats, at the Cellier Saint-Hilaire you step downwards into medieval history. This 12thC, high, vaulted, stone basement has atmosphere – cauldrons of it – and, in summer 2002, a new team was setting culinary standards that more than complemented their surroundings. The lunchtime *autur d'un plat* is a delightful light meal. Your *amusette* might be a fine hot meat salad and the dish of the day, chicken in a delicious cream sauce, with fresh fruits, exquisitely presented, to follow. With a glass of wine – Haut Poitou perhaps – and coffee included, it is excellent value at 14.50 euros.

CLOSED Sun, Mon; first 2 weeks Jan
CARDS AE, DC, MC, V

Our price bands
€ under 30 euros €€ 30-50 Euros
€€€ over 50 euros for a menu

Pons
◆ Hôtel de Bordeaux
€€ Fr

1 avenue Gambetta, 17800 Pons, Charente-Maritime
Tel 05 46 91 31 12 Fax 05 46 91 22 25

As you tour the famous Cognac vineyards, each village seems to be home to at least one producer. Wondering how many different labels there are is an obvious question. You get a clue to the answer as you walk into the spacious dining room at the Bordeaux, where a polished round table groans under the weight of some 150 bottles of spirit old and new: a modest selection, they say. At tables in the adjoining enclosed courtyard, you can enjoy the careful cuisine of Pierre Jaubert, who places great emphasis on his daily search for fresh produce, and whose specialities include *poitrine de veau rôti aux épices douces et caviar d'aubergines* and *tranche de carré de veau grillée à la moutarde violette de Brive.*

❛ *You could have a different Cognac after every meal for 11 weeks* ❜

CLOSED never
CARDS AE, DC, MC, V

● *You can have a wonderful dinner at Auberge Pontoise in Pons (05 46 94 00 99), where Hélène and Frédéric Massiot are the delightful new owners.*

Port de Salles
◆ La Grimolée € – €€

port de Salles, 86150 le Vigeant, Vienne
Tel 05 49 48 75 22 Fax 05 49 48 59 99

In a river port about 18 km (11 miles) as the crow flies due north of Confolens and just south of l'Isle Jourdain, this glass-fronted rural restaurant overlooks a placid section of the Vienne. Book a table before setting out, because it is very popular with young men from the nearby motor racing circuit: Circuit Automobile du Val de Vienne. The menu is unusual in offering all the dishes on five different menus as individually priced *à la carte* items as well: such dishes as *filet de dorade au vin de pays Charentais, magret de canard à la moutarde violette de Brive La Gaillarde* and *minute de Saint-Pierre aux copeaux de jambon de Vendée.* The portions are lavish; beware the desserts in particular. For example, the *macaron à la crème d'amaretto brulé, au sirop d'amandes grillées* fully justifies its name and comes with a fruit salad as well.

CLOSED Sun dinner, Mon; Jan–Mar
CARDS AE, MC, V

La Rochelle
◆ André € – €€€

2 rue St Jean de Pérot, 17000 La Rochelle, Charente-Maritime
Tel 05 46 41 28 24 Fax 05 46 41 64 22

This bar-restaurant succeeds because of its size. On the quayside in the height of summer its tables and chairs jostle with those of many other diverse establishments trawling for tourists. Go a short step around to the stern (an appropriate term for a 'Grande Brasserie de Poissons' – as it styles itself), and you will find refrigerated tables of oysters on the arcaded pavements and a quiet, cave-like room packed with marine artefacts, in which to appreciate the fruits of the ocean. The printed menu offers a wide selection of seafood and fish with a range of set menus offering various combinations of oysters, crabs, prawns etc. Blackboards offer the morning market's selection of fish.

CLOSED never
CARDS AE, DC, MC, V

La Rochelle
◆ Le Boute en Train
€ – €€

*7 rue des Bonnes Femmes, 17000 La
Rochelle, Charente-Maritime
Tel 05 46 41 73 74 Fax 05 46 45 90 76*

Le Boute en Train translates as a live-wire
or the life and soul of the party. Certainly
the buzz inside and outside this bistro
comes mostly from locals crowding the market hall or relaxing over their meals. Quite a
walk from the sights and souvenirs of the old
port, this restaurant is reassuringly 'the real
France'. The menus, on blackboards, make
no particular concessions, either to the *terroir* or the sea. They are straightforward,
interesting (fresh steamed cod with
essences of rhubarb) – and well prepared.
All in all, a great antidote to the tide of
tourism that flows through this ancient harbour town.

❛ *A popular place - convivial* ❜ ...
'*Good value and good food* ❜

Closed Sun, Mon; last week Aug, first week Sep
Cards AE, MC, V

● *Grégory Coutanceau is the outstanding chef at Les Flots in La
Rochelle (05 46 41 32 51): his specialities are delicious without
being complicated, and his wine
list dazzles. A tiny romantic café,
La Solette (05 46 41 06 33), makes
a perfect lunch spot, where you
can sit in the shade and enjoy a
simple meal for less than 20 euros.*

Royan
◆ Les Filets Bleu
€ – €€€

*14 rue Notre Dame, 17200 Royan,
Charente-Maritime
Tel 05 46 05 74 00*

On special occasions you can still find
ladies and gentlemen in Edwardian
dress taking the air on the front at Royan.
On the nearby hill, almost in the shadow of a
ship-shaped cathedral, at Les Filets Bleu,
with its portholes and polished deck, you
could imagine yourself taking a voyage on a
famous liner in a gracious bygone age. The
food here is served from the open kitchen at
the front of the restaurant. As you would
expect in a French seaside resort, fish and
seafood feature strongly. A charcoal grill is
the source of several specialities, notably
the lobster *à la maison* with lemon butter,
cream and Cognac, served for something
akin to the annual salary of the kitchen
maid. The restaurant's motto is that all their
dishes are fresh, and they claim that they
would rather throw them out than serve disappointing food.

Closed Sun, Mon; 2 weeks Oct and Jan
Cards DC, MC, V

Our traditional French cuisine symbol
So many of our readers enjoy seeking out
the genuinely French eating experience
that we have used Fr to mark restaurants
which offer *cuisine du terroir*, classical
French dishes or regional dishes with an
emphasis on local ingredients, and traditional recipes.

Saint-Maixent-l'Ecole
◆ Le Logis Saint-Martin
€ – €€€

*chemin de Pissot, 79400 Saint-Maixent-
l'Ecole, Deux-Sèvres
Tel 05 49 05 58 68 Fax 05 49 76 19 93*

Le Logis Saint-Martin is a wonderful surprise. A couple of minutes' drive down a
worryingly suburban road leading off the
N11 as it leaves Saint-Maixent-l'Ecole brings
you suddenly to the green, wooded bank of
the river Sèvre, opposite an island served by
a footbridge. Bertrand and Ingrid Heintz run
this long, low 17thC stone house as a hotel-
restaurant of uncompromisingly high standards. They have a first-class chef and a passion for tip-top service. The beamed restaurant is an enticing room washed in muted
yellows and glinting with silver and crystal,
and there is a steady stream of local people
who make the pilgrimage from town, along
the river bank, to eat here (particularly at
lunchtime, when they offer a good-value

menu). This close to Cognac, you can bring your meal to a satisfactory conclusion; there is also a generous list of teas and coffees.

CLOSED Sun dinner, Mon; first 2 weeks Jan, first 2 weeks Nov
CARDS MC, V

Saint-Jean-d'Angely
◆ Le Scorilon € – €€

5, rue de l'Abbaye, Saint-Jean-d'Angely, Charente-Maritime
Tel 05 46 32 52 61 Fax 05 46 59 99 90

In an ancient town much loved by the Brits, you might expect their favourite restaurant to have a quaint exterior. Not so, it's in a plain building tucked away in a corner by the place du Pilori. Le Scorilon takes itself seriously, and their menus and *carte* seem to steer their clients towards the more expensive dishes. There is the *menu suggestion* at 25.15 euros, the *menu plaisir*, a substantial step up at 35.83 euros, the *menu découverte* at 48.78 euros or à la carte. *Entrées* include *asperges blanches tièdes* served with *une émulsion de volaille*, and main courses, *pavés de carrelet rôti, épinards, velouté de poisson* and *filet de boeuf poêlé, foie gras, pommes rösties et jus de viande à la betterave. Sablé aux pommes caramelisées, crème Anglaise* and *tarte au chocolat blanc, sauce au chocolat amer* are among the delicious desserts. Children are welcome. Pipes and cigars are not, and you pay a service charge at your discretion.

CLOSED Sun dinner, Mon; first 2 weeks Jan, first 2 weeks Nov
CARDS MC, V

Please send us reports
A guide such as this thrives on reader's reports. If you send us five usable reports, we will send you a free copy of any title in our *Charming Small Hotel Guides* series (see page 241 for France titles in the series).

The five reports should contain at least two new restaurants; the rest can be comments on restaurants already in the guide.
1 Tell us about your experiences in restaurants already in this guide.
2 Send us new reports. New reports should give the following information:

- **Region** – City, town, village or neaest village.
- **Name of restaurant** – Please double check the spelling, it's surprisingly easy to make a mistake.
- **Address** – including *département*
- **Telephone number** – plus fax and e-mail if available. Double check this information.
- **Objective description** – Try to explain simply why it should be in the guide. Remember that the guide is very selective - our entries are those one-in-five places that combine
  ● **interesting food with**
  ● **character and charm, in the building, the setting or both.**
  The guide hates tourist traps, and pretentious, dressed-up food. We like places where the French go.
  We favour places in the lower and middle price bands but there are plenty of expensive places that have our qualities, and we list those too.
- **Diner's comments** – These should be short, personal comments on features that strike you. They can be your comments, or others'.
- **Closing times**
- **Credit cards accepted**
  Don' t forget to date your report and add your name and address.
Send reports to Charming Restaurant Guides, Duncan Petersen Publishing, 31 Ceylon Road, London W14 OPY.

Saint-Martin-de-Ré
◆ Le Perroquet Noir
€ – €€

rue du Docteur Kemmerer, 17410 Saint-Martin-de-Ré, Ile-de-Ré, Charente-Maritime
Tel 05 46 01 97 75 Fax 05 46 67 74 13

The name gives a clue to the nature of this restaurant: the Black Parrot is decked out like a pirate ship, sticking with dogged steadfastness to its thematic guns. It is the rather kitsch creation of Constancin Valerie, who, in the guise of a buccaneer, sports a blouse, pantaloons and plenty of gold. But there's more to this place than kitsch. It was born out of Constancin's desire to create a restaurant with 'esprit', somewhere to feel good, be nourished, fed and restored. With this and the *art de la table* in mind, he has put together some regionally-influenced, yet highly individualistic menus. For 23 euros, you can opt for the no-choice *suggestion du pirate*, or for 38.11 euros, enjoy *le régal du pirate*. The *carte* offers a range of dishes with a similarly nautical slant, from *l'assiette de l'aventurier* and *le jardin secret du pirate* to *osso bucco à l'Espagnole* (presumably a reference to the Armada), though not as much fish as you might expect.

CLOSED 3 weeks Jan
CARDS MC, V

Saintes
◆ La Ciboulette
€ – €€€ **Fr**

36 rue du Pérat, 17100 Saintes, Charente-Maritime
Tel 05 46 74 07 36 Fax 05 46 94 14 54

Simple elegance characterizes this somewhat unusual carpeted restaurant just off the main thoroughfare. A significant part of the ground floor area is devoted to an aperitif bar, and although this limits the seating area downstairs, there's a first-floor dining room as well. Chef Jean Yves is an enthusiastic supporter of Cuisineries Gourmandes – an organization devoted to the continued perfection of French regional cuisine, based on local produce. Following their policy, he produces a dessert, an old favourite, but one rarely found in a restaurant: a rhubarb tart that any grandmother would be proud of. The more adventurous (and wealthy) can enjoy a *menu saveur* at 61 euros, where each course is accompanied by fine Champagne.

❝ *Specializes in local produce, cooked well and taken seriously* ❞

CLOSED Sat lunch, Sun
CARDS MC, V

Soudan
◆ L'Orangerie € – €€

79800 Soudan, Deux-Sèvres
Tel 05 49 06 56 06 Fax 05 49 06 56 10

Although you wouldn't guess it, this building was once a blacksmith's forge, but fire and ashes have now given way to a clean regime of cream decoration. An interesting format of menus offers children an *initiation à la gourmandise*, and vegetarians a menu that includes an avocado tart with lemon cream, a *bouquet* of courgettes with thyme and a vegetable *terrine* with saffron sauce. Otherwise, what would generally be a *menu du jour* is a *menu convivial*. Neither the *régional* nor *gourmet* menus will break the bank, and the *menu régional* often includes a *farci Poitevin* – a tasty faggot-like dish, with proportions that suggest the chef thinks he's feeding the blacksmith. Though it's on the main N11 (30 km/19 miles east of Niort), the dining room faces away from the traffic, overlooking countryside.

CLOSED Sun dinner; end Nov, early Dec
CARDS AE, MC, V

Looking for somewhere to stay?
See page 241.

Surgères
◆ Le Vieux Puits € – €€

6 rue Paul Bert, 17700 Sugères, Charente-Maritime
Tel 05 46 07 50 83

You'll either find Le Vieux Puits by accident or you'll have to ask directions. The tiny cul-de-sac is hardly more than a courtyard. Nevertheless, on a summer's day, it is a sheltered spot for outside eating. In less clement weather there are two plain but pleasant dining rooms on the ground and first floors of the restaurant. If the surroundings are not the most elegant, the food more than compensates at Le Vieux Puits. The basic three-course menu is full of surprises: it might start brightly with a colourful mosaic of vegetables; followed by salmon in an aluminium *papillote*; and, after a choice of cheese, dessert, sorbet or ice-cream, you will leave entirely satisfied. A bistro in the best sense of the word - there are no frills in the surroundings – the effort all goes into the food.

CLOSED Thu, Sun
CARDS MC, V

Taillebourg
◆ Auberge des Glycines €

17350 Taillebourg, Charente-Maritime
Tel 05 46 91 81 40

About 10 km (6 miles) north of Saintes, Taillebourg is an unexpected little gem in the Charente river valley, one of the least well known but most attractive in the whole of France. The Auberge des Glycines (which means 'wisteria') must have been a popular watering hole when commercial barges crowded the long adjoining quayside. Now local youths bathe between the pleasure cruisers and this *auberge* offers its guests a single wide-ranging menu. There seems to be something for everyone, from the exotic *cassolette d'escargots à la Charantaise* to the more prosaic sirloin steak with onions and butter (*faux-filet grillé, fondue d'echalottes au beurre*). Taillebourg is signposted from the complex road junction between exit 35 from the A10 and the D137 Rochefort road.

Closed Wed; Nov
Cards MC, V

Talmont-sur-Gironde
◆ Auberge du Promentoire €–€€

rue de l'Ancien Château, 17120 Talmont-sur-Gironde, Charente-Maritime
Tel 05 46 90 40 66 Fax 05 46 90 43 79

The north bank of the Gironde estuary is not recognized as a tourist area, but, for any visitors to the region, the tiny peninsula and village of Talmont-sur-Gironde is a jewel that makes the journey worthwhile. Amongst the cottages that huddle around the seaside church, Auberge du Promentoire provides a small outdoor eating area and a deceptively large restaurant. It is lit by a fleet of ceiling lights inside simple shades of cotton print fabric, which look rather like buoys bobbing in the sunlight. The kitchen has a glass wall, so diners can watch the preparation of their meal – a good alternative to seascapes when the weather turns nasty. Not surprisingly the *auberge* is renowned for its fish; the char-

grilled grey mullet is particularly delicious, firm but easily flaked.

❛ *Superb fish' ... 'A great discovery* ❜

Closed Tue dinner, Wed
Cards MC, V

Thouars
◆ Le Rabelais €

3 rue Saint Médard, 79100 Thouars, Deux-Sèvres
Tel 05 49 67 93 63

With its shop front, striped awning and round back metal chairs, Le Rabelais has something of the atmosphere of a 1950s tea shop, but genteel ladies and gentlemen would be hard pressed to understand the unusual format of the menu. Indeed, at first sight it seems that only an advanced mathematician or bookie's clerk could sort out the permutations on offer. It's worth taking a moment to resolve the apparent complexity. Once you have done so, you'll find a flexible system, offering outstanding value for money from an ambitions kitchen. The bargain is even more attractive as each menu includes at least one glass of a named local wine.

Closed Mon dinner, Tue
Cards MC, V

Vouille
◆ Cheval Blanc €–€€

3 rue de la Barre, 86190 Vouille, Vienne
Tel 05 49 51 81 46 Fax 05 49 51 96 31

Two river channels almost make an island of the Cheval Blanc, and swans, geese and ducks are quite likely to greet your arrival at the car park. In the quiet village centre, this hostelry has three dining rooms and a large patio with a fixed roof, which extends into a further riverside terrace. A *timbale* of shrimps and mussels is in fact a seafood chowder; the *tournedos du canard Rossini* is recommended; but the outstanding dish, guaranteed to send you for a *siesta*, is the pear and almond flan, set on curved quarters of red and cream fruit *coulis*.

Closed Sun dinner
Cards AE, MC, V

CENTRAL FRANCE

THE REGIONAL CUISINES

• PAYS DE LA LOIRE • CENTRE • BOURGOGNE •
• FRANCH-COMTE • POITOU-CHARENTES • LIMOUSIN •

PAYS DE LA LOIRE

'Loire Country' refers to the western reaches of France's longest river where it finally empties into the sea. (The region now called Centre is the one that encompasses the Loire Valley with its famous châteaux). Pays-de-la-Loire stretches inland from the Atlantic coast to encompass the *départements* of Vendée, Loire-Atlantique, Maine-et-Loire, Mayenne and Sarthe. Each one has a distinct identity; indeed Loire-Atlantique, whose capital Nantes is now capital of the whole region, was formerly part of Brittany and still considered Breton. Taken as a whole, however, this is, like its neighbour Centre, a mild, gentle region: in its landscape, its climate, and its gastronomy. One thinks of *sauce beurre blanc*, cream and mushrooms, freshwater fish, poultry, fruit, buttery biscuits, creamy cheeses and subtle, refreshing wines.

Stretching along the Atlantic coast, the Vendée mixes meadows full of grazing

Centre: Auberge de Kerbourg, St-Lyphard.
Below: A familiar scene on the Loire and its tributaries.

cattle with heather and gorse and – in the south, on the border with Poitou-Charentes – the Marais Poitevin, once the bay of Poitou, now a region of watery marshland including the Venise Verte, where visitors and market gardeners alike get around by boat.

Along the coast, the mussels and oysters from L'Aiguillon-sur-Mer and La-Tranche-sur-Mer are prized, as well as *pommes-de-terre de Noirmoutier* and beef raised on the Marais. Look out too for ducks from Challans and for *mojettes*, white beans much enjoyed by locals and often eaten on their own with a knob of butter or spread on garlicky bread. *Brioche*, perfumed with orange flower water or *eau-de-vie*, is also a speciality, as are *vins des fiefs Vendéens*: wines traditionally produced by Vendée fiefdoms as far back as the Middle Ages.

Loire-Atlantique includes Nantes, the largest city in Western France with the second largest wholesale market after Rungis, and, in contrast, the low-lying Parc Naturel de Brière and salt marshes of Guérande, criss-crossed by numerous canals and channels. Nantes has several culinary claims to fame, including the invention of the *petit beurre* biscuit, originally made by local bakers to keep seafarers happy. Of the original six sugar-cane refineries in Nantes only one, Béghin-Say, is still active, but they were responsible for the local boiled sweet, *berlingot* and for the fruit-centred *rigolette*. Then there is *gâteau Nantais*, made with butter and

Centre:Vineyard near Saumur.
Below: White-fronted geese in the rough grasslands of the Mayenne valley.

rum, and of course *sauce beurre blanc*, properly made with a reduction of Muscadet, vinegar and shallots and served with the plentiful freshwater fish of the region. Mâche Nantaise is just one of the many vegetables grown in the region's numerous market gardens. In the marshes minute elvers, civelles, appear in abundance in spring, while pimpeneau, a non-migrating eel, is smoked over peat; salicorne, preserved in vinegar, is served as an accompaniment to meat or fish; and sea bass is cooked in a salt crust. The addition of Guérande salt creates the unique local butter. Cockles, mussels and oysters from Le Croisic, and sardines from Turballe are best savoured with a glass of Muscadet or Gros-Plant from the Nantais vineyards.

In the historic region of Maine and Anjou — today comprising the *départements* of Maine-et-Loire, Mayenne and Sarthe – the beautiful *manoirs* and châteaux are not paraded along the banks of the Loire, as they are further inland, but hidden away down country lanes in romantic parks. The Loire Valley here is full of orchards, market gardens and vineyards, while further north, the quiet Mayenne valley makes a perfect setting for a peaceful stay, and for river trips. Gastronomic highlights include *rillettes* of pork, goose and even rabbit, capons from Le Mans, poultry from Loué and delicious *reinette* apples. Local beef goes into the pot roast *cul-de-veau à l'Angevine*. Mushrooms, known as *champignons de Paris*, are cultivated on a huge scale in the region's chalk caves. They turn up with cream as a sauce for chicken, as in *poulet à l'Angevine*. Freshwater fish such as salmon and the far more rare shad are also often served with a sauce of cream and sorrel. *Crémets d'Anjou* are creamy moulds of fresh cheese served with puréed fruit. Amongst wines, look out for Quarts-de-Chaume (sweet), Coulée de Serrant and Saumur-Champigny from Maine-et-Loire, and Vin de Jasnières from Sarthe.

Below: Auberge de Kerbourg, St-Lyphard.

CENTRE

The bland but geographically accurate name accorded to this region gives little away, but 'The Loire Valley', which is what this area is, instantly gives a far more vivid picture. First, of course, one thinks of magnificent châteaux ; then of the fruit, vegetables and flowers of the 'garden of France'; of troglodyte villages — semi-subterranean dwellings carved from the tufa limestone; of the cathedrals of Blois and Chartres; of Tours and Orléans; and of the woods and lakes of the Solonge, a paradise for anglers and hunters.

With its rich and colourful history, one might imagine that the gastronomy of the Loire Valley would be equally flamboyant; in fact it is low key. The royalty and nobility who occupied the great châteaux may have feasted off meat and other luxuries, but the ordinary inhabitants had to make do with whatever they could grow that was edible, and the cuisine is more about ingredients than about distinctive ways of cooking them. It was largely thanks to King Charles VIII that fruit and vegetables were found to thrive so well in the mild climate, when, in the spirit of the Renaissance, he imported gardeners along with artists and architects to Amboise. In this region, superb ingredients including freshwater fish, fruit and vegetables are prepared with simplicity. Some would call it a delicate cuisine, others bland.

The Tourangeaux (inhabitants of Touraine) have a thing about prunes, which probably dates back to the Crusades, when they were brought back from Damascus. They turn up in all sorts of dishes, both sweet and savoury, but are particularly good with pork and cream. Fruit tarts are hugely popular and can be admired in every *pâtisserie* window, while

Below: Spring comes to woodlands near Domaine de la Tortinière, Montbazon.

229

Lamotte-Beuvran is the home of the famous upside-down *tarte Tatin*. Legend has it that the two Tatin sisters, proprietors of the local hotel, created the caramelized apple tart quite by mistake. Pithiviers, is the home of *gâteau Pithiviers*, puff pastry filled with almond paste (as well as the much more dubious lark pâté). From the Gâtinais comes delicate saffron, clear, richly coloured honey, walnuts, mushrooms, and Montargis pralines, still sold from the building where they were invented. Nearby Orléans is celebrated for its vinegars and for *cotignac d'Orléans*, melt-in-the-mouth quince jelly.

Where meat or poultry appears on a traditional regional menu, it often does so in a delicate sauce of cream and mushrooms, such as *géline à la Lochoise* or *beuchelle Tourangelle*. Game naturally makes a strong showing in the Sologne, while Tours has its own version of *rillettes*

(potted meat), either served with bread or in *tarte Tourangelle*, a type of quiche. In the north of the region, surrounded by mile upon mile of wheat fields, Chartres has a love affair with pâté, which was said to have been started by an appreciative Attila the Hun.

The region's cheeses are predominantly goat's, including Crottin de Chavignol and Saint-Maure, but there are some fine cow's milk cheeses too, such as Cendré d'Olivet and Saint-Benoît. Amongst its celebrated wines, diversity is the key, ranging from sweet whites to excellent reds, including some wonderful sparkling wines, and the smoky, fruity Sancerre and Pouilly-Fumé.

Above: La Tonnnellerie, Tavers.
Below: Terrace overlooking the parkland of Domaine de la Tortinière, Montbazon.

BOURGOGNE

Conveniently situated just south of Paris and *en route* for Provence and the Côte d'Azur, Burgundy combines the best of France – in its history, its medieval buildings, its varied landscape, its superb wines and, of course, in its fine traditional cuisine. Together with its southern extension, the Rhône-Alpes

Aligoté, followed by a properly made *coq au vin* in which oceans of the local red wine, perhaps Chambertin, has been reduced to create the cooking liquid.

There is much to do until it's time to eat and drink once more. You can visit neat villages with legendary names floating in a sea of immaculate vines in the

Above: Vézelay, Burgundy pilgrimage centre.

region centred on Lyon, this is the gastronomic heart of France.

Good wine and plenty of it makes for good food. Burgundian recipes are a perfect marriage of local ingredients and local wine – even poached eggs turn up in red wine – and as a result the dishes manage to be both satisfying and sophisticated. Here perhaps more than anywhere, it's important to seek out purveyors of *cuisine de terroir* in preference to the plethora of fancy restaurants that insist on playing tricks with the food. Nothing could beat a dish of *escargots à la Bourguignonne* cooked in a *court-bouillon* of Chablis or

Côte d'Or. Or you can admire the world-class art in the Musée des Beaux Arts in Dijon; the spectacular Hôtel-Dieu with its amazing multi-coloured roof in Beaune; the Romansque masterpieces of Vézelay, Cluny, Autun and Fontenay; the charming country churches of pastoral Brionnais; the rugged, thickly wooded terrain of Morvan. The Palais des Ducs (now housing the Musée des Beaux Arts) in elegant Dijon is the clue to both the region's good fortune and its good cooking. In medieval times it was the seat of the powerful Grand Dukes of Burgundy who ruled over a vast swathe of western Europe from the North Sea to the Loire, and from the Loire to the Rhine. It also contains the impressive and, for its time, innovative kitchen that was added in the 15th century. Art, culture and good food all arrived in Burgundy at this time.

Burgundy's illustrious Charolais beef (in point of fact tough in texture and mild in flavour) is best suited to slow-cooked dishes such as the classic *boeuf Bourguignon*, *boeuf en daube* or *boeuf à la mode* (braised with vegetables). Ham from Morvan is excellent and often appears as *jambon persillé* (with parsley in aspic), or as a *saupiquet* (sautéed with a spiced cream sauce). Game is always worth looking out for – you might see sanglier and marcassin as well as *lièvre*, perhaps marinated with grapes, and *lapin de la garenne* (wild rabbit) – while Bresse, south of Dijon in the Rhône-Alpes region, produces France's most prized poultry. The Bresse chicken is a special breed, large, white of flesh and feather, with bluish legs. It must conform to the strictest of rules to qualify as a proper – and expensive – *poulet de Bresse*, including being free-range, fed on a special diet of cereals and weighed before and after dressing. They are at their best simply roasted with butter in the French fashion.

The region is awash with rivers — principally the Saône – and waterways, and freshwater fish makes a celebrated appearance in *pauchouse*, or *pochouse*, a

mixture of fish cooked in white Burgundy. Crayfish are happily in evidence, perhaps poached in Chablis or, not uncommonly, served with chicken.

Though the true *escargot de Bourgogne* (*Helix pomotia*) is a rarity these days, snails from wherever still feature large on the menu. Look out for dishes other than the usual *escargots à la Bourguignonne*, stuffed with garlic and parsley butter.

Most cooking in Burgundy involves a good drenching in the local wine. And why not? Even eggs don't escape when poached *en meurette* with a thickened sauce of young red wine. Eggs are important hereabouts: this is the home of *gougère*, delicious cheese-flavoured choux pastry.

Although by no means all *moutarde de Dijon* is made at Dijon these days, the city is as famous for its mustard as it is for its Burgundian dukes and its art museum. Mustard seed was said to have been brought to the

Centre: lobster on the menu at Lameloise, Chagny.
*Below: Canal boat (*peniche*) for hire on the Burgundy Canal.*

region by the Romans, and found to suit the climate perfectly. It has been made since the 13th century (the dukes loved it) with wine, sour grape juice, herbs and spices. Any dish 'à la Dijonnaise', such as veal or kidneys, is flavoured with Dijon mustard. Two other specialities of Dijon are *pain d'épices* (bread made with spices and honey) and *cassis*.

The cheeseboard is likely to be superb. Local cheeses include feisty goat's cheese from around Mâcon such as Chevreton de Mâcon and Boutons-de-Culottes; Chaorce, Soumaintrain and Saint-Florentin from the border with Champagne; and the powerful, gooey, Epoisses, its rind washed in Marc.

Burgundy wines are amongst the greatest. The soil, the grapes (principally chardonnay and pinot noir, and to a much lesser extent aligoté and gamay), the climate and the winemakers' skill combine to produce exceptional results. From near Auxerre comes white Chablis, from the Côte de Nuits classic reds such as Chambertin and Clos-de-Vougeot, from the Côte de Beaune whites such as Montrachet as well as reds, from the Côte Chalonnaise white Rully and red Givry, and from the Mâconnais white Pouilly-Fuissé as well as reds and rosés. Plots of vines – first cultivated by Cistercian and Cluniac monks – change hands for vast sums of money, especially those called climats, top quality named plots from within a production area, for example Gevrey-Chambertin Premier Cru Clos Saint-Jacques. Each autumn a world-famous wine auction is held in Beaune's flamboyant Hôtel-Dieu.

Above: Burgudian cheeses and snails.
Below: Gougères of chicken.

FRANCHE-COMTÉ

Alpine, Alsatian and Burgudian cooking all have their influences on the traditional table in Franche-Comté, but this relatively little visited region – gently rolling country to the north, wild, mountainous and forested with torrents of water to the south – has a distinct culinary character, and a distinctive wine too. The name Franche-Comté - literally 'free country' - is still of course proudly borne, and refers to the fact that the region survived waves of invaders and attempts at annexation.

In the south of the region the Jura shares a similar cuisine to that of Savoie, but often using the local mild blue cheese Gex, rather than Gruyère in raclette. Cheese also appears in the ever-popular fondue, and wrapped in ham and fried on skewers, with bacon on toast, in choux pastry puffs, with ham in *escalope de veau belle Comptoise*, even baked with chicken, as in *poulet au Comté*.

Dairy farming in Franche-Comté has long operated on the co-operative principle in small factories called *fruitières*. *Comté* is its most distinguished cheese, followed by Vacherin du Mont d'Or and Morbier with its thin black line in the middle. Amongst puddings, look out for *papette Jurassien*, a brioche or pastry tart with vanilla- or orange flower- flavoured cream. And amongst Jura's wines, grown principally around Arbois, try the sherry-like Vin Jaune, made in Château-Chalon from the Savagnin grape. With a deep yellow colour and nutty flavour, it is matured for six years in oak casks, then bottled in special waxed *clavelins*. Drink as an aperitif or with cheese. The much rarer Vin de Paille can be kept for 50 years. And try the region's liqueurs, made from gentian, pine, cherry and plum, as well as Marc and Hypocras, a spiced red wine.

Right: imported spices vie with local ingredients in Franche-Comté markets.

After a cheesy start, the classic main course to choose in Franche-Comté would be *coq au Vin Jaune or poulet aux morilles*, made with vin Jaune. The chicken may come from nearby Bresse in the neighbouring Rhône-Alpes region but the pitted, intense morel mushrooms will certainly be from carefully-guarded forest sites in Franche-Comté, where *cèpes, girolles* and other edible mushrooms grow in abundance. *Charcuterie* plays an important role: *brési* (thinly sliced cured beef), Jésus de Morteau , and cumin-spiced *saucisse de Montbéliard* are specialities.

The many rivers, streams and lakes of Franche-Comté yield plenty of freshwater fish, always prominent on local menus. Trout is good when cooked in vin Jaune, and a mixture of fish goes to make the Burgundian fish stew with white wine called *pauchouse* or *pochouse*.

A once-staple, now little known speciality of Bésançon is *gaude*, a soupy mixture of cornmeal and milk or cream. And frog's legs soup is a feature of Doubs.

Below: Franche-Comté markets groan with fruit and vegetables.
Bottom: The stall specializing in foie gras of duck or goose straight from the producer is a universal attraction.

POITOU-CHARENTES

Mild and serene, Poitou-Charentes is a landscape of softly rolling hills, fertile pastures and marshland. There are canals and fens, wide horizons, wooded valleys, hills and vineyards – and 300 miles of sunny coast whose highlights include the delightful and gastronomic port of La Rochelle and the islands of Ré and Oléron. The culinary stars of the region are distinct: melons, oysters, mussels, snails, marsh-fed lamb, beef, butter, goat's cheese and, to drink, Cognac and Pineau de Charente.

Charentais melons with their sweet, blushed-orange flesh are grown in many parts of France, but the finest are found here, and are especially good when served with a dash of the local aperitif Pineau de

Left: Seaside markets of Poitou-Charentes can offer deep water game fish such as swordfish alongside more predictable species.
Below: freshest local fare.

Charentes. Amongst vegetables, *mojettes* (white beans) are served in a garlic-infused cream sauce; cabbage is either stuffed or stewed in butter; fat green beans are sautéed in butter, and leeks called *jaunes de Poitou* are widely used in seafood dishes such as lamprey stewed in red wine and La Rochelle's *porée*.

Oysters from the Marennes-Oléron Basin are the best in France in terms of both quality and quantity, thanks to the combination of fresh (from the Seudre river) and salt water and a warm, sunny climate. Oysters and oyster-farming is a science in itself, with several museums in the area devoted to the subject. The best way to eat them (throughout the year) is simply: raw and freshly opened, with lemon juice or a shallot-flavoured vinaigrette. They may also come as a soup, stuffed with savoury butter, as a gratin or on a kebab. In restaurants you will find mussels in *mouclade*, stewed with saffron and cream, but probably not in *éclade*, flambéed over pine needles (best done at home or on the beach), while the local clams (*palourdes*) are also excellent. A traditional way of using a mixture of local Atlantic seafood is in the splendid fish soup *chaudrée*.

In Poitou, *petit gris* snails are called *lumas*, in Charentes, *cagouilles*. They were once found in abundance in the vineyards, but since local demand is still high they are now mostly imported. They come in all sorts of guises: braised with red wine, chopped in omelettes, dressed in vinaigrette, even as soup.

Local lamb is tender with light, well-marbled flesh, for example *agneau de Poitou-Charentes* is raised around Montmorillon and Confolens. The beef, from a long tradition of breeding Limousine and Parthenaise cattle, is also excellent, perhaps in a *daube* with calf's foot or with sorrel and bone marrow. You might also come across hare, often stuffed and braised, and pig's head soup.

Charentes butter rivals that of Normandy, some say it is even better. It was not always so: as phylloxera wiped out the vineyards a century or more ago, and the land was put to grass and dairy farming. Another bonus is the cheese, mainly from goats: there are 50 types of Chabichou alone.

After phylloxera, only a small area of vines was left in Charentes, and even those are of poor quality. Tended with the utmost care, they produce the king of *eau-de-vie*, Cognac, and the aperitif Pineau, always served chilled.

Above: 20 or more different sizes, shapes and colours of olive are a feature of markets here and all over France.
Left: The fresh flower stall.

LIMOUSIN

With its swathes of high meadows, its dense forests and great stands of oak, chestnut and beech, Limousin is a mosaic of green, cut everywhere by crystal-clear water. Limoges, set in particularly beautiful countryside, is a great porcelain centre, and Aubusson similarly for tapestries, while Brive-la-Gaillard stands out for its market (Tuesdays, Thursdays and Saturdays).

The gastronomy of Limousin is a perfect complement to the surroundings, with soups, superb beef and *charcuterie*, hearty stews, thick batter puddings and fruit liqueurs that combine the need to make do with what is available with the French flair for fine, well-balanced flavours. There are no local wines.

Since the region is thick with chestnut forests, it's not surprising that they turn up so often in the cooking, as in *soupe aux marrons*, a thick purée of chestnuts cooked in broth with cream added, and ladled on to slices of toast. Another local soup is *bréjaude*, spoon-standing thick with vegetables and accompanied by rye bread. Typical peasant dishes still found on country menus are *farcidure*, which can refer to a type of potato cake or to dumplings, rye pancakes (*galettes*, *galetons* or *tourtons*), *potée* (cabbage stew) and *cassoulet* (pork, beans and *confit*).

Beef and veal raised on the lush meadows of the Limousin plateau are celebrated for their tenderness and full flavour, while the air is just right for drying *charcuterie*, including excellent *saucisses*, *andouille* and *boudin*, the latter flavoured

Below: The Limousin plateau.

with chestnuts. Boudin (black pudding) is *Limousin cattle* often accompanied by red cabbage and chestnuts. Ham is roasted with chestnuts, breast of veal comes stuffed with chestnuts and rabbit is stuffed and served with a chestnut *coulis*. There are walnuts, hazlenuts and almonds too: look out for walnut bread and walnut and hazlenut cake, and almond cake from Creuse, as well as *gâteau de miel aux noisettes*. The region is also renowned for its mushrooms, particularly its *cèpes*, which are both used in cooking and served on their own, sautéed in a little onion and garlic with

cream - perfection.

Local cheese is in short supply in Limousin, since most cattle are reared for meat rather than for their dairy products, but you may find Brach, a type of Roquefort. Puddings are a different matter: it is Limousin that is responsible for the great *clafoutis* (traditionally made with cherries, but any fruit can be used) as well as for apple-flavoured *flaugnarde*, another batter-based dessert.

Above and bottom: Limousin is aregion of rivers, streams and waterfalls.
Below: At Collonges-la-Rouge, Limousin.

VISIT
charmingsmallhotels.co.uk

Duncan Petersen's travel website is the internet's most interesting database for places to stay with character and charm. It is based on the publisher's *Charming Small Hotel Guides*.

Many of the best hotels and other places to stay in Britain, France and Italy are featured on the site, with new destinations are being added all the time.

Locate places to stay with ease by clicking on maps or scanning geographical listings. Each hotel is illustrated with a colour photo and a full description plus essential facts for booking,

For most entries there's an onward link direct to the hotel's own website, which in turn offers online booking.

THE CHARMING SMALL HOTEL GUIDES

The biggest and the best special accommodation guide series published internationally: no hotel pays for an entry.

Four titles in the series will especially interest travellers in France as companions to this restaurant guide:

CHARMING SMALL HOTEL GUIDES
FRANCE

CHARMING SMALL HOTELS AND RESTAURANTS
SOUTHERN FRANCE

CHARMING SMALL HOTELS AND RESTAURANTS
PARIS

CHARMING SMALL HOTEL GUIDES
FRANCE'S MOST DISTINCTIVE
BED & BREAKFASTS

NORTH AMERICAN READERS

This series is published by Interlink Books and is available at all good bookstores or directly by visiting www.interlinkbooks.com

U.K. READERS

From all good booksellers, or order through charmingsmallhotels.co.uk

LIMOUSIN

B ordered by Poitou-Charente to the west, Auvergne to the east, Centre to the north and Aquitaine to the south, Limousin is full of trees and water. Lakes, rivers, granite, heather, chestnut forests and wide open spacesdefine this green region, whose capital Limoges, surrounded by lovely countryside, is famous for its porcelain, while Aubusson is celebrated for its tapestries.

Crozant 245
La Souterraine 249
Mortemart 247
POITOU-CHARENTES
Saint-Léonard-de-Noblat 248
Limoges 246
Saint-Ybard 248
AQUITAINE
Brive-la-Gaillarde 244
Collonges-la-Rouge 245
Turenne 249

CENTRE

Boussac 244

N145

Gueret 246

Saint-Hilaire-
le-Château 247

D941

AUVERGNE

LIMOUSIN

A89

N120

Tulle 249

N120

Beaulieu-sur-
Dordogne 244

MIDI-
PYRENEES

Beaulieu-sur-Dordogne
◆ Auberge des Charmilles €€ – €€€

*20, bd Saint Rodolphe de Turenne, 19120
Beaulieu sur Dordogne
Tel 05 55 91 29 29 Fax 05 55 91 29 30*

The Boulevard St Rodolphe, despite its central location, seems to be more of a residential suburb than the location of a restaurant. However, on entering this converted country house you will appreciate the peaceful setting: the restaurant backs on to a branch of the Dordogne, and in summer you can eat on the terrace with the water at your feet and in the shadow of the great trees opposite. For quick (and inexpensive) visits there is a simple *Autour un Plat* – a main dish followed by cheese or dessert. The standard menu offers a choice of two dishes in both starter and main course, followed by cheese and dessert. Or you could venture into other more elaborate and expensive dishes. The Charmilles has eight sunny and spacious guest rooms, each of them named after a variety of strawberry grown in the Beaulieu region. Beaulieu is a medieval town that is known for its 'Strawberry Day', when a huge strawberry tart is divided between thousands of visitors. The town square has a strawberry field where 800kg of the fruit is picked for the enormous tart.

❛ *Riverside peace in the heart of a vibrant town* ❜

Closed Tue, Wed; Christmas Day
Cards AE, MC, V

Our price bands
€ under 30 euros €€ 30-50 Euros
€€€ over 50 euros for a menu

Boussac
◆ Relais Creusois
€ – €€€

*rte de la Châtre, 40 la Maison-Dieu, 23600
Boussac
Tel 05 55 65 02 20 Fax 05 55 65 13 60*

Among a row of houses on the left-hand side of the hill as you leave the town centre, this upmarket Relais does nothing to draw attention to itself, despite the baffling vertical green rods that clad the front of the building. Neither the location nor the bistro-style furnishings of this restaurant, with its views across a lush green valley, seem to do justice to the aspirations of chef Jean-Jacques Tulleau. His menus are named after some gastronomic giants – Escoffier, Brillat-Savarin and Lucullus, and ranged in price from 20 to nearly 60 euros as we went to press. Jean-Jacques' own recommendation for a *plat du terroir* is farmed pigeon with *millefeuille* of potatoes and mushrooms.

Closed Sun, Mon; first three days Jan, Ten days Feb, 2 weeks Aug
Cards MC, V

Our price bands
Rather than giving actual prices (which are prone to change) we indicate the cost of a three-course meal for one person, without wine, by means of price bands. They are as follows: € under 30 euros €€ 30-50 euros €€€ over 50 euros. Where we give more than one price band, for example €– €€€, this indicates that in that restaurant a meal can be had at a range of prices. As well as the cost of *prix fixe* menus, our price bands also take into account the cost of an average selection from the *à la carte* menu.

Brive-la-Gaillarde
◆ Chez Francis
€ – €€€ **Fr**

*61 av de Paris, 16100 Brive la Gaillarde
Tel 05 55 74 41 72 Fax 05 55 17 20 54*

This slightly eccentric restaurant is situated in a busy street of bars and restaurants on the fringe of Brive's city centre, and is very popular with the locals. A black bowler-hatted statue (of the kind that would once have stood outside the restaurant to draw in passers-by), now greets you inside among other early 20thC catering equipment and nick-knacks, from bacon slicer to a vast copper coffee percolator. Mme Tessandier rules the busy restaurant efficiently, but even so it took a long time for the aperitif to arrive, before the modestly priced *repas* including a beef, lentil and onion starter; fresh mackerel; and the local speciality of *crème brulée fleur d'oranger*.

❝ A great place to soak up an atmosphere - as long as you're not in a hurry ❞

CLOSED Tue evenings; Wed (except July and Aug); every evening (except by reservation) Oct to May; one week June; Jan, Feb
CARDS MC, V

Looking for somewhere to stay? See page 241.

Collonge- la-Rouge
◆ Relais de St Jacques de Campostelle € – €€

19500, Collonges la Rouge
Tel 05 55 25 41 02 Fax 05 55 84 08 51

It's easy to miss Collonges la Rouge on the D38 from Brive to Beaulieu sur Dordogne, an attractive drive. As an open stretch of road skirts a hillside, the sign indicating 'One of France's Prettiest Villages' seems a little over the top when all you can see is a few functional buildings. But stop and venture down a little lane and you'll find the quaintest of medieval settlements, tucked into a fold of the valley. The Relais was created in the 1950s when M. and Mme Richier were enticed to this red sandstone toy-town-like village and took charge of a 15thC house. Now under the directorship of M. and Mme Guillaume, the Relais offers two modern dining rooms and a pleasant dilemma – do you prefer the view over the countryside, or over the village? In summer it can be easily resolved by eating on the garden terrace. The smart bedrooms also offer a choice of delightful views.

CLOSED mid-Nov to mid-Mar
CARDS AE, DC, MC, V

Please send us reports
A guide such as this thrives on reader's reports. If you send us five usable reports, we will send you a free copy of any title in our *Charming Small Hotel Guides* series (see page 241 for France titles in the series).

The five reports should contain at least two new restaurants; the rest can be comments on restaurants already in the guide.
1 Tell us about your experiences in restaurants already in this guide.
2 Send us new reports. New reports should give the following information:
- **Region –** City, town, village or neaest village
- **Name of restaurant –** Please double check the spelling, it's surprisingly easy to make a mistake
- **Address –** including *département*
- **Telephone number –** plus fax and e-mail if available. Double check this information.
- **Objective description –** Try to explain simply why it should be in the guide. Remember that the guide is very selective - our entries are those one-in-five places that combine
- **interesting food with**
- **character and charm, in the building, the setting or both.**
  The guide hates tourist traps, and pretentious, dressed-up food. We like places where the French go.
  We favour places in the lower and middle price bands but there are plenty of expensive places that have our qualities, and we list those too.
- **Diner's comments –** These should be short, personal comments on features that strike you. They can be your comments, or others'.
- **Closing times**
- **Credit cards accepted**
  Don' t forget to date your report and add your name and address.
Send reports to Charming Restaurant Guides, Duncan Petersen Publishing, 31 Ceylon Road, London W14 0PY.

Crozant
◆ Auberge de la Vallée € **Fr**

Auberge de la Vallée, 23160 Crozant
Tel 05 55 89 80 03 Fax 05 55 89 83 22

The high promontory at the confluence of the rivers Creuse and Sédelle is the site of the ruins of a massive medieval fortress. Life is laid-back here, in the heart of rural Limousin. Even so, the windows of the Auberge de la Vallée groan under a profusion of commendations and memberships of culinary organisations. Evidently the cuisine is taken seriously and they have made efforts to create an atmosphere (if you like that kind of thing) by dressing the waitresses in traditional market-day costume. Try pigeon cooked in pastry and lamb cutlets 'Baronet of Limousin' with garlic and grain mustard.

CLOSED Mon evening;Tue (except July to Aug); Jan
CARDS AE, MC, V

Our price bands
Rather than giving actual prices (which are prone to change) we indicate the cost of a three-course meal for one person, without wine, by means of price bands. They are as follows: € under 30 euros €€ 30-50 euros €€€ over 50 euros. Where we give more than one price band, for example €– €€€, this indicates that in that restaurant a meal can be had at a range of prices. As well as the cost of *prix fixe* menus, our price bands also take into account the cost of an average selection from the *à la carte* menu.

Gueret
◆ Hotel Auclair € – €€

19 Avenue de la Sénaterie, 23000 Gueret
Tel 05 55 41 22 00 Fax 05 55 52 86 89

This restaurant, situated conveniently in the city centre, must have soothed many a furrowed brow over the years. High-ceilinged and spacious, with white tablecloths and cool colours, it's an ideal place to exchange confidences or seek assurance while enjoying fine food. You can also relax in one of the 30 bedrooms, or while cooling off in the swimming pool. With a menu that changes daily, you need never eat the same dish twice. Recently on the menu was asparagus in puff pastry, leg of lamb en croûte and apple tart with caramel sauce.

CLOSED never
CARDS AE, DC, MC, V

Limoges
◆ L'Escapade du Gourmet
€ – €€ **Fr**

5 rue de 71 Mobiles, 87000 Limoges
Tel 05 55 50 06 94 Fax 05 55 32 11 95

The Escapade du Gourmet is unashamedly a stylish brasserie with decoration rooted in the Belle Epoque and is conveniently located between Galerie Lafayette and the Cathedral of St Etienne. Walls are clad in mosaics of tiles in the style of Mucha and the lighting shines through great patterns of stained glass in the ceilings. All too frequently menus across France seem cast in stone and remain almost unchanged from year to year, despite a sincere devotion to fresh produce. This place is different, and at the time of a recent visit the Menu de l'Escapade was genuinely seasonal with a tasty roulade of veal filled with autumn vegetables and fresh chestnuts playing no small part in the triangular dessert of three different flavours.

❛A happy mix of sophistication and the country market❜

CLOSED Sat lunch; Sun evening; Mon
CARDS MC, V

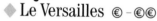

charmingsmallhotels.co.uk
Visit Duncan Petersen's travel website, the best online search tool for places to stay that combine character and charm. Currently features Britain, France, Italy and Ireland, with other destinations being continuously added.

Limoges
◆ Le Versailles € – €€

20, place d'Aine, 87000 Limoges
Tel 05 55 34 13 39 Fax 05 55 32 84 73

This is a well-named restaurant: Parisian in style and feel and yet, like the palace, not quite in Paris. It is on the edge of the semi-pedestrianised old city centre of Limoges, amongst chic and expensive boutiques of porcelain and the churches and the market hall. It's a stylish and formal brasserie, with mirrors, fawn and cream decoration and the Sun King symbol on the glass frontage. Cyril Boissier and his team offer two three course menus well within our lowest price bracket (together with even cheaper two course variations). They (and the *carte*) are replete with interesting dishes – *crème de haricots paimpolaise, huile de noix; epaule d'agneau farcie et des pommes au jus* and *Osso Bucco de dinde mitonné aux olives vertes* to name but three. You might also try one of the succulent beef dishes certified to be of Limousin stock. The Versailles puts on a special Beaujolais Nouveau evening in November, with a good-value menu of dishes designed to go with the grapey new wine, such as Limousin beef hot pot with chunky vegetables.

❝ Why bother with Paris and its prices? ❞

CLOSED May 1st
CARDS MC, V

Please send us reports
A guide such as this thrives on reader's reports. If you send us five usable reports, we will send you a free copy of any title in our *Charming Small Hotel Guides* series (see page 241 for France titles in the series).
    The five reports should contain at least two new restaurants; the balance can be comments on restaurants already in the guide. **Send reports to** Charming Restaurant Guides, Duncan Petersen Ltd, 31 Ceylon Road, London W14 0PY.

Mortemart
◆ Le Relais € **Fr**

*le Relais, 87330 Mortemart
Tel 05 55 68 12 09*

The exterior of this hotel and restaurant does not stand out as being anything special. In fact, you'll pass many a Relais not dissimilar to that at Mortemart the length and breadth of France. The interior, on the other hand, has been renovated to an exceptional standard. The dining room is smart, with bare stone walls and clean white table linen. French doors open on to a pretty terrace and garden for summer eating. The most basic menu offered a Limousin salad (green leaves, croutons, roast chestnuts, baby tomatoes and onions), followed by an outstanding salmon *feuillette* with deep green *sorrel* sauce. The ice cream dessert is the creation of a Limoges ice-cream-maker who can claim to be a craftsman in his field.

CLOSED phone for details
CARDS MC, V

Our traditional French cuisine symbol
So many of our readers enjoy seeking out the genuinely French eating experience that we have used Fr to mark restaurants which offer *cuisine du terroir*, classical French dishes or regional dishes with an emphasis on local ingredients, and traditional recipes.

Saint-Hilaire-le-Château
◆ Le Thaurion
€ – €€ **Fr**

*Le Thaurion, 23250 St Hilaire le Chateau
Tel 05 55 64 50 12 Fax 05 55 64 90 92*

Marie-Christine and Gérard Fanton have created a smart modern hotel and restaurant by renovating a terrace of old stone houses set back from the main road, without losing the atmosphere of the buildings. Exposed beams have become a cliché in most old-world buildings, but here the massive timbers really are something. And chef Gérard's cooking is excellent, both for traditional and modern dishes. His menu is inexpensive, yet everything on the menu is carefully prepared and perfectly executed. Try salmon salted for one night in a sauce of *yoghurt à la greque* or sichuan pepper for a starter; golden leg of duck with Limousin potatoes and elder jelly as a main course; followed by crème brulée with vanilla and tiny cakes for dessert. *❝ This place is the perfect blend of rustic charm and modern style ❞*

CLOSED Thu; Wed lunch
CARDS AE, DC, MC, V

Saint-Léonard-de-Noblat
◆ Grand St-Léonard

€ – €€€

23 avenue de du Champ-de-Mars, 87400 St Leonard de Noblat
Tel 05 55 56 18 18   Fax 05 55 56 98 32

Approach from the east and the Grand St-Léonard hotel stands supreme at the crossroads where you enter this old town. You could be at an Alpine resort or a British spa – the building seems like a relic of the first age of mass travel. The simple daily menu will satisfy most diners, but if you are prepared to edge into our middle price bracket you will be well rewarded. Jean-Marc Vallet's specialities include a crown of boiled eggs with cèpes, Langoustine pie, and filet of lamb flavoured with garlic, followed by cheese and dessert.

CLOSED Mon and Tue lunch (except July to Aug)
CARDS AE, DC, MC, V

Please send us reports
A guide such as this thrives on reader's reports. If you send us five usable reports, we will send you a free copy of any title in our *Charming Small Hotel Guides* series (see page 241 for France titles in the series).

The five reports should contain at least two new restaurants; the rest can be comments on restaurants already in the guide.
1 Tell us about your experiences in restaurants already in this guide.
2 Send us new reports. New reports should give the following information:
- **Region** – City, town, village or neaest village.
- **Name of restaurant** – Please double check the spelling, it's surprisingly easy to make a mistake.
- **Address** – including *département*
- **Telephone number** – plus fax and e-mail if available. Double check this information.
- **Objective description** – Try to explain simply why it should be in the guide. Remember that the guide is very selective - our entries are those one-in-five places that combine

● **interesting food with**
● **character and charm, in the building, the setting or both.**
The guide hates tourist traps, and pretentious, dressed-up food. We like places where the French go.

We favour places in the lower and middle price bands but there are plenty of expensive places that have our qualities, and we list those too.
- **Diner's comments** – These should be short, personal comments on features that strike you. They can be your comments, or others'.
- **Closing times**
- **Credit cards accepted**
Don't forget to date your report and add your name and address.
Send reports to Charming Restaurant Guides, Duncan Petersen Publishing, 31 Ceylon Road, London W14 OPY.

Saint-Ybard
◆ Auberge St Roch
€ Fr

St Ybard, 19140 Uzerche
Tel 05 55 73 09 71   Fax 05 55 98 41 63

This is everyone's dream of what a country *auberge* should be. Situated on the crest of a hillside, opposite the church on the village square, what might otherwise be called a local café and bar extends through three small dining rooms where the Mouliniers serve food that is far better than average country fare. Three menus are offered – all within our lower price bracket, but which would not be out of place in a much more expensive restaurant. Typical offerings are a fan of trout with Chanterelle mushrooms from the cheapest; Limousin beef in a creamy cèpes sauce from the middle-priced; and simple roast pigeon on a nest of mushrooms from the most expensive. The middle-priced menu features a Trou Normande: a measure of Calvados to clear your palate for the next course. St Ybard is awarded its own exit sign on the N20 but after leaving the motorway junction and the following turning left, be alert for a right turn at the crux of a well marked 900 bend to the left. The St Ybard sign is small and almost overgrown in the hedge.

CLOSED Sun evening, Mon; Christmas holidays
CARDS MC, V

La Souterraine
◆ La Gondole sur le Toit
€

8 pl St Jacques, 23300 la Souterraine
Tel 05 55 63 03 08

The town of la Souterraine gets few plaudits in the guidebooks but, while it's short of monuments and museums, it does have Mario di Pasquale's mythical gondola (which arrived via Paris) on the roof of a tall ivy-clad building on the edge of a small square. Mario regularly emerges from his kitchen to bring food to tables and to quip with his customers. Only six items on his menu betray his Italian origin: try the *filletto di pollo val d'aosta* with spaghetti - it drew admiring glances from the adjacent table of mature locals, who were possibly regretting that they had stayed safely with the Menu du Jour.

❛ *A lively setting for authentic Italian food* ❜

CLOSED Wed
CARDS MC, V

Fr French regional or classical French dishes on menu.

Tulle
◆ La Toque Blanche
€ – €€ Fr

29 rue Jean-Jaures, 19000 Tulle
Tel 05 55 26 75 41 Fax 05 55 20 93 95

The glass frontage of la Toque Blanche overlooks a large car park and the channelled river beyond it in this long, thin town of steep hillsides. It's a well-lit restaurant with pristine white tablecloths and attentive service, and it can really brighten up your visit to an otherwise drab Prefecture town. For a starter a fan of thinly sliced cantaloupe melon served with little rolls of cured ham turned up on a square glass plate. As specialities chef Bruno Estival lists

a fantasy of hot and cold foie gras with fresh truffle-flavoured pasta. But you might be just as happy with the generous fricasse de Volaille, pieces of poultry and game formed into a star shape, with lots of vegetables. Bedrooms available.

CLOSED Sun evening, Mon (except July to Aug); mid-Jan to mid-Feb
CARDS AE, MC, V

Our traditional French cuisine symbol
So many of our readers enjoy seeking out the genuinely French eating experience that we have used Fr to mark restaurants which offer *cuisine du terroir*, classical French dishes or regional dishes with an emphasis on local ingredients, and traditional recipes.

Turenne
◆ La Maison des Chanoines € – €€€

rte de l'Eglise, 19500 Turenne
Tel 05 55 85 93 43

It's worth trying to approach Turenne from the south in order to experience the superb view as the old town emerges on its conical hill at the head of the valley. Turenne is steeped in the religious conflicts that shaped much of the region's history. This restaurant is in a building - a solid, stone house with a spiral staircase and vaulted ceilings - that played its part in the conflicts. The cooking here is generally innovative and original, and dishes are well presented. It's no surprise that a restaurant of this calibre cites local produce as the cornerstone of its success, but you have to wonder just how local we are talking when mussels in green walnut juice is a favourite speciality. But why quibble when the alternative lamb or veal (often spit-roasted) is superb, and doubtless from nearer to home. In summer you can eat in the little garden across the road. Six bedrooms.

❛ *Great ambience* ❜

CLOSED Wed; Tue and Thu lunch (except July to Aug); Nov to Easter
CARDS MC, V

POITOU-
CHARENTES

Gironde

Pauillac 265

Arcins-en-
Médoc 253

Saint-Emilion
267

Bordeaux

Garonne

Saint-
Macaire 268

Sauternes
269

AQUITAINE

Mimizan 262

Sabres 266

Sainte-Maure-
de-Peyriac 268

Uza 271

Saint-Justin
267

Azur 254

Grenade-sur-
l'Adour 260

Saint-Sever 269

Aire-sur-
l'Adour 252

Hossegor 261

Montfort-en-
Chalosse 263

Eugénie-les-Bains 259

Amou 252

Aydie 253

Biarritz 255

Guéthary 260

Espelette 259

Lembeye 262

Biriatou 255

Aïnhoa 252

Pau 264 265

Sare 269

Barcus
254

Bosdarros
256

Saint-Etienne-
de-Baïgorry 267

Esquiule
259

Larrau 262

ESPAGNA

AQUITAINE

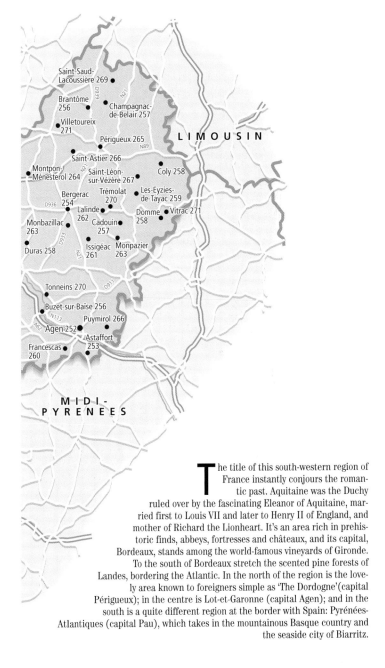

Saint-Saud-Lacoussière 269
Brantôme 256
Champagnac-de-Belair 257
Villetoureix 271
Périgueux 265
LIMOUSIN
Saint-Astier 266
Montpon-Ménestérol 264
Saint-Léon-sur-Vézère 267
Coly 258
Bergerac 254
Trémolat 270
Les-Eyzies-de-Tayac 259
Lalinde 262
Domme 258
Vitrac 271
Monbazillac 263
Cadouin 257
Duras 258
Issigéac 261
Monpazier 263
Tonneins 270
Buzet-sur-Baïse 256
Puymirol 266
Agen 252
Astaffort 253
Francescas 260

MIDI-PYRENEES

The title of this south-western region of France instantly conjours the romantic past. Aquitaine was the Duchy ruled over by the fascinating Eleanor of Aquitaine, married first to Louis VII and later to Henry II of England, and mother of Richard the Lionheart. It's an area rich in prehistoric finds, abbeys, fortresses and châteaux, and its capital, Bordeaux, stands among the world-famous vineyards of Gironde. To the south of Bordeaux stretch the scented pine forests of Landes, bordering the Atlantic. In the north of the region is the lovely area known to foreigners simple as 'The Dordogne'(capital Périgueux); in the centre is Lot-et-Garonne (capital Agen); and in the south is a quite different region at the border with Spain: Pyrénées-Atlantiques (capital Pau), which takes in the mountainous Basque country and the seaside city of Biarritz.

Agen
◆ Mariottat €€

25 rue Louis-Vivent, 47000 Agen, Lot-et-Garonne
Tel 05 53 77 99 77 Fax 05 53 77 99 79

Agen's top restaurant occupies a lovely, elegant 19thC town house with high ceilings, chandeliers and large windows, hidden in the back streets to the south of the town's Jacobin church. Part of the garden has been requisitioned for car parking, but there's still a pleasant gravelled terrace to one side for outdoor dining. As far as the food is concerned, there's no mistaking the fact that you are in the heart of duck country; indeed, the speciality dish is *c'est tout un art d'être un canard* – a feast of duck in all its many guises. Other notable dishes include *croustillant de calamars à la biscaïenne* and *filet de limande-sole, sauce au fenouil*. The wine list is lovingly put together by Christiane Mariottat (her husband Eric is the chef) and it usefully includes, among many choices, an unusually good selection of half bottles.

Closed Sat lunch, Sun dinner, Mon; first week Feb
Cards AE, MC, V

Our price bands
€ under 30 euros €€ 30-50 Euros
€€€ over 50 euros for a menu

Aïnhoa
◆ Ithurria €€ Fr

place du Fronton, 64250 Aïnhoa, Pyrénées-Atlantiques
Tel 05 59 29 92 11 Fax 05 59 29 81 28

In a picturesque village on the pilgrim route to Santiago de Compostela, this is an excellent, long-established and family-run hotel-restaurant with a fine reputation for Basque food and a vast wine cellar. The attractive dining room has a huge fireplace for cool days and hand-made tiles on the floor. There is a lovely garden for summer eating, and a pool.

Closed Wed Sep-Jun; Nov-Easter
Cards AE, MC, V

Aire-sur-l'Adour
◆ Chez l'Ahumat € Fr

rue Pierre-Mendès-France, 40800 Aire-sur-l'Adour, Landes
Tel 05 58 71 82 61

In the vibrant market town of Aire, with the pretty river Adour running through it, this is a bustling restaurant, packed with locals, tourists and business people. The food is simple and good value: well cooked, efficiently served, and inexpensive. The daily changing *menu du jour* might start with *charcuterie* or salad, followed by roast beef and potatoes, and dessert. There is a carte too, with an extensive menu of local meat and fish dishes.

Closed Sun dinner, Mon Oct-Mar; three weeks Feb, early to mid-Nov
Cards AE, DC, MC, V

Our traditional French cuisine symbol
So many of our readers enjoy seeking out the genuinely French eating experience that we have used Fr to mark restaurants which offer *cuisine du terroir*, classical French dishes or regional dishes with an emphasis on local ingredients, and traditional recipes.

Amou
◆ Darracq € Fr

Hôtel Le Commerce, 40330 Amou, Landes
Tel 05 58 89 02 28 Fax 05 58 89 24 45

A busy hotel-restaurant with friendly service on the edge of a small Landais village. From the large terrace, shaded by an awning, you can watch village life and enjoy traditional cooking, choosing from a carte or from *prix fixe* menus at varying prices.

❛ Not an exceptional gourmet experience but pleasant surroundings and enjoyable food. Busy with passing tourists, travelling professionals and retired folk ❜

Closed Sun dinner, Mon Oct-Mar; Feb, Nov
Cards AE, DC, MC, V

Arcins-en-Médoc
◆ Le Lion d'Or € **Fr**

place de la République, 33460 Arcins-en-Médoc, Gironde
Tel 05 56 58 96 79

Handily situated on the D2 Bordeaux Route du Vin not far north of Margaux, the Lion d'Or is as popular with locals as it is with the passing tourist trade, particularly for its excellent value lunchtime menu. The decoration is definitely a cut above the usual village restaurant, and there is even a small garden, but patron Jean-Paul Barbier's food remains traditional, unfussy *cuisine du terroir*: fresh fish from the Gironde, local lamb, tripe, lamprey, *tête de veau* or just a simple, perfectly cooked omelette. During the grape harvest, pigeon, hare and other game feature strongly. One particularly pleasing innovation is that you can take along your own bottle of wine (the wine list concentrates on local reds). A well-deserved Bib Gourmand from Michelin.

Closed Sun, Mon; Christmas, New Year, Jul
Cards AE, MC, V

Astaffort
◆ Le Square – Michel Latrille € - €€€ **Fr**

5-7 place de la Craste, 47220 Astaffort, Lot-et-Garonne
Tel 05 53 47 20 40 Fax 05 53 47 10 38

Warm ochre and Sienna-washed exteriors, blue shutters and striped awnings on a little *place* filled with roses and pergolas really make you feel you are heading south. Here is a great combination: a sweet little hotel with a simple but excellent restaurant, run by Agen chef Michel Latrille and his vivacious wife Sylvie. No expense has been spared on the high quality renovation of two adjoining village houses and the smart Kenzo fabrics, painted furniture, modern uplighting - and nooks and crannies filled with interesting detail imbue the place with a sense of easy informality. Outside dogs bark, old men play *boules* and children scamper in the square. Inside, or on the large, leafy terrace on the first floor, you can enjoy Michel's sublime versions of the

regional cuisine. Menus start at 20 euros (at the time of going to press), or you can eat from the more expensive carte. The cheapest menu is excellent value.

❛ We loved this place ❜

Closed Sun dinner, Mon, Tue lunch, two weeks Jan, one week May, one week Nov
Cards AE, DC, MC, V

Please send us reports
A guide such as this thrives on reader's reports. If you send us five usable reports, we will send you a free copy of any title in our *Charming Small Hotel Guides* series (see page 241 for France titles in the series).
  The five reports should contain at least two new restaurants; the balance can be comments on restaurants already in the guide. **Send reports to** Charming Restaurant Guides, Duncan Petersen Ltd, 31 Ceylon Road, London W14 0PY.

Aydie
◆ Le Relais d'Aydie € **Fr**

64330 Aydie, Pyrénées-Atlantiques
Tel 05 59 04 00 09

High up in the Madiran hills, the region famous for the Madiran and Pacherenc wines, this is a completely unpretentious restaurant frequented mostly by local artisans and farm workers. Simple, both in decoration and food, it offers friendly service and honest, earthy, unadulterated dishes. At 10 euros (at the time of going to press) the lunch menu – which changes every day – offers exceptional value. Or you can choose from the à la carte menu. Either way, you will be presented with hearty, wholesome, home-grown produce on simple platters: perhaps an award-winning *garbure*, followed by a delicious omelette full of cep mushrooms, then *confit de canard* or local sausage and lentils, a generous cheeseboard with salad, and a choice of *croustade* or gâteau Basque for dessert. You might accompany your food with a superb local Madiran wine, although the carafe wine from a neighbouring farm is quite acceptable. To find Aydie, follow signs from Madiran, Viella or Lembeye.

❝ To our mind, a perfect meal ❞

CLOSED 3 weeks Oct-Nov
CARDS MC, V

Azur
◆ Auberge du Soleil
€ – €€   **Fr**

64 route du Lac, 40140 Azur, Landes
Tel 05 58 48 10 17

In the Landais pine forest, 5 miles (8 km) from the coast, and near a lake for fishing, rowing and windsurfing, this simple Logis offers a warm welcome and good, local, home-cooked food. The country-style restaurant with large fireplace is pleasant enough, but it's the superb terrace, shaded by trees, that really appeals.

CLOSED phone for details
CARDS MC, V

---

charmingsmallhotels.co.uk
Visit Duncan Petersen's travel website, the best online search tool for places to stay that combine character and charm. Currently features Britain, France, Italy and Ireland, with other destinations being continuously added.

Barcus
◆ Chilo €€

64130 Barcus, Pyrénées-Atlantiques
Tel 05 59 28 9079 Fax 05 59 28 93 10

The expertise of three generations have created in Chilo a place of welcome, comfort and wonderful food. The attractive building harmonizes with the surrounding village, with a delightful garden and children's play area. The L-shaped dining room with open fireplace, the main dining room with picture windows on to the garden and the large sitting room with bar are reminiscent of an English country inn. This is the setting for a memorable meal. Each morning the freshest and best of local produce is delivered straight from the market, ready to be transformed by Pierre Chilo into dishes of exceptional refinement and quality.

❝ A refreshing, reasonably priced, efficient and very enjoyable stopping place'…The Chilos specialise in a warm Basque welcome ❞

CLOSED Sun dinner, Mon, Tue lunch Oct to May; Jan, two weeks Feb
CARDS AE, DC MC, V

● *For places to eat in Bayonne you should try Le Chistera (tel 05 59 25 93), a popular canteen-style bistrot run by a champion pelota player with good value Basque food; and Auberge du Cheval Blanc (tel 05 59 59 01 33): gastronomic Basque food, friendly ambience.*

Bergerac
◆ L' Enfance de Lard
€ – €€

place Pelissière, 24100 Bergerac, Dordogne
Tel 05 53 57 52 88 Fax 05 53 57 52 88

This restaurant's odd name is a play on words. The normal phrase is *l'enfance de l'art*, meaning child's play or kid's stuff, but also a certain simplicity, an essence that comes across in the cooking and the presentation. On the fun side, the wine list is pasted on to a jeroboam and the menu is fronted by a framed picture. The speciality is meat (*magret*, veal, beef, lamb in generous quantities) grilled over vine clippings on the open fire in an intimate, stone-walled room – particularly cosy in winter. The dining room is in upmarket country-kitchen style, with antique mirrors and homely clutter, which marry perfectly with mellow jazz and opera arias on the sound system. There's just one room (on the first floor) with six or so tables, so it's wise to reserve. The one set menu consists of three courses (a choice of two starters, two main courses, and then a selection of scrumptious home-made tarts such as apple or *crème brûlée* with raspberries) and coffee or infusion (selected by their own herbologist). Or you can choose from the limited carte: tomato salad with onion and eau de vie; grilled *magret;* chicken breast with garlic *confit;* lamb with mint sauce. The patrons, André Morant and Michael Barnes-Wortley also host regular dinner concerts.

❋ This is 'slow food' at its best, everything completely fresh, simple but of excellent quality ❜

CLOSED lunch Mon–Sun; Tue
CARDS MC, V

Our price bands
Rather than giving actual prices (which are prone to change) we indicate the cost of a three-course meal for one person, without wine, by means of price bands. They are as follows: € under 30 euros €€ 30-50 euros €€€ over 50 euros. Where we give more than one price band, for example €– €€€, this indicates that in that restaurant a meal can be had at a range of prices. As well as the cost of *prix fixe* menus, our price bands also take into account the cost of an average selection from the *à la carte* menu.

Biarritz
◈ Tantina de Burgos
€ – €€ **Fr**

2 place Beaurivage, 64200 Biarritz, Pyrénées-Atlantiques
Tel 05 59 23 24 47

There is always a bustling, buzzing atmosphere in this delightful restaurant. The menu, chalked up on a blackboard, is the first indication that what is on offer is the best of whatever is in season. The strong Basque influence is evident in both the cooking and the decoration, with red check tablecloths and simple table settings, bistro chairs and bold paintings hung against exposed stone walls. Strings of garlic dangle all around, the busy kitchen is open to view, and a continuous stream of locals stand at the bar enjoying drinks and tapas while they wait for a table. On the menu, entrées usually feature Spanish ham served on crusty toasts with tomato; stuffed peppers; grilled mussels; *calamari;* omelette with ceps; grilled or marinated anchovies, and mixed

salads. The fish is sensationally fresh, simply baked or grilled with rock salt and olive oil. You might choose a single fish such as *dorade* or *cabillaud* or opt for a *parrillada* (mixed platter). Meat eaters will enjoy succulent rack of lamb, milk fed pork, *axoa d'espellette*, grilled *boudin* or *côte de boeuf.*

❋ One of our favourite places on the Basque coast...simple, generous cooking ❜

CLOSED Sun, Mon
CARDS MC, V

Biarritz
◈ Les Viviers des Halles
€ **Fr**

8 rue du Centre, 64200 Biarritz, Pyrénées-Atlantiques
Tel 05 59 24 58 66

In a large warehouse on a road running up from the fish market, Les Viviers has a spacious modern interior with a long bar where you can have an aperitif while waiting for a table. The atmosphere is one of animated bustle, and the food is the day's catch: fish soups, seafood platters, oysters, sardines, prawns, *gambas*, crab, lobster and so on. The 24.50 euro menu (at the time of going to press) consists of: *soupe de poissons ou assiette de fruits de mer; homard grillée ou poisson du jour; dessert aux choix.*

CLOSED Sun, Mon
CARDS MC, V

Biriatou
◈ Bakéa €€€

64700 Biriatou, Pyrénées-Atlantiques
Tel 05 59 20 76 36 Fax 05 59 20 58 21

Ten minute's drive from the beach at Hendaye, Corine and Eric Duval have created a haven of civilized calm at the edge of the village of Biriatou, and a welcome escape from the bustle and crowds of the coast. An inviting terrace overlooks the wide Bidassoa valley, whose river here defines the border between France and Spain. Bakéa is a reliable hotel but it is the restaurant that particularly appeals, with menus that represent good value and a wine list with an interesting selection of French, Basque and Spanish bottles, including Jurançon *sec* and Irouléguy. Eric Duval's cooking merits a Michelin star and his signature dishes include *lasagne d'anchois frais marinés au basilic* and *salade de ris d'agneau aux parfums de pays.*

CLOSED Mon and Tue lunch Easter to Oct, Sun dinner, Mon Oct-Easter; Feb
CARDS AE, DC, MC, V

Fr French regional or classical French dishes on menu.

Bosdarros
◆ Auberge Labarthe
€ – €€

64290 Bosdarros, Pyrénées-Atlantiques
Tel 05 59 21 50 13 Fax 05 59 21 68 55

Bosdarros is a beautiful little village high up on a ridge, 7.5 miles (12 km) south of Pau, with far reaching views of the Pyrenees. All the village houses are well kept with pretty gardens and local stone architecture. Auberge Labarthe is an old coaching inn which has been converted into a restaurant offering a welcome stop for weary travellers, and a rendezvous for local professionals. It's well worth a trip: the village and the surrounding countryside are exceptionally beautiful, and the restaurant is charming, with window boxes full of tumbling geraniums. Inside, there is a little reception room with an open fireplace where you can have an aperitif at the bar before you go to your table. The dining room is simply decorated, with pale limewashed walls, and pretty tables set with starched linen. The cooking is taken seriously here, although the swift and professional service is undertaken in a particularly friendly and unpretentious way. The chef-patron and his team prepare seasonal produce with innovation and flair. Regional influences can be felt in the traditional *magret de canard* and *filet de boeuf* with a slice of *foie gras*, de-boned pigeon and fish dishes including fresh *bar* and *langoustines*. This is fine food, beautifully presented. Ask the Labarthe's knowledgeable *sommelier* to recommend the local wines.

CLOSED Sun dinner, Mon, Tue Sep-Jun; 2 weeks Jan
CARDS AE, MC, V

● *For a bistro in Bordeaux: La Tupina (tel 05 56 91 56 37) serves great regional dishes with an equally good wine list; for gastronomic cooking in cosy, elegant surroundings: Didier Gélineau (tel 05 56 52 84 25).*

Brantôme
◆ Le Moulin de l'Abbaye
€€ – €€€

1 route de Bourdeilles, 24310 Brantôme Dordogne
Tel 05 53 05 80 22 Fax 05 53 05 75 27

The setting is the thing. The shady riverside terrace, illuminated in the evening, is an idyllic place for a drink or a meal while admiring Brantôme's unusual angled bridge, the tower of the abbey or the swans gliding by. Traditional Périgord dishes with a creative touch earn the restaurant a Michelin star. The dining room makes an excellent setting for such dishes as *petits-gris à la crème de persil* and *pied de porc confit farcis aux cèpes.*

❝ We arrived (on motorbikes) late and without a booking but were warmly welcomed'...'Lovely setting but we could raise no enthusiasm for the 'Monet-style' colour scheme in the dining room ❞

CLOSED Mon-Fri lunch Sep-Jun, Mon lunch Jul, Aug; Nov-May
CARDS AE, DC, MC, V

Buzet-sur-Baïse
◆ La Vigneron
€ – €€

boulevard de la République, 47160 Buzet-sur-Baïse, Lot-et-Garonne
Tel 05 53 84 73 46 Fax 05 53 84 75 04

This unpretentious village restaurant makes a good adjunct to a visit to the nearby Buzet wine cooperative. The restaurant is popular with locals, businessmen and tourists alike. There's a choice between eating on the front 'terrace' (a small seating area on the quiet main street, surrounded by plants), the simple dining room, which has a more airy extension at the rear, and the back terrace overlooking vegetable plots. It's not a fancy place: the dining room is plain, with pale yellow walls and a few pot plants. The main attraction is the food, which offers excellent value for money in the grand tradition of village restaurants. Even the cheapest *menu du jour* (14 euros at the time of going to press; not available on Sunday), which really does change every day, offers four courses: soup, a *chariot of hors-d'œuvre*, a main course (always a choice of meat and fish, but focusing on local cuisine, including dishes such as *confit* of duck and wild boar stew) and a *chariot* of desserts. The wine list features local wines, too, so it's a good opportunity to sample Buzet, and you don't have to buy a bottle; they also offer well-priced pitchers. All the food is above average, but the strong point is the choice of desserts. House special is a gâteau de crêpes, comprising crêpes layered with a *pâtisserie* cream filling, the whole coated in meringue and baked. It's sublime – and served in huge wedges.

⁶ The service couldn't have been more helpful and efficient – make sure you save room for the desserts ⁹

Closed Sun dinner, Mon
Cards DC, MC, V

Cadouin
◆ Restaurant de l'Abbaye
€ Fr

24480 Cadouin, Dordogne
Tel 05 53 63 40 93 Fax 05 53 61 72 08

No fireworks here, but an unpretentious, family-run country inn harking back to the old days: floral tablecloths, solid cutlery and plenty of glassware. In fine weather you can sit out under a vine, across the road from Cadouin's famous abbey. In winter there's a good log fire. All the menus start

with a large helping of the local garlic soup. The weekday lunch menu represents particularly good value. Simple local dishes shine: *tourin*, *foie gras au torchon*, various presentations of duck, and roast leg of lamb. There is a good cheese platter (the sort where you choose your own rather than getting a few wedges presented on a plate), and the chocolate and walnut tart is a perennial favourite with regulars.

⁶ We love the feel of this restaurant. Its friendly welcome and the no-nonsense home cooking keep drawing us back ⁹

Closed Sun dinner, Mon
Cards MC, V

Our traditional French cuisine symbol
So many of our readers enjoy seeking out the genuinely French eating experience that we have used Fr to mark restaurants which offer *cuisine du terroir*, classical French dishes or regional dishes with an emphasis on local ingredients, and traditional recipes.

Champagnac-de-Belair
◆ Moulin du Roc
€€€

24530 Champagnac-de-Belair, Dordogne
Tel 05 53 02 86 00 Fax 05 53 54 21 31

This delectable old walnut mill with its Michelin-starred restaurant belongs to that rare breed of hotels that gives you the sense of being pampered without costing a fortune. The setting on the banks of the Dronne is truly romantic: the gardens are lush, secluded, shady and bursting with colour. Inside the rough-stone 17thC building, oak beams, stone fireplaces, mill machinery, rich fabrics and a wealth of antiques – oil paintings, silverware and solid Périgord dressers – combine with abundant flower arrangements to create an intimate yet highly individual style. Some may find it slightly heavy. The same cannot be said for the food: in the land of *foie gras*, Alain Gardillou manages to build on culinary traditions to produce remarkably light and inventive dishes such as *tarte chaude moelleuse de langoustines* and *pâtes fraîches aux truffes et escaloppe de foie gras*. Herbs and vegetables come from the restaurant's gardens and there is a dazzling choice of wines.

Closed Tue, Wed lunch; Jan–Mar
Cards AE, DC, MC, V

Looking for somewhere to stay? See page 241.

Coly
◆ Manoir d'Hautegente
€€€ – €€

24120 Coly, Lot-et-Garonne
Tel 05 53 51 68 03 Fax 05 53 50 38 52

Tables set out beside the mill-race with the lovely vine-covered manor house – once a forge – as backdrop, not to mention the superb cuisine (Périgord with a modern twist) makes this a great venue for a splurge. The current chef worked in Dubai for two years and brings a creative use of spices to his cooking, particularly his sauces. As well as excellent fish, the meat dishes are particularly recommended, for example, duck married with turmeric and sesame. If you can't decide which dessert to plump for, there's an assorted platter. The set menu changes weekly; otherwise there's a carte to choose from and, for those with a big appetite, a *menu dégustation* for a min-imum of two people. The dining room is made up of several small rooms, decorated with antiques but in a homely way (faded gilt mirrors, old bookcases, lots of flowers), and you can take aperitifs in the old forge – a stone-vaulted room with a huge fireplace. The family-run Hautegente has long been one of the most appreciated hotels in the region, according to regular readers of our *Charming Small Hotel Guide to France*.

❛ A dream location...I particularly appreciated the chef's subtle use of spices, and his sorbets were out of this world ❜

Closed Mon, Tue, Wed, Thur lunch; Nov–Mar
Cards AE, DC, MC, V

Domme
◆ L'Esplanade €€€

15-20 L'Esplanade, 24250 Domme, Dordogne
Tel 05 53 28 31 41 Fax 05 53 28 49 92

A well-practiced husband and wife team (he cooks, she runs front-of-house), and a happy marriage of the traditional and the innovative in the dishes (duck *foie gras* grilled with raspberries, *ragôut* of lobster, *profiteroles* with ginger ice cream and a warm *coulis* of apricots flavoured with Armagnac) have ensured the reputation – and a Michelin star – for this hotel and restaurant in the busy tourist village of Domme. And the view from the terrace across the river is scintillating.

❛ We were so put off by the sour receptionist when we dropped in, that we decided to go elsewhere for dinner. What did we miss? ❜

Closed Wed lunch, Mon; Nov to mid-Feb
Cards AE, DC, MC, V

Duras
◆ Hostellerie des Duc
€ – €€ **Fr**

boulevard Jean-Brisseau, 47120 Duras, Lot-et-Garonne
Tel 05 53 83 74 58 Fax 05 53 83 75 03

More than twenty years ago the Blanchet family fell in love with a semi-ruined convent in the castle town of Duras. They have painstakingly converted it into a com-fortable hotel with a highly-rated restau-rant. In summer tables are set up in the flower-filled garden; in winter there's a fire to welcome you. It's traditional, but not rus-tic, with pink tablecloths, gleaming glass-ware and cutlery, pot plants and flowers. The cuisine is largely regionally based – duck, *foie gras*, prunes, walnuts, garlic – and locally sourced, and the very drinkable Duras wines feature strongly on the wine list. As is normal at this type of establish-ment, the variously priced menus change with the season. For autumn there's a *ter-rine de foie gras* with prunes, duck *Rossigny* with *foie gras* and salmon with ceps. For a light weekday lunch the *formule* consists of a main course, dessert, glass of Duras wine and coffee.

❬ The flavour of southwest France just as you imagine it'...'There's no better way to sample the 'local wines than over a meal here ❭

CLOSED Sun dinner, Mon Oct-Jun; Mon lunch Jul-Sep
CARDS AE, DC, MC, V

Espelette
◆ Euzkadi € **Fr**

285 route Karrika-Nagusia, 64250 Espelette, Pyrénées-Atlantiques Tel 05 59 93 91 88 Fax 05 59 93 90 19

Espelette is famous for its red peppers, and they are everywhere to be seen, including on the plate, at this much-loved hotel-restaurant. André Darraïdou and his wife Michèle, the patrons of Euzkadi, put a modern twist on traditional Basque recipes. This is real Basque cooking: if you want to know what *tripotxa*, *axoa*, and *elzekaria* taste like, come to this vast restaurant – you won't be disappointed. It is immensely popular, though, so it is wise to book in advance. Free aperitif.

CLOSED Mon; Tue winter; Nov to mid-Dec
CARDS MC, V

Fr French regional or classical French dishes on menu.

Esquiule
◆ Chez Château € **Fr**

Esquiule, 64400 Oloron-Sainte-Marie, Pyrénées-Atlatiqes Tel 05 59 39 23 03 Fax 05 59 39 81 97

A great local institution, full of wine, music and song, and locals enjoying the warm atmosphere created by the friendly chef-patron and his enthusiastic team. Excellent regional offerings on the kindly-priced menus include hearty *garbure* and *garburade*, as well as gamey dishes of duck and pigeon. You could also try the sweet and sour duck salad with oyster mushrooms. There is a good choice of wines at fair prices.

CLOSED Sun dinner, Mon
CARDS MC, V

Eugénie-les-Bains
◆ La Ferme aux Grives
€€ – €€€ **Fr**

40320 Eugénie-les-Bains, Landes Tel 05 58 05 05 06 Fax 05 58 51 10 10

The approach is a formal herb garden full of lavender, rosemary and thyme, with a garden path leading to the restaurant – a beautiful converted barn with a modish sophisticated-yet-rustic feel, with exposed stone walls. In summer, tables and chairs are set in the garden as well. Many of the dishes are cooked on the grill in the monumental open fireplace, in front of which is a vast kitchen table piled high with fresh fruit and vegetables, and baskets of bread. Jars of *confit*, barrels of wine and kitchen utensils abound, as well as hams hanging from a ceiling pulley which allows them to be pulled down and sliced to order. Before your meal, you can have a drink in the bar in front of the fire – perhaps a glass of house wine from Michel Guérard's own estate – for La Ferme aux Grives is the baby sister restaurant to his famous Les Prés d'Eugénie. As for the food, it is simple, well cooked country fare, served without frills (but at sophisticated prices). You might have chestnut soup followed perhaps by milk-fed pork, or a casserole or *gratin* served with ramekins of vegetables. Desserts are equally simple: *crème brûlée*, baked bananas, apple tart, chocolate *fondant*, homemade icecreams or local *brébis* cheese.

CLOSED Wed, Thu Sep-Jun
CARDS AE, DC, MC, V

Les-Eyzies-de-Tayac
◆ La Grange du Mas € **Fr**

Le Mas de Sireuil, 24620 Les Eyzies-de-Tayac, Dordogne Tel 05 53 29 66 07 Fax 05 53 30 39 67

This *ferme-auberge* on the hills above Les Eyzies has been open for twenty years and the farm in the same family for four generations. The present owners, Michel and Marie-Noëlle Descamp, make a great team, Marie-Noëlle in the kitchen rustling up honest country-cooking (*foie gras* with verjuice, or rabbit casserole served with the local *pommes sarladaise* – potatoes fried in duck or goose fat and laced with garlic), while Michel fulfils the role of jovial host. They spend the winter preparing the *foie gras*, *confit*, *rillettes* and *pâté* for the next season; the majority of the produce comes from the farm itself. The dining room is pretty, with beams, exposed stone walls and a mezzanine floor, though nothing special. The main thing is the quality of the cooking, the location and the opportunity to sample a *ferme-auberge*. Reservations are obligatory. In addition to the four set menus, of which there is a good choice, you can also opt for a *plat du jour* or eat à la carte. The farm is signposted off the D47 near the village of Sireuil and between LesEyzies-de-Tayac and Sarlat.

❛ I simply couldn't resist a second helping of dessert – a melt-in-the-mouth fromage blanc. The pâté – truly a pâté de campagne – really hit the spot too. We bought several tins to take home ❜

Closed Tue lunch; Oct-Easter
Cards MC, V

Francescas
◆ Relais de la Hire
€€ – €€€

47600 Francescas, Lot-et-Garonne
Tel 05 53 65 41 59 Fax 05 53 65 86 42

It's well worth driving out of your way to eat at this fine, welcoming resaurant in a charming old 18thC house in the placid litle village of Francescas, 6 miles (10 km) south-east of Nérac. The food – like the decoration – is a successful blend of modern and traditional, and the presentation truly memorable. The desserts in particular are works of art, though all the dishes come garnished with flowers or sprigs of aromatic plants from the restaurant's garden. You may be regaled by such dishes as a delectable soufflé of artichoke and *foie gras*, follwed by sea bream roast with olives. The wine list is innovative and helpful, with suggestions for accompanying each dish on the menu. And you will be dazzled by the tremendous choice of Armagnacs with which to finish.

❛ Delicious food in a lovely old house – the place for a treat ❜

Closed Sun dinner, Mon
Cards AE, DC, MC, V

Grenade-sur-l'Adour
◆ Pain Adour et Fantaisie €€€

14-16 place des Tilleuls, 40270 Grenade-sur-l'Adour, Landes
Tel 05 58 45 18 80 Fax 05 58 45 16 57

One half of this distinguished riverside hotel-restaurant was an 18thC *maison de maître* and boasts a superb stone staircase and fine oak panelling and carved fireplace in part of the dining room. The other half is 17thC, with original arcading on to the market square and half-timbered walls. Antique furniture, original paintings and fine mirrors abound inside, while on the south side is a handsome wide terrace overhanging the river, with elegantly-laid tables and green-and-white parasols. Philippe Garret is the chef, and his food, which has a Michelin star, easily lives up to the lovely setting.

❛Dinner on the terrace on a warm summer's evening was truly romantic ❜

Closed Mon, Wed lunch, Sun dinner; one week Feb, one week Nov
Cards AE, DC MC, V

Guéthary
◆ Alcyon €€ – €€€ Fr

Guéthary, 64210 Pyrénées-Atlantiques
Tel 05 59 26 55 72

To reach this charming old fishing port between Biarritz and Saint-Jean-de-Luz you must descend a precarious lane which serves only one car at a time. Once there, the views of the coast from Biarritz to the Pyrenees are spectacular. The village is rich in Basque architecture, with a *fronton* for the passionate game of *pelota*. There are three small al fresco restaurants down the lane, all specialising, of course, in the freshly-caught fish. Alcyon has a superb position right on the ocean. It is very basic: a deck with simple chairs, no trimmings, and open to the elements. The kitchen is small and most of the food is grilled on an outside grill. The menu consists of a range of salads and tapas-style starters as well as grilled sardines, grilled fish, prawns, baked lamb and *confit de canard*. If the weather is bad opt for the Restaurant Txamara next door which offers more protection from the elements.

❦ Brace yourself for the sea breeze and enjoy an aperitif while the sun sets over the sea and surfers fade to silhouettes on the famous breakers'...'We opted for pan tomate and stuffed peppers with morue and dorade; the children got what they wanted: fish and chips ❩

CLOSED Mon-Sun lunch; Oct-Apr
CARDS none

Hossegor
◆ Les Huîtrières du Lac
€ – €€

1187 avenue du Touring-Club, 40150 Hossegor, Landes
Tel 05 58 43 51 48 Fax 05 58 41 73 11

As you might expect, the restaurant of this little hotel in a pleasant setting specialises primarily in fish and seafood, although there are alternatives. The larger dining room has a view over the adjacent lake and the oyster beds. Dishes include *foie gras* with peaches, sea bass in a salt crust and pigeon flavoured with honey.

CLOSED Mon, Tue winter
CARDS AE, MC, V

Issigéac
◆ Chez Alain € – €€ Fr

Tour de Ville, 24560 Issigéac, Dordogne
Tel 05 53 58 77 88 Fax 05 53 57 88 64

On Sunday mornings, after the market, brunch is served in this popular village restaurant – a skillfully restored old building with several dining rooms and a terrace around a fountain. Alain Commeinhes cooks local specialities including freshwter fish and game in season. A pleasant spot.

CLOSED Sun dinner, Mon Sep-May; mid-Jan to mid-Feb
CARDS DC, MC, V

Lalinde
◆ Le Château €€

1 rue de Verdun, 24150 Lalinde, Dordogne
Tel 05 53 61 01 82 Fax 05 53 23 74 60

Squeezed on the edge of the Dordogne, the setting of this odd little turreted castle is spectacular. The decoration is quirky and modernistic (it's a hotel; some rooms have balconies overlooking the fast-flowing river). The affable patron, Guy Geneau, rides a motorbike and stuffs snails with walnut butter. The riverside setting is great; it is reported that his cooking can be erratic, but not without its merits.

CLOSED Sun dinner, Mon Nov-Mar; Mon Apr-Jun, Sep-Oct; Mon and Tue lunch Jul, Aug; one week Sep; mid-Dec to mid-Feb
CARDS MC, V

---

charmingsmallhotels.co.uk
Visit Duncan Petersen's travel website, the best online search tool for places to stay that combine character and charm. Currently features Britain, France, Italy and Ireland, with other destinations being continuously added.

Larrau
◆ Etchemaïte €

64560 Larrau, Pyrénées-Atlantiques
Tel 05 59 28 61 45 Fax 05 59 28 72 71

This is a great place: a warm welcome awaits you from the Etchemaïte family (who also offer 16 simple bedrooms), plus superb home cooking (the place has been handed on from father to son for generations) at unbeatable prices, with wonderful mountain views from the restaurant's rustic dining room.

❛ *We loved this place'...'Enchanting and peaceful* ❜

CLOSED Sun dinner; Mon Feb-May; mid-Jan to Feb, mid-Nov to Dec
CARDS MC, V

Our traditional French cuisine symbol
So many of our readers enjoy seeking out the genuinely French eating experience that we have used Fr to mark restaurants which offer *cuisine du terroir*, classical French dishes or regional dishes with an emphasis on local ingredients, and traditional recipes.

Lembeye
◆ Restaurant de la Tour
€ – €€

29 place Marcadieu, 64350 Lembeye,
Pyrénées-Atlantiques
Tel 05 59 68 54 94

In the market square of this country town, the Restaurant de la Tour is distributed over two rooms in a very old building. Each room has an open fireplace with log fires, and one has exposed stone walls and is open to the kitchen, The others look out towards the road and square and has more eclectic decoration, with orange-washed walls and bold art. The service is friendly and efficient, the atmosphere pleasantly bustling. The traditional menus (of two, three or four courses) offer simple, fresh local food: large salads, *magret de canard*, duck hearts, as well as good pizzas with proper bases. Main courses come with a carefully prepared vegetable dish to accompany them.

CLOSED Wed
CARDS MC, V

Mimizan
◆ Au Bon Coin du Lac
€€ – €€€

29 avenue du Lac, 40400 Mimizan, Landes
Tel 05 58 09 01 55 Fax 05 58 09 40 84

Jean-Pierre Caule is the third generation of his family to run this hotel-restaurant beside a large freshwater lake away from the noise and bustle of the seaside town. Both he and Mme Caule, who runs front of house with a ready smile, maintain exacting standards, and his excellent cooking merits a Michelin star. In the light and welcoming dining room, with a terrace outside shaded by trees and awning, you might enjoy such dishes as *sole soufflée aux langoustines* or *pot-au-feu de la mer.*

CLOSED Sun dinner, Mon Sep-Jun; Feb
CARDS AE, MC, V

Monbazillac
 ## La Tour des Vents
€€

Moulin de Malfourat, 24240 Monbazillac,
Dordogne
Tel 05 53 58 30 10 Fax 05 53 58 89 55

The modern building in which this restaurant is located – part of a decommissioned windmill – may be nothing to shout about, but the menus at the Tour des Vents represent excellent value, the welcome is warm and the views are superb. You are perched high above the vine-clad Dordogne valley directly south of Bergerac; ask for a table on their pleasantly shaded terrace or, failing that, beside the dining room's big picture windows. *Foie gras* and duck feature prominently, of course, on Marie Rougier's menu, as do the local Bergerac and sweet Monbazillac wines on the wine list, but there's also plenty of fresh fish and even a vegetarian menu. A perennial favourite is a dish of scallops sprinkled with balsamic vinegar and walnut oil – if you are feeling rich, you order it with truffles.

CLOSED Sun dinner, Mon Sep-Jun, Mon lunch Jul; Jan
CARDS AE, DC, MC, V

Monpazier
Privilège du Périgord €

60 rue Notre-Dame, 24540 Monpazier,
Dordogne
Tel 05 53 22 43 98 Fax 05 53 22 98 85

Jean-Michel Lovato and his wife Marie-Josée have established an excellent reputation for this little restaurant tucked in a corner of Monpazier, one of the region's best-preserved *bastides*. The quiet, creeper-clad courtyard is particularly alluring in fine weather, its tables set with blue and white checked cloths. Inside, the decoration leans towards the casual – a very mellow, laid-back *bistrot* – as you'd expect from a jazz fanatic (the restaurant hosts Friday night jazz concerts from April to October). The classic dish here, invented here 14 years ago, is *foie gras* topped with a fried egg, but there's plenty else to tempt you: *civet* of goose with ceps cooked in local Pécharment wine; *cassoulet* of three *confits* – duck, sausage and pork ; *pot-au-feu* of cod with *aïoli*. The *menu dégustation* makes a good light lunch: a *foie gras* starter followed by omelette with ceps and *pommes salardais* (sliced potatoes fried in duck fat with parsley and garlic) with a side-salad sprinkled with local walnuts.

'The enchaud (pork confit), here served hot with a prune stuffing, was absolutely delicious '

CLOSED Tue; two weeks Oct; mid-Nov to mid-Dec; early Jan to Mar
CARDS MC, V

***

Our price bands
€ under 30 euros €€ 30-50 Euros
€€€ over 50 euros for a menu

***

Montfort-en-Chalosse
Aux Tauzins €

52 rue Royale, 47270 Puymirol, Lot-et-Garonne
Tel 05 53 95 31 46 Fax 05 53 95 33 80

A solid, two-fireplace Logis in its third generation of family ownership, Aux Tauzins is an honest, comfortable and very pleasant family-run place in which to both stay and dine, with white walls and green shutters and excellent views over the countryside. In summer meals are taken on the wistaria-shaded terrace. The good value regional dishes include *tournedos Landais, fricassée* of monkfish, chicken dishes and local mushrooms, and the cooking merits a Bib Gourmand from Michelin. You will find Aux Tauzins on the D2 to Baigts and Hagetmau, just outside the village of Montfort-en-Chalosse.

CLOSED Sun, Mon winter; early to mid-Oct, Jan
CARDS MC, V

Montpon-Ménesterol
◆ Auberge de l'Eclade
€ – €€

24700 Montpon-Ménesterol, Dordogne
Tel 05 53 80 28 64 Fax 05 53 80 28 64

Menus that represent very good value and cooking (of chef-patron Christian Martin), which is both traditional and creative, using regional produce, mark out this attractive, homely, country-style restaurant. Michelin awards a Bib Gourmand. The weekday lunch menu at just 13 euros (at the time of going to press) is very good. Dishes include *escalopines de foies de canard* with asparagus tips with a sesame-flavoured sauce. The *auberge* is signposted in Ménesterol, approached by the D708.

CLOSED Tue dinner, Wed; Mar, Oct
CARDS MC, V

Please send us reports
A guide such as this thrives on reader's reports. If you send us five usable reports, we will send you a free copy of any title in our *Charming Small Hotel Guides* series (see page 241 for France titles in the series).

The five reports should contain at least two new restaurants; the balance can be comments on restaurants already in the guide. **Send reports to** Charming Restaurant Guides, Duncan Petersen Ltd, 31 Ceylon Road, London W14 0PY.

Pau
◆ Le Berry € – €€

4 rue Gachet, 64000 Pau, Pyrénées-Atlantiques
Tel 05 59 27 42 95

This splendid place is a typical old fashioned brasserie still in the hands of the original family. There is no booking; you must be prepared to wait in line for a short while until you are seated. The tables are very close together and there are no frills, just plenty of bustle as an eclectic mixture of diners come and go. There's never a table free for more than a few minutes. The extensive menu offers simple, fresh, inexpensive brasserie food: liver and onions, *steak frites*, great *filet mignon* with a generous portion of *foie gras*. There are also copious regional salads and a fresh fish dish or two, plus a delicious onion soup with melted cheese. Desserts are old fashioned: chocolate mousse and homemade tarts and pastries.

❝*An institution*❞

CLOSED one week May
CARDS MC, V

Pau
◆ La Michodière
€ – €€

34, rue Pasteur, 64000 Pau, Pyrénées-Atlantiques
Tel 05 59 27 53 85 Fax 05 59 27 76 86

This restaurant, selected for the quality of its freshly prepared food and a warm welcome, is tucked away down a little side street behind the Brocante market. It's in a pretty stone building dating from around 1700 with a simple interior and a slightly formal atmosphere. At lunchtimes you will be offered a set menu (excellent value at 13 euros at the time of going to press) that usually features fresh fish for the main course and a delicate starter and choice of desserts. The kitchen is open to view, so you can see the chef-patron preparing your meal. His signature dishes include *raviolis* of *langoustines* or lobster, *feullantine de bar, sauce aux truffes* and *l'eventail de magret aux pommes et sa sauce parfumée aux Calvados*. The day's catch of fish as well as live lobsters are proudly presented.

❝*On my last visit I had salad of wild mushrooms and gesiers sautéed until caramelised and deglazed with sherry and balsamic vinegar, then panaché of fresh fish garnished with freshwater crayfish, and a delicious raspberry bavaroise...I wasn't disappointed!*❞

CLOSED Sun; late Jul to late Aug
CARDS MC, V

Pau
◈ Spàgo Ristorante
€ – €€

*8 rue Adoue, 64000 Pau, Pyrénées-
Atlantiques*
Tel 05 59 98 48 62

Recently opened, this Italian restaurant (in a road running down to the boulevard des Pyrénées and opposite the church near the Château *quartier*) has already made an impression on the Pau restaurant scene. The decoration is modern and refined with a Venetian slant. The innovative cooking is brave, inspired by the cuisine of northern Italy and using the freshest produce. Though chef-patron Marco is a native of Pau, he brings a wealth of experience from 25 years in the United States where, as a top chef with Giuseppe Sansone, an Italian restaurateur in New York, he developed his passion for Italian food. Today, together with his wife and a team of trendy waiters and waitresses, he offers tantalizingly fresh produce assembled stylishly on oversized plates. His Italian stall in the local Pau market is a key to the quality and freshness of the ingredients. The evening menu is particularly representative of northern Italy. Chef's specials include *salade Spago* and shellfish flambéed in *grappa*, with pasta.

'We had very good calamari and octopus, as well as carré d'agneau à la Lombarde '

CLOSED Sat and Sun lunch
CARDS MC, V

Pauillac
◈ Château Cordeillan-Bages €€€

*route des Châteaux, 33250 Pauillac,
Gironde*
Tel 05 56 59 24 24 Fax 05 5659 01 89

There is something of the feel of an English country house about the elegant dining room and intimate sitting rooms of this smart Relais & Châteaux hotel and restaurant in the heart of the Médoc. Built in the purest 17thC style, its restaurant and terrace look directly out on to rows of vines

– neighbours are Latour, Lafite, Mouton-Rothschild and many other distinguished names in the history of wine. The château is home to the Ecole de Bordeaux, which offers a wide choice of courses for both professional and amateur wine lovers and organizes visits to other vineyards in the area. The hotel slightly lacks the character it might have in private hands, but it is a charming house and the high standard of service lives up to its four star expectations. In the kitchen, chef Thierry Marx uses his skills to create new dishes based on seasonal produce, as well as traditional regional food. Specialities include *presse d'anguilles fumées terre et estuaire* and *pigeon en coque de pois chiches*. Two Michelin stars.

CLOSED Sat lunch, Mon, Tue lunch; mid-Dec to mid-Jan
CARDS AE, DC, MC, V

Our price bands
Rather than giving actual prices (which are prone to change) we indicate the cost of a three-course meal for one person, without wine, by means of price bands. They are as follows: € under 30 euros €€ 30-50 euros €€€ over 50 euros. Where we give more than one price band, for example €– €€€ , this indicates that in that restaurant a meal can be had at a range of prices. As well as the cost of *prix fixe* menus, our price bands also take into account the cost of an average selection from the *à la carte* menu.

Périgueux
◈ Le Clos Saint-Front €

*5 rue de la Vertu, 24000 Périgueux,
Dordogne*
Tel 05 53 46 78 58 Fax 05 53 46 78 20

This up-and-coming restaurant in central Périgueux has developed a well-deserved reputation for the excellent value and inventiveness of its food. The style tends towards *nouvelle*, but the flavours are rich and so beautifully balanced that you won't leave the table dissatisfied, however light the dishes. There is a limited menu – always a good sign – which changes monthly, plus a selection of speciality dishes, including an absolutely exquisite *foie gras* served warm with a spicy caramel sauce. The service is impeccable without being grand and the staff are exceptionally accommodating. Last but not least, in warm weather you can eat in the haven of the palm-filled courtyard.

❜ We stumbled on this place by chance, and as luck would have it, a table was free (unusual apparently); we couldn't believe our good fortune'... 'the dishes don't change, but what they do, they do very well. Satisfying ❜

Closed Sun, Mon; two weeks Jan, one week Jun, one week Sep
Cards AE, MC, V

Our traditional French cuisine symbol
So many of our readers enjoy seeking out the genuinely French eating experience that we have used Fr to mark restaurants which offer *cuisine du terroir*, classical French dishes or regional dishes with an emphasis on local ingredients, and traditional recipes.

Puymirol
◆ Les Loges de l'Aubergade €€€

52 rue Royale, 47270 Puymirol, Lot-et-Garonne
Tel 05 53 95 31 46 Fax 05 53 95 33 80

In a little fortified village, Les Loges de l'Aubergade is a handsome former residence of the Counts of Toulouse, dating from the 13th century. The lodestones to Puymirol are chef Michel Trama (two Michelin stars) for his superb food, wine and cigars, and his wife Maryse, with whom he has created this international-class hotel and restaurant. The building has stone walls, high ceilings, beams, a 17thC oak staircase and is decorated in impeccable style. The extensive kitchens are impressive and full of activity, with M. Trama very much in personal charge. A special feature is a large smoking room with a glass-fronted, fully humidified cabinet containing a collection of the very best Cuban cigars – not for show but for smoking. A terrace garden, leading off the dining room, has attractive canvas umbrella sunshades and is discreetly illuminated through trees and bushes after dark. As for the food, specialities of the house include *papillote de pomme de terre à la truffe* and *pot-au-feu de canard au foie gras et au jus de truffe*, so you can see that truffles and *foie gras* are firmly in evidence.

Closed Mon lunch Jul, Aug, Sun dinner, Tue lunch Sep-Jun; Feb
Cards AE, DC, MC, V

Sabres
◆ Auberge des Pins
€ – €€€ Fr

rue de la Piscine, 40630 Sabres, Landes
Tel 05 58 07 56 74 Fax 05 58 07 56 74

The restaurant in this excellent country hotel – a chalet-style building in lovely, pine-scented surrounding – caters as much to locals as it does to visitors. In an attractive dining room, Michel Lesclauze cooks simple, regional dishes with aplomb: *pigeonneau roti et truffeé sur la peau et son risotto de jeunes légumes; aumônière de pied de porc sur sa compôtée d'oignons.* There is a widely priced range of menus to choose from, plus a similarly widely-ranged à la carte menu.

Closed Sun dinner, Mon; Jan
Cards MC, V

Saint-Astier
◆ La Palombière
€ – €€

7 place de l'Eglise, 24110 Saint-Astier, Dordogne
Tel 05 53 04 40 61 Fax 05 53 04 40 61

Consistent quality and excellent service keep people coming back to this little restaurant opposite Saint-Astier's 12thC church – the summer terrace overlooks the church square. As so often, it's the food rather than the decoration that is the attraction here, though it's pretty enough, in the stone-walls, pink-tablecloth genre. The main feature is a large ornamental fireplace. There is also a non-smoking room. A wide range of menus are offered. The weekday lunch menus, at three or four courses without choice, offer exceptional value, otherwise there are two *menus gourmets* offering four and five courses respectively, with a choice of dishes, and two *menus gastronomiques*. Firm favourites are *sandre aux morilles* and *foie gras* pan-fried with fruits of the season. There is always a good showing of game in autumn, of which the signature dish is the regional speciality, *salmi de palombe*.

❛ I love the way they do foie gras with a raspberry coulis. Attentive, friendly waitresses ❜

Closed Tue dinner, Wed; three weeks Feb, two weeks Jun, two weeks Sep
Cards V

Saint-Emilion
◆ Francis Goullée
€€ **Fr**

27 rue Guadet, 33330 Saint-Emilion, Gironde
Tel 05 57 24 70 49 Fax 05 57 24 70 49

For somewhere traditional and honest, as opposed to the rather chi-chi restaurants in this part of the world, head down this narrow street and enjoy the excellent regional dishes of Francis, and the friendly welcome of his wife Annie. Pigeon, ceps, *foie gras, magret de canard* and *brandade de morue* all feature. Affordable wine list.

Closed Sun dinner, Mon; three weeks Dec
Cards MC, V

Saint-Etienne-de-Baïgorry
◆ Arcé € – €€ **Fr**

64430 Saint-Etienne-de-Baïgorry, Pyrénées-Atlantiques
Tel 05 59 37 40 14 Fax 05 59 37 40 27

The setting – by a river in a typical Basque village – is a magical one, best appreciated from the dining terrace, which juts out over the water and is sheltered by a canopy of chestnut trees. Nestled there, one feels both intimate and secluded and nothing could be more pleasant than a relaxed lunch or dinner, enjoying good local cooking, with

the emphasis on fresh ingredients, together with an interesting wine list at reasonable prices. In cooler weather there is a smart dining room with picture windows, and a beamed library with books in a variety of languages. Arcé makes a lovely place to stay; some of the bedrooms are impressively large, others have small terraces with mountain views, and there is a blue-tiled swimming pool hidden in a green enclosure on the far side of the river.

❛Arcé has now been run by five generations of the Arcé family, creating a consistency 'that can be palpably detected'...'We've returned time and again, and never been disappointed ❜

Closed mid-Nov to mid-Mar
Cards DC, MC, V

Saint-Justin
◆ Hôtel de France
€ – €€ **Fr**

place des Tilleuls, 40240 Saint-Justin, Landes
Tel 05 58 44 83 61 Fax 05 58 44 83 89

In fortified Saint-Justin, which dates from the 13th century, this typical, honest, old-fashioned hotel stands at its centre. In a tranquil atmosphere, in the hotel's dining room or on the arcaded terrace, the local *bourgoisie* tuck in to *cuisine du terroir* that is a cut above: duck, suckling pig with *ratatouille, foie gras*, ceps, goose cooked in red wine and so on.

Closed Sun dinner, Mon, Thu dinner; mid-Nov to mid-Dec
Cards MC, V

Saint-Léon-sur-Vézère
◆ Le Petit Léon € **Fr**

24290 Saint-Léon-sur-Vézère, Dordogne
Tel 05 53 51 18 04 Fax 05 53 51 18 04

Midway along the lush Vézère valley with its world-famous prehistoric caves, the exquisite little riverside village of Saint-Léon (complete with elegant château and little Romanesque church) makes a perfect pit stop. The shaded and walled garden of Le

Petit Léon looks out over one of the village's two châteaux, while in cooler weather you eat in an elegant, stone-vaulted dining room. On offer are four well-priced menus in addition to a limited carte: house specialities include mushroom-stuffed *magret de canard* topped with *foie gras*, and an unusual dish of *gésiers* fried with mushrooms – much better than it might sound. British visitors will no doubt be tempted to end with a generous slice of mouth-watering lemon meringue pie.

Closed Sun dinner, Mon May–Jul, Sep; Nov–Apr
Cards AE, DC, MC, V

Please send us reports

A guide such as this thrives on reader's reports. If you send us five usable reports, we will send you a free copy of any title in our *Charming Small Hotel Guides* series (see page 241 for France titles in the series).

The five reports should contain at least two new restaurants; the balance can be comments on restaurants already in the guide. **Send reports to** Charming Restaurant Guides, Duncan Petersen Ltd, 31 Ceylon Road, London W14 OPY.

Saint-Macaire
◆ L'Abricotier €€

rue Bergoeing, 33490 Saint-Macaire, Gironde
Tel 05 56 76 83 63 Fax 05 56 76 28 51

The location of this little restaurant – on the main N 113 as it skirts north of Saint-Macaire – may not appear too promising, but don't let that put you off. Once inside, you discover a pretty walled garden where, among the heady scents of roses and jasmine, all is peace and calm. Furthermore, as many locals will tell you, this is one of the best eating places in the area. The reason is simple: the young owners, Alain and Michèle Zanette, are sticklers for using only the freshest and highest quality ingredients. In doing so, they offer a limited menu, but one that changes almost every week, with a strong showing of fish – including delicacies such as lamprey, shad

and eels from the nearby Garonne river – and plenty of game in season. The wine list is as well-judged as the food.

Closed Mon, Tue dinner; mid-Nov to mid-Dec
Cards V

Sainte-Maure-de-Peyriac
◆ Ferme-Auberge du Boué € Fr

47170 Sainte-Maure-de-Peyriac, Lot-et-Garonne
Tel 05 53 65 63 94 Fax 05 53 65 41 80

This working farm, lost in the depths of the countryside, is a good example of a *ferme-auberge*, where the majority of produce served must come from the farm itself or, in the case of the wine and Armagnac, for example, from the local area. It's best to arrive at lunch time when you can enjoy the journey and the surroundings. Reservations are obligatory. Jean-François Boitard, Jehanne Rignault and their children give visitors a warm welcome. They are more than happy to talk about the farm and – most importantly – the food. The cheapest menu (14 euros at the time of going to press) is a feast; don't plan anything too active afterwards. You may, for example, be presented with a tureen of garlic soup, followed by Jean-François' award-winning *rillettes* to eat with home-made bread rubbed with garlic, *magret de canard* served with potatoes crispy-fried in duck fat and a *gratin* of courgettes, a slice of plum and pear tart and coffee. Before you commence, you are proffered a generous glass of greengage aperitif. On the 18.50 euro menu you will be served *foie gras* and *cassoulet*, plus Armagnac with the coffee. Most of the clients are French, some staying here in the farm's *gîtes*. You eat at big pine tables with bench seats - not the most comfortable set-up. The dining room is functional rather than cosy. There is a *plan d'eau* for fishing, and wooded grounds for walking. The farm is signposted off the D109 between Sos and Sainte-Maure-de-Peyriac.

❛ We were treated like family – the Armagnac bottle was just left on the table for us to help ourselves'...'Jean-François is a real character ❜

CLOSED Sun dinner, Mon; Mon-Fri Apr, May, Sep, Oct; Nov-Easter
CARDS MC, V

Saint-Saud-Lacoussière

◆ Hostellerie Saint-Jacques €€ **Fr**

24470 Saint-Saud-Lacoussière, Dordogne
Tel 05 53 56 97 21 Fax 05 5356 91 33

The front of the creeper-clad 18thC building gives little clue to what lies within – or, more to the point, what lies behind: owners the Babayou's 'summer sitting room', which consists of lovely sloping gardens, with masses of colourful flowers, a swimming pool and tennis court. Inside there is an unusually large dining room/bar decorated in bright blue and yellow, with big windows which open on to the terrace above the garden. If you are staying, there are comfortable bedrooms above, several of which can accommodate families. The food, in the capable hands of Thierry Mancelly, son-in-law of patron Jean-Pierre Babayou, is accomplished *cuisine du terroir*, rich, varied and satisfying. Occasionally there are lively evenings with dancing and games, or communal dinners devoted to the exploration of regional cuisine. Not your cup of tea? Give it a try; you might be surprised once you join in with the fun and games.

CLOSED Mon; Sun dinner, Mon, Tue lunch; Nov-Mar
CARDS AE, MC, V

---

charmingsmallhotels.co.uk
Visit Duncan Petersen's travel website, the best online search tool for places to stay that combine character and charm.
Currently features Britain, France, Italy and Ireland, with other destinations being continuously added.

Saint-Sever

◆ La Table des Jacobins € **Fr**

11 place de Verdun, 40500 Saint-Sever,
Landes
Tel 05 58 76 36 93 Fax 05 58 76 36 93

In a little side street opposite the church in this pretty tourist town, La Table des Jacobins is a small narrow café-style restaurant frequented mainly by local business people. It serves excellent value, simple home cooking, and the three course *menu du jour* (which changes daily) goes for just 10 euros (at the time of going to press) with wine. A good address to know, as Saint-Sever is worth a visit but lacks places for lunch.

CLOSED Mon-Sun dinner; Sat, Sun lunch
CARDS none

Sare

◆ Arraya €€

64310 Sare, Pyrénées-Atlantiques
Tel 05 59 54 2046 Fax 05 59 37 40 27

With its timbered, white-painted houses adorned with red or green shutters, Sare can claim to be the prettiest of all the extremely pretty Basque villages. In the heart of the village, this 17thC house was once an overnight resting place for pilgrims on their way across the Pyrenees to Santiago de Compostela. Behind the slightly severe frontage lies a country-style hotel and restaurant of great character, now run by the third generation of the charming Fagoaga family. Inside, all is spick and span – airy and light, with much old, dark, burnished wood. The beamed sitting room and dining room are filled with glorious old Basque furniture: sofas and chairs are comfortable and inviting and flowers are everywhere. The regional cuisine is generally of a high standard, although there can be slips; a well-chosen wine list accompanies the food. In summer, meals are taken on the attractive terrace.

CLOSED Sun dinner, Mon lunch Apr-Jul, Sep-Nov; Nov-Apr
CARDS AE, MC, V

Sauternes

◆ Le Saprien €€

11 rue Principal, 33210 Sauternes,
Gironde
Tel 05 56 76 60 06 Fax 05 56 76 69 97

Overlooking the vineyards that produce the great Sauternes wine, this stone-built house makes an elegant setting for a glass or two (it is offered by the glass as well as by the bottle) accompanied by the good food of chef M, Garrigues. Sauternes sauces accompany such dishes as lamprey and veal sweetbreads, and you can also eat *terrine de foie gras à la gelée de Sauternes* as well as meat grilled simply over vine clippings.

CLOSED Sun dinner, Mon, Wed dinner
CARDS AE, DC, MC, V

Tonneins
◆ Côte Garonne € – €€€

36-38 cour de l'Yser, 47400 Tonneins, Lot-et-Garonne
Tel 05 53 84 34 34 Fax 05 5384 31 31

Côte Garonne's new chef (since March 2002), Christian Papillon, was born locally but lived in Réunion for a while, an influence which is clear in his beautifully conceived – and presented – dishes, such as beef served with *morilles,* garlic *confit* and cardamom, and especially when it comes to the lip-smacking desserts: baked banana drizzled with a liquorice sauce and served with a mango and ginger sorbet, *poire William* poached in wine and saffron, served with prunes soaked in Armagnac and green tea. This is a gastronomic restaurant, but the three-course menu (20 euros at the time of going to press) is remakably affordable. Or you can really go to town with the 61 euro *menu côte epicurien* (a *menu surprise*), which must be ordered 24 hours in advance. There is a good choice of local wines on the extensive wine list, and even a cigar cellar. Solid teak chairs, ochre walls and white cloths create a clean, cool – slightly oriental – ambience, enhanced by big picture windows overlooking the Garonne and the farmland beyond. The restaurant consists of threee riverfront houses that have been knocked together.

❛ Undoubtedly one of the leading restaurants in Lot-et-Garonne, Côte Garonne always has something unexpected – and inspiring – on the menu'... 'The meal costs more than we normally care to pay, but it was well worth every last euro and we can't wait to return ❜

CLOSED Mon, Tue and Sat lunch, Sun dinner
CARDS MC, V

Trémolat
◆ Le Bistro d'en Face
€ Fr

24510 Trémolat, Dordogne
Tel 05 53 22 80 69 Fax 05 53 22 84 89

Set in a lovely quiet village among walnut orchards on a huge meander in the Dordogne river, this bistro is a cheaper and livelier alternative to its parent, the nearby Vieux Logis (see below). It's a cheerful, bustling place with blue-and-yellow cloths where you eat in one of two stone-walled rooms or in the glass-fronted extension. Your companions are as likely to be from the Dordogne's large ex-patriot community as French. The food is produced out of a tiny kitchen, part of which is open to the restaurant, so this is simple fare, with little choice, but high quality. Service can take a long time when the place is busy. On weekdays there is a good-value (11.50 euros at the time of going to press) lunch menu of three courses and a *pichet* of wine per person. There are two more slightly more expensive menus. The carte features fish from the Dordogne (perch, sander or eel, according to what's available). Other dishes include vegetable terrine, omelette with ceps, rabbit stew, home-made ice creams and sorbets.

❛ Our friends, who chose from the carte, found the portions a bit small, but we were more than happy with our set menus ❜

CLOSED Wed Oct to mid–Apr
CARDS MC, V

Trémolat
◆ Le Vieux Logis
€€€

24510 Trémolat, Dordogne
Tel 05 53 22 80 06 Fax 05 53 22 84 89

The Giraudel-Destords family have lived in this complex of farm and village houses for over 400 years. Today it is one of the most civilized hotels in the region, with a fine galleried dining room, recently redecorated in a much warmer and more intimate style that previously, with views over the green and flowery garden. Current chef Vincent

Arnould had an impressive training in Alsace and Provence and has brought new ideas and flair to the cooking while still respecting local traditions.

CLOSED Mon-Fri lunch Sep-Jun; Jan-Mar
CARDS AE, DC, MC, V

Uza
◆ Le Cottage €

Le Bourg, 40170 Uza, Landes
Tel 05 58 42 82 98

Just inland from the Atlantic coast, Uza is a small Landaise village, and Le Cottage is a simple lakeside restaurant with friendly service and home-cooked food: *bouill-abaisse*, lasagne, pizzas, tarts, plainly cooked fish and so on. Nothing exceptional, but enjoyable, in pleasant surroundings.

CLOSED Mon-Fri Jan-Apr; phone for further details
CARDS MC, V

Villetoureix
◆ Le Vieux Frêne
€ Fr

Les Deux-Ponts, Villetoureix, 24600 Riberac, Dordogne
Tel 05 53 91 09 74

Le Vieux Frêne is one of a fast-disappearing breed: a simple restaurant with red-checked tablecloths and a four-course *menu du jour* (lunchtime Tuesday to Friday only; 11 euros at the time of going to press) including a carafe of wine. It kicks off with a good *hors-d'œuvre* buffet, then main course, cheese and dessert. It's a favourite of local artisans at lunch, but it's a cut above basic. The dining room is rustic (strings of garlic and hams hanging from the beams) and it's cosy. There's a riverside terrace in summer and the whole place is surrounded by greenery, even though you are by a fairly main road just across the Dronne from Ribérac. It's a popular place to eat after browsing round Ribérac's famous Friday market. Expect hearty, no-nonsense fare, with the emphasis on grilled meats.

❛ *We were delighted when the chef came out to chat with his regulars and greet us newcomers. It was a*

real throwback to how French restaurants used to be'...'Adorable – a place that's real rather than pretending to be ❜

CLOSED Mon, Wed dinner
CARDS DC, MC, V

Our price bands
Rather than giving actual prices (which are prone to change) we indicate the cost of a three-course meal for one person, without wine, by means of price bands. They are as follows: € under 30 euros €€ 30-50 euros €€€ over 50 euros. Where we give more than one price band, for example €– €€€, this indicates that in that restaurant a meal can be had at a range of prices. As well as the cost of *prix fixe* menus, our price bands also take into account the cost of an average selection from the *à la carte* menu.

Vitrac
◆ La Treille
€ – €€€

Le Port, 24200 Vitrac, Dordogne
Tel 05 53 28 33 19 Fax 05 53 30 38 54

The cooking of Philippe Latreille of hotel-restaurant La Treille near Sarlat, puts an unusual spin on standard dishes, many incorporating the regional delicacy, *foie gras*: a *pot-au-feu* of *foie gras* flavoured with sage; *foie gras* poached in Bergerac and served on a bed of caramelised, slightly spicy turnips; goose stuffed with duck *foie gras* in a bitter-sweet cherry sauce. In 1999 he won an award as young chef of the year in the Aquitaine region. The setting is simple but attractive, with a small dining room and a covered terrace surrounded by luxuriant vegetation on the banks of the Dordogne, though you can't see the river from the tables. The service efficient and friendly.

❛ *It' the restaurant that steals the show. The cuisine is superb, and very reasonably priced too* ❜

CLOSED Sun dinner, Mon; Jan, Feb
CARDS AE, DC, MC, V

MIDI-PYRENEES

S ituated in the heart of south-west France, the government region of Midi-Pyrénées
extends from the wooded hills of the Dordogne in its far north to the great river valleys (Lot, Tarn, Garonne and Aveyron) at its centre and the majestic Pyrénées in
the south. It is one of the largest regions in the country, with a landscape of simple agriculture, ancient towns, fortified villages, castles, Romanesque
churches and a past that goes back to pre-history. It comprises no
less than eight départements. The department of Lot covers
the popular Lot valley, the town of Cahors and the old
region of Quercy. Its rocky, limestone plateaux,
known as causses, extend into rural Aveyron and
industrial Tarn (principal towns Rodez and
Albi) in the old regions of Rouergue and

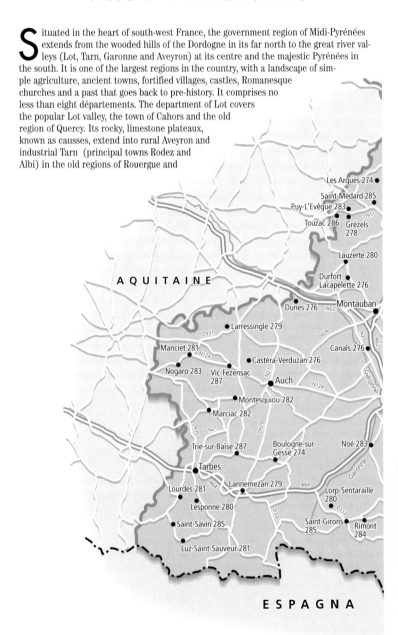

Les Arques 274

Saint-Médard 285

Puy-L'Evêque 283

Touzac 286   Grézels
278

Lauzerte 280

AQUITAINE

Durfort-
Lácapelette 276

Dunes 276   Montauban

Larressingle 279

Manciet 281

Canals 276

Nogaro 283   Vic-Fezensac
287

Castéra-Verduzan 276

Auch

Montesquiou 282

Marciac 282

Trie-sur-Baïse 287

Boulogne-sur-   Noé 283
Gesse 274

Tarbes

Lourdes 281   Lannemezan 279

Lorp-Sentaraille
280

Lesponne 280

Saint-Savin 285

Saint-Girons   Rimont
285   284

Luz-Saint-Sauveur 281

ESPAGNA

Albigeois. In the centre of the Midi-Pyrénées, Haute-Garonne and Tarn-et-Garonne mark the progress of the river Garonne past the region's dynamic capital, Toulouse, once the capital of the Haute-Languedoc kingdom. Gers is Gascony and Armagnac country, while mountainous Haute-Pyrénées, including the shrine of Lourdes and rugged Ariège, 'Cathar country', both meet the border with Spain.

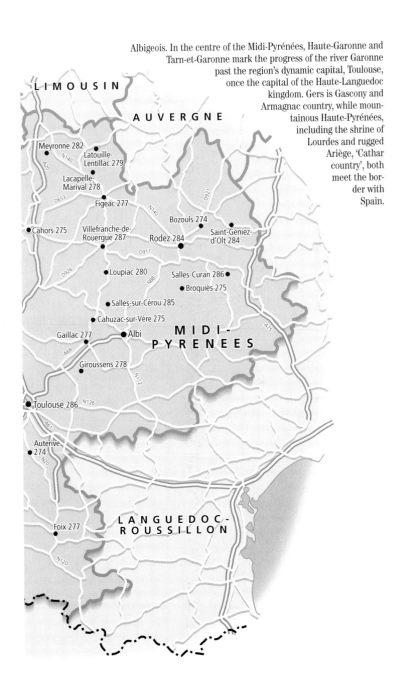

LIMOUSIN

AUVERGNE

Meyronne 282

Latouille-Lentillac 279

Lacapelle-Marival 278

Figeac 277

Cahors 275

Villefranche-de-Rouergue 287

Bozouls 274

Rodez 284

Saint-Geniez-d'Olt 284

Loupiac 280

Salles-Curan 286

Broquiès 275

Salles-sur-Cérou 285

Cahuzac-sur-Vère 275

Gaillac 277

Albi

MIDI-PYRENEES

Giroussens 278

Toulouse 286

Auterive 274

LANGUEDOC-ROUSSILLON

Foix 277

Les Arques
◆ La Récréation € Fr

46250 Les Arques, Lot
Tel 05 65 22 88 08

This appealing restaurant occupies the old village school in the pretty, sleepy hamlet of Les Arques, whose other claim to fame is its museum to the Russian sculptor Ossip Zadekine. Meals are served in the dining room (where the friendly English-speaking owner exhibits the work of local artists), in the courtyard, or on the small wisteria-covered terrace. The menus are quite limited in choice, but use produce from the garden wherever possible (in, for instance, stuffed courgette flowers). The set *menu du jour* is excellent value at 11 euros, including wine and coffee. The price for other menus rises to 23 euros, without wine. The cuisine is typical regional French, with the occasional twist (for example, *cabecou* in filo parcels). Although the all-French wine list lacks breadth, it has a good range of medium-priced Cahors. As the restaurant is popular with both holiday-makers and locals, it's important to book a table. Even at its busiest, you will not be rushed and the service remains calm yet efficient.

❛ **The perfect setting for a long lazy lunch. Quiet, rustic, timeless surroundings** ❜

Closed Wed, Thu lunch, Thu eve Sep-Jul, Mon; Dec-Mar
Cards MC, V

Auterive
◆ Les Murailles € – €€ Fr

route de Grazac, 31190 Auterive, Haute Garonne
Tel 05 61 50 76 98 Fax 05 61 50 76 98

It's unlikely that by chance you would stumble across this charming restaurant in a lovely and immaculately restored old stone and brick building. But it's well worth planning a visit, and you must book in advance. Menus, ranging from 15 to 38 euros, are all characterized by Hélène and Philippe Tourniants' mission to provide simple, tasty, traditional dishes, based on poultry and home-produced ingredients, with fierce regard to reputation. The dining room has an enormous chimney, beams, exposed brickwork, and some interesting ornaments, including a quirky collection of ducks. It is set in well-tended gardens, with tables on the patio and deep countryside beyond. A glance at the visitors' book will reveal that it is not completely undiscovered: Tony and Cherie Blair ate here on a recent trip to France. To the south-west of Auterive, it is off the D28E to Grazac.

❛ **Discreet and very peaceful** ❜ ... ❛The enthusiastic patrons are committed to their cuisine and their clients❜

Closed Mon; mid-Sep to early Oct
Cards MC, V

Boulogne-sur-Gesse
◆ Le Nizors € Fr

route de Blajan, 31350 Boulogne-sur-Gesse, Haute Garonne
Tel 05 61 88 20 68

Tucked away off a minor road (the D633 south of Boulogne), this small, remote *auberge* offers simple traditional food. Choose between three well-priced menus of four to five courses or the very reasonable *plat du jour*. A large conservatory, decorated with sheaves of wheat, seats most diners at colourful tables, laid with prettily patterned crockery and napkins of different colours, which add to the cheerful atmosphere. You can also sit outside on the terrace, overlooking a wooded valley. Le Nizors is recognized by the 'Auberge du Pays' organization, which supports small rural restaurants committed to regional catering.

Closed Thu
Cards MC, V

Bozouls
◆ A la Route d'Argent
€ – €€

route d'Espalion, 12340 Bozouls, Aveyron
Tel 05 65 44 92 27 Fax 05 65 48 81 40

The charm of this restaurant doesn't lie in its rather nondescript location on the edge of Bozouls village, but in the elegantly decorated dining room and the quality and presentation of the food. Beneath a tented fabric ceiling, silver gleams on tables covered in crisp white linen, decorated with fresh flowers, and standing on a polished marble floor. Menus range from 14.50 to 37 euros, and there is no à la carte. The style of the cooking is regional, tending to gourmet, with a basis of good quality ingredients, though the sauces might be over-seasoned for some tastes. The range of desserts is very attractive (fresh fig tart and excellent homemade vanilla ice-cream, for example). The wines are predominantly from the southwest of France and very reasonably priced. At lunchtime the restaurant is a favourite with local business people and, though staff are generally polite and friendly, service can be brusque when it's busy.

(A memorable meal in elegant, contemporary surroundings)

CLOSED Sun dinner, Mon lunch; Jan–Mar
CARDS AE, MC, V

---

charmingsmallhotels.co.uk
Visit Duncan Petersen's travel website, the best online search tool for places to stay that combine character and charm. Currently features Britain, France, Italy and Ireland, with other destinations being continuously added.

Broquiès
◆ Le Pescadou
€ – €€€ **Fr**

Pont du Navech, 12480 Broquiès, Aveyron
Tel 05 65 99 40 21 Fax 05 65 99 48 04

At the north end of a bridge over the Tarn, about 2 km (1 mile) outside the hilltop village of Broquiès, this modest hotel-restaurant is a converted farm. It has a plain dining room but a delightful wisteria-covered first-floor terrace, which looks over the swimming pool, orchard and lush river valley. The menus are based on classic peasant cooking, and though the food comes with the minimum of frills, the chef chooses good quality ingredients and treats them simply and sympathetically. Stick to the reasonable menus; à la carte could mean a bill of more than 50 euros, which would be expensive for a restaurant such as this. Service is friendly

and unhurried but a little lacking in polish.

(Good uncomplicated food. A very pleasant setting)

CLOSED mid-Oct to mid-Mar
CARDS not accepted

Cahors
◆ Le Rendez-Vous
€ – €€

49 rue Clément Marot, 46000 Cahors, Lot
Tel 05 65 22 65 10 Fax 05 65 35 11 05

Tucked away down a narrow pedestrian alley in the heart of the historic quarter, a few steps from the cathedral of Saint-Etienne, this restaurant is a stylish blend of old and new – ancient exposed stonework and a flagstone floor combined with colour-washed walls hung with modern art. The interior is surprisingly light and airy, and a mezzanine level, used to exhibit paintings by local artists, means that it can seat more people than would seem at first sight. Offered on a good value two-course set lunch menu and a three-course menu, as well as à la carte, the typical modern French cuisine is well presented and so popular – especially with the locals – that it's always advisable to book. The service is efficient without being pressing.

CLOSED Sun, Mon; first 2 weeks May, first 2 weeks Nov
CARDS MC, V

Cahuzac-sur-Vère
◆ La Falaise € – €€€

routes de Cordes, 81140 Cahuzac-sur-Vère, Tarn
Tel 05 63 33 96 31 Fax 05 63 33 96 31

You wouldn't guess from the outside of this small restaurant on the outskirts of the sleepy little village of Cahuzac, how superb the standard of its cooking is. Whether you eat in the old dining room or the modern extension, the surroundings are pleasant, and the food and service excellent. Specialities, such as Cantal cheese with a reduced cherry *confit*, *rouget* with squid, and *langoustine* with an avocado *salpicon*, are refined versions of traditional regional dishes, carefully prepared and presented. As you might expect, local Gaillac wines (starting at 13 euros) are well-represented on a first-class list. The advice on wines is very knowledgeable and well-judged.

> *6 Clear flavours; careful cooking; excellent results' ... 'The well-matched local wines are a bonus 9*

CLOSED Sun dinner, Mon, Wed lunch Apr-Oct, Wed dinner Nov-Mar; first 3 weeks Jan, first 2 weeks Dec
CARDS DC, MC, V

Canals
◆ L'Ancre Marine € – €€

RN20, 82170 Canals, Tarn et Garonne
Tel 05 63 02 84 00 Fax 05 63 02 84 01

In a dullish corner of Tarn et Garonne, a Breton-style seafood restaurant might be the last thing you'd expect to find. The immediate location is nothing special: near a busy main road, a few kilometres south of Montauban, but the dining room is quiet. Both it and the garden marquee are decorated predominantly in cool shades of blue and white, with a relentless nautical theme. Even the platters of seafood arrive in large blue plastic boats. Good-value seafood and regional specialities comprise the menus, and though the ingredients are fresh and well-cooked, dishes tend to be uninspired (desserts are more interesting than main courses). The wine list concentrates on local wines from the south west and, though modest, is fairly priced. The clientele is mainly French, including businessmen and women at lunchtime, which might account for the attentive yet slightly impersonal service.

CLOSED Sat lunch, Sun dinner, Mon dinner
CARDS MC, V

Castéra-Verduzan
◆ Le Florida € – €€€

32410 Castéra-Verduzan, Gers
Tel 05 62 68 13 22 Fax 05 62 68 10 44

Opened by the current patron's grandmother in 1935, this restaurant has earned a reputation for high standards and exciting specialities, with the emphasis on duck. If you're not tempted by duck, you might start with a warm black pudding salad with golden apples and Bezolles mustard or

foie gras with figs, followed by roasted rack of lamb with a garlic, anchovy and parsely crust, or Provençal-style monkfish medallions. There is a bargain lunch-only menu for 12 euros; otherwise menus range from 21 to 40 euros, or you can choose à la carte. The decoration is tastefully restrained: terracotta-tiled floors, white walls, old oak beams and strategically hung mirrors. Outside it is equally attractive, with flower-filled borders, a palm and tables on the terrace, shaded by a chestnut tree and umbrellas.

> *6 Well-established, and proud of its tradition' ... 'Perfect duck 9*

CLOSED Sun dinner, Mon; 2 weeks Feb
CARDS AE, DC, MC, V

Dunes
◆ Les Templiers
€ – €€€€

82340 Dunes, Tarn et Garonne
Tel 05 63 39 86 21 Fax 05 63 39 86 21

In a 16thC house on the main arcaded square of this tiny quiet 13thC *bastide* village, Les Templiers is a pretty restaurant, with a smart, rustic modern dining room, decorated in shades of yellow. The food is modern French, offered on a range of menus, which means that you can keep your meal simple by choosing the 18-euro menu or push the boat out with the *menu dégustation* for 52 euros. Fresh local produce is well-prepared with interesting sauces and accompaniments. Wines are from all regions of France, but with the emphasis on the south west. Service is quiet and efficient.

> *6 A delightful restaurant in a delightful bastide setting 9*

CLOSED Sat lunch, Sun dinner, Mon, Tue dinner
CARDS MC, V

Durfort-Lacapelette
◆ L'Aube Nouvelle
€ – €€€

82390 Durfort-Lacapelette, Tarn et Garonne
Tel 05 63 04 50 33 Fax 05 63 04 57 55

In the beautiful Quercy Blanc countryside, this surprising *auberge* stands alone on a small ridge. From the outside, you could be forgiven for thinking that you had come across a farm in need of renovation, but once you step inside, you will find a smart dining room, recently redecorated in shades of yellow and terracotta. The menus reveal the Belgian origins of the proprietor, who moved here as a child, and, amongst other dishes, feature *lapin à la Flamande* and *waterzooi* of fish. The desserts are rather disappointing in comparison with the other courses. The *auberge* is one km (half a mile) north of the village off the D2, and is a regular watering hole for Swiss tour companies as well as being popular with other holidaymakers and locals.

CLOSED one week Jan-Apr
CARDS AE, DC, MC, V

Figeac
◆ La Puce à l'Oreille
€ – €€ **Fr**

5-7 rue Saint-Thomas, 46100 Figeac, Lot
Tel 05 65 34 33 08 Fax 05 65 34 33 08

Converted 15thC stables in the heart of old Figeac provide a cool oasis for this comfortable restaurant with character. High ceilings and old stone arches looking out to a small green courtyard give it an ecclesiastical air. It also feels relaxed, partly because the tables are at different levels and partly due to the friendly, competent staff. The restaurant's claim to be '*gastronomique*' is a slight exaggeration: the food is typical of the region, competently prepared and presented, but not outstanding. Unusually, dogs are welcome; even given a bowl of water. The downside is that the house cat can sometimes excite the dogs. There is an excellent value 12-euro menu (available only at lunchtime) and a reasonable selection of fairly priced French wines, with the emphasis on Cahors.

❛ *Unpretentious, genteel and slightly old-fashioned' … 'It's rather like eating in a medieval monastery chapel* ❜

CLOSED Sun dinner and Mon Apr-Aug; Sep-Apr
CARDS MC, V

Foix
◆ Le Phoebus € – €€

3 cours Irénée Cros, 09000 Foix, Ariège
Tel 05 61 65 10 42 Fax 05 61 65 10 42

Unprepossessing when viewed from the main road entrance (after a walk up from the railway station where you can park), this restaurant has two winning points: a highly acclaimed menu and a terrific view. Stewed rabbit with blueberry sauce and baked apple stuffed with Roquefort, with cinnamon ice-cream, are amongst the specialities. There is also a vegetarian menu. The furniture and beams are of dark old oak, offset by crisp white tablecloths, with the glazed terrace and its view as backdrop. From the terrace you can look down over the river (ignoring the railway line) and across to the dramatic castle perched high on the rocks opposite. When it is lit at night, it looks even more impressive.

❛ *Come here just for the view* ❜

CLOSED Sat lunch, Mon; sometimes mid-Jul to mid-Aug
CARDS DC, MC, V

Our price bands
€ under 30 euros €€ 30-50 euros
€€€ over 50 euros for a menu.

Gaillac
◆ Les Sarments
€ – €€€

27 rue Cabrol, 81600 Gaillac, Tarn
Tel 05 63 57 62 61 Fax 05 63 57 62 61

In the heart of the narrow medieval streets of old Gaillac, this atmospheric restaurant is housed in a vaulted 14thC winery. Restored eight years ago from ruins, it retains its old beams and the exposed narrow brick arches typical of the region, both of which lend the dining room a particular charm and character. (There is a separate vaulted annexe for functions.) The wine list has selections from each of the French regions, but specializes in the local Gaillac vintages (with 50 priced between 15 and 20 euros). The cooking is high-quality traditional cuisine, stylishly presented, with original touches. The chef, Bernard Bisson, and his wife, Sylvie, pay great attention to detail: even the aperitifs are garnished, and the *kir* arrives with a few liqueur-marinaded blackcurrants floating in it. Though the service can be cool at first, it warms up once you've broken the ice, and staff are very knowledgeable and efficient. The cheapest menu is not offered on Saturdays.

❛ *Excellent food in a special setting - don't miss the chance to eat here* ❜

CLOSED Sun dinner, Mon, Wed dinner Sep-Jul; mid-Dec to mid-Jan, mid-Feb to mid-Mar
CARDS DC, MC, V

Giroussens
◆ L'Echauguette
€ – €€ Fr

81500 Giroussens, Tarn
Tel 05 63 41 63 65 Fax 05 63 41 63 13

In a 13thC building on the ramparts of Giroussens, this restaurant with four rooms has a splendid panoramic view of the surrounding countryside from its terrace. The village is well-known for its many families of potters (there are at least 24 living here), some of whose work – together with local paintings and sculptures – adorn every nook and cranny of the establishment. The owner is a fanatic about food, wine and art, and will enthusiastically discuss, or proffer advice on, any of these topics with his guests. The food is honest *cuisine bourgeoise*, using good ingredients from local sources wherever possible, though puddings don't quite come up to the standard of the rest of the meal. The south west of France is well represented on an admirable wine list.

❛ *Welcoming, friendly and relaxed'* ... *'Memorable for the food and art* ❜

CLOSED Sun dinner and Mon Sep-Jul; last 2 weeks Sep, 3 weeks mid-Feb
CARDS AE, DC, MC, V

Grézels
◆ La Terrasse € Fr

46700 Grézels, Lot
Tel 05 65 21 34 03

La Terrasse is one of those wonderful old-style family restaurants which you won't find in the guides and where there's no menu – you just sit down and the food begins to appear. A mellow, neatly kept building in a peaceful village, it has a long, stone-walled dining room with an enchanting view from the window at one end. Tables and chairs are unpretentious but comfortable. The no-choice lunch is notable value, its five daily changing courses typically including a simple vegetable broth with noodles, tuna fish salad, perfectly cooked steak and sautéed potatoes, cheese and apple tart. Flavours show through simply and honestly. M. Pignères, the patron, gives unhurried but good service, looking after the whole dining room. He might pull a long face if you ask for white instead of red wine, and you'll probably forgive him because this is one of those places where you happily forget choice and instinctively trust the Gallic genius for food.

CLOSED dinner and Mon lunch Sep-Jul, Sat dinner and Sun dinner Jul-Sep; 2 weeks Sep, one other week (not fixed)
CARDS MC, V

Lacapelle-Marival
◆ La Terrasse € – €€€

près du Château, 46120 Lacapelle-Marival, Lot
Tel 05 65 40 80 07 Fax 05 65 40 99 45

In a village that claims – somewhat erroneously – to be one of the prettiest in France, this hotel-restaurant has a pleasant position near the impressive old castle, now the town hall. Though an eccentric mixture of styles, it is smartly decorated and seems to work well. The tables near the windows overlook an attractive terraced garden leading down to a small stream and, wherever you sit, there are views of the castle keep and church. The smoked bacon *quennelles* in asparagus sauce are recommended on menus, priced from a lunchtime-only 12 euros to 33 euros, whilst à la carte dishes include a duo of *foie-gras* and pan-fried crayfish with a cardamom *nage* (and your dinner could exceed 50 euros). No detail is forgotten: nibbles with your aperitif, a *bouche de maison* and excellent home-made bread rolls. Expect some innovative ideas, such as the delicious strawberry *parfait* with a green-tea-infused *sauce Anglaise*. The wine list is exclusively French, but quite extensive; ask the knowledgeable *patronne* for her recommendations – the Gaillac Perlé is a splendid choice for a lunchtime wine.

❛ Fresh ingredients, carefully prepared and presented' ... 'Clear and subtle flavours ❜

CLOSED Sun dinner, Mon, Tue lunch Sep-Jul; Jan-Mar
CARDS MC, V

Lannemezan
◆ Le Pré Vert €–€€

250 rue du Dr Uberschlag, 65300 Lannemezan, Hautes-Pyrénées
Tel 05 62 98 58 77 Fax 05 62 98 58 77

Going to a golf course just to eat might not seem an obvious option, but you will be warmly welcomed at Le Pré Vert, which offers both brasserie and restaurant meals. In a fairly modern, purpose-built building, the restaurant section is pleasantly done out in peach and pine-green. Here you can choose from a range of reasonably priced menus, including a speciality 'Bigourdan' version, or à la carte. The chef-patron likes to be personally involved, insisting on serving some dishes at table himself. Though the brasserie is more informal, with tile-top tables and rush-seated chairs, there are also plenty of tasty dishes to choose from, and portions are substantial. Spanning both sections is a large terrace, overlooking the lush, green, wooded golf course, where you can eat or just sit and have a drink.

❛ Its charm lies in the tranquil setting and personal attention ❜

CLOSED Sun dinner, Mon, Tue dinner
CARDS MC, V

Larressingle
◆ Auberge de Larressingle €–€€ Fr

Larressingle, 32100 Condom, Gers
Tel 05 62 28 29 67 Fax 05 62 68 33 14

This former farm, built of honey-coloured stone, is now a comfortable restaurant with character. The dining room is tastefully understated, whilst outside you can dine on a terrace shaded by vines and bamboo. At weekday lunchtimes only, you can have a generous helping of a regional dish and glass of Gascon wine for 11 euros: usually beef in red wine, *cassoulet* or game stew – you take 'pot luck'. For 15 euros, you can lunch or dine on the 'pilgrim's menu' (three courses, limited choice), also only available on weekdays unless you are a pilgrim on the Santiago de Compostella road, in which case you can also have it at weekends. Two more expensive menus and à la carte suggest starters such as cold puréed aubergine with smoked salmon, and prawns with Armagnac and fennel cream for a main course amongst other interesting options. However, this restaurant's unique charm lies in its setting: Larressingle is a tiny, beautifully preserved 13thC fortified village. A little huddle of buildings surround the church, enclosed by ramparts, through which there is only one entrance, by bridge and gate-tower. Just outside, the *auberge* is surrounded by gardens and vineyards, and has a marvellous view up to the imposing fortifications.

❛ A special setting and peaceful atmosphere' ... 'Traditional, generous cuisine ❜

CLOSED Mon low season
CARDS MC, V

Fr French regional or classical French dishes on menu.

Latouille-Lentillac
◆ Gaillard €–€€ Fr

46400 Latouille-Lentillac, Lot
Tel 05 65 38 10 25 Fax 05 65 38 13 13

In a small village buried in a verdant valley, this typical village restaurant is somewhat nondescript from the outside, but the dining room is pleasant and smartly decorated, with a delightful view of the valley's many different trees. It is clearly a favourite with the locals – and is used for village functions and celebrations – but its real strength is the traditional French *cuisine bourgeoise*. Specialities include local trout, *foie gras* and wild mushrooms on menus that run from 12.50 to 25.50 euros (with a special Sunday lunch menu that offers six courses and includes wine for 20.60 euros). The wine list is solidly French, with a reasonable selection of local and Bordeaux vintages. The house wine is good value but basic.

❝ A traditional French village restaurant. Eat here and you'll feel like one of the locals ❞

CLOSED one week Jun, Nov
CARDS AE, MC, V

Lauzerte
◆ Hôtel du Quercy € Fr

faubourg d'Auriac, 82110 Lauzerte, Tarn-et-Garonne
Tel 05 63 94 66 36 Fax 05 63 95 73 21

The restaurant of this unpretentious country hotel on the edge of Lauzerte is definitely going places. Chef Frédéric Bacou has built up a loyal following, not least because he continues to offer excellent value for money and a range of menus to suit every budget. As to his cooking, M. Bacou brings a light, imaginative touch to local dishes featuring duck and *foie gras*, local lamb, sander and game in season. Imaginative they may be, but he is careful not to produce anything which is over-sophisticated: he understands the importance of retaining the authentic tastes of simple country fare, and he strikes a happy balance. Equally true to the region is the well-chosen list of southern wines. With only a small dining area and roadside terrace, it's worth booking in advance.

CLOSED Sun dinner, Mon; one week Feb, early to mid-Oct
CARDS DC, MC, V

Lesponne
◆ Domaine de Ramonjuan € Fr

Lesponne, 65710 Campan, Hautes-Pyrénées
Tel 05 62 91 75 75 Fax 05 62 91 74 54

This ivy-clad Pyrenean farmhouse, converted to a hotel a few years ago, has recently enlarged its restaurant and is now able to feed non-residents. There is a three-course set menu and a single sitting for dinner at around 7.30-8pm, for which it is essential to book ahead. The food is local and wholesome, and best accompanied by wine from an excellent list of reds (there are fewer whites and rosés). The homely dining room has a warm colour scheme, original beams and intimate lighting, with extra seating provided by a conservatory and terrace overlooking the grounds and steep green valley beyond. The Domaine also has a number of bedrooms and apartments, and a charming, attentive family at the helm. It is one km (0.6 miles) beyond Lesponne, up the valley on the right.

❝ A warm family atmosphere ❞

CLOSED Sun dinner, Mon
CARDS MC, V

Lorp-Sentaraille
◆ Côté Jardin € – €€

route de Toulouse, 09190 Lorp-Sentaraille, Ariège
Tel 05 61 66 26 80 Fax 05 61 66 26 08

The modern Hôtel Horizon 117 has within it a well-regarded restaurant with a character that belies its age. The spacious dining room has a large fireplace, dark wood, brass and copper pieces, and manages to avoid feeling the slightest bit fake. It opens out on to a large covered terrace, looking over tranquil lawns and a swimming pool, with a panoramic view of the Pyrénées. The menus include rich regional specialities, such as garlicky roast pigeon, sautéed *suprême* of guinea fowl with rosemary and mountain honey, and a pear pastry, caramelized with a local spiced aperitif and served with a raspberry *coulis*. Less regionally based dishes include ravioli of snails with garlic cream and rum cake and ice-cream.

CLOSED Sat lunch and Sun dinner mid-Sep to mid-Jun; late Oct to mid-Nov
CARDS AE, DC, MC, V

Loupiac
◆ Le Mûrier de Viels
€ – €€

12700 Loupiac, Aveyron
Tel 05 65 80 89 82 Fax 05 65 80 89 82

An old Quercy farmhouse and its outbuildings on a steep hillside above the Lot provide an idyllic setting for this rather eccentric restaurant with rooms. The delightful owner has worked wonders in the last couple of years converting the ruins – including the transformation of the old cowshed/ tobacco store into a smart restaurant with a splendid terrace. He has taken particular care with the decoration, including yellow leather dining chairs and sculptures of swans' feathers. The 200-year-old mulberry tree that gives the restaurant its name stands at the entrance, but first you pass a tree from which hang yellow plastic bananas and various sculptures of twisted, rusted iron. The eccentricity has made its way into the kitchen too. *Carré d'agneau* seems to be from an oversized sheep rather than a lamb; lavender ice-cream is sprinkled with a too generous helping of lavender seed heads; and sorbet of *coquelicot* is luminous violet in colour and tastes of violets as well. Despite this, the ingredients are fine quality, prepared well and presented in dishes that are reinterpretations of regional favourites. Prices are a touch on the high side, and the all-French wine list is limited. To get here, follow the signs from the D922 Figeac to Villefranche road.

CLOSED never
CARDS DC, MC, V

Lourdes
◆ Relais de Saux ⓔ - ⓔⓔ

*Saux, route de Tarbes, 65100 Lourdes,
Hautes-Pyrénées
Tel 05 62 94 29 61 Fax 05 62 42 12 64*

The choice of places to eat in Lourdes is overwhelming, though most are charmless and noisy. After a day in the crowds – just a couple of kilometers away but worlds apart – you can escape to this gem of a restaurant in an old ivy-clad hotel (don't be put off by the approach if you drive in the back way). A cosy atmospheric dining room with subdued lighting shares dramatic views to the mountains with the dining terrace. Menus at a range of prices, reflected in the number of courses (from three to six), feature a good choice of seafood including whole lobster with fresh *fettucini* and bitter orange *julienne*, beef tenderloin in an aged red wine sauce with potato cake, and other meat and poultry dishes, none of which would raise the bill for three courses to the level of our most expensive price bracket.

❛ *A haven of charm and tranquillity' ... 'A lovely setting with panoramic views of the Pyrénées* ❜

CLOSED Mon; mid-Nov to early Dec
CARDS AE, DC, MC, V

Luz-Saint-Sauveur
◆ Hôtel de Londres ⓔ

*8 rue du Pont de Luz, 65120 Esquièze Sère,
Hautes-Pyrénées
Tel 05 62 92 80 09 Fax 05 62 92 96 85*

A dramatic setting, lively ambience, interesting, good-value menu and friendly, efficient service ensure that this restaurant is always busy – even mid-week – so it's advisable to book a table in advance. From the covered terrace above the river there are spectacular views of the Pyrénées. Here and in the pale salmon pink dining room, the tables are quite closely placed, lending an atmosphere of conviviality rather than intimacy, but not affecting the quality of service. The middle-priced menu presents four courses: perhaps an *hors d'oeuvre* of melon, ham, beetroot and tomato, followed by fresh river trout or snails, five well-considered choices for a main course, and desserts and cheese to finish, all imaginatively prepared and delicious.

CLOSED early Oct to Christmas
CARDS MC, V

Manciet
◆ La Bonne Auberge ⓔⓔ Fr

*place Pesquerot, 32370 Manciet, Gers
Tel 05 62 08 50 04 Fax 05 62 08 58 84*

An outstanding address in a region of France noted for its fine food, this country inn (it also has 14 bedrooms) is much appreciated by customers from near and far. Its hosts are Simone and Pepito Sampietro, both welcoming, she elegant, he with something of the Musketeer about him. Reflecting the character of its proprietors, La Bonne Auberge is elegant yet cosy, with warm colours, old stone walls, candle and lamp light, and rows of Armagnacs glinting in their glass display case. Pepito's cooking is satisfyingly rooted in the region, and changes with the seasons. You are presented with a short *carte*, plus three menus: 'Bonheur et poésie de la Gascogne', 'La magie des saveurs du terroir', and 'La part des anges au parfum d'Armagnac'. Armagnac features strongly on the menus, as do (as you would expect) *foie gras*, truffles, duck and game in season.

CLOSED Sun dinner, Mon winter; Feb
CARDS AE, DC, MC, V

Marciac
◆ Le Coin Gourmand €

7 rue Juillac, 32230 Marciac, Gers
Tel 05 62 09 38 74 Fax 05 62 09 38 74

Not far from La Petite Auberge (see below), Le Coin Gourmand is only open when the *auberge* is closed on Wednesdays and Thursdays. On the other days, they're busy with outside catering but, on request, will open for parties of four or more. The cooking is a blend of local and *nouvelle*, with expertly prepared ingredients and very stylish presentation; evident in specialities such as *magret de canard au miel et gingembre*, *lotte rôtie à la tomate* and *filet de boeuf façon Rossini*. The interior is delightful: traditionally elegant but with an eclectic style. Each table is unique, laid with fine china and cutlery, candelabra and large white damask napkins. Quirky antiques are dotted all around the room.

❝ Delicious food in a charming, unusual interior ❞

CLOSED Fri-Tue (may open on request)
CARDS MC, V

Marciac
◆ La Petite Auberge €€ Fr

place d'Hôtel de Ville, 32230 Marciac, Gers
Tel 05 62 09 31 33

Famous for its annual jazz festival, Marciac is a delightful *bastide* town with arcades surrounding the square. Here La Petite Auberge – favourite among the locals – surprises you with its successful blend of ancient and modern. Inside, past the shaded terrace under the arcades, in contrast to the handsome exposed stonework and rustic artefacts, a cool contemporary patio with a

vast glass atrium has been incorporated, and looks very striking. There are set menus at a range of prices; the least expensive should satisfy the most demanding of quality and quantity. A popular main course is their splendid version of *cassoulet*, made with the tenderest broad beans. Other specialities include duck and *foie gras* dishes, crayfish in cream and roast pigeon.

❝ Hearty food in the Gascon tradition, but with an edge' ... 'Informal, friendly service ❞

CLOSED Thu
CARDS MC, V

Meyronne
◆ La Terrasse €€ Fr

46200 Meyronne, Lot
Tel 05 65 32 21 60 Fax 05 65 32 26 93

Set on a low rise overlooking the Dordogne, it is the vine-shaded terrace of this 11thC château, once the summer residence of the bishops of Tulle, that really appeals. In cooler weather, however, the main dining room of this hotel-restaurant is pleasant too, and in quiet periods food is served in another intimate, stone-vaulted room. In whichever setting, diners are regaled with beautifully presented regional fare: melt-in-the-mouth *foie gras*, lamb raised on the Quercy's uplands, earthy truffles, and *cabécou*, the smoky-sweet goats' cheese from nearby Rocamadour. There is also an interesting choice of fish dishes – perhaps you might try an excellent filet of sea bass roasted on a bed of fennel – and a daily changing selection of desserts that are hard to resist.

CLOSED late Nov to Mar
CARDS AE, DC, MC, V

Montesquiou
◆ Le Haget € – €€

32320 Montesquiou, Gers
Tel 05 62 70 95 80 Fax 05 62 70 94 83

Deep in rural Gascony, in the stable block of a château, this restaurant is a cosy, tranquil place to eat lunch or dinner out of season, and is well worth seeking out. In summer there's a lively buzz as people staying in the château or in the grounds (in chalets or camping) come to eat here as well as the regulars. You dine in a series of small interconnected rooms, done out with rustic charm, which open on to a large terrace. The genuine value menu is inventive and the specialities, carefully prepared: lamb with thyme honey sauce, *foie gras* freshly baked and excellent seafood dishes. A few choices need 24 hours' advance notice. An unusual feature is the menu 'Surprise' – you don't know what you're getting, but the surprise should be a pleasant one. To find the restaurant, turn south of the D943 on to the D34 to Monclar, then first right and the entrance is on the left.

(*Gourmet dishes at reasonable prices' ... 'Friendly service in a peaceful setting*)

Closed Mon and Tue Sep-Jun; mid-Jan to Mar
Cards MC, V

Our price bands
Rather than giving actual prices (which are prone to change) we indicate the cost of a three-course meal for one person, without wine, by means of price bands. They are as follows: € under 30 euros €€ 30-50 euros €€€ over 50 euros. Where we give more than one price band, for example €-€€€, this indicates that in that restaurant a meal can be had at a range of prices. As well as the cost of *prix fixe* menus, our price bands also take into account the cost of an average selection from the *à la carte* menu.

Noé
◆ L'Arche de Noé € – €€

31410 Noé, Haute-Garonne
Tel 05 61 87 40 12 Fax 05 61 87 06 67

Conveniently situated in the centre of a little village, just off the A64 Toulouse-Tarbes motorway (between exits 28 and 29), this hotel-restaurant has kept its impressive old arched coach entrance. Go through it and you reach an inner courtyard and garden, a little haven from the bustle outside. Indoors there's a cool tiled dining room, or you can eat under the arcades to one side of the courtyard, where oil paintings for sale

are exhibited on the walls. Tables are also set out in the open, on the small tree-shaded lawn. Menus are priced between 15 and 33 euros. The cheapest offers such choices as warm goats' cheese salad with almonds and honey to start, followed by salmon with Champagne *sabayon*. More choices and more courses as the price goes up.

(*A serene stop-off' ... 'Refined cuisine with emphasis on authenticity and quality*)

Closed Sun dinner
Cards MC, V

Nogaro
◆ Le Commerce €

2 place Cordeliers, 32110 Nogaro, Gers
Tel 05 62 09 00 95

Although the tables on the terrace are rather too close to the main road at one side of the square, inside all is calm and agreeable. The soft green and pink decoration hasn't yet discouraged the many commercial travellers for whom this is a much favoured stopover. The restaurant's chief attraction lies in its interesting menus. The cheapest includes veal and duck dishes, while more exotic offerings – crown of scallops with white leek and tomato, duck with mandarins and wild boar stew – feature on the more expensive menus and the *carte*. The service is pleasant and courteous.

Closed never
Cards MC, V

Puy-L'Evêque
◆ Côté Lot €€ – €€€ Fr

place de la Truffière, 46700 Puy-L'Evêque, Lot
Tel 05 65 36 06 60 Fax 05 65 36 06 61

The Hôtel Bellevue has two restaurants: a stylish bistro with tables that spill out on to a terrace, facing Puy-L'Evêque's main square, and Côté Lot, a smart, formal restaurant at the rear of the old stone building. This dining room perches high above the Lot, and has been designed to take advantage of the stunning panoramic views over the river and its valley far below. The cooking is rooted in the region; first-rate local produce – *foie gras*, duck, pigeon, asparagus in season – is skilfully prepared so that the flavours subtly emerge. Wines are solidly French, with a good local Cahors selection from 13 euros a bottle. The cost of dinner can rise sharply if you stray à la carte, but the menus are quite reasonably priced, and in season this is a haunt of holidaymakers and second-home owners. Staff are polite, friendly and efficient.

❢ Worth a visit for the view alone - the meal is a bonus ❣

Closed Sun dinner, Mon, Tue low season
Cards MC, V

Rimont
 Au Bon Accueil € Fr

avenue de la Résistance, 09420 Rimont, Ariège
Tel 05 61 96 30 70 Fax 05 61 96 30 70

The little village of Rimont has three restaurants more or less in a row; this one provides the best value and the best view. Built of the unusual pink-coloured local stone, with flower-filled window boxes, it has a large glassed-in terrace at the back, overlooking the garden and steep valley beyond. The floor is of honeycomb mosaic tiles, and you sit on bentwood chairs at tables covered in pink and white linen. The menus start at 10 euros for three courses, including wine (limited choice, but speedy service), and go up to 23 euros for four courses. The signature dish is duck breast with slices of pan-fried *foie gras*.

❢ A simple, convenient staging post for authentic cooking using local produce' ... 'Warm attentive service ❣

Closed Mon dinner, Tue
Cards MC, V

Rodez
 Gouts et Couleurs €€

38 rue de Bonald, 12000 Rodez, Aveyron
Tel 05 65 42 75 10 Fax 05 65 42 75 10

Head for this little side street close to the pink sandstone cathedral for an hour or two of 'taste and colour'. In the intimate, pastel-shaded restaurant (there is also a pretty terrace for outdoor eating), you will encounter truly individual and inventive cooking. Jean-Luc Fau gives his imagination full rein, especially on his *menu dégustation*, but he rarely loses the plot: his dishes successfully mingle the *cuisine de terroir* with the modern and the exotic. How about *tajine de volaille en gelée aux citrons confits et confiture de courge à la cannelle*, or *carpaccio de gambas à l'huile de fluer de sureau*, or *sushis de fraises à la citronelle et lait de coco*? Certainly, this is the most inventive cooking in Rodez, indeed perhaps in all the Massif Central.

Closed Sun, Mon; Jan, Sep
Cards MC, V

Looking for somewhere to stay?
See page 241.

Saint-Geniez-d'Olt
 Le Rive Gauche
€ – €€€

place du Général de Gaulle, 12130 Saint-Geniez-d'Olt, Aveyron
Tel 05 65 47 43 30 Fax 05 65 47 42 75

Offspring of the Hostellerie de la Poste, this restaurant is in a modern building just across an alley from the hotel. You can eat in the dining room, on the covered terrace, or the upstairs verandah overlooking the swimming pool and slopes of the valley. It describes itself quite rightly as a '*restaurant gastronomique*': the chef creates imaginative specialities from top quality ingredients – *écrévisses, foie gras*, local veal – and presents them superbly. Even the bread is delicious. Leave room for pudding; the *fondant au chocolat* is a must for chocolate-lovers. The trolley of local cheeses arrives with an unusual onion and strawberry *compôt*, which tastes better than it sounds. The cheapest menus (13 and 15 euros) are only offered at lunch. The most expensive costs 45 euros, though you could spend double by choosing à la carte. The wine list leans to the south west (good-value vintages from Gaillac and Marcillac). This restaurant is particularly popular for family celebrations.

Closed Dec-Mar
Cards MC, V

Saint-Girons
◆ La Clairière €-€€€

avenue de la Résistance, 09200 Saint-Girons
Tel 05 61 66 66 66 Fax 05 34 14 30 30

This hotel-restaurant is housed in a modern chalet with shingle-clad sloping sides, set in wooded grounds including a poolside terrace. Its individuality and elegance are enthralling. Each table is set with square glass dishes, unusual cutlery and a large natural stone, drilled out to take a single flower. Candles on the tables are augmented by wall lights, made from large wood-carved skeleton leaves. The leaf motif is picked up in the full-length chair covers, and on the menus and wine list, which offers more than 200 vintages. There are six menus, including a vegetarian one, ranging from 14 euros (weekday lunchtimes only) to 64 euros, for which you receive two starters, two main courses, cheese, dessert and four different wines. Among the specialities on the à la carte menu are a *foie gras* starter and a whole shoulder of Pyrenean lamb (for two). The chef, Paul Fontvieille, is responsible not only for this superb cuisine, but the distinctive style and ambience as well.

❝Modern, distinguished, tasteful – adjectives that apply equally to cooking and decoration❞

Closed Sun dinner, Mon Dec-Apr
Cards AE, DC, MC, V

Saint-Médard
◆ Le Gindreau €-€€€

46150 Saint-Médard, Lot
Tel 05 65 36 22 27 Fax 05 65 36 24 54

Le Gindreau, located in a former village school, isn't the sort of place you stumble across, but it's worth going out of your way to discover this superb restaurant which, over nearly 30 years, has been developed by Alexis and Martine Pélissou into one of the best in the region. (Prices, however, remain surprisingly affordable.) M. Pélissou's cuisine is anchored in authenticity and tradition, while at the same time creating fresh, light dishes which appeal to the modern palate. Each course is a work of art, and the desserts are so delectable they seem

almost a shame to eat. The same exacting standards are seen in the wine list, with a strong showing of local dark, peppery Cahors. You eat either in the high-ceilinged 'classrooms' or on the geranium-bedecked terrace under towering chestnut trees. Service is attentive, yet discreet.

Closed Mon, Tue lunch, Tue dinner Sep-Jul; first 2 weeks Mar, mid-Oct to mid-Nov
Cards AE, DC, MC, V

Saint-Savin
◆ Le Viscos €€ Fr

65400 Saint-Savin, Hautes-Pyrénées
Tel 05 62 97 02 28 Fax 05 62 97 04 95

In a mountainside village near Lourdes, this six-generation family-run restaurant (and simple hotel) has been in the capable, and capacious, hands of Maître-Cuisinier de France Jean-Pierre Saint-Martin. To his inheritance of old family recipes based on top quality local produce, including mountain herbs, he has introduced inventiveness and lightness of touch. Mouthwatering menus include *galette de touradisse au foie gras, palombie en cocotte aux cèpes, merveille fourée de fruits au Jurançon*. The food is served in a large rectangular dining room with huge picture windows, or on an attractive terrace, both with superb mountain views. Your host, who runs cookery courses and displays his talents as guest chef in top hotels abroad, has an expansive personality, full of bonhomie.

Closed Dec
Cards AE, DC, MC, V

Salles-sur-Cérou
◆ Aux Berges du Cérou €-€€

rue du Pont, 81640 Salles-sur-Cérou, Tarn
Tel 05 63 76 40 42

Behind the blue shutters of this old stone house in a sleepy village on the banks of the Cérou is a small contemporary restaurant. The decoration is simple yet effective: cool natural colours and materials provide a background for African masks and black and white photographs. The chef has his own very distinctive and original style of cooking and presentation. A starter of marinated anchovies, served in a flaky pastry bun with a dab of mint sorbet, a tomato and mozarella salad that arrives as a parcel, wrapped in thin slices of aubergine, then fried, and the *feuillantine* chocolate dessert with sheeps' milk ice-cream are among his more inventive contemporary dishes. Although there is a range of menus, none offers a huge choice. The vegetarian and most expensive menus both have to be ordered in advance, and the children's menu simply offers smaller portions of the adult version, and might be over-sophisticated for young children. The wines mostly come from the south west, and there are only one or two half-bottles on the *carte*. Efficient, friendly staff.

❛ *An up-and-coming chef' ... 'Some dishes look too pretty to eat* ❜

Closed Mon, Tue-Fri Apr and Oct; Nov-Apr
Cards AE, DC, MC, V

Salles-Curan
◆ Hostellerie du Lévezou
€ – €€€ **Fr**

12410 Salles-Curan, Aveyron
Tel 05 65 46 34 16 Fax 05 65 46 01 19

This splendid ivy-clad building was the summer palace of the bishops of Rodez in the 14th century. Now it houses a hotel-restaurant with an impressive stone-vaulted dining room and a paved inner courtyard shaded by a large chestnut tree. It is smart, yet full of atmosphere, and the chef produces food, of which the bishops would certainly have approved: classic and regional dishes, with the emphasis as much on hearty as gourmet (vis. pork knuckle in a sweetened sauce). Prices are on the high side, but not excessive given the surroundings. The cellar has a good spread of French wines, with the south west and Bordeaux well represented. There are no real bargains but the local Marcillac is reasonably priced. Staff are friendly and helpful.

❛ *The food was full of flavour, generous and satisfying* ❜

Closed Sun dinner, Mon, Tue dinner, dinner one other day high season; Oct to Easter
Cards AE, DC, MC, V

Toulouse
◆ La Bohème € **Fr**

3 rue Lafayette, 31000 Toulouse, Haute Garonne
Tel 05 61 23 24 18

Centrally situated near the Capitole, this simple restaurant is in the basement of a 17thC Toulousaine rose red-brick building, which affords welcome relief from the heat of the summer and cosy warmth in cooler seasons. It specializes in hearty regional cuisine. The duck- and goose-based dishes, *cassoulet* and fish are all well cooked and offered on an attractive menu at reasonable prices. With plenty of character in the dining room's decoration, a busy, relaxed atmosphere and its convenient location, La Bohème is an ideal place to break for lunch during a day in the city.

Closed Sun
Cards AE, MC, V

Our traditional French cuisine symbol
So many of our readers enjoy seeking out the genuinely French eating experience that we have used **Fr** to mark restaurants which offer *cuisine du terroir*, classical French dishes or regional dishes with an emphasis on local ingredients, and traditional recipes.

Touzac
◆ La Source Enchantée
€ – €€ **Fr**

lieu-dit 'La Source Bleue', 46700 Touzac, Lot
Tel 05 65 30 63 18 Fax 05 65 24 65 69

This handsome, stylish restaurant is a converted 17thC barn in the extensive grounds of La Source Bleue hotel (itself a conversion of two old water mills). The shady yet airy building is split into two rooms by a large, central fireplace. The style is 'modern rustic': exposed stoneware, beams and carefully chosen *objets d'art*. At one end is a minstrels' gallery. The cooking is anchored in the region, using its finest fresh produce and preparing it with care in regional recipes with a modern touch. Expect to see *terrine* of *foie gras*, freshwater crayfish and duck on a range of menus from 16 to 37 euros (for the *menu gastronomique*). Vegetables are not just accompaniments but, carefully chosen and cooked, and taken seriously in their own right.

❝ A chic address' ... 'The food doesn't disappoint ❞

CLOSED Mon lunch, Wed; Jan–Mar
CARDS MC, V

Trie-sur-Baïse
◆ De la Tour €–€€

1 rue de la Tour Carrée, 65220 Trie-sur-Baïse, Hautes-Pyrénées
Tel 05 62 35 52 12 Fax 05 62 35 59 92

Part of a hotel, off the town's main square and next to its historic fortifications, this restaurant overlooks a quieter square at the back, where there is a medieval monastery. (The cloisters of this monastery have been reconstructed stone by stone in New York.) The dining room is beamed, with a fireplace, and overlooks the small hotel garden. In warmer weather, tables are placed outside next to the garden, providing a pleasant place to eat. Menus start at 9.90 euros for the bargain midday menu, which includes three courses with wine, and rise to 32 euros or there is the *carte*. With 48 hours' notice, a 'plateau' of seafood (six or seven varieties) can be ordered for 29 euros. Be warned: arrive at the beginning of August and Trie, a town of about 1,000 people, which styles itself as 'the most important pork market in Europe', holds a pig festival, and you could be caught up in 'The pig squeal imitation contest' or 'The best pig disguise contest', amongst various others.

❝ A good range of well-priced dishes' ... 'Central yet calm. ❞

CLOSED Mon lunch
CARDS MC, V

Vic-Fezensac
◆ Le Bistrot d'en Pace €

2 place Julie Saint-Aint, 32190 Vic-Fezensac, Gers
Tel 05 62 06 45 45

In the corner of a flower-filled square, this is essentially a popular lunchtime bar-restaurant that is also open on Friday and Saturday evenings in summer, when à la carte choices are available. You can either sit at one of the tables outside the bar under the arcades or upstairs in a jaunty yellow room, the tables draped in aubergine-coloured cloths. The *menu du jour* represents great value for money at 10 euros, with a choice of three dishes for each of the three courses, and includes wine. If it's featured, the cheese tart is a delicious starter, and you might try the tender guinea-fowl and bruléed rice pudding to follow.

❝ A simple, unpretentious place, with a surprisingly sophisticated menu at this price ❞

CLOSED Sun dinner to Thu dinner summer, dinner winter
CARDS MC, V

Villefranche-de-Rouergue
◆ L'Assiette Gourmande
€–€€ Fr

place André Lescure, 12200 Villefranche-de-Rouergue, Aveyron
Tel 05 65 45 25 95

A pleasant traditional little restaurant in a 13thC house on a quiet street, just off the arcaded medieval place Nôtre-Dame. In the atmospheric beamed dining room, or on the pavement outside, you can enjoy deliciously robust regional specialities, such as *tripe de Rouergue* and *aligot* (a cheese and potato dish). All the meat is grilled over oak in the huge old fireplace. You can pay between 12.50 and 28 euros for the set menus, but if you're interested in 'gourmet' dishes, you must choose from the à la carte menu. The reasonably priced wines are predominantly from the south west, with the house wine good value for money at 2.50 euros a bottle.

❝ An old-fashioned, atmospheric dining room, a perfect backdrop for the regional cuisine' ... 'Excellent meat grilled on the open fire ❞

CLOSED Sun, Tue and Wed dinner low season; 2 weeks Apr, Oct
CARDS DC, MC, V

AUVERGNE

A t the heart of France, the Massif Central is a rugged plateau of granite and hardened lava, scarred and pitted by volcanic peaks and deep gorges. This is the Auvergne, a mixture of rustic countryside and dramatic landscape, appreciated for its remoteness, traditions and outdoor life. In the centre, the regional capital Clermont-Ferrand, mixes busy industry with history, and a whiff of the south. The Auvergne's Puy volcanic mountain chain runs to the south, with an incomparable view from its highest peak, Puy-de-Dôme. In the south-west of the region are the gentler Monts du Cantal, where the cattle graze on pastures to produce the famous Cantal cheese. To the east, across the Monts de la Margeride, are the high reaches of the great river Loire and the religious centre and, nearby, departmental capital, Le-Puy-en-Velay. Here, as in Clermont-Ferrrand, Orcival, Issoire, Saint-Nectaire, Saint-Saturnin and Brioude, there is an austerely beautiful example of an Auvergne Romanesque church.

Saint-Bonnet-Tronçais 293

Bourbon-L'Archambault 290

Monluçon 291

Saint-Gervais-d'Auvergne 293

Chamalières 290

Clermont-Ferrand

LIMOUSIN

Laqueuille 291

AUVERGNE

Le Theil 295

Pailherols 293

Aurilla

Vitrac 295

Boisset 290

Montsalvy 292

Calvinet 290

MIDI-PYRENEES

BOURGOGNE

N79

N1079

N7

N9

N7

N209 • Vichy 295

RHONE-
ALPES

D906

A72

D906

Sarpoil 294

St-Etienne •

Lavaudieu 291

D906

N88

N102

Tence 294 •

Le-Puy-en-Velay • Saint-Bonnet-le-Froid
293 •

Saint-Julien-Chapteuil 294 •

Moudeyres
292

Boisset
◆ Auberge de Concasty
€ – €€ **Fr**

15600 Boisset, Cantal
Tel 04 71 62 21 16 Fax 04 71 62 22 22

Set on a farm in splendid hiking country, and with magical views over the pasture where the patron's cattle graze, this remote, attractive *maison de maître* radiates country charm. Madame (Martine Causse), who couldn't be friendlier or more welcoming, cooks unpretentious but mouthwatering Franco-Auvergnat dishes, according to the season. *Cèpes, foie gras*, fish and Salers beef are among her favourite ingredients. The Causses also have 15 pretty bedrooms, all different and named after wild flowers.

❛ We ate like kings ❜

Closed Mon, Tue-Sat lunch; mid-Nov to mid-Mar
Cards AE, DC, MC, V

Bourbon-L'Archambault
◆ Grand Hôtel Montespan-Talleyrand
€ – €€ **Fr**

2-4 place des Thermes, 03160 Bourbon-
L'Archambault, Allier
Tel 03 21 38 03 73 Fax 03 21 38 17 39

The name originates from the visits of the VIPs (Madame de Montespan and Talleyrand), who used to come here to take the thermal waters, for which Bourbon-L'Archambault is famous. In fact, the 'Montespan room' is still kept for those taking the spa treatments. The fine historic building has now been transformed into a stylish hotel, with views across the rooftops to the turrets of the town's château and a well-regarded restaurant. Robust homemade regional food – including superb pastries, meat and game pies, and fruit tarts – is served in an elegant beamed dining room, which looks out to a huge, green courtyard garden, where you can sit with your drink in summer. In winter, there's a glossy pale-coloured bar with an open fire.

Closed late Oct to Apr
Cards AE, DC, MC, V

Calvinet
◆ Puech € – €€

route de Maurs, 15340 Calvinet, Cantal
Tel 04 71 49 91 68 Fax 04 71 49 98 63

Like those of many of his fellow gourmet chefs, Louis Bernard Puech's bywords are 'produce', 'tradition' and 'seasons'. Born and bred in the Cantal region, he is passionate about the local *terroir*, and considers his daily visit to the market to shop for ingredients to be an art. Whether or not his cooking is an art is not a question for the food-lovers who flock here from all over the country. Of the deceptively simple dishes that he prepares with imagination and flair, he lists his specialities as *bouillon de poularde et châtaignes, rapée de truffes blanches d'Alba, gaufre de foie de canard, caramel à la gentiane* and *côtelette de cochon paysan cuit sous la couenne, pommes de terre farcie au pied de porc*. And he keeps the prices for his menus remarkably honest. The hotel, the Beauséjour, that is this restaurant's home is an inconspicuous modern building with 12 bedrooms, which Louis Bernard's parents built and he revamped when he took over.

❛ Sublime, original cooking ❜

Closed Sun evening, Mon and Tue lunch low season; mid-Jan to Mar
Cards DC, MC, V

Chamalières
◆ Le Radio € – €€€

43 avenue Pierre-et-Marie-Curie, 63400
Chamalières, Puy-de-Dôme
Tel 04 73 30 87 83 Fax 04 73 36 42 44

The building dates from the 1930s, when it was built in Art Deco style on the theme of the radio, a new invention and symbol of the time. The hotel still has its original mosaic floor, wrought-ironwork, mirrors and radios, and the restaurant has been renovated in similar style. For a long time, it was run by the enthusiastic and totally dedicated Michel Mioche, who won it its Michelin star and was dubbed '*père de la cuisine Auvergnate*', and his wife. Their daughter, Caroline, is now in charge – having abandoned a career as a journalist to carry on the family tradition – with the help of her very talented young chef, Frédéric Coursol. He started working here under Michel in 1994, and is just as passionate about his job as his predecessor. Also like Michel, Frédéric combines classic French, regional and contemporary cuisines to create a style that is quite individual. He handpicks his ingredients, and his imaginative menus show a bias towards fish, which he confesses to loving above everything. If you can, try his *queue de homard bleu saisi à la plancha*.

❝ *Gorgeous Art Deco decoration'* ... *The tartare de lapin au serpolet was sublime* **❞**

CLOSED Sat lunch, Sun, Mon lunch; early Jan to late Feb, one week Nov
CARDS AE, DC, MC, V

Fr French regional or classical French dishes on menu.

● *Cinq Claire (04 73 37 10 31), a useful address in Clermont-Ferrand, is recommended for its honest regional cuisine – aiguillettes de canard, rouelle de porc, and a gigantic board of mainly local cheeses.*

Laqueuille
◆ Auberge de Fondain
€ Fr

Lieu-dit Fondain, 63820 Laqueuille, Puy-de-Dôme
Tel 04 73 22 01 35 Fax 04 73 22 06 13

It's easy to spot this country house from miles around, as it stands four-square and four storeys high in the middle of a plain near the Parc Naturel Régional des Volcans d'Auvergne. A barrier of trees provides protection from the elements, and, in spring, the surrounding meadows are filled with wildflowers. A delightful mother-and-daughter duo (Danielle Desboudard and Sophie Demossier) took over a few years back, lending a feminine touch to everything from the simple, tasteful decoration in the six-room hotel (white walls, parquet and a scattering of antiques) to Sophie's delicate versions of traditional Auvergnat cuisine. You eat *poitrine de veau farcie* or *trio de cochon vinaigrette* at scrubbed wooden tables in front of a huge chimney in the pretty rustic dining room, with views of the garden through French windows.

CLOSED Sun evening, Mon; one week Mar, first 2 weeks Nov
CARDS MC, V

Lavaudieu
◆ Auberge de l'Abbaye
€ Fr

Lieu-dit Fondain, 43100 Lavaudieu, Haute-Loire
Tel 04 71 76 44 44

The quintessential village inn, Auberge de l'Abbaye is perfectly placed to catch Sunday worshippers as they pile out of church, since it's just opposite. Decorated in country style, it is appealing and snug, particularly in winter when the open fire is lit. Laurent Coupry is the chef, who has made a name for himself, promoting local lamb, specifically the Bizet breed, and you can hardly come here without tasting it, perhaps after a plate of delicious *charcuterie d'Auvergne*. If you're not a meat-lover, there are usually traditional-style dishes based on fish and lentils on his interesting regional *menu 'planchette'*.

CLOSED Sun evening low season, Mon
CARDS MC, V

Montluçon
◆ Le Grenier à Sel
€ – €€€

10 rue Sainte-Anne, place des Toiles, 03100 Montluçon, Allier
Tel 04 70 05 53 79 Fax 04 70 05 87 91

So drenched in ivy is the impressive 16thC building that houses this four-star hotel and restaurant that it's almost impossible to see its façade. Above, it sprouts a collection of roofs that look like little pointed hats, and is surrounded by a small but ravishing garden with some ancient trees that provide useful shade. Inside the hotel is comfortable and elegant, furnished with good antiques and paintings. But it's the restaurant that is the real draw. Jacky Morlon, one of the Maître Cuisiniers de France, returned home to the Auvergne several years ago, after working with some of the best chefs elsewhere in France. His specialities – *chaussons de morilles à la crème de champignons des bois, pâté aux pommes de terre, filet de sardines au caviar d'aubergines, canette fermière à la Duchambais* – are simple yet exciting and, as you would expect, anchored in the region. To accompany them, there is a wonderful selection of Bordeaux. Meals are served in a pretty dining room, or on the terrace overlooking the garden, floodlit at night and a gloriously romantic setting for summer dinners. Madame Morlon is a great asset 'front of house'.

❝ An excellent dinner ... the terrace looked beautiful at night ❞

CLOSED Sun evening, Mon winter; Feb hols
CARDS AE, DC, MC, V

Our price bands
Rather than giving actual prices (which are prone to change) we indicate the cost of a three-course meal for one person, without wine, by means of price bands. They are as follows: € under 30 euros €€ 30-50 euros €€€ over 50 euros. Where we give more than one price band, for example €–€€€, this indicates that in that restaurant a meal can be had at a range of prices. As well as the cost of *prix fixe* menus, our price bands also take into account the cost of an average selection from the *à la carte* menu.

Montsalvy
◆ Auberge Fleurie
€ – €€ **Fr**

place du Barry, 15120 Montsalvy, Cantal
Tel 04 71 49 20 02

Despite redecoration, this delightful, creeper-covered village inn has a refreshingly traditional air. Half the building is taken up by a busy *café tabac*, a lunchtime and evening watering hole for many locals. But the focal point is the restaurant, in two attractive rooms, all polished wood dressers, gleaming copper, red-check tablecloths, open fireplace and oak beams. Here Jean-Pierre Courchinoux produces his distinctive, lively brand of Auvergnat cuisine on remarkably modestly priced seasonal menus. Specialities concentrate on *foie gras*, duck, pork, rabbit, mushrooms and chestnuts. The 11 bedrooms have a fresh and (unlike the public rooms) contemporary look, but they face on to a main road. Staff are attentive and helpful.

CLOSED mid-Jan to mid-Feb
CARDS MC, V

Looking for somewhere to stay?
See page 241.

Moudeyres
◆ Le Pré Bossu € – €€

43150 Moudeyres, Haute-Loire
Tel 04 71 05 10 70 Fax 04 71 05 10 21

Moudeyres is a remote village of thatched stone cottages and farm buildings, high (1,200 m/365 ft) in the volcanic Mézenc massif, surrounded by fields of wildflowers in the spring and mushrooms in the autumn. It is a long way off the beaten track and very difficult to get to – the terrain is very rugged – but it's worth the journey. The conscientious Flemish owners, the Grootaerts, have worked extremely hard to create an attractive and comfortable hotel with a good restaurant. To original beams, wooden floors and old-fashioned, open fireplaces, they've added antique dressers, lace curtains, wild flowers when they are available – dried flowers when they are not – and books. Pots of home-made jam and other products are (subtly) for sale. Carlos Grootaert is passionate about gardening and grows many of the vegetables and herbs that he uses in his Flemish-influenced cuisine. His imaginative vegetarian menus are evidence of how highly he rates vegetables.

❝ Rarely have I seen a more beautiful location' ... 'The vegetables were simply delicious ❞

CLOSED Mon-Sat lunch; Nov to Easter
CARDS AE, MC, V

Pailherols
◆ Auberge des Montagnes € Fr

15800 Pailherols, Cantal
Tel 04 71 47 57 01 Fax 04 71 49 63 83

The countryside of the Pailherols plateau
that surrounds this village inn is wild,
rugged and starkly beautiful. It lies between
two mountain ranges (the Aubrac and the
Puys), and is magnificent walking country.
This aptly named *auberge* is owned and run
by the warmly welcoming Combourieu family, who are fourth-generation inn-keepers.
At its heart in a bright, cheerful room, the
restaurant is devoted to producing an excellent *cuisine de terroir*. Local specialities,
many featuring mushrooms, dominate the
menus, the most expensive of which is only
21 euros. The *pavé de boeuf du Cantal* is
wonderfully succulent, and you are almost
obliged to try their famous pudding *'noiseti-
er sous la neige'*.

❢ *Delicious regional food … unbeatable prices' … 'Charming owners* ❢

CLOSED Tue low season; early Oct to late Dec
CARDS MC, V

Saint-Bonnet-le-Froid
◆ Auberge et Clos des Cimes €€€

43290 Saint-Bonnet-le-Froid, Haute-Loire
Tel 04 71 59 93 72 Fax 04 71 59 93 40

This stylish country-style restaurant is
one of the most prestigious and justifiably expensive in the area (with menus
ranging from 51 to 100 euros). The man
responsible for its reputation is Régis
Marcon, a dynamic, intuitive chef, and pos-
sessor of two Michelin stars and 19 Gault
Millau *toques*. He has not, however,
allowed success to go to his head, and still
chooses his ingredients himself, with rigor-
ous care, for a cuisine based on the native
region he loves and its traditional early
20thC recipes. His subtle, innovative versions favour mushrooms, rare herbs and
vegetables, lentils, river fish, farm poultry
and local organic meat. You will be made
welcome by Régis' courteous wife, Michèle.

CLOSED Mon evening Oct-Jun, Tue, Wed lunch; Jan to
mid-Mar
CARDS AE, MC, V

Saint-Bonnet-Tronçais
◆ Le Tronçais
€€ – €€€

avenue Nicolas-Rambourg, Tronçais, 03360
Saint-Bonnet-Tronçais, Allier
Tel 04 70 06 11 95 Fax 04 70 06 16 15

On the edge of the forêt de Tronçais and
a stone's throw from the historic Route
de Jacques Coeur, this former forge-
owner's house is set in a tranquil garden of
lawns and trees. It has 12 large, comfortable
bedrooms, and hotel guests can fish the
well-stocked lake and river that border the
grounds. Both lake and river also provide a
number of the tasty and delicate specialities
featured on the menu (pike, zander and
trout). You eat either in the enchanting
restaurant or outside, on the gravel at the
front of the hotel, where tables, chairs and
parasols are set out in the summer months.

❢ *Charming service … excellent fish* ❢

CLOSED Sun evening and Mon low season; mid-Dec to
mid-Mar
CARDS MC, V

Saint-Gervais-d'Auvergne
◆ Castel €€ – €€€

*rue du Castel, 63390 Saint-Gervais, Puy-
de-Dôme*
Tel 04 73 85 70 42 Fax 04 73 85 84 39

The Castel is one of two restaurants in the
Castel Hôtel 1904. The 1904 refers to the
date in which this château-style house was
turned into a hotel; the remarkable thing is
that the same family has owned it ever since.
The present incumbent, Jean-Luc Mouty is a
gourmet chef, whose delicate, interesting
style of cookery pulls the crowds from miles
around. Well-priced menus (13 to 46 euros)
include such appetizing specialities as *salade
à l'ail d'escargots panés et noisettes car-
mélisées, pavé de sandre de la Truyère aux
coings* and *cuissot de sanglier à la moutarde
pourpre*. The chic dining room makes an ideal
setting to enjoy his cuisine: light streams in
through the many windows, dressed with long

peach-coloured curtains, on to the starched white tablecloths and polished wood floor. In the evening, the room looks cosy, lit by table lamps and wall lights. For lighter meals, there's a rustic bistro, Comptoir à Moustache (open every day), which serves simple regional dishes. The rest of the hotel (there are 17 bedrooms) has a genuine old French feel, and is well renovated and furnished with antiques.

CLOSED Mon, Tue; mid-Nov to late Mar
CARDS MC, V

---

charmingsmallhotels.co.uk
Visit Duncan Petersen's travel website, the best online search tool for places to stay that combine character and charm. Currently features Britain, France, Italy and Ireland, with other destinations being continuously added.

Saint-Julien-Chapteuil
◆ Vidal ⓔ – ⓔⓔⓔ

43260 Saint-Julien-Chapteuil, Haute-Loire
Tel 04 71 08 70 50 Fax 04 71 08 40 14

There's a jolly atmosphere in Jean-Pierre Vidal's mellow restaurant, fitted out almost entirely in wood. At friendly round tables, you will be served the light, creative dishes that are Jean-Pierre's specialities; always simple, never pretentious, and revealing his preoccupation with the local *terroir*. You might choose a *salade tiède d'andouille du pays*, followed by *galette de pied de porc à la purée de cèpes* or *pièce de boeuf gras du Mézenc* on the seductive *menu du marché*.

CLOSED Sun evening and Tue Sep-Jul, Mon; mid-Jan to Mar
CARDS AE, MC, V

Sarpoil
◆ Bergerie de Sarpoil
ⓔ – ⓔⓔⓔ

Sarpoil, 63490 Saint-Jean-en-Val, Puy-de-Dôme
Tel 04 73 71 02 54 Fax 04 73 71 02 99

An ideal stopping-off place from the A75 north-south *autoroute*, this restaurant is just as charming in winter when you eat in the large dining room, made snug by its cheerful log fire, as it is in summer, when you can laze away the hours on the terrace in the shade of a huge oak tree. The excellent food here is the result of a happy collaboration between two chefs, Laurent Jury and Eric Moutard. They offer a range of good-value menus, which respect both region and season. You might start with a cep tart with garlic and cep tapenade (in season), followed by milk-fed pork with hot *foie gras*, served with roast *ratte* potatoes and vine peaches, and rum baba to finish. On the *carte de vins*, it's best not to stray from the local wines.

❛ *A fantastic restaurant in spitting distance of the motorway* ❜

CLOSED Sun evening, Mon and Tue Sep-Jun; 3 weeks Jan
CARDS AE, MC, V

Fr French regional or classical French dishes on menu.

Tence
◆ Hostellerie Placide
ⓔ **Fr**

1 route d'Annonay, 43190 Tence, Haute-Loire
Tel 04 71 59 82 76 Fax 04 71 65 44 46

In a sleepy village in the lush Velay region, this former post house was built in 1900 and is very attractive; the outside smothered in ivy, the inside restored with taste and character. It has been in the Placide family for four generations. Pierre-Marie and Véronique are currently in charge. He is a first-class chef who has raised the reputation of the restaurant; she has a dual role, looking after the guests and the cellar. Pierre-Marie combines unusual flavours with delicacy and imagination on a variety of regional-style menus. The decoration is traditional; leather and wood furniture complementing beams and panelling.

❛ *Regional food with a modern twist* ❜

CLOSED Mon and Tue Oct-May; mid-Nov to mid-Mar
CARDS AE, MC, V

Le Theil
◆ Hostellerie de la Maronne ⓔ - ⓔⓔ

Le Theil, 15140 Saint-Martin-Valmeroux, Cantal
Tel 04 71 69 20 33 Fax 04 71 69 28 22

This elegantly furnished 19thC *hostellerie*, surrounded by lovely gardens and sweeping countryside, makes a fine, peaceful retreat. Much has changed during Alain Decock's tenure, including the building of a smart new dining room into the hillside. Food is taken seriously with first-class results, and a growing reputation. Mme Decock is the chef, and she puts her feminine imprint on a range of menus (reaching up to *gastronomique* levels) as well as a reasonable *carte*. Her specialities include *escalope de sandre aux mousserons*, *risotto d'orge perlé aux cèpes et au lard grillé* and *tarte tiède aux marrons et chocolat amer*. If you're keen for a spell away from it all, it's an appealing place to stay, with 21 fresh, comfortable bedrooms and apartments, all with gleaming new bathrooms.

CLOSED Nov-Mar
CARDS AE, DC, MC, V

Please send us reports
A guide such as this thrives on reader's reports. If you send us five usable reports, we will send you a free copy of any title in our *Charming Small Hotel Guides* series (see page 241 for France titles in the series).

The five reports should contain at least two new restaurants; the balance can be comments on restaurants already in the guide. **Send reports to** Charming Restaurant Guides, Duncan Petersen Ltd, 31 Ceylon Road, London W14 OPY.

Vichy
◆ L'Alambic ⓔⓔ

8 rue Nicolas-Larbaud, 03200 Vichy, Allier
Tel 04 70 59 12 71 Fax 04 70 97 98 88

This miniscule restaurant near the Parc des Souces in the city centre has great charm, but can only seat 14, so you must book in advance; if at first you can't get a table, it's worth persevering. Accolades have been heaped on L'Alambic, including a Gault Millau heart and 16/20 points. In this intimate setting, Jean-Jacques Barbot and Marie-Ange Tupet make a dynamic combination, preparing fabulous, fresh food with control and sensitivity. Choose from dishes such as *panaché d'escargots*, *lardons et artichauts en petits feuilletés à la sauge* and *mijotée de lapin et crème de lentilles du Puy à la moutarde de Charroux*, and don't forgo one of the mouthwatering desserts, for example, *nougat glacé au miel d'arbousier*. Staff are friendly yet discreet.

❛ *Friendly local restaurant in a peaceful country setting* ❜

CLOSED Mon, Tue; mid-Feb - mid-Mar, mid-Aug - mid-Sep
CARDS MC, V

Vitrac
◆ Auberge de la Tomette ⓔ - ⓔⓔ **Fr**

15220 Vitrac, Cantal
Tel 04 71 64 70 94 Fax 04 71 64 77 11

In an exceptionally pretty village in the middle of the chestnut groves of the southern Cantal, this jolly whitewashed and shuttered inn has been much expanded and improved over the past 18 years, without the loss of its essential appeal. With its large garden, where trees and parasols provide plenty of shade, and lawns plenty of space for running around, it is the perfect place for families with children. Wood-panelling gives a rustic feel to the cosy dining room, where every day a vase of freshly picked garden flowers is placed on each of the pink-covered tables. In summer, meals are served on a lovely terrace, part of which is covered for those who prefer to eat in total shade. The menus are dominated by simple, hearty, local dishes: *filet de truite aux noisettes*, *ris de veau crémaillère*, *crépinette de pied de cochon*, as well as a variety of sweet and savoury tarts.

❛ *Cheerful, good-value, family inn* ❜

CLOSED Jan-Apr
CARDS AE, MC, V

RHONE-ALPES

Eight départements makes up the Rhône-Alpes government region, which stretches, as its title suggests, eastwards from the Rhône Valley into the high Alps, culminating in Mont-Blanc. Situated mid-way between Paris and the Côte d'Azur, just south of Burgundy, the Rhône part of the region is dominated by France's second city, Lyon, as famous for its food and wine as for its long history . The

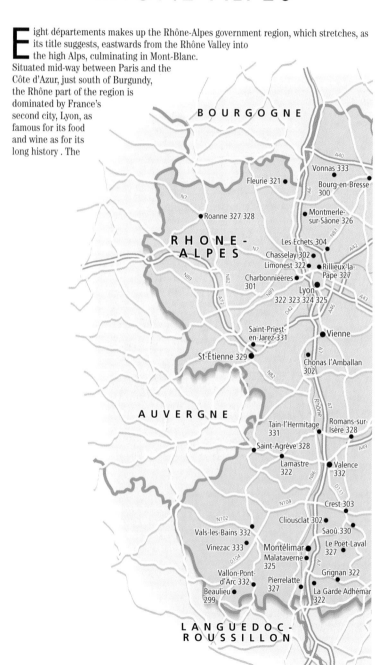

BOURGOGNE

RHONE-ALPES

AUVERGNE

LANGUEDOC-ROUSSILLON

Vonnas 333
Fleurie 321
Bourg-en-Bresse 300
Roanne 327 328
Montmerle-sur-Sâone 326
Les Echets 304
Chasselay 302
Limonest 322
Rillieux-la-Pape 327
Charbonnieères 301
Lyon 322 323 324 325
Saint-Priest-en-Jarez-331
Vienne
St-Étienne 329
Chonas l'Amballan 302
Tain-l'Hermitage 331
Romans-sur-Isère 328
Saint-Agrève 328
Lamastre 322
Valence 332
Crest 303
Cliousclat 302
Vals-les-Bains 332
Saoû 330
Vinezac 333
Montélimar
Le Poët-Laval 327
Malataverne 325
Vallon-Pont-d'Arc 332
Pierrelatte 327
Grignan 322
Beaulieu 299
La Garde Adhémar 322

area known as Lyonnais stretches around it, bisected by the Rhône. To the north liethe départements of Ain and Loire (principal towns Bourg-en-Bresse and Saint-Etienne), to the south Drôme and Ardèche (principal towns Valence and Privas). East of the Rhône is the region known as Dauphiné. From here the mountains pile up into Savoie and Haute-Savoie.

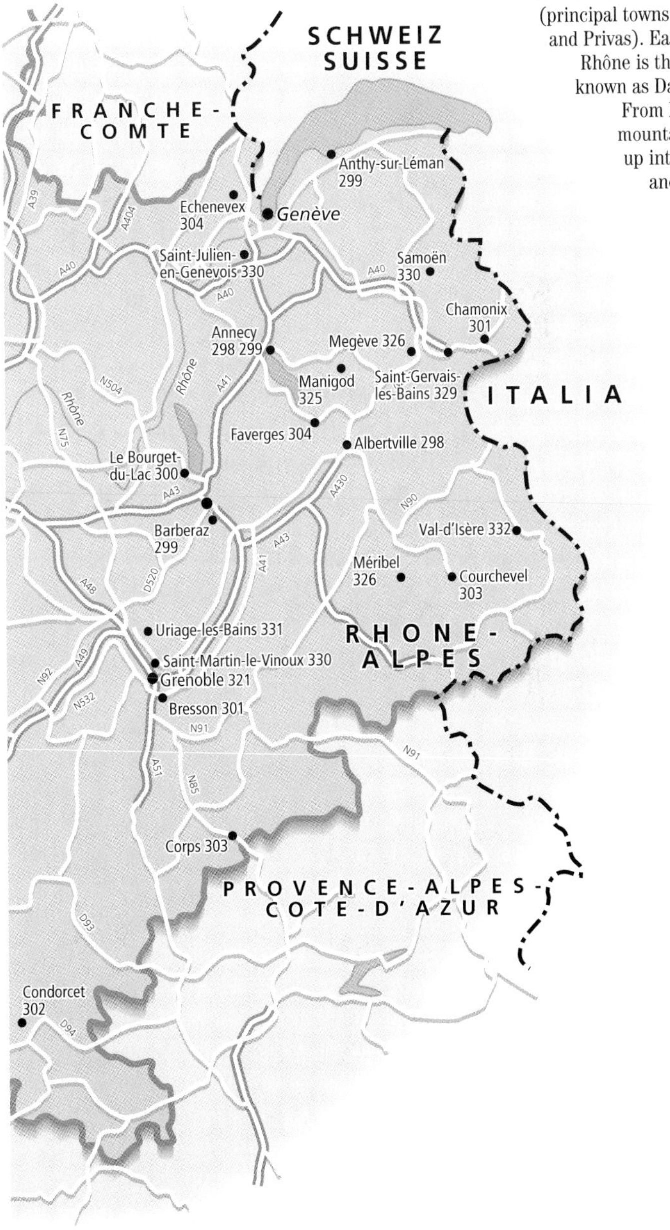

SCHWEIZ
SUISSE
FRANCHE-COMTE
Anthy-sur-Léman 299
Echenevex 304
Genève
Saint-Julien-en-Genevois 330
Samoën 330
Chamonix 301
Annecy 298 299
Megève 326
Manigod 325
Saint-Gervais-les-Bains 329
ITALIA
Faverges 304
Albertville 298
Le Bourget-du-Lac 300
Barberaz 299
Val-d'Isère 332
Méribel 326
Courchevel 303
Uriage-les-Bains 331
RHONE-ALPES
Saint-Martin-le-Vinoux 330
Grenoble 321
Bresson 301
Corps 303
PROVENCE-ALPES-COTE-D'AZUR
Condorcet 302
Rhône
A39
A404
A40
A41
A43
A430
N90
N504
N75
A48
D520
A49
N92
N532
N91
A51
N85
D93
D94

Albertville
◆ Le Chalet des Trappeurs € Fr

col de Tamié, 73200 Albertville, Savoie
Tel 04 79 32 21 44 Fax 04 79 31 24 34

An attractive, rustic old Alpine chalet, this is a great place to stop before heading up the mountain, or indeed to celebrate a successful run down. Traditional and simple, it has a convivial dining room, where day or night, you can while away happy hours in the warmth of the generous hearth, where a wood fire burns. The food too is generous: try the grills, the *civet de porcelet* or the rabbit with the delicious, delicate black wild mushrooms that the French, rather worryingly, call *trompettes de mort*, though, be assured, they are completely safe. As with all Alpine retreats, they also offer *fondues*, *raclettes* (*au feu du bois*) and many other cheese specialities, as well as some delicious local sausages called *diots*. If you have wined and dined late into the night, which is only too easy in the authentic, welcoming, country atmosphere, you could order a helicopter to fly you home (there's a convenient heliport next door).

CLOSED Wed
CARDS MC, V

Albertville
◆ Million €€ – €€€

8 place de la Liberté, 73200 Albertville, Savoie
Tel 04 67 94 20 87 Fax 04 67 21 38 40

This elegant hotel was named after its first owner, Philippe Million, who guided it to Michelin stardom. A few years ago he handed over the reins to José de Anacleto, who had long worked in his kitchen, and who, with his charming wife, Su-Chan, continues the Millions' tradition, style and reputation. Three menus are offered in a gracious 19thC dining room – or better still in summer on the attractive terrace beside lawns: a simple no-choice three-course menu at 26 euros; a 'menu Caccia' (four courses at 45 euros); and the six-course 'Ambroise' at a staggering 84 euros. The food is classically gastronomic and not exclusively Savoie, as with the *homard rôti, en croûte*

d'amandes au poivrons confits au fumet d'oranges, and the *filet de turbot poêlé, légumes 'belles Niçoise' tartine à la tapenade*. The welcome and attention to detail are faultless, and they will lay on a programme for hotel guests, introducing them to the cuisine and culture of the area, including cooking with M. de Anacleto.

CLOSED Sat lunch, Sun dinner, Mon
CARDS AE, DC, MC, V

Our traditional French cuisine symbol
So many of our readers enjoy seeking out the genuinely French eating experience that we have used Fr to mark restaurants which offer cuisine du terroir, classical French dishes or regional dishes with an emphasis on local ingredients, and traditional recipes.

Annecy
◆ Le Belvédère
€€ – €€€

7 chemin de Belvédère, 74000 Annecy, Haute Savoie
Tel 04 50 45 04 90 Fax 04 50 45 67 25

There's a good reason why this *restaurant perché* is called Le Belvédère: the panoramic views across the lake to the mountains are fabulous. It is one of the best vantage points in Annecy. Vincent Lugrin is an inventive audacious cook, and the combination of his imagination and use of fresh, excellent quality produce makes eating here a delightful adventure. The experience is not just confined to the senses of taste or sight; he also uses aromas to tease and excite: take the *purée de pomme de terre parfumée aux sapins de nos montagnes*, or *dos de féra du lac Léman saisi, jus court au café torréfié*, or – even more original – *grenadin de veau parfumé au cigare de la havane Montecristo No 4*. It is 2 km (1 mile) out of the town centre via rue des Marquisats and boulevard de la Corniche.

❢ Well worth a visit if you enjoy imaginative cuisine ❢

CLOSED Sun dinner, Tue dinner, Wed; Jan to late Feb
CARDS AE, DC, MC, V

Annecy
◆ Le Clos des Sens
€– €€€

13 rue Jean-Mermoz, 74000 Annecy-le-
Vieux, Haute Savoie
Tel 04 50 23 07 90 Fax 04 50 66 56 54

With its light, bright dining room looking over the old town of Annecy and its shady terrace with another splendid view, this attractive restaurant is run by the Petits – he in the kitchen, she 'front of house' – with a young team of willing servers. They share an appealing enthusiasm and energy. The lunchtime menu is very reasonably priced (considering they have a Michelin star), and there's also a 'haché menu' de fera, only available from February to September. Laurent's cuisine is delicate and well thought out, with excellent sauces, in whose creation he's not afraid to experiment, sometimes combining a beef sauce with fish, for example.

❛ A recommended lunch stop while exploring the old quarter of Annecy ❜

CLOSED Sun dinner Sep-Jul, Mon, Tue lunch; first 2 weeks Jan, first 2 weeks Sep
CARDS AE, DC, MC, V

Anthy-sur-Léman
◆ L'Auberge d'Anthy
€ – €€ Fr

74200 Anthy-sur-Léman, Haute Savoie
Tel 04 50 70 35 00 Fax 04 50 70 40 90

This delightful village auberge has been offering le bien manger since 1927. It's also the bar-tabac, so it really is the heart of the village. The husband and wife team of Claude and Catherine Duboulez run a busy, thriving restaurant with zest and energy. Claude's cooking is based on lake fish, which he grills, fries, roasts or steams to bring out every gram of freshness and flavour. If you really want to take advantage of this, order (in advance) the 'Bacouni menu', in which you can savour the générosité du lac in all its diversity. It's not only fish that is served here however: charcuterie, poultry and pork – all local – are also on the extensive menu,

as are delicious mountain cheeses (try the soufflé au fromage d'Abondance). The wines continue the Alpine theme, chosen by Catherine from independent vignerons including ones in Piemont, Geneva and Savoie.

CLOSED Sun dinner, Mon low season
CARDS AE, DC, MC, V

Barberaz
◆ Mont Carmel € – €€€

1 rue Eglise, Barberaz, 73000 Chambéry,
Savoie
Tel 04 79 85 77 17 Fax 04 79 85 16 65

In an ancient village house next to the church, this restaurant has a lovely terrace with a spectacular panorama over the mountains. It serves fairly classic food (filet de pigeon rôti aux choux et foie gras and ravioles d'écrevisses for example), cooked with loving care, which is why it is so popular locally. The menus are reasonable, and it's advisable to book in advance. It is one km (0.5 miles) south-east of Chambéry on the D912 and then the D4.

❛ The glorious terrace makes this a great stopping place in the summertime ❜

CLOSED Sun dinner, Mon, Wed dinner
CARDS AE, MC, V

Beaulieu
◆ La Santoline € – €€

07460 Beaulieu, Ardèche
Tel 04 75 39 01 91 Fax 04 75 39 38 79

Residents of nearby villages still speak of the big, old, stone Santoline as 'le château' – a reference to its 15thC origins. As time passed, it was used as a hunting lodge and remains a secluded place well off the beaten track. On warm evenings guests dine outside on a flower-filled terrace and watch the sun set behind the Cévennes. The mountain view is exhilarating, and there is little to disturb the peace here, except birdsong and the occasional braying of a donkey. It is difficult to imagine a more relaxed setting. The inside dining room is also appealing, with a fine stone-vaulted ceiling and tiled floor. Since opening their hotel and restaurant (there are eight rooms) in 1991, the Espenels have gathered a very loyal clientele by striking the right balance between easy-going conviviality and discreet attentiveness. The popular restaurant provides a menu of regional fare, which changes daily, and affordable wines of the Ardèche.

CLOSED Oct to late Apr
CARDS MC, V

Bourg-en-Bresse
◆ L'Auberge Bressane
€ – €€€ **Fr**

166 boulevard de Brou, 01000 Bourg-en-Bresse, Ain
Tel 04 74 22 22 68 Fax 04 74 23 03 15

If there's one thing that Bresse is famous for, it's chicken; and this typical local restaurant certainly favours this fowl – not just on the menu (with its skin delicately flavoured with truffles), but also as the principal motif in the decoration of its attractive dining room. Prices vary from the excellent value 22-euro *menu simple* to *l'été à Brou*, considerably steeper at 66 euros, though it does include *foie gras* in Sauternes jelly, grilled lobsters on a *gratin* of crayfish, followed by the ubiquitous *poulet de Bresse* in a *morille* sauce. The menus are carefully constructed with limited choice, but the *carte* is more extensive and includes a selection of ways to cook the revered chicken, one of which is whole, roast on a spit. One chicken feeds four people, but it does entail a wait.

❛ The chicken was mouthwatering'
... 'A meal we won't forget ❜

CLOSED Tue
CARDS AE, DC, MC, V

Bourg-en-Bresse
◆ Chez Blanc € – €€ **Fr**

19 place Bernard, 01000 Bourg-en-Bresse, Ain
Tel 04 74 45 29 11 Fax 04 74 24 73 69

Another runaway success from the Georges Blanc stable, this busy, popular bistro is the latest in an ever-growing stable (see page 333). It is a welcoming place, where the staff are young, the food excellent

and the atmosphere congenial. Try and eat on the *véranda rétro*, which is quieter than the elegant dining room. Generous local specialities are cooked by Blanc's apprentice, David Pageau – piles of frogs' legs, juicy Bresse chicken, roast pigeon in Beaujolais sauce or *boeuf Vigneronne* – all as tender as they are aromatic. The wine list is impressive and reasonably priced, although much of the wine is sourced from the Macon estate of Domaine d'Azenay, owned by – guess who? Yes, you're right – Georges Blanc.

CLOSED never
CARDS AE, DC, MC, V

Our price bands
€ 15 Euros or less €€ 30-50 Euros
€€€ 50+ Euros for a menu.

Le Bourget-du-Lac
◆ Le Bateau Ivre

73370 Le Bourget-du-Lac, Savoie
Tel 04 79 25 00 23 Fax 04 79 25 25 77

Standing proudly over the Lac du Bourget, with terrific views to Mont Revard on the other side, this mansion from the early 1900s houses the Hôtel Ombremont and Le Bateau Ivre, with its lovely bright yellow dining room and a wooden terrace that stretches out to the water below. The menus are directed by Jean-Pierre Jacob, who draws his inspiration, not surprisingly, from the lake, especially with his *lavaret* (a lake fish), cooked with truffles, mushrooms and tomato *confit* in a light artichoke sauce. What he calls merely *'l'oeuf'* is a wonderful dish of roasted *langoustine* crowned with an egg, on a melting base of onions and potatoes. Incredibly, the frogs' legs in garlic sauce are de-boned, confirmation that care, time and effort, and love are the bywords in this kitchen. (If you want to catch this extraordinary chef in winter, head for the Bateau Ivre restaurant in the Pomme de Pin hotel in Courchevel, where he takes up residence from late December to mid-April.)

❛ A stunning setting for fabulous food ❜

CLOSED Mon dinner, Tue lunch, Thu lunch; Nov–May
CARDS AE, DC, MC, V

Bresson
◆ Chavant €€ – €€€ Fr

38280 Bresson, Isère
Tel 04 76 25 25 38 Fax 04 76 62 06 55

You can eat one of the excellent two 'basic' menus in the oak-beamed restaurant of this creeper-clad country *auberge*, or in its tranquil gardens, or you could splash out on one of the menus based on Jean-Pierre Charant's great love: lobster. For 105 euros, you could savour *homard et sa gelée de pommes vertes*, followed by *homard au Champagne et caviar*, followed by *tronçon de homard au Bouzy*, and then *petit soufflé de homard*. But if lobster is not to your taste, you'll find plenty of other interesting dishes to choose from at kinder prices. The *auberge* has been owned by the Charant family since 1852, so many of the classic recipes have been handed down through the generations. Its reputation extends to its wine cellar, where you can taste and buy under the passionate tutelage of Jean-Charles Pouzeratte.

❝ A family-run inn amidst peaceful countryside' … 'One of the best dinners of our trip ❞

CLOSED Mon, Sat lunch, Sun dinner
CARDS AE, DC, MC, V

Chamonix
◆ Auberge du Bois Prin
€€ – €€€ Fr

69 chemin de l'Hermine, Les Moussoux,
74400 Chamonix, Haute-Savoie
Tel 04 50 53 33 51 Fax 04 50 53 48 75

Despite elegant local competition, the Bois Prin stands out for being rooted in the traditions of the region, for its stunning views across the steep-sided Chamonix valley to the spires and glaciers of Mont Blanc, and for being a deeply cosseting place to visit – or indeed, stay. The Carrier family have run this classic, dark-wood chalet since it was built in 1976 by the present owner's parents. It stands in a pretty, flowery garden close to the foot of the Brévent cable-car on the north side of the valley. The first impression may be of a surprising degree of formal-

ity, with crisply dressed staff. But in fact you quickly find that the informal and friendly approach of the young owners sets the tone. The food is excellent with a good choice of menus (specialities include *aile de poularde de Bresse et farçon* and *filet de féra aux écrevisses du lac Léman*) and a wonderful cheeseboard.

❝ Luxurious, yet at the same time homely and cosy ❞

CLOSED Mon lunch, Wed lunch; mid-Apr to early May, Nov
CARDS AE, DC, MC, V

---

charmingsmallhotels.co.uk
Visit Duncan Petersen's travel website, the best online search tool for places to stay that combine character and charm.
Currently features Britain, France, Italy and Ireland, with other destinations being continuously added.

Charbonnières-les-Bains
◆ L'Orangerie de Sébastien € – €€

domaine de Lacroix Laval, 69280 Marcy-l'Etoile, Charbonnières-les-Bains, Rhône
Tel 04 78 87 45 95 Fax 04 71 87 45 96

In the parkland of Lacroix Laval, 8 km (5 miles) north-west of Lyon, this beautiful restaurant and its gorgeous terrace are especially popular when the weather starts to become spring-like. The young chef, Sébastien Bégouin, is busy making a reputation for himself for creating delicate dishes with an imagination which does not rely on complexity. He is also to be congratulated for keeping his prices admirably honest for the high standard of cuisine that he presents. His *foie gras* is excellent – whether accompanied by fresh figs or artichokes – and he prepares a fabulous *filet de bar à la plancha*, delicately flavoured with passionfruit, and a whole bass with truffles (for two, to be ordered 48 hours in advance). This enchanting place has only been open since April 1998, but it is already an established gastronomic magnet for the Lyonnais.

CLOSED Sun dinner, Mon
CARDS MC, V

Chasselay
◆ Guy Lassausaie
€€ – €€€

rue Belle-Cize, 69380 Chasselay, Rhône
Tel 04 78 47 62 59 Fax 04 78 47 06 19

A marriage made in heaven lies behind this restaurant: a Michelin-starred chef, whose wife is a professional and talented *sommelière*. Guy Lassausaie is a perfectionist in the kitchen, and his whole establishment – recently redecorated – reeks of style and good design. Although he has run it since 1984, he is in fact the fourth generation to do so, and it has been in his family since the beginning of the 20th century. He has brought his own style to the tradition of *'la maison'*. His signature dish is famous: pigeon cooked in hay. He is not only imaginative, but also takes into consideration colour, contrasts of texture and fascinating combinations of flavour, although sometimes he goes a flavour too far (in for example fillet of red mullet, roasted in olive oil, served with ginger polenta and rhubarb sauce with pink pepper). His desserts are a triumph, not surprising from a one-time finalist in the 'Championnat de France du Dessert'. Marie-Annick Lassausaie has created an admirable wine list to complement her husband's excellent cuisine.

❛ Dishes that are as beautiful as they are sublime' ... 'Expensive, but worth it ❜

CLOSED Tue, Wed
CARDS AE, DC, MC, V

Chonas l'Amballan
◆ Domaine de Clairfontaine €€ – €€€

38201 Chonas l'Amballan, Isère
Tel 04 74 58 81 52 Fax 04 74 58 80 93

O nce the 'rest home' of the bishops of Lyon, this lovely 18thC house is surrounded by several hectares of stunning parkland, whose serenity is only interrupted by the cries of the peacocks or the flapping of a swan's wings. The chef-patron, Philippe Girardon, has a Michelin star and offers four gourmet menus (priced between 42 and 85

euros). His signature dish is *nénuphar de homard*, offset by a *tartare* of *tomate cru en millefeuille* and *mousseline d'avocats*. His puddings are deliciously creative; try the *Stradivarius au chocolat*, both for its sumptuousness and its perfect presentation. Laurence Girardon is an excellent hostess, who clearly enjoys her *métier*.

CLOSED Mon, Tue; 3rd week Aug, mid-Dec to mid-Jan
CARDS AE, DC, MC, V

Looking for somewhere to stay? See page 241.

Cliousclat
◆ La Treille Muscate € Fr

26270 Cliousclat, Drôme
Tel 04 75 63 13 10 Fax 04 75 63 10 79

T his charming ivy-covered inn with green shutters in a small perched village is infused with the spirit of Provence from its sunny ochre walls and cheerful Provençal fabrics to the deliciously simple regional food. Inside, floors are tiled, furnishings are wrought-iron, and dried flowers add a touch of colour. Outside, there is a glorious shaded terrace with expansive views of the Rhône valley. The chef specializes in homemade, seasonal cooking, featuring the same dishes on his menus and *carte*: dishes such as *tarte fine au thon et fenouil confit*, *joues de cochon au citron et au gingembre* and *aumônière d'agneau confit au picodon*, for which he insists on only using the freshest ingredients.

CLOSED Wed; mid-Dec to Mar
CARDS MC, V

Condorcet
◆ La Charrette Bleue € Fr

route de Gap, 26110 Condorcet, Drôme
Tel 04 75 27 72 33 Fax 04 75 27 76 14

I t is well worth driving the extra 7 km (5 miles) from Nyons (via the D94) to find this pretty white farmhouse, where the staff not only welcome you warmly but serve first-class local food at very reasonable prices. At lunch there is a superb 16-euro *menu du marché* (weekdays only), and there are three other menus which are hard to beat for value. And it's not as if they stint on their ingredients: their specialities are *foie gras de canard maison et sa gelée de Muscat, carré d'agneau rôti en croute d'ail aux herbes* and *demi-pigeon desossé, farci, rôti*. The well-chosen wine list is firmly rooted in the Côtes du Rhône. What's more, the dining room is prettily decorated in bright Provençal colours, and they speak English.

❛ A pretty dining room. An excellent meal at a bargain price ❜

Closed Tue Sep-Jul, Wed and Sun dinner mid-Sep to Apr
Cards MC, V

●*Hôtellerie Beau Rivage in Condrieu (04 74 59 52 24) has a splendid position beside the Rhône and a Michelin star.*

Corps
◈ Hôtel de la Poste €€

place de la Mairie, route Napoléon, 38970 Corps, Isère
Tel 04 76 30 00 03 Fax 04 76 30 02 73

There is a warm, intimate and friendly atmosphere at this notable hotel and restaurant in Corps, a busy tourist centre within reach of ski-ing and walking. The exterior sets the happy tone, with its pink walls, blue awnings and bright geraniums in window boxes. Nothing inside disappoints. The two dining rooms are cosy and welcoming, with antique country furniture, colourful fabrics and paintings on the walls. Service is smiling, and the cooking of M. Dulas draws people from miles around (and a Bib Gourmand – good food at moderate prices – from Michelin). You might choose *pantagruélique farandole de hors d'oeuvre avec saladiers de palourdes*, followed by *gigot d'agneau*, roast quail or smoked duck salad, with a delicious *pâtisserie* for dessert. There's an inexpensive wine list.

Closed Jan to mid-Feb
Cards AE, MC, V

Courchevel
◈ Le Genépi € – €€

rue Park City, 73120 Courchevel, Savoie
Tel 04 79 08 08 63 Fax 04 79 08 08 63

Amid the chic of Courchevel, it is a delight to find a bustling little bistro with an impeccable range of local menus, impeccably cooked. In the wood-panelled dining room, warmed by a wood fire, you sit beneath horse bridles and straw-filled mangers, looked after by the charming Cécile Mugnier. Her husband, Thierry, one of the 'jeunes restaurateurs d'Europe', cooks five menus with energy and passion. Alongside his excellently turned-out 34-euro three-course menu, he offers the inevitable *fondue Savoyade* and *tartiflette*. There's also a tasty *menu végétarien* – something of a rarity in France. Although it includes some local vintages, the extensive, but highly marked-up wine list is orientated towards Bordeaux. There's a terrace for warm days.

Closed Sat and Sun May-Nov; Jul-Sep
Cards AE, MC, V

Our price bands
Rather than giving actual prices (which are prone to change) we indicate the cost of a three-course meal for one person, without wine, by means of price bands. They are as follows: € under 30 euros €€ 30-50 euros €€€ over 50 euros. Where we give more than one price band, for example €–€€€, this indicates that in that restaurant a meal can be had at a range of prices. As well as the cost of *prix fixe* menus, our price bands also take into account the cost of an average selection from the *à la carte* menu.

Crest
◈ Porte Montségur
€ – €€€

avenue des Trois Becs, 26400 Crest, Drôme
Tel 04 75 25 41 48 Fax 04 75 25 22 63

The reason for choosing this old farm-house is not only its admirable position beside the Drôme river – particularly desirable in summer, from the pleasant shade of the terrace – but also for its mouthwatering menus. Claude Allier enjoys creating novel and interesting dishes, according to what he can find at the market and to the mood he is in that day. Eating here is therefore an adventure as well as a pleasure. There is a bargain lunchtime menu (under 20 euros), which is hard to beat. It also has eight attractive bedrooms.

❛ Great value for money' … 'Fresh ingredients, delicious dishes ❜

CLOSED Wed and Mon low season
CARDS AE, DC, MC, V

Echenevex
◆ Auberge des Chasseurs
€€

Naz-Dessus, 01170 Echenevex, Ain
Tel 04 50 41 54 07 Fax 04 50 41 90 61

At the foot of the Jura mountains, facing the Alps (with views over Lac Léman to Mont Blanc), this is a handsome converted farmhouse with a warm welcome. It has been in the family of its owner, Dominique Lamy, since the mid-19th century, and thanks to the attentions of a Swedish decorator is now dressed in a Scandinavian-inspired coat of paint effects, which includes patterned beams, painted ceilings and doors adorned with flowers and inscriptions. The satisfying food has its origins in the region, and includes *foie gras*-based dishes, *volaille fermière aux morilles à la crème* and a *trilogie de poissons marinés à cru*. It is served in the stylish dining room, or on the flowery terrace, complemented by an impressive, well-priced wine list.

❛ A chic setting for an excellent, reasonably priced meal ❜

CLOSED Sun dinner and Mon Sep-Jul; mid-Nov to mid-Apr
CARDS AE, MC, V

Les Echets
◆ Jacques et Christophe Marguin € – €€€

916 route de Strasbourg, 01700 Les Echets, Ain
Tel 04 78 91 80 04 Fax 04 78 91 06 83

Just 20 km (12 miles) from Lyon, this marvellous, elegant restaurant has been an institution in Les Echets for four generations. The current chef, Christophe Marguin, follows the classical style of his father and grandfather, employing local ingredients with a refined simplicity, although he is not afraid of importing flavours from other cuisines, which results in inventive combinations. His *volaille à la crème* is faultlessly juicy, and he usually has a *grenouille* dish on his menu. The atmosphere is warm, and there is a seductive terrace for summer dining.

❛ Not only a delightful place to stop, the menus offer good value too ❜

CLOSED Sun dinner, Mon
CARDS AE, DC, MC, V

---

charmingsmallhotels.co.uk
Visit Duncan Petersen's travel website, the best online search tool for places to stay that combine character and charm. Currently features Britain, France, Italy and Ireland, with other destinations being continuously added.

Faverges
◆ Au Gay Séjour € Fr

Le Tertenoz de Seythenex, 74210 Faverges, Haute-Savoie
Tel 04 50 44 52 52 Fax 04 50 44 49 52

A simple, honest and much admired inn that stands in a secluded spot not far from Lac d'Annecy en route to the major ski resorts. The sturdy 17thC former farmhouse has been in the dedicated hands of the Gay family for generations. Chef-patron Bernard Gay was taught to cook by his grandmother and will one day hand over the running of the place to his son, who is training as a chef. Food is at the heart of the house, with plenty of fish dishes, both from local lakes and the sea, as well as local specialities such as truffles in season. There are 12 simple and spotless bedrooms.

❛ A gloriously remote traditional inn, where peace and quiet are assured ❜

Continued on page 321

SOUTHERN FRANCE

THE REGIONAL CUISINES

AQUITAINE ‹ MIDI-PYRENEES ‹ AUVERGNE ‹
RHONE-ALPES ‹ LANGUEDOC-ROUSSILLON ›
PROVENCE-ALPES-COTE D'AZUR ‹

AQUITAINE

This much appreciated, gastronomically rich region takes its name from the Dukedom of Aquitaine, acquired by the English when Eleanor of Aquitaine married Henry II of England in 1152. To the west, it encompasses Bordeaux and its surrounding vineyards, and Landes, the long strip of sand and pine that runs the length of the Atlantic Coast from below the bay of Arcachon to the Pyrenees. Here, in the far south-west corner of France at the border with Spain, is Basque country, mountainous yet cool and green and characterised by brightly coloured, half-timbered villages. In the centre is Périgord, cut by the lovely river Dordogne. To the south, the river Lot runs into the Garonne on its way to the Atlantic.

The cooking of the Pays Basque is a highly flavoured, highly individual meld of France and Spain. Peppers feature prominently in dishes such as *pipérade* (scrambled eggs, peppers and ham, simple but tricky to pull off successfully), and *poulet*

Basquaise. Fish is readily available in the form of tuna, sardines, anchovies, squid (chipirones – cooked in its own ink) and cod, which mostly appears salted as in morue Basquaise, again with peppers and tomatoes. The local – fiery – fish stew is called ttoro. The famous *jambon de Bayonne* is salted, dry cured and smoked to a time-honoured recipe: try it with eggs, a perfect combination. Maize, introduced from America via Spain, remains an important staple: white cornmeal is the main ingredient in *millas*, a sweet flan flavoured with orange flower water. *Gâteau Basque*, with its trademark lattice tracery on the surface, is a rum-flavoured, cream-filled tart. The tasty cheese, such as Ardi-Gasna and Iraty, is mainly of ewe's milk (*fromage de brébis*).

Moving inland, the Basque country becomes Béarn, the region around Pau where Henry IV, King of Navarre and later King of France was born in 1553. His desire to put 'a chicken in every pot' is still remembered in the local speciality of *poule au pot*, while the belief that he was christened with a drop of Jurançon wine has given it the epithet 'the wine of kings'. Other regional wines are the reds of Irouléguy in Pays Basque and the light, fruity reds and rosés of Béarn. Apart from the ubiquitous sauce Béarnaise, Béarn is also noted for its vegetable, ham and *confit* soup, *garbure*, and for *salmis de palombes*, wood pigeon stewed in red wine.

Unlike Burgundy and the region around Lyon, the traditional dishes of Bordeaux are no match for its stupendous wines (which is not to say you won't eat

Below: Foothills of the Pyrenees.

well). Lacking even in cheese, the perfect partner for red wine, its greatest contribution to the national cuisine is *sauce Bordelaise* (made with Bordeaux wine of course), most famously served with an *entrecôte* steak. Red wine will crop up in seafood dishes such as *moules à la Bordelaise* and *lamproie à la Bordelaise*, while your *huîtres à la Bordelaise*, or *huîtres d'Arcachon* will come with tiny truffled sausages called *crépinettes*. But the wine is the thing: nearly 40 *appellations controlées* or designated wines, a large number of the finest crus, and a host of names to savour (and save up for), including Château Lafite-Rothschild, Château d'Yquem, Margaux, Mouton-Rothschild, Pétrus....

In Périgord, the countryside around the Dordogne produces quantities of well-known everyday table wines such as Côtes de Bergerac and the increasingly well-regarded Côtes de Duras, as well as the delicious sweet white Monbazillac. As for food, as in neighbouring Quercy (see Midi-Pyrénées) you are back in the land of truffles, mushrooms, *foie gras* and *confit d'oie* (food is often cooked in goose fat, which gives it a delicious taste). Look out for *sauce Périgueux* (truffle sauce), *pommes sarladaises, oeufs brouillés aux truffes, miques* (plump dumplings made with salt pork), *pieds de cochon farcis* (stuffed pigs' feet) and *tourin* (garlic soup served with egg).

Above: Wine for sale in a vente direct.
Below: Wine cellars near Duras.

MIDI-PYRENEES

The region called the Midi-Pyrénées embraces central south-west France and no less than eight *départements*: Lot, Tarn, Tarn-et-Garonne, Haute-Garonne, Aveyron, Gers, Hautes Pyrénées and Ariège. To its north lie the limestone plateaux or causses of Lot, Tarn and Aveyron, cut by river valleys of the same names. In the centre of the region, the Garonne runs down from the Pyrenees through Haute Garonne to the 'pink city' of Toulouse, before making a left turn to continue through Lot-et-Garonne on its

Below: *Le Pont Valentré, Cahors.*

way to the Atlantic. It marks the northern boundary of Gascony and the *département* of Gers, with its soft, rolling countryside and fortified *bastides*. Gradually, the foothills pile up into the Hautes-Pyrénées, with Lourdes acting as a gateway to the high passes and valleys. At the opposite end of the range, the mountains begin their descent towards the plains of Languedoc-Roussillon and the Mediterranean in Arìege, still marked by the austere fortresses that remind visitors of the tragic Cathar religious movement.

In western Languedoc, around Toulouse and Carcassonne, easily the most famous traditional dish is *cassoulet*, in which pork, beans and preserved goose (*confit d'oie*) are slowly cooked together. In Rouergue and Albigeois (the *départements* of Tarn and Aveyron) you will find plenty of *charcuterie*, including wonderful *jambon de sanglier* (wild boar). As in the Auvergne, you may come across *tripoux* (tripe parcels) and *aligot* (potatoes mashed with Laguiole cheese) as well as tasty crackling (*fritons*), *fricandaux* (hashed meats), and *fouace* (circular bread with a dusting of sugar). Look out, too, for the prettily blushed *ail* (garlic) rose de Tarn. Amongst *les douceurs*, don't miss the delicious *croustillants de noisettes* of Cordes-sur-Ciel, and look for the *gimblettes*, navettes and *petits janots*

Above: La Terrasse at Grézels.

of Albi, and the *marquises* and *dragées* of Toulouse. There are wines too, notably the flinty whites of Gaillac, but also the dry whites of Etraygues (vin du Fel), the rosé of Estaing, and the rough red of Marcillac. The cooking of Quercy (covered by the *départements* of Lot and Tarn-et-Garonne), dominated by duck, goose and truffles, and

Above: Ail Rose *(pink-tinged garlic), a Tarn speciality, seen in local markets.*
Below: Summer grazing, high Pyrenees.

accompanied by the dark red wines of Cahors, is much the same as that of neighbouring Périgord (see Aquitaine). *Gâteaux de noix* can be found in markets across the region and cheeses such as Bleu des Causses, Bleu de Quercy, Laguiole, the little goat's cheeses Cabécou de Rocamadour and the strongly flavoured Passe-l'An.

Around Toulouse and in Gascony, apart from *charcuterie* (including the famous *saucisse de Toulouse*) and *cassoulet*, plain or fancy, the emphasis is on goose and duck (*oie en daube, confit d'oie, confit de canard, magret de canard* and, of course *foie gras d'oie* and *foie gras de canard*). Truffles, game and poultry also feature on the traditional menu.

Gascony is Armagnac country: the brandy is produced in three areas: Bas-Armagnac, said to be the best; Ténarèze, in the centre; and Haute-Armagnac. As well as bottles of Armagnac, aged in oak barrels for up to ten years, you can buy fruits preserved in Armagnac.

South of Gascony the Pyrenees rise to snow-capped peaks. To the west stretch the regions of Béarn and Pays Basque (part of Aquitaine). To the east is Ariège. In the country – dotted with prehistoric caves – around rock-like Foix, you may find such traditional dishes as *rousolo* (a savoury cake of pork, bacon and egg), *estouffade de Pamiers* (pork and haricot beans) and *croustade* (thin, crispy leaves of pastry filled with fruit). Foix is also home of the multi-coloured almond paste sweet, *touron*. There are few other specialities, except some cheeses: Monségur, Les Orrys, Saint-Lizier and Bethmale.

AUVERGNE

At the heart of France lies the Massif Central, a vast granite and hardened lava plateau slashed by deep gorges and crowned by volcanic peaks. A sense of isolation and self-sufficiency pervades, especially in the thrilling mountain landscape around Puy de Dôme, the extinct volcano, which rises to 1,465 m (4,807 ft). In times past, many inhabitants of this area would leave to seek their fortune in Paris, often as *bougnats* (coal and wood merchants), but would always dream of home, and one day return. Today, outdoor pursuits, including downhill and cross-country skiing, are what draw visitors to the Auvergne, as well as austerely beautiful Romanesque

churches, notably Notre-Dame-du-Port in the capital Clermont-Ferrrand, and at Le Puy, Orcival, Issoire, Saint-Nectaire, Saint-Saturnin and Brioude.

The cooking of the Auvergne suits the terrain perfectly, the emphasis being on simple warming fare and on cheese from the cattle which graze on the mountain pastures. (You can still occasionally see *burons*, the stone houses with large living quarters for the cows and smaller ones for the farmer and his family). The hearty

Below: Produce of Auvergne's southern département of Cantal.

pork, cabbage, potato, sausage, onions and *potée Auvergnate* is typical, combining pork, cabbage, potato, sausage, onions and leeks in a cross between soup and stew. *Truffade* is a mixture of mashed potato and cheese shaped into cakes then fried with bacon and garlic. Cabbage features prominently, for example, stuffed with chopped seasoned meat in *choux farci*. Leg of lamb is simmered with vegetables for four hours or more in *gigot brayaude*. Ham and bacon mixed with chard or spinach beet become a dense pie in pounti. Potatoes and Tomme or Cantal cheese, crème fraîche and garlic become *aligot*. Parcels of tripe are simmered in white wine in *tripous*. Look out

for *fritons*, crispy pork scratchings, delicious when added to salad; and for *rissoles de Saint Flour*, filled with cheese.

As you see, it's the dishes, rather than the ingredients, that distinguish the gastronomy in the tough conditions of the Auvergne, though the outstanding *lentilles de Puy* are a notable exception (they often appear with the excellent local salt pork in *petit salé aux lentilles*). Also exceptional are the cheeses, of which no less than five are accorded A.O.C. status: Saint Nectaire, Fourme d'Ambert, Bleu d'Auvergne, Cantal and Salers. The wines are not A.O.C. Côtes d'Auvergne are best drunk young when they are pleasant and fresh.

Above left: Auberge la Tomette, Vitrac.
Above right: Le Pre Bossu, Mondeyres.

Centre: Wild mushrooms, including cèpes, *on the menu at Puech, Calvinet.*

RHONE-ALPES

The name of this region is self-explanatory, covering as it does two very different landscapes: the Rhône valley and surrounding hills north and south of Lyon (*départements* of Loire, Rhône, Ain , Ardèche and Drôme) and the French Alps (*départements* of Isère, Haute Savoie and Savoie). In Lyonnais are found some of the greatest chefs and the highest gastronomic aspirations in France; in Savoie the food reflects the simpler ways of mountain life.

A happy combination of superb local ingredients – the famous poultry from Bresse (see Bourgogne), *pâtés*, *terrines*, *charcuterie*, freshwater fish from the Domme lakes, fruit, vegetables, cheese and wine – and an instinctive love and appreciation of good food has made Lyon the gastronomic rival of Paris, with hundreds of restaurants, and dozens of superb ones. Though culinary fireworks are in evidence all round, the traditional dishes allow the fine basic flavours to shine. They include *saladier Lyonnais* (salad of herring); *tablier de sapeur* (breaded tripe with tartare sauce); Lyon sausage served with a warm potato salad, wrapped in brioche or in a Beaujolais sauce; *quenelles de brochet* (pike dumplings); chicken with truffles , cooked in a pig's bladder (*poularde en vessie*) or with tarragon vinegar; *entrecôte Beaujolaise*; and *cardons à la moelle* (cardoons cooked with beef marrow). From nearby Dauphiné come the great potato dish *gratin*

Below: Produce of the Rhône valley.

Above: Le Tour Rose in Lyon.

Above: Outside Le Manoire du Raveyron at Vallon-Pont-d'Arc.

Dauphinois, ravioli and walnuts, and from Nantua, the crayfish *sauce Nantua*, served with *quenelles*. The *charcuterie* of Lyon is superb. Look out in the shops for the pure pork *cervelas Lyonnais*, *rosette de Lyon*, *Jésus de Morteau*, *saussicon à l'ail*, and *judru*, flavoured with marc, as well as for *boudin* and *andouille*. Regional cheeses include Saint-Marcellin, Claqueret, Lyonnais, Chamberand, Arômes, Fondue aux Raisins and Picodon. The *pâtisseries* of Lyon are filled with such local delicacies as *cocons*, *coussins*, *marrons glacés* and *pâté d'amande*, while Montélimar is world-renowned for its nougat. As for wine, the Rhône area can draw on the great vineyards of Beaujolais and the Côtes du Rhône, while those of Burgundy are close at hand: Pouilly-Fuissé, Juliénas, Fleurie, Crozes-Hermitage are just a few of the fine regional wines.

Traditional Alpine cooking is filling and warming, with emphasis on cheese and potato dishes, and on cured meats, including fine smoked mountain hams and sausages (look out for spiced *pormonier*). There is cheese fondue of course, while *gratin Savoyard* mixes cheese and potatoes. Hearty meat dishes include *potée Savoyarde* and *diots au vin blanc* (pork sausages in white wine). Freshwater fish include char –

perhaps baked with wine and mushrooms – and salmon trout.

Several of the great cow's cheeses of France come from these mountains, including unpasturised Reblochon, which was once given to the monks in exchange for the blessing of the peasants' fields. Beaufort is a close relative of Swiss Gruyère and comes in two varieties, summer and winter. Then there is supple, nutty Tomme de Savoie and its regional varients, and sharp, blue-veined Bleu de Tignes and Bleu de Sainte-Foy. Amongst desserts and *pâtisserie*, *gâteau de Savoie*, the featherlight sponge cake said to have been invented at the court of the Count of Savoy in the 14th century, takes pride of place, but look out too for *matefaims* (pancakes) and liqueur-flavoured chocolates and *bonbons*. Liqueurs are important, most famously Chartreuse, invented by the monks, and the deliciously dry vermouth from Chambéry. Mountain wines include pleasant still and sparking white Vins de Savoie, as well as Crépy, Seyssel and Roussette de Savoie.

Centre: On the dessert menu at Auberge d'Anthy at Anthy-sur-Léman.

LANGUEDOC-ROUSSILLON

C aught between the wide sweep of the Mediterranean Golfe du Lion and the hills and peaks of the Cévennes and the Pyrenees, the Languedoc-Roussillon region exudes a strong southern character, especially in Catalan Roussillon, but also in sun-frazzled, vine-clad Languedoc.

Strewn across the region are eloquent reminders of the medieval past, with many Romanesque churches as well as fortified towns – most famously Carcassonne (though what you see today is a 19thC interpretation of what might have been).

The food is southern too. Olive oil, garlic, tomatoes, anchovies, fish and herbs from the stony *garrigue* all play a part as they do in Provence, but the cooking of the region around Toulouse in Midi-Pyrénées (see 286) is also evident around Castelnaudry and Carcassonne, with smoked hams, *foie gras*, *charcuterie* and their own versions of *cassoulet*.

In Roussillon, close to the Spanish border, Catalan dishes feature prominently. You may find stuffed red peppers, partridge and pigeon, tuna, *civet de langouste* (lobster stew) and *saucisse*, all served *à la Catalan*, which means plenty of tomatoes, garlic, herbs and perhaps Banyuls wine and orange peel. *Boles de Picoulat* are piquant meatballs in a tomato sauce.

Collioure is justly famous for its anchovies, while the local fish stews are *pinyata* and *boullinade*.

The gentle coastline of Mediterranean Languedoc, with its lagoons and marshes, yields plenty of fish, as well as mussels and oysters from the Etang de Thau. The main port, Sète, is known for its *bourride*, served with *aïoli* (garlic mayonnaise) and for its *moules farcies Sétoises*, when they are stuffed with sausagemeat and served in a sauce of tomatoes and olive oil. Further east, around Aigues-Mortes in Gard, look out for *boeuf à la gardiane*, *brandade*, asparagus, *brasucades* (grilled mussels) and *sardinade* (sardines grilled on vine cuttings).

Centre: Fresh lobster for the pot at La Littorine, Banyuls-sur-Mer.

Inland, salt cod, in the form of a purée (*brandade*) is a local favourite, especially around Nîmes, as are snails. Cooked *à la Languedocienne*, they will turn up in a sauce, perhaps of anchovy and walnut; *en cargolade* they are grilled over vine stalks. The herb butter sauce, with anchovies and capers, *beurre de Montpellier*, makes a delicious accompaniment to fish or meat. From Pézenas come sweet mutton pies, *petits pâtés de Pézenas*. Containing a mixture of mutton, beef suet, lemon peel and brown sugar, they have been baked here since their first appearance with returning Crusaders.

Where the region pushes into the impoverished Cévennes, in the *département* of Lozère, the cooking is at its simplest, relying on tripe, *charcuterie*, game and mushrooms.

Regional cheeses are all but non-existant, except for Bleu de Causses, produced in Lozère and Herault, Bossons Macérés, found in local markets north of Alès, and Pelardon, a soft goat's cheese from the Cévennes. Sweet things are better represented, often flavoured with aniseed, pistachio, almond, orange and lemon. Though vines dominate much of the landscape, the wines have largely been considered poor, producing the bulk of French 'plonk'. Recently they've improved, especially Côtes du Roussillon-Villages and Corbières. The sweet wines of Banyuls and the sparkling Blanquette de Limoux make good aperitifs.

*Centre:
L'Orangeraie,
Argelès-sur-Mer.
Below: Vieux
Pont, Belcastel.*

PROVENCE-ALPES-COTE D'AZUR

Imagine Provence and you might see yourself sipping a pastis in the shade of a giant plane tree, watching old men in berets play *boule*, and allowing yourself to be lulled by the grating cicadas and the hot perfumes of lavender and thyme. Or you may think of cool, wooded Mont Ventoux and Cézanne's spectacular Mont Sainte-Victoire, bathed in the clearest of light and constantly changing in colour. Or the cities of Aix, Arles and Avignon, with their Roman past and their festivals of music and art. Or perhaps the Lubéron, no longer a backwater, but full of chic visitors, smart restaurants and restored villages. Or you might think of Marseille, with its famous port; and of the flamingos and white horses of the Camargue.

Further east, the Côte d'Azur, the overcrowded coast between Marseille and Monte Carlo, still remains one of Europe's most beautiful: a succession of rocky headlands and wooded coves, strung with palms and cypress trees, cacti and flowers. Despite the overexposure, it has an undeniable draw: sweeping seafront boulevards, little harbours crowded with yachts, magnificent beaches, hotels and restaurants. It makes a striking contrast with the mountainous hinterland, serene and mostly unspoilt.

The cooking of Provence and the Côte d'Azur is just as it should be: colourful and aromatic, imbued with the flavours of garlic, herbs and olive oil, with an emphasis

Below: Provençal sun gives tomatoes and other market produce colour and flavour that supermarkets can rarely match.

Above: Colombe d'Or, Saint-Paul-de-Venice.

on sun-loving vegetables and on fish. Traditionally it is simple, but it lends itself well to modern adaptations and the vagueries of fashion.

As a general rule, anything described as *à la Provençale* is cooked with tomatoes, olive oil, garlic, onions and herbs, while *à la Niçoise* indicates the inclusion of capers, anchovies and olives. The cooking of Nice shows the Italian influence in dishes such as ravioli, canneloni, gnocchi and *pissaladière* (onion bread pizza with anchovies and olives). Other great Niçoise dishes are *salade Niçoise*, *pan bagna*, *stoficado* (salt cod or stockfish stew); *soupe au pistou* (with a basil sauce, much like pesto) and ratatouille.

Apart from ratatouille, vegetables – fat, sun-ripened tomatoes, aubergines, artichokes, and fennel amongst others – crop up in dishes such as *tian* (cooked in a traditional gratin dish called a *tian*), *artichauds à la barigoule* (braised in wine with vegetables and sometimes stuffed with ham or mushrooms); or stuffed, fried, baked or grilled. *Crudités* are served with the pungent garlic sauce, aïoli; other local sauces are *tapenade*, with olives, *rouille* (with chilli and garlic), *anchoïade*, with anchovies, and *raito*, with red wine and walnuts.

The great fish soups of the Midi are found all along the coast, although traditionally *bouillabaisse* belongs to Marseille and bourride to Mediterranean Languedoc. *Bourride* is served with *aïoli*, and *bouillabaisse* (really a stew); and smooth, brown-orange *soupe de poissons*, with *rouille*. Amongst fish dishes, look out for the local speciality, *loup au fenouil* (sea bass with fennel), and also for

rougets à la Niçoise or *au fenouil*.

Amongst traditional meat dishes, the great beef *daube of Provence* – slow-cooked with red wine, tomatoes, orange peel and perhaps olives – stands out. Anchovies and beef are a surprisingly good combination, as in *estouffade de boeuf Provençal*, while lamb is also popular, and particularly prized if from the area around Sisteron where they graze naturally on wild herbs.

Cheeses make a limited appearance in the form of Banon, wrapped in chestnut leaves, and Picodon as well Brousse and Tomme from Bouches-du-Rhône, and Annot from Var.

The wines of the Midi fall into two distinct types, since technically the southern part of the Côtes du Rhône wines fall into the *département* of Vaucluse, which is in Provence. Names include Gigondas, Châteauneuf-du-Pape, Lirac and Tavel (the great majority of Côtes-du-Rhône are reds) as well as the sweet white Muscat de Beaumes-de-Venise (the perfect foil for *foie gras*, as well as for desserts). Then there are more southern wines: the reds and rosés of Côtes du Ventoux; the wines of Lubéron, and nearby Aix-en-Provence; the reds and dry, fruity rosés of Côtes de Provence, including those from north of Nice, made with the rare Bellet vine; and the refreshing wines of Cassis and Bandol on the Provence coast.

Top: La Maison, Beaumont-du-Ventoux.
Centre: La Bonne Etape, Châteaux-Arnoux.

Continued from page 304

CLOSED Sun dinner, Mon; mid-Nov to mid-Dec
CARDS AE, DC, MC, V

Fleurie
◆ Le Cep €€

place de l'Eglise, 69820 Fleurie
Tel 04 74 04 10 77 Fax 04 74 04 10 28

"**I** have decided to devote my cooking entirely to the cuisine de terroir," says Chantal Chagny, who sites Brillat-Savarin as her inspiration. "I would only want to serve *langoustines* if I lived by the sea." She has dropped a Michelin star (she now has just the one plus a well-deserved Bib Gourmand good value symbol) since her change of direction, but we ate a truly memorable lunch, including the best *coq au vin* we have ever tasted. Not surprising: it takes 60 litres of wine and days to prepare, with all the ingredients separately cooked in goose fat. The hand-written menus are a marvellous introduction to the cuisine of the whole region.

❝ *Simple, friendly dining room'* ... *'Old-fashioned charm'* ... *'Smart waiters* ❞

CLOSED Mon; Sun dinner, Tue Lunch; mid-Dec to mid-Jan, one week Feb, one week Aug
CARDS AE, MC, V

La Garde Adhémar
◆ Le Logis de l'Escalin
€€ – €€€

26700 La Garde Adhémar, Drôme
Tel 04 75 04 41 32 Fax 04 75 04 40 05

An ideal stopping place, off the A7 south of Montélimar, this beautiful old farmhouse is just outside the fortified medieval village of La Garde Adhémar. You are now in Provence, as the pretty dining rooms, terrace and seven charming bedrooms bear witness. The menus also veer in a southerly direction, but with great originality and style, starting with an *amuse bouche* of *mousse de bloody Mary fraîche*. Dishes are created from fresh market produce – take *melon à la gelée de Beaumes de Venise et copeaux de jambon de Parme* or *pièce d'ag-*

neau, or légumes longuement mijotés au jus de beaurre d'escargots - and there's plenty of choice. The selection of menus is topped by the *menu dégustation*, served to the whole table. It comprises 12 courses, but all *délicatesses servis en petites portions*.

❝ *The menu dégustation is to die for* ❞

CLOSED Sun dinner, Mon
CARDS AE, DC, MC, V

Grenoble
◆ Auberge Napoléon €€

7 rue Montorge, 38000 Grenoble, Isère
Tel 04 76 87 53 64 Fax 04 76 87 80 76

The famous general-emperor stopped here on his return from Elba at the beginning of his infamous 100 days, so this restaurant is dedicated to Napoléon. The dining room is decorated with Napoleonic bees and frescoes based around the revolutionary calendar. It is a fascinating and attractive building, appropriately done out in Empire style. There is just one menu, at 40 euros for four dishes, designed by the talented young chef, Agnès Chotin, who is very happy to give customers the recipe for her *plat de signature*: *le gourgouillon de caille*, but it is so incredibly difficult that it's much better to come here to taste it than try to cook it yourself.

❝ *The quail was superb* ❞

CLOSED Sun, Mon lunch, Tue lunch, Wed lunch
CARDS AE, MC, V

Grenoble
◆ Bistrot Lyonnais
€ – €€€ Fr

168 cours Berriat, 38000 Grenoble, Isère
Tel 04 76 21 95 33 Fax 04 76 21 95 33

As you would expect from its name, this rustic *auberge*, not far from the station, offers you specialities from Lyon – *andouillettes*, sausages, *boudins* and superb *charcuterie*, to say nothing of the incomparable *tarte tatin*. But the food is not the only attraction here: the lovely courtyard dazzles with the blue of its ancient, tumbling wisteria, which has apparently been classified as historically important by the town of

Grenoble, and you are assured a warm welcome from the cheerful staff.

> *'An oasis in town with a beautiful courtyard' ... 'A great find'*

Closed Sat, Sun
Cards AE, MC, V

● *For good-value bistro food, you can't do better in Grenoble than Le Petit Paris (04 76 46 00 51).*

Grignan
◆ Le Poème €–€€

montée du Tricot, 26230 Grignan, Drôme
Tel 04 75 91 10 90

In the town made famous by the Marquise de Sévigné, this little restaurant lies by the château where she is buried. Its literary name pays tribute to this lady of letters, and appropriately the restaurant is surrounded by bookshops. However, they are planning to move soon – staying in Grignan and keeping the same telephone number – so check the address before setting out. The food is essentially Provençal in style, beautifully presented and based on local ingredients. Specialities include a truly delicious rabbit *en croute aux girolles avec un jus au thym.*

> *It's as pretty and delicious to look at as the food it serves*

Closed Tue and Wed winter
Cards MC, V

Lamastre
◆ Hôtel du Midi
€€ – €€€

place Seignobos, 07270 Lamastre, Ardèche
Tel 04 75 06 41 50 Fax 04 75 06 49 75

At the heart of this hotel is a Michelin-starred restaurant, serving a very successful blend of traditional and modern dishes. With his variations on classic regional dishes – his *salade tiède de foie gras de canard et champignons des bois,* his *pigeon rôti à l'ail servi avec des lentilles vertes du Puy* and his *poularde de Bresse en vessie,*

for example – chef Bernard Perrier is giving his loyal clientele exactly the kind of cuisine they want. He is well-known for treating his ingredients with the greatest respect. Côtes-du-Rhône dominate the wine list, which is strong but expensive, as are the menus. The dining rooms are rather plain, but intimate, and the service is mostly helpful and friendly, though recent critics have accused the Midi of relying too much on its reputation. There are 12 tasteful, comfortable bedrooms in a separate building a minute's walk away.

> *The soufflé glacé aux marrons just melts in your mouth*

Closed Sun dinner, Mon, Fri dinner; mid-Dec to Feb
Cards AE, DC, MC, V

Limonest
◆ Gentil'Hordière
€ – €€€

route Mont Verdun, 69760 Limonest, Rhône
Tel 04 78 35 94 97 Fax 04 78 43 85 45

In summer it is a pure pleasure to sit out in the shade of the majestic plane trees on the terrace outside this *auberge*. In winter the dining room is as warm and inviting as the welcome. The chef, José Godart believes in basing his dishes on the freshest local produce he can find. They are fairly classically based, but always with an inventive twist (*cassolette de grenouilles aux champignons des bois*). As it's 13 km (8 miles) north of Lyon, this is a great place to break your journey from the UK to the Côte d'Azur (or vice versa). Take exit 22 off the A6 and follow the D42 to Limonest.

Closed Sat lunch, Sun dinner, Mon; 3 weeks Aug
Cards AE, MC, V

Lyon
◆ Les Adrets € – €€ Fr

30 rue de Boeuf, 69005 Lyon, Rhône
Tel 04 78 38 24 30 Fax 04 78 42 79 52

This bustling little bistro exudes the atmosphere of Old Lyon, and a warm welcome awaits guests in its rustic dining room, where the ceiling is beamed and the floor tiled. They specialize in splendid, suitably traditional fare at prices that offer excellent value for money, particularly at lunchtime, when the 13-euro menu must be the best bargain in town. The locals certainly think so, because it is packed out from midday, so be sure to book. In the evening, there are four menus (ranging from 19 to 38 euros). The most expensive offers no choice, but a fabulous five courses of *foie gras*, *cassolette de queues d'écrevisses et ravioles* (a speciality of the house), *filet de boeuf* with truffles, cheese and dessert. On the other menus, there's a choice of three or four dishes, and the fish is a particular treat, here in the heart of charcuteried Lyon. As you'd expect, the wine list is centred on the Rhône.

❝ *A real discovery ... excellent food at bargain prices* ❞

CLOSED Sat, Sun; Aug
CARDS MC, V

Lyon
◆ **Auberge de l'Ile** €€€

place Notre-Dame, l'Ile Barbe, 69009 Lyon, Rhône
Tel 04 78 83 99 49 Fax 04 78 47 80 46

On a verdant little island in the Saône river – a haven of tranquillity, this fairytale 17thC house has been beautifully modernized. The decoration reeks of elegance and simplicity, while the menu is just pure elegance without the simplicity. Jean-Christophe Ansanay-Alex joined this establishment ten years ago, celebrating his tenth anniversary with the reward of a second Michelin star. Don't be deceived – it is pricey (75 euros for the main menu; 60 euros if you decide against the lobster or caviar dishes). But the cooking is 'inspired by emotion' and totally original, evident in his confident, creative combinations of ingredients: warm salad of lobster in vanilla oil with mango, avocado and passionfruit; *turbot grillé sur un raviole de tapenade, tomate confite, et beurre d'agrumes*; and *nage d'huitres et Saint-Jacques avec un chantilly de caviare*. There is a set menu during the week, and menus change monthly.

❝ *Mouthwatering menus'...'A special place – ideal for romance* ❞

CLOSED Sun dinner and Mon Oct-Jun, Mon Jun-Oct
CARDS AE, DC, MC, V

Lyon
◆ **Bistrot du Palais** €

220 rue Duguesclin, 69003 Lyon, Rhône
Tel 04 78 14 21 21 Fax 04 78 14 21 22

What is it about Lyon that makes the people here so loyal to their *terroir* and so proud of the quality of their food? What accounts for the large numbers of good chefs and restaurants? Perhaps it all starts with Bocuse and Léon, who train so many chefs, who then go out into the world to 'carry the word' but rarely stray far from home. Olivier Belval, the Bistrot du Palais' extraordinarily talented chef, ran Léon de Lyon's kitchen before breaking out on his own ten years ago, when he joined this bright, attractive Lyonnaise restaurant with a magnificent covered terrace. His 20-euro menu changes daily, although he likes to keep his popular speciality *tartare de boeuf assaisonné par nos soins, et pommes grenaille*. He also offers the opportunity of ordering a single *plat du jour* with a green salad for 11 euros.

CLOSED Sun, Mon dinner
CARDS AE, MC, V

Lyon
◆ **Brasserie Georges** €

30 cours Verdun, 69002 Lyon, Rhône
Tel 04 72 56 54 54 Fax 04 78 42 51 65

Little has changed at this lively, much loved local restaurant since it opened in 1836. Huge and bustling, it is one of the oldest *brasseries* in Europe. The setting is still attractively and brightly Art Nouveau, and the cooking is based on local produce, with a northerly influence, evident in its speciality, *choucroute*. (It appears in *The Guinness Book of Records* for producing the largest ever *choucroute*, weighing 1.5 tonnes.) It offers a good selection of beers – its motto is: 'Bonne bière et bonne chère depuis 1836' – in addition to an excellent-value wine list. The Brasserie Georges has an attractive terrace, and has been a haunt of the rich and famous since Hemingway, Rodin, Sartre and Zola were customers, more because it is an address which is sought after by 'those in the know', than because of its low prices.

CLOSED never
CARDS AE, DC, MC, V

Lyon
◆ Café des Fédérations ⓔ **Fr**

8-10 rue du Major Martin, 69001 Lyon, Rhône
Tel 04 78 28 26 00 Fax 04 72 07 74 52

If you're after the ultimate Lyon *bouchon*, look no further than this café. It is the genuine article, from its checked tablecloths to the *charcuterie* over the bar. And the simple menu offers food that is the most typical Lyonnais in the whole of Lyon. Steer clear if you're vegetarian, watching your cholesterol or are not partial to pork. *Charcuterie, terrine, civet de joue de porc, tripes maison, andouillettes* in mustard sauce, *tête de veau, poulet au vinaigre* number among dishes that could not be more typical of the city and make a refreshing change from the inevitable *grasse double à la Lyonnaise*. Book ahead – the real Lyon is in great demand.

CLOSED Sat, Sun, Aug
CARDS DC, MC, V

Our traditional French cuisine symbol
So many of our readers enjoy seeking out the genuinely French eating experience that we have used Fr to mark restaurants which offer *cuisine du terroir*, classical French dishes or regional dishes with an emphasis on local ingredients, and traditional recipes.

Lyon
◆ La Meunière ⓔ **Fr**

11 rue Neuve, 69001 Lyon, Rhône
Tel 04 78 28 62 91

At first glance you might walk past this old-fashioned little *bouchon*, still decorated as it was when it opened in the 1920s, but venture in and you will find that the food on offer is of such quality, and that the customers are greeted with such warmth and affection, that they return time after time. There are three lunchtime menus and two more comprehensive ones available at dinner. They cite as their most triumphant

dishes the *daube de joues de boeuf* and the veal kidneys roasted with shallots.

❝*A little place with a great reputation*❞

CLOSED Sun, Mon; late Jul to late Aug
CARDS MC, V

Lyon
◆ Le Passage ⓔ – ⓔⓔ

8 rue Plâtre, 69001 Lyon, Rhône
Tel 04 78 28 11 16 Fax 04 72 00 84 34

The food is excellent here, not heavily Lyonnais in style, but based in Lyon while lightening it with influences and ingredients from all over France. The menu includes salads and a wide variety of meat and fish dishes that are all extremely appealing. It's not just for the food, however, that Le Passage is so popular in Lyon, it is also for its style and theatre. In the small upstairs dining room, you will sit in the velour chairs that once lined the Eldorado Theatre, surrounded by dramatic decoration and *trompe l'oeils*. And in the courtyard, sink into the comfort of armchairs that came from the Majestic Hotel in Cannes. This is the style and individuality that the Lyonnais seek when they come here – again and again. Booking essential.

CLOSED Sun, Mon
CARDS AE, DC, MC, V

Lyon
◆ Petit Léon ⓔ

3 rue Pleney, 69001 Lyon, Rhône
Tel 04 72 10 11 11 Fax 04 72 10 11 13

Jean-Paul Lacombe made his name at the two-rosette Léon de Lyon, the smart, prestigious, expensive address, renowned throughout the centre of France. But the simple charms and low prices of the Petit Léon, which he has opened next door, are far more appealing. It is one of the cheapest and most convivial bistros in the city. The formula is simple: there is one menu (at 16 euros) with a choice of *entrées, plats du jour* and cheeses or desserts, which changes daily according to the market. It is only open for lunch, and it is essential to book, because this cosy little room, decorated with old advertising posters, buzzes – mostly with locals – every lunchtime. The food is as delicious as you would expect from Lacombe's kitchen: fairly Lyonnais in style, and excellent quality.

Jean-Paul Lacombe is a genius

CLOSED dinner, Sun, Mon
CARDS AE, DC, MC, V

Lyon
◈ Le Tour Rose €€€

22 rue du Boeuf, 69005 Lyon, Rhône
Tel 04 78 37 25 90 Fax 04 78 42 26 02

Philippe Chavent, a Lyon chef with a Michelin star, is something of a Renaissance man. In Saint-Jean, the old quarter, he has renovated a mainly 17thC building to create a dramatic, exclusive small hotel and restaurant. The atmosphere rekindles that of the great Florentine bankers' and merchants' residences, with balustraded galleries, ornamental ponds with waterfalls, terraced gardens and, at its heart, a pink tower. The dining room is in the 13thC chapel of a former convent, with a cobbled terrace and a fabulous glass extension, which opens to the sky in the summer. M. Chavent's cooking is a perfect complement to the architecture, equally innovative, harmonious and beautifully presented. His signature dish is *saumon mi-cuit au fumoir servi tiède au naturel*, and the wine list reads like a textbook of classic vintages. Try to have an aperitif in the bar, where the fireplace was rescued from a condemned château and the panelling comes from the law courts at Chambéry.

CLOSED Sun, lunch Aug
CARDS AE, DC, MC, V

Malataverne
◈ La Domaine du Colombier €€ – €€€

route de Donzère, 26780 Malataverne, Drôme
Tel 04 75 90 86 86 Fax 04 75 90 79 40

Meticulously restored and full of flowers and colour, this pleasing 14thC stone building, once a coaching inn where pilgrims stopped on the road to Santiago de Compostela, remains an ideal place for travellers to break their journey (largely due to its position near the *autoroute*, yet in the countryside). With its vine-clad façade, stone staircases, tiled roof, wrought-iron railings and penchant for flowers, you really feel that you're on the road to the south. Wild flowers, gathered in the grounds, brighten every table, and service is efficient and professional. When the weather is favourable (and the infamous mistral is not blowing) guests dine on the terrace, which is, again, packed with flowers and enchanting in the evening glow of lamplight. There is also a large restaurant with a vaulted ceiling, where the food, based on local specialities, has acquired a solid reputation.

CLOSED never
CARDS AE, DC, MC, V

Manigod
◈ Chalet Hôtel de la Croix-Fry €– €€€ Fr

rue du Col de la Croix-Fry, Manigod, 74230 Thônes, Haute-Savoie
Tel 04 50 44 90 16 Fax 04 50 44 94 87

At the highest point of an alpine col, its terrace overflowing with flowers, this wooden mountain chalet is run with great pride by a third generation of Veyrats – the chalet was once shared in the summer by the family and their cows. Cosy and welcoming, the restaurant, under the direction of Marie-Ange Veyrat, whose brother Marc is one of Savoy's culinary celebrities (see La Ferme de mon Père, below) serves nourishing mountain food (smoked ham, rabbit with wild thyme and a bilberry tart that has many admirers). There are also spectacular views of the surrounding peaks and valleys, but what really impresses is the evident pride of the family and the effort they make to ensure that their guests enjoy their food. The Veyrats love running their small hotel (it has just ten rooms) and restaurant, and the pleasure shows.

CLOSED Mon low season, Tue lunch; mid-Sep to mid-Dec, mid-Apr to mid-Jun
CARDS AE, MC, V

Megève
◈ La Ferme de mon Père
€€€

367 route du Crêt, 74120 Megève, Haute-Savoie
Tel 04 50 21 01 01 Fax 04 50 21 43 43

Ask any Frenchman about Marc Veyrat and he will have a story and a knowledgeable opinion. Arguably the most brilliant contemporary chef, and certainly the most eccentric, self-willed and passionate about his patrimony, he now possesses six Michelin stars: three for his Auberge de l'Eridan near Annecy and three for this new venture, which is part gastronomic centre, part museum. His dream was to recreate the farm in which he had been brought up, and to this end he bought a large chalet, ripped out the interior, and uses it as a backdrop for his culinary theatricals. Black hat on head, he strides across the Savoyard mountains in search of gentians, violets, hysop and crocus pistils, and experiments with mosses and shrubs to create stunning combinations, always different, imaginative and virtually impossible to describe. Caviare jelly, mandarin-flavoured scampi and *foie gras* sorbet can appear on his *menu symphonie* or *menu sonate*. Savour these extraordinary delights in the huge wooden salon with sheep and chicken staring up at you through glass panes in the floor from the *bergerie* below. The dairy, multi-coloured bee hives, stables, cider press, farm objects and windmill have all been painstakingly reconstructed by this mad philosopher-poet-maverick-genius-artist-chef to give you the most unforgettable experience of your holiday, even though it will put a serious dent in your credit card.

❛ *An incomparable experience* ❜

Closed Mon; May-Dec
Cards AE, DC, MC, V

Megève
◈ Flocons de Sel
€ – €€€

75 rue Saint-François, 74120 Megève, Haute-Savoie
Tel 04 50 21 49 99 Fax 04 50 21 68 22

In the heart of the village, this 19thC farmhouse is an extraordinarily pretty place with a Michelin star (so you must book a table). Emmanuel Renaut is a Marc Veyrat disciple, who set out to create his own style just four years ago, and has quickly made a reputation for his light, fine cuisine and beautiful presentation. There is a good-value lunch menu and, in the evening, two *sel au sucre* menus, full of innovation and real class. One of his favourite inventions is *langoustines rôties sur leur consommé en gelée, émulsion de jus de maïs et coulis de coriandre*. The dessert menu is also unique.

❛ *A country-style restaurant ... wonderfully different food* ❜

Closed Tue and Wed low season
Cards MC, V

Méribel
◈ Allodis € – €€€

Le Belvedère, BP43, 73552 Méribel, Savoie
Tel 04 79 00 56 00 Fax 04 79 00 59 28

At 1,800m (6,000ft) high, in winter you can ski right down to the doors of this attractive chalet hotel, and either eat in the elegant restaurant or on the broad, bustling, sunny terrace. Alain Plouzané presents four menus, based on traditional local dishes, but spiced up by his ever-fertile imagination, evident in his specialities: *pigeonneau rôti en croûte de noisettes* and *tatin de cèpes de Méribel et petite salade de beatilles*. For 59 euros, he will also offer a seven-course *menu découverte – élaboré au moment par le chef* – but only if the whole table orders it. The hotel's excellent facilities include a small indoor swimming pool, fitness centre and half-tennis court.

❛*Extremely good food and very comfortable* ❜

Closed Sep to mid-Dec, late Apr to Jul
Cards MC, V

Montmerle-sur-Sâone
◈ Emile Job €€ Fr

12 rue de Pont, 01090 Montmerle-sur-Sâone, Ain
Tel 04 74 69 33 92 Fax 04 74 69 49 21

The terrace, in the shade of huge lime trees, is the principal charm of this pleasant restaurant in the Hôtel du Rivage beside the river Sâone. Although the plate-glass entrance is rather off-putting, once inside the feeling is of a *bourgeoise* country house, and the food, cooked by M. Job and M. Lépine (the husbands of the two couples who run the hotel-restaurant) is typical of the region. Their *grenouilles persillées* are meltingly good, as is the *poulet de Bresse à la crème aux morilles*. Rather ambitiously they cover six menus – the 19 and 26 euro ones are available at weekday lunchtimes only. A warm welcome and courteous service make this an extremely agreeable stop; and the home-made puddings are irresistible.

CLOSED Mon, Tue lunch high season, Sun dinner low season
CARDS AE, MC, V

Pierrelatte
◆ Le Gourmand Gourmet €€ – €€€

6 place Eglise, 26700 Pierrelatte, Drôme
Tel 04 75 96 83 10 Fax 04 75 96 46 18

Next to the church in the old town, this pretty Provençal-style yellow-walled restaurant is actually carved out of an ancient stone-fronted abbey. They describe their food as *'une cuisine gastro-créative soignée'*, born out by the excellent and refreshingly different dishes created by the imaginative young chef, Frédéric Dumoulin. In his *carpaccio de boeuf* and *médaillon de lotte*, with a *beurre de tomates*, he experiments not just with local traditions, but borrows from other areas in France and elsewhere in an attractively eclectic way.

❛The service is attentive but not intrusive ❜

CLOSED Fri lunch, Sat lunch, every second Sat dinner
CARDS AE, MC, V

Le Poët-Laval
◆ Les Hospitaliers
€€€ – €€€€

Le Poët-Laval, 26160 La Bégude-de-Mazenc, Drôme
Tel 04 75 46 22 32 Fax 04 75 46 49 99

This distinctive hotel and restaurant has an unusual position within the ramparts of a 13thC castle above a perched medieval village. The attractive old stone buildings were formerly part of a stronghold of the Knights of Malta (the Maltese cross is the hotel's emblem). From the terrace, where meals are served in fine weather, there are spectacular views across wooded countryside to hills beyond. Owner Bernard Morin's father was an art dealer, which accounts for the interesting collection of pictures decorating the walls of the restaurant. Tables are laid with fine china, white linen and candles. The service is hard to fault, and the food is excellent. Bernard is the cook, and he uses the freshest produce available for his menu, which changes daily. His younger brother is the *sommelier*, in charge of a wide-ranging cellar, and the welcome from the entire family is warm and genuine.

CLOSED Mon and Tue low season; mid-Nov to Feb
CARDS AE, DC, MC, V

Rillieux-la-Pape
◆ Larivoire €€ – €€€€

26 chemin des Iles, 69140 Rillieux-la-Pape, Rhône
Tel 04 78 88 50 92 Fax 04 78 88 35 22

Ten minutes from the hurly-burly of the city centre, you can be relaxing on the terrace of this ancient rose-coloured restaurant beside the Rhône. The husband-and-wife team of Bernard and Chantal Constantin will look after your comfort and taste-buds with great attention and style. Bernard (a Maître Cuisinier de France) changes his menu four times a year, but, by popular re-quest, his *carte* always includes his magnificent starter of *oeufs en cocotte aux langoustines et morilles*. He is a chef who lets his imagination and instinct lead him; in-deed, there is a *menu dégustation*, which you are vociferously encouraged to try, consisting of four dishes (each of small portions), created according to *'l'imagination du moment'*.

❛An absolutely lovely place'...
'Every dish is an event ... certainly merits its Michelin rosette ❜

CLOSED Sun dinner, Mon dinner, Tue; last 2 weeks Aug
CARDS AE, MC, V

Roanne
◆ Auberge Costelloise
€ – €€€

*2 avenue Libération, 42120 Coteau,
Roanne, Loire
Tel 04 77 68 12 71 Fax 04 77 72 26 78*

There are three good reasons for visiting this attractive restaurant: its pleasant Loire-side setting (which you can enjoy to the full on the small but pretty terrace), its beautiful Art Deco decoration, and the superb food. There is an excellent-value lunch for 14 euros, rather misleadingly called a *menu rapide*, because nothing is skimped in Christophe Souchon's kitchen. It is often referred to as 'the best restaurant in Roanne', though the competition is exceedingly steep. It has one Michelin star, richly deserved by the largely classical cuisine: river fish and Christophe Souchon's famous *risotto de poulet fermier*, which truly melts in the mouth.

❛ *This restaurant on the right bank of the Loire is well worth a detour'
... 'Excellent value and quality* ❜

Closed Sun, Mon Jul-Sep
Cards AE, MC, V

Roanne
◆ Château de Champlong
€ – €€€

*100 chemin de la Chapelle, 42300 Villerest,
Roanne, Loire
Tel 04 77 69 69 69 Fax 04 77 69 71 08*

At the helm of this elegant 15thC château, surrounded by glorious parkland in the heart of the *pays Poannais*, the Boizets make a formidable partnership. She (Véronique) is a perfect hostess: charming and accommodating, calling herself 'la fée du domaine'. He (Olivier) learned his trade at the feet of Maximin and Georges Blanc, (see Chez Blanc p300 and Georges Blanc p333) and and he is a superb cook. They bought the château ten years ago and have restored it beautifully. The 17-euro weekday lunchtime menu is irresistibly good value, but, if you feel more indulgent, there is an incredible array of other tempting versions.

Alternatively you can try Olivier's *menu surprise*: *au gré de mes humeurs*, which he will create from scratch when he knows which wines you have chosen. This takes time, of course, because: "La cuisine est un art et tout art est patience." Olivier favours ceps in autumn, Jerusalem artichokes and truffles in winter, asparagus in spring and tomatoes in summer. He sees himself as an instinctive, artistic chef, and relies heavily on vegetables – a great rarity in France.

❛ *A glorious spot, delicious food and smiling, personal service – you could hardly ask for more* ❜

Closed Sun dinner, Mon, Tue Sep-Jul
Cards AE, DC, MC, V

Romans-sur-Isère
◆ La Fourchette   € – €€

*8 rue de Solférino, 26100 Romans-sur-Isère, Drôme
Tel 04 75 02 12 94 Fax 04 75 05 07 61*

This pretty oasis right in the heart of Romans-sur-Isère is an 18thC house with an attractive little dining room and, more importantly, a delightful garden. Here, you can relax in the shade of the huge, old trees, perhaps after a busy morning sight-seeing (you might end up in the extraordinary Musée de la Chaussure next-door). You can tell that La Fourchette is family run the moment you walk through the door and are greeted by a friendly, welcoming smile. The food ranges from simple classic fare – excellently cooked and presented – to more ambitious ingredients such as lobster and *foie gras*. Whatever your mood or your appetite, you should find something to suit your palate (and your wallet) in this calm relaxing spot.

Closed Sun dinner, Mon, Thu dinner low season
Cards MC, V

Saint-Agrève
◆ Domaine de Rilhac
€ – €€€

*lieu dit Rilhac, 07320 Saint-Agrève, Ardèche
Tel 04 75 30 20 20 Fax 04 75 30 20 20*

If you like chic bustle, then the Domaine de Rilhac is not for you. However, if you're looking for peace and quiet, and light, fascinating food, then you will love this place. Lost in the Ardèche countryside, this old farmhouse is run by Ludovic Sinz, who trained under such illustrious chefs as Chibois (see Bastide Saint-Antoine, page 360) and Alain Ducasse (see Hostellerie de l'Abbaye de La Celle, page 356), and has one Michelin star. His specialities, he claims, are his *salade de truite*, *carpaccio de boeuf au Cornas* and *nougat glacé aux marrons confits*, but his menus (from 21 to 66 euros) all reflect true Ardèchois traditions and styles. The wine list is strongly Rhône-orientated, happily including many small *vignerons*, rather than *negotiats*. There are also eight bright, pretty bedrooms.

Closed Tue dinner, Wed, Thu lunch
Cards AE, DC, MC, V

Fr French regional or classical French dishes on menu.

Saint-Etienne
◆ Bistrot de Paris €

7 place Jean-Jaurès, 42000 Saint-Etienne, Loire
Tel 04 77 32 21 50

As the name suggests, this is a simple but charming bistro, where the food is impeccably cooked and then served in a real *brasserie* ambience. The Stephanois (as the people of Saint-Etienne call themselves) have been flocking to this little gem of a place for all of its 20 years' existence, enjoying, in particular, the excellent steaks from local herds. The very reasonable 21-euro menu also offers many other delights, including some Italian specialities. In summer, the terrace, in the stylish, attractive surroundings of place Jean-Jaurès, comes into its own.

❬ *One of the best steaks I've eaten in France'* ...
... *'A delightful, bustling bistro with excellent service* ❭

Closed Sat lunch, Sun, Mon Sep-May
Cards AE, MC, V

Saint-Etienne
◆ du Musée €

Musée d'Art Moderne, 42000 Saint-Etienne, Loire
Tel 04 77 79 24 52

If you are visiting the fabulous Museum of Modern Art in Saint-Etienne, don't hesitate to take a break half way round in its stylish, modern restaurant. Run by an enthusiastic young team with a philosophy of offering good quality, adventurous food at affordable prices. You can choose from a variety of delicious light dishes, but their mouthwatering fish recipes are worth a special mention.

❬ *Excellent value, excellent quality* ❭

Closed Sun dinner
Cards none

Our price bands
€ 15 Euros or less €€ 30-50 Euros
€€€ 50+ Euros for a menu.

Saint-Gervais-les-Bains
◆ Chalet Rémy € Fr

le Bettex, 74170 Saint-Gervais-les-Bains, Haute-Savoie
Tel 04 50 93 11 85 Fax 04 50 93 14 45

In sharp contrast to the glossy chalet hotels and restaurants of nearby Megève (see pages 325-326), this chalet is as simple – and as genuine – as you could hope to find, with all the associated charm and character. With breathtaking views across to Mont Blanc, it's a traditional 18thC stone and log farmhouse, with its original woodwork and an interior that seems to have been frozen in time for at least 50 years. Traditional, satisfying dishes are served in a candlelit dining room, and there's a fine terrace with views overlooking the garden and the mountains.

❬ *Charmingly old-fashioned'* ...
'Arrive with an appetite – the food is robust, portions are large ❭

Closed never
Cards MC, V

Saint-Julien-en-Genevois
◆ La Ferme de l'Hospital
€€ – €€€

rue Molard, Bossey, 74160 Saint-Julien-en-Genevois, Haute-Savoie
Tel 04 50 43 61 43 Fax 04 50 95 31 53

Once the farm that supplied its produce to Geneva's main hospital, this one-Michelin-rosette restaurant has gained a justifiably high reputation for superb, creative food at prices that are honest, if not exactly cheap. It is run by Sylvie and Jean-Jacques Noguier – he in the kitchen, she in the pleasant, bright, bay-windowed dining room, or on the pleasantly green verandah, with views of Mont-Salève. The menus start at 32 euros and offer delectable combinations; many based on the 'fruit of the lake' (*écrevisses* or *féra*) and the 'fruit of the mountains' (Beaufort cheese, beef and ceps), used creatively and instinctively with a rare degree of finesse. You must book as it's extremely popular with locals and, as it's only a few minutes from Geneva (5 km/3 miles east of Saint-Julien via the N206), the Noguiers have little problem filling their elegant tables with eager customers.

CLOSED Sun, Mon
CARDS AE, DC, MC, V

Saint-Martin-le-Vinoux
◆ Pique-Pierre €€

1 rue Conrad Kilien, 38950 Saint-Martin-le-Vinoux, Grenoble, Isère
Tel 04 76 46 12 88 Fax 04 76 46 43 90

In its mirrored dining room or on the lovely terrace, this restaurant is popular for its country feel (despite its proximity to Grenoble and the *autoroutes*) and for its superb cooking. There are excellent menus at 30 euros (four courses) and 42 euros (five courses), and the *carte* is also attractive and inviting, given the interesting and commendable idea of pricing for both *petits appétits* and *grands appétits*. The puddings are sublime, especially the calorie-laden chocolate *puck* and *chartrousien*. They sometimes hold wine study evenings, and choose interesting selections as 'wines of the month', reflecting a rounded gastronomic approach.

CLOSED Sun dinner, Wed dinner; Mon
CARDS AE, MC, V

Samoëns
◆ Gite du Lac de Gers € Fr

74340 Samoëns, Haute-Savoie
Tel 04 50 34 44 83 Fax 04 50 89 52 92

Probably the most unusual restaurant in this guide and certainly the hardest to get to, this pretty wooden Savoyarde chalet is hidden away from civilization on the tranquil lake Gers, a haven of peace and beauty. There are three methods of access: across country in a 4x4; in summer, by parking your car either at Leddedien, near Samoëns, and walking for an hour and a half, or at Englène, near Sixt, and walking for two hours along the beautiful GR96; and, in winter, on skis by the *piste bleu des cascades* and the *piste noir de la combe de Gers*. If this sounds complicated, telephone the delightful Cottets, who will give you reassurance and more detailed directions. Pam is Scottish and her husband, the chef, Jean-Maurice, comes from Samoëns. The food is fairly simple, but absolutely authentic Savoy fare – *fondues*, *raclettes*, *reblochonnade* and *braserade*, plus two excellent-value menus. It is a perfect spot for nature lovers, hikers and skiers. Surrounded by Alpine flowers, chamois, eagles and marmots, you find the stresses of the world will melt away. In summer they offer *gite* accommodation.

❢ *A little paradise in the Alps - truly uncommercial and welcoming* ❢

CLOSED May
CARDS none

Saoû
◆ L'Oiseau sur sa Branche € Fr

la Placette, 26400 Saoû, Drôme
Tel 04 75 76 02 03 Fax 04 75 76 05 02

An excellent little café-restaurant in a very pretty village, appealing not just for its low prices and warm, bistro atmosphere, but for its lack of pretension and its family feeling. The food is simple but irresistible, and if they have their splendid *caillette de l'oiseau et ravioles de la mère Maury, pâtes à l'ail et tomates fraîches* on their menu, don't hesitate to order it. Even the local goats' cheese, *picodon du roc*, is remarkable; and it's not often that you stop and savour goats' cheese.

❛ This lovely place is definitely worth making a detour to ❜

CLOSED Mon and Tue Sep-Jul
CARDS none

Saint-Priest-en-Jarez
◆ Le Clos Fleuri
€ – €€€

*76 avenue Albert Raimond, 42270 Saint-Priest-en-Jarez, Saint-Etienne, Loire
Tel 04 77 74 63 24 Fax 04 77 79 06 70*

As you would expect from its name, this elegant restaurant is surrounded by a lovely garden, so its terrace is a delight. Patrick Mathis is the chef, and he suggests his signature dish of *foie chaud poêlé au pain d'épice*. They buy the *pain d'épice* – like so much of their fresh produce – from a local producer; in this case, from a beekeeper in the gorges of the Loire. Patrick creates five menus. None has any choice, because he believes in putting together a perfect combination when he creates each menu. Although there are some possibilities for vegetarians, the options are pretty limited, so it's advisable to telephone in advance to warn them.

CLOSED Sun dinner, Mon dinner, Wed
CARDS AE, MC, V

Tain-l'Hermitage
◆ Rive Gauche
€ – €€

*17 rue Joseph Péala, 26600 Tain-l'Hermitage, Ardèche
Tel 04 75 07 05 90 Fax 04 75 07 05 90*

When Pierre Reboul used to leave his famous *escalope de foie gras poêlée, pomme passion* off the menu, his customers would revolt, so now it is a permanent feature in this restaurant bordering the Rhône.

As you would expect from its riverside setting, the menus have a bias towards fish and shellfish, but always cooked with originality and style; for instance, in the *boudins de tourteaux et langoustines*, the lobster *sushi* and the *Saint-Pierre en croute de meringue et d'épices*, which comes beautifully presented on a sea of beetroot juice. There is a terrace for summer dining, which gives a pleasing view over the medieval town of Tournon, with its château, and the restaurant itself is decorated in the style of an old river steamer. The *carte des vins* is both excellent and extensive, geared to the Rhône, but also with intelligent choices from Burgundy, Bordeaux and even Chile and Spain, although it's unlikely that anyone would want to accompany a Rhône meal beside the Rhône river with a Spanish wine.

CLOSED Sun dinner, Mon, Wed lunch Jun-Oct, Wed dinner Oct-Jun
CARDS MC, V

Uriage-les-Bains
◆ Les Terrasses
€€ – €€€

*le Grand Hôtel, 38410 Uriage-les-Bains, Isère
Tel 04 76 89 10 80 Fax 04 76 89 04 62*

This restaurant is part of a fabulous hotel in a huge, peaceful park. As it is also a 'cure', it makes a great stop on the way back from the Alps, so that you can rest your aching muscles in the spa waters. Even non-skiers will enjoy the brilliantly innovative cuisine of Philippe Brouisseau, especially when they can enjoy it on the agreeable summer terrace. The menus are not cheap, but considering the generosity and style of the dishes, they constitute real value – especially the 46-euro *menu des découvertes*, which offers three smaller portions of the specialities, plus a dessert, and a mountain of *amuses gueules* to start. The cheese platter is perfect, representing the entire area with integrity and at the peak of maturity.

❛ A gorgeous place' ... 'Expensive, but worth it ❜

CLOSED Sun and Mon and Tue-Thu lunch Sep-Jul, Wed Jul-Sep; late Aug to early Sep
CARDS AE, DC, MC, V

Val-d'Isère
◆ La Becca €€ – €€€

*le Laisinet, 73150 Val-d'Isère, Savoie
Tel 04 79 06 09 48 Fax 04 79 41 12 03*

Something different from Val-d'Isère's massed ranks of fast eateries and formulaic restaurants, La Becca is in a charming spot, outside the hubbub of the town centre (but still only three minutes away by car) in a renovated old farming settlement at the foot of 'L' and Mattis *pistes*. There is an informal *après-ski* atmosphere in the stone and pine dining room, where the food on offer strikes an excellent balance between local dishes and ones from elsewhere. Though pricey, it is considered by some to be the most serious food in the valley, and worth the cost if you're tired of what the town centre restaurants are offering.

❢ *Chunky medallions of duck and subtle cod flavoured with fennel* ❢

CLOSED early May to late Jun, late Aug to Dec
CARDS AE, DC, MC, V

Looking for somewhere to stay? See page 241.

Valence
◆ Maison Pic €€€

*285 avenue Victor Hugo, 26001 Valence, Drôme
Tel 04 75 44 15 32 Fax 04 75 40 96 03*

Despite the death a decade ago of Jacques Pic, son of its founder, this remains (under his daughter Anne Pic-Sinapian) one of the best restaurants in the country, with two Michelin stars – yet remains delightfully modest (not a word you could apply to the prices though). The cuisine is, as you would expect, classic, employing ingredients of the highest quality. On her menus and *carte*, Anne retains the traditional *grands plats*, on which Pic's reputation was based, but with her own inimitable stamp. *Filet de loup au caviar 'Jacques Pic'*, *palourdes et seiches en jus de bouillabaisse* and *rougets de roche en barigoule* are among her specialities. The cellar contains some superb Côtes-du-Rhône.

CLOSED Sun dinner, Mon; 3 weeks Jan
CARDS AE, DC, MC, V

Vallon-Pont-d'Arc
◆ Le Manoir du Raveyron € Fr

*rue Henri Barbusse, 07150 Vallon-Pont-d'Arc, Ardèche
Tel 04 75 88 03 59 Fax 04 75 37 11 12*

It sounds grand, but it is nothing of the sort: this is the sort of rustic village *auberge* that is the bedrock of French innkeeping – a two-fireplace *logis* offering simple accommodation, modest prices, a warm welcome and excellent wholesome food (visit the place on a Sunday and you'll find it bursting at the seams with lunching families). It faces an ugly modern building, but the surroundings do not intrude, because the old stone building is set well back from the street, behind gates and a large, leafy courtyard garden.

❢ *Cosy family inn ... delicious home-cooked food* ❢

CLOSED Nov-Mar
CARDS MC, V

Vals-les-Bains
◆ Hôtel du Vivarais €€ – €€€

*5 avenue C. Expilly, 07600 Vals-les-Bains, Ardèche
Tel 04 75 94 65 85 Fax 04 75 37 65 47*

You might not realize it, but there are five 'great traditional varieties of chestnut' found in the Ardèche: the Sardonne, the Aguyane, the Comballe, the Bouche Rouge and the Merle. And behind the pink façade of the Hôtel du Vivarais, built at the turn of the 20th century, with wonderful terraces fringed with flowers, Christiane Bossi-Brioude (the fifth generation of chefs here) pays homage to chestnut cuisine with real energy. There is a 38-euro *tout chataigne* menu, including chestnut soup (with chestnut bread) or ham dried with chestnut flour, followed by pigeon stuffed with chestnuts, and – guess what – a frozen soufflé of chestnuts with chocolate and *marron glacé*.

There are two other menus, which weave in and out of the chestnut theme, and a gastronomic *carte*. It is a cuisine of passion and takes pleasure in all ingredients Ardèchois.

CLOSED Feb
CARDS AE, DC, MC, V

Vinezac
◆ La Bastide du Soleil

€€ – €€€

l'ancien Château, 07110 Vinezac, Ardèche
Tel 04 75 36 91 66 Fax 04 75 36 91 59

With its views over the lavender, vines and olive groves of the Cevennes, this beautifully restored 17thC château is a splendid place to stop for a meal while visiting this stunning part of the country (leave the A7 at Montélimar or Bollène). You might even be tempted to stay as the village is medieval and car-free, and the château has six glorious, huge bedrooms. The restaurant, at the top of the monumental staircase, is another delight, with dishes invented by Fabien Loszach, who trained under Ducasse among others. He relishes fresh simplicity, is influenced by the south, but is not constricted by style or price. His summer menu features an extremely rich lobster *entrée* with a peppered iced accompaniment. It also offers a refreshing and far more affordable *salade de fleurs et herbes amères* and a huge salad (*du moment*) in truffle oil. His fish selection is impressive, and his meat dishes are usually topped by a fabulous *méridionale de râble de lapin girolles et salade d'herbes*.

CLOSED Mon-Wed Sep-Jul, Thu-Sat lunch; mid-Nov to Easter
CARDS AE, DC, MC, V

Vonnas
◆ L'Ancienne Auberge

€ – €€ **Fr**

place du Marché, 01540 Vonnas, Ain
Tel 04 74 50 90 50 Fax 04 74 50 08 80

If you want to sample George Blanc's cuisine and style at half the price of the eponymous flagship of the empire (see this page), the Ancienne Auberge offers you the chance. Reconstructed to look like the original inn owned by the Blancs in 1872, it is pretty with a *brasserie* style and a delightful flowery inner courtyard. The food is regional, and the prices fair. Frogs' legs and *poulet à la crème* are the more famous elements of the 17 and 40-euro menus. It is always busy and popular, and no wonder.

❝ *Wonderful traditional food'* ...
'*Make sure you book* ❞

CLOSED never
CARDS AE, DC, MC, V

---

charmingsmallhotels.co.uk
Visit Duncan Petersen's travel website, the best online search tool for places to stay that combine character and charm. Currently features Britain, France, Italy and Ireland, with other destinations being continuously added.

Vonnas
◆ Georges Blanc €€€

place du Marché, 01540 Vonnas, Ain
Tel 04 74 50 90 90 Fax 04 74 50 08 80

The Blanc dynasty broke into catering in 1872 when Georges Blanc's great-grandfather set up as an innkeeper in Vonnas. From such modest beginnings, it has blossomed into a grand gastronomic empire with this three-Michelin star restaurant-hotel as its stunning flagship. Flowers abound in the pretty village, the beamed salon and around the stone-flagged dining room, which overlooks a tranquil park. You could describe the style as 'farmhouse chic', and the Georges Blanc watchwords are 'tradition, imagination and conviviality. The cuisine is largely Bressane, and one of the signature dishes is *poulet de Bresse comme au G7 avec gousses d'ail et sauce foie gras*, originally created to please the palates of the G7 heads of state in 1996. The menus are mouthwatering, but beware, this place is only for those with a healthy appetite and a healthy bank balance. *Foie gras*, caviar and lobster abound on the menus, served by a succession of charming waiters. There is, as you would expect, a superb wine list.

CLOSED Mon-Wed lunch (except bank hols)
CARDS AE, DC, MC, V

LANGUEDOC-ROUSSILLON

S tretched between the peaks of the Pyrénées and the Cévennes and the Mediterranean coastline of the Golfe du Lion, Languedoc-Roussillon bears the traces of many civilizations that have gone before. Strong reminders of the Middle Ages exist in the Cathar fortresses, in towns like Carcassonne, Aigues-Mortes, and in the wealth of Romanesque churches, while Nîmes is still imbued with its Roman past. At the border with Spain, Pyrénées-Orientales and its capital Perpignan continue to celebrate its Catalan lifestyle. All across this sun-frazzled southern region of France there are vineyards, as well as memorable gorges, creeks and caves. In the centre is the dynamic regional capital, Montpellier, famous for its university and medical school.

MIDI-PYRENEES

Toulouse

Olargues 345

Saint-Pons-de-Thomières 348

Magalas 342

Castelnaudary 339

Bize-Minervois 338

Béziers

Carcassonne 338

Ouveillan 346

Narbonne

Ornaisons 346

Bages 337

LANGUEDOC-ROUSSILLON

Gincla 341

Perpignan 346

Molitg-les-Bains 344

Banyuls-sur-Mer 337

Argelès-sur-Mer 336

Port-Verdes 347

ESPAGNA

Céret 339

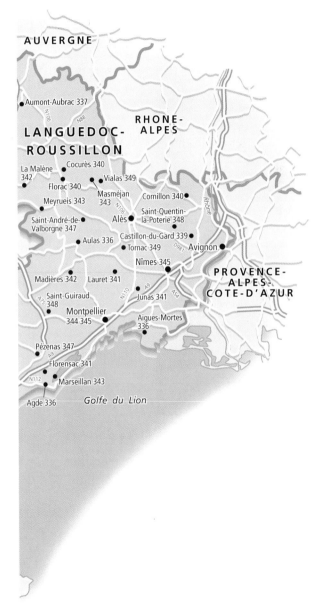

AUVERGNE

• Aumont-Aubrac 337

RHONE-
ALPES

LANGUEDOC-
ROUSSILLON

La Malène   • Cocurès 340
342
    • Florac 340   • Vialas 349
Meyrueis 343   Masméjan   • Cornillon 340
                343
Saint-André-de-•   Saint-Quentin-
Valborgne 347   Alès•   la-Poterie 348
    • Aulas 336   Castillon-du-Gard 339 •
            • Tornac 349   • Avignon •
            Nîmes 345•

Madières 342   Lauret 341
    Saint-Guiraud   Junas 341
    348•   PROVENCE-
    • Montpellier   ALPES-
        344 345   • Aigues-Mortes   COTE-D'AZUR
                    336

• Pézenas 347
    • Florensac 341
    • Marseillan 343
Agde 336   *Golfe du Lion*

Agde
◆ La Tamarissière
ⓔ – ⓔⓔ

21 Quai Théophile-Cornu, 34300 Agde,
Hérault
Tel 04 67 94 20 87 Fax 04 67 21 38 40

Started in 1882 by the great grandmother of the current patron, Nicolas Albano, in the old Greek city of Agde, this once modest wooden house has been transformed into a first-class hotel and restaurant. Nicolas' cooking is based on delicious seafood dishes, though the menu changes with the season. In the autumn, you dine on *gibier*, whilst lobster in a wealth of different guises dominates the menu all summer long. Nicolas' son Lionel is the *sommelier*, and he will suggest fine local wines from the well-respected list. Reservations are recommended.

❛ *A relaxing, light atmosphere'* …
'*Superb cuisine and cellar* ❜

Closed Sun dinner, Mon dinner, Mon lunch Oct to mid Jun; Nov, early Mar
Cards MC, V

Aigues-Mortes
◆ Le Maguelone ⓔ **Fr**

38 rue République, 30220 Aigues-Mortes,
Gard
Tel 04 66 53 74 60 Fax 04 66 80 87 65

Inside the medieval walls of the 13thC town of Aigues-Mortes, Le Maguelone is a pretty little restaurant with a cosy air. You can sit on the terrace under a sky-blue awning and eat a plate of wonderfully fresh seafood, a large salad or a tender *toro* (bull) steak whilst enjoying the view of the majestic ramparts. Although the town, established by Louis IX as a Mediterranean port, is a huge tourist destination, this restaurant has succeeded in avoiding the tackiness. Apparently untouched by the 21st century and its mass marketing, it takes you back to a bygone age. The food is excellent and the service elegant and pleasantly formal.

❛ *Well worth discovering* ❜

Closed Sun dinner, Mon; variable winter closing times (phone to check)
Cards DC, MC, V

Argelès-sur-Mer
◆ L'Orangeraie
ⓔⓔ – ⓔⓔⓔ

21 rue Arthur-Rimbaud, 66700 Argelès-sur-
Mer, Pyrénées-Orientales
Tel 04 68 81 07 33 Fax 04 68 81 59 69

The Chaîne des Albères is the last gasp of the Pyrénées before they reach the Mediterranean and Argelès-sur-Mer is virtually the last stop in France before the Spanish border. L'Orangeraie belongs to Le Cottage, a modern hotel in a residential area between the village and a broad sandy beach, with splendid views. It has a calm, stylish dining room, decorated in pale colours, which opens on to an enchanting garden where dinner is served on summer evenings. (The restaurant is closed for lunch, except on Sundays.) Over the years, it has developed a name for the delicate touch that chef Eric Normand brings to Mediterranean cooking (in, for example, his *dorade farcie au caviar d'aubergines* and his *glace au miel de lavande*) and the strength of Mickael Grégoire's regional wine list. Combined with candlelight on the linen-clad tables under the palms on a starry night, they make a heady mix.

Closed lunch Mon-Sat, Mon dinner late Sep to mid Jun
Cards AE, MC, V

Aulas
◆ Auberge Le Mas Quayrol ⓔ – ⓔⓔ

Les Molières, 30120 Aulas, Gard
Tel 04 67 81 12 38 Fax 04 67 81 23 84

Even on a chilly day you can sit inside this simple rustic restaurant and admire the spectacular panorama over the entire Aulas valley to the foothills of the Cévennes: a huge picture window stretches along one side of the building. Here chef Patrick Chabert specializes in a *cuisine du terroir*, in which he blends fresh Cévenol produce with spices, as in *brochettes de Saint-Jacques au beurre à l'ail parfumé au curry*. He cooks his original recipes with spirit and dash, and has acquired quite a following. This, together with the stunning view, affable staff and reasonable prices, means that in high season you must book a table (especially if you want to sit in front of the window). You can also sit outside.

CLOSED Nov-Apr
CARDS MC, V

---

charmingsmallhotels.co.uk
Visit Duncan Petersen's travel website, the best online search tool for places to stay that combine character and charm. Currently features Britain, France, Italy and Ireland, with other destinations being continuously added.

Aumont-Aubrac
◆ Grand Hôtel Prouhèze
€€ – €€€ **Fr**

2 route du Languedoc, 48130 Aumont-Aubrac, Lozère
Tel 04 66 42 80 07 Fax 04 66 42 87 78

Just off the old pilgrim route to Santiago de Compostella and surrounded by stunning countryside between the Aubrac plateau and the Margeride massif, Guy Prouhèze reinvents local cuisine with panache. Inspired by the region's traditional recipes and flavours, his innovative dishes use natural products such as mushrooms, wild flowers, herbs and meat produced by local farmers. Among the most delicious of his specialities are artichoke hearts with *petits gris* snails, fresh *foie gras* in a stew with spring vegetables, and those including mushrooms – young morel, cep, truffles and other varieties. The beamed dining room is stylishly furnished with chandeliers, upholstered chairs and crisp white tablecloths. Guy's wife, Catherine, was responsible for the decoration and the transformation of what was a family house into this charming three-star hotel, with 27 pretty bedrooms. But it's the restaurant that is its *raison d'être* and, as it is almost always busy, you should book in advance.

❛ *Delicious meal ... enchanting restaurant* ❜

CLOSED Sun and Mon dinner and Tue lunch Sep-Jul, Mon lunch Jul-Aug
CARDS AE, MC, V

Bages
◆ Le Portanel €€

passage Portanel, 11100 Bages, Narbonne, Aude
Tel 04 68 42 81 66 Fax 04 68 421 75 93

Eight different dishes featuring eels are part of the repertoire of Didier Marty, who runs this exceptional fish restaurant in a village house with his wife Rose-Marie. Take your choice: perhaps *l'anguille en persillade* or *l'anguille en bourride*. Whichever, the eels could not be fresher, coming as they do straight from the Etang de Bages, the lake which stretches from Narbonne to the sea and which the little fishing village of Bages overlooks. If you don't like eels, there are plenty of other fish to choose from, equally fresh, and oysters from Bouzigues. Try your fish *en croûte de sel*, or perhaps *le lessou cuit sur la peau au suc de volaille*, or *figuette Narbonnaise*. There are non-fish dishes too, including free-range chicken and other local produce. In warm weather you eat on a terrace overlooking the lake.

❛ *The fish – fresh from the lake – was out of this world* ❜

CLOSED Sun dinner, Mon; mid to late Nov
CARDS AE, DC, MC, V

Banyuls-sur-Mer
◆ La Littorine €€

plage des Elmes, 66650 Banyuls-sur-Mer, Pyrénées-Orientales
Tel 04 68 88 03 12 Fax 04 68 88 53 03

This restaurant belongs to the Hôtel Les Elmes, on the winding coast road just outside Banyuls-sur-Mer, with its own little beach. The large airy dining room has huge picture windows, a soothing atmosphere and attentive service. For outdoor eating, there is a shady terrace overlooking the sea. Jean-Marie Patroux's range of menus presents a wide choice of stylish Catalan dishes, which typically combine fish and meat in surprisingly successful ways: warm oysters with artichokes, or baby squid with *morilles* sauce and parmesan to start; or a main course of cod with *palourdes* (tiny clams), *boudin noir* and *fruits de mer*, or pigeon with *gambas* (large prawns). Fish is especially recommended as the fish market of Port Vendres is just down the road.

CLOSED Jan, Nov
CARDS AE, DC, MC, V

Belcastel
◆ Le Vieux Pont €€ Fr

12390 Belcastel, Lozère
Tel 05 65 64 52 29 Fax 05 65 64 44 32

The name refers to a medieval cobbled bridge linking the two components of this much-lauded restaurant-with-rooms. On one side of the river stands a solid rough-stone house, the Fagegaltier sisters' childhood home and now the restaurant; on the other side the sisters have rescued a tumbledown building next to the church to create seven comfortable, stylish bedrooms. Above, Belcastel's picture-postcard houses cling to a cliff with a castle crowning its summit. Michèle Fagegaltier is the manager, while her sister Nicole and Nicole's husband Bruno Rouquier are responsible for the cooking. Their subtle, imaginative versions of local dishes, such as rabbit with mushrooms, hazelnuts, homegrown spices and garlic, and *boeuf de l'Aubrac à la réduction de Banyuls*, served with *un concassé de pommes de terre à la ventrèche et au Roquefort*, have won them much praise, including a Michelin star and a Gault Millau heart and 16 points. Through picture windows diners can spot trout rising if the Aveyron isn't flowing too fast.

❛ *A delightful, bucolic setting'* ...
❛*Phenomenal value ... more than lived up to its reputation* ❜

CLOSED Sun dinner and Tue lunch Sep-Jul, Mon
CARDS AE, DC, MC, V

Bize-Minervois
◆ Auberge des Templiers € Fr

place aux Herbes, Porte Saint-Michel,
11120 Bize Minervois, Aude
Tel 04 68 46 39 72

Quaintly decorated in old French bistro style and with bonsai trees filling the interior courtyard, this intimate little inn has a delightfully old-fashioned charm. It is the perfect place for summer dining or for lunch after browsing in the local *brocantes*, or exploring the ruined Tower of Boussecos, which overshadows Bize. This region is renowned for producing some of the finest olives and olive oil in France, a fact that is reflected in the menu here. You should also find some tempting seafood dishes such as *coquille de mer*, and wonderful duck. The food is simple, yet lovingly prepared, designed to be eaten with one of the delicious Minervois wines from their *carte de vins*, and in a warm, friendly atmosphere. The owner is gracious and welcoming, and the staff superbly professional. You can choose to dine inside or out and, as the restaurant is popular with locals and intrepid tourists who choose to roam off the beaten track, it's wise to book.

CLOSED never
CARDS MC, V

Our traditional French cuisine symbol
So many of our readers enjoy seeking out the genuinely French eating experience that we have used Fr to mark restaurants which offer *cuisine du terroir*, classical French dishes or regional dishes with an emphasis on local ingredients, and traditional recipes.

Carcassonne
◆ Le Languedoc €€

32 allée Iena, 11000 Carcassonne, Aude
Tel 04 68 25 22 17 Fax 04 68 47 13 22

When you have had enough of the tourists, the trinkets and the unreal perfection of Viollet le Duc's 19thC restoration of Carcassonne's medieval walled *Cité*, head for the less crowded *ville basse* and this relaxing retreat. Surrounded by a pretty garden, the flowery patio, complete with fountain, makes a cool, refreshing setting for a lingering meal. If the weather does not permit, don't be put off – the warmly decorated dining room is pleasant too. Either way, smiling waiters will serve you with Didier Faugeron's reasonably priced classic cuisine, set out in three fixed-price menus, including a brilliant *cassoulet Languedoc au confit, entremets de fraises en feuilleté*, and (in season) quail with *foie gras*. The wine list offers some of the better local Minervois.

> 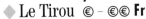 *A peaceful setting, away from the bustle' ... 'The fondant au chocolat was heavenly*

CLOSED Mon lunch, Sun dinner and Mon Sep-Jun; mid-Dec to mid-Jan
CARDS AE, DC, MC, V

Castelnaudary
◆ Le Tirou € – €€ Fr

90 avenue Mgr Delange, 11400 Castelnaudary, Aude
Tel 04 68 94 15 95 Fax 04 68 94 15 96

This fine city, the most important in Lauragais, owes its fame to *cassoulet*, as it's one of several places that claims to be the dish's rightful home. This robust stew of mutton, pork and beans has assumed such a significant role in local history that an academy of *cassoulet* has been established for people who prepare and like it. The place to come to sample this speciality is Le Tirou, just outside the centre, not far from the Chapel of Notre-Dame-de-Pitié. Here Pierre Dac prepares an excellent version, which he takes extremely seriously and for which he uses tip-top ingredients. One of the regional red wines from the list would be the ideal accompaniment. You might precede the *cassoulet* with *rillettes à l'oie* and then, if you have room, finish with the *marquise au chocolat*.

CLOSED Sun dinner, Mon, Wed dinner Sep-Jul; early Jan to early Feb, late Jun to early Jul
CARDS MC, V

Castillon-du-Gard
◆ Le Vieux Castillon
€€€

Rue Turion Sabatier, 30210 Castillon-du-Gard, Gard
Tel 04 66 37 61 61 Fax 04 66 37 28 17

The obvious thing to do with a cluster of medieval houses above a breathtaking view of the vineyards of the Ventoux valley is to leave one or two charming ruins as conversation pieces and turn the rest into a lux-

urious (Relais et Châteaux) hotel and restaurant, well defended outside against the mistral (by walls) and inside from the summer heat (by air conditioning). The quality of the cooking in the handsome beamed restaurant, or on a large, peaceful terrace, is consistently excellent – deserving of its Michelin star, and backed up by an agreeably broad offering of Côtes du Rhône. On the menu, you might find *langoustines en croûte de pommes de terre* and *carré d'agneau* roasted in a garlic purée, with that local delicacy *calisson*, served warm with raspberries to follow. But keep an eye on the bill, this is a notoriously pricey place.

CLOSED Mon lunch, Tue lunch; early Jan to late Feb
CARDS AE, DC, MC, V

Our price bands
€ 15 Euros or less €€ 30-50 Euros
€€€ 50+ Euros for a menu.

Céret
◆ La Cerisaie €€

route de Fontfrède, 66400 Céret, Pyrénées-Orientales
Tel 04 68 87 01 94 Fax 04 68 87 39 24

La Terrasse au Soleil is a heavenly rural hotel in an 18thC *mas*; La Cerisaie is its restaurant. With a young chef from Paris, an enviable reputation, a stunning setting, higher up the hillside than nearby Céret, and splendid views over unspoiled country, it could hardly fail. There is plenty of individuality in the interior design – much of it the legacy of Charles Trenet (the house at one time belonged to his agent and was a haunt of show-business personalities). Try to have a pre-dinner drink in the large bar, decorated with African carvings, and if the weather is fine, tables are usually put out on the terrace where Picasso is said to have sat to savour the view of Mont Canigou. Local specialities on the two seasonal menus are cooked to perfection: among the most typical are *soufflé de foie gras* with local violet artichokes and truffle *vinaigrette*, *médaillon de rosé de veau des Pyrénées* with morel and Rivesaltes Muscat wine, *petit Charolais* with shallot flan and truffle sauce, followed by *crème brûlée Catalane* with orange blossom or perhaps their famously mouthwatering *mille-*

feuille. At lunchtime, there is a tempting *carte brasserie* as a lighter alternative to the more serious food served at dinner.

> ❛ One of my favourite restaurants' … The view is spectacular ❜

CLOSED Mon-Fri lunch
CARDS AE, DC, MC, V

Cocurès

◆ La Lozerette € – €€ Fr

48400 Cocurès, Lozère
Tel 04 66 45 06 04 Fax 04 66 45 12 93

In the heart of the Cévennes, this peaceful, friendly alpine-style inn has a large dining room with a low wood-panelled ceiling, wicker chairs, cheerful yellow curtains, and a surprisingly intimate atmosphere. It has been in the same family for three generations. Today it is Pierrette Aguilhon who owns and runs it with her father, and their culinary collaboration produces a wide selection of hearty regional dishes that reflect a lifetime in this area. Many combine homegrown ingredients, or feature the prized local ceps, various kinds of game and wild boar, which appeal to the robust local appetite for meat, and trout from nearby rivers. The menu is exceptionally good value and so highly regarded that it keeps the restaurant almost permanently full (it's advisable to book). Leave your choice of wines to Pierrette, who – in addition to her other talents – is a qualified *sommelier*.

CLOSED Tue and Wed lunch, Tue dinner Sep-Jul; Easter to early Nov
CARDS AE, DC, MC, V

Cornillon

◆ Vieille Fontaine €€

30630 Cornillon, Gard
Tel 04 66 82 20 56 Fax 04 66 82 33 64

This family-run restaurant-with-rooms has a fabulous location on the ramparts of a Cathar fortress in the centre of a tiny, tranquil jewel of a medieval village, high above the Cèze valley. The superb terrace gives views over the sweeping vineyards below and, if you come here for dinner, of sunsets *par excellence*. Charmingly renovated, the hotel has a stunning swimming pool and gar-

dens built into the steep terraces below. The menu in the restaurant doesn't change very often, but the food is carefully prepared. The speciality that regularly crops up is *moules farcies à la diable*, a very imaginative dish, in which fat Mediterranean *moules* are stuffed, one by one with a pork and herb *farce*, and then each is tied with string. The *rognons de veau* in a white truffle sauce are equally delicious. Most of the wines on the carefully chosen wine list are Côte du Rhône, including Saint-Gervais. Try the Château de Bastet Viognier as an aperitif – an excellent wine at excellent value. Cars are banned from the centre, so park in the nearby square.

> ❛ A delicious spot overlooking 200 hectares of vineyards ❜

CLOSED Sun dinner, Wed; Nov to mid-Mar
CARDS AE, DC, MC, V

Looking for somewhere to stay?
See page 241.

Florac

◆ La Source de Pêcher € Fr

1 rue de Remuret, 48400 Florac, Lozère
Tel 04 66 45 03 01 Fax 04 66 45 28 82

You cannot help but be charmed by the location of this pretty mill-turned-bistro, its terrace poised just above the water, where you can sit and watch the plump trout. The regional menus are a collaboration between the owner, Pascal Paulet, and talented chef, Jean-Louis Huc, who give pride of place to *produits du terroir*: *nectar de myrtilles*, *agneau*, *truite de Lozère*, *fromages affinés sur place* and *gâteau à la châtaigne*. Jean-Louis transforms these ingredients into such tasty, subtle dishes as *émincé de canard aux myrtilles* and *pélardon frais gratiné au miel de châtaignier*. For wine, you're spoiled for choice – there are some 100 Languedoc vintages on the list, and for dessert, the *salade de fruits rouges au vin rouge* is deliciously refreshing.

CLOSED Wed Sep-Jul; Nov to Easter
CARDS none

Florensac
◆ Léonce €€ Fr

2 place de la République, 34510 Florensac,
Hérault
Tel 04 67 77 03 05 Fax 04 67 77 88 89

Another wonderful family-run establishment, this hotel-restaurant was founded
in 1929 by the eponymous Léonce Fabre and
is now run by his grandson Jean-Claude with
his wife Josette. In the centre of Florensac,
it is simply yet elegantly decorated, reflecting Jean-Claude's artistic talent. On his seasonal menu you will encounter game in the
autumn – deer in a *gibier* sauce, for example
– but house specialities, such as the succulent pigeon, are available throughout the
year. The presentation is as stylish as the
interior decoration, blending contemporary
flair with old-world charm.

❛ *A warm, contemporary ambience'*
... 'Great service and superb region-
al food ❜

CLOSED Sun dinner, Mon in winter
CARDS MC, V

Gincla
◆ Hostellerie du Grand
Duc € Fr

2 route de Boucheville, 11140 Gincla, Aude
Tel 04 68 20 55 02 Fax 04 68 20 61 22

The Grand Duc is the eagle owl, presiding
(stuffed) over the fireplace in the large
beamed dining room of this delightful, modest little *logis*. A refurbished *maison de*
maître (the *maître* made his living from the
surrounding forests), it was opened as a
restaurant by Bruno Bruchet, a chef whose
father is a wine inspector from Burgundy.
The restaurant's rustic decoration – whitewashed walls, plenty of natural stone and
exposed beams – complements Bruno's creative country-style cooking. On a short, but
appealing menu, the majority of dishes are
made from locally produced ingredients
(such as river trout, lamb and young vegetables). There is a superb modern kitchen,
where they make their own bread, and a
romantic terrace, looking on to a fountain
and old lime trees, where you dine in summer by candlelight.

CLOSED Wed lunch Sep-Jul; early Nov to Apr
CARDS MC, V

Junas
◆ Can Peio € – €€

Gare de Junas-Aujargues, Junas, 30250
Sommières, Gard
Tel 04 66 77 71 83 Fax 04 66 77 71 83

The old waiting room of a renovated railway station has been transformed into
this open and airy Catalan restaurant, carefully done out with tiles and painted woodwork. Through the original ticket office window, you can see the chef, Peio, hard at
work, preparing Catalan delicacies and outstanding *tapas* at very reasonable prices. He
is inspired by the traditional recipes of the
area, and uses them as a basis for his own
experiments. The menu changes almost
every day, according to what is available,
although a staple is the fresh seafood, served
with heavenly sauces and baby vegetables.
There is a wide choice of Catalan wine, and
if you don't finish the bottle, they will give
you a cork, so that you can take it home with
you. It's wise to reserve in advance.

❛ *Heaps of atmosphere ... terrific*
food ❜

CLOSED Sat and Sun lunch Jul-Aug, Sun dinner, Wed; first
week Sep, late Dec to mid-Jan
CARDS MC, V

Lauret
◆ Auberge du Cèdre €€

34270 Lauret, Hérault
Tel 04 67 59 02 02 Fax 04 67 59 03 44

If you want to escape from the world, this
is the spot. A handsome country house on
the Domaine de Cazeneuve wine estates in
the midst of the Pic Saint Loup vineyards is
the setting for this highly regarded restaurant, which draws a host of diners from
locals and visiting families, to motorcyclists
on tours of the region and international travellers. Most of them are hotel guests; the
restaurant is only open to non-residents for
dinner on Friday to Sunday. The simple seasonal menu has its roots in Catalan cuisine,
evident in the dominance of olive oil,
Mediterranean herbs, goat's cheese, *tapas*,

white beans and seafood. Almost more important than the food however is the wine: the restaurant has more than 100 varieties to choose from and is a wine lover's paradise. In particular, you can sample many outstanding vintages from the Languedoc region. The *auberge* is quite secluded and restrictions on non-residents make it essential to reserve a table in advance. If you are tempted to stay, there are 19 chic bedrooms, a two-acre (five-hectare) park and a glorious swimming pool.

*‘ Very romantic - a terrific getaway'
… 'Spectacular poolside views ’*

Closed Mon-Thu, Fri-Sun lunch; Jan-Mar (winter closing times may vary)
Cards MC, V

Our traditional French cuisine symbol
So many of our readers enjoy seeking out the genuinely French eating experience that we have used Fr to mark restaurants which offer cuisine du terroir, classical French dishes or regional dishes with an emphasis on local ingredients, without modern influence or presentation.

Madières
◆ Château de Madières s
€€ – €€€

Madières, 34190 Ganges, Hérault
Tel 04 67 73 84 03 Fax 04 67 73 55 71

An exciting blend of ancient and modern beauty characterizes this 14thC fortress in a spectacular position, perched above the Vis river gorge. The view is especially impressive through the arched windows of the vaulted dining room, which juts out from the main building and has a terrace above. The ambience is relaxed and casual. The walls are of rough stone, the floor is terracotta tiled, and attractive print cloths cover the tables. The chef, Marc Daniel, came from the famous Parisian restaurant Lasserre and, though he only took over a few years ago, has dramatically raised the reputation of the food here. Among his imaginative versions of some of the region's favourite dishes are *terrine de chèvre frais* and *artichauts aux herbes*, *daurade royale*

à la vinaigrette de légumes and *poule au pot*. The accompanying wine list is impressive and not overpriced. 12 bedrooms

‘ An ideal place to relax both mind and body ’

Closed Nov to late Mar
Cards AE, DC, MC, V

Magalas
◆ Boucherie of Magalas
€ – €€

place d'Eglise, 34480 Magalas, Hérault
Tel 04 67 36 20 82

Owned by a former trapeze artist and a dancer, the Boucherie of Magalas – as you might have guessed from its name – is a butcher's shop for most of the day and a bistro-style restaurant at noon and in the evening. Set in the quiet streets of this small hilltop village between Béziers and Bédarieux, it is a carnivore's dream. Only the best cuts are served with fresh vegetables and an excellent choice of *vins de pays*. Try the excellent *carpaccio*, *côte de boeuf* or *rouelle d'agneau*. Posters and photographs of circus life line the walls, harking back to the fun-loving owners' colourful past.

‘ Simple, quaint and lots of fun - not to be missed ’

Closed Sun dinner, Mon, Sun lunch Sep-Jul
Cards MC, V

La Malène
◆ Manoir de Montesquiou € – €€

48210 La Malène, Lozère
Tel 04 66 48 51 12 Fax 04 66 48 50 47

Set dramatically between two sheer rock faces in the Gorges du Tarn, this attractive 15thC manor house is family-run and stands out for its warm welcome, traditional charm and excellent value. Castle-like and heavily creepered, it has an inner courtyard, stunning views and a reliable restaurant, where the owners Bernard and Evelyne Guillenet have been providing tasty regional fare for as long as they have been running the Manoir, which is more than 30 years (though they now receive a helping hand from their three daughters). On one of three menus, you might spot specialities such as *mille-feuille aux deux truites, crème ciboulette et baies roses, carré d'agneau de Lozère aux épices* and for dessert *poire à la poitrine fumée, sauce au bleu des causses*. The portions are as robust as the flavours, and the wine list is eclectic.

CLOSED Nov to Apr
CARDS DC, MC, V.

Marseillan
◆ Chez Philippe € – €€

20 rue de Suffren, 34340 Marseillan, Hérault
Tel 04 67 01 70 62 Fax 04 67 01 70 62

In a back street, not far from the quay, Chez Philippe offers imaginative eclectic dishes made with delicious but humble ingredients, for which they charge exceptionally low prices. You can either dine on a charming outside terrace or indoors, where the cheerful decoration is in light, earthy colours. There is only one menu for lunch and dinner, with a choice of five or six dishes for each of the three courses, plus a daily special. You might find yourself choosing between *anchois frais marines, compotée d'aubergines, tarte à l'envers de legumes et chèvre frais* and *potage de crabe au safran*, followed by *rognon de veau, chorizo et zestes d'orange confits, daube de joues de porc, frites de polenta* or *daurade royale, legumes caramelisés*. Portions are modest so you might have room for one of the exquisite desserts: the rum baba, the banana and lime tart, or perhaps the *dessert du jour*. Open, airy and fun, the restaurant has an expert staff and a first-rate cellar; in fact this is a gastonomic gem in Marseillan.

CLOSED Sun, Mon, and Tue lunch and Wed lunch Sep-Jul
CARDS MC, V

Masméjan
◆ Chez Dédé
€€ – €€€ Fr

Masméjan, 48220 Saint-Maurice-de-Ventalon, Lozère
Tel 04 66 45 81 51 Fax 04 66 45 80 91

Frequented by locals and nature-lovers, this remote and rustic restaurant, set in glorious mountain terrain, specializes in simple but delectable country cooking. It's a real treat to come here after a day of hiking or cross-country ski-ing. A fixed-price menu of three to four courses features a choice of three different dishes for each course, delicious desserts and a selection of outstanding local cheeses. Specialities such as wild boar, venison and assorted *charcuterie* make it particularly appealing to meat-lovers. Just ensure that you're hungry, as portions are exceedingly generous, and eating tends to be a lengthy business – you will need at least three hours for lunch. There is an impressive list of wines to accompany the food.

> ❛ *Simple and charming ... Honest country cooking'* ... *'A wonderful discovery* ❜

CLOSED Wed and dinner winter
CARDS none

Fr French regional or classical French dishes on menu.

Meyrueis
◆ Château d'Ayres
€ – €€

48150 Meyrueis, Lozère
Tel 04 66 45 60 10 Fax 04 66 45 62 26

This lovely stone, mainly 18thC, white-shuttered château, on the site of a 12thC Benedictine monastery, is in the heart of the Cévennes National Park and in its own beautiful wooded grounds, with mature sequoias and oaks. The vaulted dining room is traditional in look with high-backed wooden chairs and crisp tablecloths, but with a convivial atmosphere. The food is excellent. The chef, Jacqui Joubi, specializes in classic Languedoc recipes using plenty of prime local ingredients. Look for *filet de boeuf poêlé sauce au Roquefort, langoustines au beurre d'orange* and *soupe tiède au chocolat et crème glacée au miel des Cévennes* on Jacqui's daily changing menu. The principally female staff are very friendly and helpful, and the owner M. de Montjou is a knowledgeable *sommelier*. The *château* is just over 1 km (0.6 miles) south-east of Meyrueis.

CLOSED Sun and Mon dinner and Tue lunch Sep-Jul, Mon lunch Jul-Aug
CARDS AE, MC, V

Molitg-les-Bains
◆ Grand Hôtel Thermal €

66500 Molitg-les-Bains, Pyrénées-Orientales
Tel 04 68 05 00 50 Fax 04 68 05 02 91

Hardly charming, but nonetheless amusing, this is a spa hotel in a craggy mountain gorge, with exotic gardens surrounding a huge lake, marble spa rooms, a swimming pool and 1930s salon, complete with cane chairs and grand piano. The restaurant shares a chef with the adjoining Château de Riell, long famous for its stylish cuisine, but the trick is to dine here – not at the château – where you will eat well and pay less. The marble terrace is perfect for summer eating, but the dining room, full of clients taking the cure, can be a bit hushed, and the service is invariably slow. Still, excellent value menus more than compensate. They feature local produce and fresh herbs: perhaps *gambas* grilled with pesto, served with green pepper *coulis*, followed by salmon with coriander, or a succulent *confit de canard*.

CLOSED Dec-Mar
CARDS AE, DC, MC, V

Montpellier
◆ Les Bains € – €€ Fr

6 rue Richelieu, 34000 Montpellier, Hérault
Tel 04 67 60 70 87 Fax 04 67 60 54 68

A romantic, secluded spot in the very centre of Montpellier, the terrace of this restaurant is one of the prettiest in the city, with its palm trees and private fountain, perfect for a quiet lunch or dinner *à deux*. In the *cuisine bourgeoise* tradition, the food is excellent and reasonably priced. The *tarte Niçoise* is particularly delicate and satisfying. The bar is reminiscent of a New York lounge, a place where trendsetters sip aperitifs or fine regional wines. Between 3pm and 6.30pm, Les Bains' *salon de thé* offers a selection of fine imported teas in a contemplative setting, almost as romantic as dining on the terrace.

❛Tranquil, charming, romantic❜

CLOSED Sun
CARDS MC, V

Montpellier
◆ Le Bazar €€

448 rue de la Rogueturière, 34000 Montpellier, Hérault
Tel 04 67 02 15 40 Fax 04 67 02 15 40

Tucked away from the bustle of Montpellier, Le Bazar is another city restaurant with a charming, peaceful terrace, where you dine under pine trees. But this restaurant specializes in dishes from the *cuisine du sud*. There is a fixed-price menu for lunch, a choice of delicious *entrées* at dinner, including duck and fresh seafood, and an exciting regional wine list. The staff is lively and more than willing to recommend a delicious Muscat to go with your dessert. Inside, it is warmly decorated in a rustic style, and in winter a fire burns in the huge fireplace, heating the whole dining area. The restaurant fills up so it is advisable to book.

❛A lovely, cosy atmosphere' ... 'We ate like kings❜

CLOSED Sun, Mon
CARDS MC, V

Montpellier
◆ Le Jardin des Sens €€€

11 avenue Sainte-Lazare, 34000 Montpellier, Hérault
Tel 04 99 58 38 38 Fax 04 99 58 38 39

Twin brothers and sons of a winemaker, Jacques and Laurent Pourcel are the draw of Le Jardin des Sens, a four-star restaurant where the food is superb and the prices are reasonable. It has a chic, open, airy, modern design with a three-sided glass dining room overlooking a small amphitheatre of a garden. The brothers' cooking is intense in flavour yet light, surprisingly simple and delicious. Their menu is refined, inventive and constantly evolving. They understand how to blend the products of the region from seafood to spices, creating a gastronomic mosaic of textures and flavours in dishes such as *bonbons de foie gras croustillants aux pommes de terre avec une salade à l'huile de colza grillé* and *filets de pigeon rôtis et pastilla de ses abats*. Although the food is wonderful and to eat here is quite an experience, sadly the ambience lacks warmth and personal attention.

CLOSED Sun, Mon lunch, Wed lunch; three weeks Jan
CARDS AE, DC, MC, V

Montpellier
◆ Le Saleya €

place du Marché aux Fleurs, 34000 Montpellier, Hérault
Tel 04 67 60 53 92

You can only eat outside at this charming, lively restaurant in the heart of Montpellier, where the terrace makes a perfect setting for relaxing beneath large umbrellas and enjoying one of their delicious salads as you watch the people that throng the square. The cuisine is imaginative, using only the freshest of ingredients, and the wine list reflects a wide choice of local vintages. This is a place to stop for a light lunch and a glass of wine between seeing the sights or during a break from shopping, where you can watch others go about the business of city life.

❛*Fun and energetic' ... 'Very social – you're bound to make new friends*❜

CLOSED Sun, Mon; variable winter closing times
CARDS MC, V

Nîmes
◆ Vintage Café € – €€

7 rue de Bernis, 30000 Nîmes, Gard
Tel 04 66 21 04 45 Fax 04 66 21 04 45

You are guaranteed a warm welcome from the small staff at this charming, informal little café bistro in the centre of Nîmes, between the arena and the Maison Carrée. There is a choice of two menus: one, displayed on a blackboard, offers three courses of specialities that blend ingredients with style, or the main menu, which usually includes an assortment of seafood and *ratatouille* with rice. Most wines on the shortish

list are honest regional vintages. This is a gem of a bistro, ideal for a spontaneous stopover – as long as it's not full.

❛*Fun, casual, great value*❜

CLOSED Sat lunch, Sun, Mon
CARDS MC, V

Our price bands
Rather than giving actual prices (which are prone to change) we indicate the cost of a three-course meal for one person, without wine, by means of price bands. They are as follows: € under 30 euros €€ 30-50 euros €€€ over 50 euros. Where we give more than one price band, for example €–€€€, this indicates that in that restaurant a meal can be had at a range of prices. As well as the cost of *prix fixe* menus, our price bands also take into account the cost of an average selection from the *à la carte* menu.

Olargues
◆ Domaine de Rieumégé €€ Fr

route de Saint-Pons, 34390 Olargues, Hérault
Tel 04 67 97 73 99 Fax 04 67 97 78 52

In a superb natural setting of hills, rock, water, trees, shrubs and soft green grass, this sensitively restored 17thC stone house is in the middle of the Parc Régional de Haut Languedoc, close to Olargues, one of the villages classed as the most beautiful in France. It is now a 14-room hotel, where deep calm prevails, with an attractive high-ceilinged, beamed restaurant, which retains – even after restoration – its country barn origins. The emphasis of the cooking is firmly on classic regional dishes (*petite caille farcie aux noix et aux raisins* and *tarte fine aux pommes à la cannelle et au miel* for instance), well-prepared, beautifully cooked, and served by a courteous staff.

❛ *Impressive views' ... 'Excellent food and pleasant, relaxed service*❜

CLOSED Sat and Sun Sep-Jul; Nov-Apr
CARDS AE, DC, MC, V

Ornaisons
◆ Le Relais du Val d'Orbieu
€€ – €€€

11200 Ornaisons, Aude
Tel 04 68 27 10 27 Fax 04 68 27 52 44

This charming old mill; which has been cleverly extended with sympathetically designed red-roofed buildings, arranged to enclose a lush, secluded cloister; is now a hotel with 20 bedrooms, a swimming pool, and a fine restaurant. You eat in an airy, yellow and white dining room or on the flowery terrace, lit at night by a combination of lanterns and candles. The food from classic regional menus is excellent, especially the fish and seafood dishes (*la queue de lotte en aïoli léger et légumes printaniers, le pavé de truite de mer marinée, cuit au four,* or *le croustillant de gambas au gingembre*); vegetables and herbs, home-grown in the large garden, also feature prominently. Stocked with an impressive selection of Corbières wines, the cellar reflects the personal passion of the owner Jean-Pierre Gonzalvez, the son of a *vigneron.*

Closed lunch, Sun dinner low season Nov-Feb; Dec
Cards AE, DC, MC, V

Ouveillan
◆ Relais de Pigasse
€€

RD5, Domaine de Pigasse, 11590 Ouveillan, Aude
Tel 04 67 89 40 98

A 17thC posting house on the banks of the Canal du Midi has been renovated in simple, chic and cutting-edge style. Cool lighting, Italian leather furniture and modern art and sculpture combine happily with the old stones and rustic views. It is the brainchild of English *vigneron* Bertie Eden, and makes a wonderful way to sample his excellent Minervois wines. Dine – in the cool vaulted interior or beside the tree-shaded canal – on accomplished dishes, which interpret authentic regional recipes with panache, each served with an appropriate wine. Try unctuous *foie gras* with Limoux Bégude, or rabbit stuffed with snails with

Saint-Chinian Château de Combebelle, and a gorgeous Muscat sorbet and red fruits with the delicate Muscat of Saint-Jean-de-Minervois. All of the wines and vegetables are *biologique.*

Closed Mon
Cards MC, V

Perpignan
◆ La Casa Sansa € Fr

3 rue Fabrique Nadal, 66000 Perpignan, Pyrénées-Orientales
Tel 04 68 34 21 84

Casa Sansa is a Perpignan institution, and the best place in town to sample authentic Catalan food. Tucked away in one of the narrow streets around the Castillet, the restaurant makes a good stop either for *tapas* and drinks, or a full lunch or dinner. It's best to arrive early at lunchtime since it is very popular with the locals and quickly fills up. The atmosphere is warm and lively, and the decoration idiosyncratic and artistic, with every inch of the walls covered in paintings and cartoons, and lovely old Spanish tiles lining the bar. Typical dishes include a rich Catalan-style *ratatouille, pintade* with figs or rabbit with *aïoli.* They also serve a luxurious house *foie gras,* which is a meal in itself, and a truly delicious *crème Catalane,* subtly perfumed with orange.

❝An authentic Catalan restaurant' … 'Terrific food at reasonable prices ❞

Closed Sun, Mon
Cards AE, DC, MC, V

Perpignan
◆ La Villa Duflot €€

109 avenue Victor-Dalbiez-rond point Albert Dannezan, 66000 Perpignan, Pyrénées-Orientales
Tel 04 68 56 67 67 Fax 04 68 56 54 05

A charming couple, André and Laure Duflot own and run this luxurious four-star hotel and restaurant set in a vast and beautifully lush park, filled with trees, flowers and birds. Water spouts from an Italian fountain all day long, and time seems to stand still. The garden is so private and tranquil that Perpignan feels much further away than 3 km (2 miles). Apart from this glorious setting, the restaurant enjoys a first-class reputation for its light, contemporary, Catalan-influenced cuisine. For all the dishes, including the *foie frais de canard poêlé aux raisins et Muscat* and a range based on *morue* (cod), only the best and freshest ingredients are selected. As you would expect, the wine list is as impressive as the menu, concentrating on Roussillon wines but ranging from *vins de pays* to *crus classés*. Try to dine here on a balmy evening, when candlelit tables cluster around the floodlit swimming pool and it is hard to imagine a more romantic spot.

Closed never
Cards AE, DC, MC, V

Our price bands
€ 15 Euros or less
€€ 30-50 Euros
€€€ 50+ Euros for a menu.

Pézenas
 Les Goutailles €

6 rue Saint-Alban, 34120 Neffiès, Pézenas, Hérault
Tel 04 67 24 07 86

If you were going to drive along the road from Neffiès to Vailhan via the Barrage des Olivettes, on one of the most beautiful roads – if not the most beautiful road – in south-west France, with a view to eating at the Auberge de la Presbytère – don't. Though the view is fantastic, the food is frozen. Instead, do the drive in reverse and eat in the small and intimate Les Goutailles, a *maison particulier* opposite the square, with exposed stone and wood and cheery red tablecloths, all lovingly restored by owners, Karene and Didier. The best seat in the house is on the tiny Juliet balcony, where there is room for a maximum of six.

> ❝ *Good food, pleasant atmosphere ... hospitable service* ❞

Closed Mon-Sat lunch and Sun dinner in season; check for winter closing times
Cards none

Port-Verdes
◆ Ferme Auberge des Clos de Paulilles
€€ **Fr**

Baie de Paulilles, 66660 Port-Vendres, Pyrénées-Orientales
Tel 04 68 98 07 58

Escape the busy restaurants of Collioure for this enchanting sanctuary on a small bay surrounded by vineyards just beyond Port-Vendres. Run by the vineyard, with a fixed menu to showcase the Paulilles wines, the restaurant is comfortably chic, with Spanish tiled floors and banquettes, Catalan-striped fabrics and art on the walls. A large tiled patio looks out on to vineyards and the sea, and the beach is only a stroll away. Each course is accompanied by a different wine; cooling *gazpacho* with a Collioure *rosé*, home-reared chicken and polenta with a selection of rich reds, *manchego* cheese and orange *confit* with a Rivesaltes Muscat, and for dessert *tarte au chocolat noir* matched by a rich sweet Banyuls. End your meal with one of the superb *vieille* Banyuls you can see maturing in glass flagons; the cheese is on sale, and you will want to buy some to take home.

Closed Mon-Sat lunch; Sep-Jun
Cards none

---

charmingsmallhotels.co.uk
Visit Duncan Petersen's travel website, the best online search tool for places to stay that combine character and charm. Currently features Britain, France, Italy and Ireland, with other destinations being continuously added.

Saint-André-de-Valborgne
◆ Bourgade €€

place de l'Eglise, 30940 Saint-André-de-Valborgne, Gard
Tel 04 66 60 30 72 Fax 04 66 60 35 56

Trained by celebrity chefs Patrick Pagès and Alain Ducasse, dashing Alain Bourgade honed his skills while cooking for the French Ambassador in Washington DC. In 1998 he came home to renovate and run his family's 17thC coaching inn. It stands beside the fountain on this mountain village's main square, with tables outside on all but the chilliest evenings. Inside, there is a soothing pastel colour scheme. Among the imaginative specialities on the fixed-price and *à la carte* menus are wheat risotto, wild mushrooms and meat juice, beef *carpaccio* with coriander, capers and shallots, grilled lamb steak with Guérande sea salt and veal shank cooked in its own juice. If you can't face the drive home, there are ten attractively decorated bedrooms.

CLOSED Mon-Thu dinner Sep-Jun; mid-Nov to mid-Apr
CARDS MC, V

Our traditional French cuisine symbol
So many of our readers enjoy seeking out the genuinely French eating experience that we have used Fr to mark restaurants which offer *cuisine du terroir*, classical French dishes or regional dishes with an emphasis on local ingredients, and traditional recipes.

Saint-Guiraud
◆ Le Mimosa €€–€€€

34725 Saint-Guiraud, Hérault
Tel 04 67 96 67 96 Fax 04 67 96 61 15

Combine a savoury menu with a beautiful, calm atmosphere in a restored medieval house and you've discovered Le Mimosa. Relaxed and comfortable, it is simply decorated with beautiful antique furniture and warm lighting. Close to Lac Salagou and Clermont l'Hérault, it perches on top of the village of Saint-Guiraud, overlooking a spread of vineyards below. The owners are a charming couple: David Pugh, a former violinist, and his wife, Bridget, who was a ballet dancer and is now a top-flight *cuisinière*. She prepares her delicate and refined dishes daily from organically grown products; rabbit stuffed with pistachios and sage, for example, and *tellines* (a Mediterranean delicacy of tiny clams, garlic, parsley and olive oil). David devotes much of his time to stocking his cellar with local wine good enough to match Bridget's cooking. The couple own an elegant hotel nearby at Saint-Saturnin-de-Lucian, Ostalaria Cardabela, which has seven bedrooms and provides

free transport to and from the Mimosa.

6 A memorable dinner in a stunning dining room with charming service 9

CLOSED Mon, Tue-Sat lunch, Sun dinner Sep-Jul
CARDS DC, MC, V

Saint-Pons-de-Thomières
◆ Les Bergeries de Pondérach €€ – €€€

route de Narbonne, 34220 Saint-Pons-de-Thomières, Hérault
Tel 04 67 97 02 57 Fax 04 67 97 29 75

Saint-Pons-de-Thomières is a pleasant little town in the Parc Régional de Haut Languedoc, in an area of gentle wooded hills. This restaurant-hotel in an 18thC farmhouse is just under a kilometre (0.6 miles) outside the town, with large grounds, a charming courtyard, peaceful rural surroundings and much of its character intact. M. Lentin, the proprietor, used to own an art gallery and paintings are a major feature of the attractive dining room. But they don't detract from the food, which is the high point. There are four menus from which to choose, the cheapest offering excellent value for money. Fresh local produce, especially pork, takes precedence, and the wine list has an interesting selection of country wines. There are also seven smart, bright double bedrooms.

6 A marvellous meal. Wonderful warm hospitality, very fair prices 9

CLOSED Dec-Mar
CARDS AE, DC, MC, V

Saint-Quentin-la-Poterie
◆ La Table de l'Horloge €€ Fr

place de l'Horloge, 30700 Saint-Quentin-la-Poterie, Gard
Tel 04 66 22 07 01

Halfway up the church square, La Table de l'Horloge, a tiny restaurant with just 30 covers, is the perfect place for an intimate *dîner à deux*. Thibaut Peyroche d'Arnaud, the chef, offers a daily changing menu that concentrates on local vegetables, fruits, a variety of meat and irresistible desserts. He shops daily at the farmers' market in Uzès for the freshest produce, including asparagus grown in the sandy fields nearby and truffles for his *paté de foie gras*. Inside, the restaurant is warmly decorated with sand-coloured walls, subdued lighting and polished antique furniture. The food arrives as beautifully arranged as works of art on locally made ceramic plates. On warm summer nights, you can have a candlelit dinner in the garden with Uzès, a stunning silhouette in the background. You must book.

❝ *Superb beautifully presented food'* ... *'One of the most enjoyable meals of our holiday* ❞

Closed Wed, Thu
Cards MC, V

Tornac
◆ Demeures du Ranquet
€€ – €€€

route Saint-Hippolyte-du-Fort, Tornac, 30140 Anduze, Gard
Tel 04 66 77 51 63 Fax 04 66 77 55 62

Set among pines and scrub oak in the peaceful foothills of the Cévennes, the Demeures du Ranquet is the kind of place that lingers in the memory for all the right reasons. The restaurant is in the main building, a long, low, beautifully restored farmhouse, and is simply decorated. Black and white photographs jostle for space with colourful paintings on plain walls. In summer the tables sally forth on to the terrace and out under the trees where hammocks also lie in wait to help you through the heat of the afternoon. Anne Majourel's cuisine is a real treat. Borrowing from the local *cuisine du terroir*, specialities such as *ratatouille de ma grand mère avec les mouillettes de saucisses d'Anduze, carpaccio de lapin à la tapenade, galette de polenta* and *queue de baudroie rôtie, bourride d'herbes, cannellonni de petits gris au gratin* are adventurous, original and fresh, and supported by an excellent wine list, which Anne's husband Jean-Luc will help you navigate. Ten comfortable bedrooms are in chalets scattered amongst the trees

on a slope above the swimming pool.

❝ *A magical place* ❞

Closed Tue dinner and Wed mid-Sep to mid-Jun; Oct-Apr
Cards DC, MC, V

Please send us reports
A guide such as this thrives on reader's reports. If you send us five usable reports, we will send you a free copy of any title in our *Charming Small Hotel Guides* series (see page 241 for France titles in the series).

The five reports should contain at least two new restaurants; the balance can be comments on restaurants already in the guide. **Send reports to** Charming Restaurant Guides, Duncan Petersen Ltd, 31 Ceylon Road, London W14 0PY.

Vialas
◆ Hostellerie Chantoiseau
€€ – €€€

48220 Vialas, Lozère
Tel 04 66 41 00 02 Fax 04 66 41 04 34

Christiane and Patrick Pagès have turned this rustic 17thC *relais de poste* into a gastronomic jewel, hidden away in the mountains of the Cévennes. Patrick is passionate about the region and its cuisine. His cooking was known to cause President Mitterand to jump into his private helicopter to sample his game specialities and fine wine. And although celebrities don't come here every day, you are guaranteed to eat like a king at a reasonable price. The food is filling, so arrive famished, especially if you plan to choose the outstanding *menu gastronomique*. The beamed dining room is cosy and welcoming; the colours are warm, the walls of natural rough stone, and the lighting is subtle. The Chantoiseau has one of the most attractive dining terraces, where you eat beneath the shade of a huge chestnut tree or an umbrella while admiring this region's spectacular wild scenery.

Closed Tue dinner, Wed dinner; mid-Oct to Apr
Cards MC, V

PROVENCE-ALPES-COTE-D'AZUR

Caught between the Mediterranean and the Alps, this captivating, sun-drenched region – also known as the Midi – is full of colour, heady scents, history and diverse landscapes and architecture. Bisected by the lower valley of the Rhône, Provence comprises the départements of Vaucluse – including Avignon and the mountains of Vaucluse and Lubéron – and Bouches-du-Rhône, which takes in the Camargue, the regional capital Marseille and Aix-en-Provence. The region marches east to the Italian border, first taking in the département of Var, which stretches inland from Toulon and Saint-Tropez. Then comes the famous

RHONE-ALPES

Saint-Disdier 371

D994

D994

Mison 364

Mondragon 365

Sérignan-du-Comtat 374

Séguret 374

Aubignosc 353

Piolenc 368

Gigondas 359

Beaumont-du-Ventoux 354

LANGUEDOC ROUSSILLON

Châteauneuf-du-Pape 356

Le Beaucet 354

Le Pontet-Avignon 368

Avignon 353

L'Isle-sur-la-Sorgue 360

Apt 353

Manosque 362

Rhône

Bonnieux 355

Saignon 370

Saint-Rémy-de-Provence 373

Saint-Andiol 371

Cucuron 358

Verquières 376

Lourmarin 361

Maussane-les-Alpilles 364

Arles

Rognes 369

Aix-en-Provence 352

Ventabren 376

Le Tholonet 374

Saint-Maximin-la-Sainte-Baume 372

Rove 370

Marseille 363 364

Cassis 355

La Ciotat 357

Bandol 354

French Riviera, or Côte-d'Azur, which spans the coast from Cannes and Nice to Monaco. Lying just below the foothills of the last Alpine chain, its hilly hinterland is distinguished by dozens of charming old villages perchés. To the north, Alpes-de-Haute-Provence (principal town Digne) is the département that rises north through increasingly dramatic landscape towards the high Alps.

ITALIA

Villeneuve-la-Salle 377

Gap 358

Barcelonnette 354

PROVENCE-ALPES-COTE D'AZUR

Roure 370

Digne 358

Châteaux-Arnoux 356

Moustiers-Sainte-Marie 365

La Turbie 375

Villefranche-sur-Mer 377

Peillon 368

Menton 364

Saint-Paul-de-Vence 373

Monaco

Tourrettes-sur-Loup 375

Saint-Jean-Cap-Ferrat 371

Grasse 360   Opio 367

Nice 366 367

Villecroze 376

Valbonne 376

Saint-Laurent-du-Var 372

Mougins 365

Pégomas 367

Antibes 352

La Napoule 365   Golfe Juan 359

Cotignac 357

La Napoule 365   Cannes 355

Correns 357   Lorgues 361

Saint-Raphaël 373

La Celle 356

Collobrières 357

Saint-Tropez 374

Toulon 375   Hyères 360

Le Pradet 369

Porquerolles (Ile de) 369

Aix-en-Provence
◆ L'Aixquis €€

22 rue Victor Leydet, 13100 Aix-en-Provence, Bouches-du-Rhône
Tel 04 42 27 76 16 Fax 04 42 33 10 61

Benoit Strohm is Alsacien by birth but his cooking is very Southern in flavour. He insists on absolute freshness, changes his menus every 15 days without fail, and cooks every dish to order. This sometimes entails a wait, but it is always worth it. In winter he favours game; in summer, fish and shellfish, all served with light, imaginative sauces, and often with black or white truffles. His originality is evident in the different ways he prepares lobster: warm in a salad, with pine nuts, blended with vanilla, in an infusion of Mediterranean herbs, and even with cocoa beans. The restaurant is elegantly decorated with pale marbled and frescoed walls and muted lighting, perfect for romantic dinners.

❛ Flair combined with excellent value ❜

CLOSED Sun, Mon; first week Jan, first 3 weeks Aug
CARDS AE, MC, V

Looking for somewhere to stay? See page 241.

Aix-en-Provence
◆ Le Formal € – €€

32 rue Espariat, 13100 Aix-en-Provence, Bouches-du-Rhône
Tel 04 42 27 08 31 Fax 04 42 27 08 31

Although it only opened in June 2001, this exciting restaurant (the latest venture of Breton chef Monsieur le Formal and his Dutch companion Yvonne Kruithof) is rapidly becoming a favourite with the Aixois. In an atmospheric stone-vaulted cellar, its walls are covered with works of art and its nooks filled with art books. The cooking is innovative, combining sweet and savoury flavours in, for example, the *tatin de poire avec foie gras*, a stunning main course. Puddings are equally delicious: in the *moelleux au chocolat et griottes, son jus d'orange au safran,*

the saffron delicately lifts the richness of the dish. Everything is beautifully presented on square or triangular white plates, and the service is caring and professional. No dogs.

❛ The scents and flavours are intoxicating ❜

CLOSED Sun, Mon
CARDS MC, V

Aix-en-Provence
◆ Laurane et sa Maison €

16 rue Victor Leydet, 13100 Aix-en-Provence, Bouches-du-Rhône
Tel 04 42 93 02 03 Fax 04 42 93 02 03

A unique, fun restaurant, decked out like a courtyard belonging to an untidy but clean 19thC brothel. Washing lines sporting bloomers and corsets are suspended above the diners' heads and the walls are a clutter of knick-knacks and laundry paraphernalia. The room is bright and airy, with wrought-iron tables and chairs, and manages to create an impression of being outside, even at night. The chef, Martine Barbesier, specializes in dishes from the South West, so duck and *cassoulet* are on the menu. She favours spices, and the *tagines* are recommended, as well as the wonderful dishes based on fresh lamb from Aveyron, one of her favourite ingredients.

❛ Cheerful venue, cheerful food, cheerful service' ... 'Good value and good fun' ❜

CLOSED Sun, Mon
CARDS MC, V

Antibes
◆ La Jarre €€

14 rue Saint-Esprit, 06600 Vieil Antibes, Alpes-Maritimes
Tel 04 93 34 50 12 Fax 04 93 34 50 12

This delightful restaurant is only open for dinner in high season and is exceptionally popular, so you must book in advance. There are two very good reasons for its popularity. One is its pretty patio with flowers in pots under the shade of an ancient fig tree, attractively lit in the evening. The second is the quality of chef-*patronne* Hélène Moro-Veziano's gastronomic spread. The dishes change daily, and, whilst everyone raves about the *tiramisu*, opinions differ as to which dish is her finest: the *soupe d'escargots* married with baby spinach or the *gambas au gingembre*; the pigeon or the veal kidneys. The wine list is excellent, and features a few Italian wines in addition to an unusual Provençal selection.

CLOSED lunch; mid-Oct to Apr
CARDS AE, MC, V

Apt
◆ Bistro de France €€

67 place de la Bouquerie, 84400 Apt, Vaucluse
Tel 04 90 74 22 01

Hardly a discovery (it featured in Peter Mayle's *A Year in Provence*), though it certainly feels like one the first time you eat in (or on the pavement outside) this basic town centre café with its dark, old-fashioned street frontage, and when a slightly battered saucepan of something delicious is placed on your table for you to help yourself. The cooking is plain and Provençal and mostly very good. Some dishes can be a disappointment, such as an overcooked, unimaginatively sauced pasta, but others are excellent. In summer, for example, they serve a delicious *aïoli* with a big bowl of vegetables and a sharp knife to cut them; in winter, a *brouillade de truffes* (the house speciality) and game. Service is fast and to the point at lunch; you need to book for dinner.

❛ *Congenial town café' ... 'Honest regional fare* ❜

CLOSED Sun lunch; Nov to mid-Mar
CARDS MC, V

Aubignosc
◆ La Magnanerie
€ – €€ **Fr**

Les Fillières, N85, 04200 Aubignosc, Alpes-de-Haute-Provence
Tel 04 92 62 65 30 Fax 04 92 62 63 05

The word *magnanerie* means a silk worm factory, which is exactly what this attractive old house beside the Durance river was. Nowadays it is owned by the Paroche family (mother, father and two sons), who cook local ingredients and present them in four expertly balanced menus. You will, of course, be offered lamb from Sisteron, roasted with garlic and rosemary, pigeon, kid, pork and eggs, all from Durance valley farmers and breeders, and a selection of cheeses from the nearby Jabron valley. There is a pleasant summer terrace, but even in winter (and winters can be hard in this area), the warmth of Stephanie Paroche's welcome and her brightly painted dining room soon banish the chill of the Mistral. It is 5 km (3 miles) outside the village on the N85 towards Sisteron.

CLOSED Sun dinner (except summer), Mon; first 3 weeks Jan
CARDS MC, V

Avignon
◆ La Fourchette €

17 rue Racine, 84000 Avignon, Vaucluse
Tel 04 90 85 20 93 Fax 04 90 85 57 60

Behind the opera house in the heart of historic Avignon, this pretty little bistro is not only popular with tourists but also a favourite haunt of the Avignonnais. You can't count on turning up and finding a free table; you have to book. 'Warm', 'generous' and 'unpretentious' are the three words that best describe Danièle Hiély's welcome; the atmosphere in the animated, packed dining room (decorated with a collection of forks and models from the Festival); and the food, presented on a single menu, but with plenty of choice. Dishes prepared by Danièle's husband, Philippe, with verve and gusto, have a southern bias. The *ravioli de légumes, emulsion de poisson rouge, filet de lapin à la sauge et jus d'olives, sauté d'agneau* in capers and *daube à l'Avignonnaise* are all excellent. The lack of pretension also extends to the prices and, given the high standard of the cuisine, this attractive place offers excellent value for money, particularly at lunchtime. The wine list is small but well-researched, concentrating on reasonably-priced wines from individual producers on the Rhône.

Bandol
◆ L'Auberge du Port
€ – €€€

9 allée Jean-Moulin, 83150 Bandol, Var
Tel 04 94 29 42 63 Fax 04 94 29 44 59

This seafront restaurant is a place for fish lovers. There is a limited meat menu (including a superb *foie gras*), but the fish is the real attraction here. As you walk inside, you are greeted by a charming waiter and a wooden boat full of ice, where the 'catches of the day', morning-fresh, are on show. Monkfish, sea bream, lobster, *gambas* and all the Mediterranean fish – *daurade, chapon* and *Saint-Pierre* – are served, grilled with fennel, pan-fried, or baked in an impressive salt overcoat, which is smashed in front of you to reveal the succulent, juicy flesh inside. As you would expect, they also serve *bouillabaisse* and *bourride*, as well as fish pasta, *paella* and an unusual fish couscous. The ambience is relaxed and, if it is windy, transparent windbreaking walls will keep you warm. If you stick to the menus, the value is good, but prices rise steeply once you venture on to the carte.

❛ One of the coast's leading fish restaurants' ... 'A very special place but prices are starting to soar ❜

CLOSED never
CARDS AE, MC, V

Barcelonnette
◆ La Mangeoire Gourmande € – €€

place des Quatre-Vents, 04400 Barcelonnette, Alpes-de-Haute-Provence
Tel 04 92 81 01 61 Fax 04 92 81 01 61

Nothing is hidden in this charming restaurant, decorated in yellow and blue and occupying 17thC stables: Didier Le Mar prepares the food for his happy clientele in the open kitchen, proud for them to see the care with which he treats his market-fresh ingredients. Open to all flavours, he uses spices inventively, and changes his imaginative

menus every three months. On the basic menu, for instance, you might find *lasagnes de morue fraîche aux senteurs de Provence et de Saïgon* and, on the gourmet one, *tournedos de magret de canard au caramel d'épices, crème de châtaignes*. Appropriately *foie gras de canard frais, gelée au Muscat* is a speciality of the house.

CLOSED Mon, Tue in low season; Nov-Dec
CARDS MC, V

Le Beaucet
◆ Auberge du Beaucet €

84210 Le Beaucet, Vaucluse
Tel 04 90 66 10 82 Fax 04 90 66 00 72

In a beautiful spot in a *village perché*, 11 km (7 miles) south-east of Carpentras (on the D4 and D39), with troglodyte caves dug into the cliff, this pretty *auberge* serves traditional dishes prepared with loving pride from carefully chosen ingredients. They bear the stamp of the female chef, Brigitte Pizzecco. There is only one menu, but it offers plenty of choice and terrific value. They are particularly proud of the *lapin aux morilles et polenta* and the Landes duck *au miel de La Roque*. Try and leave room for one of the meltingly light hot desserts. Pierre Rouby has built up a first-class wine list, starring well-selected *Côtes du Rhônes*. You must reserve a table.

❛ The puddings are to die for ❜

CLOSED Sun, Mon; Dec-Feb
CARDS MC, V

Beaumont-du-Ventoux
◆ La Maison €

84340 Beaumont-du-Ventoux, Vaucluse
Tel 04 90 66 10 82 Fax 04 90 66 00 72

From the outside, La Maison looks like dozens of other pretty Provençal houses – creeper-covered stone walls, blue window-shutters and doors, white wrought-iron tables and chairs, parasols and plants in terracotta pots on a shady front terrace – but a surprise lies in store. The restaurant, opened by Michèle Laurelut in June 1993, is as chic as the owner herself with the kind of sophistication that you would hardly expect to find on the edge of a sleepy rural village like Beaumont, in the shadow of Mont Ventoux. The decoration is stylishly simple: ochre-washed plaster walls, terracotta-tiled floor and heavy cream curtains at the windows. It is furnished like a private house, with massive table lamps, cushions to sit on, well-spaced tables, and artfully arranged pictures and ornaments. The focal point is an immense stone fireplace where a fire burns on chilly nights, to be replaced by a bank of hydrangeas when the weather improves. Mme Laurelut offers a short seasonal good-value menu (specialities might include *tian d'agneau, aubergines confites à la Provençale* and *petits farcis de saison*), and you can keep your bill down if you stick to the excellent local wine. To save driving home after dinner, you could stay in one of the four large, modest bedrooms.

CLOSED Mon and Tue Apr-Jun, Sep and Oct, lunch Mon-Sat Jul-Sep; Nov-Apr
CARDS MC, V

Our traditional French cuisine symbol
So many of our readers enjoy seeking out the genuinely French eating experience that we have used Fr to mark restaurants which offer *cuisine du terroir*, classical French dishes or regional dishes with an emphasis on local ingredients, and traditional recipes.

Bonnieux
 Fournil €

5 place Carnot, 84480 Bonnieux, Vaucluse
Tel 04 90 75 83 62 Fax 04 90 75 96 19

In a tiny room hewn out of Bonnieux's rocky hillside, Le Fournil is the locals' favourite restaurant. Guy Malbec's Provençal food is neither fussy nor fancy, just consistently good. It's a very individual place, both cosy and bohemian, with rough irregular walls, vibrant modern paintings and a yellow and green chequerboard tiled floor. In summer, tables are set outside around a handsome fountain. The cheap menu is a terrific bargain and the main menu is fairly priced, considering what it offers. They typically include lentil terrine with *foie gras* or aubergine and

tomato *mille-feuille* as starters, followed by roast duckling, rabbit, veal or pork, cooked simply with seasonal vegetables, and accompanied by an excellent selection of local wines. There are very few covers, so it is essential to book.

CLOSED Mon, Tue lunch, Tue dinner Sep-Dec and early Feb to Apr; Dec to early Feb
CARDS MC, V

Cannes
 Mère Besson € – €€ **Fr**

13 rue Frères Pradignac, 06400 Cannes,
Alpes-Maritimes
Tel 04 93 39 59 24 Fax 04 92 18 93 11

This simple little family bistro in the middle of town has a pretty yellow-walled dining room and a delightful terrace. It doesn't have a swish Croisette address, but that is why we like it. Modest and traditional, it offers a welcome relief from the posing and the pretension evident elsewhere in Cannes. The straightforward fresh flavours of Mère Besson's expert cooking, viewed in this area as the mother of true country cuisine, take you back to how Provençal meals used to be. Made from the freshest ingredients, typical dishes are *pieds et paquets* and *suprême de volaille*, but with that extra something that raises each dish from the ordinary to the remarkable. The *salade Niçoise* is food writer Patricia Wells' favourite version.

❛ You can feel the expertise in the kitchen and the enjoyment of the diners ❜

CLOSED Sun; lunch Jun-Sep
CARDS AE, DC, MC, V

Cassis
 Nino €€

Port de Cassis, 13260 Cassis, Bouches-du-Rhône
Tel 04 42 01 43 72 Fax 04 42 01 43 72

The last of the restaurants and cafés strung out around the pretty port of Cassis with its bobbing boats and jolly seaside air, Nino is also the most sophisticated and the most amusing, with the distinct air of an Italian *trattoria*. You sit on a terrace above a wall dripping with bougainvillea and beneath a blue awning in a simple, white-walled room decorated with paintings and photographs. The Italian influence extends to the friendly, prompt waiters as well as to the food. On the short, mainly fish menu you will find *antipasto Nino* and spaghetti dishes as well as Provençal staples such as *bourride*, *bouillabaisse* (very good) and *soupe de poissons*. The lively atmosphere, good fish and fair prices make it just the right place for the setting – perfect between a morning lazing on the beach and an afternoon boat trip to the *calanques*.

CLOSED Sun in winter, Mon; mid-Dec to mid-Feb
CARDS AE, DC, MC, V

La Celle
◆ Hostellerie de l'Abbaye de la Celle €€

place Général de Gaulle, 83170 La Celle, Var
Tel 04 98 05 14 14 Fax 04 98 05 14 15

Two big names, top chef and hotelier Alain Ducasse and local chef/entrepreneur Bruno Clément, came together to create this restaurant, opened with great fanfare in 1999. Together they restored an ancient pilgrim's hostel, abandoned for three centuries, to its present breathtaking architectural splendour. It stands in a tiny village nestling under the Roc Candelon, flanked on one side by the Maison des Vins for Coteaux Varois, on the other by the restored abbey, its cloisters filled with spreading mulberry trees. When the restaurant's garden has fully matured, perfection will have been achieved. The cuisine of Benoit Witz, overseen by Ducasse and Clément, matches the surroundings, with menus that change daily, and are full of flavour and delicacy. Wonderful breads and *madeleines* with coffee. Thoughtful service.

CLOSED never
CARDS AE, DC, MC, V

Châteaux-Arnoux
◆ La Bonne Etape €€€

chemin du Lac, 04160 Château-Arnoux, Alpes-de-Haute-Provence
Tel 04 92 64 00 09 Fax 04 92 64 37 36

From the outside, this former coaching inn in an unremarkable small town gives little hint of what lies within – one of the most satisfactory blends of refinement and hospitality to be found in the region. Although the kitchen lost its second Michelin star, we would re-award it if we could. Chefs Pierre and Jany Gleize (father and son) make innovative and stylish use of largely home-grown ingredients. The house speciality is Sisteron lamb (raised on mountain pastures): try it with a deep-red Vacqueyras Côte du Rhône. Tables in the formal dining room have fresh flowers; Bach plays in the background. There are serious eaters here, many alone. The atmosphere is slightly hushed, but the waiters are helpful and friendly. There is a charming bar with painted beams. The Gleize family are warmly welcoming hosts, happily committed to their work (the inn has 19 rooms); they also own a simpler restaurant nearby.

6 Exceptional food' ... 'Impeccable service 9

CLOSED Mon Oct-Mar, Tue lunch; mid-Nov to mid-Dec, Jan to mid-Feb
CARDS MC, V

Châteauneuf-du-Pape
◆ Mère Germaine
€ – €€ Fr

3 rue Cdt Lemaitre, 84230 Châteauneuf-du-Pape, Vaucluse
Tel 04 90 83 54 37 Fax 04 90 83 50 27

This bright, sunny, bustling brasserie is a delight. It stands in the centre of town beside a fountain, immortalized by a painter and now reproduced on the placemats (on sale at the bar), with spectacular views over the valley's famous vineyards. As you would expect, its wine list is a splendid reflection of local specialities, including Mont Rédon, the new-style, drink-young Châteauneuf-du-Pape – from one of the modern producers. The food is not merely an accompaniment to the wine, but wonderfully rustic traditional country cooking, using heaps of tomatoes, aubergines and, above all, garlic. This makes a great stop-off between vineyard visits.

CLOSED Sun dinner, Tue dinner, Wed; Feb
CARDS MC, V

La Ciotat
◆ RIF Chez Tania €─€€

Calanque de Figuerolles, 13600 La Ciotat,
Bouches-du-Rhône
Tel 04 42 08 41 71 Fax 04 42 71 93 39

The RIF stands for République Independante de Figuerolles and this little wooden cabin right at the tip of Provence, hovering over a tiny narrow creek, is one of the most eccentric restaurants on the coast. The family who own and run it are Russian, and bring a real Russian spirit to their service and style. In summer they serve fish dishes on the pretty terrace, and in winter transform it into a mini *'dacha'*, called 'Tania', serving *borscht, blinis* and lashings of vodka. The food is excellent – the chef, Pascal Barthelet, trained under M. Troigros – though there is almost too much of it (the *côte de boeuf* between two is enough to challenge the heartiest appetites). Fish forms the mainstay of the menu, from the superb *carpaccio de la mer* (swordfish, salmon and tuna) to the *navarin de daurade* with fresh spring vegetables. At night the *calanque* is lit and the views are magical. To find it, follow signs south of La Ciotat to Calanque de Figuerolles. When you arrive, park your car and walk down the steps to the southernmost point.

❨ *A magical spot' ... 'The friendliest welcome I've had in France. I'm thinking of applying for citizenship'* ❩

CLOSED Tue and Wed Dec–Mar
CARDS MC, V

Collobrières
◆ La Petite Fontaine € Fr

83610 Collobrières, Var
Tel 04 94 48 0012

The very best time of year to visit La Petite Fontaine is on a warm autumn day when you can sit outside in the little square, under the turning trees and the washing strung out across the balconies above. Then you can savour the freshly gathered chestnuts for which the village, wedged in the Maures

Massif, is renowned, as well as the booty from *la chasse* – *gibier* plays an important part on the menu of this family-run restaurant. All is rustic warmth and hospitality, where pretension plays no part. The wine is from the local co-operative, and the food (there are just two menus written on blackboards) is local too. Every dish is explained with passion and relish by the Fontana family, whether it be a simple starter such as *terrine* or *tarte à l'oignon*, or a more complex main dish, followed by a plate of ripe cheeses and a delicious dessert. Perfection.

CLOSED Sun dinner, Mon; mid-Feb, mid-Sep to Oct
CARDS MC, V

Correns
◆ Auberge du Parc €€

place du Général de Gaulle, 83570 Correns,
Var
Tel 04 94 59 53 52 Fax 04 94 59 53 54

One of a clutch of notable restaurants in this region owned by larger-than-life Bruno Clément, the Auberge du Parc stands in the centre of Correns, which has proudly styled itself the first *'village biologique'* in France. The street entrance opens on to a pretty but perhaps too fussily decorated Regency-style dining room and a smart terrace at the rear. The clientele is knowing, and not necessarily local, and the lunchtime menu breaks the mould for people spoiled for choice: there is none. You begin with four or five dishes to share, followed by a meat course, again shared from a large platter, then a dessert. Most reports have been of convivial and tasty meals, though some have mentioned dissatisfaction with the choice on offer and 'tough meat'. There is a little creeper-covered arbour, perfect for lovers. If you can, approach Correns along the delightful Sourn valley.

CLOSED Tue, Wed; Nov–Apr
CARDS AE, MC, V

Cotignac
◆ La Table de la Petite Fontaine €─€€

27 cours Gambetta, 83570 Cotignac, Var
Tel 04 94 04 79 13 Fax 04 94 04 79 13

This restaurant is right in the centre of the pretty town and, in summer, spills out into the shady square around the eponymous fountain. Jean-Luc Delandemare is in charge of the excellent kitchen, while his graceful wife attends to the 'front of house'. The menus change quite often – they have to because there is a very loyal clientele here. Among the most memorable dishes are a *gratin of moules* with spinach and spatch-cocked quail in a sauce delicately flavoured with carrots (both on the cheapest menu). Relaxing in the pretty, busy square, eating Provençal food, accompanied by a well-selected local wine, with the town accordionist, dressed in traditional stripey shirt and beret, belting out his rendering of *La Vie en Rose* – this is the real Provence.

❝ *The sort of place you can while away the whole afternoon* ❞

Closed Sun dinner Sep-Jun, Mon; mid-Nov to mid-Dec
Cards DC, MC, V

---

charmingsmallhotels.co.uk
Visit Duncan Petersen's travel website, the best online search tool for places to stay that combine character and charm. Currently features Britain, France, Italy and Ireland, with other destinations being continuously added.

Cucuron
◆ La Petite Maison
€€ – €€€

place de l'Etang, 84160 Cucuron, Vaucluse
Tel 04 90 77 18 60 Fax 04 90 77 18 61

Beautifully restored and furnished, this compelling restaurant in the heart of the lovely village of Cucuron suits its surroundings perfectly, and has a pleasant relaxing summer terrace. There are three menus: *du terroir*, which has four courses; *dégustation*, which has five, including a stunning *râble de lapin de ferme farci de ses rognons*; and, for the true gourmet, an appetizing and imaginative truffle menu. Michel Mehdi claims as his specialities *risotto d'épautre de Sault* and *pieds et paquets en cocotte de fonte*, but everything is well chosen and prepared. Even the bread is baked daily from flour specially

selected from a small independent local mill. There is a limited but intelligent list of mostly Provençal wines.

❝ *Warm and friendly' ... 'Food which is simple but so succulent* ❞

Closed Mon, Tue; mid-Nov to mid-Dec, 2 weeks Jan
Cards MC, V

Digne
◆ Le Grand Paris
€ – €€€

19 boulevard Thiers, 04000 Vieil Digne,
Alpes-de-Haute-Provence
Tel 04 92 31 11 15 Fax 04 92 32 32 82

The bustle of Digne just fades away once you are inside the walls of this splendid hotel and restaurant in a 17thC monastery, where it is claimed Napoleon once stayed. This is a family business: the daughter, Noémie, manages the hotel and the organization of the dining room, with her father, Jean-Jacques Ricaud, at the helm in the kitchen, as he has been for many years, building a strong and respected reputation. His menus, based on local ingredients, are classically gastronomic, and over time he has created certain signature dishes like his *mignonettes d'agneau 'Casimir Moisson'*, his *ragoût* of truffles, and his hot lime *soufflé*. For all the rich ingredients, the prices are not inflated, either for the food or the wine on a superb, comprehensive list. This is a true refuge, as peaceful as it was in olden times, but with the sort of cuisine the monks would never have encountered.

Closed Sun dinner, Mon in winter; Dec-Feb
Cards AE, DC, MC, V

Gap
◆ Le Patalain € – €€

2 place Ladoucette, 05000 Gap, Hautes-
Alpes
Tel 04 92 52 30 83 Fax 04 92 52 30 83

The joy of this restaurant in a handsome town house is the choice you have between two dining rooms and two entirely different styles. On the one hand, the comfortable *bourgeois* dining room offers a gastronomic menu, where the specialities might include *foie gras* with apples and cinnamon prunes, and a fabulous seafood couscous or risotto. On the other, there is a simple bistro with a cheap, straightforward menu of wonderfully tasty dishes to go with the surroundings. The chef-patron, Gérard Perinet is justifiably proud of what he has created here. If you go in summer, book a table in the delightful shady garden.

CLOSED Sun, Mon; first 3 weeks Jan
CARDS AE, DC, MC, V

Our price bands
Rather than giving actual prices (which are prone to change) we indicate the cost of a three-course meal for one person, without wine, by means of price bands. They are as follows: € under 30 euros €€ 30-50 euros €€€ over 50 euros. Where we give more than one price band, for example €– €€€, this indicates that in that restaurant a meal can be had at a range of prices. As well as the cost of *prix fixe* menus, our price bands also take into account the cost of an average selection from the *à la carte* menu.

Gigondas
◆ Les Florets €€ Fr

route des Dentelles, 84190 Gigondas, Vaucluse
Tel 04 90 65 85 01 Fax 04 90 65 83 80

Flowers abound at Les Florets: on the nearby hills in spring, in pots and vases on the terrace and in the dining room, and on the pretty hand-painted plates, each one different. The setting, alone in a fold of wooded hills east of Gigondas and facing the dramatic Dentelles de Montmirail, is glorious, and the ambience is loved by everyone who has a hankering for traditional, proud, family-run places. The Bernard family, who bought the inn (which also has 16 rooms) in 1960, have long been respected for their honest, straightforward approach, and for the good-value food served in the animated dining room or on the lovely leafy terrace in summer. Seasonal dishes of the region dominate the menu. Those based on beef, duck and game are particularly recommended, as are the cheeses. The Bernards are also winegrowers; they keep an impressive cellar, or

you can drink a bottle of their own Gigondas or Vacqueras with your meal.

❛ *A charming family and a wonderful, traditional restaurant' … 'The wine was hard to beat* ❜

CLOSED Wed; Jan-Mar
CARDS AE, DC, MC, V

Golfe Juan
◆ Tetou €€€

boulevard des Frères Roustan, 06220 Golfe Juan, Alpes-Maritimes
Tel 04 94 29 42 63 Fax 04 94 29 44 59

One of the oldest institutions on the coast, Tetou was founded in 1920 beside the newly established beach, which was already becoming fashionable for bathing. Little has changed in the intervening 80 or so years. Their pricey menu has always been built around a fabulous *bouillabaisse* – either with or without lobster – and, considering it costs an extra 15 euros, you might not think the lobster is worth it. But you don't just come here to sample the flavours of the Mediterrannean in good style, you also come here to people-watch as it's a regular haunt of the great and the grand from Cannes. One diner witnessed a poodle in a jewelled collar, its hair dyed with the same light mauve rinse as its elderly lady owner's, sitting on a cushion beside her, being fed the 15-euro lobster by a seriously ingratiating waiter. The wine list is local and includes a well-chosen selection of whites from Côtes de Provence, Cassis and Bellet, which match the fish perfectly.

CLOSED Wed
CARDS none

Golfe Juan
◆ Tetou Plage € Fr

boulevard des Frères Roustan, 06220 Golfe Juan, Alpes-Maritimes
Tel 04 93 63 23 26

Attached but not affiliated to the grand Tetou (see above), this is such a simple family place that you cannot fail to be enchanted. These neighbouring restaurants are totally different yet complement each other so well. Tetou Plage is a beach restaurant with a few tables on wooden boarding, some beach huts and 20 or so mattresses in the sun. But what makes it special is the dynamic and fairly young family who own and run it. Evelyne does the cooking – simple but superb; her husband, Dédé, takes care of bookings and the beach. Their son, Thomas, who speaks fluent English, trained for years in Surrey. They usually only offer two dishes on the basic menu, for instance, salad followed by *filet de boeuf* or *gambas Provençales*, plus dessert. You need to book in high season because locals flock here – and usually stay all afternoon, chatting away.

❝ You'll probably end up being kissed goodbye; it's that sort of place. Join in – become part of the family ❞

CLOSED Oct to Easter
CARDS none

Fr French regional or classical French dishes on menu.

Grasse
◆ Bastide Saint-Antoine
€€ – €€€

48 avenue Henri-Dunant, 06130 Grasse, Alpes-Maritimes
Tel 04 93 70 94 94 Fax 04 93 70 94 95

In summer the bougainvillea that tumbles down the outside of this fine *bastide*, in the hills above the busy Riviera, and on to the paved terrace is so bright that you reach for your sunglasses. The whole place is beautiful, stylish and light. As you realize when a uniformed lackey steps out to park your car for you, it is not a casual place, but somewhere to be pampered. It can be a very expensive treat indeed, especially for dinner, but the three-course lunch menu, a gastronome's delight, offers much better value (not served at weekends). The *bastide* is the creation of the famous Jacques Chibois. He names as his *plats signatures*, the *papillon de langoustines en chiffonnade de basilic*, the *loup de Mediterranée nouvelle vague à l'huile d'olive vanillée* and the *fraises cuites au vin d'epice avec leur glace à l'huile d'o-live*. This is a hint: M. Chibois is justifiably proud of his olive oil, which he makes from the trees that shade his own property. It is

such a passion that he bases his cuisine on it. There are also beautiful but expensive rooms and a lovely pool.

❝ A very special place' … 'A fantastic experience – one of the best meals I've ever had ❞

CLOSED never
CARDS AE, MC, V

Hyères
◆ La Colombe €€ Fr

663 route de Toulon, La Bayorre, 83400 Hyères, Var
Tel 04 94 35 16 Fax 04 94 35 37 68

The ochre of this pretty *auberge* catches the eye, signalling a restaurant where the cooking is equally outstanding. It is Pascal Bonamy who has turned this house into the success that it is today. He believes in consistent excellence in his kitchen, which is open to the bright, sunny dining room. Passing food fads and newfangled crazes are not for him; he uses Provençal produce to create uniquely Provençal flavours – *petits légumes confites*, lamb with local herbs, or in a potato crust, *mignon de veau poêlé* – and light, delicate desserts. You'll find it 5 km (3 miles) west of Hyères on the road to Toulon, and there is a particularly attractive terrace for those long summer evenings.

CLOSED Mon in high season, Tue lunch
CARDS DC, MC, V

L'Isle-sur-la-Sorgue
◆ Bernard Auzet €€ – €€

Petit Palais, 84800 L'Isle-sur-la-Sorgue, Vaucluse
Tel 04 90 38 09 74 Fax 04 90 20 91 26

One of the smallest restaurants – if not the smallest – featured in this guide, Bernard Auzet serves only 15 clients at each sitting. Three years ago they deliberately reduced capacity, to increase the family feeling and personal service and to allow Bernard to produce masterpieces of rare quality. Coming in through the pretty garden entrance, you will be welcomed by Sophie who will show you either to the elegant dining room or the glorious terrace. Menus change daily and with the season.

Specialities such as quail's eggs poached in *foie gras, fricassée of baudroie aux langoustines* or *estouffade d'agneau du Lubéron aux olives.* Everything, from the *apéritif feuilletés* to the bread and ice-creams, is made by Bernard, who believes passionately in local ingredients from *culture raisonnée* producers. A jewel of a place, but make sure you book. It is 6 km (4 miles) south-east of L'Isle-sur-la-Sorgue on the D3.

(*Fabulous use of herbs' ... 'Although service can be slow, the food is well worth waiting for*)

Closed Sun in winter, Tue dinner, Wed
Cards MC, V

Our price bands
€ under 30 euros €€ 30-50 Euros
€€€ over 50 euros for a menu

Lorgues
◆ Le Chrissandrier €

18 cours de la République, 83510 Lorgues, Var
Tel 04 94 67 67 15 Fax 04 94 67 67 15

For a perfect morning, pay a visit to Lorgues' Tuesday market, one of the best in the area, followed by lunch at this delightful restaurant in the town centre. Small and intimate, charmingly decorated (with a cabinet of antique wine decanters in the dining room), it is filled with tables all through the building, under bright umbrellas on the busy roadside pavement and on the pretty terrace at the back. Owners, Christophe and Sandra Chabredier (he is the chef, she smiles welcomingly at front of house) describe their cuisine as 'faite de passion et de sincérité', and you really do feel that this keen young couple are giving their all. They offer a simple and inexpensive lunchtime menu, and a surprisingly extensive *carte*. Interesting vegetables to accompany, such as *petits légumes servis avec un jus d'orange aux olives Niçoise*. The wines are local.

(*A terrific find, run by a charming, dedicated young couple*)

Closed Wed
Cards MC, V

Lourmarin
◆ Auberge la Fenière
€€€

route de Cadenet, 84160 Lourmarin, Vaucluse
Tel 04 90 68 11 79 Fax 04 90 68 18 60

You are guaranteed a gourmet dinner at this Michelin-starred restaurant in a converted *mas,* where the chef is a talented, self-taught and charming woman, Reine Sammut. The feminine touch is easy to detect in such dishes as *foie gras* sautéed in honey, a tart of sea bass topped with caramelized apples, or *pigeonneau fermier* eaten in the fingers, accompanied by Camargue rice. Reine's husband is front of house, overseeing service that is as smooth as you would expect from a slick operation like this, but it lacks heart. If you stay the night – there are seven smart modern bedrooms and two kitsch gypsy caravans. Breakfast is also a gourmet experience.

(*The cooking was wonderful – light and delicate*)

Closed Mon, Tue lunch mid-Oct to Jul; mid-Nov to Feb
Cards AE, DC, MC, V

Lourmarin
◆ Moulin de Lourmarin
€€€

rue du Temple, 84160 Lourmarin, Vaucluse
Tel 04 90 68 06 69 Fax 04 90 68 31 76

The presence of Edouard Loubet, the precocious chef of this old olive mill turned chic restaurant, during one of his splendid meals will live forever in your memory. A description has to begin by stating how excellent the food is, richly deserving of its two Michelin stars. The sauces are exquisite and each dish is presented with pride and panache. Many chefs in this region talk about their dedication to the flavours of the local terrain, the *terroir*. None is as passionate or devoted as Loubet, who presides over his kitchen garden as fiercely as he presides over his kitchen, uses every type of hedgerow plant, and even decorates his plates with crumbs of earth from his garden. "It is dirt!" he exclaims, daring you to question his audacious genius. Eating here is certainly expensive, but it is an experience you will never forget, not just for the fabulous food – each year surpasses the last – but for the awesome personality of the chef. The knowlegeable *sommelier* will direct you skilfully through the excellent Lubéron-dominated wine list.

CLOSED Tue, Wed lunch; mid-Jan to mid-Mar, late Nov to early Dec
CARDS AE, DC, MC, V

Manosque
◆ La Barbotine €

5 place de l'Hôtel de Ville, 04100 Manosque, Alpes-de-Haute-Provence
Tel 04 92 72 57 15

An entirely feminine welcome awaits customers at this charming ochre-walled restaurant, owned, run and staffed by women. Heavy old oak beams and worn tiled floors characterize this generous oasis, a much-appreciated discovery in an area where there are many restaurants, but not many, frankly, to recommend. Gisèle and Mireille Rey are the creators of La Barbotine, and they offer a fabulous seasonal, if simple, menu featuring Provençal vegetable dishes, fresh pasta, *pâtisseries à la maison* and – in summer – superb salads which are a meal in themselves. And look out for the delicious and sumptuous grills on the *viande* menu. There are just two menus, one featuring meat, the other vegetarian. There is a pretty terrace for outdoor dining, and a *salon de thé* on summer afternoons.

> ❝ One of the few restaurants in France where you can savour being vegetarian ❞

CLOSED Sun
CARDS MC, V

Manosque
◆ Dominique Bucaille €€

43 boulevard des Tilleuls, 04100 Manosque, Alpes-de-Haute-Provence
Tel 04 92 72 32 28 Fax 04 92 72 32 28

In a handsome beamed 17thC mill, Dominique Bucaille (whose passion, he

declares, is for vegetables) orchestrates his kitchen in full view of his customers. As well as the excellent medium-priced *carte*, there are two special menus. *Autour de la pomme de terre* is an extraordinarily creative and delicate collection of dishes, where the *tubercule délicat* first arrives as a cappuccino soup, followed by a dish of *foie gras* on smashed potato, then as a *galette* with lamb. The *tout homard* menu is more expensive but mouthwatering tempting. The wine list is intelligent and extensive with only the Burgundies showing a weakness as most have been bought from *negotiants*, whereas the Southern wines are all Château bought and carefully chosen.

> ❝ Superbly delicate dishes. His passion for vegetables shines through everything – so rare in Provence ❞

CLOSED Sun (except bank hols), Wed dinner; mid-Jul to mid-Aug
CARDS AE, DC, MC, V

Manosque
◆ Hostellerie de la Fuste €€ – €€€

Lieu-dit la Fuste, route d'Oraison, D4, 04210 Valensole, Alpes-de-Haute-Provence
Tel 04 92 72 05 95 Fax 04 92 72 92 93

Elegantly set in a shady garden, this old post house has now been in the steady, capable, loving hands of Daniel Jourdan for some 40 years, and throughout that time has been considered one of the best tables in Provence. Whether you are sitting out on the terrace under the ancient plane trees in summer, eating crayfish or the local Sisteron lamb roasted with thyme; or in the gilded dining room in winter, sampling partridge, hare or *foie gras* flecked with truffle; you are likely to enjoy a traditional Provençal feast at the Hostellerie de la Fuste. There is a huge wine list, which tends to be overpriced, but even this doesn't deter loyal fans of M. Jourdan's cooking and warm, charismatic personality. The *hostellerie* is 6 km (4 miles) south-east of Manosque on the D907, then the D4. It's wise to book ahead.

CLOSED Sun dinner, Mon Oct-Jun (except bank hols); one week early Jan, 2 weeks Mar, mid-Nov to early Dec
CARDS AE, DC, MC, V

Marseille
◆ Le Bar de la Marine €

15 quai de Rive-Neuve, 13007 Marseille,
Bouches-du-Rhône
Tel 04 91 54 95 42 Fax 04 91 55 00 67

Down by the old port, near the spot where the ferryboat docks, this little bar/restaurant has been done out in its original 1930s style. Amongst all the zinc and tiling are many reminders of Marcel Pagnol's characters, for it was here that the Marius films were made. Nowadays it is favoured more by locals than tourists, perhaps because they relish the familiar service as well as the generous portions and robust cooking. There are usually two or three dishes of the day, numerous vast salads, plus some fish and bistrot dishes. It is always busy and congenial and can become rather squashed inside, but there is an outside terrace too.

❛ No-fuss food, simple wine list, great atmosphere' … 'Feels like being whisked back in time ❜

Closed never
Cards none

Please send us reports
A guide such as this thrives on reader's reports. If you send us five usable reports, we will send you a free copy of any title in our *Charming Small Hotel Guides* series (see page 241 for France titles in the series).

The five reports should contain at least two new restaurants; the balance can be comments on restaurants already in the guide. **Send reports to** Charming Restaurant Guides, Duncan Petersen Ltd, 31 Ceylon Road, London W14 0PY.

Marseille
◆ Le Lunch €€

Calanque de Sormiou, 13008 Marseille,
Bouches-du-Rhône
Tel 04 91 25 05 37

The *calanque* is wild and stony, the sea clearer than you will ever have seen, and this little restaurant sits beside the lapping waves. They serve simple grilled fish – quite pricey but wonderfully appropriate as you relax and soak up the magic of this remote spot. The *bouillabaisse* (for a minimum of two people) is special and should be ordered in advance. Otherwise the menu includes an *entrée* and grilled sea bream, monkfish or whatever has been the 'catch of the day'. It is advisable to book in high season. To get there, follow signs for Baumettes and Sormiou from the southern quarter of Marseille. Between mid-June and mid-September, it is important to phone the restaurant in advance to arrange a pass to allow you through the barrier in your car. It is a long winding road on foot.

❛ The terrace must be one of the best places in the world to sit and sip a pastis ❜

Closed Nov to mid-Mar
Cards none

Marseille
◆ Les Mets de Provence
€€

18 quai de Rive-Neuve, 13007 Marseille,
Bouches-du-Rhône
Tel 04 91 33 35 38 Fax 04 91 33 35 38

One of the most atmospheric and homely places to eat in Marseille, Les Mets de Provence is long-established, having first opened in 1937, and is still justly popular. Located on the second floor of the old quayside family home of the proprietor, Maurice Brun, it's right in the heart of the old port (near Le Bar de la Marine, see opposite), best viewed, with its ferries and fishing boats, from the restaurant's big picture window. Rough wharfside steps take you away from the world of the sea and deposit you, once inside, firmly in the Provençal countryside. The rustic dining room has a large *rôtisserie* in the open hearth, and charming tables laid with prettily mismatched plates and glasses. There's no menu: M. Brun recites the offerings of the day (plenty of choice), spanning an extensive repertoire of Provençal dishes.

Closed Sun, Mon lunch; early to mid-Aug
Cards MC, V

Marseille
◆ Une Table au Sud
€ – €€

2 quai Port, 13002 Marseille, Bouches-du-Rhône
Tel 04 91 90 63 53 Fax 04 91 90 63 86

Gault Millau 2002 has picked Lionel Levy as one of its six 'chefs of tomorrow' and with good reason. Trained by Alain Ducasse, he is one of the most exciting young chefs in the area. He serves imaginative dishes, blending the spices of the Far East with the flavours of the Mediterrananean; for example, fish with ginger. His saddle of lamb with honey and lemon, served with dates and apricots, is delectable, but his sure touch reaches perfection with the magnificent desserts, particularly his famous tomato stuffed with aromatic fruits, a gloriously successful cocktail of pineapple, pear, caramelized orange, bitter citrus and cardamom. The yellow and orange dining room is airy and full of sunshine and sunflowers. Prices have increased slightly in line with Levy's reputation, but a meal here is something you won't regret.

❢ A great view along the port' ... 'This place just gets better and better ❣

Closed Sun, Mon; first week Jan, end Jul to late Aug
Cards MC, V

Maussane-les-Alpilles
◆ Margaux €€

1 rue Paul-Reveil, 13520 Maussane-les-Alpilles, Bouches-du-Rhône
Tel 04 90 54 35 04 Fax 04 90 54 35 04

This perfectly kept little restaurant, just off the attractive main square filled with plane trees and with a fine fountain in the centre, has a crisp freshness about it. You enter into a charming courtyard, where you can dine in fine weather under perfectly shaped olive trees. The dining room, for cooler days, looks as if it has just been decorated, very smart with its lemon-yellow walls and white-clothed tables. In fact it's six years old, the creation of patron Jean Metraz-Brunand-Meiffre and his wife Martine. Jean, like his name, is larger than life, both in height and character, and often chats to his guests with wry humour. The

menu is short, to the point, and well executed: *crespëou*, a terrine of Provençal vegetables, *artichauds à la barrigoule*, *poulet fermier* with tarragon, *pieds et paquets*.

Closed Tue, Wed lunch; Feb, mid-Nov to mid-Dec
Cards DC, MC, V

Our traditional French cuisine symbol
So many of our readers enjoy seeking out the genuinely French eating experience that we have used Fr to mark restaurants which offer *cuisine du terroir*, classical French dishes or regional dishes with an emphasis on local ingredients, and traditional recipes.

Menton
◆ Pierrot-Pierrette
€ – €€

place de l'Eglise, Monti, 06500 Menton, Alpes-Maritimes
Tel 04 93 35 79 76 Fax 04 93 35 79 76

Quaintly 'French farmhouse' in style and rather dark in winter, this restaurant has two great attractions: its fantastic perched position in the hills behind Menton and the excellent food, which has brought it a regular, devoted clientele. The menus comprise local specialities, with a leaning towards seafood. Their *écrevisses à la Provençale*, *notre petite bouillabaisse* and *noix de Saint-Jacques aux pointes d'asperge* are first-class, and served with such warm smiles that you feel like part of the family.

❢ The views from the terrace are breathtaking ❣

Closed Mon; Dec to mid-Jan
Cards MC, V

Mison
◆ L'Iris de Suse €
04200 Mison, Alpes-de-Haute-Provence
Tel 04 92 62 21 69

Tucked away in the shadow of the walls of a château, this ancient stone *bergerie* has been beautifully restored and turned into a little gem of a restaurant, a brilliant discovery. Convivial and welcoming, it makes you feel immediately at ease. The excellent value menus are packed with plum local ingredients, presented in tempting and innovative new recipes. Go for the stuffed rabbit, the *canard au sauce miel* or the *pintadeau* (baby guinea-fowl) stuffed with figs. The wine list is mainly local and there is a relaxing terrace. Mison is 10 km (6 miles) north of Sisteron via the N75.

CLOSED Sun in winter, Tue dinner, Wed
CARDS MC, V

Mondragon
◆ La Beaugravière €€€

RN7, 84430 Mondragon, Vaucluse
Tel 04 90 40 82 54 Fax 04 90 40 91 01

Truffles are the thing at La Beaugravière: Guy Jullien is a specialist, and during the autumn truffle season, aficionados flock to his restaurant for dishes such as *foie gras de canard rôti au jus de truffes* and *pavé de boeuf sauce au vin de Syrah truffé*. Whatever time of the year, the menu reflects classic regional cuisine, paying close attention to seasonal variations and good local produce. The wine list is strong on Côte du Rhône. In summer you eat on a shady terrace, in winter in the dining room decorated with illustrations of species of vines. Service is prompt and attentive.

CLOSED Sun dinner, Mon; mid to late Sep
CARDS MC, V

Mougins
◆ Hôtel de Mougins €€

205 avenue Golf, 06250 Mougins, Alpes-Matitimes
Tel 04 92 92 17 07 Fax 04 92 92 17 08

Mougins has so many good restaurants to choose from, led by Roger Vergé's Moulin de Mougins, that it is hard to decide where to eat. But the Hôtel de Mougins has the prettiest setting, as well as food you cannot fault and delightful service. The hotel is stylish in a very Provençal way, and the terrace where you eat is bordered by a lovely garden. The menu is also Provençal in flavour, but with subtle and imaginative variations. Compared to some of the town's other establishments, it is very reasonably

priced. It is 2.5 km (1.5 miles) out of Mougins on the road to Antibes.

❛ *Highly recommended' … 'Perfect for dinner on a summer's evening* ❜

CLOSED Sun
CARDS AE, DC, MC, V

Moustiers-Sainte-Marie
◆ La Ferme Sainte-Cécile €€

route de Castellane, 04360 Moustiers-Sainte-Marie, Alpes-de-Haute-Provence
Tel 04 92 74 64 18 Fax 04 92 74 63 51

Moustiers is blessed with wonderful restaurants, but Patrick Crespin's small farm is a particular delight. Its broad shady terrace looks down over slopes of asparagus, raspberries, lettuce and tomatoes to a riverbed below, while the two small dining rooms are charming, with cream flagstones, white chairs and tables festooned with flowers. Fresh local produce is the basis for Crespin's cuisine; as well as cultivating his own, he patronizes the local markets and farmers (vis. his *pigeonneau fermier de Valensole*, or *tomette de chèvre de L&L Martin*) and twice a week makes the 120-km (75-mile) journey to Marseille's Vieux Port fish market. An interesting innovation are his savoury ices – fresh anchovies with Ligurian olive ice cream, or roast garlic ice served with fish. Enthusiastic and knowledgeable staff.

CLOSED Sun dinner, Mon Sep-Jun; mid-Nov to mid-Dec, Feb
CARDS MC, V

La Napoule
◆ Le Bruit de la Mer €

Port de la Rague, 06210 La Napoule, Alpes-Maritimes
Tel 04 93 49 57 47

Its exterior seems unassuming enough, but this restaurant enjoys a stunning and unforgettable view over the Mediterranean. The best time to appreciate it is at dinner: it's positioned on the furthest promontory of the port, and as the sun begins to sink, the lights of Cannes across the bay begin to twinkle, against a backdrop of the looming Iles de

Lérins, and the brooding Alps in the distance. As for the noise of the sea (*bruit de la mer*), that comes to you in the guise of the gentle clank of halyards against masts in this modern but pleasant harbour. The view wins the day, but the food won't disappoint. The fish, as you would expect, is the freshest possible, and served according to the day's catch with a wide selection of sauces and accompaniments. If you can't decide, ask what the chef recommends.

CLOSED Sun-Wed, Thu eve in winter
CARDS AE, DC, MC, V

Please send us reports
A guide such as this thrives on reader's reports. If you send us five usable reports, we will send you a free copy of any title in our *Charming Small Hotel Guides* series (see page 241 for France titles in the series).

The five reports should contain at least two new restaurants; the rest can be comments on restaurants already in the guide.
1 Tell us about your experiences in restaurants already in this guide.
2 Send us new reports. New reports should give the following information:
- **Region** – City, town, village or neaest village.
- **Name of restaurant** – Please double check the spelling, it's surprisingly easy to make a mistake.
- **Address** – including *département*
- **Telephone number** – plus fax and e-mail if available. Double check this information.
- **Objective description** – Try to explain simply why it should be in the guide. Remember that the guide is very selective - our entries are those one-in-five places that combine
- interesting food with
- character and charm, in the building, the setting or both.

The guide hates tourist traps, and pretentious, dressed-up food. We like places where the French go.

We favour places in the lower and middle price bands but there are plenty of expensive places that have our qualities, and we list those too.
- **Diner's comments** – These should be short, personal comments on features that strike you. They can be your comments, or others'.
- **Closing times**
- **Credit cards accepted**
Don't forget to date your report and add your name and address.
Send reports to Charming Restaurant Guides, Duncan Petersen Publishing, 31 Ceylon Road, London W14 OPY.

Nice
 Chantecler €€ – €€€

Hôtel Negresco, 37 promenade des Anglais, 06000 Nice, Alpes-Maritimes
Tel 04 93 16 64 00 Fax 04 93 88 35 68

That famous Belle Epoque palace, the prestigious Negresco, needs little introduction to visitors to Nice. At some point, most people cannot resist a stroll through the stunning Salon Royal, its crystal dome glistening over the largest Aubusson carpet in the world, to drink in the luxury – the gold leaf, mahogany panelling and rich silks – before strolling out again on to the promenade des Anglais. But the Negresco has a secret that comparatively few people seem to know. Alain Llorca's Chantecler restaurant, which usually feeds the rich and famous from two exorbitantly priced menus (the Chantecler and a *ronde des tapas* comprising 11 *gourmandises*) has an affordable yet inspired weekday lunchtime *retour de marché* menu. It provides a chance to sample Llorca's exquisite cuisine for a mere 40 or 50 euros (including wine and coffee). Consisting of three courses, it might start with *foie gras* with peach marmelade or *Chartreuse d'asperges verte à l'oeuf mollet et mozzarella*, followed by a main course such as *daurade royale, brocolis et jus à la verveine*. The desserts are light and luxurious at the same time. Lunching here is an experience both in culinary and aesthetic terms, and is well worth the visit. Emphatically no pipes, cigars or active mobile phones.

❛ Sumptuous surroundings' … 'Dishes prepared with such style and confidence' … 'I'll never forget it ❜

CLOSED mid-Nov to mid-Dec
CARDS AE, DC, MC, V

Nice
◆ Château des Ollières
€€

39 avenue des Baumettes, 06000 Nice,
Alpes-Maritimes
Tel 04 92 15 77 99 Fax 04 92 15 77 98

The last of the fantastical follies from the Belle Epoque, this château in its own park in the centre of Nice was built by a Russian prince for the love of his wife (unfortunately for protocol, she was the wife of the French ambassador in Constantinople). After her death, it passed through various hands, but has now been in the same family for nearly 70 years, and they turned it into a hotel in 1990. It's an extraordinary place, turreted and eclectic, and inside the style is equally over-the-top: some walls covered in silk, others in leather, ceilings moulded or frescoed and everywhere you look antiques, paintings, sculptures, family memorabilia and curios. In the luxuriously draped Restaurant-Véranda, which opens on to the garden, Patrick Bor's menu is as rich and fine as the surroundings. His *mousseline tiède de crabe sur son cake d'herbes fraîches* is particularly delicious, but he is best known for his *carré d'agneau en croute d'olives et son infusion d'herbes rôties.*

❛ An extraordinary place – it feels like another world' … 'I couldn't believe how warm and unstuffy the welcome was ❜

Closed never
Cards AE, MC, V

Nice
◆ Coco Beach €€ – €€€

2 avenue Jean Lorrain, 06300 Nice, Alpes-Maritimes
Tel 04 93 89 39 26 Fax 04 92 04 02 39

This fabulous restaurant, with incredible views right across to Cap d'Antibes was started in 1936 by a local fisherman, Jean-Baptiste Coco. And it's no surprise that fish is on the menu – the freshest you'll find: grilled, fried in olive oil, and in *bouillabaisse* – a real *cuisine de la mer*. It is still run by the family, Jean-Baptiste's grand-daughter in fact, and the friendly welcome doesn't disap-

pear after the first 5 minutes but is evident throughout the meal. A popular place since the beginning, it numbered Cocteau, Picasso and Pagnol amongst its customers – and no wonder for, apart from the cooking, it probably has the best view on the whole Eastern Riviera. You can gaze out across the bay, with the ferries and yachts going in and out of Nice's port, and all the way along the coast.

❛ The sunset from this terrace was spectacular ❜

Closed Sun and Mon in winter, Sun lunch and Mon lunch in summer
Cards AE, DC, MC, V

Opio
◆ Mas des Géraniums
€ Fr

San Peyre, 06650 Opio, Alpes-Maritimes
Tel 04 93 77 70 11 Fax 04 93 77 70 11

There is something truly beguiling about lunch on the wide sloping terrace of this restaurant. As well as simple food, it once offered simple bedrooms in the house, a traditional Provençal *bastide*, but now, under chef Michel Creusot, concentrates on the food alone. It is well named, you think, as you relax at one of the tables under shady trees and awnings, surrounded by bright geraniums. Ask for one on the highest level to get the best view of the old village and the golf course below. Although there is, inevitably, a mainly Provençal flavour to the food (such as *filets de rougets à la Provençale*), M. Creusot comes from Burgundy, and therefore *escargots*, *poulet de Bresse aux morilles* and the like also make a showing on the menu.

Closed Tue, Wed, Thu lunch Jul-Aug; mid-Nov to mid-Jan
Cards MC, V

Pégomas
◆ Relais du Pas de l'Ai
€€ Fr

route de Tanneron, 06580 Pégomas, Alpes-Maritimes
Tel 04 93 60 98 47 Fax 04 93 42 81 84

If you're looking for peace and quiet, here is a tiny oasis of tranquillity amid the brazen bustle of the Côte d'Azur. Though it lies between Grasse and Cannes, it feels as though it's in the middle of nowhere, lost in a little valley which is as lovely in February, when it is covered in yellow mimosa, as it is in summer. There are fine views from the terrace. As for the food, it is described as '*gastronomique*' although it is really good standard Provençal. The delightful family who have owned the place since it started 12 years ago are endearingly enthusiastic: "La terrine de foie gras! C'est une merveille." Also notable are the *confit de canard* and *risotto de gambas*. An unpretentious place with a genuinely rural feel, where you can get away for a few hours before rejoining the madding crowd.

CLOSED Mon, Tue lunch summer, Sun and Tue dinner winter
CARDS AE, MC, V

Our price bands
Rather than giving actual prices (which are prone to change) we indicate the cost of a three-course meal for one person, without wine, by means of price bands. They are as follows: € under 30 euros €€ 30-50 euros €€€ over 50 euros. Where we give more than one price band, for example €– €€€, this indicates that in that restaurant a meal can be had at a range of prices. As well as the cost of *prix fixe* menus, our price bands also take into account the cost of an average selection from the *à la carte* menu.

Peillon
◆ Auberge de la Madone €€

06440 Peillon, Alpes-Maritimes
Tel 04 93 79 91 17 Fax 04 93 79 99 36

You may think that you have taken a wrong turning as you first spy Peillon, perched impossibly on the hillside, with little sign of any road leading up to it. Time seems to stand still in this medieval walled village, just outside which is the *auberge* with an equally stunning position. In the same family for three generations, it happily combines a sense of special hospitality with affordable prices and good honest cooking created by father-and-son team, Christian and Thomas

Millo. They use organic local ingredients in specialities such as *agneau de lait, cuit comme l'autrefois et moelleux de pommes rattes à la purée d'olive* or *brousse de vache fondante à l'huile du pays, quelques chanterelles et une farce d'herbe et de blettes, dans un feuilletage léger*. Lunch and dinner are served on the sunny terrace, under a large awning, or in the welcoming Provençal-style dining room, depending on the season.

CLOSED Wed; 2 weeks Jan, mid-Oct to mid-Dec
CARDS MC, V

Piolenc
◆ Auberge de l'Orangerie €

4 rue de l'Ormeau, 84420 Piolenc, Vaucluse
Tel 04 90 29 59 88 Fax 04 90 29 67 74

This curious little *auberge*, almost submerged by a jungle of greenery, is just off the main street of a small town that prides itself on its garlic festival. Owners Gérard and Micky Delarocque have given an original and imaginative 'retro' feeling to to an 18thC house in a gated courtyard. The lively restaurant draws in local business people at lunchtime with such dishes as *filets de rascasse à la Provençale, noisettes de gigot d'agneau au basilic frais, crabe farci au piment des Caraïbes* and their own special *struddel*. The walls display what appears to be a collection of striking Georges de La Tour pictures; they are, in fact, painted by M. Delarocque, a talented copyist (and single-malt connoisseur). Upstairs there are five bedrooms, decorated in a delightfully bohemian style.

CLOSED Mon lunch
CARDS MC, V

Le Pontet-Avignon
◆ Auberge de Cassagne €€€

450 allée de Cassagne, 84130 Le Pontet-Avignon, Vaucluse
Tel 04 90 31 04 18 Fax 04 90 32 25 09

Behind a high wall in an unprepossessing setting – a suburb of Avignon with wide, busy roads and new housing developments – is a former cottage of the nearby château. With much hard work, it has been turned into a remarkably comfortable and pleasing hotel with a locally renowned one-Michelin-star kitchen, chef from Bocuse, Philippe Boucher, and an abundant wine cellar. At dinner, you can count 20 different cheeses on the tray and 45 Côtes du Rhône reds on the wine list. Boucher's cooking mixes the classical with the regional, in for example, his *escalope de foie gras de canard poêlée et déglacé au suc de porto*. He is not without his critics, however, and the menu is undeniably overpriced. Despite this, the restaurant is a popular local gathering place, buzzing in the evenings with local custom, visitors and hotel guests.

Closed never
Cards AE, DC, MC, V

---

charmingsmallhotels.co.uk
Visit Duncan Petersen's travel website, the best online search tool for places to stay that combine character and charm. Currently features Britain, France, Italy and Ireland, with other destinations being continuously added.

Porquerolles (Ile de)
◆ Auberge des Glycines
€ Fr

place des Armes, 83400 Ile de Porquerolles, Var
Tel 04 94 58 30 36 Fax 04 94 58 35 22

As soon as you enter the courtyard, shaded by wisteria (*glycines*), fig and lemon trees and framed with peach walls and forget-me-not blue shutters, you realize this is a haven of peace off the busy main square, choc-a-bloc with tourists on bicycles (cars are not allowed), and you start to relax. *Plat du jours* include typically *Provençale cuisine*, in which, not surprisingly on an island, fish dominates: swordfish and tuna *brochettes* or *loup de mer*, flambéed at the table with fennel and grilled in a salt crust that is cracked open before serving. Specialities are *aïoli* and *bouillabaisse*, served on Provençal tablecloths under large umbrellas or before an open fire in the terracotta-tiled dining

room, depending on the season. This is a fun, casual, bright place with a charming look of stylish simplicity and 11 sunny, air-conditioned bedrooms.

❛ Pretty Provençal colours; charming welcome and service' … 'Fresh fish – pure and simple – a delight ❜

Closed never
Cards AE, MC, V

Le Pradet
◆ Chanterelle €€

Les Oursinières, 83220 Le Pradet, Var
Tel 04 94 08 52 60

In a *cul-de-sac* a stone's throw from the seafront, this little pastel-decorated restaurant looks on to a wonderfully lush garden. Filled with rampant geraniums, lavender, bougainvillea, colourful butterflies, dragonflies and the *chant de cigales*, it is the province of Corinne Perrot, Chanterelle's lovely smiling hostess, who takes care of every tiny detail. She is justifiably proud of her husband Didier, whose imaginative and interesting menus include a *ravioli* of *escargots* in a chervil sauce, topped by cinnamon-flavoured nut crumbs, *filet de maigre* (a seabass cousin), full of flavours and smokey richness, and a meaty, flakey and gently caramelized *filet de merou*, on a shallot bed. He also makes fresh, light and tasty puddings (*nougat glacé* and warm *tarte aux pommes, glace vanille*). The *carte des vins* is a marvellous reflection of superb value Provence wines, showing intelligent knowledge of the area, and the whites are cooled in a bucket containing a massive hunk of ice – much more effective than the usual eight cubes.

Closed Mon Sep to Easter; Jan-Mar
Cards MC, V

Rognes
◆ Les Olivarelles €€

route Saint-Christophe, 13840 Rognes, Bouches-du-Rhône
Tel 04 42 50 24 27 Fax 04 42 50 17 99

In the calm of the hills outside Rognes, this attractive *mas* is named after the young girls who used to harvest the olives. In winter, lunch and dinner are served in the handsome antique-filled dining room, in summer, on the delightful shaded terrace. Paul Dietrich, who has owned this popular restaurant for 25 years, is a perfectionist in the kitchen. He boasts that his cuisine is classical and light, and uses only *bons produits*. The poultry, for example, is raised in the garden, and fed only on wheat, barley and oats. The specialities on his regular menus include *foie gras*, *emincé de lapin au basilic* and meat cooked on a huge roasting spit, including suckling pig, whole lamb and duck. His desserts are seriously delicious, especially the *soufflé glacé lavende*. Every now and then they have a 'themed menu', usually based around truffles, but occasionally lobster. Though more than twice the price of the regular menus, they are famous throughout the area and draw in many loyal enthusiasts. Wines — mostly local Coteaux d'Aix and Lubéron, but sometimes Rhône Valley, Cassis or Bandol — are carefully chosen to bring out the best in each delicate course. It is 6 km (4 miles) north-west of Rognes; take the D66 then follow the signs.

❛ The truffle dinner was wonderful – there was even a magnificent truffle sorbet ❜

CLOSED Mon, Sun dinner in summer; Mon-Thu in winter
CARDS MC, V

Fr French regional or classical French dishes on menu.

Roure
◆ Auberge du Robur €

06420 Roure, Alpes-Maritimes
Tel 04 93 02 03 57 Fax 04 93 02 00 72

This is a charming restaurant in a charming spot some 70 km (44 miles) north of Nice, perched above the Tinée valley, almost lost to civilization and certainly far from the glitz of Cannes' Croisette. It's the sort of place you need to know about, because you'd never just stumble across it. Gérard Bassard, who cooks, and his wife, Patricia, offer a warm welcome and two great-value menus, generously served, and based on *cuisine du haut pays Niçois*. Their *petits choux farcis* (with terrine and *foies de volaille*) are mouthwatering, as is their *croustillant d'ag-

neau à la tapenade au fumet de pistou. Even the attractive starter of *pressé de chèvre frais, tapenade noire et poivrons rouges grillés* is worth travelling 70 km (44 miles) and climbing 1000 m (3000 ft) for.

❛ Simple, generous and unspoilt – a beautiful spot, deep in the country ❜

CLOSED Sun lunch, Wed low season; one week Christmas
CARDS MC, V

Rove
◆ Auberge de Mérou €

3 chemin du Port, Calanque de Niolon,
13740 Rove, Bouches-du-Rhône
Tel 04 91 46 98 69 Fax 04 91 46 90 06

In this tiny fishing village with the narrowest of roads, parking is incredibly frustrating, but once you get to the lovely Auberge de Mérou, and glimpse the fabulous view, all your irritation will melt away: it gives meaning to the expression 'le grand bleu'. There is a fisherman's menu to go with the setting, in which the flavours are quintessentially Mediterranean. Although the food is expertly cooked and presented (simple grilled fish or *fruits de mer flambés à l'anis*), it is the spectacular sea view that wins the day. Rove is 17 km (11 miles) north-west of Marseille off the N568.

CLOSED never
CARDS AE, MC, V

Saignon
◆ Auberge du Presbytère €

place de la Fontaine, 84400 Saignon,
Vaucluse
Tel 04 90 74 11 50 Fax 04 90 04 68 51

Towering above Apt, wedged between two huge rocky outcrops is the picturesque medieval village of Saignon with its 1,000 inhabitants, who are gradually restoring the buildings with great care and taste. So far, it has avoided becoming too much of a tourist trap. This old inn is in the heart of the village, with its brightly coloured tables set out in summer beside the huge fountain, shaded by a rare, lovely *micocoulier* (lotus) tree. You might be tempted by the perfect

Lubéron lamb, its herbal flavours enhanced by a deliciously peppery Grenache-Syrah Côtes du Lubéron from Château Saint-Pierre de Mejons. There are two menus at lunchtime on weekdays (at other times only the more expensive is available). Both are delightfully simple in choice, with excellent, well-cooked ingredients, and local cheeses at their peak. Don't dodge the desserts: the *ruche amandier*, a calorific pastry with red-currants and caramelized almonds, is a house speciality; or in summer try *soupe de pêches et menthe*, with a melon sorbet floating in it. The *auberge* is run by a friendly, happy, slightly chaotic but dedicated family.

Closed Wed
Cards MC, V

Please send us reports

A guide such as this thrives on reader's reports. If you send us five usable reports, we will send you a free copy of any title in our *Charming Small Hotel Guides* series (see page 241 for France titles in the series).

The five reports should contain at least two new restaurants; the balance can be comments on restaurants already in the guide. **Send reports to** Charming Restaurant Guides, Duncan Petersen Ltd, 31 Ceylon Road, London W14 0PY.

Saint-Andiol
◆ Le Berger des Abeilles €

RD74E, 13670 Saint-Andiol, Bouches-du-Rhône
Tel 04 90 95 01 91 Fax 04 90 95 48 26

Nicole Grenier, a celebrated cook, was born in this shuttered farmhouse that now caters for her large circle of admirers. There are nine brightly decorated bedrooms, but the action is downstairs in the equally colourful beamed dining room or out on the terrace. Charming and modest, Mme Grenier puts her heart into her *cuisine Provençale*, with specialities that include *filets de rougets cuits en brique d'argile sur fondue de légumes* and *pavé de cabillaud au beurre blanc d'estragon*. Try to leave enough room

for one of her heavenly desserts; the *mousse au miel de lavande* perhaps. The house is 2 km (one mile) north of Saint-Andiol on the N7, then the D74E towards Cabanes.

❛ *Delightful welcome. Nicole Grenier has a sure yet feminine touch* ❜

Closed Mon and Tue lunch; Jan to mid-Feb
Cards AE, MC, V

Saint-Disdier
◆ La Neyrette € Fr

05250 Saint-Disdier, Hautes-Alpes
Tel 04 92 58 81 17 Fax 04 92 58 89 95

If you are travelling in this region – a culinary desert compared with the rest of Provence – it's worth making a detour this lovely restored mill in its enchanting garden fringed by a trout lake. The food is plain but excellent, concentrating on local ingredients; not surprisingly trout is on the menu every day. It can be smoked or *meunière* or in a *morilles* sauce, but you know it will be fresh however it is served. But then everything here is fresh – the *charcuterie*, the grills, the lively welcome, and the air. The Muzzard family are responsible for this honest and delightful *auberge* with refreshingly unpretentious prices.

Closed 2 weeks Apr, mid-Nov to mid-Dec
Cards AE, MC, V

Saint-Jean-Cap-Ferrat
◆ Le Sloop €€

Port de Plaisance, 06230 Saint-Jean-Cap-Ferrat, Alpes-Maritimes
Tel 04 93 01 48 63 Fax 04 93 01 48 63

Le Sloop became an overnight celebrity when Andrew Lloyd-Webber confessed to *The Sunday Times* that it was his favourite restaurant in the South of France. What distinguishes it? Though it's one of a string of restaurants overlooking the new port, it's a clear cut above the others, both in design and cooking. It has the feel of a sophisticated cruise ship, whether you are sitting on the deck under sunshades, or inside the bright dining room. The menu offers great choice and value, and Alain Thericocq's cuisine has a knack of being unpretentious yet original. There's his *salade d'homard mozzarella et avocat au basilic*, for instance, or his *dorade entière au four à la Niçoise avec fleurs des courgettes*. Desserts include interesting combinations of *chaud-froid* using the same fruits in different ways. Service is always attentive, however busy the restaurant.

CLOSED Wed, Thu lunch; mid-Nov to mid-Dec
CARDS AE, DC, MC, V

Saint-Laurent-du-Var
◆ Calypso €‑€€

176 promenade des flots Bleus, 06700 Saint Laurent du Var, Alpes-Maritimes
Tel 04 93 14 80 25 Fax 04 93 07 21 24

The perfect stop-off when you arrive at or just before you leave from Nice airport – it's just a few hundred metres away. The approach is unprepossessing (through the huge shopping zone of Saint-Laurent-du-Var), but you emerge at a little promenade, where a dozen or so restaurants overlook a tiny beach. Calypso is by far the prettiest, with its *pieds dans l'eau* – the tables tumbling right down to the water's edge. As you would expect, the food is typically Mediterranean, but with a light, confident touch: predominantly fish, but with aubergines and market vegetables too. The service is charming, the waiters are helpful, and the dining area is pretty and pastel-coloured. If your flight is delayed, there is even water-ski-ing next door.

CLOSED never
CARDS MC, V

Please send us reports
A guide such as this thrives on reader's reports. If you send us five usable reports, we will send you a free copy of any title in our *Charming Small Hotel Guides* series (see page 241 for France titles in the series).

The five reports should contain at least two new restaurants; the rest can be comments on restaurants already in the guide.
1 Tell us about your experiences in restaurants already in this guide.
2 Send us new reports. New reports should give the following information:
– **Region** – City, town, village or neaest village.
– **Name of restaurant** – Please double

check the spelling, it's surprisingly easy to make a mistake.
– **Address** – including *département*
– **Telephone number** – plus fax and e-mail if available. Double check this information.
– **Objective description** – Try to explain simply why it should be in the guide. Remember that the guide is very selective - our entries are those one-in-five places that combine
● **interesting food with**
● **character and charm, in the building, the setting or both.**
The guide hates tourist traps, and pretentious, dressed-up food. We like places where the French go.

We favour places in the lower and middle price bands but there are plenty of expensive places that have our qualities, and we list those too.
– **Diner's comments** – These should be short, personal comments on features that strike you. They can be your comments, or others'.
– **Closing times**
– **Credit cards accepted**
Don' t forget to date your report and add your name and address.
Send reports to Charming Restaurant Guides, Duncan Petersen Publishing, 31 Ceylon Road, London W14 OPY.

Saint-Maximin-la-Sainte-Baume
◆ Hostellerie du Couvent Royal €€

place Jean-Salusse, 83470 Saint-Maximin-la-Sainte-Baume, Var
Tel 04 94 86 55 66 Fax 04 94 59 82 82

Saint-Maximin-la-Sainte-Baume usually gets missed on the motorway to the coast, but you may have glimpsed the silhouette of its grandiose basilica as you sped by. The attractive market town huddles round it (don't miss the darkened skull of Mary Magdalene in the 4thC crypt), and its adjacent 13thC convent. It's most pleasant to stroll through its lovely shady cloisters, and then to dine in the elegant restaurant in what was once the Chapter House. Stylishly restored, it has huge windows inserted into vaulted walls, giving both light and a great view of the cloisters. It's large-scale, with big tables and comfortable chairs to match. In summer you can sit outside in the cloister garden. The cooking is described as *tendance Provençale* but has a delicate touch, with a hint of the orient in its use of coriander, saffron and spices. The wines are mostly local.

CLOSED Sun dinner, Mon
CARDS AE, DC, MC, V

---

charmingsmallhotels.co.uk
Visit Duncan Petersen's travel website, the best online search tool for places to stay that combine character and charm. Currently features Britain, France, Italy and Ireland, with other destinations being continuously added.

Saint-Paul-de-Vence
◈ Colombe d'Or
€€–€€€

06570 Saint-Paul-de-Vence, Alpes-Maritimes
Tel 04 93 32 80 02 Fax 04 93 32 77 88

The trouble with the Colombe d'Or is that it is just too pretty and too famous, but somehow we can't bring ourselves to leave it out of this book – even though occasionally (only occasionally) the food can be a little eccentric. But seafood on the stone terrace under the fig trees, overlooking gardens and olive-clad slopes, the tranquillity of the place and sense of well-being are near-perfect. The moment you step into the garden, near the entrance to Saint-Paul-de-Vence, you leave behind the hurly burly and the busloads of tourists traipsing up into the old town. This is possibly the most attractive hotel and garden in the South of France. In the restaurant, start with the huge baskets and platters of *hors d'oeuvres* – *charcuterie, aïoli, crudités* and much more. Follow that (if you have room) with the *carré d'agneau des Alpes de Haute Provence* or the *filet de turbot*. However, you feed your senses here as well as your stomach, and you must venture into the hotel to see the staggering collection of early 20thC art. Picasso, Miró, Braque and Léger, amongst others, were regulars here and paid for their *carré d'agneau* with

paintings and sculptures - a rare treat to see.

❛ Full of film stars and celebrities - people can't resist coming here ❜

CLOSED 2 weeks Jan, Nov to late Dec
CARDS AE, DC, MC, V

Saint-Raphaël
◈ L'Arbousier   € – €€€

6 avenue Valescure, 83700 Saint-Raphaël, Var
Tel 04 94 95 25 00 Fax 04 94 83 81 04

The marriage of Philippe Troncy's fine cooking and his wife, Christine's vivacious welcome has made L'Arbousier the most popular and attractive restaurant in Saint-Raphaël since 1992. The two sunny dining rooms, which only seat 50 covers, have recently been done up in Provençal yellows and ochres. Outside, in the shade of awnings and thick foliage, the terrace seats another 60. The menus are carefully constructed around Provençal products and styles, with some interesting contrasts in, for example, the *carpaccio de langouste à la vinaigrette de marjolaine* and the half duckling, the breast grilled with *arômes* of liquorice, the leg in a *confit* of rosemary. The desserts are splendid, reflecting the chef's experience as a *patissier*. At lunchtime there is an excellent value three-course menu (not available on Sundays). Prices rise steeply for the two mouthwatering dinner menus, and rocket if you stray on to the *carte*, but a treat lies in store if you do.

CLOSED Mon and Tue lunch high season, Sun dinner, Tue and Wed low season; late Dec to early Jan
CARDS AE, DC, MC, V

Saint-Rémy-de-Provence
◈ Alain Assaud   € – €€

13 boulevard Marceau, 13210 Saint-Rémy-de-Provence, Bouches-du-Rhône
Tel 04 90 92 37 11

In his grange-style restaurant, Alain Assaud reigns supreme as a chef who enjoys creating fine, simple, authentic food, without fuss or frippery. He learned his trade at the feet of Troisgros and Chapel, and at the famous L'Oustau de Baumanière in Les Baux. His two well-priced menus are a tribute to local produce and custom. The *caillette d'herbe à la sauge* is bursting with flavours, while the roast pigeon with roasted shallots just melts in the mouth. His restaurant has a regular following and he is praised by all the respected critics. But, quite admirably, his menus have both remained the same price for more than two years, proof that his attitude to his food and his clients is dedicated and honest.

CLOSED Wed, Thu, Sat lunch; mid-Nov to early Apr
CARDS AE, DC, MC, V

Saint-Tropez
◆ La Ponche €€€

3 rue des Remparts, 83990 Saint-Tropez, Var
Tel 04 94 97 02 53 Fax 04 94 97 78 61

Tucked away in a tiny square overlooking the small fishing port and tiny beach of La Ponche (where Vadim's *And God Created Woman* was filmed, starring Brigitte Bardot), this cluster of 17thC houses offers a compelling combination of sophistication and warmth. What began as a simple fishermen's bar in 1937, has been steadily transformed over the years by Simone Duckstein into a stylish, arty four-star hotel and restaurant, full of personal touches. You can eat on a terrace, looking across a square to the sea, or in one of several areas indoors, including the main dining room, which is unpretentious but sophisticated. The food is memorable, particularly the seafood (*soupe de poisson* and red mullet). And because it is now so popular, the menu changes little from one year to the next.

CLOSED mid-Nov to mid-Feb
CARDS AE, MC, V

Séguret
◆ La Table du Comtat
€€€

Séguret, 84110 Vaison-la-Romaine, Vaucluse
Tel 04 90 46 91 49 Fax 04 90 46 94 27

It's certainly a business getting to this eyrie at the top of one of the region's most captivating villages. By car, you wind up the hillside, round steep, narrow streets, but once tucked into a parking space at the top, you are rewarded by magnificent views of the plain below, and by the delights of a much modernized, but essentially old-fashioned *auberge*. Built in the 15th century, it is attractively decorated and has a gorgeous terrace, which shares the view over the vineyards. The food is not cheap, but it is good. Prepared by Franck Gomez, the menus have a pleasing unity, borrowing from traditional recipes but giving them a contemporary slant. His specialities include *julienne de truffe en coque d'oeuf* and *figues pochées au jus d'agrumes*. Service is accomplished yet personal, and you leave feeling that you have found the elusive spirit of Provence.

CLOSED Feb
CARDS AE, DC, MC, V

Sérignan-du-Comtat
◆ Pré du Moulin €–€€€

route Sainte-Cécile-les-Vignes, 84830 Sérignan-du-Comtat, Vaucluse
Tel 04 90 70 05 58 Fax 04 90 70 05 62

Eight kilometres (5 miles) north of Orange, in this pretty village, is the Hostellerie du Vieux Château, which used to own Le Pré du Moulin. The restaurant has now been separated from the hotel, bought by a young chef, Pascal Alonso, and his Swiss wife, and has quickly established a reputation for delicate gastronomic delights. For once, in this region, it does not concentrate exclusively on Provençal cuisine, but aims to create light dishes simply and elegantly. In the brightly painted yellow and blue dining room, or on the terrace, you can choose wonderfully creative dishes from two very reasonably priced menus. The wine list is based on the Rhône Valley as you would expect in this area.

❢ An excellent find. ❢

CLOSED Sun dinner Oct-Apr, Mon lunch, Mon dinner winter; mid-Feb to early Mar, late Oct to early Nov, last week Dec
CARDS AE, MC, V

Le Tholonet
◆ Chez Thomé € Fr

La Plantation, 13100 Le Tholonet, Bouches-du-Rhône
Tel 04 42 66 90 43 Fax 04 42 66 90 43

Beneath the Mont Sainte Victoire, made famous by Monet, this is a delightful spot, especially in summer when you can sit out under the shade of spreading trees in the company of families from far and wide. It's a very popular place, particularly for Sunday lunch, so be sure to book. The menu – which is very Provençal and includes dishes with plenty of garlic and aubergines – is written on slate boards that are brought to each table. The chef's favourite is *epaule d'agneau farcie à la tapenade*, a fabulous combination of local flavours, and the *assiette Sainte-Victoire* combines all the flavours that Provence has to offer. The *pieds et paquets* is adored by the locals, but an acquired taste for the Anglo-American palette. The wine list is limited but local; the service is friendly.

❛ Lunch here – one of the best ways to while away a lazy afternoon ❜

Closed Mon, Tue dinner high season
Cards MC, V

Toulon
◈ Bernard €€€

Calanque de Magaud, 83000 Toulon, Var
Tel 04 94 27 20 62

Having parked your car on the main road (avenue de la Résistance), you walk down a tiny, shaded, winding path, to emerge at a beautiful little creek with stunning rocks and cliffs as a backdrop to the sea. To your right is a bright terrace, all painted in blue and yellow. The Bernard restaurant may be hard to find, but perservere, it is a lovely unspoilt quiet place with the sea lapping at your feet. The menu is limited, but sea-based: oysters, mussels, *terrine* of *rascasse*, followed by grilled catch of the day, or other fishy specialities. If you want their *plateau de fruits de mer*, *bouillabaisse* or *bourride*, you need to order 24 hours in advance. The only disappointment was the *tourte au crabe*, which contained a mixture of crab-sticks and crab, but the sauce (*crème fraîche et vin blanc*) was quite delicious. At night, the twinkling lights reflect in the silent sea, the place is bustling with Toulonnais - you must book for dinner.

❛ A wonderful welcome from Madame Impellizzeri ❜

Closed Oct to Mar
Cards MC, V

Tourrettes-sur-Loup
◈ Auberge de Tourrettes €€

11 route de Grasse, 06140 Tourrettes-sur-Loup, Alpes-Maritimes
Tel 04 93 59 30 05 Fax 04 93 59 28 66

Talented young chef Christophe Dufau and his Danish wife Katrine opened this restaurant-with-rooms in the shell of a typical village inn just a few years ago. Though it's close to the hotspots of the Côte d'Azur, Tourrettes is an unassuming village high in the hills, and from the airy open-plan restaurant with its glassed-in terrace, there are great views over unspoiled wooded hillsides down to the coast. The decoration is simple, stylish and unstuffy; clean contemporary lines, warm tiled floors, shades of white, natural linen tablecloths, much wood and an olive tree in a terracotta pot. The reasonably priced food has real flair, and uses plenty of local ingredients including herbs from the garden. Dishes might include lobster terrine *en gelée* flavoured with orange, asparagus served with parmesan chips and a delicately falvoured *mousseline*, or perhaps chicken stewed with pickled lemons.

❛ Sophisticated food' ... 'Flavours more subtle than robust' ... 'I'd certainly make the trip here from the coast ❜

Closed Mon, Tue Oct–May; mid-Jan to mid-Feb
Cards AE, DC, MC, V

La Turbie
◈ Hostellerie Jérôme €€

20 rue Comte-de-Cassole, 06320 La Turbie, Alpes-Maritimes
Tel 04 92 41 51 51 Fax 04 92 41 51 50

Once a presbytery of the Lérins monks, this is where the great Jerome was fêted as one of the Riviera's top chefs in the 1950s and 60s. Now Bruno Cirino has taken it over, lightened and brightened the decoration, and produces masterpieces in the kitchen. Cirino is passionate about ingredients (it is rumoured that he will travel 50 km/31 miles to find the right independent producer of aubergines), and he scours the locality to produce a menu that reads like a map of the Riviera – from Italy to Antibes: *gamberoni* from the gulf of Genoa; Piedmont rice; sea bass roasted with Menton lemons; vegetables from Ventimiglia; olives from Nice. Don't expect haste here; in any case, you will want to take time to savour the exquisite food in this Italian-style setting with glorious views. Although Cirino has only been open a few years, he has already won two well-deserved stars from Michelin.

Closed Mon and Tue Sep-Jun; lunch Jul-Aug; first 3 weeks Dec
Cards MC, V

Valbonne
◆ Auberge Fleurie €€€

1016 route de Cannes, 06560 Valbonne, Alpes-Maritimes
Tel 04 93 12 02 80 Fax 04 93 12 22 27

Run for many years by Jean-Pierre Battaglia, who has now been joined in the kitchen by Lionel Debon, this seductive restaurant impresses for its reasonable prices, especially for the cheapest of the *prix fixe* menus, and Michelin awards a Bib Gourmand for 'good food at moderate prices'. Signature dishes include *rosace de rougets en gelée de crustacés, Saint-Pierre cuit sur la peau à la fleur de sel*, and *pigeonneau rôti aux morilles*. You eat either (according to weather and availability) in the dining room of the old *auberge*, or – preferably – on the shady terrace. This is a popular place (book ahead), with an agreeable buzz on busy evenings.

Closed Sun dinner Sep-Jun, Mon; early Dec to early Jan
Cards AE, MC, V

Ventabren
◆ La Table de Ventabren €

13122 Vieux Village, Ventabren, Bouches-du-Rhône
Tel 04 42 28 79 33 Fax 04 42 28 87 37

Although it has recently changed hands, the new owners, Christine and Pierre Dussaud have not altered the exotic decora-

tion of this renovated village house with panoramic views across the valley. Crushed silk cloths in rich autumnal colours cover the tables; large gilt-framed mirrors and paintings decorate the stone walls (there is even a Modigliani in the toilet); all is taste and luxury. The service is equally pampering, and the food, delicious, though with limited choice. The menu changes daily according to what's available in the market. One of the great pleasures of eating here is that large dishes are brought to the table, so that all the diners can help themselves when and however often they like. A typical lunch might consist of *pâté de campagnard* with tapenade and almonds, followed by veal with fennel and roast potatoes, all faultlessly cooked. Desserts on offer are usually pies, *tatins* and tarts.

❛ Small, pretty, intimate and friendly ❜

Closed Mon dinner and Wed dinner Nov-Apr, Wed Apr-Nov
Cards MC, V

Verquières
◆ Croque Chou € – €€

place Eglise, 13670 Verquières, Bouches-du-Rhône
Tel 04 90 95 18 55

Opposite the church in the centre of the village, this striking 18thC house was originally a *bergerie*. It is now a highly regarded Michelin-starred restaurant, specializing in traditional Provençal food. The chef is Jean-Louis Ravoux, whose trademark dishes on his medium-priced menu include *galantine de gigot d'agneau* and *dorade rotie au vin rouge et fenouil braisé*. There is no terrace, but a heavenly dining room compensates. Strictly no dogs, no smokers and no credit cards. Verquières is 11 km (7 miles) from Saint-Rémy via the D30 and D29.

❛ All the flavours of Provence ❜

Closed Sun dinner Oct-Mar, Mon and Tue late Dec to Mar
Cards none

Villecroze
◆ Le Colombier € – €€

route de Draguignan, 83690 Villecroze, Var
Tel 04 94 70 63 23 Fax 04 94 70 63 23

In the charming antique-filled dining room of their country house, and on the summer terrace, the Lecontes have built a justifiably solid reputation for excellent food and excellent value. While his wife runs the restaurant with stylish ease, Claude produces classic dishes on two menus. There are three courses on the basic one, with two or three choices for each, depending on the market of the day. The menu gourmand has five courses and is fairly rich, so be sure to fast the day before. It might feature *terrine de foie gras* with a *Baumes de Venise* jelly (the house speciality) to start, followed by *noix de Saint Jacques*, then stuffed pigeon, cheese and a *moelleux au chocolat noir*. Between the middle of December and the end of March, they serve a menu specializing in local truffles, for which the area is famous. The wine list concentrates on vintages from the neighbouring *haut Var*. The house is at the edge of the village on the D557.

❨ Even the salads are beautifully made and presented ❩

Closed Sun dinner low season, Mon (except bank hols)
Cards AE, MC, V

Villefranche-sur-Mer
◆ Mère Germaine
€€ – €€€

quai Courbet, 06230 Villefranche-sur-Mer, Alpes-Maritimes
Tel 04 93 01 71 39 Fax 04 93 01 96 44

When Villefranche is mentioned, most people think of this classic fish restaurant, overlooking the fishing port, which has been in existence since 1938. It is now more sophisticated than it was in those days, but its commitment to fresh fish dishes remains the same. The simple menu is well-chosen and well-priced, but if you are tempted by the warm lobster salad, the *bouillabaisse* or the *langouste flambée façon Mère Germaine* from the *carte*, you will need to reach deep into your pocket. It is, however, such a pleasure to eat so well, especially on the terrace with a view of the *Rade*, sipping one of the wines from the long list, that you almost forgive the charming waiter bearing the bill.

Closed mid-Nov to late Dec
Cards AE, MC, V

Villeneuve-la-Salle
◆ Bidule €€

au Bez, Villeneuve-la-Salle, 05240 La-Salle-les-Alpes, Hautes-Alpes
Tel 04 92 24 77 80 Fax 04 92 24 85 51

In a picturesque little hamlet in the mountains, this chalet-restaurant used to be a sheepshed, and is still genuinely atmospheric. In winter you eat in one of two rustic dining rooms, in summer on the lovely *terrace l'été*. Bruno Cirino's *plats de signature* are the *gamberoni rôti au citron de Menton* and *rognons de veau de lait cuit entiers dans leur graine au romarin*, showing his preference for the flavours of the South. But, as you'd expect from an address in the mountains, *raclettes* and *fondues* are also on the menu and favourites with visitors. It is advisable to book, especially for lunch. They also rent out apartments for four to ten people.

❨ Feels just like a mountain farm ❩

Closed Mon and Tue Sep-Jun
Cards MC, V

Looking for somewhere to stay? See page 241.

Villeneuve-la-Salle
◆ Marotte € Fr

36 rue de la Guisane, 05240 Villeneuve-la-Salle, Hautes-Alpes
Tel 04 92 24 77 23

A tiny buzzing bistro, as full of energy and laughter as the family who run it. There is a single, very reasonably priced menu, and they are particularly proud of their terrines, main courses and desserts. Everything is made on the spot and tastes delicious. Rightly they call the food, *cuisine familiale française*. Book well in advance because the dining room is small and always crowded; and it's addictive – once you've been here, you'll keep coming back.

❨ Great value' … 'A fantastically warm welcome ❩

Closed Sun
Cards none

The city, town or village in which or near which a restaurant or restaurants is located is given first; then the region. Page numbers of regions are on page 6. Within each region, locations follow in alphabetical order.

A

Agde, Languedoc-Roussillon
Agen, Aquitaine
Agnetz, Picardie
Aigues-Mortes, Languedoc-Roussillon
Aïnhoa, Aquitaine
Aire-sur-l'Adour, Aquitaine
Aire-sur-la-Lys, Nord-Pas-de-Calais
Aix-en-Provence, Provence-Alpes-Côte d'Azur
Albertville, Rhône-Alpes
Amiens, Picardie
Amondans, Franche-Comté
Amou, Aquitaine
Ancenis, Pays-de-la-Loire
Andelys, Les, Haute-Normandie
Angers, Pays-de-la-Loire
Angles-sur-l'Anglin, Poitou-Charentes
Angoulême, Poitou-Charentes
Annecy, Rhône-Alpes
Anthy-sur-Léman, Rhône-Alpes
Antibes, Provence-Alpes-Côte d'Azur
Apremont, Picardie
Apt, Provence-Alpes-Côte d'Azur
Arbois, Franche-Comté
Arcins-en-Médoc, Aquitaine
Ardouval, Haute-Normandie
Argelès-sur-Mer, Languedoc-Roussillon
Arnay-le-Duc, Bourgogne
Arques, Les, Midi-Pyrénées
Arques, Nord-Pas-de-Calais
Arras, Nord-Pas-de-Calais
Artzenheim, Alsace
Astaffort, Aquitaine
Attin, Nord-Pas-de-Calais
Aubignosc, Provence-Alpes-Côte d'Azur
Aubigny-sur-Nère, Centre
Aulas, Languedoc-Roussillon
Aumale, Haute-Normandie
Aumont-Aubrac, Languedoc-Roussillon
Auterive, Midi-Pyrénées
Auvillars-sur-Saône, Bourgogne
Avignon, Provence-Alpes-Côte d'Azur
Aydie, Aquitaine
Azay-le-Rideau, Centre
Azur, Aquitaine

B

Baerenthal, Lorraine
Bages, Languedoc-Roussillon
Bandol, Provence-Alpes-Côte d'Azur
Bannegon, Centre
Banyuls-sur-Mer, Languedoc-Roussillon
Barberaz, Rhône-Alpes
Barbizon, Paris and Ile-de-France
Barcelonnette, Provence-Alpes-Côte d'Azur
Barcus, Aquitaine
Barils, Les, Haute-Normandie
Bar-le-Duc, Lorraine

Barneville-Carteret, Basse-Normandie
Bas-Rupts, Lorraine
Baule, Centre
Baume-les-Dames, Franche-Comté
Baume-les-Messieurs, Franche-Comté
Beaucet, Le, Provence-Alpes-Côte d'Azur
Beaulieu, Rhône-Alpes
Beaulieu-sur-Dordogne, Limousin
Beaumesnil, Haute-Normandie
Beaumont-du-Ventoux, Provence-Alpes-Côte d'Azur
Beaune, Bourgogne
Bec-Hellouin, Le, Haute-Normandie
Belcastel, Languedoc-Roussillon
Bellou-en-Houlme, Basse-Normandie
Bénodet, Bretagne
Bény-Bocage, Le, Basse-Normandie
Bergerac, Aquitaine
Bergheim, Alsace
Bernerie-en-Retz, Pays-de-la-Loire
Berry-au-Bac, Picardie
Besançon, Franche-Comté
Beutin, Nord-Pas-de-Calais
Beuvron-en-Auge, Basse-Normandie
Biarritz, Aquitaine
Biriatou, Aquitaine
Bize-Minervois, Languedoc-Roussillon
Blain, Pays-de-la-Loire
Blendecques, Nord-Pas-de-Calais
Bléré, Centre
Blois, Centre
Bagnoles-de-l'Orne, Basse-Normandie
Boisset, Auvergne
Bonlieu, Franche-Comté
Bonneuil-Matours, Poitou-Charentes
Bonnieux, Provence-Alpes-Côte d'Azur
Borne, La, Centre
Bosdarros, Aquitaine
Bouille, Haute-Normandie
Boulogne-sur-Gesse, Midi-Pyrénées
Bourbon-L'Archambault, Auvergne
Bourg Charente, Poitou-Charentes
Bourg-en-Bresse, Rhône-Alpes
Bourget-du-Lac, Rhône-Alpes
Boussac, Limousin
Bozouls, Midi-Pyrénées
Bracieux, Centre
Brantôme, Aquitaine
Bresson, Rhône-Alpes
Bressuire, Poitou-Charentes
Brest, Bretagne
Brinon-sur-Sauldre, Centre
Briollay, Pays-de-la-Loire
Briouze, Basse-Normandie
Brive-la-Gaillarde, Limousin
Broquiès, Midi-Pyrénées
Brouains, Basse-Normandie
Bruère Allichamps, Centre

Brumath, Alsace
Buzançais, Centre
Buzet-sur-Baïse, Aquitaine

C

Cadouin, Aquitaine
Caen, Basse-Normandie
Cahors, Midi-Pyrénées
Cahuzac-sur-Vère, Midi-Pyrénées
Calvinet, Auvergne
Campigny, Haute-Normandie
Canals, Midi-Pyrénées
Cancale, Bretagne
Cannes, Provence-Alpes-Côte d'Azur
Carantec, Bretagne
Carcassonne, Languedoc-Roussillon
Cassis, Provence-Alpes-Côte d'Azur
Castelnaudary, Languedoc-Roussillon
Castéra-Verduzan, Midi-Pyrénées
Castillon-du-Gard, Languedoc-Roussillon
Caulières, Picardie
Caurel, Bretagne
Celle, La, Provence-Alpes-Côte d'Azur
Celles-sur-Belle, Poitou-Charentes
Céret, Languedoc-Roussillon
Chagny, Bourgogne ,
Chalais, Poitou-Charentes
Challans, Pays-de-la-Loire
Chalon-sur-Saône, Bourgogne
Chamalières, Auvergne
Chamonix, Rhône-Alpes
Champagnac-de-Belair, Aquitaine
Champillon-Bellevue, Champagne-Ardenne
Champtoceaux, Pays-de-la-Loire
Chantilly, Picardie
Charbonnières-les-Bains, Rhône-Alpes
Charolles, Bourgogne
Charron, Poitou-Charentes
Chartres, Centre
Chasselay, Rhône-Alpes
Châteaubourg, Bretagne
Châteaubriant, Pays-de-la-Loire
Châteaudun, Centre
Château-Gontier, Pays-de-la-Loire
Châteaumeillant, Centre
Châteauneuf-du-Pape, Provence-Alpes-Côte d'Azur
Châteauneuf-en-Thymerais, Centre
Châteaux-Arnoux, Provence-Alpes-Côte d'Azur
Châtillon, Franche-Comté
Chauvigny, Poitou-Charentes
Chavignol, Centre
Chemillé, Pays-de-la-Loire
Chênehutte-les-Tuffeaux, Pays-de-la-Loire
Chenillé-Changé, Pays-de-la-Loire
Chenonceaux, Centre
Chinon, Centre
Chissay-en-Touraine, Centre
Chitenay, Centre
Cholet, Pays-de-la-Loire
Chonas l'Amballan, Rhône-Alpes
Ciotat, La, Provence-Alpes-Côte d'Azur
Clairmarais, Nord-Pas-de-Calais
Clécy, Basse-Normandie
Cliousclat, Rhône-Alpes

Cocherel, Haute-Normandie
Cocurès, Languedoc-Roussillon
Cognac, Poitou-Charentes
Collobrières, Provence-Alpes-Côte d'Azur
Collonges-la-Rouge, Limousin
Colmar, Alsace
Coly, Aquitaine
Combourg, Bretagne
Combreux, Centre
Concarneau, Bretagne
Conchers-en-Ouche, Haute-Normandie
Concoret, Bretagne
Condorcet, Rhône-Alpes
Connelles, Haute-Normandie
Cormeilles, Basse-Normandie
Cornillon, Languedoc-Roussillon
Corps, Rhône-Alpes
Correns, Provence-Alpes-Côte d'Azur
Cotignac, Provence-Alpes-Côte d'Azur
Courcelles-sur-Vesle, Picardie
Courchevel, Rhône-Alpes
Courlans, Franche-Comté
Coye-la-Fôret, Picardie
Crépon, Basse-Normandie
Crest, Rhône-Alpes
Croisic, Le, Pays-de-la-Loire
Crozant, Limousin
Cucuron, Provence-Alpes-Côte d'Azur
Cussay, Centre

D

Diefmatten, Alsace
Dieppe, Haute-Normandie
Digne, Provence-Alpes-Côte d'Azur
Dijon, Bourgogne
Dissay, Poitou-Charentes
Dol-de-Bretagne, Bretagne
Dole, Franche-Comté
Domfront, Basse-Normandie
Domme, Aquitaine
Doudeville, Haute-Normandie
Ducey, Basse-Normandie
Dunes, Midi-Pyrénées
Duras, Aquitaine
Durfort-Lacapelette, Midi-Pyrénées

E

Echenevex, Rhône-Alpes
Echets, Les, Rhône-Alpes
Eguisheim, Alsace
Epernay, Champagne-Ardenne
Ernée, Pays-de-la-Loire
Erquy, Bretagne
Erstein, Alsace
Espelette, Aquitaine
Esquiule, Aquitaine
Etréaupont, Picardie
Etroeungt, Nord-Pas-de-Calais
Eugénie-les-Bains, Aquitaine
Eyzies-de-Tayac, Les-, Aquitaine

F

Falaise, Basse-Normandie
Faouët, Le, Bretagne
Faverges, Rhône-Alpes

Ferté-Bernard, La, Pays-de-la-Loire
Fierville-les-Mines, Basse-Normandie
Figeac, Midi-Pyrénées
Flagy, Paris and Ile-de-France
Flèche, La, Pays-de-la-Loire
Fleurie, Rhône-Alpes
Florac, Languedoc-Roussillon
Florensac, Languedoc-Roussillon
Foix, Midi-Pyrénées
Fontainebleau, Paris and Ile-de-France
Fontenay-le-Comte, Pays-de-la-Loire
Fontevraud-l'Abbaye, Pays-de-la-Loire
Fort-Mahon, Picardie
Fossé, Le, Haute-Normandie
Fouesnant, Bretagne
Fougerolles, Franche-Comté
Fourges, Haute-Normandie
Francescas, Aquitaine

G

Gaillac, Midi-Pyrénées
Gap, Provence-Alpes-Côte d'Azur
Garde Adhémar, La, Rhône-Alpes
Garette, Poitou-Charentes
Gavre, Le, Pays-de-la-Loire
Ger, Basse-Normandie
Gérardmer, Lorraine
Gerberoy, Picardie
Gevrey-Chambertin, Bourgogne
Gigondas, Provence-Alpes-Côte d'Azur
Gincla, Languedoc-Roussillon
Giroussens, Midi-Pyrénées
Gisors, Haute-Normandie
Golfe Juan, Provence-Alpes-Côte d'Azur
Gouesnière, Bretagne
Goumois, Franche-Comté
Gourin, Bretagne
Grasse, Provence-Alpes-Côte d'Azur
Gravelines, Nord-Pas-de-Calais
Grenade-sur-l'Adour, Aquitaine
Grenoble, Rhône-Alpes
Grézels, Midi-Pyrénées
Grignan, Rhône-Alpes
Gueret, Limousin
Guéthary, Aquitaine

H

Hardelot-Plage, Nord-Pas-de-Calais
Haute-Chapelle, La, Basse-Normandie
Herbiers, Les, Pays-de-la-Loire
Hesdin, Nord-Pas-de-Calais
Hinsingen, Alsace
Honfleur, Basse-Normandie
Hossegor, Aquitaine
Houlle, Nord-Pas-de-Calais
Hunawir, Alsace
Hyères, Provence-Alpes-Côte d'Azur

I

Ile Bouchard, L', Centre
Ile-de-Groix, Bretagne
Illhaeusern, Alsace
Illiers-Combray, Centre
Inxent, Nord-Pas-de-Calais
Isle-sur-la-Sorgue, L', Provence-Alpes-Côte

d'Azur
Isle-sur-Serein, L', Bourgogne
Issigéac, Aquitaine
Issoudun, Centre
Issy-les-Moulineaux, Paris and Ile-de-France
Itterswiller, Alsace

J

Jarnac, Poitou-Charentes
Javron-les-Chapelles, Pays-de-la-Loire
Josselin, Bretagne
Jugon-les-Lacs, Bretagne
Junas, Languedoc-Roussillon

K

Kernascléden, Bretagne

L

Lacapelle-Marival, Midi-Pyrénées
Ladoix-Serrigny, Bourgogne
Lalinde, Aquitaine
Lamastre, Rhône-Alpes
Lamballe, Bretagne
Langres, Champagne-Ardenne
Lannemazan, Midi-Pyrénées
Lanvenegen, Bretagne
Laon, Picardie
Lapoutroie, Alsace
Laqueuille, Auvergne
Larrau, Aquitaine
Larressingle, Midi-Pyrénées
Latouille-Lentillac, Midi-Pyrénées
Lauret, Languedoc-Roussillon
Lauzerte, Midi-Pyrénées
Laval, Pays-de-la-Loire
Lavaudieu, Auvergne
Leigné-les-Bois, Poitou-Charentes
Lembeye, Aquitaine
Lencloitre, Poitou-Charentes
Lépinoy, Nord-Pas-de-Calais
Lesponne, Midi-Pyrénées
Levroux, Centre
Limoges, Limousin
Limonest, Rhône-Alpes
Lisieux, Basse-Normandie
Locquirec, Bretagne
Lorgues, Provence-Alpes-Côte d'Azur
Lorient, Bretagne
Lorp-Sentaraille, Midi-Pyrénées
Loudun, Poitou-Charentes
Loué, Pays-de-la-Loire
Loupiac, Midi-Pyrénées
Lourdes, Midi-Pyrénées
Lourmarin, Provence-Alpes-Côte d'Azur
Lude, Le, Pays-de-la-Loire
Lunéville, Lorraine
Luxé, Poitou-Charentes
Luz-Saint-Sauveur, Midi-Pyrénées
Lyon, Rhône-Alpes
Lys-Saint-Georges, Centre

M

Macon, Bourgogne
Madelaine-sous-Montreuil, Nord-Pas-de-Calais
Madières, Languedoc-Roussillon

Magalas, Languedoc-Roussillon
Mailly-le-Château, Bourgogne
Maisonnais, Centre
Malataverne, Rhône-Alpes
Malbuisson, Franche-Comté
Malène, La, Languedoc-Roussillon
Manciet, Midi-Pyrénées
Manigod, Rhône-Alpes
Manosque, Provence-Alpes-Côte d'Azur
Mans, Le, Pays-de-la-Loire
Marciac, Midi-Pyrénées
Marcilly-en-Villette, Centre
Marlenheim, Alsace
Marseillan, Languedoc-Roussillon
Marseille, Provence-Alpes-Côte d'Azur ,
Martin-Eglise, Haute-Normandie
Masméjan, Languedoc-Roussillon
Mauléon, Poitou-Charentes
Maussane-les-Alpilles, Provence-Alpes-Côte d'Azur
Mayenne, Pays-de-la-Loire
Megève, Rhône-Alpes
Mélisey, Franche-Comté
Mellecey, Bourgogne
Menton, Provence-Alpes-Côte d'Azur
Mercurey, Bourgogne
Méribel, Rhône-Alpes
Mesnières-en-Bray, Haute-Normandie
Mesnil-Val, Haute-Normandie
Metz, Lorraine
Meyronne, Midi-Pyrénées
Meyrueis, Languedoc-Roussillon
Mezangers, Pays-de-la-Loire
Mimizan, Aquitaine
Mison, Provence-Alpes-Côte d'Azur
Mittelbergheim, Alsace
Mittelhausen, Alsace
Moëlan-sur-Mer, Bretagne
Moissy Cramayel, Paris and Ile-de-France
Molitg-les-Bains, Languedoc-Roussillon
Moncoutant, Poitou-Charentes
Mondragon, Provence-Alpes-Côte d'Azur
Monpazier, Aquitaine
Montbazillac, Aquitaine
Montbazon, Centre
Montbron, Poitou-Charentes
Montesquiou, Midi-Pyrénées
Montfort-en-Chalosse, Aquitaine
Montigny-sur-Avre, Centre
Montluçon, Auvergne
Montmerle-sur-Sâone, Rhône-Alpes
Montpellier, Languedoc-Roussillon
Montpon-Ménesterol, Aquitaine
Montreuil, Nord-Pas-de-Calais
Mont-Saint-Michel, Le, Basse-Normandie
Montsalvy, Auvergne
Morlaix, Bretagne
Mortemart, Limousin
Moudeyres, Auvergne
Mougins, Provence-Alpes-Côte d'Azur
Moustiers-Sainte-Marie, Provence-Alpes-Côte d'Azur
Mouzon, Champagne-Ardenne

N

Naintre, Poitou-Charentes
Nancy, Lorraine
Nantes, Pays-de-la-Loire
Napoule, La, Provence-Alpes-Côte d'Azur
Néant-sur-Yvel, Bretagne
Neau, Pays-de-la-Loire
Négreville, Basse-Normandie
Neufchâtel-en-Saosnais, Pays-de-la-Loire
Neuilly, Paris and Ile-de-France
Neuilly-Saint-Front, Picardie
Neuvy-Deux-Clochers, Centre
Nevers, Bourgogne
Nice, Provence-Alpes-Côte d'Azur ,
Nîmes, Languedoc-Roussillon
Niort, Poitou-Charentes
Nitry, Bourgogne
Noé, Midi-Pyrénées
Nogaro, Midi-Pyrénées
Nogent-le-Roi, Centre
Noirmoutier-en-l'Ile, Pays-de-la-Loire
Norroy-le-Veneur, Lorraine
Noyers-sur-Cher, Centre

O

Obernai, Alsace
Oiron, Poitou-Charentes
Olargues, Languedoc-Roussillon
Olivet, Centre
Opio, Provence-Alpes-Côte d'Azur
Ornaisons, Languedoc-Roussillon
Osthouse, Alsace
Ottrott, Alsace
Oulon, Bourgogne
Ouroux-en-Morvan, Bourgogne
Ouveillan, Languedoc-Roussillon

P

Pailherols, Auvergne
Paimpol, Bretagne
Paris, 1st Arrondissement
Paris, 2nd Arrondissement
Paris, 3rd Arrondissement
Paris, 4th Arrondissement
Paris, 5th Arrondissement
Paris, 6th Arrondissement
Paris, 7th Arrondissement
Paris, 8th Arrondissement
Paris, 9th Arrondissement
Paris, 10th Arrondissement
Paris, 11th Arrondissement
Paris, 12th Arrondissement
Paris, 13th Arrondissement
Paris, 14th Arrondissement
Paris, 15th Arrondissement
Paris, 16th Arrondissement
Paris, 17th Arrondissement
Paris, 18th Arrondissement
Paris, 20th Arrondissement
Parthenay, Poitou-Charentes
Pau, Aquitaine
Pauillac, Aquitaine
Pégomas, Provence-Alpes-Côte d'Azur
Peillon, Provence-Alpes-Côte d'Azur
Penmarc'h, Bretagne

Restaurant locations: alphabetical list

Périgueux, Aquitaine
Perpignan, Languedoc-Roussillon
Perreux-sur-Marne, Le, Paris and Ile-de-France
Perros-Guirec, Bretagne
Petites Dalles, Les, Haute-Normandie
Petit-Pressigny, Centre
Pézenas, Languedoc-Roussillon
Pierrelatte, Rhône-Alpes
Piolenc, Provence-Alpes-Côte d'Azur
Plaine-sur-Mer, La, Pays-de-la-Loire
Plougonvelin, Bretagne
Plumelec, Bretagne
Poët-Laval, Le, Rhône-Alpes
Poisson, Bourgogne
Poitiers, Poitou-Charentes
Pons, Poitou-Charentes
Pont-Audemer, Haute-Normandie
Pont-Aven, Bretagne
Pontet-Avignon, Le, Provence-Alpes-Côte d'Azur
Pont-L'Evêque, Basse-Normandie
Pontlevoy, Centre
Porquerolles (Ile de), Provence-Alpes-Côte d'Azur
Port de Salles, Poitou-Charentes
Port-Verdes, Languedoc-Roussillon
Pouldreuzic, Bretagne
Pradet, Le, Provence-Alpes-Côte d'Azur
Priziac, Bretagne
Putange-Pont-Ecrepin, Basse-Normandie
Puy-L'Evêque, Midi-Pyrénées
Puymirol, Aquitaine

Q
Quarré-les-Tombes, Bourgogne
Quend, Picardie
Quiberon, Bretagne

R
Reims, Champagne-Ardenne
Rennes, Bretagne
Révigny sur Ornain, Lorraine
Ribeauvillé, Alsace
Rillieux-la-Pape, Rhône-Alpes
Rimont, Midi-Pyrénées
Riquewihr, Alsace
Roanne, Rhône-Alpes
Roche-Bernard, La, Bretagne
Rochelle, La, Poitou-Charentes ,
Roche-sur-Yon, La, Pays-de-la-Loire
Roche-Vineuse, La, Bourgogne
Rodez, Midi-Pyrénées
Rognes, Provence-Alpes-Côte d'Azur
Romans-sur-Isère, Rhône-Alpes
Roudouallec, Bretagne
Rouen, Haute-Normandie
Rouffach, Alsace
Roure, Provence-Alpes-Côte d'Azur
Rove, Provence-Alpes-Côte d'Azur
Royan, Poitou-Charentes
Rue, Picardie
Rully, Bourgogne

S
Sables d'Olonne, Les, Pays-de-la-Loire

Sable-sur-Sarthe, Pays-de-la-Loire
Sabres, Aquitaine
Saché, Centre
Saignon, Provence-Alpes-Côte d'Azur
Saint-Agrève, Rhône-Alpes
Saint-Aignan, Bretagne
Saint-Andiol, Provence-Alpes-Côte d'Azur
Saint-André-de-Valborgne, Languedoc-Roussillon
Saint-Astier, Aquitaine
Saint-Benoît-sur-Loire, Centre
Saint-Bonnet-le-Froid, Auvergne
Saint-Bonnet-Tronçais, Auvergne
Saint-Briac-sur-Mer, Bretagne
Saint-Denis d'Anjou, Pays-de-la-Loire
Saint-Disdier, Provence-Alpes-Côte d'Azur
Sainte-Marine, Bretagne
Sainte-Maure-de-Peyriac, Aquitaine
Saint-Emilion, Aquitaine
Saintes, Poitou-Charentes
Sainte-Suzanne, Pays-de-la-Loire
Saint-Etienne, Rhône-Alpes
Saint-Etienne-de-Baïgorry, Aquitaine
Saint-Folquin, Nord-Pas-de-Calais
Saint-Geniez-d'Olt, Midi-Pyrénées
Saint-Georges-le-Gaultier, Pays-de-la-Loire
Saint-Gervais-d'Auvergne, Auvergne
Saint-Gervais-en-Vallière, Bourgogne
Saint-Gervais-les-Bains, Rhône-Alpes
Saint-Girons, Midi-Pyrénées
Saint-Guiraud, Languedoc-Roussillon
Saint-Hilaire-le-Château, Limousin
Saint-Imoges, Champagne-Ardenne
Saint-Jean-aux-Bois, Picardie
Saint-Jean-Cap-Ferrat, Provence-Alpes-Côte d'Azur
Saint-Jean-d'Angely, Poitou-Charentes
Saint-Joachim, Pays-de-la-Loire
Saint-Julien-Chapteuil, Auvergne
Saint-Julien-en-Genevois, Rhône-Alpes
Saint-Justin, Aquitaine
Saint-Laurent-du-Var, Provence-Alpes-Côte d'Azur
Saint-Léonard-de-Noblat, Limousin
Saint-Léon-sur-Vézère, Aquitaine
Saint-Lô, Basse-Normandie
Saint-Lyphard, Pays-de-la-Loire
Saint-Macaire, Aquitaine
Saint-Maixent-l'Ecole, Poitou-Charentes
Saint-Malo, Bretagne
Saint-Martin-de-Ré, Poitou-Charentes
Saint-Martin-le-Vinoux, Rhône-Alpes
Saint-Martin-Osmonville, Haute-Normandie
Saint-Maximin-la-Sainte-Baume, Provence-Alpes-Côte d'Azur
Saint-Médard, Midi-Pyrénées
Saint-Ouen, Paris and Ile-de-France
Saint-Paul-de-Vence, Provence-Alpes-Côte d'Azur
Saint-Pierre-du-Vauvray, Haute-Normandie
Saint-Pons-de-Thomières, Languedoc-Roussillon
Saint-Priest-en-Jarez, Rhône-Alpes
Saint-Quay-Portrieux, Bretagne
Saint-Quentin-la-Poterie, Languedoc-

Roussillon
Saint-Quentin-sur-le-Homme, Basse-Normandie
Saint-Raphaël, Provence-Alpes-Côte d'Azur
Saint-Rémy-de-Provence, Provence-Alpes-Côte
d'Azur
Saint-Saud-Lacoussière, Aquitaine
Saint-Savin, Midi-Pyrénées
Saint-Sever, Aquitaine
Saint-Sylvain d'Anjou, Pays-de-la-Loire
Saint-Tropez, Provence-Alpes-Côte d'Azur
Saint-Vaast-la-Hougue, Basse-Normandie
Saint-Vincent-sur-Jard, Pays-de-la-Loire
Saint-Ybard, Limousin
Salles-Curan, Midi-Pyrénées
Salles-sur-Cérou, Midi-Pyrénées
Samoëns, Rhône-Alpes
Sancerre, Centre
Saoû, Rhône-Alpes
Sare, Aquitaine
Sarpoil, Auvergne
Saulges, Pays-de-la-Loire
Saumur, Pays-de-la-Loire
Sauternes, Aquitaine
Saverne, Alsace
Savigny, Basse-Normandie
Séguret, Provence-Alpes-Côte d'Azur
Sérignan-du-Comtat, Provence-Alpes-Côte
d'Azur
Servon, Basse-Normandie
Signy-l'Abbaye, Champagne-Ardenne
Sille-le-Guillaume, Pays-de-la-Loire
Sommery, Haute-Normandie
Sorrus, Nord-Pas-de-Calais
Soudan, Poitou-Charentes
Souterraine, La, Limousin
Steenvoorde, Nord-Pas-de-Calais
Strasbourg, Alsace
Surgères, Poitou-Charentes

T

Taillebourg, Poitou-Charentes
Tain-l'Hermitage, Rhône-Alpes
Talmont-sur-Gironde, Poitou-Charentes
Tavers, Centre
Tence, Auvergne
Thannenkirch, Alsace
Theil, Le, Auvergne
Thionville, Lorraine
Tholonet, Le, Provence-Alpes-Côte d'Azur
Thouars, Poitou-Charentes
Thury-Harcourt, Basse-Normandie
Tinqueux, Champagne-Ardenne
Tonneins, Aquitaine
Tornac, Languedoc-Roussillon
Toulon, Provence-Alpes-Côte d'Azur
Toulouse, Midi-Pyrénées
Touquet, Le, Nord-Pas-de-Calais
Tourrettes-sur-Loup, Provence-Alpes-Côte
d'Azur
Touzac, Midi-Pyrénées
Trébeurden, Bretagne
Trégunc, Bretagne
Trelly, Basse-Normandie
Trémolat, Aquitaine
Tréport, Le, Haute-Normandie

Trie-sur-Baïse, Midi-Pyrénées
Troyes, Champagne-Ardenne
Tulle, Limousin
Turbie, La, Provence-Alpes-Côte d'Azur
Turenne, Limousin
Turquestein-Blancrupt, Lorraine

U

Uriage-les-Bains, Rhône-Alpes
Uza, Aquitaine

V

Valbonne, Provence-Alpes-Côte d'Azur
Val-d'Isère, Rhône-Alpes
Valence, Rhône-Alpes
Vallon-Pont-d'Arc, Rhône-Alpes
Vals-les-Bains, Rhône-Alpes
Valtin, Le, Lorraine
Vendôme, Centre
Ventabren, Provence-Alpes-Côte d'Azur
Vernierfontaine, Franche-Comté
Verquières, Provence-Alpes-Côte d'Azur
Versailles, Paris and Ile-de-France
Veuil, Centre
Vialas, Languedoc-Roussillon
Vibraye, Pays-de-la-Loire
Vic-Fezensac, Midi-Pyrénées
Vichy, Auvergne
Villaines-la-Juhel, Pays-de-la-Loire
Villecroze, Provence-Alpes-Côte d'Azur
Villedieu-les-Poêles, Basse-Normandie
Villefranche-de-Rouergue, Midi-Pyrénées
Villefranche-sur-Mer, Provence-Alpes-Côte
d'Azur
Villeneuve-la-Salle, Provence-Alpes-Côte d'Azur
Villers-le-Lac, Franche-Comté
Villetoureix, Aquitaine
Vinay, Champagne-Ardenne
Vinezac, Rhône-Alpes
Vire, Basse-Normandie
Vitrac, Aquitaine
Vitrac, Auvergne
Vonnas, Rhône-Alpes
Vougeot, Bourgogne
Vouille, Poitou-Charentes
Vouvray, Centre

W

Wihr-au-Val, Alsace
Wimereux, Nord-Pas-de-Calais

X

Xonrupt-Longemer, Lorraine

Y

Yvetot, Haute-Normandie
Yvrandes, Basse-Normandie
Yzeures-sur-Creuse, Centre

Z

Zellenberg, Alsace

PICTURE CREDITS